W9-CUF-968

EDITED BY

BURNS MANTLE

THE BEST PLAYS OF 1909-19
(*With Garrison P. Sherwood*)
THE BEST PLAYS OF 1919-20
THE BEST PLAYS OF 1920-21
THE BEST PLAYS OF 1921-22
THE BEST PLAYS OF 1922-23
THE BEST PLAYS OF 1923-24
THE BEST PLAYS OF 1924-25
THE BEST PLAYS OF 1925-26
THE BEST PLAYS OF 1926-27
THE BEST PLAYS OF 1927-28
THE BEST PLAYS OF 1928-29
THE BEST PLAYS OF 1929-30
THE BEST PLAYS OF 1930-31
THE BEST PLAYS OF 1931-32
THE BEST PLAYS OF 1932-33

Photo by White Studio, New York.

"DINNER AT EIGHT"

Larry: Eight thousand a week—that's what I got! And I was going to get ten—only the talkies came in. So don't think you're doing me a favor, giving me a part in your ratty little play—because I'm doing you one.

Stengel: I think maybe we're keeping you from your dinner, Mr. Renault.

(*Frank Manning, Sam Levene and Conway Tearle*)

THE BEST PLAYS OF 1932-33

AND THE
YEAR BOOK OF THE DRAMA
IN AMERICA

EDITED BY
BURNS MANTLE

With Illustrations

DODD, MEAD AND COMPANY
NEW YORK - - - 1933

PRINTED IN THE U. S. A. BY
Quinn & Boden Company, Inc.
BOOK MANUFACTURERS
RAHWAY, NEW JERSEY

INTRODUCTION

THE theatre season of which this volume is a record—being that of the years 1932-33—may be described figuratively as the season in which an ol' villain Depression enjoyed certain third-act triumphs.

He had our Little Nell Theatre in his power practically the whole time. Had her tied to the railroad tracks, sold into a life of shame, trussed up and ready to hurl from yonder promontory, and threatened with a fate worse than bankruptcy a score of times.

But the curtain saved Little Nell. We are at the moment impatiently awaiting the end of the intermission. So the theatre that was about to die again salutes you. I put aside the suggested caption: "Theatre Reaches New Low" and substitute: "Theatre Starts Rally. New Highs in Sight."

Commercially the theatre has been fasting and fasting cures many ills, physical and spiritual. Ask Gandhi. Artistically the drama has made progress by sustaining previously attained levels. The plays chosen to represent the season of 1932-33 average very well, I think, with those of previous lists the year book has carried. Nine of the ten are of American authorship.

The Pulitzer prize winner, Maxwell Anderson's "Both Your Houses," which heads the list because of the honor conferred, is perhaps the best of the propaganda dramas in that it does not permit its propaganda to get in the way of its entertainment. The Pulitzer committee is apparently becoming politically minded. Last season the satire, "Of Thee I Sing," ridiculing governmental stupidities and the politicians who create and sustain them. This season "Both Your Houses," heaping opprobrium upon the politicians of both parties and their grafting practices.

In the esteem of two other prize-awarding bodies, the Theatre Club of New York and the trustees assigned the job of selecting a winner for an annual prize of $500 left by the late Roi Cooper Megrue and his mother, Stella Cooper Megrue, Rachel Crothers' "When Ladies Meet" was the best play of the year. The Megrue gift, however, is not for a "best" play save in the sense that it is given annually to the play written by a member of the Author's League that seems to accomplish most in "making the audience a little brighter and a little more cheered up when it leaves the theatre than when it came in."

"When Ladies Meet" skillfully organizes a duologue between the tolerant wife and the prospective mistress of a philandering husband, without either knowing the other's interest in the man. In the midst of their exchange of viewpoints the husband walks in upon them, precipitating a crisis that is of particular interest to would-be mistresses, self-pitying wives and careless husbands.

"Dinner at Eight" may justly lay claim to the distinction of being the most expertly cast and skillfully staged drama of the year. In story appeal it is handicapped by its multiplicity of scenes, and the relative unimportance and brevity of each separate entertainment unit. The welding of the scenes into one culminating episode proved sufficiently satisfying to a majority of its patrons, however, to give it standing as one of the most popular dramas of the season.

Mr. Coward's "Design for Living," which he himself describes as being a bit thin, proved the outstanding event of the theatre year in a commercial sense. The author, with the endorsement of his co-stars, Miss Fontanne and Mr. Lunt, set an arbitrary playing period of twelve weeks on the engagement originally, but afterward extended this to fifteen and finally played seventeen weeks. The demand for seats was as heavy at the close as it was at the inception of the run. For this there were many and varied explanations, but none more satisfying than that a great many people wanted to see "Design for Living" and its three-starred trio.

S. N. Behrman's "Biography," attractively strengthened by the engagement of Ina Claire to play the chief part, that of an internationally known artist who combined romance with business to the improvement of both, proved the one outstanding success of the Theatre Guild season. The Anderson "Both Your Houses," as recorded, won the Pulitzer prize and did fairly well, but "The Good Earth," dramatized by Owen and Donald Davis; "American Dream," a first play by the poet, George O'Neil, and "The Mask and the Face," a somewhat dated comedy from the Italian, barely got through the subscription list.

Sidney Howard's two plays, "Alien Corn" and "The Late Christopher Bean," were pleasant contributions to the season. The first, an original study of frustrated character hemmed in by the depressing limitations of a woman's college in a small middle Western town, was helped considerably by Katharine Cornell's playing of the leading character.

The second play, "The Late Christopher Bean," is an adaptation from the French of Rene Fauchois. Mr. Howard practically fashioned a new play on the Fauchois framework, however, changing the locale to New England and developing the characters as typical small town representatives of rural America. A cast that included Pauline Lord, playing the heroine, Walter Connelly and Beulah Bondi, directed by Gilbert Miller, was of notable assistance to the comedy.

It has been my frequent contention that a year book of the drama, if it is fairly to represent the season, should be a collaboration of its editor's best judgment and the vote of those who actually support the theatre by attendance upon it. The editorial prerogative must be occasionally exercised, however, as a preservative of editorial satisfaction. Enough playgoers voted against "We, the People" to force its classification as a box office failure. In spite of which I believe it to be one of the important dramas of the year, a play of propaganda inspired by the very problems that lie at the root of the depression and many other social ills for which we, as a people, are seeking reasonable means of correction. I have therefore included it in this group of best plays, and rest the case with the book's readers.

I have long wanted to include a George Cohan play in this series, holding him in esteem as one of the outstanding representatives of the native theatre and the native drama. His "Pigeons and People," being something of a stunt play in that it is written in one long act and played principally by Mr. Cohan himself, is still admirably representative of the Cohan genius as playwright and comedian. It manages to include a vast amount of homely philosophy, is keenly revealing as a study of character and is dovetailed and pointed with such skill as to make it typically Cohanesque.

James Hagan's "One Sunday Afternoon" is one of those honest, simple-folk comedies that happen periodically and some way renew faith in the basic appeal of honest drama. The fact that, although it was obscurely sponsored and produced, it managed to weather the depression and came within a single vote of winning the Pulitzer prize, I hold as significant.

Plays that were seriously considered at one time or another during the season as likely candidates for inclusion in the list of ten were George Haight's and Allan Scott's "Good-by Again," J. B. Priestley's "Dangerous Corner," John Howard Lawson's "Success Story," Charles MacArthur's and Ben Hecht's "Twentieth Century," and George O'Neil's "American Dream." Some were not considered for long, and some were lively contestants at the finish. But I stand by the ten finally chosen.

This is the fourteenth volume of the Best Play annuals. With a new volume, "The Best Plays of 1909-1919," brought out last spring and in the preparation of which Garrison P. Sherwood was my esteemed and most helpful collaborator, the record of the present-day American theatre is carried forward from 1909 to 1933. We hope in time to add a 1900-1909 volume. With that addition the history of the theatre in this republic will be complete from its beginnings in the early eighteenth century, where it was taken up by Dunlap, Ireland, Prof. George D. Odell and others, to the present time.

Thanks are extended again to John Chapman, who has kept track of the song hits of the various musical comedies and operettas of the season, and to Clara Sears Taylor, who has been helpfully active in the assembling of the completed material.

B. M.

Forest Hills, 1933.

CONTENTS

ILLUSTRATIONS

THE BEST PLAYS OF 1932-33

THE BEST PLAYS OF 1932-33

THE SEASON IN NEW YORK

THIS theatre season survived on half rations. No more than half the theatres in New York were in use, something less than half the actors were employed, and virtually all bankrolls were in hiding. It quite naturally became, therefore, a season of experiments and revivals. The record of revivals, in fact, was quite startling. Almost a third as many old plays were revived as there were new plays produced. Something like fifty of them. A record season for the sale of used plays, you might call it.

A majority of the revivals were not old plays in the matter of age, however. Most of them were quite new plays. The successes of two, four, six years ago. Plays like Crothers' "As Husbands Go," Kelly's "Show-off," the Kaufman-Lardner "June Moon," and the Laurence Johnson "It's a Wise Child." Only "Uncle Tom's Cabin," "Camille" and Edward Locke's "The Climax" represented the theatre's more distant past.

The revivals were important in that they carried with them a price cut that seems to me quite certain to play an important part in whatever rebuilding of the legitimate theatre's popularity is done the next few years. Some of them were sold at prices little higher than the government tax. A majority of them at $1 and less. The best of them for no more than $1.50.

John Golden, having played Rachel Crothers' "When Ladies Meet" for three months at prices ranging from $4.40 to $2.20, brought that popular play with its original cast back to Broadway at $1. To these prices there was an immediate response. Box-office attachés reported that hundreds of people came to the theatre saying this was the first legitimate attraction they had seen in five or six years. The refusal of an international stagehands' union to coöperate made a continuance of that run impossible.

The day of the $3, $4, $5 and $6 theatre is about over. The occasional success of sensational proportions will always command a speculators' premium, but the average run of first-class offerings will sell for modest sums. This will mean a readjustment of actors' salaries, of authors' royalties, of managers' profits. It should also mean larger and happier audiences. A healthier theatre and a more prosperous theatre must logically result.

This was a season of only minor sensations. Nothing in the way of a major sensation developed, save the somewhat exciting success of Noel Coward's "Design for Living," and this may be classified as an event of commercial rather than artistic importance, as is more fully explained in later pages.

An event outside the record of the legitimate theatre, yet closely associated with it, was the opening of the two huge theatres that have been included in the Radio City activities of the Rockefellers. Here, in a master music hall, S. L. Rothafel hoped to bring about a return of old-style vaudeville, mixed with such ballets and spectacle shows as the motion picture stages have developed. The theatre, a grand affair seating 6,200 persons, serviced by an army of military ushers and soft-voiced maids, was formally opened in a steady blaze of Neon reds and searchlight whites. The beauty, fashion and remaining wealth of the town was invited. Seats for the opening sold at premiums up to $100 each. Yet the show was what Broadway dismisses expressively as a flop.

The second Rockefeller theatre, opened a week later as a home for featured screen shows, was more successful. A fortnight after its gala opening the Music Hall was also turned over to the screen and has since been conducted as the largest of the motion picture cathedrals in this part of the world.

There is a definite impression in Broadway circles that the Messrs. Rockefeller will think twice, and probably three or four times, before they have anything more to do with show business after their Radio City experience.

It naturally follows that at the peak of a depression the charity enterprises of the theatre should also be greatly increased. There were probably more benefits given in New York theatres during the season of 1932-33 than in any three seasons previously. In fact, so common did the money-raising entertainment become that a benefit racket developed, causing the actors, led by Eddie Dowling, to organize an Actors' Betterment Association as a means of protection against the promoters who organized benefits for worthy causes and then organized themselves as the worthy causes to be benefited.

Two outstanding actors' charities were the Stage Relief Fund, brought into service by Rachel Crothers, who had performed a similar work in war time, and the Actors' Dinner Club, organized by Selena Royle when hard times became pressing. By spring the Stage Relief had helped some 6,000 theatre folk and raised over $58,000 through pledges, benefits and contributions. This went for food, gas, light, medical attention and the like in the homes of the hard-hit players.

The Dinner Club served meals to the general public at $1, and spent 50 cents of that to pay for the dinner of an idle actor. By a system of tickets sold at the club and given out by the various actor organizations no one knew who paid and who did not, nor how much was paid for a meal. The club served upwards of 150,000 meals during the winter, 120,000 and more being free.

Neither the Theatre Guild nor the Civic Repertory enjoyed a normal season. The Guild had but one real success, and that S. N. Behrman's "Biography," with Ina Claire as its featured player. A second play, Maxwell Anderson's "Both Your Houses," was awarded the Pulitzer prize, but, being what the profession knows as a man's play, was of limited appeal to women playgoers.

Eva Le Gallienne scored a success for the Civic Repertory in Fourteenth street with a production of "Alice in Wonderland," in the adaptation of which she served as co-author with Florida Friebus, but the expenses incident to the preservation of the repertory idea as a whole took all her profits. Finally Miss Le Gallienne abandoned her repertory temporarily and moved "Alice" uptown for a run in the New Amsterdam Theatre. Success here made it possible for her to hold her organization together. With that same purpose in mind she is planning a tour of the country in 1933-34.

A fairly remarkable record was achieved by the Shakespeare Theatre. Taking over a playhouse originally named the Jolson by the Messrs. Shubert as a compliment to Al Jolson, comedian, Julius Hopp and Percival Vivian began a season of modest Shakespearean revivals at prices ranging from 25 cents to $1. The company was coöperative and fairly obscure, the expenses reduced to the minimum and then cut. Some weeks there were salaries and some weeks there were none. But the enterprise survived. Fifteen Shakespeare dramas were given, notably "Romeo and Juliet" with Cyril Maude's daughter Marjorie, who some years ago married and retired from the stage, playing Juliet. In all 249 performances of Shakespeare were given, which is probably an all-time record for New York. The most popular of the revivals were "The Merchant of Venice," "Midsummer Night's Dream" and "Julius Cæsar."

Picking up the record where we left it with the previous volume of "The Best Plays" we find that the summer of 1932 added nothing worth mentioning to the decimated list of holdovers from 1931-32. In mid-September we got "Flying Colors," a musical comedy featuring Clifton Webb, Charles Butterworth, Patsy Kelly and Tamara Geva, and a lively journalistic comedy by the Samuel Spewaks, "Clear All Wires," featuring Thomas Mitchell. Later the Group Theatre, one-time off-shoot of the Theatre Guild, produced a vivid drama of social criticism, with John Howard Lawson picturing the devastating influences of Gentile business methods on the o'erleaping ambitions of the Ghetto's sons. It was called "Success Story," was vividly acted by the Adlers, Stella and Luther, but ran out of audiences in three months. Earl Carroll tried another "Vanities" in September, this time at the Manhattan Theatre, but could keep it going for no more than eighty some performances.

October, as frequently happens, was the banner month of the fall. Two outstanding hits were registered early by Miss Crothers' "When Ladies Meet" and the late Edgar Wallace's "Criminal at Large." A few days later came "I Loved You Wednesday," a comedy of polished dialogue and a series of artificial situations. Grace George and her husband's daughter, Alice Brady, combined their talents and invited A. E. Matthews in to help them with an amusing light comedy from the French called "Mademoiselle." The Theatre Guild suffered its first defeat with "The Good Earth." A fortunate failure in one way for the Guild. So excited had the motion picture interests become over the success of the Pearl Buck novel, from which the play was made by Owen Davis and his son Donald, that they bid much more for the picture rights than it cost the Guild to stage the play. The Guild's hurt, therefore, was largely a matter of pride and prestige.

The George Kaufman-Edna Ferber "Dinner at Eight" put heart in the season by scoring a stirring success about this time, a record of which will be found further on.

"Dangerous Corner," was an interesting comedy by J. B. Priestley, English novelist, relating the tragedy that was drawn out of a dinner party when one of the guests refused to permit a chance remark to pass unnoticed. Refusing to turn that dangerous corner, one thing leads to another until practically every member of the party is exposed as some sort of cheat. Then the first scene is played a second time to show that had those sleeping dogs of suspicion been permitted to lie there would have been no unpleasantness—nor any play.

The first of the outstanding musical successes, and there were precious few of them the season through, was "Music in the Air," a pleasantly simple concoction by the wholesomely sentimental Jerome Kern and Oscar Hammerstein 2d. It is much in the atmosphere and style of "The Cat and the Fiddle," a Kern opus of the season before. Song hits and personal performances by Natalie Hall, Reinald Werrenrath, Walter Slezak and Al Sheean kept "Music in the Air" playing through winter and summer.

The season's importations were few and of no great importance, save in the case of a curly-headed Czech named Francis Lederer. He, having been a popular favorite in Germany and later in London, after having been born and lived most of his life in Prague, came to America for his first visit in a piece called "Autumn Crocus," a sentimental bit written by an ex-stenographer of London whose name is Dody Smith but who prefers to write under the *nom du theatre* of C. L. Anthony. Lederer won adoration from lady playgoers and respect from the men. A matinée idol who can do that has done much. "Autumn Crocus," with careful nursing, ran the better part of the season.

Gilbert Miller's second try, the first being the successful Sidney Howard adaptation "The Late Christopher Bean," was a splendidly cast and staged "Firebird," with Judith Anderson starred. It failed to stir enough audience interest to keep it going. Grace Moore, coming out of so much of a retirement as her too infrequent appearances at the Metropolitan forced upon her, returned to a light opera rôle in "The Dubarry," which she sang with sufficient charm to keep it active for eleven weeks. A rowdy musical piece, "Take a Chance," featuring Jack Haley, Ethel Merman, Jack Whiting and Sid Silvers, caught the fancy of Broadway and stayed on through the season. Then Ole Olsen and Chick Johnson, popular vaudevillians hailing from Chicago, bought an interest in the production, appointed themselves its chief comedians and took it to the Chicago Fair. "Gay Divorce," bringing Fred Astaire to Broadway for his first engagement since his sister Adele married Lord Cavendish and became a settled somebody in England, was nothing much as to story but rather good entertainment, what with the Astaire and Claire Luce dances and Luella Gear's comedy.

Beatrice Lillie, one of this volume's favorite silly sisters, did not do so well in "Walk a Little Faster." She had Clark and McCullough to help her and they did what they could, but this was somewhat short of being enough. Ina Claire, however, also a favorite stage relative, found herself playing the heroine in Sam Behrman's "Biography" a little better than she had played any other comedy rôle within the memory of this generation of playgoers. Consequently "Biography" ran on through the year and also into the pages of this book.

An incident of the season was the success of a logical depression attraction—Podrecca's "Teatro dei Piccoli." These lively wooden heads have been playing in Europe for years. They were brought over, or some of them were brought over originally for a showing in one of the "Follies." But they never got so very far until this year, when they kept all the marionette faddists excited for weeks.

Ben Hecht and Charles McArthur, having grown tired of dodging contract servers, agreed finally to finish a piece called "Twentieth Century," which numerous producers had been ready to stage as soon as they could get a third act for it. The authors finished the act, the piece went on, with Phil Dunning and George Abbott (once of "Broadway") as the producers, and stayed on for practically six months.

There had been a considerable hue and cry from time to time demanding that a star part be found for Osgood Perkins. Mr. Perkins happens to share with Walter Connolly the honor of being the New York drama critics' favorite comedian. Arthur Beckhard, who had successfully produced "Another Language," having a good ear for hues and cries, found a comedy by two new writers, George Haight and Allan Scott, called "Good-by Again," and sent for Mr. Perkins to play the chief rôle. He did. With Sally Bates helping him, he played it through the season.

George Cohan, deciding that he had been away long enough, came back with a comedy of his own which one day may be referred to as having started a vogue for long one-act plays. He wrote "Pigeons and People" and played it for two hours without an intermission, as hereafter recorded.

Elmer Rice, having things to say he believed should be said, wrote them into a drama called "We, the People." Noel Coward's "Design for Living" followed "We, the People" three days later and won the town's acclaim. "One Sunday Afternoon," scheduled for the oubliette by the wiser showmen of Broadway, went out with the Bank Holiday, but came back a week later to stay through the season. All three of these plays are included with the ten from which I have taken excerpts.

Tallulah Bankhead, Alabama's favorite daughter, having gone to London for one season and stayed for ten, decided to come home with a piece called "Forsaking All Others," written by Edward Roberts and Frank Cavett. The local boys and girls took kindly to Tallulah's efforts to entertain and she achieved quite a run.

Hall Johnson, whose colored choirs are vocally gifted above any others it is easy to call to mind (you will remember that of "The Green Pastures"), staged a strange colored drama called "Run, Little Chillun." It had to do with the black man's worship of voodoo rites in the past and his finding salvation in the camp meetings of the present, and it was rather exciting. Jimmy Durante, a popular clown on Broadway, and Lupe Velez, both of whom had been pretty busy in Hollywood, took time out for advertising and came East to play in a revue called "Strike Me Pink." Hope Williams of the Park Avenue and Wyoming Williamses, made up a starring trio. They played together successfully until Jimmy and Lupe had to go back to their cinemas.

A fairly amusing family comedy called "Three-Cornered Moon" attracted some attention, first because it was played principally by Ruth Gordon and Cicely Loftus and, second, because the authoress, whose first play it was, had promised to marry her fiancé, a young doctor named Charles K. Friedberg, if it were successful. The marriage threat sounded a good deal like a press story, but when the comedy proved successful, or at least moderately so, Miss Tonkonogy and Dr. Friedberg made good.

Lillian Gish added to her stature and her local reputation as a dramatic actress, following a none-too-successful experiment playing "Camille" earlier in the year, by her performance in "Nine Pine Street," a dramatization of the famed Lizzie Borden murder case that ran through the courts of Fall River, Mass., forty years ago, made by John Colton (co-author of "Rain") and Carleton Miles. A fiery young juvenile, Burgess Meredith, made a Broadway name for himself in a sad little reform school drama called "Little Ol' Boy." In the same play John Drew Colt gave a performance that caused his mother, Ethel Barrymore, to be prouder of him than she had been. A group of earnest youngsters produced "They All Come to Moscow," a slice of life under the Soviets in which an American engineer refused to take a Russian official's wife, even when offered. It was written by John Washburne and Ruth Kennell, who evidently knew their subject but not their theatre.

In the late spring the Players' Club, sponsoring a twelfth resurrection of a neglected classic, revived "Uncle Tom's Cabin" with Otis Skinner as Uncle Tom and Fay Bainter as Topsy heading a starry cast. The old play so surprised Broadway that in place of playing one week it was taken over by the actors and continued for three.

Which is a good place to end this account of the playing year's activities. There were, for those who like figures, 180 productions of which 110 were dramatic. This is fifteen or sixteen less than last season and something like fifty or sixty under boom-year averages. The percentage of failures was much higher than usual, as it properly should have been. There were more bad plays than usual. Short bankrolls, inexperienced producers, playwrights sold down to Hollywood—a lot of things contributed to these results.

THE SEASON IN CHICAGO

By Charles Collins
Drama Editor of the *Chicago Tribune*

THE activities of the legitimate stage in Chicago during the full year that ended in mid-June, 1933, present in general view a picture that corresponds to the economic conditions of the same period. In other words, there was a break-down which was often perilously close to complete collapse. Nevertheless the institution, although maimed, struggled on with that persistence of stamina which has kept the drama alive through the ages and which is its guarantee of survival no matter how fantastically the world may spin through its cycles of change.

When the last playbill was counted, at the arrival of the summer solstice, Chicago was beginning the fourth week of its second brilliantly successful World's Fair, officially called A Century of Progress. Thus the total includes the first bookings of productions that hoped to find a rich harvest among the exposition crowds. These early entries, it may be added, were few because the source of supply—New York hits of commanding interest—was incapable of responding in abundance to the opportunity.

The year's count of "attractions" was 50, a figure somewhat surprising to the chronic playgoers who had dragged through the period lamenting the emptiness of Chicago's theatres. The decrease from preceding years, however, was marked; 1931-1932 had brought 75, and 1930-1931 had contributed 85. The years of that halcyon time which ended in the fall of 1929, often called the "whoopee period," when the nation lived in a blue heaven of economic bliss, averaged well over 100. Thus it will be seen that, in the mere matter of counting titles of shows, Chicago's legitimate stage has shrunk to one half its former size. If one should use other indices in approaching the matter—for example, the number of theatres in more or less regular operation, or the total of performance-weeks for the full list of available playhouses—the amount of shrinkage would be much more depressing to contemplate.

The quality of productions was good in the upper brackets, where fine stagecraft, able authorship and first-class acting were to be found. Below these worthy representatives of the theatre as a fine art, however, there was an assortment of flotsam and jetsam, forlorn hopes of shoe-string promoters and provincial showmen, which ranged in quality from the bad to the ghastly.

Here is a list of the best things that the Chicago stage had to offer during the year:

"Cynara," with Philip Merivale; "Another Language," with Patricia Collinge; "Of Thee I Sing," with a second company generally believed to have been better, in most rôles, than the original; "Reunion in Vienna," with Alfred Lunt and Lynn Fontanne; "Cyrano de Bergerac," "Caponsacchi" and "Hamlet," with Walter Hampden; "The Good Earth," with Alla Nazimova; "The Cat and the Fiddle," with Bettina Hall; "The Laugh Parade," with Ed Wynn; "Show Boat," revived, with Helen Morgan; "Blossom Time" and "The Student Prince," with Allan Jones; the Abbey Theater Company of Dublin in repertory; "Yoshe Kalb," in Yiddish, with Maurice Schwartz; "When Ladies Meet"; "Pigeons and People," with George M. Cohan; "The Piccoli," Podrecca's marionette company from Rome; "Alien Corn," with Katharine Cornell; "Dinner at Eight."

In addition to the players of stellar personality named above, the distinguished visitors included Ernest Truex, Donald Brian, Cornelia Otis Skinner, Paul Muni, Ethel Barrymore, Violet Heming, Roger Pryor, Lenore Ulric and (because of his radio eminence) Jack Pearl.

Events that should be triple-starred in the catalogue of the year were: the brilliant engagement of the famous extravaganza of satire, "Of Thee I Sing," with Oscar Shaw, Harriette Lake, Donald Meek and Cecil Lean in the featured rôles; the seven weeks' run to enthusiastic patronage, through the dark and sinister time of the banking moratorium, of the Abbey Players from Dublin; and the three excellent productions of poetic drama, especially "Hamlet," by Walter Hampden.

Mr. Hampden was, I think, the hero of the year. He defied the economic auguries and the prophets who are forever croaking that the classic drama is dead. He led two successful tours across the country, the first in "Cyrano," the second in "Caponsacchi" and "Hamlet"—elaborate productions of a type that no longer travels. His pilgrimages were executed with precision; early in the fall he announced that a certain night in the following spring would find him in Chicago, and kept his date.

Changes of plan, cancelled bookings, postponed premières, broken promises were the regular procedure of a theatrical system that had apparently gone daft; but Mr. Hampden worked on schedule. The fact that he played in Peoria, Ill., for one night may not seem important, but it happens that this booking was the only one of the year by a mid-western agency which, ten years ago, supplied more than a hundred small cities of the central states with theatrical attractions. Thus it will be seen that Mr. Hampden kept the trail open along a deserted "road."

For Chicago, however, the admirable repertory players from the Abbey Theater of Dublin—second generation of the earnest disciples of Lady Gregory and William Butler Yeats—were the redeemers of the drama. They came for a two weeks' stay, just at the time when the nation passed into its financial coma. They came and conquered. Every theatre but theirs closed with the banks. The Irish kept on acting, changing the bill every night, and their many admirers clustered thickly around the box-office. But for them the Chicago stage would have descended among the dead, to arise, no doubt, in better times. But the folk-drama of Ireland, interpreted with that rich racial quality which has made the Abbey one of the most famous theatres in the world, tided over the crisis. From every point of view, this was a notable achievement.

The Abbey Company, counted only as one "attraction" in my list because of its unity of appeal, gave Chicago eight full-length plays and seven curtain-raisers. The long pieces were: "The New Gossoon" and "Professor Tim," by George Shiels; "The Far-off Hills" and "The White-headed Boy," by Lennox Robinson; "The Playboy of the Western World," by J. M. Synge; "Autumn Fire," by T. C. Murray; "The Shadow of a Gunman," and "Juno and the Paycock," by Sean O'Casy. The one-act plays were: "The Rising of the Moon," "Spreading the News" and "The Workhouse Ward," by Lady Gregory; "Riders to the Sea" and "In the Shadow of the Glen," by J. M. Synge; and "Kathleen ni Houlihan" and "The Words on the Window-pane," by William Butler Yeats. I am inclined to cite "The Far-off Hills" as the best comedy of the year.

The only theatres whose operation approached regularity and continuity were the Grand Opera House, the Harris, the Erlanger and the Apollo, these being the favored places of that organization in New York which has welded together the touring activities of the two great systems of the baronial period—Shubert and Erlanger. The Cort Theater, however, after being a mere specimen of archeology for two years, walked off with the longest run of the season. This was achieved by a little domestic comedy called "The Family Upstairs," a provincial affair in every aspect except the presence of the veteran comedian Thomas W. Ross at the head of its cast. By using cut-rate devices of every description, and thus getting the box-office tariff down to a maximum of 50 cents, this trifling show stayed for twenty-six weeks.

A characteristic of the depression period has been the passing of Chicago theatres from strong into weak managerial hands. The Shuberts, upon emerging from their protracted receivership, control four playhouses—the Grand Opera House, Apollo, Harris and Selwyn. The ancient magnificos of the Erlanger syndicate now hold only the house named after their dead overlord. Others on the list of eighteen legitimate theatres are in the hands of minor and speculative managements or have become "ghost" houses like the mining camp opera house in Central City, Colo.

The rehabilitation of the Auditorium Theater has been a promising event of the year. It has offered the "Show Boat" revival and a postscript week of "Of Thee I Sing," between occasional concerts and sporadic opera productions. Its old tradition is being restored, and although it is properly an opera house, light lyric spectacles will undoubtedly be given there with increasing frequency when the stage recovers from its long sinking spell.

The collapse of Samuel Insull's public utilities empire and personal fortune wiped out Chicago's Civic Opera Company, and left a question mark against the future of its magnificent home. This Taj Mahal of Rajah Insull's grandiose ambitions was the scene of an experiment in operetta revivals by the stock company method, but the venture, weakly capitalized and ineptly exploited, flickered out after a month of discouraging results. The pieces given, with opulent backgrounds out of the opera company's warehouse, were "Robin Hood," "The Song of the Flame," and "Katinka."

The story of the theatrical year, 1932-1933, in Chicago has not been happy reading. But the several millions of playgoers in this region hope and believe that, like Paolo and Francesca, in this book they will read no longer.

THE SEASON IN SAN FRANCISCO

By George C. Warren
Drama Editor of *The San Francisco Chronicle*

SAN FRANCISCO'S theatrical season of 1932-33 was marked by scarcity of attractions, high quality of plays and casts of those given, and an unusually large number of original plays, none of which is very important. There were weeks when no legitimate theatre was open, an extraordinary situation in a city that loves the stage and has a glorious history behind it.

The year began with Channing Pollock's "The House Beautiful" at the Alcazar Theater with Charles Ray, former screen star, and Dale Winter playing the leads. At this time Katharine Cornell came with her New York cast in "The Barretts of Wimpole Street," which crowded the Curran Theater to such an extent Miss Cornell added an extra week, rushing away after the Saturday matinée to catch a train for New York so she might make connections for her European holiday.

Belasco and Curran made a production of Robert Emmet Sherwood's "Reunion in Vienna" with Ina Claire, Donald Brian, William Stack and Ethel Griffies in the leads, and Ernest Truex came with the Eastern cast in "Whistling in the Dark" with Claire Trevor and Edward Arnold, but the public here did not know Truex and the engagement was cut to one week.

"The Cat and the Fiddle" with Helen Gahagan, Olga Baclanova, Paul Gregory, Arman Kaliz and Inez Courtney in top spots ran for nine weeks at the Curran Theater, and came back later for two further weeks. Philip Merivale came in "Cynara" with Sir Guy Standing, Phœbe Foster and Nancy Sheridan, who is a Pacific Coast woman belonging in Seattle, Wash.

Irving Kaye Davis' play, "Intermission," on which David Belasco and some other New York producers held options from time to time, was produced at the Columbia Theater with Madge Bellamy and Glenn Tryon at the head of a long cast, but the play, despite the novelty of its action, confined to the lobby of a theatre, failed to draw.

Belasco and Curran made a production of Will Cotton's comedy, "The Bride the Sun Shines On," which brought back Laura

Hope Crews to the stage, and had Kenneth McKenna, Irene Purcell and Marjorie Gateson in its cast. Gordon Davis was the director. But the public failed to appreciate its humor or its satire.

Henry Duffy made an elaborate production of "Abie's Irish Rose" with George Sidney and Charlie Murray as the Jewish and Irish fathers, but the old magic of the play was gone. It did not draw, despite the fact it had the best cast in its amazing history.

Maurice Colbourne and Barry Jones brought their London repertory company to the Columbia Theater, appearing in Robert Emmet Sherwood's "The Queen's Husband" and in George Bernard Shaw's "Too True to Be Good," in which Colbourne, as the Hermit, made up as Shaw himself, wearing a brilliant green knickerbocker suit. His resemblance to the Irish dramatist was surprising.

Louise Dresser, making a brief return to the stage, was seen at the Curran Theater in Sophie Kerr's domestic play; "A Plain Man's Wife." Charles Dow Clark, Flobelle Fairbanks, a niece of Douglas Fairbanks, and Lottie Williams, old-time star of the popular-priced circuit, were in the supporting cast.

Lilyan Tashman came from the studios to the Alcazar stage to act in "Grounds for Divorce," playing the rôle Ina Claire acted in New York seven or eight years ago. Jameson Thomas and Morgan Farley were in the cast. Duffy also brought Billie Burke from retirement to act in Noel Coward's "The Marquise," in which New York saw her five years ago. Morgan Farley was in the cast as were Alan Mowbray and William Stack. The play ran six weeks to big business.

Frank Fay and Barbara Stanwyck brought "Tattle Tales" to the Curran Theater, with Janet Reade featured, but the run, which promised to be successful, was interrupted. Belasco and Curran staged Rachel Crothers' comedy, "When Ladies Meet" with Kay Johnson, Tom Douglas, Catherine Calhoun Doucet and Catherine Willard in the cast. The play failed to please San Francisco.

Edgar Wallace's "Criminal at Large" was done by Henry Duffy with Pauline Frederick starred, and Crane Wilbur, Kay Hammond and Dwight Frye in the cast. And then at the Alcazar came Otto Kruger in "Counsellor-at-Law" with Olive Tell, Vera Gordon, Mary Doran, Nellie V. Nichols and Elizabeth Wilbur in the long cast. The run was for four weeks and might have been doubled so great was the demand for seats.

"Of Thee I Sing" with Oscar Shaw, Donald Meek, Harriett

Lake, Cecil Lean and Adrian Rosley at the head of the cast got a slow start. Sam H. Harris ordered the run cut to two weeks, and then the rush began and the satire closed to jammed houses. At the Columbia Walter Hampden divided a week between "Caponsacchi" and "Hamlet," doing a tremendous business. Pauline Frederick came to the same theatre with two plays, both new, dividing a week between them. They were "Her Majesty the Widow," a thin comedy by John Charles Brownell, and Martin Brown's slightly better drama, "Amber."

As the year closes Belasco and Curran's production of "Dinner at Eight" is doing a tremendous business at the Curran Theater, the only legitimate theatre open at the moment. The cast has at its head Hedda Hopper, Louis Calhern, Alice White and Jobyna Howland, with important picture actors in the other rôles. The run will probably go eight weeks.

Amateur organizations and university drama classes kept busy, producing a number of original plays, one or two of which promise something in the future. Aurania Rouverol, who wrote "Skidding," which had a season's run in New York, showed with "Temperamentals," tale of actors, done at the tiny Travers Theater in the Fairmont Hotel.

At Stanford University a comedy called "Parade" by Elaine Ryan Wallace, was presented, but made slight impression. Everett Glass, of the University of California, produced an excellent farce, "Marrying Virginia," a play that should have professional production. Elene Wilbur had a comedy, "She Got Away With It," produced in Palo Alto. Mrs. Wilbur has won many prizes in play contests.

Martin S. Rosenblatt, who spent many years in China, produced a play, "The Dragon Gate," embodying something of the history of the Dowager Empress Tsi An. The play was effective and with further work might have a chance on the professional stage. A comedy, "Private Graveyard," by Harold Helvenston, head of the dramatic department of Stanford University, and George Hinkle, gave promise on its production, and Sarah Newmeyer's "License" seemed ready for regular production on its trial at the Travers Theater. Helen Hayes is interested in this play, and Jed Harris had it on his list of productions two years ago.

An interesting thing done by the Little Theater of the University of California was "The Tower Beyond Tragedy," a dramatization of Robinson Jeffer's poem on Electra. Edwin Duerr made the adaptation. Another play along classic lines was "Medea" in verse, an adaptation of the Euripidean tragedy made by Henry B. Lister for his wife, Lydia Warren Lister, and produced at the California Club.

The Playmakers of Berkeley kept up their record of four programs of original one-act plays, work that is developing radio writers and such budding dramatists as Miss Newmeyer, mentioned above. The Wayfarers of San Francisco produced several original plays during the year, as well as modernized versions of "Camille" and "A Doll's House." Jack Thomas is the dramatist-in-chief of the organization which has its own theatre, seating fifty persons.

During the year there were a number of efforts made toward establishing a theatre for children. At least five organizations with that end in view worked with more or less success for this purpose. The principal persons are Ronald Telfer, who had Better Plays for Children, and Eva Smith Hackett, who produced for the Western Women's Club. Among the plays presented by these rival organizations were "Little Women," "Pollyanna," "The Little Princess," "Little Lord Fauntleroy," "Mrs. Wiggs of the Cabbage Patch," "Daddy Long Legs," and some fairy stories.

An interesting event of the year was the placing of a bronze plaque on the Telephone Building, 444 Bush Street, marking the site of the famous old California Theater. The late Emelie Melville, who was in the first stock company, originated the idea in a plea to the Drama Section of the Commonwealth Club. Funds were collected, the plaque designed by Irving Morrow, architect, and permission obtained from the Telephone Company for placing the memorial on the building.

A crowd of perhaps 200 persons stood in the street during the brief ceremonies which included addresses by President James A. Johnston of the Commonwealth Club, Lyle M. Brown, division manager for the Telephone Company, and the writer, chairman of the drama section of the Commonwealth Club at the time the placing of the plaque was planned.

THE SEASON IN SOUTHERN CALIFORNIA

By Edwin Schallert

Drama Editor of the *Los Angeles Times*

WHETHER the low ebb has finally been reached in Southern California theatricals cannot at this moment be determined, but certainly the season of 1932-33 has been the poorest in volume of attractions, and one of the most erratic in quality. Everything intruded that was possible to disturb any genuine development, though conditions here, in the final analysis, but reflected those that prevailed elsewhere in the country.

The West has been no "white spot" dramatically in the tag-end of the depression. The political turnover, the bank holiday, and financial upsets all struck at the amusement business, and a good old-fashioned earthquake happened right in the midst of them. So, it is to be hoped, the dramatic career of Los Angeles and its environs has now perhaps reached the absolute nadir, and may gradually evince a reawakening.

In only one field has marked progress been disclosed—that of the community theatre. Here a marked improvement has taken place. The Pasadena Community Playhouse offered such a varied roster of plays as "Hamlet," "Richelieu," Ben Jonson's "Volpone," Ibsen's "Peer Gynt," Shaw's "The Apple Cart," and "Captain Brassbound's Conversion," Wilde's "The Importance of Being Earnest," Molnar's "Liliom," Goldoni's "The Fan," and an adaptation of "Alice in Wonderland." "Brief Moment," "Alison's House," "Foolscap," "The Devil Passes," "Green Grow the Lilacs" and "Louder Please" were among newer plays seen, as well as the revue, "Low and Behold," which was given its première. Margaret Namara, the singer, Sylvia Sidney, Douglass Montgomery, Harrison Ford, Hardie Albright, Arthur Lubin, Gordon Westcott, Frank Puglia, Morris Ankrum, Doris Lloyd and others from the professional stage and screen were seen in these productions. Montgomery starred most regularly, appearing in "Volpone," "Peer Gynt" and "Green Grow the Lilacs," while Albright was deemed a remarkable Hamlet.

The Beverly Hills Professional Theater, under the direction of Oliver Hinsdell, had its best year, with outstanding productions including "Pygmalion," "The Second Man," and Molnar's "The Good Fairy." This organization, which draws on the film colony for talent, plans to build its own theatre. Hedda Hopper, Kenneth Thomson, Richard Tucker, Martha Sleeper, Walter Byron, Marion Clayton, Mary Forbes and Crauford Kent were among the professionals seen in the plays given by this group. They also offered one new play, "The Plowboy," by Paul Fort, which was tried out at the Playbox in Pasadena, the workshop attached to the Community Playhouse.

Another group that drew attention was the Gateway Players with their offering of "The Flaming Brontes" by De Witt Bodeen, a telling excursion into the lives of a celebrated literary family, while the Padua Community Players in Claremont gave revivals of "The Importance of Being Earnest" and "Camille."

Of Mr. Mantle's ten best plays only two were given professional performance. These were "Dinner at Eight" and "When Ladies Meet," which latter opened just about the time of the bank holiday and closed after four days. "Dinner at Eight" was a notable success, as was "The Cat and the Fiddle" from last year's ten best. "Dinner at Eight," with Coast-assembled cast, and an amazing cast too, played for seven weeks. Louis Calhern, Jobyna Howland, Hedda Hopper, Frank Elliott, William Davidson, Alice White, Martha Sleeper, Huntley Gordon, Inez Courtney and Don Alvarado were among the featured names, Mr. Calhern's portrayal of the down-and-out actor being especially outstanding. Miss Howland also drew notice for her performance as the voluble ex-stage star.

"Cat and the Fiddle" shines as an enchanting memory, with Helen Gahagan as its star, while Paul Gregory and Miss Courtney were among the other principals. This Kern-Hammerstein operetta endured for eight weeks, chalking up one of the longest runs, and proving that Miss Gahagan, since she played in "Tonight or Never" last season, has become a personality attractive to local theatregoers.

Both these plays were given under Belasco-Curran management, whose productions also include "Reunion in Vienna" done with Ina Claire, Donald Brian and William Stack—a not extraordinary success; "Tattle Tales," which had its première on the Coast, and subsequently was taken to New York, with Frank Fay (Barbara Stanwyck did not appear in the piece in Los Angeles); "Another Language," which limped through two weeks with a poor cast from the East; the ill-fated "When Ladies Meet," and the beautiful "Music in the Air," which failed to catch on because of certain personnel weaknesses, and the fact that it wasn't given the fullest chance to lure out a public conservative about money-spending. At the moment (July 1) the intention is to revise this production, open it anew in San Francisco and then bring it back to Los Angeles.

The outstanding success was Elmer Rice's "Counsellor-at-Law," with Otto Kruger. This play's engagement, which lasted nine weeks, could unquestionably have gone on longer had there not been a demand for its return to San Francisco, and were not Kruger's services required for pictures by Metro-Goldwyn-Mayer, where he is under contract. This play had a splendid and memorable production, and with "The Marquise," starring Billie Burke, was the prize attraction of the Henry Duffy playhouse, the El Capitan, which enjoyed a good if spotty season, because of the fact that its price scale is at a minimum. Duffy's latest feat has been the bringing in of "Twentieth Century" with Eugenie Leontovich, and various members of the New York company. He has substituted Gregory Ratoff in the rôle of the Gest-like theatrical producer, concededly with much benefit to the production. This looks to be good for an extended run at the prevailing Duffy prices. Leontovich was seen here a few seasons ago in "Candlelight."

Miss Burke, dividing time between screen and stage, still remains a star of charm undisputed. "The Marquise," seen once before in a very poor stock production at the old Morosco Theater, thrived by virtue of her presence, and an extra matinée or two were both bidden and secured during the engagement. Eight weeks made up the run of this stage piece.

Other plays given by Duffy included a revival of "As Husbands Go," which seems to be a perennial hereabouts; "Bridal Wise," "Grounds for Divorce," with Lilyan Tashman featured, and Edgar Wallace's "Criminal at Large," with Pauline Frederick weakly cast. Miss Frederick also tried out two plays, "Her Majesty the Widow" and "Amber" at the Biltmore Theater during a single week, which failed of any acute public approval. Yet in the right kind of play she is favored. She was also seen in "As Husbands Go."

The Biltmore, home of the road show, offered few plays during the season. A belated presentation on the Coast of the Pulitzer prize musical, "Of Thee I Sing," ran right into the bank holiday, and, at best, but a reserved show of enthusiasm for its merits, which had lost their luster of timeliness. Had this very original creation by George Kaufman, Morrie Ryskind and the brothers Gershwin been given last season it would undoubtedly have survived even the bank closings, and been an enormous success. Staging lacked glamor. A road show out here is still a road show, and does not compare with the productions staged within the Coast's own area, except in important items of running smoothness and tempo.

Walter Hampden brought his very fine "Caponsacchi" and "Hamlet," during the same week the Pasadena Community gave the Shakespearean tragedy. "Cynara," with Philip Merivale, won almost no attention during its two weeks' engagement, but in view of the fact that the film version with Ronald Colman did not fare well either, it would appear that the title and the subject of the play, despite its excellent literary quality, exerted no magnetism for the audience.

The Biltmore also tried a comic opera revival, offering Victor Herbert's "The Only Girl" in a very pleasing production. Such songs as "I Want What I Want When I Want It," from "Mlle. Modiste" and "Sweethearts" from the Herbert creation of that name were interpolated, but even these transplanted solos and a cast of ability could not arouse the public to the merits of a work so obviously dated. Herbert music may charm over the radio, but his librettos will have to be rewritten completely for the Southern California showgoers, who evidence small concern over the resuscitation of past glories of the stage. A star name seems to be about the only justification for any revival, and few stars mean aught here aside from the most brilliant and the long established. Movie fame is another reliable means of exciting interest, but a stage reputation must generally accompany that.

While not a single theatre remained open right straight through the season, the Belasco and El Capitan maintained a very consistent record, especially El Capitan. Everything else was sporadic. A play called "Privilege Car" was tried out with Betty Compson in the lead, aimed for the movie mart. Louise Dresser appeared in "A Plain Man and His Wife," Lucille LaVerne staged one of her revivals of "Sun-Up," Alexander and Nat Carr were seen in "Business Before Pleasure" (Abe and Mawruss) and attempts were made to give various other plays on a trial basis, or coöperatively, with little or nothing added to show world history. Among those were "Rose of Flanders," "Hedda Gabler" (poorly done), "The Golem," "Young Ideas," etc.

A real movement has begun just lately, though, under the sponsorship of George K. Arthur, the film actor, which may lead somewhere. He started by giving a series of Grand Guignol plays including "Something More Important," "The Old Woman," "Eight O'Clock" and "A and O.A" and followed this with a remote English comedy, "I *Am* So Sorry," and "Middle Watch." The enterprise has gotten along fairly well with these offerings at the Music Box Theater, and more recently following a transfer to the Hollywood Playhouse, with George Bernard Shaw's "O'Flaherty, V.C." and "Androcles and the Lion," and "The Sport of Kings." Philip Merivale is now slated to appear in "The Tale of Two Cities." Arthur is well known in Hollywood, and by diligent personal effort is adding to his list of patrons.

The Second Music Box Revue (Coast venture) coöperative in

spirit and in fact, was in town for six or seven weeks with Eddie Lambert, John T. Murray and Vivien Oakland, and others, endeavoring to make its ribald humor palatable. They didn't quite succeed, and the show didn't even compare with "Tattle Tales," which suffered much from back-stage difficulties. Frank Fay is enough of a favorite here almost to carry the weight of a musical, but he left the cast after a very brief session, and did not rejoin it until shortly before the production moved to San Francisco. At best, "Tattle Tales" had a troubled lifetime.

Much more unusual among the revues is "Low and Behold," which embarks on professional seas on the other side of that longitudinal line which divides seasons here—a purely imaginary line, by the way. Sponsored by Leonard Sillman, this revue has a modernistic aspect which does not conflict with the handsomely appointed movie theatre prologues given in this locality. It proffers one real talent discovery—Betzi Beaton, the daughter of K.C.B. the columnist. She is a strangely casual comedienne with rare poise and a remarkable and *outré* manner and personality. The chances are Broadway will see her ere the next season is over.

Whatever talent Southern California offers on the stage is quickly snapped up by the studios, as a rule. Sheer stage talent that can be divorced from pictures did not show up surprisingly during the year. The studios constantly watch the community theatres and very few finds escape them, which is one thing that helps to sustain the community fever at its present height.

From the studio standpoint, economic considerations enter into this. The picture magnates know that they do not have to pay as high for "undiscovered" personalities as for those who enjoy Broadway acclaim, and such personalities are also more easily molded to the screen's needs.

Incidentally Los Angeles has been gradually losing some of its producers of former years to pictures. Dickson Morgan and Arthur Collins are both directing dialogue, while Edward Everett Horton finds film engagements more and more enticing. Sid Grauman is again the impresario of the Chinese Theater, première Mecca of the movies. He it was who very notably gave the public here "Once in a Lifetime," "Street Scene" and other plays a season or so ago. Without contributions from these men, theatres have been dark more of the time than usual, for almost no one of equal competency and ambition has taken their places. Oliver Morosco has talked of producing plays again, but naught has come of this, and he also is engaged at present in a film undertaking.

Belasco and Curran, and Henry Duffy (there seems a gradual uniting of the Duffy and Curran interests) follow safely in the wake of the New York success. One or the other has been considering presentations of "Biography," "The Late Christopher Bean" and "One Sunday Afternoon." Right now, though, it is a case of marking time, with some anticipations of a genuine revival during the fall season.

Even such permanent institutions as the Mission Play and the Pilgrimage Play have been in the doldrums. So far this season the Mission Play, an annual event, has not matured, despite that its author, John Steven McGroarty, has been hailed as the poet-laureate of California. Pilgrimage Play will start late if at all. It played last summer. An outdoor performance of "David," a pageant play contrived under religious auspices, failed to win the audience, notwithstanding the presence of William Farnum in the rôle of Saul.

The future lies momentarily with the community theatre, until the professional can summon reserves and capital to reënter the tourney. The only exceptions are the few producers here—really only two consistently—who have demonstrated faith with the theatregoing public, and the sledding even for them, isn't easy. The greatest hope is that next season will bring a new deal for the show world.

BOTH YOUR HOUSES

A Drama in Three Acts

By Maxwell Anderson

THE fourth production of the Theatre Guild's season was Maxwell Anderson's "Both Your Houses," a propaganda play deriving its title from Mercutio's compliments to the Montagues and Capulets in his dying speech as Romeo's fiery defender. "A plague o' both your major political parties" is Mr. Anderson's implied paraphrase.

Propaganda plays are not, as a rule, popular with the American theatregoer. He has a natural human resentment of being told of social or political weaknesses for which he, in his heart, feels a certain personal responsibility. But Mr. Anderson's argument is so soundly based in reason and so substantially buttressed by provable facts, and withal so fair and forthright and entertaining in statement that it inspired immediate favor with a thinking minority. Even its conspiring public enemies among the pilloried politicians are amiable, likable villains.

The Guild had two commercial failures, and one success, to its credit when "Both Your Houses" was presented. Owen and Donald Davis' "The Good Earth" and George O'Neil's "American Dream" had proved disappointing. "Biography," thanks in part to Ina Claire's brilliant playing of the heroine's rôle, was a success.

The Anderson play was produced March 6. In May it was awarded the Pulitzer prize as the outstanding American play of the year. This was Playwright Anderson's first award, though he had been numbered as a serious contender with "Saturday's Children" the season of 1926-27. There were many who thought he and Laurence Stallings should have shared the prize with "What Price Glory?" the season of 1924-25.

The scene at the opening of "Both Your Houses" is the reception room in the offices of the Chairman of the Appropriations Committee in the House Office Building, Washington, D. C.

Marjorie Gray, an attractive young woman in her early twenties, secretary to and daughter of the Committee Chairman, Simeon Gray, is at work at her desk. Greta Nillson, a more definite secretarial type, and known by her nickname of Bus, is in to report that she has been fired. A tall blonde, who has never been in Washington before, reports Bus, but who is a friend of the steel lobby, has her job. The blonde, so closely as Bus can figure, has been engaged to help Eddie Wister, who was Bus' boss, with his home work. It is entirely possible, she thinks, that "illicit passion has raised its pretty tousled head." Bus is pretty sure she can get another job, but if she does it probably will be with one of those new Congressmen who has never been away from home before.

"All they know about having a secretary is what they've learned from the moving pictures," declares Bus. "They try holding you on their laps the first day and assault the second."

Eddie Wister, arriving shortly, is quick to assure Bus that she has not been fired. There will be work enough for two secretaries with his committee, and he is going to need Bus to finish the work on the new bill. Bus, however, is not interested.

Solomon Fitzmaurice, an old-time Congressman, florid of face and genial of manner, joins the group with an expressed objection to finding the office filled with wenches.

"In the old days when government was government, a couple of men could sit down over a jug of whiskey and decide something," protests Sol, opening the lower drawer of the filing case and replacing an empty jug with one he has brought in his satchel.

The janitor, Marjorie warns him, is complaining about carrying out empty jugs from that office. She wishes Sol would leave his empties in his own waste basket. In reply to which Sol takes the empty jug and casually drops it out the window.

"Let 'em sweep it up, the Soviets!" he growls. "You got to bear with an old man, Clover. The changes of this world are too much for him, and he's growing testy and short-tempered."

Now Simeon Gray has arrived. He, too, is a veteran in service, tall, spare, businesslike. Simeon is not in a particularly good mood at the moment. Sol has failed him in needed committee work. They are a week late with the deficiency bill and there is a new member to reckon with—a new member who is certain to be asking a lot of questions.

This new member, Simeon further reports, is already causing trouble. He has been dodging the party whip. They are going to need a solid caucus to push the bill through the committee. Somebody had better get hold of the new member.

"I never saw him in my life," admits Simeon; "but as the case was presented to me, it looked like a set-up. He was from the district of the dam, he'd have to vote for it, and he wouldn't dare add any more to it."

"What did you say his name was? McClean?" asks Sol.

"Yes, Alan McClean."

"McClean. There's a McClean owns a newspaper in Nevada—used to sow a lot of headaches around here. Any relation?"

"Yes. This is his son," reports Marjorie.

"If he's anything like the old man, you'd better keep him under your cold speculative eye, Dizzy," Sol suggests to Congressman Levering, who has joined the others.

Everyone, it appears, has been trying to tack something onto this appropriation bill. And everyone, as Sol sees it, has succeeded excepting himself. All he has asked for is that the Atlantic Fleet spend its vacation near what Gray calls Sol's real estate development at Rocky Point, Long Island. The fleet has to go somewhere, argues Sol, and it might as well be Rocky Point as Hampton Roads. The liquor is better and the girls of Long Island are a lot fresher than at the naval base, "where the gobs have been chasing them since 1812."

"I don't know anything else you've balked at," protests Sol to Simeon. "The bill started out as a forty million dollar appropriation to finish that goddam dam which was supposed to cost four hundred million over all—"

"You're telling me—"

Sol—And which has already come to seven hundred and ninety on account of the inside gouging you stood for! Why, damn it, Simeon, you've let 'em pile odds and ends of boodle onto this last forty million until you've run it up to two hundred and seventy-five—and still going strong! There isn't a lobby in Washington that hasn't got a section all to itself! Dell's in it, Eddie's in it—

Eddie—I am like hell—

Sol—Well, you will be if I know you! Everybody has a cut in it except old Sol himself, who did all the work. I'm the contact man for the whole kit and caboodle in this dirty House—I spend my days soft-soaping the middle-westerners and my nights drinking with the Southern colonels and my mornings eating apple pie with leather-bellies from New England—and what do I get? A rain-check—come back tomorrow!

Gray—Too bad about you, Sol!

Sol—I'm getting to be an old man, Sime—we've worked together a long time, and I don't ask much. All I need's a jug of liquor every day and a lot of hard work. But I've got to make a little to retire on. Why, goddam it, I haven't even paid last year's income tax yet.

GRAY—Save the goddams for the radio. Listen, Sol, a lot of that junk's coming out, and coming out today. You've got to help me. They've got it loaded down till the old man'll have to veto his own measure. Anyway, we're not going to be caught short in front of any new member—

They now seek further report on the troublesome new member. Merton, a sharp-faced young man, has come in answer to their summons. McClean, Merton reports, was a teacher in an agricultural college in Nevada. He had kicked up a row over the misappropriation of endowment funds and got himself fired. His father had made an issue of that in his newspaper and as an upshot young McClean was elected to Congress. But he wouldn't have been elected if a lot of contractors had not got back of him and put up the funds.

"He's straight," admits Merton. "It never enters that head not to be straight. But the farmers out there are waiting for water, and he promised them he'd work to get the Nevada dam finished. He'll be for the bill. You needn't worry about that."

"Good."

"What's he like?"

"Serious. Wears mail-order clothes. Reads Thomas Jefferson. He came down to Washington three months ago, and he's spent all his time in the Congressional Library."

And the funny thing about it, adds Merton, is that the reason McClean has not kept any appointments since he has arrived in Washington is that he has been spending all his time having his own election investigated. He has had a detective agency look it up—

"Comes from Nevada, intellectual, reads Jefferson, having his own election investigated," injects Sol. "Simeon, call your meeting to order and for God's sake muzzle him. This is William Jennings Bryan!"

Other members of the committee are assembling. Sneden, Dell, Miss McMurtry, Wingblatt, Farnum and Peebles. They are all there now, and all wrangling about what they didn't or did get as their bit in the bill.

The committe has filed into its meeting when Alan McClean arrives. He is a tall, thin, serious young man in his late twenties. He is not particularly disturbed when Marjorie tells him of the search that Levering has been making for him. Alan has known about that, but there was some information that he had been trying to verify and it took time.

MARJORIE—Well, you are late, but it can't be helped now. You'll have to walk in and sit down and tell them who you are.

ALAN—I think I'd better meet your father first and get started regularly. I'm not at all sure I know how to deal with these facts I've gathered. That's why I tried to see him yesterday.

MARJORIE—He simply couldn't manage it, Alan. He'd just got back and didn't have a free moment. Most of this bill was framed while he was ill and away, and it was a day's work checking up on it.

ALAN—Then—there might be some clauses he hasn't had time to look into?

MARJORIE—Oh, that's possible—There are an awful lot of clauses.

ALAN—I see. I'd better see him before I sit on the committee.

MARJORIE—You mean—you mean you aren't going in today?

ALAN—No, I don't think so.

MARJORIE—Merton's been advising you, hasn't he? They know about you, Alan. And if some of them didn't have a lot of faith in you why would you be here at all?

ALAN—I wouldn't be too sure that's the reason. They may have wanted somebody that looked easy and didn't know too much.

MARJORIE—Do you think you're like that?

ALAN—I probably don't know how to be very dangerous, even if I do know more than they think I do. And appointments are made that way sometimes, aren't they?

MARJORIE—All the time. I played among the pork barrels as a child! That's what one learns. In fact, you're quite right. Yours was made that way.

ALAN—Well, I don't like it—really, Marjorie.

MARJORIE—Dad will take you right under his wing, Alan, and help you any way he can. He's like that.

ALAN—I know—I know. I've been counting on him.

Levering has found Alan at last. He has been worried. He had wanted to have a chat with Alan before the new member took up his duties with the committee. Levering doesn't know what Alan's ideas are, but he does know that a good party man does not make important decisions without consulting his party leaders. He realizes that Alan was elected on a reform ticket, but he feels sure he does not want to be counted as one of the sons of the wild jackass. Alan admits that he does not like the name.

"But you don't coöperate, McClean," protests Levering. "We knew you were a sensible, reliable young man, and we put you on the Appropriations Committee for that reason. I had one talk with you and then you disappeared. I haven't seen you. You've either avoided me, or I've had unbelievable luck with the telephone service. Now what's the matter?"

"I guess I've just been uncertain of a number of things—and I didn't want to try to talk about them till I felt sure—"

LEVERING—That's a good answer, I can see your point of view. But if you're puzzled, just put your questions to me. Now the caucus this morning is considering the deficiency bill for the Nevada dam. You're naturally for that project; it'll make a nice start for you.

ALAN—Well, I don't know—

LEVERING—You don't know what?

ALAN—I've discovered that some of the people who backed me for office were the contractors who have handled the work on the whole project.

LEVERING—Can you be sure of that?

ALAN—Oh, yes. I've looked it up and they don't really need forty millions to finish it. There's a lot of water in this business besides what's to be used for irrigation.

LEVERING—If you're sure of that, we ought to go over it. We certainly should. And I want to do it.

ALAN—But I didn't want to go over it with anyone, Mr. Levering. And I felt almost certain that if I went over it with you, it would lead to a compromise.

LEVERING—You amaze me, McClean. There could be no question of compromise in such a case. This comes of your working alone and taking no advice.

ALAN—It puts me in a sort of hyphenated position, because I realize I owe it to the people who elected me to put the dam through. But I also ran on an economy platform, and that concerns the whole country. I've been thinking about it a good deal and the two things just don't go together. But I guess I'll just have to decide that for myself.

LEVERING—The dam must go through, of course.

ALAN—But why must there be so many expensive and unnecessary things attached to it?

LEVERING—You wouldn't break your word to the people?

That would be flatly dishonest.

ALAN—But isn't the whole affair dishonest?

Levering has gone back to his office. He will expect Alan later, and Marjorie has a minute to repeat her warning. Alan must keep on good terms with Levering, she says. Levering is the presidential mouthpiece, the official whipper-in of the administration.

"I could bring myself to dislike him," admits Alan, with some spirit. "I don't like taking advice from him and I don't like his face. And I certainly don't care to be—whipped in."

Suddenly Alan comes to a decision. He will sit with the committee after all. He hopes there will be an extra chair. Afterward he and Marjorie will have lunch together.

"Alan, you aren't a wild radical, are you?" asks Marjorie, a little anxiously, as he starts for the committee room.

"No, just a farmer."

"Well, this first time it might be better just to listen."

"All right," he says, as he goes into the room. The curtain falls.

Inside the committee room Simeon Gray is taking up the provisions of the debated appropriations bill item by item. The committee members, seated around a long table, are accepting with such grace as they can muster his decisions and fighting for their individual rights whenever they decide that these have been attacked.

Chairman Gray would, for example, strike out Section 42 in toto, but Congressman Peebles, recognizing that as the Big Belly Creek improvement, reminds the chairman that the committee was forced to include that item to insure the support of a majority for the Iowa drainage proposition, which is the jackass Senator's pet notion.

Well, if Section 42 has to stay in then Section 74, enlarging the nursing force under the Department of the Interior, must go. Even if it does give Miss McMurtry the appointing of the nurses and means much to the maternity bureau, it also means the appropriation of fifteen thousand dollars for the dissemination of birth control information and contraception. That's out.

Miss McMurtry is prepared to fight for the birth-control provision. Her investigations have satisfied her that there are too many children. Nor does she consider it a subject for jesting, as other members of the committee seem to do, "especially at a time when so many men are unemployed and are constantly at home, and women don't know how to protect themselves, and the result is even more mouths to feed and even greater destitution."

"I declare that angle never occurred to me before," admits Peebles.

"There are a lot of things that don't occur to men," replies Miss McMurtry, "but women know that during periods of unemployment the men have nothing else to do and no other outlet for their energy."

Nevertheless, Section 74 is out, Chairman Gray announces. Also the section favored by Congressman Farnum appropriating money to establish a national park around the home of Joaquin Miller. Who was Joaquin Miller, anyway? Did he write poetry or a jokebook? And Section 65—establishing a patrol of the Canadian border for the Japanese beetle—that's out.

Not, however, if Congressman Wingblatt can help it. That Japanese beetle section is very important to some of the Non-Partisan and Farmer-Labor members. And they need those Non-Partisan votes. Sol Fitzmaurice would also say a word for the Non-Partisan claims and a border patrol of farmers.

"Those pretty little golden bugs are a godsend," insists Sol. "They're coming down like a plague from the northwest, and it gives us a chance to control the Non-Partisans by voting a little something to exterminate 'em."

"They're coming from the southwest, Sol, not the northwest," corrects Congressman Dell. "There are no Japanese beetles along the Canadian border."

"Well, what of it?" retorts Sol. "Is this geography or politics?"

But out go the beetles. Chairman Gray has promised the President the committee will bring the bill down under two hundred millions and they're going to do it if he has to go on the floor and attack it.

"By God, if there's anything I hate more than store liquor it's an honest politician," explodes Sol at this announcement. "There's something slimy about a man being honest in your position. You spend your days and nights arranging deals among a pack of thieves, and just because you won't take anything for yourself, you think your hands are clean. . . . The whole damn government's a gang of liver flukes, sucking the blood out of the body politic—and there you sit, an honest liver fluke, arranging the graft for everybody else and refusing to do any blood sucking on your own account! God, it makes me sick!"

"Mr. Fitzmaurice," protests Miss McMurtry, "there are some

of us here who would rather not be compared to animal parasites —and moreover the government is here for the good of the people! It does a great deal of good—"

"It does a four billion dollar business in taxes, and I'll say that's pretty good. For God's sake why don't you folks admit it, and take your bribes like men and go home and invest 'em?"

The door opens and Alan McClean hesitantly enters the room. He does not want to disturb anything, he tells them, after he has introduced himself. The committee proceeds.

Chairman Gray would not throw out Section 57, but that happens to provide for a new veterans' hospital at Baton Rouge and Member Dell would warn the chairman of their very definite talk with Klein—and remind him of what the Legion had said—

The Baton Rouge hospital will have to stay in, agrees Gray. Something else will have to suffer. There's still about thirty-three millions to be cut— And it is coming out, one way or another.

When they reach Section 200, "appropriating an additional million for extending irrigation service from the Nevada dam," Alan takes a hand in the proceedings. He does not want to argue about that particular appropriation, he assures them, but he would like to ask a few questions.

Is it true that two hundred millions is the total which the bill will carry? It is. Is it also the committee's intention to put the bill in final shape at that session? It is.

"Oh—well, I just want to say, Mr. Chairman, that I'm in sympathy with you on this," the new member begins. "When you say the bill ought to be cut down, I agree with you. But I'd go farther than that. I think the whole bill—and I hope you'll realize that I say this quite sincerely—not for effect at all—and I know it's a radical suggestion—but I think the whole bill ought to be dropped."

Sol—Now that's something! (*There is a general gasp.*)

Wingblatt—You'll have to take that up somewhere else, sir.

Alan—I think it ought to be dropped right here and now.

Gray—You've made a study of this, I presume?

Alan—I've been looking into it for some time, Mr. Chairman.

Gray—I have been in charge of House appropriations for something like fifteen years, sir, and I say that this bill can't be dropped, and it's like sweating blood to get it down within limits. If you have any suggestions along that line—

Alan—I come from an agricultural district, Mr. Chairman, where the farmers haven't got any money, and they're taxed beyond what they can stand already. Not only that but in the town I come from there used to be thirty-eight stores on the main street. There are now fifteen—because people have no money to buy. When stores get judgments against the farmers and put up their cattle and machinery at auction, nothing is sold. And the whole country's like that. Nobody can buy anything at any price. Now, I was elected and sent here because I told my people I'd do what I could to reduce taxes and cut down even necessary expenditures. And there's nothing in this bill that can't be done without. So I'm against it.

GRAY—We'll take the vote later. If you wish to vote against it, that's your privilege. Meanwhile, we have little enough time, and I'd like to proceed with the business in hand.

ALAN—I beg your pardon, Mr. Chairman, but I thought this was the business in hand.

GRAY—At the moment you're out of order.

WINGBLATT—Do you expect to run the House and dictate to the government the first time you step into a committee room?

ALAN—It may be that I've had exceptional opportunities for studying this particular bill. You see, in looking up a certain matter that concerned me closely I was astonished to come upon several instances of lobbyist influence. There's private graft in this bill, Mr. Chairman.

SOL—My God, that's a bombshell!

Asked what he means Alan explains that he has learned of at least three people, all members of the committee, who are asking for certain appropriations from which they will benefit in a monetary way. He prefers, however, not to make his charges more concrete at that time.

Congressman Dell would also remind Alan that he (Alan) has pledged himself to work for the completion of the Nevada dam and this bill was framed for the special purpose of providing funds for that enterprise.

Alan is free to admit that this is true, but he has changed his mind. He is no longer in favor of it. "I have discovered that my backer and campaign manager had an understanding concerning the contracts. Naturally that puts a different face on the scheme."

Congressman Fitzmaurice grows facetious in the face of all these revelations, but Alan stands his ground. Even after Congressman Sneden has taken pains to explain to him that if the committee should drop the bill it would mean the virtual abandonment of a half billion dollar investment which the government has made in the dam.

"But I say there's an understanding with the contractors! That forty million is too much because the work could be done for less if the bidding were honest! And even if the whole forty millions were necessary, why must the bill carry over two hundred millions for other projects—most of them quite unnecessary—"

WINGBLATT—How unnecessary?

ALAN—Wasteful, useless, extravagant, ridiculous—

WINGBLATT—And how are you going to pass a bill giving forty millions to Nevada if the rest of the country gets nothing out of it? Nobody'll vote for it but Nevada's own Congressmen and, by God, you'd look pretty lonely.

ALAN—Does Congress have to be bribed to pass a bill?

SOL—Boy, they're laughing at you. Maybe I'm laughing at you myself. Don't you know about the government of the United States?

GRAY—That's enough, Sol.

SOL—Sime, this boy is suffering!

GRAY—I say it's enough.

SOL—Wait a minute. Let me put it to him in two words. Mr. McClean, you can't do anything in Congress without arranging matters. Everybody wants something, everybody's trying to put something over for his voters, or his friends, or the folks he's working for. So they all get together, and they put all those things in bills, and everybody votes for 'em. All except the opposition. They don't vote for 'em because they don't get anything. That's all there is to it. That's the whole government. Is that crooked?

ALAN—Yes, it is.

SOL—That's what I say. I've been saying it for years. (*The committee laughs.*) What are you laughing at? You all came up to this Congress fighting mad, full of juice and high purpose—just like him. Well, look what happened to you. You run into people making deals! Money changers in the temple of public righteousness!

MCMURTRY—Indeed!

SOL—Yes, and it happened to me too, and I was shocked and I started making radical remarks. Why, before I knew where I was I was an outsider. I couldn't get anything for my district, I couldn't get recognized to make a speech—I couldn't even get into a poker game. My constituents complained and I wasn't going to be reëlected. So I began to play ball, just to pacify the folks back home. And it worked. They've been reëlecting me ever since—reëlecting a fat crook because he gets what they want out of the Treasury, and fixes the Tariff for 'em, and sees that they don't get gypped out of their share of the plunder. That's what happened to every man of us here, but that's the way the government's run. If you want to be in Congress you have to do it. You let us finish that dam for you, and you'll be reëlected—talk against it and you won't be.

McMurtry—I won't listen to this! (*Half the committee is standing.*)

Alan—What right have I to be thinking about being reëlected?

Sol—I'm saying it only because you're going to make yourself a lot of trouble, boy. If you don't fall in line and help pass the pie—and do it quick—you'll be no better than a ghost in these historic halls. Nobody'll see you or hear what you say—and when you leave it'll be as if you'd never been here.

Alan is not convinced. Whatever may have been true in the past cannot possibly be true now. Times have changed. He is sorry the matter came up as it did, sorry if, intending to sit and listen, he has gone at everything wrong end to and broken all the rules. But he would still like to know if they do not think, seeing the desperate situation the country is in about taxes, it would not do more good than harm to cancel the bill?

"Well, this country has long been in need of some bright young college graduate who was willing to take over the burdens of the administration," sneers Sneden. A moment later Simeon Gray has adjourned the meeting.

Most of the committee have gone. Sol and Gray remain. Gray thinks perhaps Alan would like to talk things over with him, but Alan prefers to be alone for a little. Sol would give the young man a drink, but Alan doesn't want that, either.

When Chairman Gray and Alan are later alone Alan ventures a second apology for the mess he has made of things. There is a matter, however, about which he would very much like to talk to Mr. Gray—a matter of evidence that might seem to reflect on even Gray's integrity.

"I realize that you were away at the time the bill was framed," says Alan, "but I have it on fairly competent authority that you own stock in a Culver bank, which is in shaky condition, and that the location of a penitentiary there and the spending of

Photo by Vandamm Studio, New York.

"BOTH YOUR HOUSES"

"You have an eminent nerve!" protests Bus, spiritedly facing Sol. "We may be just beginners, Sol; we may be putty in your hands, but we know better than that!"

(*Walter Kelly, Shepperd Strudwick and Mary Phillips*)

federal money would probably save it."

Gray is not disturbed. It had slipped his mind entirely that the penitentiary went to Culver. If there is anything wrong with that he would be glad to go over it with Alan any time. But not just now.

Marjorie has heard a part of the conversation. After Alan leaves she, too, seeks confirmation of it. Her father admits that the facts are pretty much as Alan has stated them. The papers would be quite sure to go after him like a pack of wolves and plenty of people would have fun believing that he was crooked. But it is too late now to change anything. The penitentiary deal is hooked up with too many agreements and promises.

Alan has come to take Marjorie to lunch. With her father gone he finds her in no very friendly state of mind. She doesn't know, she says, just what Alan thinks he is there for, but he has forfeited her respect for whatever it is.

"And it's not that he's my father," she protests, "but he's the one person who's really on your side! He's fought all his life to cut down appropriations and maintain a standard of honesty! And he's never got anything out of it."

"But I always believed that, Marjorie."

"But the first step you take in your campaign is to turn on him! Threatening to expose an innocent coincidence that would make it impossible for him to go on with his work!"

It is Marjorie's conviction that every form of corruption in the country would take on new life if her father were to be crowded off the committee. Every lobbyist in the city is waiting for just such a chance.

Still, Alan insists, if Gray has made himself so much a part of the system that no part of it can be attacked without attacking him, there isn't anything to be done about it. He realizes, as well as she, that it is hard to keep up a reputation like Gray's in Washington over a long period of years.

Gray has returned and Marjorie has gone to lunch with him, in place of Alan. Bus Nillson has come in. She is prepared to sympathize with Alan, but he must realize that to oppose Marjorie's father is no way to win a girl.

BUS—I wish I'd met somebody like you when I was young and inflammable. I'd be a better woman today. However, now that I'm here, let me congratulate you on your disgraceful conduct in the committee. You were swell.

ALAN—Was I?

BUS—I haven't heard such a row since the debate over taking the couches out of the House Office Building. That was an uproar.

ALAN—I suppose I might as well go ahead with it.

BUS—With what?

ALAN—Well, I'm against this bill—it's crooked from beginning to end—and I've got enough information to kill it.

BUS—Where, if I may ask, did you get all this stuff?

ALAN—Well, I was having my election investigated.

BUS—I heard that—I didn't believe it.

ALAN—Well, I was. And day before yesterday I got some extra pages from the bureau—and they weren't about myself—they were about some of the others on the committee.

BUS—Someone else is doing some investigating.

ALAN—Yes. Well, they sent right over for the pages but not before I'd read them. I didn't realize at first how important it was, but now that I do, I'm certainly going to use it.

BUS—How?

ALAN—On the floor of the House, if necessary.

BUS—But what gave you the idea they'd let you make a speech?

ALAN—Why not?

BUS—They've got machinery down here especially designed for keeping people from speaking. No, you won't get a chance to open your mouth. The Speaker'll be tipped off, the parliamentary experts will have your number, they'll know everything you're planning to say before you say it. Why, damn it, your own secretary is working for them and turning in regular reports.

ALAN—My secretary? Merton?

BUS—Yes, Merton.

ALAN—But that can't be.

BUS—It is, I assure you.

ALAN—And you think I won't be allowed to speak?

BUS—I know you won't. Alan, you're up against a gang of professional empire wreckers. If you added up the conquerors of all time, from Alexander to Napoleon, the lump of what they got wouldn't touch what's dragged down annually by this gang out of our national treasury. And that being the case, do you think they'd hesitate to make things difficult for you? So far as they're concerned, you just aren't here. You don't exist. You aren't even a fly in the ointment. And the ointment business around here runs, believe me, into something staggering.

ALAN—I guess I might just as well go home.

BUS—You might just as well. It's a bad time for idealists. I'm out of a job myself.

Alan can't understand it. Can't understand how things can be run that way with someone on the inside giving all the orders. Well, they are not going to run Alan that way, nor drive him out, either. He'll not go home! He will stay and fight them! *He* knows how the country feels if *they* don't.

Bus doesn't give him much encouragement. But, she confesses, as his enthusiasm flares and his fighting spirit mounts, there is something about him that vaguely begins to appeal to her. If he needs help she needs a job. She knows enough about everything to help him a lot.

"What I've forgotten is plenty for both of us," she assures Alan, when he admits that he has no definite plans; "and if we could include the setting off of a few bombs, I'd find it a fascinating and congenial occupation."

"Go on!" says Alan feverishly.

BUS—The House is split just about fifty-fifty on this bill. A little finegling here and there, and a few promises, and you might —yes, sir, you might find yourself with the deciding vote in your own little hands.

ALAN—I wouldn't know how to do that.

BUS—But I would. Oh, they made a foolish move today. They left the Non-Partisans out of this bill. There are four or five of 'em and they could swing Congress if they could stick in a lump for once. If we could find—Beetles!!

ALAN—What?

BUS—Beetles! The committee didn't give 'em their beetles, Mr. McClean.

ALAN—Oh, I begin to get you!

BUS—Of course you do. Now you go out and talk with a few Non-Partisans and you'll find yourself among friends.

ALAN—You think it will work?

BUS—I'm sure it will!

ALAN—Listen—you're hired!

BUS—Salary?

ALAN—Whatever it's been. (*She puts out her hand. He takes it.*)

BUS—Shall we go to lunch?

ALAN—Why not? I'm hollow. (MERTON *enters from the office.*)

MERTON—Oh, Mr. McClean, I wondered where you'd escaped to. I thought perhaps you'd like to lunch with me—

ALAN—What do you mean by escaped, Mr. Merton?

MERTON—Why—uh—we have several things to talk over—

ALAN—I rather doubt that. You're fired.

MERTON—Sir?

ALAN—I said, you're fired.

MERTON—I don't quite get it—

ALAN—Maybe you're a bit slow in the head. You're fired!

MERTON—But, Mr. McClean! I've been secretary to the Congressmen from your district for many years now—if there's been any mistake made which I could rectify—

ALAN—You'd have to go back too far! You'd probably have to talk to your father and mother. You'd also have to make a lot of changes in your education and subsequent career. I said you're fired, and when I said it, I meant it good and plenty! (*He turns to* BUS.) Are you ready, Miss Nillson?

BUS—Hello, Merton!

THE CURTAIN FALLS

ACT II

In the office three days later Sol Fitzmaurice is protesting colorfully and profanely against the injustices of an iniquitous income tax bureau that has soaked him forty-five thousand dollars extra.

"Those web-footed, ass-faced, water-drinking, ossified descendants of a bad smell! What have you got to be in this carrion government to get your income tax fixed? A Secretary of the Treasury?"

"That helps. It helped before."

"God, what a government! It's bad enough to have to have it, but imagine having to pay for it!"

They're ruined, protests Sol, and the bill isn't going to pass. "It's a rebellion," he insists. "This McClean's a little David, Marjorie, and he's got six strings on his harp, six Farmer-Labor and Non-Partisan Leaguers lined up with him to control the House and ride our bill to destruction. And he'll do it, Marjorie, he'll do it!"

According to Sol's figures, there are eighteen members who can go either way, and those eighteen have been talked to. At the moment McClean is only one vote behind. Another vote against them will constitute a majority. And it is Simeon Gray who has put the ammunition in Alan's hands.

Wingblatt and Levering join them. They, too, are excited about the situation, each blaming the other for some part of it. The one vote they need is that of Congressman Trumper, and he has been closeted with McClean for an hour. If McClean gets Trumper he's over the line. Gray will have to postpone the meeting to give them more time.

Chairman Gray is likewise disturbed by the news of McClean's gains and by Sol's reiterated belief that the time has come when in place of cutting any more from the bill they have got to start building it up if they hope to get it passed.

"I tell you," warns Sol, "this boy prodigy from Nevada is lifting every stone in Washington and tipping the worms off to their big chance. And they're turning, Sime."

If Gray had been wise enough to give the Farmer-Laborers their Japanese beetles all might have been different, insists Sol. Merton and Levering are of the same mind and finally Gray gives in. Let Wingblatt go to work on Trumper and let Sol promise the Farmer-Labor group their beetles.

"I don't think it will do any good," sighs Sol. "They say even God has his price—but there's no arguing with these Scandinavians!"

There is still more trouble. Eddie Wister has arrived with news for Gray that the "Cuttlefish" has threatened to withdraw his support, and that may mean the whole Middle West will be against them. The cuttlefish, it appears, is a member of the Committee of 48 on National Defense, which is another name for "about forty-eight steel companies." They're sore about being left out of the omnibus bill and are yelling for the rehabilitation of two battleships, which means an additional fifteen millions. This, according to Gray, is quite insane.

"A battleship's no damn good any more—in peace or war," insists Gray, "and they know it. And yet they spend fortunes to wreck disarmament conferences and keep the high seas cluttered with their antediluvian tin cans."

Even though Eddie is convinced it means his defeat at the next election Gray will not give in to the battleship item. Nor will Eddie take no for an answer. Everybody else is in on the bill: The river-dredging crowd, the Veterans' Bureau, the Massachusetts crowd—and the penitentiary at Culver! Why should that be in?

"Who's the majority stock holder of the Culver bank?" demands Eddie, insinuatingly. "Who knows that it's bound to crash?"

Now Gray knows the truth. It wasn't McClean who had been looking him up. It was Wister—and he thought Wister was his friend.

"You were looked up," admits Eddie, "but not by me. Sprague had it done for the company."

"It comes to the same thing," answers Gray, bitterly. "You're Sprague's hired man."

"Well, where do you get this stuff of walking around here as if you were God's favorite archangel dispensing favors in the lower regions! It's rather nice to know that you're just one of us after all!"

Again Gray is beaten. Eddie can have his battleships. Let him take his fifteen millions—and his rake-off out of it—but let him know what Gray thinks of him. . . .

The office is clear when Alan McClean arrives. He finds Bus there and is excited in giving his report about the talk with Trumper. Trumper, insists Alan, is crazy. Demanding free seeds and free silver! Well, demands Bus, why not give them to him? Give him free seeds and free silver and free gasoline and fiat money, if he wants them. They need his vote.

"You don't know what I've let myself in for with the rest of them to get the votes we've got," sighs Alan. "I've had to pledge myself to an increased tariff on lumber and an increased tariff on wheat, a new system of land-banks, an embargo on circus animals—including Siamese cats!"

BUS—Cats and beetles! Well, what of it? What we want is to defeat this bill. You don't need to worry about those promises, because you'll never be called on to deliver. Why, not one of them will even get out of committee.

ALAN—But, Bus—

BUS—We've done everything but give it the final push-over! You're not going to fall down on that! What's a promise or two—this is Washington!

ALAN—Bus, this is funny up to a point—but I simply will not and cannot go near Trumper again. I can't work this way.

BUS—Well, what are you going to do?

ALAN—I don't know, but I've got to think of someone else.

BUS—Why? Trumper's ideal—he's a jellyfish!

ALAN—But there's nothing ideal about the way you want me to get him. You've been swell, Bus—I couldn't have got started at all without you, but our methods turn my stomach over.

They're just like everyone else's, and I'm calling in a halt right now.

BUS—There is no other method in this place, Alan.

ALAN—God, what happens to people here?

BUS—You'll find out some day. You can't just go to a Congressman and say, "Please, mister, vote on our side because it's honest!"

ALAN—I'm not quite that naïve. But there must be a few here who see—as well as I do—that this régime is damn near over! There must be a few who're sick of the way things are being done and ready to take a chance for once.

BUS—For instance—who?

ALAN—Well—Sol, for one!

BUS—Sol!

ALAN—Yes, Sol! He knows it! And more than that he has a damn good reason to be sore right at the moment!

BUS—Alan, the strain's begun to tell on you!

ALAN—No, I've got to do this my way. It may seem crazy to you but it doesn't to me! I'm going to talk to him!

BUS—Alan, you're in for a terrible headache!

Sol Fitzmaurice is prepared to admit that Alan has him worried. It was a smooth piece of work he did in picking up Bus. And what luck did he have with Trumper?

Alan admits he can have Trumper's support if he is willing to sell out to him. But he had rather make a deal with Sol.

"You remember what you said to me in the committee room, the first time I saw you? You said when you first came to Washington, you were young and a radical and the whole system made you sick—didn't you?" Alan is earnest.

"You aren't making an appeal to my virtue, Alan? My lost virtue?"

"I'm saying that you know I'm right about this thing—and you're wrong."

"There's a simple formula for deciding what's right and wrong in politics, lad. It comes down to one rule! God's always in the money. He don't lose."

"But suppose God's changed sides! The thing you'd better start worrying about is that you're going to wake up some morning and find yourself an old man—and not only old, but out—down and out."

Sol is willing to admit that Alan's eloquence shakes him, and Sol hasn't been shaken for a long time. But he doesn't believe, as Alan does, that people are changing.

"It's been my firm conviction," says Sol, "fortified by thirty years' experience, that the people don't change—and they seldom or never wake up. In fact, I have found no word in the English language and no simile or figure of speech that would express the complete and illimitable ignorance and incompetence of the voting population. But maybe I don't go back far enough. Maybe it's a longer cycle than I take in."

"They're awake now—and they're going to throw you all out—all of you," says Alan.

Sol pours himself a drink. He would hear more of Alan's proposition. Vote against the bill? Help Alan control the House and wreck the machine? Help Alan show them there are more honest men than thieves for once? There Sol stops. That isn't true. There aren't half as many honest men as thieves and never have been.

"There's just one fallacy in this argument of yours," says Sol. "Would it be your plan, in case we get control, to run this government honest—as being the best policy?"

"Why not?"

Sol—Then there wouldn't be anything in it for anybody, would there? Nothing beyond his salary?

Alan—Well—no.

Sol—You see, that's the fatal flaw!

Alan—You want to come with me, Sol. You know you do. And I'm counting on you.

Sol—You're counting on me! I'd better tell you about myself, boy, before you say any more! Long ago when I was slim and eagle-eyed, I had a good angel. You wouldn't believe it to look at me now, but old Sol had a good angel by his side back there in the morning of time. And when a question like this came up this angel of light would come shouldering around him, arguing for righteousness, arguing against evil courses and the selling of his soul. If I was going to do wrong I had a wrestle with that angel. Like Jacob of old I wrestled with him in the night, and like Jacob of old I often came out ahead. It got so that the angel didn't have a chance with me, Alan, and after a while he got tired. Temptation would come upon me and I'd look around for this here spirit to wrestle with, and he wouldn't be there. He ought to be here wrestling with me now, Alan, but he's quit me. He don't even brush his wings by me, let alone give me a struggle. So I'm just an old man soaked in tobcaco and fusel oil, and no help to anybody. No, if it's up to me to stop the bill, it'll pass. You'll never get anywhere by taking things away from people, Alan. You've got to give them something.

ALAN—Why?

SOL—Because the sole business of government is graft, special privilege and corruption—with a by-product of order. They have to keep order or they can't make collections.

Now it is Alan who has seen the light. Sol may be right, after all. Perhaps, as Sol says, you've got to steal in a big way. "Steal apples and they put you in jail—steal a nation and the hosts of heaven come down and line up under your banners." That's Sol's conviction.

A moment later Wingblatt has come in, a little radiant. He has news. He has been making promises—promises of free seeds and free silver! They have no more than left the office than Alan leaps to the telephone.

"Get me Mr. Wister's office!" he calls; and a second later: "Hello! Bus?—Alan! Are you where you can talk?—No, you were right about Sol. And they've grabbed Trumper too!—No, I'm not licked! But I've got another idea! No, no—I don't like what it means a damn bit. It's as rotten as every other method in this place, but it's the only chance I've got left. I want you to get copies of everything ever proposed for H.R. 2007. I'm going to use my information—you know what— Oh, God, Bus, I know that! I know it's a dirty thing to do! I have more reasons than you have for not liking it! But I've got to do it, and nobody's going to stop me! Oh, let's not talk about it! Just get me the copies of those things, and get 'em here quick!"

Sol is back, smiling triumphantly. Wingie has brought Trumper into camp and they've got Alan licked! It may be possible Alan has been conducting his life on too high a moral plane.

Alan admits that, too. Perhaps he can't expect to get anything unless he is on the inside. He thinks now he, too, will ask for something in the bill. He'll ask for that extra million for Nevada irrigation. Why not? Dell's in it and Sneden and the veterans' lobby—and even Mr. Gray! That Culver prison is Gray's.

Sol can't believe that Gray is in, but Alan convinces him. The Culver bank is mainly Gray's, and the money is badly needed. Alan had come on that information accidentally, and it is going to get him anything he asks for. Sol might as well profit from it, too.

"Boy, when I look at you and reflect on how I wasted my young time!" ejaculates the veteran, who is by way of being shaken a second time. "The cunning of the serpent with the outward appearance of the dove! By God, I've never been up against it before!"

"But Sol, if I'm going to make capital of it, you may as well do the same."

SOL—No. No, I can't use it on Simeon, Alan. You go in and make your own deal. I'm not a man to take an unfair advantage of a friend—never was a man to do that.

ALAN—Well, don't use it if it's against your conscience.

SOL—No, no! I couldn't do it. Not to save my soul from perdition! On the other hand—I ought to do it, Alan. This generation that's growing up now, it's a generation of vipers. You can't compete with 'em without being a viper. Why, they're born with teeth and claws now-a-days. I'll just step in and see him a minute.

ALAN—You really might as well.

SOL—Not about that. Just in a friendly way.

ALAN—Surely.

SOL—And I stood there telling you about my angel. An old man's got to look out for himself. He's got to. (*He goes into the office.* BUS *enters.*)

BUS—Well?

ALAN—Are they complete copies?

BUS—Solid pork! What are you up to?

ALAN—I've been talking to Sol. He's in there getting his navy right now.

BUS—What?

ALAN—I'll catch the rest of them when the caucus meets, and advise them to ask for anything they want. They won't be refused.

BUS—What are you going to do?

ALAN—I'm going to overload the bill! I'm going to fill that thing with rubbish till no one will have the face to vote for it. Till it's a monstrosity and no one will dare sponsor it!

BUS—And this came to you all by yourself? Let me gaze on you, Alan. Let me contemplate the contours of that Nevada profile!

ALAN—Oh, you don't think it will work out?

BUS—On the contrary, I think it might. I think it will if you can carry it off. I resign, Alan. I abdicate. Take my hand and lead me. I'm a little child!

THE CURTAIN FALLS

In the Committee Room an hour later there is still considerable excitement. The bill, with the help of Marjorie and Bus, has been pasted together and several of the committee members, Dell, Sneden, Wingblatt, Peebles and Miss McMurtry, are going over it. It is Chairman Gray's wish that they note the accepted items and make it possible to take a vote on them immediately. Too much time has been wasted already.

There are, Gray admits, a few changes. He has been over the bill with the President. The veterans' hospital has been eliminated, and so has the Iowa drainage item.

This news is mightily displeasing to Congressman Dell and Congressman Peebles. How did Sol Fitzmaurice happen to get in his Atlantic Fleet? And what does this "naval rehabilitation" item mean? Sneden would like to know that. Surely not the fifteen million slice Eddie Wister has been trying to get?

"That's it, and I couldn't avoid it," explains Gray. "Those two and the Japanese beetle, which we had to have for the Dakota vote, are the only items the committee hadn't concurred in."

"Damn swell items, if you ask me!" comments Wingblatt, and with this angry conclusion the others are in complete sympathy. How do these things happen? How does Sol get his navy and Eddie slip things in after the deadline?

Alan McClean has come in and quietly taken a seat during the jawing. Now he, too, has something to suggest. He has, as they know, been engaged, whether mistakenly or not, in trying to defeat the bill. Now it seems the bill is likely to pass, and he has come to look at several matters concerning it in a different way.

Alan would, for one thing, like to include the Nevada irrigation item which has been put over. Also he would like to add to the bill, as it stands, a list of *all* those requests which previously had been denied. With Miss Nillson's help he has got them all together and he finds, somewhat to his amazement, that they are "practically all measures of considerable value, calculated to relieve a great deal of unemployment."

"Now, my point is simply this," concludes Alan; "these appear to me to be reasonable and justifiable proposals, quite as applicable to the present state of the country as any now incorporated. In consequence I am reversing my previous stand in the committee on this subject, and hereby move that this list, which I now offer, be added to H.R.2007 in due form."

The other committee members are fairly startled. Chairman Gray finds it difficult to believe that McClean is asking him seriously to restore all that junk to the bill, after all the grief he has been through getting it out. The bill is in shape, insists Gray, and is going to the House just as it is. Who, incidentally, put Alan up to this, anyway?

He is acting, Alan insists, entirely on his own initiative, and he would call the Chairman's attention to the fact that he is putting his request in the form of a motion. He is, he repeats, in favor of putting back every item that has been taken out. The decision rests with the majority of the committee.

Now the members are becoming more and more excited. In Alan's list Sneden has found his veterans' hospital. Dell has located his appropriation for postal employees' uniforms.

"The appropriation for the nursing bureau—has it been included in this version?" Miss McMurtry is eager to know.

"God, yes!" answers Wingblatt. "All the infant industries are in it—including bastardy! I tell you it's all here, boys! If anything was ever complete, this is!"

"What's the total, Mr. McClean?" inquires Peebles, ignoring Chairman Gray's suggestion that they should have had enough of all this tom-foolery.

"Including everything, four hundred and seventy-five millions."

Sneden—That's impossible. It's a lovely dream, but it's not for us.

Alan—It's not impossible! I give you my word, gentlemen, that if you pass the motion Mr. Gray will do everything in his power to see that the bill is made law. He's pledged himself to get this dam completed.

Gray—Are you making promises for me, now?

Eddie—What do you mean, McClean? You give your word?

Gray—Can't you see what he's trying to do? He's trying to hang enough junk on this thing to sink it!

Alan—Pardon me, Mr. Gray—I'm merely trying to follow your lead—when you included the navy and the steel company—

Sol—Oh, you feathered serpent! That's what you were doing!

Gray—Are you setting up as an expert now?

ALAN—I hardly think, Mr. Gray, that you were functioning as an expert when you allowed those two items to be included.

GRAY—Oh, you don't?

ALAN—No, sir.

GRAY—Perhaps you consider this maniacal proposal of yours a constructive solution?

ALAN—I am not trying to be constructive, Mr. Chairman—merely logical.

SNEDEN—Wait a minute! You call a four hundred and seventy-five million dollar bill for a forty million dollar appropriation logical?

ALAN—Not at all. I only say that if it is logical to include Mr. Wister's rehabilitated battleships on this bill, it is just as logical to include your veterans' administration.

SNEDEN—Well, that sounds reasonable.

SOL—Boys—he's slipping something over on you!

The committee is in a state of turmoil. One thing leads to another; Farnum accusing Fitzmaurice; Gray questioning the general sanity; Alan calmly refusing to budge from the stand he has taken. Out of the turmoil Chairman Gray finally brings the question to a vote, on motion by Alan that the bill be accepted with all added clauses and appropriations included.

Again discussions, punctuated with charges and counter charges, hold the floor. And again there are calls for a vote—first on the question as to whether the bill should be submitted without the additions—

Only Eddie and Sol vote Aye to this. The rest of the committee counter with an emphatic No!

Facing this situation Chairman Gray would entertain a motion for adjournment. But again Alan calls for a vote on his motion to include all discarded items in the current copy of the bill. At which point Chairman Gray takes the floor.

"If Mr. McClean will pardon me," says the Chairman, "I'll do a little talking myself about his inspired suggestion. It's obvious that he has nothing in mind except to make this bill look like a raid on the treasury. You all know my position in such matters. I am the one man among you who has given his time to government finances over a period of years. I've carried the work and made the decisions because I know what can and what cannot be done. Now McClean has come in here with the deliberate intention of stampeding you into a log-rolling vote that will look like an organized steal, and he thinks he can get away with it—and he thinks I don't dare say anything because he's discovered that I have stock in a bank at Culver, and Culver is affected by one of the allotments in this bill. That's his whole case. If that gives him status as an expert and puts him in control here, why, pass his resolution. If you still trust my judgment or think my word's any good, you'll send the measure to the House as it stands."

Again there are objections. If Sol and Eddie are to have their fleet maneuvers and their new battleships, why should the others be left out? They refuse to believe Gray when he insists that if the bill goes to the White House with any more changes it will not be signed. They demand the question, and when it is put they vote a firm Aye—all but Sol and Eddie.

Miss McMurtry, a little frightened, thinks that perhaps after all it would be well to reconsider, but she gets practically no support from the others. Sol is still grumbling about his stupidity in falling into Alan's trap, and there is general agreement that news of the bill's progress should be kept from the reporters until it is read.

They have all gone now except Alan, Marjorie and Gray. As Alan is starting for the door Gray stops him.

"Just a moment, Mr. McClean," Gray calls. "You've beaten me here this afternoon, and made a good job of it. No doubt it looks to you as if no man with a remnant of honesty would have the face to present the thing to the House."

"Yes, that is the way I feel, Mr. Gray."

Gray—That is one way of looking at it, McClean. But you once told us about a little town where the people had no money to buy. I want to tell you about another town. I grew up in Culver and I know the people there—the storekeepers and the professional men and the people in the street. I know them by their first names—and I know what they've been through. They've lost nearly everything they had. Business is gone and two banks have failed. The third one's mine, and people think it's sound, and what money is left is in it. But the bank isn't sound; and if the bill's defeated and the penitentiary doesn't go to Culver, the bank will fail, and a lot of people will lose their life savings and their jobs.

Alan—But, Mr. Gray, isn't it a little unfair to support Culver by taxing other places which are just as badly off?

Gray—Yes, it is unfair! But I'm here to represent a certain district, McClean, and they need what I can do for them as they've never needed it before. I don't hold what you've done against you, but I'm going to fight you. I'm going to fight you every inch of the way. You've made it damn difficult! You've dumped 275 extra millions on the bill, and you expect that to kill it in the house. But I don't intend to let that kill it. This fight hasn't even begun. I'm not asking you to call off your dogs, and I'm not apologizing. I'm going to use every weapon I can lay my hands on, and I won't be very squeamish where or how I find them.

ALAN—You don't leave me much choice, do you?

GRAY—And you leave me no choice!

ALAN—That's going to make it very interesting! (*He goes out.*)

MARJORIE—Dad, what is it?

GRAY—Nothing!

MARJORIE—If you'd wanted to make him believe the worst possible about you— What does it mean? Why do you want that bill to pass as much as all that?

GRAY—It's nothing that concerns you, Marjorie.

MARJORIE—It does concern me. If I didn't believe in you right now, more than anything in the world, I'd be with Alan against you.

GRAY—Perhaps you should be!

MARJORIE—It isn't fair to tell me just that much! I want an answer! You must give me an answer!

GRAY—The Third National Bank of Culver is not merely in difficulties, Marjorie. It has borrowed twice on federal securities. In its vaults are three packages of bonds which, if examined, would prove to be blank paper. If the bank fails those securities will be examined at once. I am chairman of the board. I was away when it was done, but I've known of it for some time! To put it baldly, I'm guilty. So you see, if I don't get my penitentiary one way, I'll get it another! Does that answer your question?

THE CURTAIN FALLS

ACT III

The evening of the third day after the adoption of the deficiency bill by the Appropriations Committee Congressmen Sneden, Dell and Wingblatt are in the Committee Room listening to a report from Congressman Peebles, just back from the floor of the House.

Peebles has been trying to get a promise from the Rhode Island crowd to vote for the bill, but the Rhode Islanders are cagey. They will vote for the bill, they say, if it looks like it is going through. Which is not going to help a great deal.

The President also is bringing patronage pressure to bear, according to Dell. The President wants the bill sent back to the Committee to be scaled down, but with twenty thousand telegrams received favoring the bill the last two days, insists Sneden, there will be no scaling down.

Editorial attacks on the "plunderbund at the Capitol," on the other hand, have been increasing. Practically all the papers are talking the same way, and Dell, for one, does not enjoy being spanked in public.

Now the report is that although the Massachusetts crowd are all right, putting the sponsors of the bill four votes ahead, Illinois is not all right, which puts them four votes behind. And roll call no more than an hour off!

Sol Fitzmaurice is downstairs at a conference of the manufacturing states. Farnum and Eddie Wister are with him. And the Speaker has sent word that he cannot keep the debate going more than another half hour.

Mark, the colored boy, has brought in another basket of telegrams, but "Dizzy" Levering is not swayed by the sight of these. "Don't confuse the country with the people that still have money left to send telegrams," he advises his party followers. "They represent a very small fraction of the country." Yet, as Wingblatt points out, every state in the union stands to benefit by the passage of the bill.

Congressman Ebner, a radical member, is in looking for Alan, and remains to gloat a little. "You're in a hole, you boys," he ventures, with some emphasis, "McClean put you there, and we're going to keep you there. Personally I think you never will get out of it—and I think we'll blow this government higher than a kite before you know what's happened to you! I guess you never heard of a revolution, did you? Well, you're going to hear of one. And you can write that on your list, or print it on the wall, or put it up in lights over the Capitol."

"He's been reading the life of Trotsky in two volumes," sneers Sneden, after Ebner has left.

"They've got an organization now, boys. They think this McClean's a new Bob La Follette!" warns Dell.

Now Sol Fitzmaurice has come in, reciting rather cheerfully as he swings through the door:

"And how can man die better
Than facing fearful odds
For the ashes of his fathers
And the altars of his gods?"

They are upon him in a second, demanding the news and the bill's prospects. Now Farnum and Eddie also come barging happily through the door. There is a good deal of nervous tension tossing about.

"Sol, what happened?" demands Marjorie Gray, excitedly.

"Well, Clover," answers the veteran, "the situation called for a good deal of oratory!"

"Oratory!" shouts Farnum. "What do you say to Pennsylvania?"

MARJORIE—What do you mean? Did they come over?

EDDIE—What do you say to Indiana and Illinois?

FARNUM—What do you say to that vast and glorious Empire State—New York to you!

WINGBLATT—Cut the comedy!

EDDIE—They came over!

FARNUM—Sol brought 'em over!

MARJORIE—We've got a majority?

FARNUM—A majority? We've got the damnedest, sweetest, most beautiful majority I ever saw delivered in one package! (MARJORIE *runs out.*)

EDDIE—The whole blatting conference voted to go for it solid!

SNEDEN—The rosy-fingered dawn appears!

LEVERING—That's Sol's work?

EDDIE—Sol's work!

FARNUM—And beautiful!

LEVERING—What did you do to 'em, Sol?

SOL—I talked to 'em. Where are appropriations supposed to originate in the government of the United States? In the House of Representatives. Then by what right does the President try to dictate how much we can appropriate, or where, or how? That's all.

DELL—What did you do? Give 'em your word of honor?

SOL—Honor? Pennsylvania gets twenty-one millions. Illinois gets those Lake Michigan docks—

SNEDEN—How can you promise docks on Lake Michigan?

WINGBLATT—Yeah, who gave you authority to do that?

SOL—It's in the bill!

DELL—Sure. Don't you remember?

SNEDEN—No, I do not. And I'll never believe it.

SOL—This is an extraordinary bill! It will keep a million people out of bread lines!

LEVERING—If it isn't vetoed. (GRAY *and* MARJORIE *enter from the office.*)

GRAY—Well, I hear we've got a majority!

DELL—We certainly have!

WINGBLATT—What's the news from the White House, Sime?

GRAY—Well, no news is good news, I suppose. So far he hasn't said a word. Collier promised to let me know if there was any decision. (*The buzzer sounds twice.*)

DELL—There goes the buzzer. Half an hour, Disraeli! How do we vote?

WINGBLATT—My God, is there any question any more? To hell with the country. We're climbing on the bandwagon!

FARNUM—Come on, Dizzy, don't hold up the procession.

PEEBLES—How about it?

LEVERING—How much of a majority have we got?

DELL—Fifty-five or sixty to the good!

LEVERING—We're breaking with the President, Sime!

GRAY—With that majority it's an act of God. He can't blame us for going along.

LEVERING—O.K., boys, we're voting "Aye."

There is a general sigh of relief at this announcement as the crowd goes back to the House. Both Marjorie and Simeon Gray feel that Sol is entitled to their congratulations and Sol induces Marjorie to take a wee nip from his flask by way of celebration. At which moment a Presidential secretary telephones that if the bill passes the President will veto it. Which, as Sol figures it, leaves them about twelve votes shy of a two-thirds majority.

How to get those twelve votes, with only half an hour to do it in! Yet, they must be brought in some way! If Alan were to forget his principles it could be done! Sol thinks an appeal to Alan is worth trying, even though Gray is against it.

"Nobody could deliver fifteen men in the time that's left," says Gray. "And that being the case, I'd rather you didn't mention the subject. I don't particularly like the idea of people feeling sorry for me."

Bus Nillson is also anxious. She has come to compare notes with Sol. It looks to Bus, from the tone of Sol's voice and the nature of his queries, that the bill stands in grave danger of a veto. An admission which Sol is forced to make. Alan and his middle western bloc can still hold them up.

A moment later the news has been passed on to Alan, and he, too, is jubilant. It surprises him that Sol should even think that he would consider releasing the votes of the middle western bloc.

"You have an eminent nerve!" protests Bus, spiritedly facing Sol. "We may be just beginners, Sol; we may be putty in your hands, but we know better than that."

"Alan, you're going to wish you had. Sometime you're going to wish as you've never wished anything before."

"Threats?"

Sol—No, not threats. But you've got some people in a jam, Alan, and I can't get them out of it. Houdini couldn't get them out of it, but with your influence I think maybe you could.

Alan—Who?

Sol—Simeon.

Alan—I'm sorry, Sol, but I don't see why you come to me about this.

Sol—I only want to say one thing—you won't reform anything by defeating this one bill. Parties may come and parties may go—administrations come in and go out, but the graft varies only in amount, not in kind. Now you can defeat this one appropriation bill, just for your own noble satisfaction, but you won't reform anything, and it might be more to the point to be human —this once. I had a share in it, Alan, I helped you wreck him. Neither one of us knew what we were doing, but by God, we ought to do what we can to take it back.

Alan—Just what do you mean by wreck, Sol?

Sol—I mean something you won't rest easy knowing, Alan. I mean a term in jail.

Alan—What?

Sol—I mean just what I said.

Ebner, the radical, is back. His fellows are waiting for Alan. A few of them, admits Ebner, are wavering. "It's hard for some people to turn down patronage when it is offered on a silver platter," says Ebner. It will be just as well if Alan sticks close to the boys. "We'll go down in history," prophesies Ebner. "This is the day the Old Guard meets its Waterloo!"

Ebner has gone on ahead, a little worried for fear Alan is letting himself be talked to. Alan is listening now to Marjorie's plea for help.

"I don't know whether you will ever forgive me or not, Alan," she says. "I'm going back on everything I believed, but things look different when there is a prison staring someone in the face. I don't care any more whether it's honest or not. I don't want him to go through with it."

ALAN—But what has your father done?

MARJORIE—I've loved him and almost worshiped him—because he was honest and just, and they couldn't corrupt him—somebody had to be honest in this place, or you couldn't breathe the air—and he isn't really guilty even now.

ALAN—Guilty of what, Marjorie?

MARJORIE—Something at the bank, Alan. Some misuse of funds that he wasn't concerned in at all. Only it falls on him. (*The buzzer sounds twice.*)

ALAN—I'm afraid it's impossible even if there were time.

SOL—There must be two or three key men, Alan, who could bring the others around if you worked with them.

ALAN—Worked with them? Go to those farmers and ask them to vote for the bill, after what I've done to it?

BUS—We've wasted a week's work, Alan. You'd better turn those votes loose.

SOL—We're counting on you! (*The buzzer sounds three times.*)

ALAN—Counting on me! Why, I couldn't find words to say it to them. I'm sorry, Marjorie, but I can't think of any one person now. I'm not fighting you or your father. I'm fighting this machine!

MARJORIE—But think what it means to him!

ALAN—I hope you're wrong about it and the blame doesn't fall on him, but even if it does, I can't stop now. If I were wiser, I might know how to compromise. I may be sending an innocent man to prison and I wish to Christ I knew how to avoid it, but I don't! (*The buzzer sounds four times.*)

MARJORIE—Alan! Alan!

ALAN—Don't ask it of me and don't tell me what I've lost! I know what I've lost from all of you. And it's not my choice to lose it—but I'm in a fight that's got to be won—and you're asking for something I've no right to give.

THE CURTAIN FALLS

It is later that evening. The door of the Committee Room is burst open and Sneden, Farnum, Peebles, Wingblatt, Eddie Wister, Sol and Dell file in. They are staging a sort of disorganized parade. There are many liquor bottles, there is modest cheering and some singing.

"Take it away, my boys—take it away!
When we get started everybody has to pay,
Pay, pay, pay!
Take it away, my boys—take it away!
We hear the eagle screaming:
Pht the army! Pht the navy! Hey!"

"Well, boys—who won?" shouts Farnum.

"We did!"

"Who lost?"

"Nobody!"

"Have you all got your bribes? Everybody satisfied?" queries Sol. "Hold up your hands, them that didn't get their bribes!"

Now Bus and Marjorie have come to hear the news. The bill is passed. And by a safe two-thirds majority. Alan had not released his votes. His farmers stuck together, but they were not enough. Not near enough. It was a landslide. The whole House went crazy! And, as Sol says, it was Alan who did it!

Now Alan comes and his fellow members, with mock sincerity, would thank him in person. This delegation, says Sol, would have Alan feast with them at their expense, feast on sparkling Burgundy and venison pie.

"Boy," says Sol, "it was a stunning job. You give everybody what he wants, including the opposition, and lo! there ain't no opposition!"

"It can be applied to all appropriation bills!" echoes Dell.

"Yes, and I'm willing to bet it will be," chimes in Wingblatt.

Alan knows he has lost. No one has to tell him that. Nor is he interested in their sympathetic admission that he had damned near beaten them. They know that he had put the things he did in the bill to kill it. He had added his own extra million, it is true, Alan admits. But he had a personal reason for doing that.

"We all had personal reasons," insists Wingblatt. "Sol had his navy! Farnum had his national park! And I had—I won't say what I had, but it was damn good and personal!"

Levering would have Alan come in and work with the party. Wingblatt suggests that he try it a couple of months. But Alan can see through that invitation. They want him with them because he knows too much and may tell what he knows.

"Don't be a sorehead," protests Wingblatt. "We're quite willing to listen to suggestions. What do you think we ought to do?"

"I think we all ought to get up and go home!" snaps Alan. "We've cost the country about four hundred millions today, and the least we can do is to clear out of here before we cost them any more."

"You're suggesting that we all resign?"

"I am!"

They never have heard such talk. Or such foolishness. To suggest, as he does, that this governing body has made itself a laughing stock the length and breadth of the country is plain treason. Alan must be just another red.

"And I'm not a red," Alan answers. "I don't like communism or facism or any other political patent medicine! If I did, I'd say what Ebner says—go right ahead the way you're going. You're doing all you can to bring it on."

"There's never been a better government on the face of the earth," shouts the excited Farnum. "Our forefathers fought and died to give us the government we have today!"

"And look at it now!" answers Alan.

Now Chairman Gray has entered the discussion. He is calmer than the others. He respects what Alan is trying to do. He respects it profoundly and if Alan knows anything better he would like to work for it, too. Gray does not care for the system any more than Alan does.

"Is honesty possible here at all?" asks Alan.

"I'd say that honesty was so rare as to be almost unknown in any government and impossible under our system," admits Gray. "Our system is every man for himself—and the nation be damned!"

Sol—And it works! It works when you give it a chance. Do you want me to point you the road to prosperity? Loot the treasury, loot the national resources, hang fortunes on the Wall Street Christmas tree! Graft, gigantic graft brought us our prosperity in the past and will lift us out of the present depths of parsimony and despair!

Dell—You're pushing it a little far, Sol!

Sol—I'm understanding it! Brigands built up this nation from the beginning, brigands of a gigantic Silurian breed that don't grow in a piddling age like ours! They stole billions and gutted whole states and empires, but they dug our oil-wells, built our railroads, built up everything we've got, and invented prosperity as they went along! Let 'em go back to work! We can't have an honest government, so let 'em steal plenty and get us started again. Let the behemoths plunder so the rest of us can eat!

LEVERING—Oh, turn it off, Sol!

DELL—That don't sound so good!

GRAY—Allowing for Sol's usual exaggeration—it is true!

ALAN—Then aren't you against it?

GRAY—I am.

ALAN—And isn't it time to say that it can't go on?

FARNUM—Can't go on?

PEEBLES—Who's going to stop it?

WINGBLATT—Don Quixote!

SOL—Take it easy, boys. I heard Alan say once before that something couldn't go on, and the hell he raised gave you all heart-failure. If you've got anything on your mind, Alan, give us fair warning.

ALAN—More people are open-minded nowadays than you'd believe. A lot of them aren't so sure we found the final answer a hundred and fifty years ago. Who knows what's the best kind of government? Maybe they all get rotten after a while and have to be replaced. It doesn't matter about you or me. We had a little set-to here over a minor matter, and you've won, but I want to tell you that I'm not even a premonition of what you're going to hear crashing around you if the voters who elect you ever find out what you're like and what you do to them. The best I can do is just to help them find it out.

EDDIE—Let him shoot his mouth off. He'll start talking wild and the papers won't give him three lines.

SOL—That's true too, Alan. Nobody'll believe you. What happens here is incredible, absolutely incredible.

ALAN—I'm not the person to give you a warning. I'm not a politician. I'm a Nevada school-teacher. I don't know your tricks—you showed me that tonight, and I won't forget it. But I didn't lose because I was wrong. I lost because I tried to beat you at your own game—and you can always win at that. You think you're good and secure in this charlatan's sanctuary you've built for yourselves. You think the sacred and senseless legend poured into the people of this country from childhood will protect you. It won't. It takes about a hundred years to tire this country of trickery—and we're fifty years overdue right now. That's my warning. And I'd feel pretty damn pitiful and lonely saying it to you, if I didn't believe there are a hundred million people who are with me, a hundred million people who are disgusted enough to turn from you to something else. Anything else but this. (*He turns and goes out.*)

GRAY—And good luck to him! (*He goes into his office.* MARJORIE *goes out after* ALAN.)

LEVERING—Think the papers'll give him a break, Sol?

BUS—They'll give him a break! On every front page in the country!

SOL—They'll have to—if he hands them that line.

PEEBLES—May be a little nasty for some of us.

SOL—It'll blow over, it'll blow over. As a matter of fact, the natural resources of this country in political apathy and indifference have hardly been touched. They're just learning how to pay taxes. In a few more years you'll really give 'em taxes to pay.

WINGBLATT—You think so?

SOL—I know it. On the other hand, he's right about you. I always told you boys you were a bunch of crooks, and you are. The whole blistering blasphemous batch of you! And some day they're going to catch up with you.

WINGBLATT—Well, how about yourself, you two-faced swindler?

SOL—I'm too old, Wingie. They won't get me. No—I don't hardly expect it in my time. (*He pours himself a drink.*)

BUS—Maybe.

THE CURTAIN FALLS

DINNER AT EIGHT

A Drama in Three Acts

By George S. Kaufman and Edna Ferber

THE employment of the turntable stage, fairly common in European theatres, was a novelty in the American theatre when it was introduced by Arthur Hopkins and Cohan and Harris for the production of Elmer Rice's "On Trial" fifteen years back. It was again revived with effective results when "Grand Hotel" brought the drama of multiple scenes to its most successful issue in 1930.

The use of the turntable stage adds to the coherence and excitement of "Dinner at Eight," which was a late October sensation in the New York theatre. In this instance, however, considerable improvement is shown in the mechanical ease with which the scene changes are made.

While the action of the drama is episodic, calling for successive changes in the locale, the continuity of story is well sustained. This serves to minimize the handicap of a frequently broken interest on the auditor's part.

The episodic drama must always suffer from being unable to create a cumulative sympathy, but if it is able to build in interest what it misses in sympathy to the satisfaction of the audience, as "Dinner at Eight" has done, the result as entertainment is as happily achieved. Only those older playgoers, accustomed to the set forms of an earlier drama, were disappointed in the lack of emotional sweep inspired by "Dinner at Eight." Playgoers, trained in the ways of the motion picture and the story of frequently broken sequences, admired it greatly. It also gained much praise for the skill with which it had been cast and directed by George Kaufman, who collaborated with Edna Ferber in the drama's writing.

The upstairs sitting-room in Oliver Jordan's house, which is the setting of the opening scene of "Dinner at Eight," is "a luxurious and rather feminine room." It is 10 o'clock in the morning and sunlight is streaming in at the window.

Millicent Jordan, "a pretty, rather vapid woman of thirty-nine," is breakfasting in a negligee and dividing her attention between her orange juice and her mail. Her interest in the morning paper, which happens to be the *Times,* is confined to the news of the society page, to which she frequently turns.

Mrs. Jordan's day is starting busily. There are orders for Gustave, the butler, a good-looking light-haired Scandinavian. Mrs. Jordan will not be home to lunch. Both she and Mr. Jordan will be out for dinner. Miss Paula may or may not be home. And Mrs. Jordan would like to see Ricci before he drives Mr. Jordan to the office.

There is a moment for a formal morning greeting when Oliver Jordan appears. "He is in his early forties, quiet, well bred, sensitive. You are rather surprised to learn that he is in business."

Mr. Jordan is carrying his top coat and hat and is about to leave for the office. He is surprised to find Mrs. Jordan up so early. If he had known they might have had breakfast together, unless Mrs. Jordan thinks perhaps that might have set people talking.

"What's on for tonight?" Oliver wants to know. "We're home, I hope."

"Oh, now, darling, you know perfectly well tonight's the Hilliards' costume party."

OLIVER—Oh, look here, Millicent. D'you mean I have to go as something?

MILLICENT—Oh, you'll love it. I got you Richard the Conqueror, and I'm a Florodora Girl.

OLIVER—Makes an ideal couple.

MILLICENT—I wanted Tarzan for you, but it's so draughty at the Hilliards'.

OLIVER—Look here—it's a late affair. We can have dinner at home, h'm?"

MILLICENT—Oh, dear, no! We're dining with the Cartwrights and going on from there.

OLIVER—And I have to go through dinner in that armor!

MILLICENT (*a soothing smile*)—Well, we're home tomorrow night.

OLIVER—Thank God!

MILLICENT—The Martins are coming in for bridge. (*His look says, "And you call that an evening at home!"*)

OLIVER—Oh, well—

GUSTAVE (*carrying radiogram on a small tray*)—This just came, Mrs. Jordan.

MILLICENT—Oh, good! Wait a minute, Oliver. (*Opens and*

reads radio to herself.) Delighted . . . Friday . . . Listen to this, Oliver. I've got the Ferncliffes!

OLIVER—What?

MILLICENT—Lord and Lady Ferncliffe. They get in this morning—on the *Aquitania*. I sent them a radio last night, and they're coming to dinner Friday. Wasn't that bright of me?

OLIVER—Yes—if you want the Ferncliffes.

MILLICENT—Want them! Why, you know everybody'll pounce on them. Besides, we've got to have them. They entertained us in London.

OLIVER—Yes, and very dull it was, too.

MILLICENT—Oh, I don't know. I like those formal English dinners.

OLIVER—Not that one. All family portraits and Australian mutton and fox-hunting and Lloyd George. And the guests! A lot of people who had been buried for years, and who got up just for that dinner.

MILLICENT—Don't be American, Oliver. It's a great coup for me to get them. Friday. That gives me just a week.

OLIVER—Friday! . . . I was taking Paula to the opera. That Russian singer.

MILLICENT—I'm giving up Bori this morning! The Plaza musicale. All this phoning.

OLIVER—Bori—in the morning! To sit on a little gold chair and listen to Bori in the morning. Where's the glamour?

MILLICENT—Oh, Oliver, do be sensible and keep your mind on this a minute. After all, it's just as much your dinner as mine. And the Ferncliffes are terribly important. I should think you'd like to talk to him. Hasn't he got something to do with shipping?

OLIVER (*a little genuflexion*)—Mr. Oliver Jordan accepts.

Mrs. Jordan thinks it should be just a small number—ten perhaps. She thinks she will ask the Talbots and perhaps Carlotta Vance. Carlotta is an old friend of Oliver's and may have known the Ferncliffes, though she goes with a much faster set than they on the other side.

Oliver has a suggestion about guests, too. If Millicent is looking for another couple he would like her to ask Dan Packard and his wife. At first Millicent thinks he is joking. The Packards! With the Ferncliffes! That Mrs. Packard— The idea is preposterous!

But Oliver is quite earnest. There are reasons. Packard has become a big man in the last year or so. Besides, the Ferncliffes will probably like the Packards. The English always like that two-fisted Western stuff, and as for Mrs. Packard—they will probably find her very refreshing. And it is damned important—

Paula Jordan is in. She is nineteen, modern, chic, and dressed for the street. Her father surveys his daughter approvingly. Her mother would know her plans for the day. Will she be able to meet her mother and see about the monogramming she has been putting off for weeks? Paula should remember that she is being married in three months and so far she hasn't a stitch of trousseau. For an engaged girl she is certainly casual!

But Paula is not worried. She will get everything when the time comes. And Ernest understands. Calls her "a flawless fiancée." About last night? Well, Paula had come home with Ernest about ten, suffering with a terrific headache. Then she had taken three aspirins, her headache disappeared and, some of her crowd calling up about a marvelous party, she had gone to that.

"Well, I hope you've got charm enough to explain that to Ernest," observes Millicent. "Where was the party?"

"Oh—around. We went over to Twenty-one . . . Look, darling, I've just got to run. I'll be home before dinner. I'm going out with Ernest. Will you be here?"

"I suppose so."

Paula has gone. Millicent is in her own room, looking for a pink gown she wants Dora, her maid, to send to the cleaner's. Gustave is back for the breakfast things. Gustave would take advantage of Mrs. Jordan's being out of the room to reassure Dora of his interest in her, and she would be willing to listen if she did not fear discovery.

A moment later Ricci, the chauffeur, has appeared. Ricci "is a tall, saturnine Italian, slim, graceful and a little sinister." He, too, would detain Dora, but the maid is apparently as eager to evade him as she was to encourage Gustave.

Now Ricci has received Mrs. Jordan's instructions as to a number of errands he is to do. He is to take a box to Charvet; return and take Mrs. Jordan to lunch; stop at Cartier's for some stationery and at Thorley's for flowers—two dozen long-stemmed Talisman roses—which he is to take over himself to the Waldorf-Astoria for Lady Ferncliffe.

That much attended to, Millicent can get back to her dinner and her telephoning. She is at her desk now, shuffling address notes and dialing for numbers. After a missed digit or two she gets the Talbots—

"Is this Dr. Talbot's home? . . . Is Mrs. Talbot there? This is Mrs. Oliver Jordan. I want to speak to Mrs. Talbot. . . . [She is turning the pages of her own private address book, hunting down certain telephone numbers as she waits.] Lucy! . . . This is Millicent. . . . How are you? . . . Oh, I'm fine. . . . Listen, Lucy dear, I'm giving a little dinner for Lord and Lady Ferncliffe. You know they're here from England. I want you and the Doctor to come. A week from tonight—Friday. . . . That'll be lovely. I'm only asking a few people whom I know they'd like. I'm inviting you informally like this because the time's so short, and anyway it's just a small dinner. . . . Yes, that's right. Friday, the twenty-third, at eight o'clock."

Hattie Loomis is in. Hattie is Mrs. Jordan's sister, "a few years older than Millicent and attractive-looking in spite of a harassed and rather bitter expression. . . . Her clothes are modish enough, but not too new."

Millicent finds it distracting to be bothered at this particular moment, with a big dinner on her hands and little time to organize it, but she does send Dora for the gown. Then she goes back to looking for an extra man. She needs an extra man—

"I've got the Ferncliffes, of course," she explains to Hattie. "That's what makes it so difficult—you see, she's so deaf you have to yell your head off, and all he knows is Parliament and grouse."

"Gives you a nice start," suggests Hattie.

Millicent—That isn't the worst; Oliver's got some business thing up his sleeve and insists on my asking those Packards. *You* know who they are. All the money in the world, and bellows at the top of his lungs.

Hattie (*brightly*)—Put him next to Lady Ferncliffe.

Millicent—And as for *Mrs.* Packard! They say she was a check-room girl, or something. Commonest little piece. She's his second wife—years younger. Of course it was his money.

Hattie—It gets better and better. Tell me more about her.

Millicent—I met her at the races once. She was beautifully dressed. But the bracelets and the perfume and the make-up—they gave her away at fifty yards. And when she opened that little rosebud mouth—well, she spoke pure spearmint.

Hattie—Ferncliffe'll be crazy about her. He'll probably divorce the old girl.

Millicent—There's one good thing—I've got the Talbots. They are sweet. And a doctor always fits in. Of course, lately, he's always trying to analyze you. And at dinner, no matter what you talk about, it leads right back to your inhibitions. When it comes to that, he ought to concentrate on his wife. You know Lucy! Talk about inhibitions!

HATTIE—I like Lucy—I think she's got brains.

MILLICENT—Nonsense! If she had any brains she'd have been on to him long ago. That bedside boy! Carrying on with every pretty patient he's got. . . . I think I'll put him next to Carlotta Vance.

HATTIE—Oh, I didn't know she was here. When did she come over?

MILLICENT—A few days ago. I ran into her at the Colony. Of course I think she's poisonous, but I've got to have her here some time. When I think of the way she behaved that summer at Antibes. Trying to steal Oliver under my very nose. You'd think a woman of her age—

HATTIE—Why, she can't be so old.

MILLICENT—Oh, Hattie!

HATTIE—How old was she when she played "La Valliere"? Remember how beautiful she was, and how thrilled we were!

MILLICENT—Well, she doesn't thrill me now—but I've got to have her. We were in and out of her house all that summer. Everybody was. Sunning on her rocks and sprawling on her terrace. It's really astonishing, the people she gets around her over there. Michael Arlen and Willy Maugham and Charlie Chaplin—even Shaw came in one day. I've got to have her.

HATTIE—Yes, have her—if you're sure you don't like her. She just fits in.

MILLICENT—Oliver's fond of her. She was one of his college crushes. He says she's a child about business and advises her now and then. If you ask me I think she's a man-eating shark. Look at the fortune she got out of old Stanfield. And that theatre named after her. It's hers, you know.

HATTIE—I wish somebody'd name a theatre after me—The Hattie Loomis.

MILLICENT—You know, 'way down deep I'm really rather glad to have her. I want to show her there are some people she could never hope to meet over there, but that she *can* meet in my house.

HATTIE—I see. Who has the choice of weapons?

Millicent is too busy looking up the Packards in the phone book to answer. The number found and dialed, Mrs. Packard is soon accepting and Mrs. Jordan registering pleasure with set teeth—

". . . Oh, that'll be lovely . . . I'm so pleased. . . . Well, I'm delighted. . . . Don't you want to know the date? . . . It's a week from tonight. Friday, the twenty-third. I'm inviting you informally like this because the time's so short, and anyway, it's just a small dinner. . . . Friday, the twenty-third. Dinner at eight. I thought we'd all go to the theatre afterward, and see a play. Though perhaps you and Mr. Packard would prefer a musical comedy. I'll see what there is, and perhaps we can go to one of those . . ." [The lights which have been gradually fading go out.]

The private office of Oliver Jordan, head of the Jordan line, is on the fifth floor of an old-fashioned red brick office building on State Street, facing the Bowery. "With the possible exception of a flat-topped desk, the furnishings of the room are those of the day of old Oliver Jordan, grandfather of the present head of the steamship line." Old mahogany bookcases are stuffed with thick volumes on maritime law etc., and on the wall there is a portrait of old Oliver Jordan, "showing him to be a rather handsome and rockbound old gentleman with side-whiskers and a good deal of watch-chain and collar."

Miss Copeland, "a spare and spinsterish forty-eight," at the telephone, is busy explaining that Mr. Jordan has not returned from lunch. It has been a busy morning for Miss Copeland, a good part of it spent in trying to get in touch with a Mr. Dan Packard, who has himself been out of touch with his own office in the Empire State Building. Mr. Packard's secretary has been chasing him by phone from Mr. Untermeyer's office, to Amalgamated Copper, to the Jockey Club, to Al Smith's office, to the New York Athletic Club—

Which irritates sixty-year-old Fosdick, clerk, "a relic of the old Jordan régime." "Like to know what they have offices for," grumbles Fosdick. "Commodore used to get here eight o'clock every morning and stayed till seven. You could set your watch by him. Now it's down at eleven, two hours for lunch, and home at four."

Now Oliver Jordan is back from lunch and he has news for Fosdick. The *Castilian* isn't sailing the next day. She hasn't enough cargo to keep her down in the water, and there's no use sending her out, despite the fact that no Jordan boat has missed a trip in sixty years. Times have changed.

Oliver sinks rather heavily into his desk chair, with "a little absent-minded rubbing of his chest, a deep sigh," but he pulls himself together, assures a Mr. Kingsbury over the phone that Jordan stock is just as good today as it ever was, allowing for the times. He hopes, however, that anyone owning any will hold it until after the next scheduled stockholders' meeting. They are pretty sure to regret hasty action.

And then Carlotta Vance calls. "Carlotta is a battered beauty of perhaps fifty-three. She cannot be said to be faded, for there still is about her a magnificent vitality and zest. Her figure is gone, for she likes good living, and in the past twelve or fifteen years she has given up the struggle. There clings to her, intangibly, much of the splendor, the success, the élan of the old days when she was a famous theatrical beauty and the mistress of millions."

"Oliver! Ducky! How are you? How simply marvelous to see you! I never was so glad to see anyone in all my life!"

Carlotta's greeting is hearty and she kisses Oliver dramatically on both cheeks. Oliver, on his part, is quite as excited to see Carlotta, and as surprised.

Carlotta, it appears, has been to the Customs office where she has had some difficulty convincing a certain son of the race named Greenbaum that it is altogether reasonable that she should own six fur coats! Seeing the Jordan sign she had come over. Now that she is here she is prepared to confess that she is also broke.

"Oliver, darling, I'm as flat as a mill pond. I haven't a sou," she tells him.

OLIVER—Oh, now, come, Carlotta! How about all those gilt-edged securities? And your theatre! Why, that theatre alone ought to bring you enough to live on.

CARLOTTA—That's my chief reason for coming over. To try to get rid of that rat trap.

OLIVER—What's the matter with it?

CARLOTTA—May I take you for a stroll down Forty-second Street and a little look at the Carlotta Vance Theatre? It's between the Flea Circus and a Hamburg-and-onion Eatery. It's had six weeks of booking in the past two years. And what were they! Special matinées of a Greek actress named Maria Koreopolous playing Sophocles' "How Are You?" in the original Greek. *That* filled a long-felt want. Then there was a movie week. A big educational film called "The Story of Evolution, or: From Ooze to Hoover" in ten reels. It then swung back to the legitimate with a little gem entitled "Papa Love Mamma?" Three days. For the past six months they haven't taken the lock off the door. It's now known as the spiders' rendezvous, but you can't collect rent from *them!*

OLIVER—Well! Then it's not bringing in a cent.

CARLOTTA—So my little problem is to find somebody I can sell it to. Though I don't know what they'd do with it, unless they flood it and use it for a swimming pool. (*A sudden thought.*) I wonder if I couldn't sell it back to the Stanfield estate. There's an idea. You know, when he gave me that theatre I thought it was pretty magnificent of the old boy. I wish now I'd taken a sandwich.

OLIVER—Oh, now, Lotta, you always exaggerated. I'll bet you're rolling in wealth.

CARLOTTA—What've I got? Railroads, oil, cotton. That's what they gave you in my day. I could only take what they had. You know what's happened to *those* things.

OLIVER—Well, you *are* down to cases. "International Beauty Returns to Stage?"

CARLOTTA—Never. I'll have my double chins in privacy. I've seen too many hardened arteries dragged out to make a first-night holiday. Though I must say I saw Julia Cavendish last night and she looked wonderful. Forty-five if she's a day.

OLIVER—Look here, Carlotta. Your stuff must bring you in a little something. It can't cost you an awful lot to live over there.

CARLOTTA—Oh, no—but you saw what it was like in Antibes —you and Millicent. Ten and twenty for lunch—cocktails— most of them stay for dinner. And the house in London. They drop in there. Noel, and Winston, and now and then Wales. I've really done pretty well for a little girl from Quincy, Illinois, but it runs into money. And unless you've salted down your million! Look at Lily Langtry! Not half my looks, but she got her Edward. I picked the wrong period. Too young for Edward and too old for Wales. I fell right between princes.

OLIVER—Why don't you get rid of all that? Live over here for a while. Get a little apartment, simplify everything.

CARLOTTA—Oliver, I've been in New York four days. It's the first time I've been back in ten years. I'm lost already. Everything's changed. I'd die here. I belong to the Delmonico period. A table by the window, facing Fifth Avenue, with the flower boxes and the pink lamp-shades and the string orchestra. Oh, I don't know—willow plumes and Inverness capes, dry champagne and snow on the ground—God, they don't even have snow any more.

Oliver is distressed by Carlotta's worries, though he believes them exaggerated, but he hopes she is not thinking of selling her Jordan stock. He'd much rather she wouldn't. Not just at this time. She would be pretty certain to lose on it, things being as they are.

"It's like this, Carlotta," Oliver explains. "You, perhaps, don't understand. Jordan stock has never been on the market. It's held very closely. Only six or seven people in all. Of course, you've got a very small block. What did you pay for it, anyway? Remember?"

"Sixty-one thousand, two hundred and fifty dollars."

"Carlotta, you're wonderful."

"No, I remember because it's the only stock I ever bought for myself. You said it was a good thing, and it has been, too, for twenty years. Of course, in the last year or two . . . You wouldn't want to buy it back yourself, would you?"

"I'd like to, but it would be pretty difficult just now."

Carlotta is surprised at that news. She had always thought of Oliver as having all the money in the world. Oliver had thought of himself that way once. Those days when he was what they called a stage-door Johnny and he used to meet Carlotta at the theatre. Oliver was very much in love with Carlotta then. She would always let him read his plays to her. He was at her feet, but so was all New York.

"If you took supper at a restaurant it was made," Oliver recalls to her. "If you wore a certain hat it became the rage."

"I was rather gorgeous, wasn't I?" recalls Carlotta. "Remember they named everything after me—cigars and race horses, and perfumes and battleships?"

The day he was twenty-one Oliver had asked Carlotta to marry him, and she had thought it very sweet. She had even wept a little, because, as she says, they didn't often ask her to marry them in those days. It was that refusal that took Oliver out of the theatre. If he could not have Carlotta the theatre could have none of his plays. So he went back to the shipping business. . . .

Dan Packard has arrived. He can be heard booming his way through the outer office before he is seen. Packard "is one of those big, vital men, bellowing, self-important, too successful. His clothes are noticeable. He seems never to sit down; ramps and gesticulates as he talks, and he talks a great deal. He is always in the midst of a big deal, and curiously enough it really is a big deal. Every now and then, in his talk or in his manner, there crops up a word or gesture reminiscent of his Western mining days."

The name of Carlotta Vance stirs reminiscence in the Packard breast, too. He can remember when her pictures helped to paper the walls of every mining shack in Montana, along with that of John L. Sullivan.

When they get down to business, after Carlotta has left them, Dan Packard is quick to report that he hasn't much time. He's in a terrible rush. Got to get down to Washington. The President, being worried, has asked a little crowd of them for a breakfast conference.

When Oliver mentions that what he wants to see Packard about is the Jordan line Dan is suddenly reminded that he must call his office, and the connection is made for him.

"Hello! Is that you, Miss Brice?" he calls. "Two or three things before I go. I won't be in. When's that directors' meeting? . . . Monday morning. . . . Wait a minute . . . [His quick eye sweeps the desk, he snatches a piece of paper which is an important letter, begins to make notes on it. Oliver instinctively flings out a hand to salvage it. Too late.] . . . Coast State Waterways, oh, yeh. . . . Did you send that South American cable? . . . Good. . . . Did the Governor call me? Tell him I'll be back tomorrow. . . . And get me ten good seats for the 'Vanities' show tomorrow night. And you know—I don't want to sit back of the second row. . . . Now! I want you to send a case of Scotch, with my compliments, to District Attorney Michael G. Slade, Presbyterian Hospital . . . Cancel my seats for the fight tonight. . . . And get this. This is important. Call up the stables down in Maryland and tell O'Rourke I'm changing the feed on Streak-o'-Lightning. Tell him to try half bran mash from now on. . . . BRAN MASH! MASH! That's all. [Hangs up. Turns to Oliver.] Now then, Jordan, what's on your mind?"

Having the Packard attention again, Oliver explains that at the moment the Jordan line, strictly a freight-carrying enterprise from New York to Southern Coast points, has been fairly hard hit. And, if recovery does take a little longer than they figured, would Packard and his associates sort of tide them over? Oliver wouldn't like to part with more of his holding than he has to, nor disturb any of the other stockholders, most of whom inherited their stock.

Packard doesn't know. Looks to him as though the Jordan line may have gone to seed. But, when Oliver resents that implication, he is quick to apologize.

"Tell you what I'll do," says Dan Packard. "You get together some figures on this thing! Can you do that?"

"Why—I could."

PACKARD—Balance sheets, assets—total tonnage, and when the boats were built—list of stockholders—not many of them, you said?

OLIVER—No, no. It's held quite closely.

PACKARD—Well, let me have a list of them. Now, when do you want to send this to me?

OLIVER—Oh—it won't take long. You understand, Packard, this is confidential.

PACKARD (*getting into his coat*)—Sure! Sure! Of course I've got to lay it before my people.

OLIVER—Another thing. We've got a stockholders' meeting on November twenty-sixth. That's a week from Monday.

PACKARD—You give me that dope early next week, and I'll let you have an answer in a few days.

OLIVER—That's very kind of you. (*Vaguely rubs his chest.*)

PACKARD—What's the matter there—got a pain?

OLIVER—No, no. Little indigestion.

PACKARD—Juice of half a lemon—I get it all the time—half a lemon in hot water. (*A hasty glance at his watch.*) Jumping Jupiter! I've got to travel. You'll send me that stuff? Do what I can for you, anyway. God knows! (OLIVER *has accompanied* PACKARD *to the door. He now stands a moment, his hand on the knob of the shut door. The other hand passes once more over his chest, absently. Then, slowly, he starts to walk toward his desk.*)

The lights dim.

Kitty Packard's bedroom in the Packards' apartment "is a rather startling room done in the modernistic manner by the newest and most fashionable decorator. The color is white—all the shades of white from cream, through ivory to oyster. Kitty has just had it done and finds she doesn't like it very well."

Kitty Packard, "a pretty woman of twenty-nine, the slightly faded wild-rose Irish type," is propped up in the center of a large and luxurious bed. It is after four in the afternoon. Kitty has been in bed all day. "There is, in her face, the petulance of the idle and empty-headed wife. . . . All about her, on the bed, on the table and even on the floor, are the odds and ends that have accumulated for her amusement during the long day."

At the moment Kitty is working with a puzzle game in a pasteboard box and when she fails to make it come right she tosses it aside pettishly. Neither does she find distraction in the movie magazine she tries to read. And there is further irritation in the report of Tina, her maid, "a somewhat hard-faced, capable and shifty girl of twenty-five or six," that she had called Dr. Talbot but did not know when he would be over.

Kitty is able to amuse herself for a few minutes with a large box of candy and then with a new hat that has arrived. She is still surveying the hat from a variety of angles in her elaborate hand mirror when Dan Packard walks into the room.

Mr. Packard is, as usual, in a hurry. He has come to have John pack his over-night bag, and is slightly irritated to find Kitty in bed again. Encouraged, however, to find her wearing a hat. That may mean she is going out. That's what Kitty needs, according to Dan—to get out and do things. Look at him! He's never been sick a day in his life.

But, as Kitty explains, Dr. Talbot is sure that she, being an introvert, needs quiet a good deal of the time to reflect in.

"Reflect in!" echoes Dan. "What have you got to reflect about? I've got to think and act at the same time! Do you know why I'm going to Washington tonight? Because the President wants to consult me about the affairs of the nation! That's why!"

"What's the matter with them?" asks Kitty.

PACKARD—Everything's the matter with them! That's why he's sending for me! And I'll tell you something else, if you want to know. It wouldn't surprise me a bit if he offered me a Cabinet job, and what do you know about that?

KITTY (*busy with her own thoughts*)—Where'd that buffer get to?

PACKARD—You ought to be married to some of the guys that I see. That'd give you something to reflect about. Why, I went into an office this afternoon—fellow begging me to—and it turns out he can't even keep a little bit of a business going! I juggle fifty things and he can't handle one! And here's the blow-off! I've been trying to get hold of just his kind of layout for the last two years, and the damn fool hands it to me! Only he don't know it. I give him a song and dance—he's sending me a full list of stockholders—I buy up what I need—and it's all over but the shouting! Little Dan Packard owns the best shipping line between here and the tropics, and Mr. Oliver Jordan is out on his ear.

KITTY (*bringing that fine mind of hers to bear*)— We're going there for dinner next Friday, and I'm going to wear my new pink.

PACKARD—We are what?

KITTY—Mrs. Oliver Jordan called me up, and they're giving a swell dinner, and we're invited.

PACKARD—Oh, that's what he was driving at—well, we're not going.

KITTY—The hell we ain't! Why not?

PACKARD—I can't go and eat his dinner! If he's a sucker that's his funeral! Business is business, but I can't go walking into his house!

KITTY—No! Presidents and Washington, and all those rummies, but you can't go anywheres with *me!* Once in our life we get asked to a classy house, and I've got a new dress that'll knock their eye out, and we're going!

PACKARD—We are *not* going!

KITTY (*now on her knees in the bed, the hat still on her head. In a high rage*)—We are so! You big crook, you pull a dirty deal and it ruins my social chances! Well, you can't get away with it!

PACKARD—Oh, go lay down! You tell me what I can do! Well, we're not going and that's all there is to it.

Kitty decides upon a change of tactics. In a honeyed voice she takes to baby talk. This does not have noticeable effect upon Mr. Packard until she mentions the names of Lord and Lady Ferncliffe. He knows about them. Ferncliffe, says Dan, is one of the richest men in England and he has been trying to meet him for years. Of course he'll go to the Jordans' dinner now—and just to make it look right he will buy up the Jordan stock through dummies. The Packard name will never appear in the deal.

"Ferncliffe!" ejaculates Dan, as he grabs his hat and coat and is ready for a quick good-by; "God, what a break! 'By, Kitten! See you tomorrow!"

With the announcement that Dr. Talbot is waiting Kitty comes quickly to life. She must have her other bed jacket, the one with the feathers, and she must have her pearls. The room must be straightened, too. Tabloid newspapers and candy box go under the bed. Then, after she is powdered and her lipstick has been freshened and the bed and the air have been sprayed with an atomizer, Kitty is ready for the doctor.

Dr. Talbot "is happy in the possession of a good figure, a

conventionally handsome face, a dark neat mustache, a reassuring bedside manner. Perhaps forty-six." His greeting is friendly but formal until Tina has left the room. Then, in response to Kitty's charge that he never comes to see her unless she sends for him, although he must know how desperately she needs him, he answers that he is a very busy man.

"I know. You're tired of me!" pouts Kitty.

"No, I'm not, dear," the doctor replies. "But—"

"Oh, Wayne, darling!" cries Kitty, throwing her arms suddenly about him.

Dr. Talbot responds to her embrace a trifle reluctantly as the lights are quickly dimmed.

It is late afternoon and Dora has just finished lighting several of the stand lamps in the Jordan sitting-room. A moment later Gustave, taking a message at the phone that a Mr. Townsend will be unable to attend Mrs. Jordan's dinner, manages a meeting with Dora for which he evidently has been hungrily impatient.

Gustave is very much in love with Dora, and she is free to admit that she only feels safe when she is with him, like this, close in his arms. The rest of the time she is constantly worried about Ricci. The chauffeur lately has taken to grabbing hold of her very roughly and saying things in Italian which she can only suspect are terrible. Dora does not like Ricci, but, before Gustave came to the Jordans she had let him take her to the movies sometimes.

Ricci, Gustave insists, is a snake and also an *ausverflugter Hund*. It is he who loves Dora. It is he who adores Dora. In fact Gustave is mad for Dora and he cannot understand why at night she will insist on locking her door against him, when she knows how much he loves her.

Dora is not convinced. If Gustave loves her as much as he says he does he would want to marry her. She has been brought up strict and believes in marriage. Dora is beginning to believe that Gustave is just as bad as Ricci and is much inclined to hate him.

Even the appearance of Paula cannot entirely stem the force of Gustave's protest against this injustice. And as soon as Paula has gone to her room Gustave has returned passionately to Dora to declare that if marriage is her test of love then he will marry her. He will marry her next Thursday, when they are both off. That makes Dora very happy, and very pleased with the success of her campaign.

Now Gustave and Dora have returned to their jobs and Mr. Jordan, supported by Ricci, has come into the sitting room. Mr. Jordan has found the stairs a little more difficult than usual, but he refuses to sit down and rest. He will go to his room. He would not have Mrs. Jordan know—

Dora, in some excitement, has been attracted by the voices. She, too, is sworn to secrecy. Mr. Jordan will get to his room by himself and he does not want anything said about his momentary weakness.

Ricci has turned on Dora with an ardor that is frightening. He is not going to let her treat him as she has been doing since that Gustave, that Australian pig, in Ricci's estimation, has been in the house. Ricci will show Dora—

He has taken Dora violently in his arms and when she pounds him with her clenched fists and threatens to scream he twists her wrists and claps his hand over her mouth. When she tries to free herself by sinking her teeth in his hand he slaps her face soundly. She is staggering and weak when Millicent Jordan's voice is heard in the hall.

Millicent and her sister Hattie have been shopping for Paula's trousseau, and Hattie has stopped in for a reviving cup of tea. She is therefore able to help Millicent with suggestions about an extra man for the dinner when Gustave reports Mr. Townsend's inability to come. Finding an extra man in New York is just too hard.

"I'll bet if I called one man this morning I called ten," declares Millicent. "Would you believe it, there just isn't an extra man in all New York?"

"I never could understand why it has to be just even—male and female," counters Hattie. "They're invited for dinner, not for mating."

MILLICENT—Don't be Bohemian, Hattie. I've got to have a balanced table. Now, who is there? I've tried everybody—Morty Beeman and Aleck Fraser, and Bob Randolph and Courtland Hudson—

HATTIE—Good heavens! Is Courty still around? He must be ninety.

MILLICENT—Well, he's a man.

HATTIE—Anybody can get by these days. So long as he's unmarried, owns a dinner suit, and can still sit up.

MILLICENT (*with her little book listing Extra Men*)—Now,

here's the list. There are the good ones. I've tried them all.

HATTIE—I know. It's like one of those boxes of candy. You begin with those luscious chocolate creams and at the finish you're down to candied violets and spit-backs. What becomes of all the men, anyhow? You see men on the street. They're well dressed, they're attractive-looking. Do they set them out in the morning and take them in at night?

MILLICENT (*tossing the book onto her desk*)—Well, I don't know what I'm going to do. There just isn't anybody, that's all.

HATTIE—Why don't you try a little new blood? They have to be those same old set pieces. Don't you know any prize-fighters or politicians or playwrights? Your dinner sounds pretty deadly to me—except for Carlotta. Get a little excitement in it.

MILLICENT—I'd love to have someone exciting—that is, if they'd fit in with the Ferncliffes.

HATTIE—Nothing exciting fits in with the Ferncliffes. Get somebody that'll go with Carlotta. Give *her* a little fun. Get an actor, or something.

MILLICENT (*thoughtfully*)—An actor. Of course, it would have to be one that's not acting. Let me see . . .

HATTIE—A *movie* star! Aren't there any movie stars around?

MILLICENT (*snaps her fingers in triumph*)—Larry Renault! He'd be marvelous. I wonder if he's still in town.

HATTIE—He was yesterday.

MILLICENT—How do you know?

HATTIE—Ed. Ed, the movie hound. Read me an interview with him in last night's *Telegram*. He's leaving pictures and going into a play.

Millicent doesn't know Larry Renault very well, but he knows Carlotta. The Jordans had met Renault three years ago in Antibes. He was a social sensation there. It was just after he had made a picture about the sins of something—

Now Hattie has remembered that Larry is stopping at the Versailles and Millicent has the hotel on the wire. If she can get Larry she will put him next to Carlotta, and Dr. Talbot on the other side. And next to Dr. Talbot she might put Mrs. Packard—but she is almost sure they would not get along together—

"See if you can get him first and let nature take its course," suggests Hattie.

Paula is in for a cup of tea while her mother is still holding the phone and Paula starts perceptibly when she hears Millicent say that she is waiting for Larry Renault. She is even more concerned when Renault answers.

MILLICENT—Is this Mr. Renault? Mr. Renault, this is Mrs. Oliver Jordan. I don't know if you remember me . . . Yes! . . . Antibes . . . Why, you're wonderful! . . . Mr. Renault, I'd like it so much if you could come to a little dinner I'm giving a week from tonight. Just a tiny dinner. Lord and Lady Ferncliffe are coming, and Carlotta Vance—of course you know Carlotta . . . Well, that's so nice. Friday the twenty-third, at eight o'clock. . . . That's right. . . . What? My daughter? . . . Well, what a memory! . . . (*To* PAULA.) He remembers *you*, Paula. . . . (*Into phone.*) She's right here, and very flattered. . . . Oh, no, she won't be at the dinner. She isn't invited. But she's quite grown up now. . . . Wait a minute. Won't you say hello to her? I know she'd be thrilled to death. . . . (*To* PAULA.) Here, Paula . . . go ahead! Don't be silly. (*Turns the receiver over to* PAULA. *Reluctantly* PAULA *takes the receiver.*)

PAULA—Hello! . . . Yes, this is Paula Jordan. . . . Indeed I do. . . . Well, people don't forget *you*, do they? . . . Now, you're just being whimsical, Mr. Renault.

MILLICENT (*as she flutters off—in a loud whisper*)—Be nice to him. I want to see how Dad is.

PAULA (*telephone*)—Oh, no, I'm not.

MILLICENT (*as she goes into the hallway*)—Oliver, I didn't know you weren't feeling well.

PAULA (*very intense, into the telephone*)—You're insane! . . . You can't come here. . . . No, she's gone. . . . No, I can't. I tell you I can't tonight. I've got to go out with Ernest. . . . No, it won't work again. He's furious about last night. . . . Larry, you've been drinking. Listen, I'll call you later on another phone. . . Of course I love you. . . . Of course. . . . Good-by. (*Hangs up quickly. Takes a darting look to see if anyone could have been within earshot. Sits a little huddled figure in the chair.*)

THE CURTAIN FALLS

The sitting room of Larry Renault's apartment in the Versailles hotel is bright, tastefully arranged and comfortable. The furnishing is French and in excellent taste. There are large chairs and a luxurious davenport couch, with many cushions and several small tables for cigarettes. In two rather huge silver frames are pictures of Paula Jordan and of Renault himself in one of his favorite, and more youthful, poses.

Renault is not to be seen until the door buzzer brings him from an inner bedroom. "He is a handsome man in his early forties, with the perfect profile that so gracefully lends itself to a successful motion-picture career. His figure still passes, but about the whole man there are the unmistakable marks of middle age, abetted by pretty steady drinking, increasing failure, and disappointment. It is a vain weak face, but not unappealing."

Renault is wearing a black moiré dressing gown with the initials L R in white on the left side. A second buzzing takes him to the door and he admits Eddie, a bellboy. Eddie brings with him a bottle of liquor but no change. It was necessary, he explains, to go to another place and pay a half dollar more—a story that Renault is forced to accept, whether he believes it or not.

A moment later Paula Jordan is at the door. She comes gayly, a little excitedly, into the room. She has come to be reassured as to Mr. Renault's love for her and to know if he would very much mind giving a hungry girl a cup of coffee. Paula has been having lunch with Ernest in a speakeasy—a liquid lunch. She had had three double Martini cocktails and Ernest had been content with a double lamb chop and spinach. There was also a quarrel—which is another reason Paula is there. She can't stand seeing Ernest again that day. She wants Larry to take her for a drive up the river—

What Paula has forgotten is that this is the night Larry is to go to her mother's for dinner— Well, if Larry does have to go to the Jordan dinner, let him please be careful not to drink— Not at her mother's. Paula would have her mother's guests see him at his best. And Larry would have her please refrain from getting maternal—

"All right, all right!" Paula shouts gayly. "My darling, my darling! Let's talk about something else. Tell me what you've been doing. Tell me everything you've done since yesterday. Did you see Baumann? Who'd he get for your leading lady? When d'you go in rehearsal? I want to know everything. Only first I want to be kissed, and kissed, and kissed."

"My sweet! My marvelous little girl!" Larry has taken her in his arms.

"You love me, don't you, Larry? I know—but *say* it!"

"Yes, yes. You know I worship you. I adore you!"

"Oh, Larry! Darling! Wouldn't it be lovely if we could just

stay here all evening. We'd pretend it was our house. We'd order up dinner, and pretend I'd cooked it, and we'd light the gas logs and pretend they were real, and we'd sit together in the firelight, you with a movie magazine, and me with a bit of sewing—doesn't it sound terrible!"

"It sounds very charming."

"Just a home boy!"

Now there is talk about business prospects. Paula is keen to know what progress is being made about the play. Larry is pleased to report that Max Kane is even then on his way over to report. Max, being an agent, practically runs Larry and it is his idea that it will be a good thing for Larry to have a season in the legitimate before he goes back to pictures. And Larry is agreed that it probably would be a good thing for him to be seen again.

Now Larry would pour himself another drink, and again Paula protests and another misunderstanding is threatened. Paula smooths it over. She can't stand another quarrel, she says, after the one with Ernest. Ernest is being sent over to London and he expects Paula to go with him. She can't stand the thought of it. She can't stand the thought of pretending to love Ernest any more. She is even a little hysterical about it. Larry has to speak sharply to quiet her.

The waiter has come with Paula's coffee, which she drinks black and at a gulp. It fails to quiet her mind. She is determined that she should tell Ernest everything and dismiss him. "Why, less than a month ago I thought I was in love with him. And you were just one of those million-dollar movie stars. Only a month ago! That was another girl—a different person. What a very young person!"

Larry—Now listen to me, Paula. I want to tell you something.

Paula—I know, I know. Ernest is just the sort of man I ought to marry. And you're the sort that girls are always warned against. Well, I don't care a hoot what people say. I know your life is different from mine; I know all the things you've done; I know all the times you've been married—

Larry—But I'm still married.

Paula—I don't care! I'm sick of hiding my love for you—I'm sick of scheming and pretending. What do I care about my prim little life—Miss Hickson's-on-the-Hudson—"one, two, three—*turn!* One, two—" I tell you I don't care! I want to give it up! I hate it!!

LARRY—You're out of your mind!

PAULA—Do you think I could still love Ernest after all this! After what we've been to each other! Oh, Larry!

LARRY—Paula, I've reproached myself a thousand times. If only I'd never touched you.

PAULA—Oh, Larry, don't talk to me as though I were the little country girl, ruined by the city slicker. I knew what I was doing. I'm proud of it.

LARRY—Paula, for the first time in my life I'm thinking of the other person. (PAULA *turns away with a look of impatience.*) You don't know anything about me. Not a thing. You've read about me in the papers. You've known me a month.

PAULA—But, Larry, how can—

LARRY—I know. It's been a beautiful month. But you don't really know me. You know less about me than—the waiter who just went out of this room.

PAULA—We've been together every day.

LARRY—Yes—as lovers. But we've hardly spoken a sensible word to each other. You know that I don't like pink, and I eat my oysters without cocktail sauce. That's all right for a month. But that isn't me.

PAULA—All right. Tell me you murdered a man in Alaska.

LARRY—That's what I mean. You're not even grown up. You're a kid of nineteen. You're nineteen and I'm forty-t—I'm almost forty.

PAULA—All the more reason. College boys in coonskin coats—I hate them!

LARRY—It isn't just age—it's everything. You've never known anything but Park Avenue and butlers, and Pierre's—

PAULA—That's not true. I've got a job. I go to work every day.

LARRY—It's the fashion to have a job in your crowd. You don't know what it means to be up against it. To be fighting 'em every second. To pull yourself up, hand over hand, and have them waiting up there with a knife to cut the rope. Well, I'm not through yet! I'll show them! If they think I'm finished!

PAULA—But, Larry! What's that got to do with it? What's that got to do with our love!

Paula can't see what Larry's ambition has to do with their love. And Larry answers quickly that love, real love, has gone out of his life. He loves Paula as much as he is capable of loving any woman—but he has loved a hundred others and he has had three wives.

There was Violet, who was a vaudeville hoofer and probably still is. They fought like wildcats, and when Larry broke into pictures he left Violet. There was Edith, who was crazy about his profile. Edith was society, like Paula. But Hollywood, its parties and liquor, got Edith and she drove her car over a cliff when she was drunk. Finally there was Diana. Diana is a big picture star now, and she had knifed Larry to help her get to the top of the heap.

"Well, there they are, the three of them," he concludes. "Pretty picture, isn't it? I won't tell you about the others. They swarmed on me—every kind and age and description. And I—oh, what the hell do you want with me?"

"I love you, Larry," Paula answers, simply.

"You're young and fresh. I'm burned out," he persists. "I've got nothing left to give. For God's sake, Paula, this is the first decent thing I ever did in my life. Listen to what I'm telling you!"

"I won't listen! I love you! Ernest and London and Mother and Dad—I love *you,* Larry! Nothing else matters in the whole world!"

Nor can anything he says induce Paula to change her mind. She is still insisting, a little shrilly, that she is going home, tell everybody everything and smash up her life if she wants to when the arrival of Max Kane interrupts them.

Max, "a small, tight, eel-like man in his thirties; swarthy, neat and very Broadway," has come with news that is not too good. He has seen Baumann, and Baumann, in place of being interested in the play they thought he was doing, has decided to go South for his health.

Larry is furious at the news. He is in favor of taking the play away from Baumann. There are other producers.

There are, Kane admits, and one of them is Jo Stengel, to whom Baumann has turned over the play. And Stengel, it develops, has his own idea as to the actor he wants to star in the piece.

"Who's going to play the part?" demands Larry, after a further and rather violent explosion of anger.

"Cecil Bellamy," reports Max.

"Ha! That piffling little— Why, he's English in the first place."

"Well, the part says English explorer."

"All right!" storms Renault. "I can be English! I can be as

English as anybody." He is pacing up and down the room. "I've waited for this play for six weeks. I could have had a million things."

Max is sure Larry is right, but, still, there are a lot of picture actors looking for a chance to work on the stage again. And it is easy for people to forget an actor. They forget overnight sometimes. Larry should get out and act again, Max thinks. Act anything. And he has an idea that there is a second part in this play—short part, but a fine chance for the right actor. The part of the beachcomber!

The suggestion is enough to send Renault into a towering rage. To suggest that he should play a part like that! He, Larry Renault! He is about to throw Max out the door before his rage has spent itself. Slowly he reconsiders.

"What makes you think the other part isn't right for me?" Larry demands.

"It's no good," eagerly explains Max. "They'll get tired of him. But this *other* fellow! Comes on once—hell of a scene—goes off—they keep waiting for him to come back, and he never does! What a part! . . . It's the high spot of the show. You know what'll happen? At the finish this what's-his-name'll be trying to take bows, and they'll all be yelling 'Renault! Renault!' "

The picture pleases Larry. It might be all right if Max were to suggest to Stengel that Larry play the beachcomber—but not let him think that he (Larry) knows anything about it. Of course, if he should play the part he would expect to be featured, and to get his regular salary. After all he is a star. He has drawn as much as $8,000 a week in pictures. Furthermore it won't do Max any good to go to Stengel and fix up an appointment. Larry Renault is not one who goes to managers with his hat in his hand. Let Max bring Stengel to him.

Suddenly Larry is convinced that he cannot go through with it. He cannot play that beachcomber part. He can't humiliate himself—

There is a buzz at the door. It is Mr. Hatfield, the assistant manager of the hotel. Mr. Hatfield has come to suggest, very politely, that Mr. Renault pay his bill. The cashier would like to balance his books.

Now Max has gone, after discovering that he hasn't got the five dollars Larry would like to borrow for taxi fare. And the waiter is in for the table. The waiter, too, would be glad to bring Mr. Renault some coffee and a caviare sandwich, but his orders are that if Mr. Renault intends signing for any more food it is not to be served.

Which sends Renault into another explosion of rage. He will call the office! He will show them! Now he is calm again. He would like to have them send up Eddie, the bellboy, to go on an errand.

Resignedly Larry takes the cuff links from his shirt sleeves and the gold buckle from his belt and puts them in a little pile. Looking for something else he spies the silver frame around Paula's picture. He has wrapped that in a piece of newspaper and has poured himself another generous drink when the dimming lights shut out the scene.

Dr. Talbot's office is oval in shape, "pine-panneled, restful, simply and tastefully furnished as a doctor's consulting room."

At the moment Miss Alden, the nurse attendant, is straightening up the doctor's flat-top table. This done, she returns to the reception room. A moment later, just as a clock in the hall is chiming the hour of five, Dr. Talbot arrives. "His whole aspect is that of a man wearied almost to the point of exhaustion."

Miss Alden returns to report that there are six in the waiting room and that a Mr. Trowbridge has telephoned about his sinus. Also Mrs. Talbot is anxious to have a talk with the doctor—

The telephone ring is answered by Miss Alden. The inquirer, when the nurse is able to get her name, is Mrs. Packard and Dr. Talbot's part of the conversation would indicate that, being summoned, he is quite unable to respond. These are his office hours, and nothing can be done about that.

"I've got a whole roomful of— . . . There's nothing the matter with you. . . . Take an aspirin. . . . I'll see you tonight at the Jordans'. . . . Of course you can go. There's nothing the matter with you—"

At which point Mrs. Talbot, "a wren-like, somewhat faded little figure, but possessed of a quiet power, too, as well as poise and gentle breeding," comes through the door from the Talbot house. She hesitates a moment, and then, while the doctor is still frantically trying to wind up his conversation, she shuts the door back of her with sufficient firmness to attract his attention.

". . . Of course I do," the doctor is saying. "I think you're very sweet. . . . Other women! Of course there's no other woman. . . . Kitty, you're driving me. . . ."

Mrs. Talbot has advanced a few steps into the room. The conversation at the phone quickly takes on a professional note.

"Yes, I think you'd better rest for an hour and then take a

mild bromide—say an aspirin. . . . Well, I have patients in the office. You must excuse me. There's no cause for alarm."

Lucy Talbot's attitude is that of a good friend who understands. She knows all about the doctor's unreasonable women patients. Of course he might prescribe an apple a day— But she is not going to make a scene. She always has behaved nicely about it when it was Mrs. Whiting, and the Dalrymple girl, and Dolly—and now—

"I knew when it started, and I knew when you began to tire of her," says Mrs. Talbot. "They came at about the same time, didn't they? And now she is at the insistent stage. It's a great bore, isn't it, darling? Don't think that I don't mind, Jo," she goes on, as he turns his eyes away guiltily. "I pretend not to—but I do. But I can't let it tear me to pieces the way it did that first time. It was just before Wayne was born—remember? I thought the world had come to an end. The noble young physician was just a masher."

"Surely, a little more than that."

"A great deal more, Jo. That's what makes it so pathetic. You are really two people. One is so magnificent, the other so shoddy."

There is a reason, thinks Talbot. Son of a railroad brakeman, brought up by an old maid aunt. Perhaps if his mother had lived he would have been different.

"I don't love anyone but you, Lucy," he says, earnestly. "I never have. Those other women— It's like gambling or drinking or drugs. You just keep on."

Out of this talk grows a closer bond than has existed for years between the Talbots. Lucy remembers now that the real purpose of her visit was to read her husband part of a letter she has from their son who is fourteen and has already decided upon a career. He is going to be a doctor. He has read the Hippocratic oath and it has greatly impressed him. He quotes it in his letter:

". . . In purity and holiness I will guard my art, keeping myself free from all wrongdoing. Now if I keep this oath, and break it not, may God be my helper in my life and art, and may I be honored among all men for all time. But if I forswear myself, may the opposite befall me."

As she finishes Talbot's head has dropped. He is reaching out timidly until his hand covers that of his wife when Miss Alden comes hurriedly from the reception room. Oliver Jordan, the nurse reports, is outside and seems quite ill. Could the doctor—

They have helped Jordan into the office. "Obviously he has had an acute attack from which he is just emerging." The pain, he indicates, when they have helped him into a chair, is in the region of his heart. Quickly they have given him a sniff of nitrate of amyl and now the doctor's stethoscope has located the trouble. There is a quick exchange of glances between the doctor and the nurse.

The attack, Jordan reports, came on suddenly and there is no reason that he can see why he should have had it. He had started to walk home from the Athletic Club, had suddenly felt—well, funny—and had managed to get into a taxicab.

The doctor thinks he had better be careful of his diet for a few days and, if he can manage it, he had better come in the next day for a more thorough examination. For the present, if he can sneak out of Mrs. Jordan's dinner that night and go to bed, Dr. Talbot thinks it would be as well. And it will be a lot better if he can avoid excitement or emotional strain for awhile.

Jordan, feeling better, makes his way to the reception room door. With a knowing smile he turns. "I'm—I'm not fooled," he says.

"How bad is it?" asks Miss Alden, as Jordan disappears.

"Coronary artery. Thrombosis."

"How long will he live?"

"A few months—weeks—days, even."

"You're sure?"

"Positive," replies the doctor. "You can tell it like that." A snap of the finger serves as emphasis.

Dr. Talbot has returned to his desk now. Miss Alden has resumed her professional manner. The doctor being ready to receive patients she goes to the door and calls:

"All right, Mrs. Beveridge!"

She is holding the door open. The doctor is at his desk. "His head comes up, his face assumes the professional look for the next patient." The lights dim.

The butler's pantry at the Jordans' is a rectangular room, its walls, wood work and curtains done in pale yellow. The room is lined with cupboards filled with dishes and glassware. There is a built-in refrigerator, and a small portable radio which, at the moment, is going full blast.

Dora, assembling plates for the approaching dinner, is happily humming such parts of the radio tune as she remembers. "There is about her an elation and bloom, the reason for which now becomes apparent. From her apron pocket she takes a handkerchief, in one corner of which is knotted a ring. She undoes this knot with fingers and teeth, slips her new wedding ring on the third finger of her left hand, and holds the hand, thus ornamented, up to her own enchanted gaze."

Mrs. Wendel, the cook, is Swedish, but without an accent, "an ample woman in her mid-fifties, dressed in white; . . . her natural amiability is clouded at the moment by a bad tooth, and her face is tied up in a great toothache bandage." Mrs. Wendel is also active in the dinner preparations, but she has taken a minute out to bring in the mail. A letter for Gustave from Switzerland, in a woman's handwriting, and one for herself from a brother in Sweden. Brother wants fifty dollars, which doesn't surprise Dora. "Letters from your folks is always money," says she.

Mrs. Wendel has not been fooled at all by Gustave and Dora. She knew they were married the minute she looked at Dora's face. She's hoping the Jordans will go to the country Sunday, and that Ricci will drive them. Then they can have a celebration in the kitchen and she will bake a wedding cake.

Dora is fearful about what Ricci might do if he learns about the wedding. She has sworn everybody to secrecy and she puts the wedding ring back in the handkerchief knot.

Preparations for the dinner go on. Mrs. Wendel has made a big lobster aspic, worked two hours on it, and is rather proud of the result.

Gustave is back with a tray of tea things and has Dora in his arms as soon as he can lay the tray down. There is joy in the meeting of the bride and groom, and resentment that they have to go on working with the dinner. That dinner will be served fast, Gustave declares, as he puts an edge on a vicious-looking carving knife. He will not even take time now to read his letter.

"It will be the same story," he decides. "They must buy a new plow—my brother-in-law is sick—there is another baby coming."

Dora would like to see Europe some day, but Gustave is convinced it would cost too much and he doubts if Dora would like it anyway.

Mrs. Wendel has brought in the lobster aspic and deposited it proudly on the table. It is not only the grandest she has ever made, but she has done it with a toothache. Any other cook would have walked out and let them get dinner for themselves.

Gustave has found a decanter of brandy and poured a glass for Mrs. Wendel. Brandy held in the mouth is good for the toothache. While they are about it he pours brandy for himself and Dora, too. Mrs. Wendel's toast is to the bride and groom. Dora has turned on the radio and she and Gustave are marching importantly around the room when the swinging door is kicked open and Ricci dramatically takes a step inside.

Ricci's first attack is upon Dora, who cowers back of Gustave. He has heard about the secret trip to City Hall from the girl next door. As he has advanced into the room his hand comes in contact with the carving knife on the table.

"If Ricci not have her, then no one will have her!" he announces, brandishing the knife. The women are hysterical. Gustave orders the chauffeur to put the knife down, but Ricci advances the more threateningly.

Gustave has armed himself with a huge, three-tined fork and, pushing off the women, is crouched to meet the attack of Ricci. The women are screaming for help, as the men approach each other warily. There is a second's silence through which the radio plays a lively tune. Then Gustave makes an unexpected attack, taking Ricci off guard. Ricci, forced back, crashes against the table. Dishes, wine glasses, plates and lobster aspic crash to the floor.

Gustave and Ricci grapple, the knife and fork flashing as each tries for an effective blow. There is a particularly wild scream from Dora as the men roll on the floor. The lights go out.

It is six o'clock the evening of the Jordan dinner. Millicent Jordan, at the phone, is completing her instructions to the musicians. She wants a particular three; she does not want them to play for dancing; just through dinner. She wants the violinist with the black mustache surely, though she does not want him to come into the dining-room and play at the guests.

The musicians will wear their red coats, insists Mrs. Jordan, and confine themselves to Hungarian music. Especially one piece that is so well known—the one that goes like—

Millicent is giving quite an exhibition of trying to trill the popular air in question when Dora appears to ask an audience for the cook. Mrs. Wendel, in a state of tension, the bandage removed from her aching tooth, has come to report the failure of the lobster aspic. It wouldn't set. It must have been the gelatine. Nor can she save the lobster, either. There was something wrong with that, too. Mrs. Wendel thinks maybe they had better send to Schultze's for some crabmeat. She could cook it Newburg. But Ricci can't go for it, as Mrs. Jordan suggests. Ricci isn't feeling so good. He's hurt himself. He slipped and fell and hit something. Schultz will have to send over the crabmeat.

Now Dora is back to announce Carlotta Vance in the hall below. Carlotta wants to see Mr. Jordan. Dora had gone to the door because Gustave isn't feeling very well. He had hurt himself.

No succession of accidents like this has ever happened to Millicent before. She thinks perhaps she is going mad—

Carlotta has come to see Oliver Jordan. She has been a little naughty, she fears, and has come to confess. But what she needs most at the moment is a whiskey and soda, because she has had a devastating day.

"Oh! What a city!" sighs Carlotta as she sinks into a chair and slips off her pumps. "I left the hotel at eleven this morning, a young and lovely girl, and now look at me! An old woman! I took on ten years just trying to get from the Barclay to Times Square. Then when we reached my building there was a crowd outside worse than Bank Holiday. It took me five minutes to fight my way through it, and it turned out to be a man selling rubberless garters at two for a quarter. I told the taxi driver to wait and he said, 'Lady, I ain't got time to wait—I got three children.' Then I had a nice, restful luncheon with four lawyers —it was up on the eighty-eighth floor of the Whatsis Building— the Sky Club—a cloud floated right into my soup plate."

MILLICENT—Isn't it awful! But we get used to it.

CARLOTTA—The minute I've seen Oliver I'm going right home and pop myself into bed and not get up until noon. Thank God I don't have to go to some dreadful dinner tonight.

MILLICENT (*in a tone of ice*)—Why—you're coming here.

CARLOTTA—Am I! So I am. How simply enchanting! Why, of course—the Ferncliffes. That means a cozy little game of bridge. Well! I can always stay awake for that.

MILLICENT—But we're going to the theatre.

CARLOTTA—Oh, how delightful! I always enjoy a new play. What are we seeing?

MILLICENT—We're going to see "Say It With Music."

CARLOTTA—Oh—charming! I thought it was *so* amusing.

MILLICENT—You've seen it?

CARLOTTA—Oh, I don't mind seeing it again. . . .

Dora has brought in a large box of Talisman roses, their long stems protruding from the end of the box. They are from Lord and Lady Ferncliffe and Millicent is quite properly impressed. Carlotta, however, is a little surprised. She knows "Bunny" Ferncliffe, and she never knew him to loosen up for flowers in that fashion.

"Once he dropped a shilling down the grating and he made them dig up Piccadilly to get it," reports Carlotta.

Gustave, with two strips of adhesive tape on his face, brings in a tray with Carlotta's whiskey and soda on it and she recognizes him, too. Gustave had been her waiter for weeks and weeks at the Bauer-au-lac in Lucerne. How is Gustave, and how are his darling wife and children, Carlotta wants to know.

"He's got three of the most—"

Dora has dropped a vase which interrupts the conversation momentarily. The next moment the girl has rushed blindly from the room. Gustave is sent to discover what the trouble is.

Oliver Jordan is surprised to find Carlotta there when he arrives. And noticeably disturbed when she confesses that she has sold her Jordan stock. She knew he wanted her to hold it, but she was just that stony, and she had such a nice chance to sell—A man named Baldridge, James K. Baldridge, bought it.

Over the phone Oliver learns of another block of stock that has been sold that afternoon. The Satterlee sisters had sold their holdings to a Mr. Whitestone.

Carlotta is pained to see Oliver taking business so seriously. The strained expression on his face as he takes her to the door is disturbing to her.

"Now, Oliver," she warns him, "you shouldn't take business so seriously. Smile! Don't be so American! Really, you never used to be . . ."

There is a phone call for Millicent. It is from Lord Ferncliffe's secretary and it causes a good deal of excitement on Mrs. Jordan's part, an excitement bordering on absolute frenzy—

"But they can't go to Florida!" she is saying. "They're coming here for dinner. . . . But it's not possible. I'm giving the dinner *for* them. . . . They've gone! When? . . . But people don't *do* things like that! . . . But letting me know at this hour —I don't care how sudden it was, you should have let . . . (PAULA JORDAN *enters. She is wearing the costume in which we have seen her at* LARRY RENAULT'S *apartment. She takes off her hat with a little gesture of something like defiance. Stands, tense, waiting for her mother to finish at the telephone.*) Well, all I can say is, I never heard of such a thing in all my life! Never! (*Bangs the telephone on the hook.*)

PAULA—Mother, I want to talk to you!

MILLICENT—What!

PAULA—It's about Ernest and me! I want to talk to you! I can't—

MILLICENT—Paula, don't bother me now! For pity's sake, don't bother me! I don't want to listen to your silly little—

PAULA—But, mother, you don't understand! This is terribly important! Ernest—

MILLICENT—Paula, shut up! Shut up, I tell you! (*Her hand pressed to her head.*) Let me think! (PAULA *is stunned into momentary silence by her mother's tone and words.* MILLICENT *stands, seething, her thoughts concentrated on her own problem. Into this brief pause* OLIVER *enters quietly from the hall.*)

OLIVER—Millicent, dear, do you mind if I don't go to the theatre? I'm feeling pretty rotten. If I could just go to bed—

MILLICENT (*as though unable to believe her ears*)—What's that you're saying!

OLIVER—I say, I'm feeling pretty rotten—(*His hand on his chest*)—and I'm up against a business thing that—

PAULA (*sympathetically*)—Oh, Dad, I'm—

MILLICENT (*in a mounting hysteria*)—Business thing! At a time like this you talk about a business thing! And feeling rotten. This is a nice time for you to say you're feeling rotten! You come to me with your—(*Turning to* PAULA)—and *you,* whimpering about Ernest! some little lovers' quarrel! I'm expected to listen to Ernest and business and headaches when I'm half out of my mind! Do you know what's happened to *me!* I've had the most hellish day that anybody ever had! No aspic for dinner—and that Vance woman coming in—and Gustave looking like a prize-fighter—and sending for crabmeat—*crabmeat*—and now, on top of everything, do you know what's happened! (*Quivering with rage and bafflement as she prepares to launch her final thrust.*) The Ferncliffes aren't coming to dinner! They call up at this hour, those miserable cockneys—they call up and say they've gone to Florida! Florida! And who can I get at this hour! Nobody! I've only got eight people! Eight people isn't a dinner! Who can I get? And you come to me with your idiotic little—*I'm* the one who ought to be in bed! I'm the one who's in trouble! You don't know what trouble is—either one of you!

Millicent storms out of the room to her bedroom. Oliver and Paula stand in silence, their eyes following her as the curtain falls.

In Kitty Packard's bedroom at 7:30 that evening the Packards are finishing dressing, Kitty at her dressing table putting the last finishing touches to her makeup. Dan in his own room whistling through the last of his shaving rites.

Dan is anxious as to the progress his Kitten is making, but he picks a wrong time to inquire. Kitty is applying mascara to her eyelashes and it makes her furious to be interrupted. She has told him at least a million times not to do that.

Packard is too full of his most recent deal to keep quiet long. He sings a little and then is back to announce that he would give a thousand bucks if he could see the expression that is going to spread over Jordan's face when he walks into his stockholders' meeting on Monday and finds Baldridge and Whitestone there each with a big hunk of Jordan stock in his fist.

"And when they begin to count noses," Packard concludes with a gesture and a whistle indicating all is over, "little Oliver can go buy himself a rowboat and start all over again."

Kitty's only interest in the announcement is that it probably means they will never be invited to dinner at the Jordans' again, but her husband assures her that his part in the deal is completely covered.

"Jordan'll never know," insists Packard. "Didn't I tell you? I stick in Whitestone for president, Baldridge is the treasurer, my name never appears. We can go there to dinner as long as they've got anything to eat."

"You're so smart you're going to land in jail some day," she warns him.

Kitty continues her dressing, with the help of Tina, and Packard's tale of conquest makes but little impression upon her. Even his prediction that he will make Washington yet does not move her.

"How'd you like to be a Cabinet member's wife," inquires Dan; "mingling with all the other Cabinet members' wives, and senators' wives and ambassadors', and even the President's wife? What'd you think of that! Huh?"

"Nerts!" replies Kitty.

"You don't know what you're talking about. There isn't a woman living wouldn't break her neck to get in with that bunch."

"Yeah! You don't drag me down to that graveyard. I've seen

their pictures in the papers—those girlies. A lot of sour-faced frumps with last year's clothes on. Giving medals to the Girl Scouts, and pouring tea for a lot of D.A.R.'s, and rolling Easter eggs on the White House lawn. A hell of a lot of fun I'd have! You go live in Washington. I can have a good time right here."

The quarrel gains impetus. If Dan Packard goes to Washington his wife is going with him, says Dan. And if he thinks so he is mistaken, says Kitty. He can't boss her around and she can yell just as loud as he can.

With a snarl of rage Packard has disappeared into his own room. A moment later he is back, more dressed, still raging.

"You've been acting damn funny lately, my fine lady," he shouts. "And I'm getting good and sick of it."

"Yeah? and so what?"

PACKARD—I'll tell you what. I'm the works around here. I pay the bills. And you take your orders from me.

KITTY—Who do you think you're talking to? That first wife of yours out in Montana?

PACKARD—You leave her out of this!

KITTY—That poor mealy-faced thing, with her flat chest, that never had the guts to talk up to you!

PACKARD—Shut up, I tell you!

KITTY—Washing out your greasy overalls, cooking and slaving for you in some lousy mining shack! No wonder she died!

PACKARD—God damn you!

KITTY (*gesticulating with the hairbrush*)—Well, you're not going to get me that way! You're not going to step on my face to get where you want to go—you big wind-bag!

PACKARD—Why, you cheap little piece of scum! I've got a good notion to drop you right back where I picked you up, in the check room of the Hottentot Club, or whatever the dirty joint was.

KITTY—Oh, no, you won't!

PACKARD—And then you can go home and live with your sweet-smelling family, back of the railroad tracks in Passaic. That drunken bum of a father and your jailbird brother that I'm always coming through for. The next time he can go to the pen, and I'll see that he gets there.

KITTY—You'll be there ahead of him—you big crook!

PACKARD—And get this! If that sniveling, money-grubbing mother of yours comes whining around my office once more, I'm going to give orders to have her thrown the hell out of there and right down sixty flights of stairs, so help me God!

Tina is back with Mrs. Packard's evening bag, but she does not get far with it. Packard snatches it out of her hand, throws it on the floor and gives Tina a shove toward the door.

Now Kitty has faced him, white with rage, and ordered him to pick up the bag. He gives it a violent kick into the corner of the room. In answer to which Kitty pulls off a three-quarter-inch jeweled band from her wrist, throws it to the floor and kicks it after the bag.

"That shows what you know about women," she screams. "You think if you give me a bracelet— Why do you give 'em to me? Because you've put over one of your dirty deals and want me to lug these around to show what a big guy you are! You don't do it to make me feel good; it's for *you!*"

PACKARD—Oh, it is, is it! What about this place and all these clothes and fur coats and automobiles! Go any place you want to, money to throw away! There ain't a wife in the world got it softer than you have! I picked you up out of the gutter, and this is the thanks I get!

KITTY—Thanks for what? Dressing me up like a plush horse and leaving me to sit alone, day after day and night after night! You never take me anywheres! Always playing poker and eating dinners with your men friends—or say you are.

PACKARD—That's a nice crack.

KITTY—You're always either coming in or going out, blowing what a big guy you just been, or going to be. You never think about me, or do any of the nice little things that women like—you never sent me a flower in your life! When I want to wear flowers I got to go out and buy 'em! What woman wants to buy theirself flowers! You never sit and talk to me, or ask me what I've been doing, or how I am, or anything!

PACKARD—Well, go and find yourself something to do! I ain't stopping you!

KITTY—You bet you ain't! You think I sit home all day looking at bracelets! Hah! Of all the dumb bunnies! What do you think I'm doing while you're pulling your crooked deals! Just waiting for Daddy to come home!

PACKARD—What're you driving at, you little—

KITTY—You think you're the only man I know—you great big noise! Well, you aren't! See! There's somebody that just knowing him has made me realize what a stuffed shirt you are!

PACKARD—Why, you—you—

KITTY—You don't like that, do you, Mr. Cabinet Member! Somebody *else* put over a deal.

PACKARD—Do you mean to tell me you've been putting it over on me with some man!

KITTY (*she is in for it now. Means to go through with it.*) Yes! And what're you going to do about it, you big gas-bag!

Packard has Kitty by the wrists trying to force a confession from her. Now he has released his wife and turned to Tina. Who has been coming to see Kitty that he doesn't know about? he wants to know. Nobody but the doctor, insists Tina. She ain't seen a soul but him—

Nor does her husband's threat to divorce her frighten Kitty. He can't prove anything, and he'd better think twice before he gets his detectives busy, if he wants to go to Washington and be a big shot and tell the President where to get off.

"I know about politics," says Kitty. "And I know all about the crooked deals you bragged about. God knows I was bored stiff—but I was listening. Stealing from Delehanty, and the Thompson business, and gypping old man Clarke, and now this Jordan thing. Skinning him out of his eye teeth. When I tell about those it'll raise a pretty stink. Politics! You couldn't get into politics. You couldn't get in anywhere. You couldn't get into the men's room at the Astor!"

"You snake, you!" answers Packard in kind. "You poisonous little rattlesnake! I'm through with you. I've got to go to this Ferncliffe dinner, but after tonight we're through. And I wouldn't go there with you, except that meeting Ferncliffe is more important to me than you are. I'm clearing out tonight, get me? Tomorrow I send for my clothes. And you can sit here and get flowers from your soul-mate. We're through."

Packard has stalked into his own room and slammed the door. For a moment Kitty stands looking sullenly after him. Then she drops into a chair at her dressing table. She calls Tina to pick up the bracelet. Tina has an idea. She thinks that, considering everything, perhaps Mrs. Packard would like to give her that bracelet—

"What are you driving at?" demands Kitty.

"Nothing," answers Tina, looking at her with a hard and meaningful eye. "Only, I thought with you having so many you might want to give me one."

Tina is powdering Kitty's back, the bracelet still in her left hand. The expression on Kitty's face as she turns her head and looks at the girl shows that the sinister meaning of Tina's remark has penetrated. The lights are dimmed.

It is a quarter of eight. Larry Renault's apartment in the Hotel Versailles is in considerable disorder—"a disorder reflecting the befuddled mind and uncoördinated movements of its occupant."

Renault himself, in full evening dress, his silk hat tilted rakishly on the side of his head, is pacing the room. He is worried about the time. He must telephone the office to find out what it is.

Presently a knock at the door announces Max Kane, the agent. With him comes Jo Stengel, the producer. "Jo Stengel is about sixty; his hair is well grayed; he is kindly looking; time has refined his features; his eyes are shrewd; his manner quiet."

Larry and Stengel parry familiar commonplaces, Max interrupting a little excitedly whenever he fears the turn of the talk is not favorable to the matter in hand. Renault is inclined to give his imagined social and racial superiorities a ride, but Stengel is amused rather than impressed. He would, if he could, cut short the actor's account of the famous eating places of the continent on which he dotes.

STENGEL (*rising*) Well, look, Mr. Renault, I haven't got an awful lot of time—

MAX—Yeah, Larry. Suppose we get down to brass tacks.

LARRY—All right, my good fellow. . . . Well, Stengel, you're going to produce this play, h'm? And you want me to act in it?

STENGEL (*a bit taken aback*)—Well, I—(*His alarmed eye goes to* MAX.)

MAX (*hurriedly*)—This is just getting acquainted, Larry. (*With his spurious good nature, to* STENGEL.) You see, he's crazy to play the part.

LARRY—Just a minute! Let's get this straight. I understood from Mr. Kane, here, that you wanted to know if I would be willing to portray the beach-comber in this thing.

STENGEL—Wait a minute! Not so fast, there.

MAX (*comes quickly between the two*)—Now, now! What's the difference which one is—*he* wants to *do* it—and you *want* him to do it—so what's the difference—

LARRY—A lot of difference.

MAX—Now, Larry!

LARRY—In the first place, if I decide to accept this part—and I don't say I will—it'll have to be built up.

MAX—There's the actor for you! No matter how good the part is, right away they want it built up.

STENGEL—Built up! The fella's got one scene, and they find him dead on the beach. This ain't a spiritualism play.

LARRY—No? Well, you're forgetting one thing, Stengel. Don't forget I'm Larry Renault.

MAX—Larry, for God's sake!

LARRY—Shut up! Now listen, Stengel. I'm a Name, and I know it. And so do you. And I'm not going to go on and play second fiddle to any cheap English ham.

MAX (*in a frantic half-whisper*)—Larry!

LARRY—Eight thousand a week—that's what I got. And I was going to get ten—only the talkies came in. So don't think you're doing me a favor, giving me a part in your ratty little play—because I'm doing *you* one. (MAX, *desperate, turns away.*)

STENGEL—I think maybe we're keeping you from your dinner, Mr. Renault.

Max can avoid the clash no longer. Now Larry, admitting that he is drunk but insisting that he knows what he is saying, has refused to have anything to do with Mr. Stengel's rotten show. And because why? "Because I'm an important artist and you're a cheap push-cart producer," sneers Renault, following the departing Stengel to the door to emphasize the epithet, "Pushcart!"

When Max returns a second later Renault transfers his insults to him. It's Max now who did him out of the part. It's Max who has conspired with Baumann and Stengel—Max, the double-dealing Kike—

Max will not stand for that. He has done his best for Renault and kept the truth from him. Renault is through. That's the truth of it.

"You think I told you all the things I tried," says Max. "No. Because I couldn't come to you and tell you what they said. I was too sorry for you. . . . Why, every time I walked into the booking office they leaned back and roared. Called me Maxie, the grave-snatcher. And the radio—remember I told you I hadn't seen the right fellow! I saw him. Only he saw me first. Last night I sent another wire to the Coast. I knew it was no use, but I sent it anyway. Do you want to see the answer?"

"No."

" 'When we are in the market for extras we will let you know.' That's the telegram."

"Of course, you never were an actor, but you did have looks," Max continues, savagely. "Well, they're gone. And you don't have to take my word for it. Look in the mirror. They don't lie. Take a good look. Look at those pouches under your eyes. Take a look at those creases. You got wattles under your chin. (*His taunting hand is up, pointing at this, at that.* LARRY *slaps it down like a frightened child.*) You sag like an old woman. Get a load of yourself. (*At the door as he claps his hat on his head.*) What's the matter? Afraid? You ain't seen nothin' yet! Wait till you start tramping round to offices, looking for a job. No agent'll handle you. Wait till you start sitting in anterooms, hours and hours. Giving your name to office boys who never heard of you. You're through, Renault. You're through in pictures, and plays, and vaudeville, and radio, and everything! You're a corpse, and you don't know it. Go get yourself buried."

Max has slammed the door behind him. Larry, dazed, stands staring into the room, passing his hand over his head. His hat falls to the floor. He doesn't notice it. Noting the mirror he lunges unsteadily toward it. Max's descriptions are true. Larry shudders at the sight of them. Now he has found the crumpled telegram on the floor. One look at it confirms that awful message. It is sickening.

Eddie, the bellboy, is at the door. He has come back with the silver frame, the belt buckle and the cuff buttons. "They don't want this junk. They wouldn't give me nothing on it," says Eddie.

Eddie is a liar, snarls Larry. Eddie is a rat. But calling him so does not help. Larry is apologetic the next minute. Apologetic and pleading for liquor. Eddie is cold to that plea too.

"I've got to have it!" pleads Larry. "I've got to! I'll pay you back. I'll pay you tomorrow!"

"Tomorrow!" sneers Eddie. "You won't be here tomorrow!"

The door has closed behind Eddie. Terror is descending on Larry Renault as he searches the room for whiskey in the hope there may be a few drops left in the empty bottle.

Again there is knocking at the door. This time it is the suave Mr. Fitch, manager of the hotel, followed by the echoing Mr. Hatfield, who had called before. Mr. Fitch has come on a rather embarrassing errand. Some old tenants of the hotel, Mr. and Mrs. Sherman Montgomery, have just notified Mr. Fitch that they are coming back to New York and are particularly eager to have their old quarters at the Versailles. Under the circumstances it will be a great favor if Mr. Renault will let the hotel have his rooms by, say, noon next day.

Other rooms? For Mr. Renault? Mr. Fitch is terribly sorry, but there again he is placed in an awkward situation. There are no other rooms. And of course old customers must be taken care of first—

"That's—that's all right," protests Larry. "Funny, I was just about to tell your office I was leaving. Some friends of mine—Palm Beach—private car—When do you want me to—"

"No hurry," says Mr. Fitch. "Shall we say—tomorrow morning?"

Again Larry is alone, standing dazedly in the center of the room. He notes the window and strides toward it with quick determination. As he throws it open a rollicking tune played by a hurdy-gurdy in the street comes floating up to him. It gives him a new thought. He runs back to scrape together seventeen cents in change—all there is left—wraps it in a crumpled bit of paper and leans far out to throw it down to the hurdy-gurdy man.

The sight of the drop is too much for him. He slams the window down and comes back into the room. He is leaning against the mantel-shelf, gazing into the room, sick and desperate. He notes the gas-log in the fireplace. Quickly he has leaned down and turned on the jet. The hiss of escaping gas greets him. He turns it off quickly, "in a kind of triumph."

Now he has rushed to the front door, pulled off his dress coat and stuffed it around the base of the door. From the bedroom he fetches his trousers and stuffs them around the bottom of the bedroom door. He takes the sofa pillows and chair cushions to hold the heavy curtains close around the windows.

Now he has scribbled a few lines on a bit of paper and stood it up by Paula's photograph, and now he has stumbled over to the telephone and told the clerk that he does not want to be disturbed until he lets them know.

Away from the telephone he pauses, swaying a little, to survey what he has done. The vanity of the actor is still strong. He must have a good exit. He smooths his hair, straightens his crumpled collar. Notes his shirtsleeves and puts on his monogrammed dressing gown. He drags one of the heavier chairs to the fireplace. He considers with some care which side of his famous profile will look best on discovery.

Now he has staggered to the switch and turned off all the lights save that of the floor lamp alongside the chair. A sharp hiss is again heard as he turns on the gas jet. He settles himself in the armchair.

"The chair is so turned that we see the back of his head, a glimpse only of the famous profile, one arm over the side of the chair, as he has previously rehearsed his position." The lights fade out.

At 8 o'clock that evening in the Jordans' drawing room, "a large, gracious and rich room, well balanced and furnished with distinction," three Hungarian musicians in red coats are just finishing their first selection when Millicent Jordan enters. Millicent is in evening dress and is having a little trouble fastening and adjusting her pearl necklace. It is her last tour of inspection before the guests arrive and she is particular about the location of the ash trays and the display of flowers.

Hattie Loomis and her husband Ed are the first to arrive. "Ed Loomis would be one of those insignificant grayish-looking men if it were not that he is distinguished a trifle by his air of irascibility, due, probably, to faulty digestion and the world in which he finds himself."

Mr. Loomis' irascibility is in evidence at the moment. He resents having been summoned to Mrs. Jordan's dinner, nor can Hattie's promise that it isn't going to be so terrible mollify him.

"Not so terrible," he echoes. "Calling up at quarter to seven, just when we're sitting down to dinner—and I got to get into this uniform and come over here and meet a bunch of fatheads I don't want to know, and eat a lot of fancy food I can't digest, and miss that Greto Garbo picture I've been waiting two months for up at Eighty-sixth Street!"

Nor does the possibility of meeting Larry Renault and Carlotta Vance stir Ed. Renault is a has-been and so far as Carlotta is concerned, she might as well be a contemporary of Jenny Lind.

The Packards appear next. "Dan's linen seems more expansive, more glistening, his broadcloth richer, than that ordinarily seen. Kitty's dress is the ultimate word in style and a bit beyond that in cut. When later she has occasion to turn her back one modifies one's first impression of the front decolletage, which now seems almost prudish."

Millicent is formally glad to see Mrs. Packard again and Mrs. Packard is sure it is nice of Mrs. Jordan to have her. Mr. Packard is pleased to meet the Loomises. At first he thought perhaps

Mr. Loomis was Ferncliffe.

"You were close," admits Ed. "I'm pinch-hitting for him!"

At which revelation he receives a nudge in the ribs from his wife. The bad news being out Millicent is quick to confirm it.

"Yes, isn't it too bad?" she says, glibly, "Lord Ferncliffe was taken desperately ill late this afternoon. Neuritis. The doctors said he must have sunshine."

"Say, that's too—Wait a minute! Do you mean he's not coming?" demands Mr. Packard.

"Oh, impossible. They rushed him right down to Florida on a special train."

Kitty is forced to emit a single high shriek of malicious laughter, but quickly subsides as the others, startled, stare at her inquiringly.

The conversation turns naturally to Florida. Millicent loves Florida but they are not going this year. The Packards are also uncertain. In fact hardly anybody is going this winter.

"Looks as though the sailfish are going to get the vacation this year," thinks Dan Packard.

When Oliver Jordon appears "there is about him an air of detachment—he seems to be no part of the room and its occupants." No one notices him until he joins the circle, and then his reception is hearty. Packard, especially, is effusively glad to see Oliver.

Now Dr. Talbot and Lucy Talbot have arrived, and are introduced. Millicent is a little surprised to discover that the doctor and Mrs. Packard know each other even professionally.

"Yes, she's getting along very well without me—aren't you, Mrs. Packard?" ventures the doctor.

"I get along better when you are looking after me," answers Kitty.

"You mustn't become too dependent on Jo," advises Mrs. Talbot, not unkindly. "He might fail you."

Now the guests have formed separate groups and there is a babble of conversation that ranges from golf to the theatre and takes in the utter impossibility of keeping track of one's friends in New York. In the midst of a rally Carlotta Vance appears in the doorway, "a resplendent figure, and, for good measure, a Pekinese dog which she carries under one arm."

"Millicent darling, do forgive me," pleads Carlotta, as her hostesses' eyes fall on the dog. "I am *so* sorry. He *wouldn't* stay home. He cried and cried. I just *had* to bring him. He's so spoiled since I brought him to America. Aren't you, Mussolini? He won't be a bit of trouble. He's as good as gold. He'll just sit under my chair as quiet as a mouse. You'll never know he's there. Just throw him a bit of lobster."

"Isn't he sweet? Carlotta, have you met—"

"What do you think of Ferncliffe! Isn't Bunny a swine? Running off to Florida and ruining your whole dinner!"

Lucy Talbot and Hattie Loomis do what they can to step up the conversation and cover Millicent's discomfiture. Carlotta is taken over temporarily by Mr. Jordan.

"Oliver darling, you haven't said a word to me. Aren't you glad to see me?"

"You know I love you, Carlotta."

"Then you're not cross with me." She has turned to Packard. "You'd have thought I'd done something terrible. Just because I sold my Jordan stock. I was stony broke, and a man came along and made me the most wonderful offer, right out of the blue—well, I grabbed it! That wasn't so terrible, was it?"

"What do you think, Packard? Was that so terrible?" asks Oliver, his gaze fixed on Packard.

"Well, business is business," answers Packard. "Every fellow's got to look out for himself. That's the kind of a world it is."

The conversation has again been broken up by groups. Now Dora and Gustave are in with the cocktails and the canapes. "Dora is deathly pale, her eyes reddened from weeping, her whole face a mask of tragedy. Gustave, too, is pale, his expression stricken and guilty. The adhesive tape bandages are still on forehead and cheek."

When they pass each other, going from group to group, Dora and Gustave come face to face and for a second exchange meaningful glances, Dora's accusing, Gustave's beseeching. Then they resume their serving.

Now Millicent has noticed that everybody is there excepting Larry Renault. It may be Larry has forgotten. Carlotta is of the opinion that he is just staging an entrance.

Paula Jordan appears in the doorway. She is on her way out to dinner with Ernest and is in evening clothes. She searches the group anxiously. Spying her, Millicent brings Paula into the room and calls the attention of the group to her. Her young man, Paula explains, is waiting in the car outside, having gone shy on her. She, too, had thought Mr. Renault was going to be there.

"She's hanging around to see the movie star," suggests Packard, jovially. "The rest of us don't stand a chance."

Again the conversation is taken up by groups, with the cocktails, and another five minutes passed. Then Millicent decides not to wait longer for Mr. Renault. He probably has been delayed. She hopes he will not be offended.

The guests move on through the arched doors toward the dining room. Bits of their conversation float back. Paula is at the back, anxiously watching the door.

LUCY—Millicent, I hope you haven't got too good a dinner, or mine will suffer by contrast.

KITTY (*to* CARLOTTA, *as they move on*)—Isn't he cute! I've had a lot of Pekineses, but I don't have any luck with them. They die on me.

PACKARD—We used to swarm around that cook shack like a bunch of locusts. And the way those beans and biscuits vanished—boy! The guy who was late was out of luck. Believe me, he could eat grass.

MILLICENT—My dear, I'm just having the simplest meal in the world. I couldn't have less.

ED (*looking at his wrist watch*)—Half-past eight. We won't get to that show till the second act.

HATTIE—I thought you didn't want to see it.

ED—If I've got to go I don't want to get there in the middle.

OLIVER (*ushering his guests ahead of him*)—I think New Yorkers ought to have their dinner after the theatre instead of before. They do it in Vienna, and Paris, and Berlin. Much more comfortable.

KITTY—I love to eat late. We went to Spain once, Dan and I, and in Madrid they eat dinner at ten o'clock, and the shows don't begin until twelve.

CARLOTTA—Really! What time is sunrise? Noon? (OLIVER *is just behind* KITTY *and* CARLOTTA, *bringing up the rear. The others have ascended the steps and disappeared in the foyer, in the direction of the dining-room.* PAULA *remains the sole occupant of the room, nervous, distrait, looking toward the foyer in the direction from which the late guest would come.*)

OLIVER—What's the matter, Paula? Something wrong?

PAULA (*pulling her wrap up about her shoulders*)—No, no. I'm just going, Dad.

OLIVER (*comes back to her. Pats her cheek tenderly, just a touch, passes a hand over her hair.*)—Good night, my dear. (OLIVER *goes. The guests being out of the room, the music slowly comes up in volume.* PAULA, *on the steps, turns and peers fixedly out in the direction from which* LARRY *would come. Turns a step or two toward the room. Sees the cocktail tray, goes quickly to it, snatches up a full glass, drains it. Turns, wavers with indecision, then, with a rush, goes. Through this we have heard, faintly, the conversation and laughter of the guests on their way to the dining room. Now a burst of laughter comes up at some special sally. For some fifteen or twenty seconds, while the stage is empty, the music plays on, a romantic, throbbing Hungarian waltz.)*

THE CURTAIN FALLS

WHEN LADIES MEET

A Comedy in Three Acts

By Rachel Crothers

THERE was rejoicing in the theatre set when Rachel Crothers brought her comedy, "When Ladies Meet," to the Royale Theatre in early October. There always is rejoicing at the first definite dramatic hit of a new season, and this particular season had seemed pretty empty up till that time.

With "When Ladies Meet" eager defenders of the legitimate drama again had a play to which they could point with satisfaction and not a little pride. Critics found it worthy their columns and their arguments that all the theatre demands is intelligent treatment of human problems to hold its proper place among the expressive arts.

The lay public, quick to react to such general praise, proceeded to adopt the Crothers comedy as its own, and for the next three months it was played to a series of sold-out houses.

In this comedy Miss Crothers continues her studies of the human family as it is variously domesticated in America. She plays with the familiar triangle of two women and one man who are seeking either an adjustment or confirmation of their sleeping arrangements that shall keep them both morally content and legally secure.

Her primary object, as indicated by the comedy's title, is to bring two ladies who are most deeply interested in one man to a meeting in which they shall individually air and justify their claims of possession without either being conscious of the other's identity. One lady is the man's wife, the other his passion.

It is after five o'clock on an afternoon in spring when the action of "When Ladies Meet" begins. The scene is a wide balcony that has been built on the back of Mary Howard's West Tenth Street apartment in New York. It is a nice balcony with a gay striped awning over it and comfortable wicker chairs and a table on it.

At the moment the balcony is occupied by Miss Howard and Jimmie Lee. Mary "is an extremely pretty woman about thirty-two. Her spring clothes are smart and alluring." Jimmie "is perhaps thirty-eight, plain almost to homeliness, but with a smile that makes him almost good looking. His clothes are right but careless in effect, and there is a general air of unorthodoxness about him."

These two are "relaxed with spring laziness, cigarettes and cocktails." The topic of their conversation is evidently one that they have been over again and again. It concerns Jimmie's consistent determination to marry Mary, and Mary's conviction that it would be much better if he could only convince himself that they are not going to marry each other—ever.

"You're too lazy to give me up," avers Mary, passing Jimmie another cocktail. "I'm a habit with you."

"If I'd rather stick around *you*—knowing you're not going to marry me—than some other woman who'd give her eyebrows for me—that's my business. *N'est-ce pas?*" answers Jimmie.

Furthermore Jimmie cannot quite understand why Mary is so insistent with her advice this particular afternoon. Is there a new reason? As for Jimmie and the sort of girl Mary thinks he should marry, Jimmie knows that one too.

"What could be more nauseating than somebody around who's damned fool enough to think you're better than you are?" demands Jimmie.

"You ought to be better than you are."

"What's the use? You wouldn't marry me if I was—were."

The fact is apparent that Mary is dissatisfied. Neither her attractive home, nor the adoration of her friends, nor her success as a novelist is enough. There is still that old, old question—a woman for a man and a man for a woman.

"It's true—and it's hell!" admits Jimmie. And adds that Mary is much too choosey. No man on earth could live up to what she expects. She analyzes and criticizes and—

"I wouldn't if—if I fell in love," answers Mary.

Jimmie—And the harder it hit you the more you'd hate him when it was over.

Mary—But it wouldn't *be* over—if it *really* happened.

Jimmie—It's *always* over. That's why I say *liking's* the greatest—why, I've seen you get sick of somebody *like that*—(*Snapping his fingers.*) right under your nose while he's talking to you. Somebody you've been all het up about—and all of a sudden—bing—you're through. The way he sits—or his shoes—or the way he eats his soup—

Mary (*smiling affectionately at* Jimmie)—Or his voice.

JIMMIE—Oh, God, yes—the *voice!* Many a poor fool has lost you because he wouldn't take voice lessons.

MARY (*laughing softly*)—*Ears* are the worst of all. That's one thing that makes *you* last so long, Jimmie. Your *ears* are *right.*

JIMMIE—That's *terrible!* There you go. Every time I see you now I'll think, good God, how are my ears today?

MARY—You're sweet, Jimmie. I wish I *were* in love with you. I *do* love you.

JIMMIE—Try me—then if you don't want me—I'll get out. You've got yourself in this damned snooty—

MARY—You don't know anything about me—really.

JIMMIE—Don't I!

MARY—Just because I haven't happened to *know* the right man—doesn't mean there *isn't* one. Oh—it's all so— When the right people *do* find— (*She checks herself.*)

JIMMIE—It's all wrong—uh?

MARY—I don't know what I was going to say.

JIMMIE—Have *you* found him?

MARY—I haven't found *anything.* Except to know that I haven't *got* anything that really *counts.* Nobody *belongs* to me —nobody whose very existence depends on me. I am completely and absolutely alone.

JIMMIE—It's your own fault.

MARY—No, it isn't. Loneliness is something we can't help. If nothing comes that *completes* us—what can we do?

There is a pause and then Jimmie inquires, casually, about Rogers Woodruff. Woodruff's married, isn't he? Mary is sure he is. And Woodruff is sure her new book is the best thing she has ever done, isn't he? He is, agrees Mary.

"It's funny to me that as big a publisher as Woodruff wouldn't *know* it's artificial stuff and *tell* you so," says Jimmie.

Which leads to further argument. When Mary first began to write, insists Jimmie, her stuff was "as real as a crooked tree" because she wrote about something she knew about. Now, in the new book, she not only shows that she knows nothing about men, but her woman is wrong. No decent woman would take a man away from his wife—

That, insists Mary, is just what her hero doesn't do. He never did love his wife the way he is capable of loving. It was all over with them before the other woman came into his life. It is the way he loves this other woman that makes him a big person.

And if their creator doesn't know these people, who does? demands Mary.

"You made 'em up. Manufactured the situation. It isn't *true,*" insists Jimmie. "That kind of a woman doesn't fool around with a married man."

MARY—You don't even know what it's about—that kind of love. It *made* her too. Changed them both from just *people*—into something *fine*.

JIMMIE—All right—I grant you they both might be hit right in the snoot with it. The woman might think she had to have him or bust—but when it came right down to going to bed with him—*no*—she wouldn't.

MARY—You don't know any more about women than—

JIMMIE—I know a damned sight more than you do.

MARY—Don't be silly.

JIMMIE—Certainly I do. I know all kinds—good and bad—straight and loose. Some of the loose ones are the best ever—because they're *honest*. If a woman pretends to be decent and *isn't* she's the worst kind of a—

MARY—You put them in pigeonholes and tab them—a man's idea of women. There are just as many reasons and conditions for women as there are for men.

JIMMIE—Nope! If a woman's good—she's good—and if she isn't—she *isn't*.

MARY—That's the greatest bunk in the world. It's just what the book is *about*. You don't even *get* it— Damn you!

JIMMIE—Well—would *you* do it?

MARY (*after a pause—her back turned to* JIMMIE)—Do what?

JIMMIE—What she does in your book.

MARY—I can't talk to you about it, Jimmie—because that kind of love—

JIMMIE (*with ironical eloquence*)—The kind that makes the music of the spheres—

MARY—Isn't in your ken—at all.

JIMMIE (*going closer to* MARY)—Maybe not. But let me tell you what I *do* know. Man is a *very law-abiding animal when it comes to decent women*. He wants a decent woman to *stay* decent—and if she *doesn't* he cusses her out for doing the *very* thing he told her was the greatest thing a woman *can* do—*giving him all for love*. If your woman did what you make her do the man would be so damned sick of her after a while he'd want to shoot her. God—I've persuaded so many women and hated 'em afterwards!

MARY—You're talking about common—sordid—

JIMMIE—I'm talking about men—as *is*—and if Woodruff's told you you've got the man *right* in your book he's a damned liar.

The discussion is ended with the arrival of Bridget Drake and Walter Manners. "Bridget is probably more than forty, but doesn't look it. She is small, round and rather pretty. . . . She speaks in a quick, sputtering sort of way—knowing as well as anyone that she isn't saying anything." Walter Manners "is thirty, good looking, well dressed and a trifle languid in manner."

Bridget is crazy about Mary's flat, and the balcony, but she never would dare live as far down town as this because no one would ever come to see her. Just now Bridget is remodeling a house in Connecticut, or Walter has remodeled one for her. She has asked Mary up for this week-end. When Jimmie has gone for more cocktails she suggests that she might ask Jimmie, too.

Mary is not particularly keen for that. She sees Jimmie every day. But, if there isn't anyone in particular, Mary thinks perhaps it would be nice if Bridget were to ask Rogers Woodruff. They have certain work to do on the book—Mary has a chapter to rewrite. She will probably be unable to go herself—unless it is possible for Mr. Woodruff to come, too. She has to work with her publisher.

Bridget doesn't see just how she could ask Mr. Woodruff without asking his wife, even if it is business. Surely she should ask someone else and she doesn't know anybody decent enough to have in the house and at the same time broad-minded enough to think it would be all right to have Mary—and—

"And *why* are you saying all that stuff to *me*—pray?" demands Mary, finally.

"What stuff?" answers Bridget, sharply. "I'm not saying *anything*. I don't mind just having Woodruff and you—if you don't. But it is sort of hard to keep it from looking—*you* know."

"I do not know. What are you talking about? It's *business*."

BRIDGET—You're so *heavy*, Mary. If you were perfectly frank about it nobody would think anything about it.

MARY—You're *insane*. I don't know what you're talking about. Rogers Woodruff? Just because he publishes my books—and I *see* him occasionally? What do you *take* me for, Bridgie?—He's *a married man!*

BRIDGET—Of course he is. The good ones always *are*. Somebody has always beaten you *to* it.

MARY—You're *imbecile,* Bridgie! Where in the name of heaven did you get such an idea?

BRIDGET (*carefully renewing her powder and lip rouge*)—I haven't an idea. I'm merely saying he's a terribly attractive man who seems to drop in here terribly often and life is flying by—terribly fast—and after all—*why not?* (MARY *laughs again and stops suddenly—standing up.*)

MARY—Now listen, Bridgie. I know you don't mean a word you're saying—but don't babble on like that to *other* people. *Everybody* doesn't know me as well as you do.

BRIDGET (*very busy with her makeup*)—Of course—but after all, why control yourself? Nobody else does. Why be a Queen Mary in *this* day and age? Where does it *get* you? I know I'm a fool to be so decent—about Walter. Everybody else is doing exactly as they please. Why shouldn't I? But I don't. And the funny part of it is I actually don't know whether it's because I'm too *good*—or because I haven't got the *nerve.*

MARY—Bridgie, you're a scream.

BRIDGET—I tell you this is an awfully *hard age* for a *good* woman to live in. I mean one who wants to have any *fun.* If you've still got the instincts for right and wrong that were pounded into you when you were a girl—what are you going to *do* with 'em? Nobody *else* seems to have 'em. And they just get you mixed up—and hold you back—so you're neither one thing nor the other. Neither happy—and bad—nor good and *contented.* You're just *discontentedly decent*—and it doesn't get you *anywhere.*

MARY—Oh, Bridgie, I love you! You're an adorable idiot.

BRIDGET—And you're not getting any *younger* as the years roll by, darling. Even *Jimmie* will see that—after awhile—and if you think this man is the big thing in life and don't grab him—you're a fool.

MARY—Shut *up,* Bridget. You're talking absolute rot and you've *made it up.* What put such an idea in your head?

BRIDGET—Nothing put anything in my head. (*Looking critically at the rouge on her lips.*) This isn't so good in the daylight—is it? I mean, after all, you never *saw* his wife. It isn't as though she were one of your *friends.* They say she's a dub.

MARY—Who says so?

BRIDGET—I don't know. An intellectual dub—just what you'd *expect* a publisher's wife to be. After all, *you* can't help *that.* And don't be a *crusader,* Mary. Don't poke around and find out too much. Just take him while you've *got* him. After all, if people stop to investigate—nobody would ever marry *anybody*. There's always insanity or tuberculosis if you look far enough. Irene's just found out there's epilepsy in the Stuart family—and now of course she's waiting for Harry to throw a fit any minute—but she says they've had three awfully happy years if he *does*.

Mary is shouting with laughter, but she recovers sufficiently to explain that there is a chance Mr. Woodruff may call this afternoon. If he does Mary wishes that Bridget would get him in the other room and ask him about the week-end without letting Jimmie Lee overhear her. Then, after that, Mary wishes Bridget would manage to take Jimmie away when she and Walter go. It is hard to work with Jimmie around.

A moment later Rogers Woodruff arrives. He is "forty-two, good looking and good style, a man of the world with the poise of success—and an irresistible charm for women." Almost before the greetings are over Bridget, finding herself alone with Woodruff, has put the matter of the week-end up to him. Rogers is pleased. He would be delighted to come, and he will make coming possible any week-end.

When Mary comes back and the balcony is clear, Rogers has to be warned not to approach too close because Jimmie is around. He manages to get close enough to assure Mary that she is looking wonderful, that her new frock is perfect, and that he is ready to swear the man in her book is right and would love the heroine forever, no matter what she did.

When the others rejoin the group and the cocktails are passed the conversation ranges from Bridget's new country house to Mary's new book. Bridget adores living in the country if she can come into town two or three nights a week. It does get fearfully lonesome at times, and it is hard to get the men to come out.

As for Mary's book, that will be out in August, Mary hopes, and if anyone would like to know what it is about Jimmie can tell them. Jimmie has read the manuscript.

"It's about a perfectly good virgin who loves a married man," says he. "Great love—the real thing—and she goes to the wife and says, 'I've lived with your husband a year. Now we must find out,' she says—'all three of us—where the *greatest* love is—and who deserves who.' "

"You idiot, Jimmie!"

Now Bridget and Walter have gone, Bridget dragging Jimmie

along with them, and he calling his good-by with a reminder that Mary is to go to the theatre with him the next night.

"I adore Jimmie," Mary admits to Rogers after a pause. "I've almost married him for so long—I s'pose I ought to."

"But you won't," predicts Woodruff.

MARY (*taking his glass*)—Perhaps not—now.

ROGERS—What does—*now*—mean?

MARY—I give you one guess.

ROGERS—How much does that mean?

MARY (*kneeling in a large chair—back of which* WOODRUFF *is standing*)—I don't know.

ROGERS—I wait for this all day—and get here—and you don't tell me anything.

MARY—We'll talk—after while. Not now.

ROGERS—It's always—not *now*.

MARY—But after dinner I *am* going to say something to you.

ROGERS (*leaning over the back of the chair*)—Say it now.

MARY—No. Let's just be happy out here—now. See the new leaves coming out on that old—

ROGERS—You're not going to make me *un*happy. You're not going to say anything foolish—

MARY—Wait—

ROGERS—Because if you are—I *won't* wait.

MARY—Please, dear—after while.

ROGERS—How lovely you are! You're always a thousand times more so than I've thought you were—all day.

MARY—And you're always a thousand times more wonderful than I *knew* you were—all day.

ROGERS—I say—"She can't be as perfect as I think she is"—and I get here—and there you are—all over again—every time.

MARY—And I say—"*Does* he know so much—and understand everything I say—before I say it?"

ROGERS—And I say—"The corners of her lips *can't* be like that"—and I come—and— (*He bends close to her.*)

MARY (*holding her head back—away from him*)—And I'm very strong and say *very* intelligent things to you—and when you get here—I'm just a fool.

ROGERS—I adore you. What is it you're going to say to me?

MARY—We're going to talk—after a while.

ROGERS—I'm only going to say the same old thing. (ROGERS *is walking toward* MARY *as the curtain falls.*)

It is several hours later in the evening, after dinner. Rogers Woodruff is standing on the balcony gazing pensively into the back yard garden below. Mary is at the piano inside the apartment, singing a love song.

Presently Mary appears on the balcony. She has changed to a simple white evening frock. She comes and stands beside Rogers. There has evidently been a slight rift in the evening's conversation. Mary, insists Rogers, has been hedging and talking platitudes. Rogers, insists Mary, chooses to think that because she has been saying true things.

Mary has a feeling that she and Rogers should stop where they are and not let their friendship go any farther. She wants it to remain on a friendship basis. She cannot think of Mrs. Woodruff, nor of the Woodruff children, and feel that it could ever be right for her and Rogers to drift into a more intimate relation.

Rogers is disappointed, terribly disappointed in Mary's lack of courage after having come as far as she has. His marriage does not count. Thought of his children should not count. When she says that they can go on being just friends she is talking hot air and she knows it.

MARY—It's all my fault anyway. I had no business to *let* it get as far as this. We *were* just friends in the beginning. We can go back to that. At least we can go on working together. . . . Thanks a lot for putting the black line around the jacket. I think it has a lot more style. Don't you? (ROGERS *doesn't answer.*) And I'll go right at the last chapter in the morning. I *know* you're right about it. (*Another pause.*) How quiet it is down here! Amazing, isn't it? Just the faintest little roar. I s'pose it's late. After twelve, isn't it?—Don't you suppose?

ROGERS—I suppose so.

MARY (*trying to keep the tears out of her voice*)—I'm going up to Bridget's on *Friday* and I'll have something done for you to criticize when you come. Remember, it's the last turn that's confusing—by the little red house—but I'll write it all out. Say good-night now, Roge.

ROGERS (*standing up*)—I'm not going to the country.

MARY—What?

ROGERS—There's no half-way about it for me. If *you* can go on that way—then the whole thing doesn't mean a damn to you. (*He goes to door.*)

MARY—Roge—don't go like that.

ROGERS—I've *got* to go—like this.

MARY (*rising*)—You can't.

ROGERS—Is this all it is to you? Have you been making a fool of me?

MARY—Listen—Rogers—

ROGERS—We've said everything on earth there is to say.

MARY—It's so *hard,* dear. Can't you see?

ROGERS—I see I *love* you.

MARY (*turning to the railing*)—It isn't so easy as that.

ROGERS (*moving to right of* MARY)—We love each other. What difference does anything else on *earth* make? *Are* you a coward—after all?

MARY—Don't *say* that to me.

ROGERS—You don't love me.

MARY—Darling, *don't.* I love you.

ROGERS—If you did you wouldn't hesitate one second. Mary—dearest—I worship you. If you loved me—like that—you'd take me.

MARY—Rogers—listen. I'd give my soul if I were standing beside you like this—*forever*—never to be alone again. It's the aloneness that frightens me. You don't know—you can't even *guess.* All my life—even when I was so little I didn't know what it *meant*—I was lonely. And into that terrible emptiness *you* came. Oh, God! Oh, God!—Oh, *God!* How can it be wrong! —Anything so *right!* What shall I do? What shall I do?

ROGERS (*catching her in his arms*)—Do you love me?

MARY (*with her arms about his neck*)—Tell me it's *right,* dear. Tell me it's *right!*

ROGERS—If you love me it's the rightest thing on earth. Don't send me away *now*—dearest. Let me stay.

MARY—My life belongs to *me*—doesn't it? If I only hurt myself it doesn't matter. I surely have a right to love you. I can't *help* it. I can't give you up, Rogers. I simply can *not do it.*

There is a low whistle from the garden below. Then Jimmie Lee calls to Mary. If she's there Jimmie is going to shin up the tree. Before he is answered he has started and by the time they have discreetly moved apart he is clambering over the balcony railing.

Jimmie is in full evening dress. He has been dining with a Mrs. Guinness, who lives in one of the apartments below. Seeing Mary's light from the community garden he had thought he would call. His hat and coat are in his car outside and he will be very glad to take Woodruff along with him, if Woodruff wants to go. Jimmie hopes that he is not butting in—

Incidentally, at Mrs. Guinness' party Jimmie had met Mrs. Woodruff. Charming woman. Woodruff's place was empty. That was because he had thought the dinner was the next night, explains Rogers.

"Too bad *you* weren't there, Mary," says Jimmie. "Your hostess said you turned her down at the last minute." He turns to Rogers. "I got through pretty well because I was next to your wife at table."

"Why don't we sit down?" asks Mary.

JIMMIE—When I found out who she was I went *very high-brow*—trying to live up to her—till I saw she was bored stiff—so I shot a joke or two at her—and she *laughed*—right out loud at the party.

MARY—Anybody have a drink?

JIMMIE—*Personally* I don't *need* one.

MARY—So I see!

ROGERS—I must *go*. I have no idea what time it is.

JIMMIE—Don't let me hurry you. I've got all the time there is.

ROGERS (*stopping in the doorway*)—We're all set then—Miss Howard? You know exactly what you're doing to do—with that situation?

MARY—Absolutely!

ROGERS—Good night then.

MARY—Good night—Mr. Woodruff. (ROGERS *goes.*)

JIMMIE (*calling after him*)—Hold on—I'm with you.—I got hold of Bix. He's keen to see you. He'll phone you. Good night, Mary. I—I'll ring you up in the morning and if I can't get tickets for that show—we'll try another one.—All right? Good night. Sorry I have to hurry off like this. Oh—well, as I say—good night. (JIMMIE *goes.* MARY *stares after him as the curtain falls.*)

ACT II

At Bridget Drake's place in Connecticut Walter Manners has taken the barn, made it over into a summer living-room, and attached it to the house. The walls retain their natural roughness. The room is attractively but simply furnished.

Saturday afternoon Rogers Woodruff, Mary, Bridget and Walter are all there. Rogers is seeing the room for the first time. It is, he agrees, a lovely place and Walter has done wonders with it.

Now Bridget and Walter have cleared out so that Mary and Rogers may get to work. But after they have gone work is not what Rogers is eager to do. He must know first the state of Mary's feelings after keeping him away from her for two days.

Mary had wanted to be sure of herself. She was, she admits, momentarily sure the night that Jimmie had climbed up the tree, but if she had let Rogers stay that night it would have been emotion and not reason that would have swayed her. Now she *knows*.

"Well?" demands Rogers, eager for the verdict.

"I know it's right for me to love you," says Mary. "I know that anything that means what this does to me—*must* be right."

"Mary—"

MARY—But, Rogers—let's not fool ourselves. Other people have thought they were sure of their love too—and look at them! You've made *one* mistake. I don't want you to make another. I *will not* let you get a divorce till we know our love *is what we think it is.*

ROGERS—Dearest!

MARY—And after a while—if we *do* know—I'll marry you. This is the *only* way it's *right—for me.*

ROGERS—Mary, you're great.

MARY—I'm doing this with my eyes wide open. Oh, Rogers—you don't know—what it means—for my kind of a woman to do this.

ROGERS (*rising and standing above her*)—Oh, yes, I do.

MARY—But you don't. You can't.

ROGERS (*putting a hand on her shoulder*)—But I do—and it makes me love you—even more.

MARY—I know now my book is true. I know I could do what she does. I know she *could* go to the wife and tell her.

ROGERS (*turning away*)—That's where you lose me. I don't believe *that.*

MARY—But she would. I may do it myself—sometime.

ROGERS—And that's what I wouldn't *let* you do. I'll do my *own* telling when the time comes. When you'll *let* me. Oh, dearest, you're awfully honest—and awfully sweet—and I love you and you've got the best-looking feet in the world—*thoroughbred.*

MARY—But listen, dear—if Eileen says— "What would it do to your life to give him up?"—and the wife says—"I have to

Photo by White Studio, New York.

"WHEN LADIES MEET"

Mary: But no man could stop loving *you*. *You* aren't her kind of a woman!

Claire: We're *all* her kind of a woman. There's nothing we can do about it. It's that *terrible* getting tired of the things we're used to. Nobody can help it—really. I get tired of *him*, too—but I've *made him my man* and built my life around that.

(*Frieda Inescort and Selena Royle*)

know how much *you* mean to him before I can answer that—"

ROGERS (*going to the piano to get a cigarette*)—But I don't think wives talk like that.

MARY—But she might.

ROGERS—What *might* be isn't as important as what *is*.

MARY—But if these two women don't come together and say these things to each other my story's nothing but a hum-drum everyday affair.

ROGERS—Life *is* a hum-drum everyday affair. If you'd just make us see what love does—to average people.

MARY—But they *aren't* just average.

ROGERS—It would be so much bigger a job of writing—if they were. You want to do something *unusual* with them. You've got something in *you* that you—

MARY—That I think is *right* and I want to say it. Why write about this same old thing unless I say something *new* and *honest* —from a woman's standpoint?

ROGERS—But why try to *say* anything, dear? Just *tell your story* and let it alone. Why not make us see that these poor devils are caught by something they can't *help*—have nothing to *do* with?

MARY—But they *can* have something to do with it—not just let life do things to *them*.

ROGERS—How? I can no more help loving you than I can help breathing. And for the same reason I can't help *not*—staying—just as I *was*.

MARY—That's what I want these two women to acknowledge—about *that* man—and decide how they can keep it from destroying either of them.

ROGERS (*putting his cigarette in the tray on the desk*)—Don't be a child, Mary. She wouldn't go to the wife. She *couldn't*. And why should she?

MARY—Because she—

ROGERS—If that woman loves that man the way you make us *believe* she does—and that's the best writing in the book, Mary—she'd *take* him. She wouldn't talk about it. (*He goes to her. A pause as he looks down at her.*) I'm going to take awfully good care of you, dearest.

Rogers has leaned over and kissed Mary's hair. Bridget, a little startled to walk in upon this scene, goes out again and begins to sing by way of warning. Then she comes to report a long-distance call for Rogers.

The call, Bridget is glad to reassure Mary, sounded as though it came from an office and not from a wife. A moment later Rogers is able to confirm that conclusion, but it is a more or less imperative call none the less. He will have to go back to town. He hopes he can get back again for dinner. If not he will be there shortly after dinner.

Rogers has gone, taking Mary with him as far as the end of the lane. Walter, at the piano, is playing a soft accompaniment to Bridget's petulant worries over the situation she has put herself in by asking Mary and Rogers for the week-end. For the looks of things Bridget has decided to put Rogers in one end of the house and Mary in the other. It is looks that count mostly with Bridget. Her reasoning tells her that there isn't much for a nice woman to do after she falls in love with the wrong man but take him. She can't very well help herself.

Feeling that way, Walter can't see why Bridget will not marry him. She may insist she is ten years older than he is, but to him she is the youngest thing he ever knew. Walter is crazy about Bridget and, so far as he can see, they are only wasting time.

"Don't *tempt* me, Walter," warns Bridget. "I've just got strength of character enough not to marry you—or *anything*—but not enough to send you away forever—and I'm just *sorry* for myself I'm so *lonely*."

"I'm lonely without you, too," declares Walter.

"Oh, no, you're not. Not in the same way. Men mean a great deal more to women than women mean to men. . . . I don't care *what* strong women—like Mary tell you about loving their work and their *freedom*—it's all *slush*. Women *have got to be loved*. That's why they're breaking out so—breaking *over* I mean. They're daring to have lovers—good women—because they just *can't stand being alone*. Because I have money and can buy anything on earth I want, do you s'pose that means anything?"

Jimmie Lee appears suddenly in the doorway. He is terribly surprised to find that he is at Bridget Drake's. Jimmie is lost and he has stopped in to enquire the way. He has been at the Meadow Club and has taken what he thought was a short cut. He can't very well come in and have a drink, because he has a lady with him—a kind of cousin.

Jimmie is persuaded finally that Bridgie would really like to have him and his cousin in and goes back for Claire Woodruff. "She's about thirty-six, fairly tall, with a strong, slender body, a fine head and a very intelligent face which is sometimes plain and sometimes beautiful. Her sport clothes are severe and extremely good."

Bridget has gone to find the butler and the drinks and Walter has disappeared, so Jimmie has a chance to explain to Mrs. Woodruff that he has not told them who she is. Jimmie has a little plan about which he is rather excited. It isn't that he is embarrassed to be found lost with a strange woman, but there is another woman there about whom he is admittedly nuts and always has been. He thinks perhaps if this other woman—"I'm the dust under her feet, not the cream in her coffee," Jimmie explains—he thinks perhaps if this other woman were to see him with Claire she might sit up and take a little notice. If on the other hand he were to introduce Claire as Mrs. Rogers Woodruff—The name reminds him that Rogers Woodruff is his friend's publisher!

"Ever heard of her—Mary Howard?" asks Jimmie.

"Of course."

"Like her stuff?"

"*One* was *awfully* good," admits Claire, with real enthusiasm.

"S'pose I use just half your name—Claire. Mrs. Claire—that's slick."

"I couldn't keep it up long, but it's more fun than I've had in a blue moon," laughs Claire. "The whole day has been. You don't know it, but you've helped me through an awfully hard place."

Claire would have been stuck in town all alone if Jimmie had not strangely insisted on her coming with him. Now she knows why. He had planned it all just so this girl he is crazy about could see him with another woman. But why her? Why not a younger, prettier—

Because Mary would know that he would never fall for that type, exclaims Jimmie. Claire is just the kind—

Bridget is back and introduced to Claire by a very nervous Jimmie. Again the story of the Meadow Club and the short cut.

Now Mary is in and again the introductions to Mrs. Claire are managed with some agitation by Jimmie. Mary also hears about the Meadow Club and the short cut. Jimmie doesn't know just how he did it. Mary is not particularly impressed by the story. So far as she has observed Jimmie never does anything that he doesn't want to.

"It's the only thing I've ever seen you try that you didn't do—perfectly—Jimmie dimmie," coos Claire, smiling warmly at Jimmie. "Have you got my handkerchief—lamb?"

Taken slightly off guard Jimmie has some trouble playing up to the lost handkerchief, but, with Claire's help, he manages finally to rise to the situation. He can't find Claire's handkerchief, but he proffers a fresh one of his own.

"Take mine—snooks," he says. Mary and Bridget can only raise their eyebrows and wonder.

Everybody has settled back comfortably with the drinks. The conversation again turns to the cleverness of Walter in getting rid of the cows and making the barn into so charming a living-room. Such a nice place to work, Claire thinks. Miss Howard must find it so. Claire knows Miss Howard's books, of course, and liked "Alice" very much—so much, in fact, that she had just been reading it a second time. She likes it best, she thinks, because it is so astonishingly true, from a girl's standpoint—

"When she tells the boy *why* she loves him—and *how* she loves him—and *understands* why he doesn't love *her* in the same way— It's— Well, I think that's very fine," says Claire.

MARY—How awfully nice to hear a *woman* say that. If you think the girl was true you'll like the new one—from a *woman's* standpoint.

JIMMIE—Tell her about it, Mary, and see what she—

MARY—Jimmie doesn't like it. He says it isn't true. But *any* woman—I wish you'd tell me what you think after you've read it.

CLAIRE—I'd love to. When is it coming out?

MARY—August, I hope. As a matter of fact I've been working on the last chapter today.

BRIDGET—Why *have* you, Mary? Well—well— I didn't know that. I mean I saw you sitting around with a—a *pencil*—but I didn't know anything was going *on*. Anything *creative* I mean. This creative business is so funny. You never *do* know when it's going on. I s'pose the people themselves don't. Are you creative, Mrs. Claire? I know I would be if I'd just let go. Would you like to see the rest of the house, Mrs. Claire?

CLAIRE—I'd love to.

Taking Walter with her to explain the changes, Bridget is showing Claire the house. Jimmie leaves the group to come back to Mary. He knew Mary would like his cousin. The reason she has not seen her before is because cousin spends most of her time in Europe. Her first name, Jimmie decides when he has to think quick, is Clara. And her husband— Well, that's just it.

Anyway, Mary likes Claire enormously and can see that she likes Jimmie. So if he likes her she is obviously the woman Jimmie should marry. That would be marvelous. He'd never get tired of a woman like Clara.

"I do want you to be awfully happy, Jimmie," Mary insists, patting his shoulder.

"When a woman says that to a man it means that she's in love with another one," retorts Jimmie. "Are you, Mary?"

"Don't be silly."

"Would you tell me if you were?"

"Why not?"

Jimmie isn't satisfied. He knows Mary is in love, and he knows she is not being frank about it. He knows that Woodruff is the man and he passes over Mary's suggestion that he should attend to his own affairs, to plead with her not to let herself in for such an affair.

Mary stands firm. Yes, she is honestly in love with Rogers Woodruff. "More than I thought I ever could be, Jimmie," she confesses. "He belongs to me—nobody else. There isn't anyone else like this for *him*—never has been."

Mary would think any other woman who got herself into such an affair the biggest fool on earth, insists Jimmie. She is just insane.

Mary knows now why Jimmie has come. He has come to see if Woodruff is there. Well, he was there and he is coming back. Bridget does not have to dissemble any longer.

One thing Bridget should not do, Jimmie insists, and that is to say anything before his cousin about Mr. Woodruff's having been there.

Now Claire and Walter are back from the tour of the house and because of the rain Bridget has insisted that they shall stay to dinner, a little to Mary's irritation. Claire is willing to stay, if Jimmie insists, but she does feel that they will be an awful nuisance.

Mary is more and more agreeably impressed with Claire. And she is not a bit jealous of her. Claire, having Jimmie's ear for a moment, thinks that the time has come to tell the company who she really is, but Jimmie stops that. They must go on as they started.

"We'll have to go through with it," he protests. "I know Mary so well. If I told her now she'd be mad as a hornet because we'd put something over on her. If I tell her—*afterwards*—she'll think it's funny."

"It *is* funny. Just as funny as it can be. I'm having an awfully good time. *Clara!*"

BRIDGET (*to* MARY *at the piano*)—What'll I do if this keeps up and I have to ask them to stay *all night?*

MARY (*trying to play "Ich Liebe Dich!"*)—Well—*ask* them. Why not?

BRIDGET—If they do stay—where shall I put *her*—next to you—or up there next to Jimmie?

MARY—Next to me. I like her. Come and play this, Walter.

BRIDGET—Play loud, Walter, and drown the thunder.

WALTER—Oh, I can't play that old thing. (CLAIRE *and* JIMMIE *have moved toward the piano.*)

CLAIRE—Perhaps I can—if it isn't *too* difficult.

MARY (*getting up*)—Oh—can you? (*Over her shoulder to* JIMMIE.) I like her a *lot,* Jimmie.

JIMMIE—Yeah?

MARY (*sings "Ich Liebe Dich" in English*)—

I love thee more than any living creature.
I love thee, dear—
I love thee, dear,
For now and for eternity.

(BRIDGET, WALTER *and* CLAIRE *come into the song.* JIMMIE *listens with a sardonic expression in his face as* CLAIRE *smiles at* MARY *as they sing the words "I love thee, dear."*)

BRIDGET (*at the end of the song*)—It's a nice old song—isn't it, Jimmie? I love the words.

JIMMIE—Yeah—the *words* are swell. (CLAIRE *plays the last bars—"And for eternity"—as the curtain falls.*)

It is about midnight when Bridget Drake brings Claire Woodruff into Mary Howard's bedroom. They are on their way to the room next door, which is where Bridget is going to put Claire for the night.

Mary's room suggests "feminine charm and comfort." The bed is turned down for the night, a nightgown, dressing gown and slippers are laid out. "The covers and pillows are lacy and pink and luxurious."

While Claire is inspecting her own room Bridget has a chance to whisper to Mary that she has had Rogers Woodruff's luggage transferred to another room and that if he should get back during the night, Pierre, who sleeps over the garage, will hear him and tell him where to go.

Claire, back from her inspection, is sure she is going to sleep wonderfully in so charming a place. This adventure would be a lot of fun if it were not for the fact that the storm has prevented her from telephoning the children.

It is a happy meeting for Mary, too. She is quite taken with Claire. "You're so full of everything that's worth while," she tells her friend. "You simply *vibrate* with it—but you don't seem to know it."

"My vibrations have been a little subdued lately," Claire replies. "You and Jimmie have keyed it up some."

Their talk turns to Jimmie. Mary has not seriously thought that there was anything between Claire and Jimmie, but it would be a fine thing for Jimmie, she thinks, if there were. Claire agrees that there is good husband material in Jimmie.

"He has that rare thing in men," she explains. "He doesn't *expect* women to like him. And if he gets the one he wants—he wouldn't be looking 'round because it wouldn't occur to him that anybody else *would* want him. That makes a marvelous husband."

Mary, for her part, wouldn't want a husband no one else wants. She loves Jimmie, but she does get awfully mad at him. She is so mad at him right now she could kill him, but she has no chance to tell why.

Bridget is back with toothbrush and cold cream for her unexpected guest, and a set of her own night things. They are alluring, she admits, but she believes in keeping up her standards at night. Now she is going to bed, but if the storm gets worse, she warns them, she will be right back there to crawl in bed with Mary. Lightning does things to Bridget. She goes, but she is back in a minute with Jimmie and Walter. She had found them prowling the halls. Jimmie explains that he always likes to know the layout of a strange house before he goes to bed—in case of fire. And another thing—

"What I want to know is—why am I over in the barn—all alone?" demands Jimmie. "I'm house-broken as well as Walt!"

Bridget has to explain again that there aren't any more rooms. And Jimmie finds comfort in the thought that if the storm continues and the lightning *does* strike him he will at least be found alone.

The men and Bridget have continued on their inspection of the house. Mary and Claire have made themselves comfortable and the desire for talk is upon them. At least upon Mary. She would so like to know what Claire would really think of her book.

"Two men have told me two different things," she explains. "But I care a lot more what women think. I mean my *own kind* of women."

"Yes—of course. So would I—if I were writing. Women can't fool women—about *women.*"

MARY (*as they smile sympathetically at each other*)—You bet they can't. If you told me it rang true I'd tell these two men to go *to.* For instance one of them had the colossal masculine early Victorian nerve to say—"If a woman's good—she's good. If she's bad—she's bad—and that's all there is to it."

CLAIRE—Men are so proper and conventional about their own *"good"* women—aren't they? Much more so than the women themselves.

MARY—And they don't see any differences. It's just black and white to them.

CLAIRE—Um—y-es-s—but don't you think if a man *knows* in the first place a woman has had other men—if he *loves* her he doesn't give a damn—he just *does?* And if it's the real thing he wants to marry her. Why not?

MARY—But in my book she's perfectly straight and *she doesn't want to marry him.*

CLAIRE—Oh. Why?

MARY—He's married already.

CLAIRE—Can't he get a divorce?

MARY—She doesn't want him to.

CLAIRE—The wife doesn't?

MARY—No—the one he's in love with. That's the point to the book. She wants to be *sure* she loves him *enough* to marry him—and sure the man hasn't made *another mistake*—before she *lets* him give up the wife. So she lives with him first. Don't you think that's natural—believable?

CLAIRE (*after a slight pause*)—What kind of a woman is she?

MARY—Our kind. Right out of the top drawer. Why? Don't you think she'd do it?

CLAIRE—If she's terrifically in love she— Love mixes us up so—for a while anyway.

MARY—But she *isn't* mixed up. She does it calmly and sanely because she thinks it's the only fair—clean way to do it. Fair to herself—fair to him—and to the other woman. (*A pause.*) How about it?

CLAIRE—Everything you say sounds so sane. But living a thing is so different. It knocks so much out of us—*and* into us.

Claire agrees that, as to morals, if Mary thinks her heroine's action is right it is right—to her. But—if she is, say, approximately Mary's age, it is difficult for Claire to see how she could believe the man.

A woman always knows when a man is in love with her, insists Mary. And a man can fall as deeply and honestly in love with a woman as she with him.

"Of course," admits Claire. "And if he honestly *does* love this woman—*now*—and if the wife still loves *him*—I think it's about the most tragic thing in the world for all three of them. What in the name of God can they do? I'm curious to see what *you* do with them. Go on. What happens?"

After her heroine has lived with the man a year, explains Mary, without the wife's knowing anything about it (which is a little incredible to Claire) she goes to the wife and tells her the whole thing.

"They've both loved him—both lived with him. One phase of his life belonged to one woman—another to the other."

"And does the wife give him up?"

"Yes. Don't you think women can be big enough and intelligent enough to face this—without letting it destroy either one of them?"

Claire lightly evades the question. Of course, she says, Mary will write the story brilliantly. And she has an awfully good situation—to take these two women and put them together. But—

"How can your woman—Eileen—think the man is worth it—worth what it costs her?"

"What *does* it cost her?"

"W-ell—her place in the sun—with life—doesn't it—with him —and above all—with herself!"

MARY—I used to think that. But now I think what she loses is very little compared to what she gets. I think if she's coward enough to push *this love* away—she'd think all the rest of her life that she'd cheated herself of the greatest thing *in* life.

CLAIRE (*putting her head back against the chair*)—Y-e-s— but I think it takes an awfully big man—an awfully big nature to appreciate what she's done—and *stick*—if he hasn't married her. I think he's pretty apt to wish after a while—she hadn't been *quite* so magnificent for his sake.

MARY—Now you sound like Jimmie.

CLAIRE—Do I? I'm afraid I'm not a very good judge of this story because I happen to be married to a man who can no more help attracting women than he can help breathing. And of course each one thinks she's the love of his life and that he's going to divorce me and marry her. But he doesn't seem to—somehow.

MARY—But no man could stop loving *you*. *You* aren't her kind of a woman.

CLAIRE—We're *all* her kind of a woman. There's nothing we can do about it. It's that *terrible* getting tired of the things we're used to. Nobody can help it—really. I get tired of *him* too—but I've *made him my man* and built my life around that.

MARY—How wise and clever you are!

CLAIRE—I wasn't always so wise. When the *first* one happened it nearly killed me. I thought the end of everything had come. But when the second one bobbed up it took the sting out of the first because I knew then *one* didn't mean any more than the *other* to him. I can always tell when an affair is waning. He turns back to the old comfortable institution of marriage as naturally as a baby turns to the warm bottle.

Claire admits, too, that not only has she built her life around her man, but that, to her, he still has more charm than anybody else in the world. For years she had felt that no really vital thing was going to come between them, but just now she is not so sure. There is somebody now, and there is always the chance that this time it may be the real thing.

"I don't know where he is most of the time now and I lie awake telling myself what a *fool* I am to care," admits Claire; "But when I hear his key in the latch everything in the world is right again. I go to sleep half way happy—trying to make myself think *this* one will pass, too." She has put her hand before her eyes to hide her sudden tears.

"It will—because you are *you!*" ventures Mary. "But what if he *did*—"

"Love somebody else?"

"And she came to you honestly and told you how much she loved him. What would you do?"

"I'd loathe her with a deadly hate that would shrivel her up. I'd call her a vile brazen slut I suppose—and tell her to get out. But I don't believe she'd come."

"But in my book—she does."

"If she *did*—if she came to me and said all she has to say about the *fairness* and *rightness*—I'd like to say a thing or two to her."

"What would you say?" Mary is keenly interested.

"I'd say *of course* something *new* is interesting. *Of course* I look the same old way—and sound the same old way—and eat the same old way and walk the same old way—*and so will you*—after awhile. I'd say *of course* I can understand his loving you—but are *you prepared to stand up to the job of loving him?* Most of the things you find so irresistible in him are terribly hard to live with. You must love him so abjectly that you're glad to play second fiddle just to keep the music going for *him*."

"Yes, but don't you think *love* makes everything easy?"

"No! I think it makes everything *hard*. But of course I wouldn't say it. Those two women *couldn't* talk to each other."

"Now you sound like Roge."

"Like who?" The color has left Claire's face as she stares at Mary.

"My publisher. He was out here today working with me and he's coming back. It's this chapter between the two women that he . . . What's the matter? Is it too hot?"

"Yes—it is." Claire has risen and gone to the window. She does not want any water. A moment later she has walked back into the room and in a controlled voice she asks: "What were you going to say about your publisher?"

Mary—He says the girl is the best thing in the book. But he doesn't think the wife is real.

Claire—And does he think the man is well done—that he would stick to the other woman—after she's—lived with him?

Mary—He says it would make him love her *more*.

Claire—I suppose you've done this girl—so well—because you believe—she's *right*. You'd do it yourself.

Mary (*going slowly back to her chair*)—Yes. I think love like that comes before *everything*. She didn't go after this man or take him away from anybody! He was just *there*—and the sun itself changed. The meaning to everything was there—in him—for her—and for him—in *her*. What could they do?—it came.—It was.—That's all. (Claire *has turned to watch* Mary *—and now moves toward her.*)

Claire—You can't hold him with just yourself. I don't care how beautiful and clever and wonderful you are. *He* has to have something in *him* that will make him stick to *you*. Nothing else can pull a man and woman through the ghastly job of living together. When they . . . (*There is a soft knock at the door to* CLAIRE'S *room. The door is pushed cautiously open and* ROGERS *comes into the room.*)

ROGERS—Mary—I got back. (*As he sees* CLAIRE *he stops.*)

MARY—Rogers! What is it?

ROGERS—What are you doing here, Claire?

CLAIRE—She doesn't know who I am, Roge. (*To* MARY.) I'm Claire Woodruff.—Jimmie introduced me as his cousin—for fun—to make you jealous of me.—Isn't it ridiculous?—And now you've turned up, Roge. It's just as funny as it can be—isn't it? Miss Howard has just told me you were her publisher.

ROGERS—It's Miss Howard's book I'm working on, Claire.

CLAIRE—Yes—of course. Miss Howard asked me if I thought the two women could talk to each other.—But it seems to me it's up to the *man* to do the talking.—Don't you think so, Rogers? Don't you think he ought to tell both women which one he wants to spend the rest of his life with?

ROGERS—Certainly I do—when the right time comes.

CLAIRE—By all means—it must be the right time. (*Going to her bedroom door.*) I'm afraid I've got your room. I think they've put you over in the barn with Jimmie.—Sorry.—Go out through the hall. Don't come through this room.—I'll be asleep. (*She goes in, closing the door.*)

MARY—She *knows!*

ROGERS (*going to* MARY)—Be careful, Mary.

MARY—You must tell her exactly how it is—now—quickly.

ROGERS—Of course—but not here—not now—in this house.

MARY—But— Oh, God—how can you tell her—*ever* Rogers? It's awful for her.

ROGERS—It is—for all of us. (*He goes through the hall, closing the door.* MARY *hesitates—goes quickly to* CLAIRE'S *door—lifts her hand to knock. The hand drops and she moves back—staring at the door as the curtain falls.*)

ACT III

It is about six o'clock in the morning. Pierre is bringing in Mary's luggage. Mary is dressed for town and is busily instructing Pierre in French that he shall go to the room of M. Lee and bring M. Lee to the living-room at once. After which Pierre is to get M. Lee's car from the garage.

A moment later Jimmie comes downstairs. He is still in his

pajamas and rather mussed. Also in a state of some curiosity. He would like to know what has happened?

Mary is furious with Jimmie. She will never forgive him for the rotten, low-down thing he has done. She wants to know who suggested it and what part Mrs. Woodruff has played in it.

Jimmie is quick to absolve Claire. It was all his plan. It was he who had telephoned Rogers Woodruff and made the seemingly important engagement with him in the name of a famous novelist that took him to town. It was then that he picked up Mrs. Woodruff and brought her to Bridgie's—lost.

That, thinks Mary, was a cheap, little boy trick. And if Mrs. Woodruff was so fine, so honest, why didn't she tell Mary who she was as soon as they were alone?

"I have nothing to regret—nothing to be ashamed of!" declares Mary, defiantly.

"Well—I don't know what you're talking about, Mary," says Jimmie.

"Oh—don't you? Rogers Woodruff came back—*that's* what I'm talking about. Nobody told him his room was changed—evidently—so he went back to it—naturally. He saw the light under my door and knocked.—Why not?—No reason in the world why he shouldn't."

"Oh—I say—"

"It wouldn't have mattered in the least—*if I'd known who she was*. But this way you've made her think all kinds of— That's what you've done by your insane interference. How dare you do such a thing to me, Jimmie?—How *dare* you! And why—*why?* What did you think you were doing?"

"Trying to keep you from making a damned fool of yourself."

The fact that Mary hates him is not important, thinks Jimmie, if she has come to her senses. And if, as she says, nothing that has happened has changed things, just brought them to a crisis, what is she raising hell for?

Before Jimmie can get away to dress, Claire Woodruff walks in upon them. She, too, is expecting Jimmie to take her to town. He brought her and he can take her back.

Jimmie is willing to take them both in if they'll go. Meantime he wants to explain to Claire that he has told Mary exactly how things happened, and how he was to blame for the whole joke. Then he goes to dress.

Claire is the first to speak after Jimmie has gone. "The thing I've always thought would happen has come—and it's you," she says, looking at Mary.

"You knew last night then."

"Not at first—and when I did—I didn't seem to be able to tell you who I was—which seems very stupid this morning. I've had six hours to think."

"So have I. Everything I said last night is true. It's me—and—that's the way it is."

Still, nothing is quite as Mary had expected it to be. The only thing of importance now is how Rogers loves her, and that, Mary insists, he must tell Claire himself.

"None of us were ready last night to say what we must say," Mary says. "I'm sorry Jimmie did this ridiculous thing."

"I'm not," answers Claire, quickly. "If he hadn't I never would have known the kind of woman you are. I never would have seen it from your—"

Rogers Woodruff has walked into the room. He, too, is starting for town and is ready to take his wife with him.

CLAIRE—We're saying the things we didn't have the courage to say last night. So don't be afraid to tell the truth now, Rogers. She and I haven't lied to each other. I *know*—about *you*—and *her*.

ROGERS—Now wait, Claire. You're not going to misunderstand anything because I—opened that door last night?—Why wouldn't I?—I saw the light and thought Mary was still working, of course.

MARY (*with sudden force*)—Don't try to protect me. I want to know what is right for me to do—for you—for *all* of us.

ROGERS—You surely haven't misunderstood anything, Claire—about my friendship for Mary. We're the greatest friends in the world—and we've worked together a lot. As I told you—I came out here to get this book fin—

MARY—*Don't!* Tell her the truth, Rogers. Nothing else will do. Anything else makes it all seem *wrong*. (*A pause.*) Aren't you going to?—Is *this* the truth then—that you've always been lying to me?

ROGERS—Mary—don't. How can you?

MARY—*Have* you? (ROGERS *turns away.* MARY *looks at* CLAIRE—CLAIRE *lowers her eyes.* MARY *goes to* ROGERS.) Rogers—look at me. Have I only been a fool? (*A long pause as* MARY *looks from one to the other—the full truth coming to her. She hesitates—then goes to entrance and stops—her back to* CLAIRE.) If I *hadn't* been a fool—it wouldn't have happened. I decided what I was going to do. *He* didn't! *I* made myself think it was right. *He* didn't. It *did* seem right. It *was* right—to *me*—till I saw you. I'm one of the others—absolutely. *Nothing* more. You know that. You *see* that—don't you?—I didn't know what I was doing—to *you*. I didn't know anybody *could* love like that. (*She goes out quickly.*)

CLAIRE (*slowly and quietly*)—It never mattered before *who it was.*

ROGERS (*going to* CLAIRE)—Claire—you're the most intelligent woman in the world. You've always looked facts in the face. What is there different about this?

CLAIRE—I've *seen her*. I *know what she is.*

ROGERS—And you know I wouldn't give you up for any woman on earth. That's the point, Claire.

She had always been glad to get Rogers back before, Claire admits. But she had never seen any of the other women and thought only of him. This time it is different.

"I've seen all of her," she says, "her whole heart and soul and self. And I know *so well* how you made her love you like that."

Mary is not just one of the others, Rogers admits. She is the one and only woman he would want to marry if it were not for Claire. But there is Claire, and always will be.

"I had no idea this thing would get me like—that it would—I've made a damn fool of myself—that's all. But I've come to my senses. We've been a *success*. You've made it a success. You've taken the best of me—and let the rest go."

"This is the last time for me, Rogers," says Claire, quite calmly. And when he gives no sign of understanding she adds: "You don't even know what I'm talking about. You can't conceive that I *could* stop loving you. But that's what's happened, Rogers. It's *over.*"

"Claire—"

"As *completely* as if it had *never been.* It happened in just one second—I think—when I saw what you'd done to *her.*"

His pleading does not change her, nor his thanks to her for being the perfect brick she had been, move her.

Now Bridget has arrived in a diaphanous negligee and a state of excitement. What on earth is happening, and why at this hour? Why is Claire going back to town with Rogers Woodruff, of all people? Why not Mary, if anybody?

Soon Walter has joined the group and he, too, is slightly confused as to what is going on. Then Jimmie comes and introduces Mrs. Rogers Woodruff and gradually the light breaks and Bridget is more confused than ever.

Claire, unable to stand more, has taken Jimmie's car and driven away by herself. A moment later Rogers drives away in his own car.

There is only one sure thing that has come out of the whole mess to Jimmie, and that is that Mary is really in love with Rogers Woodruff, and in a big and clean way. If Rogers doesn't come through—Jimmie is likely to kill him. That's the way he loves Mary.

Now Mary has joined them and Pierre has brought in a tray of coffee. Everybody has tried to change the conversation without much success. Bridgie doesn't see why either Mary or Jimmie should go back to town. It's hot there, and nothing else will be changed.

"There's nothing so bad that a little physical comfort doesn't make it better," insists Bridgie. "When Frank was having affairs with other women I was always so thankful I had a good bed of *my own*—and could have my breakfast *in* it."

They have put Bridgie in the chaise-longue and covered her up with a blanket to stop her sneezing and she is babbling on with enthusiasm.

"Of course, it's happened to me *so often* I never *expect* it to turn out right—" says Bridgie. "But when a strong intelligent woman *at last* persuades herself that a man is *the* thing in life she wants—of course she's the biggest *fool of all.*"

No one is of a mind to take issue with Bridgie. Not even Mary. Which encourages her to go on.

Bridget—Why not be frank—after all *why not?* You might as well spit the truth out about *yourself*—before other people do. Of *course* I think you've been a fool, Mary—but I love you all the more for it. It makes me feel so much *closer* to you.

Mary—Keep right on, Bridgie.

Bridget—I intend to. I think you've made a rotten mess of the whole thing, Jimmie. If Mary hadn't *seen* the wife and known how darn nice she is—she wouldn't have had her on her conscience. And if Rogers hadn't had to stand up and face the *two* of you—I bet he would have taken *you*—if he could have done it—well—*quietly*—you know. Lord knows I hold no brief for *men*—but *after all*—you can't expect *too* much of them. With both women in the same room—especially *unexpectedly*—you don't think he would say—right off the bat—"I'll take *you*—not my wife"—now *do* you? (Walter *who is sitting near the chaise-longue, touches* Bridget's *elbow with his foot—making her spill her coffee a little.*) Walter's being *subtle.* He thinks it would be a good idea if I got out and left you alone with Jimmie. I *don't.* I think the raw naked nasty truth is the best thing in the world for a broken heart. Don't be ass enough to try to patch things up for Mary, Jimmie—now that you've done the *worst* thing you possibly could do to her. The only real unhappiness on earth for a woman—is losing a man. I didn't begin to suffer, when Frank *died*—as I did when he was having an affair. It's a different thing entirely. Death is—well—it's just *death*—and that's the end of it. If you lose a man that way at least you know it's not *your* fault. Death isn't nature's greatest mistake—falling in love is. If we didn't have to do that—the *real* misery would be cut right out of life—but, my God, there wouldn't be any fun either—so what are you going to do about it?

Jimmie (*sitting on the floor—his back leaning against* Mary's *knees*)—You're right, Bridgie. If I'd minded my own damned business.

Bridget—Of course I'm right.

Mary—You hadn't anything to do with it really, Jimmie.

Jimmie—What?

Mary—I should have known sometime just what she was like.

Walter—You mean you would have *known her*—sometime—through *him.*

Mary—Yes.

Bridget—You seem to be *amazingly* intelligent this morning, Walter. You'll get over it, Mary. By Christmas he'll just be on your list of casualties.

Walter—And the wife will probably take him back—by that time.

Mary—No—*never!*

Bridget—What makes you so sure?

Mary—She doesn't want him now. That's what I've done to her. I'll never forget *her eyes—what she saw.* (*They are all quiet—staring thoughtfully.*)

THE CURTAIN FALLS

DESIGN FOR LIVING

A Comedy in Three Acts

By Noel Coward

ANY editor of a theatre year book this particular season would find it fairly difficult to exclude Noel Coward's widely discussed comedy, "Design for Living," whatever his convictions might be regarding its quality as a play.

Recent theatre history offers no parallel record in which the approach of a new play was attended by quite the same excitement. There were actually requests for seats months before any theatre had been engaged or any date of production agreed upon. And for three months previous to the first performance, which was given the night of January 24 at the Ethel Barrymore Theatre in New York, following a Cleveland opening, there was a stream of certified checks, telegraph orders, money orders and frequently actual cash received in advance payment for seats.

The astonishing popularity of this particular attraction is most easily, and probably most correctly, explained by the fact that in addition to Mr. Coward's reputation for writing smart dialogue to clothe intelligent comedy plots, he had announced that this particular comedy was being deliberately written for himself and his friends, Alfred Lunt and Lynn Fontanne of the New York Theatre Guild.

Here were combined three outstanding theatre personalities. Mr. Lunt and Miss Fontanne have been at the head of the Theatre Guild's first acting company over a period of years, and have followed one personal success with another until their individual followings are unquestionably extensive. Mr. Coward likewise has grown steadily in favor with a large public.

"Design for Living," for all the fairly outrageous liberties it takes with so-called established moral standards, proved to be highly amusing entertainment to the general run of upper middle-class playgoers. The first three months of the run were played to a succession of sold-out houses. When a break did come, it was comparatively insignificant and other weeks were added.

At curtain-rise it is 10 o'clock on a bright spring morning in Paris. The scene is a rather shabby studio.

Shortly Gilda, "a good-looking woman of about thirty," appears with coffee pot and milk jug. She is placing them on a table when a knock at the door attracts her. Before answering she disappears into a second room and, returning, carefully closes the door behind her. Then she lets in Ernest Friedman. Ernest might be "any age between forty and fifty. He is rather precise in manner." He carries a good-sized picture under his arm which, he explains, he is more than eager to show to Otto. It is a Matisse and has been secured after considerable effort.

Otto, Gilda explains, is asleep. He has suffered with neuralgia all night. He is now sleeping with a couple of hot water bottles and should not be disturbed.

Ernest is disappointed. He had counted much on Otto's pleasure in seeing the Matisse. He is very fond of Otto. So, too, is Gilda. Rather vehemently certain of it this morning.

Something, thinks Ernest, seems wrong with Gilda, though she is quick to deny the suggestion. And then as quick to confirm it.

"I'm sick of this studio," she announces suddenly. It's squalid! I wish I were somewhere quite different. I wish I were somebody quite different. I wish I were a nice-minded British matron, with a husband, a cook, and a baby. I wish I believed in God and the *Daily Mail* and 'Mother India!'"

"I wish you'd tell me what's upsetting you."

"Glands, I expect! Everything's glandular. I read a book about it the other day. Ernest, if you only realized what was going on inside you, you'd be bitterly offended!"

"I'm much more interested in what's going on inside you."

Ernest is very fond of Gilda, and her present state of mind is disturbing to him. When she, a little hysterically, presents herself as a disallusioned egoist, thinking of herself to the exclusion of others, and boring herself desperately, Ernest is troubled. Suddenly he would know more.

"Will you explain one thing to me really satisfactorily?" he demands.

"What?"

"Why don't you marry Otto?"

Gilda—It's very funny that underneath all your worldly wisdom you're nothing but a respectable little old woman in a jet bonnet.

Ernest—You don't like being disapproved of, do you?

Gilda—Does anybody?

Ernest—Anyhow, I don't disapprove of you, yourself—of

course, you're as obstinate as a mule—

GILDA—There you go again! "Strong as an ox!" "Obstinate as a mule!" Just a pack of Animal Grab—that's what I am! Bring out all the other cards. "Gentle as a dove!" "Playful as a kitten!" "Black as a crow!"

ERNEST—"Brave as a lion!"

GILDA—Oh, no, Ernest! You couldn't think that, disapproving of me as you do.

ERNEST—I was about to explain, when you so rudely interrupted, that it isn't you, yourself, I disapprove of. It's your mode of life.

GILDA (*laughing slightly*)—Oh, I see!

ERNEST—Your life is so dreadfully untidy, Gilda.

GILDA—I'm not a tidy person.

ERNEST—You haven't yet answered my original question.

GILDA—Why don't I marry Otto?

ERNEST—Yes. Is there a real reason, or just a lot of faintly affected theories?

GILDA—There's a very real reason.

ERNEST—Well?

GILDA—I love him. (*She glances towards the bedroom door and says louder:*) I love him.

ERNEST—All right! All right, there's no need to shout.

GILDA—Yes, there is, every need. I should like to scream.

ERNEST—That would surely be very bad for Otto's neuralgia.

GILDA (*calming down*)—The only reasons for me to marry would be these: To have children; to have a home; to have a background for social activities, and to be provided for. Well, I don't like children; I don't wish for a home; I can't bear social activities, and I have a small but adequate income of my own. I love Otto deeply, and I respect him as a person and as an artist. To be tied legally to him would be repellent to me and to him, too. It's not a dashing bohemian gesture to Free Love: we just feel like that, both of us. Now, are you satisfied?

ERNEST—If you are.

Now Ernest has news that causes Gilda to jump a little. Leo is back and, of all places, is stopping at the George V! Evidently Leo has made a lot of money. Which causes Ernest to wonder how Gilda will feel about a successful Leo. And how will Otto feel?

"I know what you're getting at, but you're wrong, as usual," Gilda informs him. "Everybody's always wrong about Leo and

Otto and me. I'm not jealous of Leo's money and success, and Otto won't be either when he knows. That's what you were suspecting, wasn't it?"

"Perhaps."

GILDA (*turning away*)—I think you should grasp the situation a little better, having known us all for so long.

ERNEST—Otto and Leo knew each other first.

GILDA—Yes, yes, yes, yes—I know all about that! I came along and spoiled everything! Go on, dear—

ERNEST—I didn't say that.

GILDA (*sharply*)—It's what you meant.

ERNEST—I think, perhaps, you may have spoilt yourself a little.

GILDA—Distrust of women frequently sets in at your age, Ernest.

ERNEST—I cannot, for the life of me, imagine why I'm so fond of you. You have such abominable manners.

GILDA—It's probably the scarlet life I live, causing me to degenerate into a shrew.

ERNEST—Very likely.

GILDA (*suddenly, leaning over the back of his chair, with her arms around him*)—I'm sorry—about my bad manners, I mean. Please forgive me. You're a darling, and you love us a lot, don't you? All three of us? Me a little less than Otto and Leo because I'm a woman and, therefore, unreliable. Isn't that true?

ERNEST (*patting her hand*)—Quite.

GILDA (*leaving him*)—Your affection is a scared thing, though. Too frightened; too apprehensive of consequences. Leave us to grapple with the consequences, my dear. We're bound to have a bad time every now and then, but, at least, we know it. We're aware of a whole lot of things. Look at us clearly as human beings, rather peculiar human beings, I grant you, and don't be prejudiced by our lack of social grace. I laughed too loudly just now at the thought of Leo being rich and rare. Too loudly because I was uneasy, not jealous. I don't want him to be any different, that's all.

ERNEST—I see.

GILDA—Do you? Do you really? I doubt it. I don't see how anyone outside could. But I would like you to understand one thing absolutely and completely. I love Otto—whatever happens, I love Otto.

ERNEST—I never suggested for a moment that you didn't.

GILDA—Wait. Wait and see. The immediate horizon is gray and forbidding and dangerous. You don't know what I'm talking about and you probably think I've gone mad, and I can't explain—not now. But, darling Ernest, there's a crisis on. A full-blooded, emotional crisis; and when I need you, which I expect will be very soon, I shall yell! I shall yell like mad!

There are reasons why Ernest should have felt that something is wrong, Gilda admits. Much is wrong with her, with her instincts, and her damned femininity that excites in her a complete nausea on occasion. Why is it that she can go so far keeping faith with her highest standards and then suddenly go down into the mud?

"Take a look at this, my darling," shouts Gilda, standing defiantly before him. "Measure it with your eyes. Portrait of a woman in three cardinal colors. Portrait of a too loving spirit tied down to a predatory feminine carcass!"

She is still excited when a noise outside the door attracts them. It is Otto and Otto now fairly bounds into the room. He is "tall and good-looking, wearing a traveling coat and hat and carrying a suitcase and a large package of painting materials."

Otto, too, has surprised them. He has come home, without warning, because he has finished the picture he was doing, and brought the picture with him. The lady whose portrait it is had said it was out of drawing and made her look podgy, but Otto had told her that it was overeating and lack of exercise that had made her look podgy and she had practically ordered him out of the house. But, having the picture, he is content.

Now Otto has become conscious that something is wrong with them; that their greeting is strangely restrained. There must be a reason for that.

"Gilda has neuralgia," reports Ernest, wryly. "It's glandular."

And Gilda, covering a distressing nervousness, calls to Otto to keep on his hat and coat. He must go to the hotel—the George V hotel—and meet Leo! There's a surprise for him! Leo is back from America; his play is still running in Chicago, and he has sold the movie rights to Hollywood and he is at the George V!

Otto *is* surprised. Otto is also delighted! This is by way of being a super-homecoming. Leo has been away too long. Now they can all three be together again.

Ernest and Otto go now to fetch Leo. Gilda, stiffening in Otto's arms as he kisses her, has bidden him be careful.

"I love you very much, so be careful crossing roads, won't

you?" she says, smiling gayly, but with a strain in her voice. "Look to the right and the left and all around everything, and don't do anything foolish and impulsive. Please remember, there's a dear—"

"Be quiet, don't pester me with your attentions!" answers Otto. And then, with mock earnestness, he turns to Ernest: "She's crazy about me, poor little thing; just crazy about me."

Gilda is still at the outer door staring after them when the bedroom door opens and Leo appears. "He is slim and nervous and obviously making a tremendous effort to control himself."

What are they to do now? Leo wants to know. There are not many minutes to decide.

"It's nice being human beings, isn't it?" says Leo. "I'm sure God's angels must envy us."

Gilda—Whom do you love best? Otto or me?

Leo—Silly question.

Gilda—Answer me, anyhow.

Leo—How can I? Be sensible! In any case, what does it matter?

Gilda—It's important to me.

Leo—No, it isn't—not really. That's not what's important. What we did was inevitable. It's been inevitable for years. It doesn't matter who loves who the most; you can't line up things like that mathematically. We all love each other a lot, far too much, and we've made a bloody mess of it! That was inevitable, too.

Gilda—We must get it straight, somehow.

Leo—Yes, we must get it straight and tie it up with ribbons with a bow on top. Pity it isn't Valentine's Day!

Gilda—Can't we laugh a little? Isn't it a joke? Can't we make it a joke?

Leo—Yes, it's a joke. It's a joke, all right. We can laugh until our sides ache. Let's start, shall we?

Gilda—What's the truth of it? The absolute deep-down truth? Until we really know that, we can't grapple with it. We can't do a thing. We can only sit here flicking words about.

Leo—It should be easy, you know. The actual facts are so simple. I love you. You love me. You love Otto. I love Otto. Otto loves you. Otto loves me. There now! Start to unravel from there.

Gilda—We've always been honest, though, all of us. Honest with each other, I mean. That's something to go on, isn't it?

LEO—In this particular instance, it makes the whole thing far more complicated. If we were ordinary moral, high-thinking citizens we could carry on a backstairs affair for weeks without saying a word about it. We could lunch and dine together, all three, and not give anything away by so much as a look.

GILDA—If we were ordinary moral, high-thinking citizens we shouldn't have had an affair at all.

LEO—Perhaps not. We should have crushed it down. And the more we crushed it down the more we should have resented Otto, until we hated him. Just think of hating Otto—

GILDA—Just think of him hating us.

LEO—Do you think he will?

GILDA (*inexorably*)—Yes.

LEO (*walking about the room*)—Oh, no, no—he mustn't! It's too silly. He must see how unimportant it is, really.

GILDA—There's no question of not telling him, is there?

LEO—Of course not.

GILDA—We could pretend that you just arrived here and missed them on the way.

LEO—So we could, dear—so we could.

GILDA—Do you think we're working each other up? Do you think we're imagining it to be more serious than it really is?

LEO—Perhaps.

GILDA—Do you think, after all, he may not mind quite so dreadfully?

LEO—He'll mind just as much as you or I would under similar circumstances. Probably a little bit more. Imagine that for a moment, will you? Put yourself in his place.

GILDA (*hopelessly*)—Oh, don't!

They had neither been sorry for what happened the night before. They had given away utterly and, as it seemed, quite naturally. They were for the time two different beings. It was all so violently romantic and gay. The champagne, the lights, the toasts to Otto—

Nor will either let the other take the blame now. "A silly pride made me show off for you," insists Leo; "parade my attraction for you, like a mannequin. New spring model, with a few extra flounces!"

"That's my story, Leo; you can't steal it from me," answers Gilda. "I've been wallowing in self-abasement, dragging out my last night's femininity and spitting on it. I've taken the blame onto myself for the whole thing. Ernest was quite shocked; you should have been listening at the door."

"I was."

And what will happen now, when Otto comes back? Is it possible that jealousy has played a part in this situation? Is it possible there will be a row? And blows?

Leo and Otto had had a row once, when they had first known Gilda, and there had been blows. Leo had pushed Otto into a bath tub and turned on the water. Whenever Otto had tried to get out Leo had pushed him back. It was a very narrow bath—and—

They are laughing uproariously at Leo's description, fairly groaning in their effort to control themselves—when the door opens and Otto walks into the room. The laughter dies out of their faces. Leo has gone to Otto and taken both his hands in welcome. But Otto is solemn-faced.

Why had they stopped laughing so suddenly at the sight of him? Something has changed Leo. He looks different. What is the matter with them? What has happened? What is it they seem to be hinting at that's wrong?

"It's serious, Otto," says Leo. "Please try to be wise about it."

"How the hell can I be wise about it if I don't know what it is?" And then, as Leo turns away from him, he adds—"It wouldn't be what I think it is, would it? I mean, what's just dropped into my mind? It isn't that, is it?"

Their echoing confessions have registered dully on his ears, but he listens quietly as Leo, nervously and swiftly, tries to explain what had happened. He had arrived the afternoon before. He had thrown his bags in the hotel room and dashed for the studio. After that he and Gilda had dined together and he had spent the night in the studio. Nothing had been planned. Whatever was in their minds had been there for ages. True, they might have controlled themselves, but they didn't.

They might have waited until Otto came back, as he suggests, and then told him how they felt. But that would not have made it any better. Nor any more honest. They are, Leo insists, being as honest now as they know how to be. Chance had caught them, as it was bound to catch them eventually, and they were doomed to it from the first moment.

"You don't suppose we enjoy telling you, do you?" shrills Leo. "You don't suppose I like watching the pleasure at seeing me fade out of your eyes? If it wasn't that we loved you deeply, both of us, we'd lie to you and deceive you indefinitely, rather than inflict this horror on ourselves."

"And what about the horror you're inflicting on me?" queries Otto, his voice rising. "So you love me, do you? Both of you love me deeply! I don't want a love that can shut me out and make me feel more utterly alone than I have ever felt in my life before."

It is Gilda who pleads with him now to hold on to reason. He could never be shut out of their love. They have known that what has happened might have happened; they discussed it rationally and calmly. Now that it has happened they must fight it, or it will distort and overbalance everything. If only they could tide over that moment—

OTTO—Why should we tide over this moment? It's a big moment! Let's make the most of it. (*He gives a little laugh.*)

LEO—I suppose that way of taking it is as good as any.

GILDA—No, it isn't—it isn't.

OTTO—I still find the whole thing a little difficult to realize completely. You must forgive me for being so stupid. I see quite clearly; I hear quite clearly; I know what's happened quite clearly, but I still don't quite understand.

LEO—What more do you want to understand?

OTTO—Were you both drunk?

GILDA—Of course we weren't.

OTTO—Then that's ruled out. One thing is still bewildering me very much. Quite a small trivial thing. You are both obviously strained and upset and unhappy at having to tell me. Isn't that so?

GILDA—Yes.

OTTO—Then why were you laughing when I came in?

LEO—Oh, what on earth does that matter?

OTTO—It matters a lot. It's very interesting.

LEO—It was completely irrelevant. Hysteria. It had nothing to do with anything.

OTTO—Why were you both laughing when I came in?

LEO—It was hysteria, I tell you.

OTTO—Were you laughing at me?

LEO (*wildly*)—Yes, we were! We were! We were laughing at you being wedged in the bath. That's what we were laughing at.

GILDA—Shut up, Leo! Stop it.

LEO (*giving way*)—And I shall laugh at that until the end of my days—I shall roll about on my death bed thinking about it—and there are other things I shall laugh at, too. I shall laugh at you now, in this situation, being hurt and grieved and immeasurably calm. What right have you to be hurt and grieved, any more than Gilda and me? We're having just as bad a time as you are, probably worse. I didn't stamp about with a martyr's crown on when you rushed off with her in the first place; I didn't look wistful and say I was shut out. And I don't intend to stand any of that nonsense from you! What happened between Gilda and me last night is actually completely unimportant—a sudden flare-up—and although we've been mutually attracted to each other for years, it wasn't even based on deep sexual love! It was just an unpremeditated roll in the hay and we enjoyed it very much, so there!

OTTO (*furiously*)—Well, one thing that magnificent outburst has done for me is this: I don't feel shut out any more. Do you hear? Not any more! And I'm extremely grateful to you. You were right about me being hurt and grieved. I was. But that's over, too. I've seen something in you that I've never seen before; in all these years I've never noticed it—I never realized that, deep down underneath your superficial charm and wit, you're nothing but a cheap, second-rate little opportunist, ready to sacrifice anything, however sacred, to the excitement of the moment—

GILDA—Otto! Otto—listen a minute; please listen—

OTTO (*turning to her*)—Listen to what? A few garbled explanations and excuses, fully charged with a hundred-per-cent feminine emotionalism, appealing to me to hold on to reason and intelligence as it's "our only chance." I don't want an "only chance." I don't want a chance to do anything but say what I have to say and leave you both to your own god-damned devices! Where was this much vaunted reason and intelligence last night? Working overtime, I'm sure. Working in a hundred small female ways. I expect your reason and intelligence prompted you to wear your green dress, didn't it? With the emerald earrings? And your green shoes, too, although they hurt you when you dance. Reason must have whispered kindly in your ear on your way back here in the taxi. It must have said, "Otto's in Bordeaux, and Bordeaux is a long way away, so everything will be quite safe!" That's reason, all right—pure reason—

GILDA (*collapsing at the table*)—Stop it! Stop it! How can you be so cruel! How can you say such vile things?

OTTO (*without a break*)—I hope "intelligence" gave you a little extra jab and suggested that you lock the door? In furtive, underhand affairs doors are always locked—

Leo—Shut up, Otto. What's the use of going on like that?

Otto—Don't speak to me—old, old Loyal Friend that you are! Don't speak to me, even if you have the courage, and keep out of my sight from now onwards—

Leo—Bravo, Deathless Drama!

Otto—Wrong again. Lifeless Comedy. You've set me free from a stale affection that must have died ages ago without my realizing it. Go ahead, my boy, and do great things! You've already achieved a Hotel de Luxe, a few smart suits, and the woman I loved. Go ahead, maybe there are still higher peaks for you to climb. Good luck, both of you! Wonderful luck! I wish you were dead and in hell! (*He slams out of the room as the curtain falls.*)

ACT II

In Leo's flat in London eighteen months later the floor of the living room is strewn with newspapers. It is a rented flat, but comfortably furnished and the morning sun comes through French windows opening onto a balcony at the back.

Gilda is lying on a sofa reading one paper and Leo is lying face downward on the floor reading another. Leo has had a play produced the night before and these are the criticisms. The usual criticisms: "The *Daily Mail* says it is daring and dramatic and witty." "The *Daily Express* says it's disgusting." "The *Daily Mirror* is a trifle carping."

" 'Change and Decay' is gripping throughout," reads Leo from the *Daily Mirror*. "The characterization falters here and there, but the dialogue is polished and sustains a high level from first to last and is frequently witty, nay, even brilliant—"

"I love the 'Nay,' " admits Gilda.

"Old Father *Times*," reports Leo, "is 'noncommittal, but amiable,' and carries 'a minute, if slightly inaccurate, description of the plot.'

"They seem to have missed the main idea of the play," insists the author.

It is a busy, irritating morning. The telephone rings continually. Ladies inviting Mr. Moncuré to lunch. Ladies inviting Mr. Moncuré to week-ends. It is getting a little on Gilda's nerves. It may be she is growing jealous! Or it may be, as she says, that she is just a little frightened. Success is far more perilous than failure.

"Last year was bad enough," sighs Gilda. "This is going to

be far worse."

"How would you feel about getting married?" suggests Leo. "It might be rather fun. We'd get a lot more presents now than if we'd done it before."

No, Gilda is not interested in marriage. It would upset her moral principles. And as for worrying about the Eye of Heaven —that doesn't worry her except when the eye winks. There are other reasons, too. Otto is one of them. Gilda thinks Otto would hate it.

"I wonder if he would," wonders Leo.

"I believe so," says Gilda. "There'd be no reason for him to, but I believe he would."

LEO—If only he'd appear again we could ask him.

GILDA—He will, sooner or later; he can't go on being cross forever.

LEO—Funny, about Otto.

GILDA—Screamingly funny.

LEO—Do you love him still?

GILDA—Of course. Don't you?

LEO (*sighing*)—Yes.

GILDA—We couldn't *not* love Otto, really.

LEO—Could you live with him again?

GILDA—No, I don't think so; that part of it's dead.

LEO—We were right, weren't we? Unconditionally right.

GILDA—Yes. I wish it hadn't been so drastic, though, and violent and horrid. I hated him being made so unhappy.

LEO—We weren't any too joyful ourselves, at first.

GILDA—Conscience gnawing at our vitals.

LEO—Do you think—do you think he'll ever get over it, enough for us all to be together again?

GILDA (*with sudden vehemence*)—I don't want all to be together again.

There is another session with the telephone. This time it is Mrs. Borrowdale and she wants both Leo and Gilda for the week-end. Gilda will not go, but she urges Leo to. He likes Mrs. Borrowdale, likes her house. All week-ends bore Gilda. Anyway, she is sure it is much better for Leo to go alone.

"I suppose I must be more gregarious than you," says Leo. "I enjoy meeting new people."

"I enjoy meeting new people, too," snaps Gilda; "but not second-hand ones."

"As I said before, Marion's house parties are extremely amusing. She doesn't like 'second-hand' people, as you call them, any more than you do. Incidentally, she's a very intelligent woman herself and exceedingly good company."

"I never said she wasn't intelligent, and I'm sure she's excellent company. She has to be. It's her job."

"That was a cheap jibe—thoroughly cheap—"

This time the telephone announces a young man from the *Evening Standard*. He would like to talk with Mr. Moncuré, and dejectedly Leo agrees to see him.

"This is a horrible morning," decides Gilda.

"I'm sorry," apologizes Leo.

Gilda—You needn't be. It isn't your fault.

Leo—Yes, it is, I'm afraid. I happen to have written a successful play.

Gilda (*exasperated*)—Oh, really— (*She turns away.*)

Leo—Well, it's true, isn't it? That's what's upsetting you?

Gilda—Do you honestly think that?

Leo—I don't know. I don't know what to think. This looks like a row but it hasn't even the virtue of being a new row. We've had it before several times, and just lately more than ever. It's inevitable that the more successful I become, the more people will run after me. I don't believe in their friendship, and I don't take them seriously, but I enjoy them. Probably a damn sight more than they enjoy me! I enjoy the whole thing. I've worked hard for it all my life. Let them all come! They'll drop me, all right, when they're tired of me; but maybe I shall get tired first.

Gilda—I hope you will.

Leo—What does it matter, anyhow?

Gilda—It matters a lot.

Leo—I don't see why.

Gilda—They waste your time, these ridiculous celebrity hunters, and they sap your vitality.

Leo—Let them! I've got lots of time and lots of vitality.

Gilda—That's bravado. You're far too much of an artist to mean that, really.

Leo—I'm far too much of an artist to be taken in by the old cliché of shutting out the world and living for my art alone. There's just as much bunk in that as there is in a cocktail party at the Ritz.

Gilda—Something's gone. Don't you see?

Leo—Of course something's gone. Something always goes.

The whole buisness of living is a process of readjustments. What are you mourning for? The dear old careless days of the Quartier Latin, when Laife was Laife!

GILDA—Don't be such a fool!

LEO—Let's dress up poor, and go back and pretend, shall we?

GILDA—Why not? That, at least, would be a definite disillusionment.

LEO—Certainly, it would. Standing over the skeletons of our past delights and trying to kick them to life again. That wouldn't be wasting time, would it?

GILDA—We needn't go back, or dress up poor, in order to pretend. We can pretend here. Among all this— (*She kicks the newspapers.*) With the trumpets blowing and the flags flying and the telephone ringing, we can still pretend. We can pretend that we're happy.

The young man from the *Evening Standard* is in. He has brought a photographer. He would like a home picture of Mr. Moncuré and he would like to ask a few questions.

"This is not your first play, is it?" he begins.

"No, my seventh. Two of them have been produced in London within the last three years," Leo answers, patiently.

"What were their names?"

"'Swift River' and 'Mrs. Draper.'"

"How do you spell 'Mrs. Draper'?"

"The usual way—m r s d r a p e r."

"Do you care for sport?"

"Yes, madly."

"What particular sport do you like best?"

"No particular one. I'm crazy about them all."

"I see. Do you believe the talkies will kill the theatre?"

"No. I think they'll kill the talkies."

Finally Leo can stand the strain no longer. As a very great favor he asks the young man to go away and come back another time. Let him call in his photographer, get his picture and then go. Mr. Moncuré is tired.

Leo has been posed in front of his desk. Just as the photographer is to snap him Gilda is back dressed for the street. She halts proceedings briefly while she kisses Leo good-by.

"I'm going to do a little shopping," she says, and adds, softly: "Sorry, darling—"

"All right, sweet."

"Just a little smile," calls the pressman.

Leo is smiling, or trying to smile, as the curtain falls.

A few days later, while Gilda is settling to a cold supper Miss Hodge has put out on a bridge table before the couch, the door opens and Otto walks in. For a moment they can do no more than stare at each other, and then it occurs to them that they are supremely glad to see each other.

Otto is just back from New York. He had had an exhibition in New York. A very successful exhibition, Gilda can guess. His whole personality reeks of it.

Otto is disappointed that Leo is not there. Glad that Leo will be back Monday. Glad that Leo is well.

Suddenly Otto feels that he is going to cry, and he doesn't want to do that, though Gilda thinks perhaps they should both cry a little. And now they have rushed into each other's arms and are holding each other close.

OTTO—It's all all right now, isn't it?

GILDA—More than all right.

OTTO—I was silly to stay away so long, wasn't I?

GILDA—That was what Leo meant the other morning when he said he knew what was missing.

OTTO—Me?

GILDA—Of course.

OTTO—I'm terribly glad he said that.

GILDA—We were having a row, trying to find out why we weren't quite as happy as we should be.

OTTO—Do you have many rows?

GILDA—Quite a lot, every now and then.

OTTO—As many as we used to?

GILDA—About the same. There's a bit of trouble on at the moment, really. He's getting too successful and sought after. I'm worried about him.

OTTO—You needn't be. It won't touch him—inside.

GILDA—I'm afraid, all the same; they're all so shrill and foolish, clacking at him.

OTTO—I read about the play in the train. It's a riot, isn't it?

GILDA—Capacity—every performance.

OTTO—Is it good?

GILDA—Yes, I think so.

OTTO—Only think so?

GILDA—Three scenes are first rate, especially the last act. The

Photo by Vandamm Studio, New York.

"DESIGN FOR LIVING"

Leo: We want to talk to you.
Gilda: Tomorrow, you can talk to me tomorrow; we can all talk for hours.
Leo: We want to talk now.
Gilda: I know you do, but I tell you I'm tired—dreadfully tired.

(*Alfred Lunt, Lynn Fontanne and Noel Coward*)

beginning of the second act drags a bit, and most of the first act's too facile—you know what I mean—he flips along with easy swift dialogue, but doesn't go deep enough. It's all very well played.

OTTO—We'll go on Monday night.

GILDA—Will you stay now that you've come back?

OTTO—I expect so. It depends on Leo.

GILDA—Oh!

OTTO—He may not want me to.

GILDA—I think he'll want you to, even more than I do!

OTTO—Why do you say that?

GILDA—I don't know. It came up suddenly, like a hiccup.

OTTO—I feel perfectly cozy about the whole business now, you know—no trailing ends of resentment—I'm clear and clean, a newly washed lamb, bleating for company!

Gilda has found another plate and knife and fork and Otto has found the supper delicious. Soon Otto is feeling so at home he is able to criticize the furnishings, and to vote the sherry excellent. Gradually they come around to the subject of their parting eighteen months before. That was quite terrible, they are agreed. Otto was tortured with regrets for a long while. He felt that he should have knocked Leo down, though Gilda is glad he didn't. It was their laughing when he came into the room that hurt Otto most, though Gilda thinks he should have known that they could not have been laughing at him.

Otto had gone away on a freight boat after that, and sailed for thousands of miles, and been very seasick. It was a Norwegian freight boat and Otto had learned to say, "How do you do?" in Norwegian, which inspires Gilda with the hope that they will get to know some Norwegian people so that Otto may say, "How do you do?" to them.

Back to the present, Otto reports that his things are still unpacked at the Carlton and that he has come to London with several commissions for portraits of the very best people.

"I only paint the very best people," says Otto.

"They have such interesting faces, haven't they?" retorts Gilda, almost snappily.

"I don't paint their faces, Gilda. Fourth dimensional, that's what I am. I paint their souls."

"You'd have to be eighth dimensional and clairvoyant to find them," snaps Gilda.

OTTO—I'm grieved to see that Leo has done little or nothing towards taming your proud revolutionary spirit.

GILDA—He's inflamed it.

OTTO—I know what's wrong with you, my sweet. You're just the concentrated essence of "Love Among the Artists."

GILDA—I think that was unkind.

OTTO—If you were creative yourself you'd understand better. As it is, you know a lot. You know an awful lot. Your critical faculty is first rate. I'd rather have your opinion on paintings or books or plays than anyone else's I know. But you're liable to get sidetracked if you're not careful. Life is for living first and foremost. Even for artists, life is for living. Remember that.

GILDA—You have grown up, haven't you?

OTTO—In the beginning, when we were all in Paris, everything was really very much easier to manage, even our emotional problems. Leo and I were both struggling, a single line was in both our minds leading to success—that's what we were planning for, working like dogs for! You helped us both, jostling us onto the line again when we slipped off, and warming us when we were cold in discouragement. You picked on me to love a little bit more, because you decided, rightly then, that I was the weaker. They were very happy, those days, and glamour will always cling to them in our memories. But don't be misled by them; don't make the mistake of trying to recapture the spirit of them. That's dead, along with our early loves and dreams and quarrels, and all the rest of the foolishness.

GILDA—I think I want to cry again.

OTTO—There's nothing like a good cry.

GILDA—You can't blame me for hating success, when it changes all the—the things I love best.

OTTO—Things would have changed, anyhow. It isn't only success that does it—it's time and experience and new circumstances.

GILDA (*bitterly*)—Was it the Norwegians that taught you this still wisdom? They must be wonderful people.

OTTO (*gently*)—No, I was alone. I just sat quietly and looked at everything.

GILDA—I see.

OTTO—Would you fancy a little more salad?

GILDA—No, thank you.

OTTO—Then it's high time we started on the cold rice pudding.

Gilda has come to see one thing clearly, she says, and that is that she is no longer needed. It is a question of the survival of the fittest, and both Leo and Otto have found their success. Of only one thing is she glad now—she will not rail about being feminine again. For the first time she suddenly is glad that she is feminine.

There is talk of Ernest, who also has been away on a world cruise—with a lot of old ladies in straw hats—but is now back in Paris. Now Otto has finished his supper, and is reminded that he still loves Gilda very, very much.

"A nice comfortable love, without heart throbs," Gilda estimates the emotion.

"Are you trying to lure me to your wanton bed?" demands Otto.

"What would you do if I did?"

"Probably enjoy it very much."

"I doubt if I should."

"Have I changed so dreadfully?"

"It isn't you that's changed—it's time and experience and new circumstances," snaps Gilda, maliciously.

Otto has poured them modest drinks of whiskey and soda and they are visioning many things as they talk. Otto remembers the hours he spent on the deck of the freighter conjuring up pictures of Gilda. Gilda can vision the person he thought he saw, the dim figure fitted into his romance that was not Gilda at all. Here she is, now, and none of the things that Otto's illusions pictured.

"You've worked yourself up into a frenzy of sophistication," he tells her, resenting her mood. "You've decided on being calculating and disillusioned and brazen, even slightly coarse over the affair. That's all very well, but how long is it going to last? That's what I ask myself. How long is it going to last—this old wanton mood of yours?

"Don't—don't laugh at me," pleads Gilda, breaking down.

"I must—a little," he answers.

Gilda—It's an unfair advantage. You've both got it, and you both use it against me mercilessly.

Otto—Laugh, too; it's not so serious, really.

Gilda—If I once started, I should never stop. That's a warning.

Otto—Duly registered.

Gilda—What are we going to do about Leo?

OTTO—Wait and see what he is going to do about us.

GILDA—Haven't you got any shame at all?

OTTO—Just about as much as you have.

GILDA—The whole thing's degrading, completely and utterly degrading.

OTTO—Only when measured up against other people's standards.

GILDA—Why should we flatter ourselves that we're so tremendously different?

OTTO—Flattery doesn't enter into it. We are different. Our lives are diametrically opposed to ordinary social conventions; and it's no use grabbing at those conventions to hold us up when we find we're in deep water. We've jilted them and eliminated them, and we've got to find our own solutions for our own peculiar moral problems.

GILDA—Very glib, very glib indeed, and very plausible.

OTTO—It's true. There's no sense in stamping about and saying how degrading it all is. Of course it's degrading; according to a certain code, the whole situation's degrading and always has been. The Methodists wouldn't approve of us, and the Catholics wouldn't either; and the Evangelists and the Episcopalians and the Anglicans and the Christian Scientists—I don't suppose even the Polynesian Islanders would think very highly of us, but they wouldn't mind quite so much, being so far away. They could all club together—the whole lot of them—and say with perfect truth, according to their lights, that we were loose-living, irreligious, unmoral degenerates, couldn't they?

GILDA (*meekly*)—Yes, Otto, I expect so.

OTTO—But the whole point is, it's none of their business. We're not doing any harm to anyone else. We're not peppering the world with illegitimate children. The only people we could possibly mess up are ourselves, and that's our lookout. It's no use you trying to decide which you love best, Leo or me, because you don't know! At the moment, it's me, because you've been living with Leo for a long time and I've been away. A gay, ironic chance threw the three of us together and tied our lives into a tight knot at the outset. To deny it would be ridiculous, and to unravel it impossible. Therefore, the only thing left is to enjoy it thoroughly, every rich moment of it, every thrilling second—

GILDA—Come off your soap box, and stop ranting!

OTTO—I want to make love to you very badly indeed, please! I've been lonely for a long time without you; now I've come back, and I'm not going to be lonely any more. Believe me, loneliness is a mug's game.

GILDA—The whole thing's a mug's game.

OTTO—You're infinitely lovely to me, darling, and so very necessary. The circle has swung round, and it's my turn again—that's only fair, isn't it?

GILDA—I—I suppose so.

OTTO—If you didn't want me, it would be different, but you do—you do, my dearest dear!—I can see it in your eyes. You want me every bit as much as I want you!

GILDA (*with a smile*)—Yes, every bit.

OTTO—This is a moment to remember, all right. Scribble it onto your heart; a flicker of ecstasy sandwiched between yesterday and tomorrow—something to be recaptured in the future without illusion, perfect in itself! Don't let's forget this—whatever else happens, don't let's forget this.

GILDA—How easy it all seems in this light.

OTTO—What small perverse meanness in you forbids you to walk round the sofa to me?

GILDA—I couldn't move if the house was on fire!

OTTO—I believe it is. To hell with the sofa! (*He vaults over it and takes her in his arms. They stand holding each other closely and gradually subside onto the sofa. He kisses her.*)—Hvordan staar det til!

GILDA (*blissfully*)—What's that, darling?

OTTO—"How do you do?" in Norwegian. (*The curtain slowly falls.*)

It is ten-thirty next morning when Miss Hodge shows Ernest Friedman into the living-room and tries to explain to him that Gilda will be in presently.

Ernest is a big surprise to Gilda, and Gilda, apparently in another of her incomprehensible moods, is, as usual, a surprise to Ernest.

Ernest, it appears, has come from Paris to settle a slight dispute as to the authenticity of a Holbein. Having done what he could about that he is going back to Paris and expects to sail for New York the following Wednesday. He has come to say good-by to Gilda and Leo. Ernest has rented a penthouse in New York and is of a mind to make his home there permanently. He could do with a housekeeper if Gilda will come.

Leo, Gilda explains a little excitedly, is still asleep and suffering with a bad stomach. She thinks maybe the success of his play had something to do with it. Leo is so sensitive to success.

But to Ernest it is Gilda who seems likely to suffer from sensitive nerves.

ERNEST—Will you ever change, I wonder. Will you ever change into a quieter, more rational person?

GILDA—Why should I?

ERNEST—What's wrong now?

GILDA—Wrong! What could be wrong? Everything's right. Righter than it's ever been before. God's in His heaven, all's right with the world—I always thought that was a remarkably silly statement, didn't you?

ERNEST—Unreasoning optimism is always slightly silly, but it's a great comfort to, at least, three-quarters of the human race.

GILDA—The human race is a let-down, Ernest; a bad, bad let-down! I'm disgusted with it. It thinks it's progressed but it hasn't; it thinks it's risen above the primeval slime but it hasn't—it's still wallowing in it! It's still clinging to us, clinging to our hair and our eyes and our souls. We've invented a few small things that make noises, but we haven't invented one big thing that creates quiet, endless peaceful quiet—something to pull over us like a gigantic eiderdown; something to deaden the sound of our emotional yellings and screechings and suffocate our psychological confusions—

ERNEST (*weakly*)—I think, perhaps, I would like a glass of sherry after all.

GILDA (*going to the "thing"*)—It's all right, Ernest, don't be frightened! You're always a safety valve for me. I think, during the last few years, I've screamed at you more than anyone else in the world.

They have each had a glass of sherry when Gilda warns Ernest that if he is wise he will "run like a stag." She is a lone woman, a free, unattached woman. This is a day of great exaltation for Gilda, and she is going away. Where to she does not know. Just round and round the world it may be. No, she has not had a row with Leo. Or with anyone else. She has just seen the light suddenly.

"I saw it last night," she says. "The survival of the fittest, that's the light."

Seeing the light, Gilda has written a note for Leo which he will find when he wakes up. And now, "calm inside and cold as steel," she is ready to go.

"Can one be exalted and cold as steel at the same time?" Ernest wants to know.

"I can," almost shouts Gilda. "I can be lots of things at the same time; it becomes a great bore after a while. In the future, I intend to be only one thing."

"That being—?"

"Myself, Ernest. My unadulterated self! Myself, without hangings, without trimmings, unencumbered by the winding tendrils of other people's demands—"

"That was very nicely put."

"You can laugh at me as much as you like. I give everybody free permission to laugh at me. I can laugh at myself, too, now—for the first time, and enjoy it."

It is wonderful, thinks Gilda, that Ernest should have appeared this particular morning, in time for all the good-bys. Ernest has an uncanny sense of hitting upon the "right moment." First, Gilda will go to a hotel—and it will not be the Carlton. Afterward to Paris, or maybe Berlin. She has always been attached to Berlin.

Now she has recovered a dressing case from the bedroom and is leaving with Ernest. As they are passing through the door Gilda remembers that she has another note to leave and comes back to prop it with its fellow against the brandy bottle. The front door is heard to slam very loudly as she rejoins Ernest.

The telephone brings Miss Hodge in to announce that her master is still away. The noise has awakened Otto. He emerges from the bedroom wearing a dressing gown and pajamas belonging to Leo. He is in search of a cigarette, a light and Gilda. He finds the first two, but Miss Hodge comes to tell him that her mistress has gone out. It is plain that Miss Hodge does not approve the "pretty goings on" that have kept Otto there all night. Miss Hodge, counsels Otto, would do well to mind her own business. Now he has thrown himself on a couch and is smoking meditatively when Leo creeps into the room. Leo is calling eagerly to Gilda that he could stand it no longer and so has come back. That, adds Otto, sitting up on the sofa, is the way he felt about it, too. He could not stand it any longer and he has come back. He has come back and he has been there all night with Gilda.

Otto—It wouldn't be any use lying, would it? Pretending I didn't?

Leo—No use at all.

Otto—I'm not even sorry, Leo, except for hurting you.

LEO—Where is Gilda?

OTTO—She's gone out.

LEO—Out! Why? Where's she gone to?

OTTO—I don't know.

LEO (*turning away*)—How vile of you! How unspeakably vile of you both!

OTTO—It was inevitable.

LEO (*contemptuously*)—Inevitable!

OTTO—I arrived unexpectedly; you were away; Gilda was alone. I love her; I've always loved her—I've never stopped for a minute, and she loves me, too.

LEO—What about me?

OTTO—I told you I was sorry about hurting you.

LEO—Gilda loves me.

OTTO—I never said she didn't.

LEO (*hopelessly*)—What are we to do? What are we to do now?

OTTO—Do you know, I really haven't the faintest idea.

LEO—You're laughing inside. You're thoroughly damned well pleased with yourself, aren't you?

OTTO—I don't know. I don't know that either.

LEO (*savagely*)—You are! I can see it in your eyes—so much triumph—such a sweet revenge!

OTTO—It wasn't anything to do with revenge.

LEO—It was. Of course it was—secretly thought out, planned for ages—infinitely mean!

OTTO—Shut up! And don't talk such nonsense.

LEO—Why did you do it, then? Why did you come back and break everything up for me?

OTTO—I came back to see you both. It was a surprise.

LEO—A rather cruel surprise, and brilliantly successful. You should be very happy.

OTTO (*sadly*)—Should I?

LEO—Perhaps I should be happy, too; you've set me free from something.

OTTO—What?

LEO (*haltingly*)—The—feeling I had for you—something very deep, I imagined it was, but it couldn't have been, could it—now that it has died so easily.

OTTO—I said all that to you in Paris. Do you remember? I thought it was true then, just as you think it's true now.

LEO—It is true.

OTTO—Oh, no, it isn't.

LEO—Do you honestly believe I could ever look at you again, as a real friend?

OTTO—Until the day you die.

It is Otto's conviction that Leo is not hating him nearly so much as he thinks he is. He is hating the situation, which is quite different. Otto knows, having been through the experience. It had driven him out onto the high seas and there he saw the truth clearly.

"No one of us was more to blame than the other," says Otto. "We've made our own circumstances, you and Gilda and me, and we've bloody well got to put up with them!"

"I wish I could aspire to such a sublime God's-eye view!"

"You will—in time—when your acids have calmed down."

When Leo goes mechanically to answer the telephone he comes upon Gilda's two letters stacked against the brandy bottle. The telephone call is of no further interest. Leo calls Otto. Together they realize what has happened. Gilda has "escaped."

The letters are identical. "Good-by, my clever little dear! Thank you for the keys of the city!" is what Gilda has written. They are both a little stunned. Leo feels sick. Which suggests the brandy. Otto feels a little sick, too.

They toss off two full glasses of brandy. And return to wondering about Gilda. Will she come back? Of course, she must come back. But, thinks Otto, she is not likely to come back for a long time. Leo fears that perhaps it is his success that has driven Gilda away. Otto is convinced that love among the artists is always too difficult. It all comes down to one thing. Gilda has gone because she doesn't want them any more.

"All the same," says Leo, "I should like to see her just once —just to find out, really, in so many words—"

"So many words!" repeats Otto, with sudden fury. "That's what's wrong with us! So many words—too many words, masses and masses of words, spewed about until we're choked with them. We've argued and probed and dragged our entrails out in front of one another for years! We've explained away the sea and the stars and life and death and our own peace of mind! I'm sick of this endless game of three-handed, spiritual ping-pong—this battling of our little egos in one another's faces! Sick to death of it! Gilda's made a supreme gesture and got out. Good luck to her, I say! Good luck to the old girl—she knows her onions!"

They have refilled their glasses with brandy and drained them at a gulp. It may make them drunk—but why not? They take a third drink and this is a toast to Gilda. Then another drink as a toast to their immortal souls.

And now they have come back to Gilda again. To Leo's success, and to Otto's success.

"Let's make the most of the whole business, shall we?" suggests Leo, with a glint in his eye. "Let's be photographed and interviewed and pointed at in restaurants! Let's play the game for what it's worth, secretaries and fur coats and de-luxe suites on transatlantic liners at minimum rates! Don't let's allow one shabby perquisite to slip through our fingers! It's what we dreamed many years ago and now it's within our reach. Let's cash in, Otto, and see how much we lose by it. [He refills both glasses and hands one to Otto.] Come on, my boy! [He raises his glass.] Success in twenty lessons! Each one more bitter than the last! More and better Success! Louder and funnier Success!"

Again they have drained their glasses and are left gasping a bit. Their insides, thinks Leo, must be greatly astonished to have so much brandy come hurtling down upon them.

LEO—We ought to know more about our insides, Otto. We ought to know why everything does everything.

OTTO—Machines! That's what we are, really—all of us! I can't help feeling a little discouraged about it every now and then.

LEO—Sheer sentimentality! You shouldn't feel discouraged at all; you should be proud.

OTTO—I don't see anything to be proud about.

LEO—That's because you don't understand; because you're still chained to stale illusions. Science dispels illusions; you ought to be proud to be living in a scientific age. You ought to be proud to know that you're a minute cog in the vast process of human life.

OTTO—I don't like to think I'm only a minute cog—it makes me sort of sad.

LEO—The time for dreaming is over, Otto.

OTTO—Never! I'll never consent to that. Never, as long as I live! How do you know that science isn't a dream, too? A monstrous, gigantic hoax?

LEO—How could it be? It proves everything.

OTTO—What does it prove? Answer me that!

LEO—Don't be silly, Otto. You must try not to be silly.

Otto (*bitterly*)—A few facts, that's all. A few tawdry facts torn from the universe and dressed up in terminological abstractions!

Leo—Science is our only hope, the only hope for humanity! We've wallowed in false mysticism for centuries; we've fought and suffered and died for foolish beliefs, which science has proved to be as ephemeral as smoke. Now is the moment to open our eyes fearlessly and look at the truth!

Otto—What is the truth?

Leo (*irritably*)—It's no use talking to you—you just won't try to grasp anything! You're content to go on being a romantic clod until the end of your days.

Otto (*incensed*)—What about you? What about the plays you write? Turgid with romance; sodden with true love; rotten with nostalgia!

Leo (*with dignity*)—There's no necessity to be rude about my work—that's quite separate, and completely beside the point.

Otto—Well, it oughtn't be. It ought to be absolutely in accord with your cold, incisive, scientific viewpoint. If you're a writer it's your duty to write what you think. If you don't you're a cheat—a cheat and a hypocrite!

Leo (*loftily*)—Impartial discussion is one thing, Otto. Personal bickering is another. I think you should learn to distinguish between the two.

Otto—Let's have some more brandy.

Leo—That would be completely idiotic.

Otto—Let's be completely idiotic!

Leo—Very well.

Again the discussion turns to Gilda, a little hazily now, and punctuated with frequent outbursts of mirth at the least excuse. They were both damn fools, Otto concludes, ever to have had anything to do with Gilda. A fellow feels differently about such things after he has been over the world and roughed it. That's what Leo should be. Leo should get away from all this muck and rough it. Leo should get on a ship, a small ship, a freighter preferably, and not care where it's going.

The idea appeals to Leo. Suddenly he realizes that he is free. Otto is free, too. Freedom is something worth drinking to. But there isn't any more brandy! What is there to drink to freedom with? There's sherry! Why not sherry? Tastes like brown paper—but why not sherry?

LEO—Sherry's a very ludicrous word, isn't it, when you begin to analyze it?

OTTO—Any word's ludicrous if you stare at it long enough. Look at "macaroni."

LEO—That's Italian; that doesn't count.

OTTO—Well, "rigmarole" then, and "neophyte" and "haddock."

LEO—And "wimple"—wimple's the word that gets me down!

OTTO—What is a wimple?

LEO—A sort of medieval megaphone, made of linen, Guinevere had one.

OTTO—What did she do with it?

LEO (*patiently*)—Wore it, of course. What did you think she did with it?

OTTO—She might have blown down it.

LEO (*with slight irritation*)—Anyhow, it doesn't matter, does it?

OTTO (*agreeably*)—Not in the least. It couldn't matter less. I always thought Guinevere was tedious, wimple or no wimple.

LEO—I'm beginning to float a little, aren't you?

OTTO—Just leaving the ground. Give me time! I'm just leaving the ground—

LEO—Better have some more sherry.

OTTO—I'm afraid it isn't very good sherry.

LEO (*scrutinizing the bottle*)—It ought to be good; it's real old Armadildo.

OTTO—Perhaps we haven't given it a fair chance.

Now they have filled their glasses and have drunk to Leo's toast: *"Apres moi le deluge!"*

"Apres both of us the deluge!" echoes Otto.

Again they have returned to Gilda, but with open minds. Leo is happy now. Doesn't feel angry with anybody. Feels at peace. Otto feels at peace, too. They both feel like a deep pool—a deep, deep pool, with cool green rushes on it, and the wind rustling through them. The wind is momentarily disturbed by Otto's hiccup.

"Will you forgive me—for—for everything," queries Leo, his head sinking on Otto's shoulder.

"It's I who should ask you that," answers Otto, emotionally.

LEO—I'm glad Gilda's gone, really—she was very wearisome sometimes. I shall miss her, though.

OTTO—We shall both miss her.

LEO—She's the only really intelligent woman I've ever known.

OTTO—Brilliant!

LEO—She's done a tremendous lot for us, Otto. I wonder how much we should have achieved without her?

OTTO—Very little, I'm afraid. Terribly little.

LEO—And now she's gone because she doesn't want us any more.

OTTO—I think she thinks we don't want her any more.

LEO—But we do, Otto—we do—

OTTO—We shall always want her, always, always, always—

LEO (*miserably*)—We shall get over it in time, I expect, but it will take years.

OTTO—I'm going to hate those years; I'm going to hate every minute of them.

LEO—So am I.

OTTO—Thank God for each other, anyhow!

LEO—That's true. We'll get along, somehow—(*his voice breaks*)—together—

OTTO (*struggling with his tears*)—Together—

LEO (*giving way to his, and breaking down completely*)—But we're going to be awfully—awfully—lonely— (*They are sobbing hopelessly on each other's shoulders as the curtain slowly falls.*)

ACT III

Ernest Friedman's penthouse apartment in New York is luxuriously furnished and extremely modern. On a warm summer night, two years later, the windows are wide open. Beyond a terrace the lights of the city can be seen.

There are sandwiches and drinks on a table, and presently there are voices in the hall. Gilda, followed by Grace Torrence and Henry and Helen Carver, are back from the opera and ready for a highball. It has been a fairly hard evening.

"People are wrong when they say that the opera is not what it used to be," Gilda is saying, as she comes into the room. "It is what it used to be—that's what's wrong with it."

She is elaborately and beautifully gowned. "Her manner has changed a good deal. She is much more still and sure than before. A certain amount of vitality has gone from her, but in its place there is an aloof poise quite in keeping with her dress and surroundings."

Henry Carver, at Gilda's suggestion, finds drink for them. Miss Torrence is particularly interested in the apartment. Interested in hearing, too, that everything in it is for sale, except the pictures, which are Ernest's. The Carvers are confident that the paintings are also for sale—at a price. Ernest had sold Henry's father a Matisse for eleven thousand dollars, and that is still something of a scandal in the family.

It is Henry Carver's opinion, which he is free to express to his wife when Gilda takes Miss Torrence through the sleeping quarters a floor above, that Gilda's apartment has been furnished for the sole purpose of selling the things in it; that Gilda, being an interior decorator, is also as hard as nails and entirely commercial. She may have been a good friend to Helen, but she furnished the Carver apartment—and made it much too Spanish to suit Henry.

There is a ring at the doorbell which Henry is obliged finally to answer, no servant appearing. A moment later he has ushered Leo and Otto into the room and explained that Mrs. Friedman will be down as soon as she has shown Miss Torrence over the apartment.

Leo and Otto are in faultless evening dress and elaborately pleased to meet Mr. and Mrs. Carver. They are also very glad to help themselves to a drink at Mr. Carver's suggestion. They are, they report, old friends of Mrs. Friedman's, having lived with her for years.

There is some slight difficulty in maintaining the conversation, though both Leo and Otto try to be helpful. Leo remembers suddenly that he knew a man in Sumatra named Carver, but Otto recalls that the man in Sumatra was named Eidelbaum. Leo is so traveled he is easily muddled.

"Have you been married long," Leo would know of Henry.

"Two years," admits Henry.

"Oh, dear! Oh, dear! Oh, dear! Oh, dear! Oh, dear!"

"Why? What of it?"

OTTO—There's something strangely and deeply moving about young love, Mr. and Mrs. Carver.

LEO—Youth at the helm.

OTTO—Guiding the little fragile barque of happiness down the river of life. Unthinking, unknowing, unaware of the perils that lie in wait for you, the sudden tempests, the sharp jagged rocks beneath the surface. Are you never afraid?

HENRY—I don't see anything to be afraid of.

LEO (*fondly*)—Foolish headstrong boy.

OTTO—Have you any children?

HENRY (*sharply*)—No, we have not.

LEO—That's what's wrong with this century. If you were living in Renaissance Italy you'd have been married at fourteen and by now you'd have masses of children and they'd be fashioning things of great beauty. Wouldn't they, Otto?

OTTO—Yes, Leo, they would.

LEO—There you are, you see!

OTTO—The tragedy of the whole situation lies in the fact that you don't care, you don't care a fig, do you?

HELEN (*stiffly*)—I really don't understand what you mean.

What Otto means is not really very much, but it is confusing to the Carvers. So, also, is Leo's grandiloquent explanation of what a mystery the human race presents.

"It's all a question of masks, really," insists Leo. "Brittle, painted masks. We all wear them as a form of protection; modern life forces us to. We must have some means of shielding our timid, shrinking souls from the glare of civilization."

"Be careful, Leo. Remember how you upset yourself in Mombasa!"

"That was fish," petulantly answers Leo, to the further astonishment of the Carvers.

Now Gilda and Grace Torrence have come down the stairs. Gilda does not see Leo and Otto until she is at the foot of the stairs. Then she puts her hand on the balustrade to steady herself for a second. When she speaks, however, her voice is perfectly calm.

Gilda sees, as they are quick to inform her, that her friends have come back. She is pleased to introduce them and they as pleased to put the company at its ease.

"You must forgive our clothes, but we've only just come off a freight boat," smiles the immaculately dressed Leo.

"A Dutch freight boat," adds Otto, wisely. "The food was delicious."

Otto and Leo continue to do what they can to sustain their part of the conversation with little anecdotes of their trip, quite obviously to the amusement of Gilda but the further bewilderment of Helen and Henry Carver.

Something that Miss Torrence says about Paris reminds Otto that he once had a flat in Paris that was later pulled down; a "small edifice that crumbled easily." Its ruin, however, was quite as complete as though an earthquake had been responsible.

Which in turn reminds Leo that he has never been able to understand why the Japanese can remain such a cheerful race, with "all that hissing and grinning on the brink of destruction."

"The Japanese don't mind destruction a bit," explains Otto; "they like it, it's part of their upbringing. They're delighted with death. Look at the way they kill themselves on the most whimsical of pretexts."

"I always thought Madame Butterfly was over-hasty," admits Leo.

Gilda would explain to Grace that she must pay no attention to these two; they have always talked nonsense ever since she has known them. Gilda would also know about what they have been doing. They must both come to lunch one day and tell her all about themselves.

"You'll have to forgive me if I'm not quite as helpful to you as I used to be," she adds. "My critical faculties are not as strong as they once were. I've grown away, you see."

"How far have you grown away, my dear love?" Leo would know. How lonely are you in your little box so high above the arena? Don't you ever feel that you want to come down in the cheap seats again, nearer to the blood and the sand and the warm smells, nearer to Life and Death?"

"You've changed, Leo. You used to be more subtle."

"You've changed too," says Otto; "but we expected that."

It is curious the tricks memory plays, they agree. Otto has an excellent memory for names but none for faces. Leo, for his part, is best at remembering things, often trivial unattached fragments that had been significant once but no longer mean anything. "Trees in a quiet London square, for instance—a green evening dress, with earrings to match—two notes propped up against a brandy bottle—odd, isn't it?"

"Not particularly odd," thinks Gilda. "The usual litter of an over-sentimental mind."

Otto—Be careful, Gilda. An ugly brawl is imminent.

Gilda—I'm not afraid.

Otto—That's brave, when you have so much to lose. (*He glances comprehensively round the room.*)

Gilda (*quietly*)—Is that a threat?

Otto—We've come back. That should be threat enough!

Gilda (*rising, with a strange smile*)—There now! That's what happens when ghosts get into the house. They try to frighten you with their beckoning fingers and clanking chains, not knowing that they're dead and unable to harm you any more. That's why one should never be scared of them, only sorry for them. Poor little ghosts! It must be so uncomfortable, wandering through empty passages, feeling they're not wanted very much.

LEO (*to* GRACE)—You see, Gilda can talk nonsense too.

OTTO (*reprovingly*)—That wasn't nonsense, Leo; that was a flight of fancy, tinged with the macabre and reeking with allegory—a truly remarkable achievement!

LEO—It certainly requires a vivid imagination to describe this apartment as an empty passage.

GILDA (*laughing a trifle wildly*)—Stop it, both of you! You're behaving abominably!

OTTO—We're all behaving abominably.

LEO—The veneer is wearing thin. Even yours, Gilda.

GRACE—This, really, is the most extraordinary conversation I've ever heard.

OTTO—Fascinating, though, don't you think? Fascinating to lift the roofs a fraction and look down into the houses.

GILDA—Not when the people inside know you're looking: not when they're acting for you and strutting about and showing off!

LEO—How does it feel to be so secure, Gilda? Tell us about it?

GILDA (*ignoring him*)—Another drink, Henry?

HENRY—No, thanks.

HELEN (*rising*)—We really ought to be going now.

GILDA—Oh, I'm so sorry!

LEO—Watch the smooth wheels going round!

OTTO—Reach for a Murad!

GRACE (*also rising*)—I'm going, too, Gilda. Can I drop anybody?

HENRY—No, thanks, our car's outside.

GRACE—Good night, Mr. Mercuré.

LEO (*shaking hands*)—Good night.

GRACE (*shaking hands with* OTTO)—Good night. Can I drop you anywhere?

OTTO—No, thank you; we're staying a little longer.

GILDA—No! Go now, Otto, please. Both of you, go with Grace. I'm terribly tired; you can telephone me the first thing in the morning.

LEO—We want to talk to you.

GILDA—Tomorrow, you can talk to me tomorrow; we can all talk for hours.

LEO—We want to talk now.

GILDA—I know you do, but I tell you, I'm tired—dreadfully tired. I've had a very hard day— (*She winks at them violently.*)

OTTO (*grinning*)—Oh, I see.

HELEN (*at the door*)—Come on, Henry! Good night, Gilda darling; it's been a lovely evening. (*She bows to* OTTO *and* LEO, *and goes out.* GRACE *looks at* OTTO *and* LEO *and* GILDA, *and then with great tact joins* HENRY *at the door.*)

GRACE (*to* OTTO)—My car's there, if you are coming now. Good night, Gilda—ring for the elevator, Henry— (*She goes out with* HENRY.)

GILDA (*hurriedly, in a whisper*)—It was awful of you to behave like that! Why couldn't you have waited quietly until they'd gone?

LEO (*also in a whisper*)—They wouldn't go—they were going to stay forever and ever and ever! (GILDA *runs over to her bag, which is lying on a chair, and takes a latchkey out of it.*)

GILDA—Go, now, both of you! Go with Grace. She'll gossip all over town if you don't. Here's the key; come back in ten minutes.

OTTO—Intrigue, eh? A nice state of affairs.

LEO—Good old Decameron!

GILDA (*shoving the key into his hand*)—Go on, quickly! Get a taxi straight back—

"They both kiss her lightly on the lips and go out. Gilda stands still, staring after them until she hears the door slam. Her eyes are filled with tears. She strides about the room in great agitation, clasping and unclasping her hands. She stops in front of a table on which is someone's unfinished drink. She drinks it thoughtfully, frowning and tapping her foot nervously on the ground."

Then suddenly, she bangs down the glass, snatches up her cloak and bag, switches off the lights, and runs out through the door leading to the fire escape as the curtain falls.

Early next morning the bell brings Matthew, the house man, from the kitchen of the Friedman flat to the entrance hall. The summons is from Ernest Friedman. He is carrying a suitcase and has with him also a wooden crate of canvasses.

Ernest is not surprised to learn that Mrs. Friedman is not awake. He is having his coffee alone when Leo and Otto appear at the top of the stairs. They have come from Gilda's room. Both are wearing Ernest's pajamas and dressing gowns, which are too small for them, and they are in their bare feet.

The sight of them is flabbergasting to Ernest, and he is in no way mollified by the affection of their greetings. They both would embrace him, and appear to be surprised that he is not pleased to see them.

Hurriedly they explain that they had arrived the night before quite unexpectedly; that they called on Gilda and found her entertaining her smart friends; that she put them out, pressed a latchkey upon them and disappeared. They came back to the apartment, found her gone and went to bed.

The whole thing is fantastically ridiculous to Ernest. If he appears to be disagreeable there is, he thinks, every reason why he should be. And now he would like to know what they want.

"We want Gilda, of course!" Otto is quick to answer.

"Have you gone out of your mind?"

"Not at all! It's quite natural! We've always wanted Gilda!" This from Leo.

"Are you aware that she is my wife?"

"Oh, don't be so silly, Ernest," says Otto.

"Silly! How dare you!"

"You're a dear old pet, Ernest," agrees Leo; "and we're very, very fond of you and we know perfectly well that Gilda could be married to you fifty times and still not be your wife."

There is little use of Ernest continuing to think of Gilda as his wife, they insist. They know why he had married her, and if they had both been dead it would have been an excellent arrangement. But they're not dead.

"I won't lose my temper with you, because that would be foolish—" ventures Ernest.

"And ineffective," adds Otto.

Ernest—But I think you had better put on whatever clothes you came in, and go away. You can come back later, when you're in a more reasonable frame of mind.

Leo—We're in a perfectly reasonable frame of mind, Ernest. We've never been more reasonable in our lives; nor more serenely determined.

Ernest (*with great calmness*)—Now look here, you two. I married Gilda because she was alone, and because for many, many years I have been deeply attached to her. We discussed it carefully together from every angle, before we decided. I know the whole circumstances intimately. I know exactly how much she loved you both; and also, I'm afraid, exactly how little you both loved her. You practically ruined her life between you, and you caused her great unhappiness with your egotistical, casual passions. Now you can leave her alone. She's worked hard and made a reputation for herself. Her life is fully occupied; and she is completely contented. Leave her alone! Go away! Go back to Manila or wherever you came from—and leave her alone!

LEO—Admirable, Ernest! Admirable, but not strictly accurate. We love her more than anyone else in the world and always shall. She caused us just as much unhappiness in the past as we ever caused her. And although she may have worked hard, and although her life is so fully occupied, she is far from being contented. We saw her last night and we know.

OTTO—She could never be contented without us, because she belongs to us just as much as we belong to her.

ERNEST—She ran away from you.

LEO—She'll come back. (*The front door bell rings.*)

OTTO—She has come back.

Gilda is wearing a dark day coat over her evening dress. She had borrowed coat and hat from the telephone operator at the Ritz, and must be reminded to return them.

One glance at the three men and Gilda realizes that things are awkward. She had thought Leo and Otto might stay the night. She had sneaked off, as they term it, because she had to have time to think. And now what do they think is going to happen?

Ernest, for his part, is free to admit that he is extremely angry. He has found the arrogance of Otto and Leo insufferable and the things they have dared to say to him extremely offensive. He thinks that Gilda should tell them to go away. Gilda is certain that that would do no good. As for Leo and Otto, they are quick to insist that they would not go without her.

Now Gilda is free to admit defeat. She has given in. She has thrown her hand in. The game is over.

"I mean I'm going away from you, Ernest," she says. "Some things are too strong to fight against; I've been fighting for two years and it's no use. I'm bored with the battle, sick to death of it! So I've given in."

"I knew it," cries Leo. "I knew it last night."

"We both knew it," adds Otto. "We laughed ourselves to sleep."

"You're crazy! You're stark, staring mad!" protests Ernest.

"I am, I am!" admits Gilda, ecstatically. "I'm mad with joy! I'm mad with relief! I thought they really had forgotten me; that they really were free of me. I thought that they were never coming back, that I should never see them again; that my heart would be heavy and sick and lonely for them until I died!"

"Serve you right for leaving us," says Leo. "Serve you damn well right!"

There is more to be said to Ernest. More that he should, and must hear, Gilda insists, when she has quieted the somewhat exultant spirit of her two young men.

"I'm ashamed of many things, but not of this," she says in answer to Ernest's charge that she is being unbelievably vulgar. "This is real. I've made use of you, Ernest, and I'm ashamed of that, and I've lied to you. I'm ashamed of that, too; but at least I didn't know it: I was too busy lying to myself at the same time. I took refuge in your gentle, kind friendship, and tried to pretend to myself that it was enough, but it wasn't. I've talked and laughed and entertained your friends; I've been excellent company and very efficient. I've worked hard and bought things and sold things, all the time pretending that my longing for these two was fading! But it wasn't. They came back last night, looking very sleek and sly in their newly pressed suits, and the moment I saw them, I knew; I knew it was no good pretending any more. I fought against it, honestly I did! I ran away from them, and walked about the streets and sat in Childs weeping into glasses of milk. Oh, Ernest, you've understood such a lot, understand just this much more, and try to forgive me—because I can't possibly live without them, and that's that."

There is no explanation that will satisfy Ernest, and none that the other three feel is necessary. Whatever he may think about it, the situation is as they would have it. If the sight of her old friends has revived Gilda's idiotic infatuation for them, why not? If she is like a mad woman now, hasn't she been sane and still for two years?

"It's silly to go on saying to yourself that I'm different from Otto and Leo just because you want to believe it," insists Gilda. "I'm not different from them. We're all of a piece, the three of us. Those early years made us so. From now on we shall have to live and die our own way. No one else's way is any good, we don't fit."

ERNEST—No, you don't, you don't and you never will. Your values are false and distorted.

GILDA—Only from your point of view.

ERNEST—From the point of view of anyone who has the slightest sense of decency.

LEO—We have our own decencies. We have our own ethics.

Our lives are a different shape from yours. Wave us good-by, little Ernest, we're together again.

GILDA—Ernest, Ernest, be friendly. It can't hurt you much.

ERNEST—Not any more. I've wasted too much friendship on all of you, you're not worth it.

OTTO—There's a lot of vanity in your anger, Ernest, which isn't really worthy of your intelligence.

ERNEST (*turning on him*)—Don't speak to me, please!

LEO—Otto's perfectly right. This behavior isn't worthy of your intelligence. If you were twisted up inside and really unhappy it would be different; but you're not, you're no more than offended and resentful that your smooth habits should be tampered with—

ERNEST (*losing control*)—Hold your tongue!—I've had too much of your effrontery already!

GILDA (*peaceably*)—Once and for all, Ernest, don't be bitter and so dreadfully outraged! Please, please calm down and you'll find it much easier to understand.

ERNEST—You overrate my capacity for understanding! I don't understand; the whole situation is revolting to me. I never shall understand; I never could understand this disgusting three-sided erotic hotch-potch!

GILDA—Ernest!

LEO—Why, good heavens! King Solomon had a hundred wives and was thought very highly of. I can't see why Gilda shouldn't be allowed a couple of gentlemen friends.

ERNEST (*furiously*)—Your ill-timed flippancy is only in keeping with the rest of your execrable taste!

OTTO—Certain emotions transcend even taste, Ernest. Take anger, for example. Look what anger's doing to you! You're blowing yourself out like a frog!

ERNEST (*beside himself*)—Be quiet! Be quiet!

LEO (*violently*)—Why should we be quiet! You're making enough row to blast the roof off! Why should you have the monopoly of noise? Why should your pompous moral pretensions be allowed to hurtle across the city without any competition? We've all got lungs; let's use them! Let's shriek like mad! Let's enjoy ourselves!

GILDA (*beginning to laugh*)—Stop it, Leo! I implore you!—This is ludicrous! Stop it—stop it—

ERNEST (*in a frenzy*)—It is ludicrous! It's ludicrous to think that I was ever taken in by any of you—that I ever mistook you for anything but the unscrupulous, worthless degenerates that you are! There isn't a decent instinct among the lot of you. You're shifty and irresponsible and abominable, and I don't wish to set eyes on you again—as long as I live! Never! Do you hear me? Never—never—never! (*He stamps out of the room quite beside himself with fury; on his way into the hall he falls over the package of canvasses. This is too much for* GILDA *and* OTTO *and* LEO*; they break down utterly and roar with laughter. Their laughter is still echoing from the walls as*

THE CURTAIN FALLS

BIOGRAPHY

A Comedy in Three Acts

By S. N. Behrman

THE Theatre Guild began its season hopefully, even expectantly, with Owen and Donald Davis's adaptation of Pearl Buck's "The Good Earth" to stage uses.

This proved a mighty drama in bulk, and a workmanlike and intelligent job of transplantation. But either because the readers of the widely popular novel were too exacting, or because, which is the likelier reason, it is impossible to transfer successfully to the narrowed confines of the stage so spreading and voluminous a life story as that of this Chinese saga, "The Good Earth" did not prove a popular bill. It ran through the subscription list, and a little beyond, which carried it into December. On December 12th the Guild produced its second play, a comedy by S. N. Behrman simply titled "Biography."

Mr. Behrman, who has been spending a good deal of time in Hollywood these last few years, had previous Guild productions with his most successful "The Second Man" some seasons back, and again with the less successful "Meteor," which even the popular Alfred Lunt and Lynn Fontanne could not carry far. Last season he was represented in these volumes by his moderately successful "Brief Moment."

"Biography" is written in the playwright's best high comedy vein. It is a witty, sophisticated, bantering and impudent study of character. The selected humans who tell its story are varied and interesting as to type. Even though they escape into the realms of fiction occasionally and speak the language of the novelist, they never completely lose contact with humanity in the mass. The acquisition of Ina Claire as a sort of unofficial guest star to play the rôle of the heroine proved a happy selection on the part of the Guild's production committee.

The first scene of "Biography" is laid in the studio-apartment of Marion Froude in an old-fashioned building in West Fifty-seventh Street, New York, "a great cavernous room expressing in its polyglot furnishings the artistic patois of the various landlords who have sublet this apartment to wandering tenants like Marion

Froude. The styles range from medieval Florence to contemporary Grand Rapids; on a movable raised platform in the center is a papal throne chair in red velvet and gold fringes. Not far from it is an ordinary American kitchen chair. . . . The room is warm, musty, with restful shadows and limpid lights. . . . Every school is represented here except the modern. The studio has the mellowness of anachronism."

It is about five o'clock of an afternoon in November. Pacing the room, and "finishing a nervous cigarette" is Richard Kurt, a young man who has "the essential audacity which comes from having seen the worst happen, from having endured the keenest pain. . . . He has the hardness of one who knows that he can be devastated by pity, the bitterness which comes from having seen, in early youth, justice thwarted and tears unavailing . . . the intensity of the fanatic and the carelessness of the vagabond."

At the moment young Mr. Kurt is greatly put out. Having been invited to tea, and having been kept waiting, he demands an explanation that Minnie, Miss Froude's German maid, is unable to give.

A moment later a second caller, Melchoir Feydak, arrives. Herr Feydak, Austrian composer, "is forty-five, tall, hook-nosed, thin-faced, a humorist with a rather sad face." He, too, is looking for Marion Froude and will wait. Nor is he surprised to find another before him.

"Extraordinary thing—ever since I've known Marion there's always been someone waiting for her," says Feydak, genially. "There are two kinds of people in one's life—people whom one keeps waiting—and the people for whom one waits."

Young Mr. Kurt suspects that that is an epigram and he despises epigrams. He despises gallantry. He despises all generalizations. If he also resents Feydak's attempts at friendliness he is quite unable to discourage the composer.

"When I was a young man—before I achieved any sort of success—I was rude on principle," sympathizes the older man. "Deliberately rude and extravagantly bitter in order to make an impression. When it is no longer necessary for you to wait around for people in order to do them favors you'll mellow down, I assure you."

"You think so, do you?" snaps Kurt. "That's where you're mistaken! I'm rude now. When I'm successful I'll be murderous!"

Kurt has a feeling that he has known Herr Feydak somewhere. When the composer identifies himself the young man recognizes the name as that of one of his minor passions, the man who had composed the popular operetta "Danubia." He is visibly impressed. It takes Feydak some time to explain that it is not he, but his brother, who composed "Danubia." The brother is dead.

It is during Kurt's momentary embarrassment over his mistake that Marion Froude walks in. "She is one of those women, the sight of whom on Fifth Avenue, where she has just been walking, causes foreigners to exclaim enthusiastically that American women are the most radiant in the world. She is tall, lithe, indomitably alive. Unlike Kurt, the tears in things have warmed without scalding her; she floats life like a dancer's scarf in perpetual enjoyment of its colors and contours."

A sight of Feydak is enough to set Marion raving with enthusiasm. She has not seen him in years and she has thrown herself into his arms before she is conscious of Kurt's presence. Then she quickly excuses herself and as promptly asks Kurt to give her a half hour longer. It has been so long since she has seen this old friend—

With Kurt gone, and Feydak beside her on a settee, Marion is full of news and eager to hear more. It has been six years since she has seen Feydak. The last time was at his brother Vicki's funeral. She has been back in New York two weeks now. She has met many charming people but received no commissions, despite the stories that get around about her great success. That impression, thinks Marion, is due to the extreme notoriety of some of her sitters.

"Last time I came here I was awfully busy," Marion explains. "Had great réclame because I'd been in Russia doing leading Communists. Obeying some subtle paradox the big financiers flocked to me. Pittsburgh manufacturers wanted to be done by the same brush that had tackled Lenin. Now they seem less eager. Must be some reason, Feydie. But what about you?"

Herr Feydak is able to report that of his two daughters one is with him. She is Kathie, who used to hate Marion because of a natural fear that her Uncle Vicki intended leaving her most of his money. He had, as Feydak admits, left Marion half of it, but he and his family had been obliged to spend it. Now that he is on his way to Hollywood he will soon be able to pay her back.

Feydak—If it weren't for the money Vicki left me—and you!—I don't know how we should have got through at all these six years. About a month ago we reached the end of our rope—we were hopelessly in debt—no means of getting out—when the miracle happened. . . .

MARION (*excited*)—I can't bear it. . . .

FEYDAK—It was my dramatic agent on the phone. A great American film magnate was in town and wanted to see me. Ausgerechnet me and no other. Even my agent couldn't keep the surprise out of his voice. Why me? I asked. God knows, says the agent. Well, we went around to the Bristol to see the magnate. And, as we talked to him, it gradually became apparent. He thought I was Vicki. He didn't know Vicki was dead! He thought I had written "Danubia."

MARION—Did he say so?

FEYDAK—No—not at all. But as we shook hands at the end he said to me: "Any man that can write a tune like this is the kind of man we want." And he whistled, so out of tune that I could hardly recognize it myself, the waltz from "Danubia." Do you remember it? (*He starts to hum the waltz and* MARION *joins him. They hum together, then* FEYDAK *continues to talk as* MARION *continues to hum a few more measures.*) He was so innocent, so affable that I had an impulse to say to him: "Look here, old fellow, you don't want me, you want my brother and in order to get him you'll have to resurrect him!" But noble impulses are luxury impulses. You have to be well off to gratify them. I kept quiet. We shook hands and here I am. Tonight they're giving me a dinner at the Waldorf Astoria for the press to meet my brother! Irony if you like, eh, Marion?

Marion is encouraging. She knows, having known Vicki as she did, that Vicki's belief in his brother was absolute and that he would approve now this little deception that is so galling to Feydak.

"Do you know what was the terror of his life—the fear of your resenting him," she reports. "Don't resent him now, Feydie. . . . Why, it's such fun—don't you see? It's such a curious, marginal survival for him—that a badly remembered waltz-tune, five years after his death, should be the means of helping you at a moment when you need it so badly. . . . It's delicious, Feydie. It's such fun! The only awful thing is the possibility that he is unaware of it. It would have pleased him so, Feydie. Must you grudge him it?"

"You make me horribly ashamed . . ."

"Nonsense. . . . And the funny thing is—you'll be much better for them out there than he would have been."

"Surely! They'll be able to whistle *my* tunes!"

Now Feydak, filled with a new enthusiasm, is eager that Marion shall go back to Hollywood with him, but Marion has too much pride in her ability to take care of herself to want to give up her independence.

"I'm a little proud of my ingenuity," she says. "And do you know, Feydie, no matter how hard up I've been at different times something's always turned up for me. I have a kind of curiosity to know what it will be this time. It would spoil the fun for me to take money from my friends. Nothing—so much as that would make me doubtful of my own—shall we say—marketability?"

A summons at the door is thought to herald the return of Kurt, but the caller is a Mr. Leander Nolan. "He is middle-aged, ample, handsome. Looks like the late Warren Gamaliel Harding. . . . The façade is impeccable, but in Nolan's eyes you may discern, at odd moments, an uncertainty, an almost boyish anxiety to please, to be right, that is rather engaging."

Now Marion has returned from going to the door with Feydak and is curiously intent on trying to place Mr. Nolan. She knows him, of course, but why she knows him she is not sure. Was it at Lady Winchester's garden party at Ascot—or at the American Embassy dinner in Rome—that they met?

Mr. Nolan is completely astonished. If anyone had told him that he could have walked into a room and stood in front of Marion Froude and she did not know him—

But it is not until he has taken her memory back to Tennessee—to the old, old days—that she remembers Bunny Nolan! Bunny—of all people—looking so wonderful, so important, so "like a Senator or something monumental like that—"

Nolan is not too embarrassed to admit that it is entirely within the range of possibilities that he may be a Senator one day. In Washington, too. Not Nashville.

"Do you want to be a Senator, or can't you help it?" asks Marion, but the query only confuses Nolan. Now she has a better idea. She will paint Bunny. Probably with a toga, and a ferrule, and possibly as a Tribune of the People! The idea is not displeasing to Mr. Nolan.

Now there are reminiscences. To Nolan, Marion looks just the same as she did fifteen years before. Marion can also remember Bunny as he was years before he wore piping on his vest and seemed so important. She is surprised to hear him confess that he is not married. He is, however, engaged—to Slade Kinnicott, daughter of the publisher. It's Kinnicott who is backing Bunny for the Senate; Kinnicott and his string of newspapers. Not very good papers, as Marion recalls them, but of large circulation.

"You see, Marion," Nolan explains, "I've been pretty successful in the law. Tremendously successful I may say. I've organized some of the biggest mergers of recent years. I've made a fortune —a sizeable fortune. Well, one day I woke up and I said to myself: Look here, Nolan, you've got to take stock. You've got to ask yourself where you're heading. I'd been so busy I'd never had a chance to ask myself these fundamental questions before. And I decided to call a halt. "You've got enough, more than enough for life, I said to myself. It's time you quit piling up money and began thinking about your fellow-man. I've always been ambitious, Marion. You know that. You shared all my early dreams. . . ."

"Of course I did . . ."

"Remember I always told you I didn't want money and power for their own sakes—I always wanted to be a big man in a real sense—to do something for my country and my time. . . ."

"Yes. Sometimes you sounded like Daniel Webster, darling. I'm not a bit surprised you're going to the Senate."

As for Marion, there has been nothing particularly promising in her life. There is not, she feels certain, the remotest chance of her getting into the Senate unless she marries into it. She is pleased that Bunny finds her reasonably attractive after fifteen years and amused at the apparently shocking things he has heard about her life, especially with those foreigners. Some foreigners, Marion has found, are really quite nice. And one must have friends.

Marion is also conscious of "an overtone—faint but unmistakable—of moral censure." This, it transpires, can be traced to Nolan's conviction that one cannot live one's life in art "without being sexually promiscuous." And when he has admitted so much Marion does not know whether to blush or to hang her head in shame. How should one react in the face of such an appalling accusation?

If it is true, as Bunny charges, that many of her lovers have been famous men, Marion can remind him that even he, though obscure in the old days, is famous now.

"I seem to be stimulating if nothing else," she concludes.

"If I had then some of the fame I have now you probably wouldn't have walked out on me at the last minute the way you did," says Bunny, a hurt tone in his voice.

Marion would deny that she did walk out on Bunny. She does not recall the circumstances very clearly. There had been a quarrel, hadn't there?

NOLAN—I realized after you left me how much I'd grown to depend on you—

MARION—Dear Bunny!

NOLAN—I plunged into work. I worked fiercely to forget you. I did forget you— (*He looks away from her.*) And yet—

MARION—And yet—?

NOLAN—The way we'd separated and I never heard from you —it left something bitter in my mind—something— (*He hesitates for a word.*)

MARION (*supplying it*)—Unresolved?

NOLAN (*quickly—relieved that she understands so exactly*)— Yes. All these years I've wanted to see you, to get it off my mind—

MARION—Did you want the last word, Bunny dear?

NOLAN (*fiercely*)—I wanted to see you, to stand before you, to tell myself—"Here she is—and what of it!"

MARION—Well, can you?

NOLAN (*heatedly, with transparent over-emphasis*)—Yes! Yes!

MARION—Good for you, Bunny. I know just how you feel— like having a tooth out, isn't it? (*Sincerely.*) In justice to myself—I must tell you this—that the reason I walked out on you in the summary way I did was not as you've just suggested because I doubted your future—it was obvious to me, even then, that you were destined for mighty things—but the reason was that I felt a disparity in our characters not conducive to matrimonial contentment. You see how right I was. I suspected in myself a—a tendency to explore, a spiritual and physical wanderlust—that I knew would horrify you once you found it out. It horrifies you now when we are no longer anything to each other. Imagine, Leander dear, if we were married how much more difficult it would be— If there is any one thing you have to be grateful to me for it is that instant's clear vision I had which made me see, which made me look ahead, which made me tear myself away from you. Why, everything you have now—your future, your prospects—even your fiancée, Leander dear—you owe to me—no, I won't say to me—to that instinct—to that premonition. . . .

NOLAN (*nostalgic*)—We might have done it together. . . .

MARION—I wouldn't have stood for a fiancée, Bunny dear—not even I am as promiscuous as that. . . .

NOLAN—Don't use that word!

MARION—But, Leander! It's your own!

NOLAN—Do you think it hasn't been on my conscience ever since; do you think it hasn't tortured me . . . !

MARION—What, dear?

NOLAN—That thought!

MARION—Which thought?

NOLAN—Every time I heard about you—all the notoriety that's attended you in the American papers . . . painting pictures of Communist statesmen, running around California with movie comedians!

MARION—I have to practice my profession, Bunny. One must live, you know. Besides, I've done Capitalist statesmen too. And at Geneva. . . .

NOLAN (*darkly*)—You know what I mean . . . !

MARION—You mean . . . (*She whispers through her cupped hand.*) you mean promiscuous? Has that gotten around, Bunny? Is it whispered in the sewing-circles of Nashville? Will I be burned for a witch if I go back home? Will they have a trial over me? Will you defend me?

NOLAN (*quite literally, with sincere and disarming simplicity*) —I should be forced, as an honest man, to stand before the multitude and say: In condemning this woman you are condemning me who am asking your suffrages to represent you. For it was I with whom this woman first sinned before God. As an honorable man that is what I should have to do.

It is that thought that has been torturing Nolan. That he—he was responsible. A worry, Marion assures him, that he may put quite out of his mind. She would not deprive him of his little pleasure, but— Nor is she, as he further charges, an evil person.

"You know perfectly well I'm not evil," she says defensively. "Casual, maybe, but not evil. Good heavens, Bunny, I might as well say you're evil because you're intolerant. These are differences in temperament, that's all—charming differences in temperament."

Marion thinks perhaps they should have a cup of tea, if Bunny is sure his constituents would not object to his having tea with a promiscuous woman.

They come back, finally, to the question of the painting.

Nolan thinks perhaps it would be a good thing for him to be painted in oils. The picture could be used for campaign purposes, and if he should go to Washington it might help Marion there. Bunny would like to prove his loyalty to an old friend in this way.

"I'll go the limit on you, Bunny—when I get through with you you'll be a symbol of Dignity," declares Marion. "Solid man. No nonsense. Safe and sane. Holds the middle of the course—a slogan in a frock-coat. I'll make you look like Warren G. Harding—even handsomer— Get you the women's votes."

"Well, that'll be very nice of you . . ."

Suddenly and impulsively Marion has kissed Bunny, and he is very uncomfortable. Also embarrassed and thrilled. But he would have her understand that the picture is strictly business. Bunny is going to be married in a month—and he is devoted to Slade, and he is not at all Bohemian. Marion promises not to kiss him again.

There is a ring at the door. This may be a young man Marion had met on the boat come to take her to dinner, but it proves to be Richard Kurt, come back to complete his interview of a half hour before.

With some maneuvering Marion manages to get a cup of tea into the hands of both Kurt and Nolan, and they, mutually insulting because Kurt has little use for politicians and Nolan is quickly convinced Kurt is an unmannerly young person who should be horsewhipped, have agreed to be friendly.

"Having said, from our respective points of view, the worst thing we could say about each other, having uttered the ultimate insult, there's no reason we can't be friends, Senator. Damn good cake. No lunch as a matter of fact."

"That's what's the matter with him—he was hungry—hungry boy—" decides Marion.

"He probably wants to sell you some insurance," is Nolan's idea.

"Not at all," continues Kurt, with enthusiasm. "I'm not here to sell. I'm here to buy."

What it is he has come to buy Kurt refuses to state until he can see Miss Froude alone. If she is not agreeable to that arrangement he is perfectly willing to withdraw. He has already wasted an hour of valuable time. The fact that Mr. Nolan is an old friend who would likely be consulted by Marion on any business matter does not interest Kurt. He will allow Marion one minute to decide whether or not she wants to talk with him.

Photo by Vandamm Studio, New York.

"BIOGRAPHY"

"I'll go the limit with you, Bunny—when I get through with you you'll be a symbol of Dignity," declares Marion. "Solid man. No nonsense. Safe and sane. Holds the middle of the course—a Slogan in a Frock Coat. I'll make you look like Warren G. Harding—even handsomer—get you the women's vote—" . . . Suddenly and impulsively Marion has kissed Bunny, and he is very uncomfortable.

(Ina Claire and Jay Fassett)

Nolan retires with some reluctance. He does not consider it actually safe to leave Marion alone with a character like Kurt, but he goes finally.

Marion is not pleased with Kurt's behavior. It is no way for a young man to act who hopes to get on in the world. He was quite wrong about Bunny Nolan, and behaved abominably.

Kurt has no apologies for the way he has acted. To him Nolan is no more than "a stuffed shirt—flatulent and pompous," a perfect legislator. "I bet he's greedy and vicious. Anyway he's a hypocrite. When a man starts worrying out loud about unprotected women you may know he's a hypocritical sensualist," says Kurt.

Coming finally to the proposition he wishes to submit Kurt announces that he is the editor of a magazine called *Every Week*, which Marion has seen on the news stands but never remembers having read.

KURT—That is a tribute to your discrimination. We have an immense circulation. Three millions, I believe. With a circulation of that size you may imagine that the average of our readers' intelligence cannot be very high. Yet occasionally we flatter them by printing the highbrows—in discreet doses we give them, at intervals, Shaw and Wells and Chesterton. So you'll be in good company anyway. . . .

MARION (*amazed*)—*I* will?

KURT—Yes. I want you to write your biography to run serially in *Every Week*. Later of course you can bring it out as a book.

MARION—My biography!

KURT—Yes. The story of your life.

MARION (*with dignity*)—I know the meaning of the word.

KURT—The money is pretty good. I am prepared to give you an advance of two thousand dollars.

MARION—Good Heavens, am I as old as that—that people want my biography!

KURT—We proceed on the theory that nothing exciting happens to people after they are forty. . . .

MARION—What a cruel idea!

KURT—Why wait till you're eighty? Your impressions will be dimmed by time. Most autobiographies are written by corpses. Why not do yours while you are still young, vital, in the thick of life?

MARION—But I'm not a writer. I shouldn't know how to

begin.

KURT—You were born, weren't you? Begin with that.

MARION—I write pleasant letters my friends tell me. . . . But look here, why should you want this story from me—why should anybody be interested?—I'm not a first-rate artist, you know—not by far—I'm just clever. . . .

KURT (*bluntly*)—It's not you—it's the celebrity of your subjects. . . .

MARION (*amused*)—You're a brutal young man—I rather like you.

KURT—Well, you've been courageous. You've been forthright. For an American woman you've had a rather extraordinary career—you've done pretty well what you wanted. . . .

MARION—The Woman Who Dared sort-of-thing. . . . Isn't that passé?

KURT—I think your life will make good copy. You might have stayed here and settled down and done *Pictorial Review* covers of mothers hovering fondly over babies. Instead you went to Europe and managed to get the most inaccessible people to sit for you.

How did she do it? That is what Kurt wants in Marion's story. How and why? Why did she go to Russia? What has kept her going ever since? Let her write it all. He will print portraits of Lenin, Mussolini, Shaw and the others with it and print it just as she writes it.

Marion is scared. Even more scared when Kurt writes a check for two thousand dollars and puts that in her hand as a first payment. He refuses to let her think she can't do it. It wouldn't make her feel old to write a novel, and that is all this story will be—a novel of her life.

"You may be disappointed, you know," Marion warns. "You probably see headlines in your mind. The Woman of a Hundred Affairs, The Last of the Great Adventuresses, The Magda Who Wouldn't go Home. I promise you—it won't be a bit like that."

Kurt is not impressed. The story will be announced the next issue, with the first chapter following the month after that. All she has to do is to get to work. She will not have to make up anything. Just tell what happened to her.

Now Marion has become a little stirred by his enthusiasm. Richard is his first name, she discovers, so she calls him Dickie. "Dickie," she says, "I think it'll be marvelous. It'll be a knockout. And imagine—I'm going to be paid for it! Dickie, you're an angel!"

"That's me! Angel Kurt! Well, so long. I'll be seeing you."

But again Marion's fears assail her. To be left all alone with her life, like that. Besides she is beginning to feel a little superstitious about it. It will be a kind of ultimate act. "After you've written your biography what else could there possibly be left for you to do?"

"Collect material for another!"

Now Marion is wavering again and Kurt is losing patience. Very well, it was a wrong hunch. If she doesn't want to do it he is sorry to have taken her time. Besides he is beginning to feel that, if she should try to escape vulgarity her story would probably be thin anyway. She might even achieve refinement, and he would not be interested in that. No "padded episodes hovering on the edge of amour" for him.

"Young man, you're insufferable," snaps Marion, turning on him.

"And you're a false alarm!" says he.

MARION (*after a moment*)—I congratulate you! You've brought me to the verge of losing my temper! But I tell you this—you're quite mistaken about the character of my life—and about my relations with my friends. My story won't be thin and episodic because my life hasn't been thin and episodic. And I won't have to pad—the problem will be to select. I'm going to write the damn thing just to show you. Come in tomorrow afternoon for a cocktail.

KURT—Whose memoirs are these going to be, yours or mine?

MARION—Well, you're an editor, aren't you? (*She smiles at him.*) Come in and edit.

KURT—All right, I'll come. But if you aren't here I'll go away. I won't wait a minute. (*He goes out quickly.* MARION *stands looking after him, inclined to laugh, and yet affected. This is a new type even for her.*)

MARION (*speaking to herself*)—What an extraordinary young young man! (*In a moment* KURT *comes back in.* MARION *is very glad to see him, greets him as if there had been a long separation.*) Oh, hello!

KURT (*embarrassed*)—I forgot my hat! (*He can't see it at once.*)

MARION (*without moving or looking away from him, she indicates the hat on the sofa*)—There it is! Right next to mine.

KURT—Oh, yes. (*Picks up hat.*) Thanks. (*For a moment*

he stands uncertainly, hat in hand, looking at Marion *who has not taken her eyes off him. He is embarrassed.*) Well, so long!

Marion—So long.

He has gone now. Slowly Marion takes up the check. "The whole thing has a slightly fantastic quality to her. She is very happy and excited." She sits at the piano and plays over the waltz from "Danubia." Now she has recovered a pad and pencil and seated herself comfortably, prepared to write.

"I am born—" she repeats as she puts down the first words. Minnie coming for the tea things pays no attention to her mistress's irrelevancies. She is used to them.

"I am born—" repeats Marion. "I am born—I meet Richard Kurt— Well, Minnie—here's the outline—I am born . . . I meet Richard Kurt— Now all I have to do is to fill in."

"Was, Marion?"

"Fix something light, will you, Minnie. . . . I'm not going out."

But—there is the young man coming to take Marion to dinner. What is she going to do with him?

Minnie will have to send the young man away, says Marion. She is spending the evening alone with her life.—She has to get "a good, straight, clear-eyed look at it—"

Marion has returned to "I am born—" as Minnie goes to fix the dinner.

THE CURTAIN FALLS

ACT II

Three weeks later Marion, in her studio, is putting a few touches to Leander Nolan's portrait. Her studio costume is one of baggy red corduroy trousers and a worn blue smock. Frequently, thinking of something that would go well in her biography, she steps over to the piano, where her writing things are, and jots it down. These notes please her very much. Frequently she is reduced to giggles at the recollections they invoke.

Herr Feydak is an early caller. Marion is pleased to see Feydie, but distressed to hear that he has received his traveling orders and is leaving for Hollywood next day. It is going to be pretty desolate for Marion, with no one to laugh with. She thinks perhaps she will join Feydie later—on her way to China.

Their conversation leads to Richard Kurt. Marion has seen that "bumptious and insufferable young man" quite frequently, she confesses. Kurt drops in frequently to see how the biography is coming on. Also Marion has discovered that the more she sees of Kurt the better she likes him and the more she becomes convinced that his bumptiousness is largely in defense of an aggravated inferiority complex.

"He's some kind of fanatic," she says. "Social, I think. I've met that kind in Russia—quite unassailable. But I'm optimistic. . . . [They laugh.] Well, one must never despair, must one? Life is so much more resourceful and resilient than one is oneself. Three weeks ago when you came to see me I felt quite at the end of my rope. I didn't tell you quite but I actually didn't know which way to turn. I felt tired too—which troubled me. Well, now I find myself, quite suddenly [She indicates portrait.] doing Leander and— [She indicates manuscript on piano.] doing myself. New Vista. Very exciting."

Marion has been sobered a good deal as she has studied her life. She sees it now as a sort of "interminable scherzo." Sometimes she will sit for hours and nothing will come to her. Again there will be such a rush of odd, remote, semi-forgotten things from the past as to be overwhelming. . . .

The bell and Minnie have announced Warwick Wilson. Warwick is a famous film star, "handsome, explosively emotional and given to cosmic generalizations." He is tremendously enthusiastic about seeing Marion again, and thrilled to meet Herr Feydak—because of that unforgettable waltz. As Mr. Wilson hums it now it sounds very like "The Merry Widow." Minnie, representing Mr. Wilson's public, finds it difficult to drag herself back to the kitchen, but must stand staring until Marion breaks the spell.

Warwick has seen the announcement of Marion's forthcoming biography in the magazine, and this has served to remind him that for years he has been thinking of having Marion paint him. As the Dane, preferably. He is so devoted to Shakespeare he has been trying to get them to put the poet into pictures.

Now Leander Nolan has called. Leander is plainly worried about something. He carries a rolled magazine in his hand and is curt and formal accepting introductions. Marion, thinking he has come for his sitting, would hurry him into a pose while the light is still good. But Nolan is in no mood for posing. The presence of Feydak and Wilson add to his irritation. He feels, he says, as though he were being watched taking a bath. So Marion sends Feydak and Wilson away.

Free to speak his mind Nolan soon reveals the cause of his irritation. It is the announcement of Marion's biography. It is difficult for him to believe that Marion really is writing the story of her life. If she is, what is she going to put in it? Everything? Including her life as a girl in Knoxville? Including Bunny? No, no. She must leave him out of her story.

"But how can I?" Marion protests. "You are too important—think of the rôle you played in my life. By your own confession, Bunny darling, you—you started me. That's a good idea for a chapter heading, isn't it? 'Bunny Starts Me.' I must write that down."

"This is no joke, Marion. I warn you—" The Nolan tone is menacing.

"Warn me? Let me understand you. Are you seriously asking me to give up an opportunity like this just because—"

"Opportunity! Cheap exhibitionism! A chance to flaunt your affairs in a rag like this!" Nolan is down from the model stand and is pointing to Kurt's magazine on the piano. "I won't be drawn into it. I can tell you that!"

Nolan is in a towering rage, but Marion meets him calmly. There are other moral standards besides those he holds to, she tells him. Whatever the advertisements may say she knows what she is writing. Nor does a suggestion that he will get her many commissions, including one to paint his father-in-law, alter her determination. The tip isn't big enough.

"It amuses me to write my life," continues Marion. "I am pleasure-loving—you know that.—I will therefore pass up the opportunity of painting your big father-in-law. I will even give up the pleasure of painting you. And we can part friends, then, can't we? Good-by, Bunny."

Nolan is completely devastated by this attitude. His tone is pleading. Marion, he insists, does not understand what's involved. His entire career is at stake. His fiancée's father is the most powerful leader of opinion in his state.

"To have this thing bandied about now might cause a permanent rift between him and me," he says; "might seriously interfere not only with my candidacy for the Senate, but with my marriage."

"They are interlocking—I quite understand."

Nolan—A revelation of this kind—coming at this moment—might be fatal . . .

Marion—Revelation! You make me feel like—I can't tell you what you make me feel like . . . (*She laughs—semi-hysterically.*)

NOLAN (*sepulchral*)—You must give this up, Marion.

MARION—I've met distinguished men abroad—politicians, statesmen—a Prime Minister even—and this kind of "revelation" —as you so luridly call it—is no more to them than a theme for after-dinner banter. They take it in their stride. My God, Bunny, you take it so big!

NOLAN—These people I'm depending on to elect me aren't sophisticated like you or me. (MARION *looks at* NOLAN *with some surprise.*) What I mean is—they're country people essentially—my future father-in-law is sympathetic to their point of view.

MARION—Tell me—your father-in-law, is he the man with the chest-expansion?

NOLAN—He's a fine sturdy man—as you perhaps know, he makes a fetish of exercise.

MARION (*bubbling again*)—You see his pictures in shorts in health magazines.

NOLAN—There's no disgrace in that.

MARION (*sitting on arm of sofa*)—It doesn't shock me, Bunny. I was just identifying him, that's all.

NOLAN—I owe everything to Kinnicott—I wouldn't be running for the Senate right now if not for him. I can't risk offending him.

MARION—What the devil's happened to you anyway? You used to be quite a nice boy—even fun occasionally. . . .

NOLAN (*wistful—turns away*)—Maybe—if you had stuck to me . . .

MARION—Ts! Ts! Ts! Poor Bunny. I'm sorry for you. Really I am!

Now the Nolan anger has turned to passion. The touch of Marion's hand upon his arm revives the old excitement. After all, Bunny is human. He knew the minute he saw Marion again—Nor is there any use reminding him that he is engaged and is going to be a Senator. He would like Marion to forget that he ever said that.

Marion is quite touched by this confession. She would kiss Bunny again in friendly spirit to heal the hurt. But the kiss is also inflaming and must not be repeated. Bunny knows that Marion had forgotten him once and that she would humiliate him again if she got the chance.

Now there is anger in his tone as he repeats the warning that if Marion persists in putting him in her story she will regret it.

His prospective father-in-law is a powerful man—

"I must admit, Bunny, that you provoke in me all my malicious impulses," says Marion, with some spirit. "You come here suddenly and you convey to me what I've missed in not marrying you." Minnie crosses to answer back-door bell during Marion's speech. "You dangle before me the inventory of your felicities—a career, a fortune, a fabulous bride—and then, because I get a chance to chronicle my own adventures—you object—you tell me I mustn't! I have a nice nature, Bunny, or I should be angry—I should be indignant."

Richard Kurt has come in, and Marion, remembering a dinner engagement with Feydak, runs up stairs to her bedroom to dress. While she is gone she hopes Dickie will explain to Bunny that even if she wanted to do something about stopping the biography, she is powerless. She has already signed something.

Nolan's attitude toward Kurt becomes surprisingly friendly. Having been impressed by the young editor when first they met, as he admits, he would now know more of his work. What are his ambitions and his prospects? It is quite possible that the Nolan father-in-law, Mr. Orrin Kinnicott, would be interested in a young man of Kurt's abilities. Just the other day Nolan had heard Mr. Kinnicott, whom Kurt knows very well as a publisher, speak of wanting a new man in Washington.

The idea of a Washington job is alluring to Kurt, but, if he might venture a question, why is the offer being made? Why has Mr. Nolan's attitude changed so completely toward him? What, asks Kurt, is the pay-off?

Mr. Nolan is ready, though not eager, to answer that. Frankly he does not want Marion Froude's biography printed. He wants it killed. And Marion knows why.

"My God! You! You too!" cries Kurt, wounded by a sudden and devastating jealousy.

Now Marion has reappeared on the balcony wearing a dove-colored evening dress—"the gamine transformed into the lady-of-the-world." She would know how they have been getting on and what they think of her gown. Kurt is still too mad to have any thought about it. Nolan thinks it charming.

"Thank you, Bunny. With all his faults Bunny is much more satisfactory than you are, Dickie."

Kurt (*at boiling point*)—He's chivalrous, he is! His chivalry is so exquisite that he has just been attempting to bribe me to keep your story from being published. His gallantry is so delicate that he's terrified about being mentioned in it.

MARION (*coming down stairs*)—Don't be so worked up about it, Dickie. You're another one who takes it big. It's catching!

KURT (*flaring at her*)—You're not very sensitive. . . .

MARION—Why should I be? You misapprehend Bunny. If he doesn't want to be in the same story with me that's his business. And it's nothing to do with chivalry or gallantry or nonsense like that.

NOLAN—Marion—this young man. . . .

KURT (*taunting him*)—What about Washington, Mr. Nolan? Mr. Nolan, a prospective Senator, offers to bribe me with a post in Washington controlled by his prospective father-in-law. . . .

MARION—If it's a good job take it, Dickie, by all means . . .

KURT—I am afraid, Marion, that your code is more relaxed than mine . . .

MARION—Code, nonsense! I gave up codes long ago. I'm a big laissez-faire girl!

NOLAN—If this young man is an example of the distinguished company you've come to associate with, Marion . . .

MARION—Don't quarrel, children—please. It distresses me.

NOLAN—He's extremely objectionable.

KURT—What about Washington, now, *Senator?* Are you willing to expedite . . . ! (KURT *and* NOLAN *stand glaring at each other.*)

MARION (*trying to calm the troubled waters*)—Really, Dickie, you're very naughty. Don't mind him, Bunny. He's very young.

KURT—And incorruptible!

NOLAN—Marion, I claim the privilege of a friendship that antedates Mr. Kurt's by some years, to beg you, very solemnly, not to prostitute your talents to his contemptible, sensation-mongering rag.

KURT (*faces them*)—There's a Senatorial sentence!

MARION—Hush, Dickie, hush! Bunny darling, it's true that Dickie's magazine isn't the *Edinburgh Review.* On the other hand, your assumption that my story will be vulgar and sensational is a little gratuitous, isn't it?

NOLAN—You *refuse* then?

MARION (*gently but with a serious overtone*)—Yes. This—censorship before publication seems to me, shall we say, unfair. It is—even in an old friend—dictatorial.

NOLAN (*with an air of finality*)—You leave me then no alternative. I am very sorry.

KURT—Don't let him frighten you, Marion, he can't do anything.

NOLAN—I can forgive you anything, Marion, but the fact that you value my wishes below those of this insolent young man.

MARION—But this insolent young man hasn't anything to do with it! Can't you see, Bunny—it's my own wish that is involved?

NOLAN—I have explained to you the special circumstances. If you would consent to delay publication till after election . . .

The editor and Nolan are storming at each other, Nolan threatening reprisals, Kurt gloating at the opportunity the publishing of a biography will give the circulation manager of his magazine in Tennessee during the campaign.

Now Nolan has stormed out. He never wants to see Marion again, he says, which distresses Marion greatly. Still, she cannot believe that she really does control the election of Senators in Tennessee.

"How could you ever have loved a stuffed-shirt like that?" Kurt demands.

"He wasn't a stuffed-shirt," Marion answers. "That's the funny part. He was charming. He was a charming boy. Rather thin. Rather reticent. He was much nicer than you, as a matter of fact. . . . He used to work hard all day and at night he studied law. We used to walk the country lanes and dream about the future. He was scared—he was wistful. How did he emerge into this successful, ambitious, over-cautious—mediocrity? How do we all emerge into what we are? How did I emerge into what I am? I've dug up some of my old diaries. I was a tremulous young girl. I was eager. I believe I was naïve. Look at me now! Time, Dickie . . . What will you be at forty? A bondholder and a commuter . . . Oh, Dickie!"

It is Kurt's belief that he will never be forty—that he will wear himself out before then. Marion feels differently. One is perpetually reborn, she sometimes thinks. Right now she is also convinced that everyone should write his own life. Not for publication, but for oneself, as a kind of spiritual housecleaning.

Now she would know something more of Kurt, who has again drawn within himself. His life, he slowly admits, is very dull. His past has nothing of what she would call glamour. It is easy for her, and her kind, to make romantic generalizations. But they are not true.

"I had no idea you felt this way about me," says Marion. "You despise me, don't you?"

"Yes."
"Why?"
"Why did we start this?"

MARION—You're annoyed at having even momentarily revealed yourself, aren't you? I'll have your secret, Dickie—I'll pluck out the heart of your mystery.

KURT—Secret! Mystery! More romantic nonsense, I have no secret. Nobody has a secret. There are different kinds of greed, different kinds of ambition—that's all!

MARION—Oh, you simplify too much—really I'm afraid you do. Tell me—why do you disapprove of me? Is it—as Bunny does—on moral grounds?

KURT (*angrily*)—You're superficial and casual and irresponsible. You take life, which is a tragic thing, as though it were a trivial, bed-room farce. You're a second-rate artist who's acquired a reputation through vamping celebrities to sit for you.

MARION (*quietly, she continues smoking*)—Go on . . .

KURT—As an unglamorous upstart who has been forced to make my way I resent parasitism, that's all!

MARION—Isn't there in biology something about benevolent parasites, Dickie? Many great man, I believe, owe a debt of gratitude to their parasites, as many plants do . . . there are varieties. Again, Dickie, you simplify unduly. It is a defect of the radical and the young.

They return to Nolan and the problem he presents. It is quite possible, thinks Kurt, that Nolan's father-in-law can get him fired. But if he tries it Kurt knows what he will do. He will make Nolan and his athletic father-in-law, too, the laughingstock of the country.

Marion does not like that side of Kurt; not the vindictive side. Kurt doesn't care. He is still storming about Nolan as "an epitome of the brainless muddle of contemporary life, of all the self-seeking second-raters who rise to power and wield power," when the telephone rings and he is summoned. As he suspected, it is his chief and his chief wants to talk to him about the Froude story.

The thought of battle is exciting to Kurt. If his chief kills Marion's story he will tell him to go to hell and take it to another publisher. If he cannot get quick action that way he will publish the biography himself.

"Do you think I'd miss a chance like this?" he shouts to the wondering but now sympathetic Marion. "It'll test the caliber of our magazines, our press, our Senators, our morality . . ."

"All on account of my poor little story!" marvels Marion, and later she adds, ". . . I've always rather despised these contemporary women who publicize their emotions. [She is thinking out loud.] And here I am doing it myself. Too much self-revelation these days. Loud speakers in the confessional. Why should I add to the noise? I think, as far as this story is concerned, I'll call it a day, Dickie."

The thought of giving up the story is maddening to Kurt. If Marion should let him down now he would hate her. And yet, Marion repeats, he refuses to take her into his confidence, to tell her about himself and what it is he is after.

"My ambition is to be critic-at-large of things-as-they-are. I want to find out everything there is to know about the intimate structure of things. I want to reduce the whole system to absurdity. I want to laugh the powers that be out of existence in a great winnowing gale of laughter."

It is an interesting research, Marion agrees, but she finds it biased. Kurt is so apt to overlook much that is noble and generous and gentle. She has found it so and is sorry for him.

Now she has interested Kurt further in his own story. How old he is does not matter, he says. He lives alone. His parents are dead. His mother had died when he was a child. But he has a vivid memory of his father, who was a coal miner.

Marion—Oh! Won't you tell me about him? I'd like to know.

Kurt—I was a kid of fourteen. There was a strike. One day my father took me out for a walk. Sunny spring morning. We stopped to listen to an organizer. My father was a mild little man with kind of faded, tired blue eyes. We stood on the outskirts of the crowd. My father was holding me by the hand. Suddenly somebody shouted: The militia! There was a shot. Everybody scattered. My father was bewildered— He didn't know which way to turn. A second later he crumpled down beside me. He was bleeding. He was still holding my hand. He died like that. . . . (*A moment. He concludes harshly—coldly—like steel.*) Are there any other glamorous facts of my existence you would like to know?

Marion (*stirred to her heart*)—You poor boy . . . I knew there was something . . . I knew . . . !

Kurt (*hard and ironic*)—It's trivial really. People exaggerate the importance of human life. One has to die. (*Turns to her.*) The point is to have fun while you're alive, isn't it? Well, you've managed. I congratulate you!

MARION (*her heart full*)—Dickie darling—why are you so bitter against me? Why against me . . . ?

KURT—Do you want to know that too? Well, it's because . . . (*His voice rises. She suddenly doesn't want him to speak.*)

MARION—Hush, dearest—hush—don't say any more—I understand—not any more . . . (*His defenses vanish suddenly. He sinks to his knees beside her, his arms around her.*)

KURT—Marion, my angel!

MARION (*infinitely compassionate, stroking his hair*)—Dickie—Dickie—Dickie . . . Why have you been afraid to love me?

THE CURTAIN FALLS

ACT III

Two weeks later, in Marion's apartment, Minnie is answering the telephone. Richard Kurt is calling, in an effort to locate Marion. But Marion has not confided her plans to Minnie.

A moment later Leander Nolan and his father-in-law, Orrin Kinnicott, are there. Kinnicott "is a big, well-developed Southerner, about fifty-five, with a high-pitched voice. He is a superbly built man with a magnificent chest development. He is aware that he is a fine figure of a man, impeccably dressed in formal afternoon clothes."

Kinnicott and Nolan have come to tea, and they will wait for Marion. Nolan had made the engagement for four o'clock. Kinnicott is rather irritated that Marion has not been more impressed by it. But that, he suggests with some vehemence, is the way with these fly-by-night characters. Which reminds him that he would like to be perfectly sure that there is nothing in Leander's acquaintance, his present acquaintance, with this woman that he is holding back.

Both he and his daughter Slade, reports Kinnicott, have been conscious of a change in Leander since Marion has come back into his life. In fact Kinnicott was finally forced to tell Slade that Leander and Marion had been lovers fifteen years ago. Slade had not said anything, being the silent kind, but Kinnicott thinks it is pretty small of Leander to go on defending the woman who is now endangering his entire career. Especially his political career.

Nolan is beginning to show some slight irritation at his campaign manager's dictation. He is impatient to know now what Kinnicott proposes to do about the problem in hand.

Kinnicott is quite sure that he can get the young fellow, Kurt, fired, but he has an idea that Kurt may have something more up his sleeve—something much like black-mail. Whether he has or not is what Kinnicott proposes to find out from Marion. Every woman, to a man who knows the sex as well as Kinnicott, is a potential black-mailer. And Kinnicott thinks that it is time for Leander to be making up his mind as to whether he wants to go along with a black-mailing female, or with a girl like Slade. Which makes Leander pretty angry.

Now the doorbell has rung and Minnie has let in Slade Kinnicott herself. She is a "good-looking, dark, high-spirited girl, a rather inspiriting and healthy example of the generation growing up on D. H. Lawrence."

Slade is not at all perturbed by her father's excited demand to know why she is there. Perhaps she has come to have her picture painted. And she is just as anxious to "get a load" of Marion as Leander is to have her. Furthermore she is keen to have a talk with Leander's old girl.

"If you think I didn't suspect something was up ever since Froude arrived here," says Slade, "you don't know your little bride. Maybe I haven't been watching the clouds gather on that classic brow! Where is my rival? Don't tell me she's holding up two big shots like you two boys."

Kinnicott's agitation increases. He would have his daughter leave before Marion arrives. And he would not have her treat the matter as a joke. Slade is not to be moved, and she is terribly disappointed that they should want to suppress Marion's story.

"At least I hope you'll buy the *manuscript*. My God, father, I'm curious. Can't you understand that? I want to find out what Leander was like before he became ambitious. I've a right to know! This story might hurt you with the voters in Tennessee, Leander, but it's given me a kick out of you I didn't know was there! How did she make you, Leander—that's what I'd like to know. You've been pretty unapproachable to me but I sort of took it for granted National Figures were like that. Also I'd gotten to a point when I was going to suggest that we break our engagement, but this little incident revives my interest."

Nolan is furious. If it has come to the point where Slade's

interest in him requires artificial respiration he thinks perhaps they had better separate now.

SLADE (*mock tragedy*)—Father, Leander is giving your daughter the air. Do something!

KINNICOTT—I don't blame him for being irritated. You should not be here. Please go home.

SLADE (*lights cigarette*)—Don't worry, dad. I'll get him back.

KINNICOTT—This is a bad mess, Leander. And I must tell you frankly that I don't altogether approve of your attitude . . .

NOLAN—And I must tell you frankly that I don't approve of *yours*. . . .

KINNICOTT—Is that so!

NOLAN—I don't like your tone in speaking of a woman with whom at one time I had a relation of the tenderest emotion—for whom I still have a high regard. . . .

KINNICOTT—That's evident anyway!

NOLAN—When you apply to such a woman the terms you used before Slade came in, when you impute to her motives so base, you cast an equal reflection on my judgment and my character. . . .

SLADE—And that, pop, is lèse-majesté.

NOLAN—And it may be perfectly true, Slade, that knowing Miss Froude has spoiled me for the flippant modernisms with which you study. . . .

SLADE—I'm dying to ask her one thing: when you made love to her in the old days did it always sound like a prepared speech on tariff schedules?

KINNICOTT—This is getting us nowhere. . . .

SLADE—Well, dad, what do you expect? Leander and I have broken our engagement since I came into this room. That's progress, isn't it?

KINNICOTT—Your coming here at this time was most unfortunate.

SLADE—Leander doesn't think so. (*Ironically.*) He's free now to pursue the lady for whom he still has a high regard. (*Rises.*) Are we no longer engaged, Leander?

NOLAN—That's not for me to say.

SLADE (*rises and shakes hands with* NOLAN)—Gentleman to the last! And at the very moment—

KINNICOTT (*in despair—speaks as* SLADE *starts to speak*)—Slade, if you would only go home!

SLADE—*Just* at the very moment when I was saying to myself:

Well, if a brilliant and beautiful woman who has played footie with royalty in the capitals of the world loved him, maybe there's a secret charm in him that I've overlooked—just when I was saying that and preparing to probe and discover, (*Lightly*) he gives me the air. By God, Orrin, there's life for you.

At that moment Richard Kurt bursts into the room. He is white with anger. He is not surprised to find them there, and he needs no introduction to tell him who Kinnicott is. Kurt has just come from his office where he has been informed by his editor that he could make his choice between publishing Miss Froude's story or giving up his job. He had invited the editor to go to hell, and now extends the invitation to the Messrs. Nolan and Kinnicott.

Kurt has been too excited to notice Slade. Now, obviously interested in him, she comes forward and begs an introduction. Kurt is momentarily embarrassed but is soon back in the thick of the fight with the men. He would advise them that he intends publishing Miss Froude's book himself, and he promises that it will be the best advertised first book that has been brought out in some time.

There are still laws of libel, Kinnicott is eager to remind Kurt. And Kurt is hoping Kinnicott will dare invoke them. Think of what that revelation will mean to Mr. Nolan's moral constituency—

Marion is home. "She wears a long, red velvet coat and a little red cap stuck on the side of her golden head. She looks a little like Portia. She is at the top of her form."

Marion, meeting them all, would have Minnie bring them tea, or highballs. Now she has heard of the threatened libel suit from the excited Kurt and would know more of that. Whom has she defamed? The Honorable Mr. Nolan?

Marion would go right on being a hostess, however they may feel about her as a defamer. She would have Slade sit beside her on the sofa that she may tell her how pretty she is. And now she has turned her attention to Mr. Kinnicott—

"It seems so strange to see you with all your clothes on," she tells him. "It seems a pity—as an artist I must say it seems a pity—to conceal that wonderful chest-development that I've admired so often in 'The Body Beautiful.'"

Mr. Kinnicott would change that subject. Again Kurt reminds Marion that if she understood better what it is her callers are planning to do she would be less friendly, but Marion is certain she could not possibly be unfriendly "to anyone so frank and—and—gladiatorial—as Mr. Kinnicott."

"The Honorable Nolan is going to sue you for libel—" repeats Kurt.

"I'll punch your head if you say that again," shouts Nolan.

KURT—On the assumption that when you say in your story that you and he were lovers you were lying and defaming his character!

MARION—Dear Bunny, you must want to be a Senator very badly!

NOLAN (*in despair*)—I never said it, I tell you!

MARION—As a matter of fact how could I prove it? Come to think of it, are there any letters? Did you ever write to me, Bunny?

NOLAN—I don't remember.

MARION—I don't think you ever did. You see—we were always—during that dim brief period of your youth—we were always so close—letters were hardly necessary, were they? Did I ever send you any letters, Bunny?

NOLAN—I don't remember, I tell you.

MARION—Neither do I. You might look around in old trunks and places and see if you can find some old letters of an affectionate nature—I'd love to read them—they'd probably make wonderful reading now. Why is it that the things one writes when one's young always sound so foolish afterwards? Has that ever occurred to you, Mr. Kinnicott?

KINNICOTT—I don't admit the fact.

MARION—No?

KINNICOTT—No. I was looking over some old editorials of mine written in the depression of 1907 and they're just as apropos today. I haven't changed my ideas in twenty-five years.

MARION—Haven't you really? How very steadfast. Now if the world were equally changeless, how consistent that would make you. (*To* KURT.) Well, there isn't any documentary evidence.

KURT—It doesn't matter. . . .

KINNICOTT—As I said before, this is getting us nowhere. Don't you think, Miss Froude, that the only way we can settle this is by ourselves? (*She smiles at him.*) I can see you're a sensible woman.

MARION—I am very sensible.

KINNICOTT—And you and I can settle this matter in short order.

Marion has got the others out by suggesting to Kurt that he accept Slade's invitation to take her for a walk, and by sending Nolan into her bedroom—or Minnie's bedroom, as he prefers—to wait. Then she settles down comfortably for a talk with Kinnicott.

"It's funny—I feel we've put the children to bed and can have a quiet talk after a lot of chatter," she says.

"Same here," answers Kinnicott, in hearty agreement.

A moment later, by mutual agreement, they are calling each other Orrin and Marion, and Orrin has confessed that he is greatly surprised to find Marion so "folksy." Marion, just a small-town girl from Tennessee, has often wondered how she ever got so far away from the girl she was and Orrin is convinced that it is a question of metabolism.

"I always say—take most of the bad men and most of the loose women—and correct their metabolism and you'll correct them," says Orrin. "Trouble with our penology experts—so-called—is that they're psychologists—so-called—when they should be physiologists."

It is entirely probable, intimates Orrin, that Marion does not eat enough roughage. As to that Marion would not know, though perhaps she should. She agrees with him that if, as a girl, she had met him instead of Leander and had her metabolism disciplined early in life, there is no telling how far she might have gone.

Kinnicott thinks there is still time for correction and would have Marion dine with him, at his apartment, the next evenin'. They can then go over the whole matter and make a friendly adjustment. Orrin is a widower and lives in a roof apartment, and that, admits Marion, is an irresistible combination. She also agrees with him that it would probably be unwise to say anything to Leander about the date.

Kinnicott has gone into the bedroom to explain things to Leander when Kurt and Slade get back from their walk. It was not a very encouraging walk, so far as Slade is concerned. Kurt was much too serious.

Marion had got along fine with Mr. Kinnicott, she is quick to report. She is crazy about Mr. Kinnicott. When they meet to discuss their affairs he is going to teach her how she can live in a state of virtuous metabolism.

Slade would now know from Marion what it is about Bunny that is really likeable. Marion agrees there is something sweet and touching about Bunny. But she is not in love with him. She is in love with someone else.

"I thought you were," admits Slade. "He's mad about you. I envy you, Marion."

"Do you? Why?"

"You're independent. You're yourself. You can do anything you like."

"Yes, I know. But it's possible one can pay too much for independence. I'm adrift. Sometimes—you know what seems to me the most heavenly thing—the only thing—for a woman? Marriage, children—the dear boundaries of routine . . ."

"If you had married Bunny he would've given 'em to you. He's still in love with you, but he doesn't quite know it. Shall I tell him?"

"What are you talking about?"

"I wish we could change places, Marion. You can with me but I can't with you."

Kinnicott and Nolan have finished their conference. Kinnicott emerges sweetened in temper and hopeful that Kurt is the same. Can't they let by-gones be by-gones? Miss Froude has proved such a gracious friend and intercepter—

Kurt is of no mind to accept peace on those terms, and is still glaring at Kinnicott as the latter leaves and takes Slade and Nolan with him.

Alone with Marion, Kurt would know what it was that she had said to Kinnicott to put him in such good spirits, and Marion is amused to report that everything she said had had that effect. She can hardly wait for the roughage dinner.

"Well, he may be quaint to you but to me he's a putrescent old hypocrite and I don't see how you can bear to have him come near you, say less go to dinner with him!"

"You know, Dickie, I adore you and I'm touched by you and I love you, but I'd hate to live in a country where you were Dictator. It would be all right while you loved me but when you stopped . . ."

KURT—It wouldn't make any difference if I stopped—I shouldn't be that kind of Dictator . . .

MARION (*glances at him, almost sadly*)—I see you've thought of it.

KURT (*inexorably*)—What did you say to Kinnicott?

MARION—Your manner is so—inquisitorial. I haven't been able to get used to it.

KURT (*angry and jealous*)—I heard you tell Nolan to come back too . . . How do you think I feel?

MARION—Dickie!

KURT—When Nolan sat there and told me he had been your lover, I felt like socking him. Even when we're alone together, I can't forget that . . . yet you encourage him, and Kinnicott—My God, Marion, you seem to like these people!

MARION—I certainly like Slade.

KURT—Well, I don't. She's conceited and overbearing. Thinks she can have anything she likes because she's Orrin Kinnicott's daughter.

MARION—That's where you're wrong. She's a nice girl—and she's unhappy.

KURT (*bitterly*)—Maladjusted, I suppose!

MARION—Dickie, Dickie, Dickie! Studying you, I can see why so many movements against injustice become such absolute —tyrannies.

KURT—That beautiful detachment again. . . . (*He is white with fury. He hates her at this moment.*)

MARION (*with a little laugh*)—You hate me, don't you . . . ?

KURT—Yes! Temporizing with these . . . ! Yes . . . ! I hate you. (*She says nothing, sits there looking at him.*) These people flout you, they insult you in the most flagrant way. God knows I'm not a gentleman, but it horrifies me to think of the insufferable arrogance of their attitude toward you . . . as if the final insult to their pride and their honor could only come from the discovery that this stuffed shirt Nolan had once been your lover! The blot on the immaculate Tennessee scutcheon! Why, it's the God-damndest insolence I ever heard of. And yet you flirt and curry favor and bandy with them. And you're amused —always amused!

MARION—Yes. I am amused.

KURT—I can't understand such . . . !

MARION—Of course you can't. That's the difference—one of the differences—between 25 and 35!

KURT—If the time ever comes when I'm amused by what I should hate, I hope somebody shoots me.

His rage continues. He would know all that she told Kinnicott and why. Why is she so afraid of scenes? Why does she expect to go through life as though it were a beautifully lit drawing-room with modulated voices making polite chatter?

Marion thinks perhaps Dickie forgets that she is not a born martyr as he is. And she thinks a most uncomfortable thing about martyrs is that they look down on people who aren't.

Now Kurt is raging again, this time at Marion's suggestion that they give up the story. Give it up? After all he's done? So she could marry Nolan, and live happily forever after! And be amused!

He has grabbed his hat from the stand and rushed out of the room. Nor will he return when she rushes after him, calling his name. The door slams in her face and she stands for a moment very distressed and saddened. "A deep unhappiness is gnawing in her heart, an awareness of the vast, uncrossable deserts between the souls of human beings."

"Poor Dickie! Poor boy!" she murmurs to herself.

From the piano Marion has taken the manuscript of her story from its Italian folder. Slowly, as if in a trance, she walks to the Franklin stove with it. She sits in front of the stove on a little stool. Slowly she tears out a page or two and puts them into the fire. Now the rest of the manuscript has followed "and she sits there, watching its cremation. . . ."

Leander Nolan is back. He is quite excited. He has broken with Slade Kinnicott. He has broken with all the Kinnicotts. And he has been deeply moved by Kinnicott's report that he is sure he can get Marion to give up the story—

"I realized in that moment," he hurries on, "that in all this time—since I'd been seeing you—I'd been hoping you wouldn't give up the story, that you would go through with it, that my career would go to smash. . . .

"Bunny!"

Nolan—I saw then that all this—which I'd been telling myself I wanted—Slade, a career, Washington, public life—all of it—that I didn't want it, that I was sick at the prospect of it—that I wasn't up to it, that I was scared to death of it. I saw all that—and I told her—I told Slade. . . .

Marion—You did!

Nolan—Yes.

Marion—What did she say?

Nolan—She said she knew it. She's a clever girl. She's cleverer than I am. She's cleverer than you are. I'm afraid of her cleverness. I'm uncomfortable with it. Marion, I know I seem stupid and ridiculous to you—just a Babbitt—clumsy—but

I love you, Marion. I always have—never anyone else. Let me go with you wherever you go— (*Lest she think it a "proposition".*) I mean—I want to marry you.

MARION—I'm terribly touched by this, Bunny darling, but I can't marry you.

NOLAN—Why not?

MARION—If I married you it would be for the wrong reasons. And it wouldn't be in character really—neither for me—nor for you. Besides that, I think you're wrong about Slade. She's very nice, you know. I like her very much.

NOLAN—I don't understand her. I never will.

MARION—If you did you'd like her. You better have another try. Really, Bunny, I wish you would.

Leander knows that she is trying to let him down easy and is completely stunned next minute when she admits that she loves Dickie Kurt, has loved him for some time, and yet is not going to marry him.

Nolan could strike Marion for that confession, but he is able to control himself as he leaves, promising as a last request that he will tell Kinnicott Marion has been called out of town suddenly and will not be able to dine with him.

Richard Kurt is back, white and shaken. He has rushed to Marion now and embraced her "with a kind of hopeless intensity," as he pleads for her forgiveness. These moods come over him and control him and he hates himself for them. But it is because of his great love for her. Perhaps when it is all blown over, they can go away together—away from people, to be by themselves.

Marion understands and is ready—ready to go with him now. The book? She has something to tell him about the book. He must listen and hear her out and try to understand her point of view.

"You know, Dickie, I've been very troubled about you. I've been sad. I've been sad," she says.

"I was angry . . . I didn't mean . . . It was just that . . ." he stumbles in explanation.

MARION—No, you don't understand—it wasn't your anger that troubled me. It was ourselves—the difference between us—not the years alone but the immutable difference in temperament. Your hates frighten me, Dickie. These people—poor Bunny, that ridiculous fellow Kinnicott—to you these rather ineffectual, blundering people symbolize the forces that have hurt you and you hate them. But I don't hate them. I can't hate them. Without feeling it, I can understand your hate but I can't bring myself to foster it. To you, this book has become a crusade. It couldn't be to me. Do you know, Dickie dear—and this has made me laugh so to myself—that there was nothing in the book about Bunny that would ever have been recognized by anybody. It was an idyllic chapter of first-love—that's all—and there was nothing in it that could remotely have been connected with the Bunny that is now. . . .

KURT—So much the better—! Think of the spectacle they'll make of themselves—destroyed by laughter. . . .

MARION—I don't believe in destructive campaigns, Dickie . . . outside of the shocking vulgarity of it all—I couldn't do it—for the distress it would cause. . . .

KURT—You've decided not to publish then. . . .

MARION—I've destroyed the book, Dickie.

KURT—You've destroyed it!

MARION—Yes. I'm sorry.

KURT—You traitor!

MARION—It seemed the simple thing to do—the inevitable thing.

KURT—What about *me?* You might have consulted me—after what I've . . .

MARION—I'm terribly sorry—but I couldn't possibly have published that book.

KURT (*in a queer voice*)—I see now why everything is this way . . .

MARION—I couldn't . . . !

KURT—Why the injustice and the cruelty go on—year after year—century after century—without change—because—as they grow older—people become—*tolerant!* Things amuse them. I hate you and I hate your tolerance. I always did.

MARION—I know you do. You hate my essential quality—the thing that is me. That's what I was thinking just now and that's what made me sad.

KURT—Nothing to be said, is there? (*Rises.*) Good-by.

MARION (*rises*)—All right! (KURT *starts to go. She calls after him pitifully.*) Won't you kiss me good-by?

KURT—All right. (*They kiss each other passionately.*)

MARION (*whispering to him*)—I would try to change you. I know I would. And if I changed you I should destroy what makes me love you. Good-by, my darling. Good-by, my dearest. Go quickly.

Kurt has gone, "blinded by pain." Marion is left alone, "trembling a little. She is cold. She goes to the stove and sits in front of it trying to get warm. She becomes aware that her eyes are full of tears."

Minnie is in, anxious about her mistress. Perhaps the telegram she had given Marion earlier brought bad news. Telegram? Marion had forgotten. Minnie finds it again. "This is from heaven," Marion cries, reading it. "Minnie, I want you to pack right away. We're leaving!"

Now she reads the telegram aloud: "Can get you commission to paint prize-winners Motion Picture Academy—wire answer at once. Feydie."

"Something always turns up for me," Marion is shouting to the startled Minnie. "I want to get out right away. . . . This time, Minnie, we'll have a real trip. From Hollywood we'll go to Honolulu and from Honolulu to China. How would you like that, Minnie?"

"Fine, Marion!" And then, as Marion is running up the stairs she calls: "Dot crazy Kurt, he goes vit us?"

"No, Minnie—no one—we travel alone!"

THE CURTAIN FALLS

ALIEN CORN

A Drama in Three Acts

BY SIDNEY HOWARD

IT was related some years back that Arthur Hopkins had made the quickest decision then known to Broadway in the acceptance of an important play. Taking the manuscript of "What Price Glory?" home with him Saturday for a week-end reading he came back to town on Monday and made the first payment on advance royalties to the authors, the Messrs. Stallings and Anderson.

Katharine Cornell bettered that record, if it is a record, by something more than twenty-four hours when she bought "Alien Corn" from Sidney Howard. She read the script on a Friday night and contracted for the rights to the play's production Saturday morning.

However, nearly two years were to elapse before she was able to bring the play to production. First there was the insistent public demand for "The Barretts of Wimpole Street," which continued through two seasons. And then, in the fall of 1932, when she finally had set her foot down and declared that she would not go on longer with "The Barretts" she came upon what is known in the profession as "casting difficulties." Actors about whom she was particularly keen for certain rôles in "Alien Corn," notably Siegfried Rumann who played the heroine's father, were engaged elsewhere and could not arrange a transfer.

While she was waiting Miss Cornell determined to produce André Obey's poetic drama, "Lucrece." This she did, to her financial though not to her artistic cost. "Lucrece," produced in mid-December, was continued for four weeks. "Alien Corn" was then put into rehearsal and offered at the Belasco Theatre the following February 20.

With this production Miss Cornell found herself back among her older admirers. They had raved ecstatically over her Elizabeth Barrett. They had accepted, with reservations, the artistry of her characterization in "Lucrece." Now they found her Elsa Brandt in "Alien Corn" to stand somewhere between the two, but much closer to Elizabeth than to Lucrece in the matter of emotional appeal, and they were content. The play ran through to the spring, and was then taken on tour to make it possible for the actress to play a few weeks in Chicago during the World's Fair before disbanding her company for the summer.

Mr. Howard's drama is a thoroughly workmanlike job of play-writing, as most of his plays are. There is unquestioned excuse for saying that it probably is greatly dependent for popular success upon Miss Cornell. The critics were agreed in that conviction. "Nothing is commonplace when she lays hold of it," Brooks Atkinson has written. "The magnetism of her playing persuades you that life is at stake." But it will, I believe, still be found to be a good play whenever a competent and sympathetic actress takes up the rôle. There is, in other words, no possible comparison between "Alien Corn" and the sort of play that in the old days served to sustain the reputation of a popular favorite.

As "Alien Corn" opens we are ushered into the living-room of a house occupied by Elsa Brandt and her father on the campus of Conway College for Women, "an institute of learning a few hours west of Chicago." It is early February and during the mid-way examination period.

There is an atmosphere of thrifty good taste about the room, which at the moment is in the process of being settled, the Brandts having but this day moved in. We see through to the entrance hall on one side and into the corner of the dining-room on the other. Several photographs of musical celebrities have already been hung on the wall. There is a somewhat shabby baby grand piano at which a piano tuner is working industriously.

Ottokar Brandt, a big man who has "the look of strength overcome by illness," is sitting on a sofa before the fireplace gazing at a portrait of his wife as Elsa in "Lohengrin." "His left arm is almost completely paralyzed, and when he moves about he walks with a slight limp. His age is fifty, his speech Teutonic, and his crusty manner prevents his bearing any resemblance to German musicians as immortalized by Mr. David Warfield."

There are other photographs of friends and intimates in a packing case within reach and Brandt is taking these out, unwrapping and gazing at them, when Mrs. Skeats comes with a cloth from the kitchen to wipe the dust from the pictures. Mrs. Skeats, aged 40, "is kindly, eager and limited. . . . She has two great gifts, a capacity for enthusiasm and a profound knowledge of how to live on a professor's salary without any sacrifice of her self-respect."

Mrs. Skeats is duly excited by the discovery that there are many musical celebrities among Mr. Brandt's friends, somewhat to the old master's irritation. To come upon autographed photographs of Brahms and Kreisler is like looking into a new world for her, insists Mrs. Skeats.

Watkins and Stockton, two of the younger professors of Conway College, are also helping with the settling and hugely enjoying the experience. "Stockton is small, precise, gentle and ageless in the manner of the sexless saint. . . . Watkins, twice as vigorous, seems older. He is self-assured, friendly, direct and most thoroughly American."

Brandt, unable to stand Mrs. Skeats' clatter longer, calls lustily for his daughter Elsa. Soon Elsa comes down from upstairs. She "is only twenty, but an air of authority makes her appear older. The same authority invests her carriage and every movement with a mature and individual style which is communicated even to the ready-made frock she is wearing."

Elsa has gone directly to her father, talking to him in easy Viennese German. She was, as Mrs. Skeats now suspects, named for Wagner's Elsa, as was her mother before her. Brandt is a little excited in confirming the fact.

"Elsa und Elsa!" he says tremulously. "She and I stood among the great ones of the world. Now she is dead and I am finished, and only the child remains, but the child will stand among the great ones, too!"

Now Elsa is looking among the things taken from the packing case for a little red devil, a treasured souvenir that has been lost for some time.

"I got him the last birthday I was home," she explains; "you remember, papa? We all went out in the Wienerwald to celebrate and [to the others] my father shot with a little gun in a shooting gallery and never missed once. The prize was a little red devil playing a fiddle. The fiddle was a compliment to my father. I always had it by me when I ate my supper at home in Vienna. Nicht wahr, papa? I expect I lost it long ago."

"Vienna? I've been there," remembers Stockton. "It's more than many cities. It's the embodiment of all nostalgia and romance."

"Sounds very different from a Western women's college," ventures Watkins.

"Wien! Ach, Wien!" There is a note of sharp despair in Brandt's voice at the memory. "Hast du nie von Heimweh gehort?"

"Oh, ja. Ich habst. Hab ichauch," answers Elsa.

"Heimweh. That means homesickness," says Stockton.

"You cannot know what it means," answers Brandt, goaded to scorn. "No one could be homesick for America!"

Now Brandt has stood about all of Mrs. Skeats that he can. He would not have her talk as casually of his friends as she does. He would have her know that when he played the Bach concerto for two violins with Kreisler, that Kreisler was at that time pleased to play with him. Now he has launched into German that is free and slightly vituperative, the burden of it being that they cannot, any of them, understand the Brandts or their music or their Vienna. It takes a bit of discreet pacifying on Elsa's part to get her father finally up the stairs and into his room.

"Do people ever die of homesickness?" she queries, coming back. "Sometimes I think he is going to. It's the pictures. I thought he would like living in the past better than not living at all. I was wrong."

Stockton would cheer Elsa up. The house is going to be jolly, with them all together. And there will be music, with Elsa's piano, Watkins' cello and his violin!

"Yes. For this one mid-year week, perhaps," agrees Elsa, adding wearily: "Then I'll have my students again and all of them wanting to learn the Rachmaninoff prelude."

Elsa has gone to the piano, "tearing into the first Chopin prelude F major," to make sure the tuner has done his job. The others are continuing with their picture hanging and general settling. Phipps, a newspaper man of middle age "seasoned with cynicism and drink," has arrived with an armful of well-worn music albums, and there are more in his Buick outside. He would have been there earlier, but Harry Conway had held him up trying to get him to agree to start a course in journalism at Conway College next term.

The discovery of a stack of her harmony exams has cast Elsa back into a mood of hopelessness and helplessness.

"What's the trouble?" Phipps would know.

"Teaching!" answers Elsa. . . . "If anyone had told me two years ago that I'd still be here teaching . . ."

"You're only marking time."

Elsa—That's just it! My God, when you've got a talent that's been bred in you from your father and mother and beaten into you since you were a baby, you can't sit dumb, with your hands tied, teaching! Can't you understand that? Haven't you ever wanted anything, Phipps?

Phipps—There used to be times back in New York on the old

Evening Globe when I was still a radical. Our cases aren't parallel. I wouldn't be running a hick newspaper now if they were.

ELSA—It was signing my name on that lease yesterday that woke me up. The minute I did it I heard a voice scream at me: "What have you done to yourself, Elsa Brandt?" I tied myself down to teaching for five more years, that's what I've done. . . . Will I ever get back where I belong?

PHIPPS—What's stopping you?

ELSA (*after a pause*)—Security.

PHIPPS—Eighteen hundred a year that you work like hell for and feed two people on and you call it security?

ELSA—It's eighteen hundred more than I've had most years!

PHIPPS—Do you think getting started was any cinch for Harold Bauer or this boy Horowitz? Didn't they bury Mozart in the potter's field? You're no worse off than the great ones have been.

ELSA (*passionately*)—I don't say I'm one of the great ones, Phipps! All I want's a chance to find out what I am! Show me how to get my nerve back again! Cure me of this security disease before it's too late!

PHIPPS—That's easy. Jump your lease, chuck your teaching and bolt!

ELSA—Where to?

PHIPPS—There are men you could study with in New York.

ELSA—What on?

PHIPPS—Don't they have scholarships?

ELSA—It isn't as easy as that.

PHIPPS—That's so. The old warhorse is a problem. It's tough all right, but it isn't only musicians. There's plenty of us who ought to be setting the world on fire one way or another. Some of us get the chance. . . . I'll have to give your case some thought.

The front door has been opened violently to admit Julian Vardaman. "He is a young man of not unattractive appearance, myopic but too vain to wear glasses, neurasthenic, physically undeveloped." Vardaman carries a load of examination papers called blue books and inside the room pauses to announce:

"Dr. Julian Vardaman, Ph.D., instructor in English at Conway College, arrives at his new residence, thank God!"

"It's about time," suggests Elsa, as she goes out through the dining-room.

Julian is full of explanations and excuses for not having arrived sooner. Many things delayed him, including his class of "forty-six young women of varying charm and virtually no intelligence" who were slow to finish their papers on Freshman English.

A moment later Professor Skeats, "a mellifluous, elaborate party of fifty, horn rims and carrying a parcel," arrives to add his approval of the new home.

"Oh, lady art! However humble thy dwelling place, what boundless wealth do thy devotees enjoy! How fortunate the artist!" apostrophizes the professor. "You must invite Mrs. Skeats and me in some evening when Miss Brandt is playing. A feast of Beethoven, an orgy of Bach! That's what we miss out here in the Middle West even with the radio!"

Elsa has come back to greet Professor Skeats and tell him of her thanks for all that Mrs. Skeats has done.

Now they have all gone to help with the final straightening out of the kitchen—all but Julian Vardaman and Elsa.

"I wish they'd all go home!" says Julian.

"So do I," echoes Elsa.

JULIAN (*misunderstanding*)—It's been a long time, hasn't it, Elsa, darling?

ELSA—Please don't begin that again, Julian.

JULIAN—How can I help beginning it? September, October, November, December, January! Five mortal months that I've gone home to my boarding house alone and you've gone home to yours. Now we shan't have to be lonely for each other any more.

ELSA—This isn't last summer now.

JULIAN—I know that. We're not in the country. There won't be August sweetness in the air. We shan't hear the river under the window. But we'll make up for all the months we've been kept apart and make this roof sacredly our very own.

ELSA—I hoped you'd got over that. I thought you had, or I wouldn't have asked you to come in on this house with me and help me swing it.

JULIAN—Was that all you asked, Elsa? You couldn't expect us to live here with nothing between us.

ELSA—Why not, Julian?

JULIAN—After last summer? It isn't fair!

ELSA—Much better say last summer wasn't fair.

JULIAN—Don't say that! I love you.

ELSA—I'm sorry I don't love you back. But, since I don't, we can't go on with last summer as a basis.

JULIAN—You did love me!

ELSA—Did I? I'm not sure. It was exciting. I expect that's always exciting the first few times. Julian, can't you see that in my restlessness, my desperate restlessness, I was bound to do what I did last summer? Just as a refuge?

JULIAN—A refuge! But that's what I'm offering you!

ELSA—And it's just what I don't want! I've got a refuge in my job. God help me! (*Then she softens penitently.*) Don't be too hard on me. I can't keep up the unreal thing. Not once I've found out that it is unreal.

JULIAN—My love's reality! What have you got to hope for that's half as real?

ELSA—I still believe in my star, Julian. I need all my strength for my faith in that. I haven't any left over for you or any other man. I mean it. Now, if you don't want to go through on this house, it's all right. I'll let you off.

JULIAN—No one your age has any right to be like you.

ELSA—No one like me has any right to be my age!

Elsa goes on with her work upstairs. Professor Skeats comes back. He has news for Julian. He has Julian in mind for advancement. He needs more help in his own department and he thinks that next autumn he might let Julian take over the Skeats Chaucer course and the course in advanced story writing as well. In fact Julian might take them over now, after mid-year. Also he might, if he will, look over Professor Skeats' examination papers. There are not more than fifty of them. They are on the Chaucer course and Julian may as well be getting his hand in—

Julian is not pleased. It is plain the professor is trying to foist his examination papers on an overworked instructor. But, after Skeats has ominously suggested that he is sorry to have heard reports of Julian's drinking again, and of radical opinions expressed in his lectures, and intimated that probably the advancement he had in mind can wait, the younger man is ready to reconsider. Slowly he picks up the examination papers and adds them to those of his own class on the desk.

Now Professor and Mrs. Skeats are going and the professor has taken Mrs. Skeats' hand and turned impressively to address the room at large.

"My dear Elsa, if I may use your Christian name without impertinence," he is saying, "good night to you and God bless you. Oh, my friends, when I consider this house where music and literature are bed-fellows . . . well, you do sleep under the same roof, my dear . . . and when I think how that stricken artist above stairs must revel in its peace, his long Odyssey ended, his old age secure, those ringing lines of Stevenson's come to mind. "Home is the sailor, home from the sea, and the hunter home from the hill.""

The household is relieved with Professor Skeats gone. Julian Vardaman has a chance to express a little hysterically his complete disgust of the professor for having put his examination papers off on him. The others are sympathetic until Julian launches into an attack on teaching as a profession and teachers as a class. Watkins and Stockton are proud to be teachers and joy in the work. If Julian is so disgusted why doesn't he rebel, Brandt would like to know.

"Julian's no rebel," Phipps explains. "He's just another of the great army of academic refugees. They clutter up every college faculty because they're afraid to face real life."

"Leave him alone," protests Elsa. "We're in the same boat, he and I. That's what I've got myself into. Between teaching and this damned house . . ."

The front door opens and Harry Conway enters, followed by a smartly uniformed chauffeur. The chauffeur is carrying a large wicker basket covered with a napkin. Conway "is an extremely personal Princeton alumnus of thirty-five. His manner has the ease of wealth and a level-eyed impudence which is at once uncivil and engaging."

He has come over to see if they are getting on all right with the settling. Soon Phipps, taking note of the situation, manages to herd the others out into the dining-room so Conway can talk to Elsa.

Conway has brought Elsa her lease. That there can be no chance of anyone taking the house away from her he has taken it himself and she is subletting from him, he explains.

Conway is interested in Elsa's getting the house, and the good times he suspects they will have there with their music and all. With Stockton's violin and Watkins' cello she will be in command of a trio. That should make her quite the queen.

"Watkins tells me you ride roughshod over all of 'em," he says.

"They don't seem to mind," Elsa answers.

Photo by Vandamm Studio, New York.

"ALIEN CORN"

"Yes, I've heard all about Miss Brandt," Muriel says, a little coldly. "Harry's sudden passion for music simply slays me. Harry, who couldn't carry a tune across a tennis court!"

(*Katharine Cornell, Lily Cahill and James Rennie*)

CONWAY—I expect they like music. Lots of people do.

ELSA—You don't?

CONWAY—Oh, I like a tune. I leave the musical end to my wife. She sings, you know. Not professionally, thank God! From what I've seen of 'em, I don't like professional musicians much.

ELSA—You shouldn't have my father and me for tenants.

CONWAY—I guess I shouldn't have said that.

ELSA—Has anyone ever told you that you're . . .

CONWAY—Uncivil?

ELSA—Yes!

CONWAY—Frequently.

ELSA—Why do you do it?

CONWAY—Embarrassment, I expect.

ELSA—Are you embarrassed now?

CONWAY—Yes. Aren't you?

ELSA—No.

CONWAY—I don't think that's quite civil of *you.* When people who are very different meet, they ought to interest one another so much they either hit it off at once or feel embarrassed. Now, we certainly haven't hit it off, but I, at least, have the grace to be embarrassed. (*Laughs.*) I think you might meet me half way.

ELSA (*amused*)—I'll do what I can.

CONWAY (*sitting beside* ELSA)—That's better. You . . . artists are such snobs about men like me. And you're wrong. We representative citizens have our points.

ELSA—Yes, I've seen you ride.

CONWAY—I ride damn well.

ELSA—Last fall when you had the horse show at the Hunt Club I looked over the fence. I thought I'd never seen anything so exciting.

CONWAY—Like horses?

ELSA—I always want to get my hands on them.

CONWAY—Ride with me some morning?

ELSA—Me?

CONWAY—Why not? I like the idea of seeing more of you. You may need taking down. . . . There's something disturbing about you. I've noticed that every time we've met. I really came in today to find out what it is.

ELSA—Have you sized me up to your satisfaction?

CONWAY—I believe it's sex. . . . At least we can leave it at that for the moment. . . . (*Laughs.*) You know it won't be my fault if I don't see lots more of you.

The chauffeur has come into the room with the basket which Conway had forgotten. It is a basket of supper he had put up for the movers, thinking it would be better than trying to cook or go out for supper the first night.

The others are in from the dining-room when Conway leaves. They are all delighted with the basket. Lots of good things in it. Ham. Liederkranz cheese. Salami. Spaghetti. Three bottles of Zeltinger. And a bottle of brandy! Brandt is so pleased with the wine that he is impelled to break into song—"Hoch soll er leben! Hoch soll er leben! Drei mal hoch!"

Soon they are all bustling about getting their picnic supper on the table. Elsa is at the piano again, playing softly. Julian is in an apologetic mood. He wants to apologize to Elsa and to Stockton for the row he kicked up. Stockton understands. What Julian needs is morale and he knows one way to get it.

"Every man ought to excel at something for his own soul's sake," says Stockton. "Personally I am very partial to pistol practice."

"Pistol practice!" echoes Julian.

Stockton—It's difficult. It's manly. And you do it alone so you aren't self-conscious about learning.

Julian—Don't tell me you do pistol practice, Stockton!

Stockton—Indeed I do, every day of my life. (Julian *laughs.*) You may laugh all you please, but it's a perfectly sound psychological idea! Why, I had a friend who had a boy who was afraid to swim and all the other boys lorded it over him till he got in a dreadful state. So my friend had his boy taught to play the saxophone and that made all the other boys admire him so he got over his bad morale and now he's a splendid swimmer. (*Laughs.*) Up in Maine, too, where the water's so cold. (*In his enthusiasm he has forgotten to work.*) Laugh all you please. I used to be in just such a state as you because I couldn't do the manly things other men did. And that story gave me the idea of pistol practice. And the day I hit my first three bull's-eyes was the very day I got my professorship! Now I say there are plenty of men who can play golf and tennis but there aren't many better marksmen than I am!

Julian—I can't do the manly things either, Stockton! Never could!

STOCKTON—Daily pistol practice and a mild laxative now and then. . . .

The bustle over supper preparations continues. In the midst of them Phipps, looking through a newspaper, comes upon an item of interest to them all. Evelyn Bennett, a young woman who used to be a student at Conway, is dead in Berlin. Appendicitis. Phipps is forcibly struck with an idea. Miss Bennett was studying abroad on a Conway scholarship. She had only used up six months of the scholarship and another will not be awarded until June.

"Seems a pity to let six months in Berlin or Vienna go begging, doesn't it? With a career and homesickness both on the premises."

Elsa, at the piano, snaps to attention. She continues playing but "her mind is reaching for the implication of Phipps' remark."

Julian Vardaman has moved over beside Elsa and is protesting his love softly. He is even proposing marriage very tenderly and earnestly. She does not hear. Suddenly she breaks off playing and stands up. In the dining-room the men have poured the wine and are lifting their glasses when Phipps, noticing Elsa, holds up his hand for silence.

ELSA (*in a queer, strangled voice*)—Papa. . . . Papa.

BRANDT—Ja?

ELSA—Has du gehort was Phipps uber Wien gesagt hat?

BRANDT—Ya. Warum?

ELSA—Warum?!!!

JULIAN (*terrified*)—What is it, Elsa? What did Phipps say about Vienna?

PHIPPS—All I said was: it seems a pity to see six months in Berlin *or* Vienna go begging because nobody wants 'em.

BRANDT (*softly*)—Ai!

ELSA—Because nobody wants 'em!

BRANDT—Ai!

JULIAN—But, Phipps, she's just settled here!

ELSA (*her breath catching in a sort of sob*)—I? Settled?

BRANDT (*sotto voce*)—Wien. Wien. Wien.

PHIPPS—Talk to Watkins, Elsa. He's chairman of that committee. He's the boy who can swing it for you.

THE CURTAIN FALLS

ACT II

In mid-afternoon of the following day the wintry sunlight is streaming brightly through the windows of the Brandt living-room. Julian Vardaman is working on the hated examination papers at the desk. Stockton is sitting in front of the fireplace busily cleaning a .32 caliber revolver. Phipps, the newspaper man, is there and a little excited.

The talk is of Elsa's going to Vienna, and the fun of the preparations. Phipps is of the opinion that Elsa Brandt is a fine, strong name to put on any concert hall. Stockton and Julian are agreed that the celebration of the night before was jolly but wearing. Julian has a head in consequence and needs a drink. He has been out pistol shooting when he should have been recovering his lost rest.

Then Elsa comes. She, too, is prey to the excitement. The report of the scholarship committee is not known, but everybody is hopeful. Next minute Herr Brandt and Watkins have burst through the front door.

"Elsa! Wo bist du, Elsa?" shouts Brandt, casting aside coat and muffler.

"Hier," Elsa answers, motionless and almost voiceless.

"Wir haben es durch gesetzt!"

"Kann's niche glauben!"

"In vier Wochen sind wir in Wien!"

"Frei!!!"

"Frei!!!"

Now the German is flowing freely and excitedly and the other members of the faculty have caught enough to know that this is a time for congratulations.

Elsa must have the whole story. Watkins is willing to tell it and they are all eager to listen. The Committee, the President of the College and Harry Conway were at the meeting. He [Watkins] did most of the talking. It being easy to be eloquent about Elsa, Watkins was eloquent. At which point Herr Brandt must tell what he said, too.

"I said: my daughter hass an undoubted aptitude for the piano," said Herr Brandt. "With training, experience and inspiration it is quite possible she may become an artist." It were not fitting for him to say more.

Of course the scholarship is only for six months, and only a thousand dollars, they are reminded, but many things can happen in six months. Brandt thinks perhaps they can raise more money on the piano, which isn't theirs. Or the house, which isn't theirs either. Why not sell the house anyway?

"We go to an old Burgher's house that smells of mustiness and wine and soap and curry," her father tells Elsa; "with carving on the cupboard doors and windows that stick so you cannot open them and we watch the pigeons fly up when the church bells ring! Wien! Ach, Wien!"

"Suppose I'm not the real thing after all!" suggests Elsa, holding out her hands. "Suppose there isn't anything real in these!"

"That's something you'll have to find out," answers Watkins. "That's the adventure of making a career!"

Now the excitement is a little too much for Elsa. She is afraid it will make her cry. Or make her sick. Let them talk of something else! Anything!

Suddenly Herr Brandt has grabbed Elsa and is forcing her awkwardly into a wild, crippled dance for which he shouts the strains of "The Blue Danube." Julian, Watkins and Stockton are shouting all sorts of irrelevant things at Elsa to distract her attention. Now they have taken up the cry of the Valkyrie and Elsa has leaped to the piano to crash through the chords.

Julian is standing on the sofa, with one foot on the piano. As Brandt, Watkins, Stockton and Julian are "Ho-yo, To-ho"-ing vigorously the hall door opens. Harry Conway and Professor Skeats, unperceived by the celebrants, come into the room.

There is some embarrassment when they are discovered. Followed by explanations. They are just being a little foolish, Elsa explains.

"I'm afraid you've got to bear a disappointment," says Conway, ominously. . . . "It looks as though we were too optimistic just now in the committee. . . . I'm afraid you can't have this money we promised you!"

"Why can't she have it?" demands Watkins.

"Because my father, when he founded this show and endowed these scholarships . . . put a trick clause in this one for music. . . . He must have had some notion of fostering native talent because the fund's restricted to girls of American birth who hold degrees from Conway. We none of us knew. The lawyers just told us. . . . And since you, Miss Brandt, don't hold any degree from any . . ."

ELSA—Would I play the piano any better if I did?

CONWAY—I'm not talking about the piano.

WATKINS—But, good God, Harry, can't we throw in an A.B.?

SKEATS—Throw in an A.B., Watkins!

STOCKTON—That wouldn't get her by the American birth!

ELSA—But I'm American enough! I was almost born here! (*To* CONWAY.) And you told Watkins! You told my father!

BRANDT—Ja, das ist richtig!

CONWAY—I know I did. And that's just why I've come along now. Just because I did go so far at the meeting.

ELSA—But what am I going to do without this money? I was practically on the boat!

SKEATS—Surely you can put up with us for a few years longer?

ELSA—A few years?

JULIAN (*to* STOCKTON)—You weren't so far wrong about this afternoon.

BRANDT—Das darf nicht sein! (*With the utmost passion.*) Who are these lawyers? Kings? Do you know what you are doing, you and your lawyers? You are strangling my daughter's talent! Her noble, her transcendent gifts, you are strangling them! And you are murderers just as if you took her life! Because you will make her life useless to her!

SKEATS—Really, my dear Brandt . . .

WATKINS—Take it easy, Brandt!

STOCKTON—Gracious me! Gracious me!

ELSA—Papa, bitte!

BRANDT (*out of control*)—Nein, ich will nicht schweigen! It iss true what I say! I haf seen the spirit failing in my daughter! I haf seen the strength failing in her hands! (*To* ELSA.) Ja! I haf seen your talent sickening in you just like I saw my own sicken and die! (*To* SKEATS.) And talents must be used or they do die! (*To* CONWAY.) This afternoon, you opened the gates to us. The path beyond them was not easy. But in our great need, it seemed like everything! Because hope iss not like talent. Hope does not die. It sleeps only. And you wakened our hope this afternoon! For the first time since the two years we haf been here! Maybe the next time it will be too late! Because for talent once dead there is no resurrection!

ELSA—Papa, das kann aber gar nichts helfen!

BRANDT—Können die denn gar nichts begreifen?

SKEATS—With you to guide her and work with her as you've done so long . . .

BRANDT (*screaming at him*)—How can I gif her what she must haf now? I wass a violinist! She wants the inspiration of her instrument and of a master of her instrument and of a life where music means more than arguments for selling radios! Ja, and if she wass already Paderewski you would still drag her down with your teaching business. . . . That girl who died in Berlin wass a fool! Yet you gafe her this opportunity you keep back from Elsa! And why? You want American talent, you say! You are a fool. In America iss no talent! In America iss only . . .

ELSA (*tries to comfort him*)—Solche Dickkopfigkeit hab' ich nie. . . .

They quiet Brandt finally. Julian has taken him upstairs when Conway comes back. He can't quite understand why Elsa is so hell-bent on this career of hers. He knows something about musical careers these days, through his wife, and most of them, from what he has seen, are failures. Radio is playing the devil with the market. There are more soloists than there are engagements. Let Elsa consider the handicaps and the discouragements, the long, long tours, the weary grind—

Elsa is not to be discouraged. She knows all that he knows and more about what she would be getting into, and still she is determined. She wishes that he would come to the point. "I may be licked out of things, Mr. Conway, but I can't be talked out of them," she says with finality.

Conway is sympathetic. He would like to help with something he could understand and believe in. He thinks perhaps if Elsa and her father were to go home for a visit, and then if she were to come back and go on with her teaching—

Elsa loathes teaching. She loathes local talent. Perhaps if she were to play for him that would show him that she is worth helping. Conway does not think it would.

"God knows, I want to help you," he says when Elsa frankly declares that she does not enjoy begging; "but whenever I help a man it's always more for the man himself than for what he does. Perhaps if I knew more about you . . . on the human side . . ."

"On the human side. . . ." She is leaning on a chair near him as she picks up a memory of her past.

"My mother was a singer in Vienna," she says. "An opera singer. She sang mostly the lyric Wagner rôles, and the Mozart operas. They adored my mother in Vienna—my father too. I think he was the finer artist. They were very much in love. After a while, when I was coming, they were married. It didn't seem to make any difference to them. They loved each other just as much afterwards. My mother had to put off singing Isolde on my account. She was angry with me, at first, because of that.

We came to America when I was four. I can remember the hotel where we lived and the way my mother used to lie in bed and wouldn't speak all day the days she had to sing. She had a great success at the Metropolitan and my father played concertos with the orchestras. With Muck in Boston and Stock in Chicago. Then the war came and the Metropolitan stopped giving the German operas. I'm sure my father would never have done any real harm. But his sympathies were naturally with his own people and—well, you heard him this afternoon so you can imagine how he must have talked then! It must have been that that got us interned. I know that because of the way he blamed himself when my mother died of the flu in the camp in Georgia. He tried to kill himself. The day she was buried he threw himself out of the window on a pile of stones and fractured his skull. They saved his life. But his left arm was paralyzed. When they let us out at last, we were very poor. I'm afraid your government kept all our money.

"Musicians are generous to each other, though. They took me in and hired doctors for my father. It was no good. In the end he gave up and sold his violin. No matter how long I live, no matter what terrible things may happen to me, I shan't ever, shall never forget the night he sold that violin. I wasn't yet nine, but if you'd seen him eating his soup that night. How he'd lift his spoon up to his lips and put it down and lift it up again and never taste the soup!"

They should have gone back to Vienna then, she thinks, but things were so bad in Vienna Herr Brandt decided to stay on in New York and teach. That proved a failure. He could not learn to flatter his pupils. They moved out to Cincinnati and her father had a position in a conservatory until he quarreled with everyone there. They went South, to Memphis, where Brandt tried being leader of a band.

Always her father had kept her working at the piano. Once when she had whooping cough he would not call a physician for fear he would interrupt her study. Once he had spanked her when she had fallen and hurt her wrist playing hop scotch. That was to teach her how valuable her wrists were. But he had never been really unkind.

"In Memphis I broke down and he took me to Denver for my health and it was there he first spoke of going back to Europe. We had an argument about the Brahms' sonata. 'I can teach you no more!' he said. 'You must go home.' He saved forty dollars and bought a Ford. That was less than the railway fare to New York. He wouldn't let me drive. He was too sensitive. And you could drive the old Fords with one arm. We started in October two years ago, headed for New York, in hopes that my playing would interest someone enough to send me the rest of my way. That was our idea. You can feel so rich on a good idea! We drove into this town and that forty-dollar Ford just fell apart and my father's last desperate strength fell with it. That was when I took hold. I got a job in a picture theatre playing the piano. The manager let me practice mornings. That was when I met Phipps. He came in tight one night and tried to pick me up. He got me my job with your college instead. And then yesterday this scholarship idea came up. 'To everything there is a season and a time to every purpose under the heaven; a time to be born and a time to die, a time to plant and a time to pluck up that which is planted.' It's true, that verse. If you delay when you really feel that your time has come, your impulse fails, someone else does what you might have done, and your talent, even if it doesn't die, just drops behind! They say I've waited so long I can wait longer. I can't! I mustn't! When you've got a talent it's a demon that drives you and drives you and leaves you no peace! My talent is a demon child that's got to be born! But I've got to bear it! I've got to, there's no two ways . . ."

"Well," she concludes, a little apologetically, "you asked for it."

"You'll get to Vienna, if that's where you want to go," he says. "I promise."

"You are my friend. Thank you," says Elsa, giving him her hand.

"Thank *you* for a great experience," he answers. "A woman like you is the only experience a man like me gives a damn about."

Elsa would call her father, but Conway thinks it would be unwise to tell him of the new plan. It is best to be delicate about such things. But when Brandt comes they do tell him, to his evident delight. Still Conway hesitates about giving them a check.

"I rather wanted to fix things so it would look as though someone else . . . I mean people are so ready to . . . I suppose that sounds pretty . . . Hell, I will write it now!" he finishes, drawing his checkbook from his pocket.

The check, for a thousand dollars, is filled in and signed, but before it can be torn from the book the front door flies open and Phipps, followed by Mrs. Skeats and Muriel Conway, bursts into the room in a state of considerable excitement. Mrs. Conway, "hat and furs of the best style and frock that is kind to years that are nearing forty and a figure that has been kept in control," is protesting smilingly as she meets Elsa.

"I can't imagine what you must think of me, Miss Brandt, for bursting in on you this way," she is saying. "But these two strong spirits bore down upon me and simply swept me over! But, I mean, literally."

Conway has slipped the checkbook into the side pocket of his coat. He is there, he explains to his surprised wife, because Miss Brandt has just had rather a disappointment—

"Yes, I've heard all about Miss Brandt," says Muriel, a little coldly. "Harry's sudden passion for music simply slays me. Harry, who couldn't carry a tune across a tennis court!"

He has been trying to figure out what could be done to help Miss Brandt, Conway explains. And that, quickly interjects Mrs. Skeats, is exactly what they have been doing, too.

Phipps and Mrs. Skeats, it now appears, have been talking with Mrs. Conway and have hit upon a scheme to give a series of musicales at the Conway house, one a week, at a dollar or perhaps a dollar and a half a head, with Elsa playing and Mrs. Conway singing. People will have to come, simply because it is the Conway house—

Again Muriel protests that she could not think of doing it. Not that she would not love to, as she explains to Elsa, but she does not feel that she is up to it. She would die of nerves! True, she has done considerable studying—with Lilli Lehmann, a part of it in Salzburg—but—

"Muriel, I wish you'd do it," quickly interjects Conway.

"Why, Harry? Why?"

"Lots of reasons. It's the solution for Miss Brandt, of course. But more than that, it would make the old house a center of things again. As it used to be in my father's day. It would give people pleasure, too. I know I'd enjoy it."

"You, Harry?"

"Are you surprised that a man enjoys being proud of his wife?"

Muriel is greatly pleased at that. "She seems to blush over her whole body." A moment later she has tacitly agreed, though protesting that Elsa will have to do the real work. If she sings at all it will only be once or twice to make people come.

Elsa also has misgivings. Society musicales are not much in her line. But the thought of playing for perhaps two hundred people who have paid to hear her is tempting.

Now the Conways and Mrs. Skeats have left, and Phipps is

enthusiastically figuring up the possible rewards of the musicales.

"You keep 'em through the twenty-ninth of April," he calls from the desk. "That's twelve in all. At three hundred bucks apiece. Be on the safe side. Call it three thousand. If I can't make Harry Conway raise that to five! Not one year in Vienna but five years! What do you say?"

Brandt is not too sanguine. "We get away now may be from the teachers," he says, "but something don't smell so good by the amateurs."

There is great excitement now as Brandt starts immediately to build Elsa's first program. She will begin, he decides, with the Appassionata of Beethoven. No, corrects Elsa, she will begin with the Bach English suite. She will next give three Brahms intermezzos, decides Brandt. But Elsa is sick of the E flat. She'll take the sonata!

Now Elsa is at the piano, sketchily picking up phrases of her selections. She will give them Chopin, too, with the Polonaise to wind up with. And César Franck!

Brandt will not have that. His daughter will not play any French music at her first recital! The war is over, as Phipps reminds him, but still his daughter shall play no French music at her first recital! She is a German musician and she will begin her public career with German music!

"Music's music whatever country it comes from!" firmly insists Elsa.

The argument that follows between the Brandts is excitingly German, with Elsa banging out various chords at the piano to substantiate her claims.

"If only they wouldn't scream!" protests Julian. Phipps is less polite. "Shut up!" he shouts. When this command has no effect he gives up. "All right! Don't!"

Phipps has drawn the cork from a bottle of liquor and is taking a drink. Elsa and Brandt are still hammering out their argument at the piano.

"Ich will spielen César Franck! Boom!" declares Elsa.

"Kein Franzose!" protests Brandt, angrily. "Mit César Franck fangst du gar nicht an! Du spielst Kein Franzose! Weder Mittwoch noch . . ."

"Mittwoch spiel ich César Franck! Boom!"

"Wie du hammerst! Wie du hammerst—"

"Mittwoch abend spiel ich César Franck! Boom! Boom! Boom!" shouts Elsa, as the curtain falls.

It is Sunday morning. A bright, warm sun floods the Brandt living-room. Elsa is at the piano practicing feverishly. She is working at the moment with E flat and G minor scales, playing with superb velocity and a full tone. After these, for variety, she turns to the Chorale broken chords in E flat minor over which the argument of the previous scene arose. She is in the midst of this when Harry Conway appears outside the French window. He is dressed for riding.

At first he stands watching Elsa. She is not conscious of him until she stops playing. "Then some sense of him interrupts her thought." She smiles a welcome as he steps into the room. He had seen her at work twice before that morning, as he had ridden past the house, he reports. Finally he had decided that she had done enough for Sunday.

"I've done far from enough for next Wednesday night," Elsa corrects him. "But as long as you know you're interrupting. . . ." She accepts the cigarette he offers. "I like your coming in all red and healthy and smelling of horses," she adds. "I should have stopped soon, anyway. Your wife is coming in to run through her songs."

Conway is aware of that, but they still have half an hour. Why hasn't she come riding with him he would know, and Elsa answers that she is not the type. He doesn't like music and she wouldn't like sports.

Conway would also like to know just what it is he represents to Elsa. She is not quite sure. At first she had thought him attractive. Then she had decided that he was a little dull.

"That strikes me as faint praise," says he, going over to the piano by her. "We're both pretty damned sure of ourselves, aren't we? I suppose that accounts for the mutual attraction. . . ."

"Now that I've smoked my cigarette I'll get back to work," answers Elsa.

He knows that she is trying to let him out. He knows how she feels, and he is glad. He knows now that she is in love with him just as he is in love with her. He would take her in his arms, but she eludes him. He can see that she is shaky and thinks perhaps he should beg her pardon for bringing up the matter of their love. They seem to be in for it now.

"I'm in love with you and I didn't want to be," confesses Elsa.

"What are we going to do about it?" he asks.

ELSA—We're not going to do anything about it.

CONWAY—How can we go this far and back down?

ELSA—Where is there for us to go on to?

CONWAY—Almost anywhere!

ELSA—Why did you have to do this to me? Just now? Why couldn't you leave me to work?

CONWAY—How could I?

ELSA—I don't like being alone with you. Where *is* everybody?

CONWAY—I passed Stockton and your boarder 'way up the road.

ELSA—And my father's in the kitchen making beer with Phipps.

CONWAY—I didn't hear them.

ELSA—That's because you haven't any ears! Or eyes or smell, or any of your senses! And I've got too much of all five of them! At least that's how I feel now! Why in God's name did this have to happen now?

CONWAY—Thank God, it has happened! I'm in love with you! I mean it! For ten years I've been living in a cell. Doing the same things, saying the same things, thinking and feeling the same things! No. Feeling nothing. Now loving you has let me back where I belong!

ELSA—Where *you* belong!

CONWAY—I'm not just a stuffed shirt. I used to be alive. . . . We've never hit it off, my wife and I. . . . I go my way and she goes hers.

ELSA—She happens to be doing me a good turn just now.

CONWAY—She's doing it to please me, not to help you.

ELSA—Do you expect that to make me feel better? It doesn't.

CONWAY—Oh, hell!

ELSA—I'm only just getting myself out of one hole and you're not going to . . .

CONWAY—Darling! Darling!

ELSA—Don't!

CONWAY—We can't go on. . . .

Phipps and Brandt have appeared in the doorway. Phipps is carrying a glass of beer. He had heard the piano stop and he thought perhaps Conway would like to try some of the beer. It is very good beer. Phipps also would remind Elsa that they are in a small house. It is possible to hear every spoken word all over it.

"What I've said I've said," is Conway's answer to that insinuation. "I may not have taken eavesdropping into account, but—"

"I wasn't going into eavesdropping which couldn't be helped. Or into what you said which, presumably, couldn't be helped, either. And I wasn't listening, any more than you were talking for publication. I only came in because I thought that might make you go home."

"It strikes me that Elsa and I are old enough to—"

"Your half hour must be just about up, Harry," says Elsa.

Conway has gone leaving a card with his study telephone number on it. He will expect to hear from Elsa after her rehearsal.

Phipps and Brandt had heard what Elsa had said to Conway. She has little more to say to either of them now. She is in love with Conway, terribly in love with him. But she is also under obligation to Mrs. Conway, and she will remember that if it kills her.

Professor Skeats and Watkins have come in. They have been walking and working up alibis for not going to church on Sunday. A moment later Julian Vardaman has burst through the door, brandishing a service pistol and crying out exultantly that Stockton was right. Having hit three bull's-eyes in a row Vardaman has regained the captaincy of his soul. He has found his manhood.

"These sudden changes of sex aren't good for you," suggests Phipps.

Now Stockton has come excitedly after Julian, anxious to get the pistol out of his friend's hand and safely put away.

"I've had a revelation," shouts Julian over Elsa's effort to quiet him. "My spirit soared. Out of death into life which I fear no longer! . . . I saw our future, Elsa! I saw the whole adventure of our life from that day next June when we set forth together. . . . I'm so happy! Happiness! It rolls over you like a warm wave and makes your life function in every part."

It is high adventure that Julian is now prepared to offer Elsa, and Phipps is inclined to think that at the moment she might do worse than to accept it.

There is a ring at the doorbell. Mrs. Skeats is the caller. She has just come from Mrs. Conway's and she brings with her a frock that Mrs. Conway has generously permitted her to select for Elsa to wear at the recital.

Now Elsa would get them all out that she may be ready for the rehearsal, but Mrs. Conway has asked them all to stay, Stockton reports. Mrs. Conway has planned a fairly elaborate program, it further appears—a Schubert group, a modern French group and a few arias—

"She promised me two hundred people to hear me play!" says Elsa. "Now my audience is coming to hear her sing instead! When anyone can see she can't sing a note!"

"How can you tell that?" Stockton wants to know.

"By her teeth! After the way I've been working, too. And I'd made up my mind to be grateful to her!"

"Remember, Elsa, that this is Conway College and that she is Mrs. Conway!"

The information is in no way quieting to Elsa. Again she informs them that either they all get out or there will be no rehearsal. And out they go.

A moment later Muriel Conway has arrived. Her chauffeur follows her in, his arms piled with music which he puts on the piano. Muriel is surprised to find her audience gone, and more surprised that Elsa has sent them away. Nor can she quite understand why Elsa should question her selection of songs or adopt so curt a tone.

"If you'll pause to remember that I'm going to a good deal of trouble on your account," protests Muriel.

"You can easily find another accompanist," answers Elsa, turning to the music. "Shall I take these out to your car or will you call your chauffeur in?"

Muriel (*after a pause*)—I'm sorry for anything I've done that's offended you. If I've let my enthusiasm run away with me and cut your playing down too much, I'll compromise. We can split the program between us evenly. Would you do that? And not be angry? I don't want to give these recitals up. And, without you, there's no point in them. I won't pretend I was doing them for your benefit. You heard what Harry said the day we started.

Elsa—Don't tell me why you're doing them, Mrs. Conway!

Muriel—"A man enjoys being proud of his wife," he said. You must have heard him. (*She smiles sympathetically.*) Marriage isn't like music. You can't practice five hours a day to make yourself perfect in it. You have to take it as it comes.

Elsa—Don't tell me any more!

Muriel—There's nothing to tell. Harry doesn't happen to be in love with me, that's all.

Elsa—Stop! Please, stop!

Muriel—I'm not blaming him. Most of the time I've been happy with him. Other times . . . times that weren't so happy,

I went to Salzburg and studied with Lilli Lehmann.

ELSA—Please!

MURIEL—Now you see why these recitals matter to me. I want my life just as much as you want yours. And, if I can make him proud of me, that's something, isn't it? One feels so out of it without anything.

ELSA—I'm sorry I let my . . . vanity get in your way. That can be controlled. It's surprising the things we can control if we make up our minds. (*She takes* CONWAY'S *card which has been lying on the piano and looks distastefully at it—tears it and puts the pieces in the ash tray.*) We do make up our minds, though. If only for our own inner dignity . . . I'll go ahead with any program you like.

Now Muriel, too, is eager to be generous. The compromise program will certainly be best. She thinks perhaps she should start with a big number—perhaps the "Vissi d'Arte" or the Delilah aria.

Elsa feels that Muriel may be a little too ambitious and suggests a Schubert group, perhaps the "Haidenroslein" to start with. Accepting that decision, a little reluctantly, Muriel proceeds to get herself in a Schubert mood. "She takes her place by the piano, breathes deeply, clears her throat, clasps her hands in front of her, smiles, then nods to Elsa to begin."

The beginning is only fair. Muriel has some little difficulty striking the note, although she knows quite well that the key is D. They start again and she finishes one verse. That is enough to convince her that she will have to give up smoking.

Now the second verse, also with appropriate preparations, is attacked with fervor but no improvement of tone. By the time the end of it is reached Herr Brandt has burst into the room loudly protesting in German that no one shall murder Schubert in that fashion in his house. Nor can Muriel's indignant protests nor Elsa's embarrassed demands stop him.

"If I sang well enough for Lilli Lehmann I can sing well enough for you," retorts Muriel, who objects to being insulted in a language that she does not understand.

"Lilli was teaching when she was old," Brandt answers her. "To teach one must learn to flatter."

"Never mind him," interposes Elsa, demanding again that her father be still. "What arias have you got here? How's this? 'Louise'?"

" 'Louise' will do perfectly," agrees Muriel. "It suits my voice much better than Schubert."

However well the aria may suit Muriel's voice it does not suit either Brandt or Elsa. There is trouble with the G natural in the first phrase and Brandt has risen, his hands clasped over his ears to shout: "Ach, du lieber Herr Gott!!"

There is no point in going on, Elsa is agreed. The situation just isn't possible.

At the piano Elsa is playing again the broken chords of the Franck Chorale as Muriel gathers her things together.

Suddenly Elsa's playing suggests something to Muriel. The Chorale is what Harry was whistling when he came home! And he said he had been riding all morning! He had been there, hadn't he?

"He looked in. Yes," answers Elsa.

MURIEL—What did he want here?

ELSA—It doesn't matter.

MURIEL—Why didn't he stay then? Why didn't you speak of it? (*She thinks quickly.*) Yesterday. Between four and five. Was he here then?

ELSA—Yes. He was.

MURIEL—Oh, God, and you let me talk and talk!

ELSA—There's no reason why you shouldn't have talked.

MURIEL—Don't lie to me! You're not the first one of Harry's women I've met, but I've never let one of them lie to me! Not one of them!

BRANDT—No! Du seihst! Was hab' ich . . .

ELSA—Willst du schweigen! It's all so silly!

MURIEL (*picking up her coat and hurrying out*)—Silly? Silly? You call it silly!!!

ELSA—All of it! The whole business from the beginning. Scholarships, musicales, all of it!

BRANDT—Elsa!

ELSA—I don't want any help from anybody! Strings tied to every scrap of it and compromises. Give in here! Cut down there! Watch out you don't get side-tracked!

BRANDT—Ja!

ELSA—You help yourself! That's what you do!

BRANDT—Bravo!

ELSA—You must have known that! Why didn't you tell me?

(*She breaks into inarticulate German.*) Warum hast du's mir nicht gesagt? Warum, fater? Warum?

THE CURTAIN FALLS

ACT III

It is the Wednesday evening following, some time after 10 o'clock. The Brandt house is in darkness until Julian Vardaman lets himself in and switches on the lights. Shortly he is followed by Professor and Mrs. Skeats. They are all wearing heavy wraps and have felt the chill of a lingering cold snap.

Stockton and Watkins are next to arrive. Elsa and her father, they report, are walking home. Which is surprising to Mrs. Skeats. She would think Elsa would be exhausted.

"We've got to hold a council of war before Elsa gets here," Watkins announces.

"Oh, don't let's come down to earth yet!" protests Mrs. Skeats. "I've such an intensely happy feeling! Almost as though I'd participated myself this evening. To have seen her up there so calm! As though giving a first concert were the most natural occurrence! I thought her magnificent! Of course, we all knew she would be. But to have gone ahead as she did, on her own, in spite of everything and everybody's advice, and hire a hall herself and go through with it! I'm lost in admiration!"

It is no time for sentimental fancies. In books and plays, Watkins points out, these occasions are always triumphs. But it happens that in place of the two hundred patrons Phipps had expected for Elsa's recital there were just thirty-nine people in the audience.

"Elsa's lost her shirt being magnificent," concludes Watkins.

Whatever the deficit Stockton thinks they can make it up between them and Mrs. Skeats is sure the recital was a success and that Elsa will make up her losses next time. But there cannot be a next time, as Watkins sees it.

They share the depression of Elsa's tragedy. All save Julian. He is inclined to exult at the failure. There is more in life than that kind of success. He loves Elsa. He was on the verge of losing her. Now she will not be able to get away, God help her!

"But, thank God, too!" exclaims Julian. "I know I've got nothing but my weakness and my love. My meanness and my love, if you like that better. I know that and I don't mind. That's what your pistol practice has done for me. Stockton! It's made me resigned to myself to be just what I am."

When Brandt and Elsa arrive Brandt barges into the room, letting his hat, coat and mufflers fall to the floor. He drops into a chair with a deep sigh of satisfaction, "smiling like a cherub that has just eaten his fill of ambrosia." Elsa "wearing a simple but most becoming evening frock of black that more than ever accentuates the dignity of her bearing, comes forward, like her father, unconscious of the others, clasping and unclasping her beautiful, nervous hands before her."

She goes straight to the piano, "tears into the first eight bars of Bach's Toccata in D minor, playing fortissimo and with supreme brilliance."

"That's how it ought to have gone tonight," she says, breaking off as suddenly as she began. "I knew it! Why didn't I pull it off?"

The others are quick and positive with their congratulations. Elsa is pleased, too. She feels that she *was* pretty good. For the first time she had played for people who weren't just friends and she could feel them come right up on the platform to her.

Now Phipps has arrived, stopping inside the door to lean heavily against the side of the arch. Julian has brought in beer, sandwiches and glasses on a tray. . . .

"Seventy-one dollars and fifty cents," Elsa reports as the cost of the concert. They would not let her go on until she had paid the bill. "What difference does it make? I'll lose the rest of my salary on more recitals! But by the third or fourth I'll break even and after that! We'll get away to Vienna without Mrs. Conway's help. If it isn't Vienna it will be New York. It's just as good for what I want. I tell you there isn't anything can stop me now!"

They have all raised their glasses in a toast to Elsa. "Hoch soll sie lieben!" shouts Brandt. The others echo the sentiment. All save Phipps.

"I didn't come here to drink," says he. "I came to congratulate you. . . . Not on your playing. On your deliverance . . . from security."

"How do you mean?" demands Elsa, after a pause.

"Our friend Mrs. Harry Conway had the trustees in for tea this afternoon," continues Phipps, steadying himself for declamatory purposes, "and the result of their deliberations is that Miss Elsa Brandt, instructor in music, be asked to tender her resignation and move on. . . . Mrs. Conway's private secretary personally telephoned the news to the *Gazette* with the suggestion that it might be included in my review of Miss Brandt's recital appearing tomorrow morning. I wrote that review the day before yesterday, so—"

General consternation has greeted Phipps' announcement. It is unbelievable, this thing that Mrs. Conway has done.

"I can't afford to lose my job now," protests Elsa, still a little bewildered. "Don't they know what it means to take people's jobs away? Or don't trustees think about things like that? I wanted to go, of course, but not like this! Not without any money!"

Harry Conway, it transpires, was not at the meeting. He has been in Chicago since Sunday. Watkins is for action. Stockton proposes that they draw up a petition, to which the others promptly agree. All but the conservative Professor Skeats. He would avoid a public scandal. He proposes that they wait and think the thing over. Mrs. Skeats, however, is with them. When her husband would take her home before the petition is written she signs a blank sheet of paper and bids them write what they will above her name.

"I expect husbands are always surprised, Hubert, to find that their wives have minds of their own," she says, in answer to the professor's further protest.

"The editor of the *Gazette* closed his investigations by telephoning the President of Conway College," Phipps adds to his report after the Skeats have gone. "The President is willing to endorse any petition to reinstate Miss Brandt, but insists that she forthwith abandon all hiring of halls to give piano recitals in. Will, in fact, undertake no action unless Miss Brandt will solemnly guarantee to attract no further untoward attention on any account."

STOCKTON—Well! I must say that's more encouraging!

WATKINS—Why didn't you tell us that in the beginning? With the President on our side, a petition's a mere formality.

PHIPPS—The *Gazette* editor now calls upon Miss Brandt to lay the question squarely before her. (*He meets* ELSA's *eyes very steadily.*) And the question is: Does she take advantage of what may well be her final opportunity to get back where she belongs, or does she extend the past two years to include the probable balance of her life? Are you ready for the question, Elsa? (ELSA *looks at him without answering.*)

STOCKTON—Phipps! You can't mean you don't want her to stay!

Watkins—After all, tonight's concert didn't turn out such a howling success.

Phipps—Elsa tasted her first blood tonight. Do you want to stay, Elsa?

Elsa—Do you think it's fair to corner me this way?

Stockton—No one could embark on such a venture as Elsa had in mind without a certain modicum of security.

Phipps—Security!

Elsa—Leave me alone, Phipps!

Phipps—You wanted your nerve back! Why don't you take it?

Stockton—How can she, Phipps? She's got someone to think of besides herself! There's her father! He isn't as young as he was and naturally . . .

Watkins—All your tall talk can't laugh the old warhorse off!

Elsa—Why did you have to bring that up? Now he'll start screaming and . . .

Phipps—It's about time he did! (*To* Brandt.) Come on, old warhorse, you stop her from crawling down!

Elsa (*frantic*)—What else can I do? !!!

Brandt—Du kannst gehen!

Elsa—Wie ist das möglich?

Brandt—Hier bleiben nur tehren, das ist unmöglich!

Elsa—Vir haben kein Geld!

Brandt—Das macht nichts aus! Nur weg von hier!

Elsa—Nach Wien vielleicht!

Brandt—Weg non hier! Weit von hier!

Elsa—Papa, um Himmelswillen!!!

Brandt—Schweige, Kind! Hör auf! Phipps, is it for me she has stayed here these two years? Is it for my sake? Answer me!

Elsa—Eine solche Prage . . .

Brandt—You do not answer! So! Ja! Now I see! (*His head bent back in agony.*) Ach, wir Eltern! Wir Eltern!

Their efforts to quiet and reassure Brandt are of no avail. He is determined. Now they will go. Elsa and he will go to New York, to his friends. Whether they remember him or not, he still has one good arm left. He can play a bass drum in a German band. Better that he starve, as they predict he will, than that Elsa should betray all the hopes he has in her.

"I can't stand any more," cries Elsa. "For God's sake, Watkins! Write your petition, or I'll write it myself!"

"Now that we've got back where we started I *will* take a drink," says Phipps, emptying the contents of a flask into an empty beer glass, and tossing it off. "Any objection to me lying down some place for an hour or two?" he says to Elsa. "You wouldn't make me drive after a drink like that?"

"I suppose you're through with me for good!" says Elsa.

"You can't help being human. I can't help wanting you to be something more. . . ."

The petition is finished and signed. Signatures will be added in the morning. Watkins, the old campus politician, will see to that.

"Now we don't have to fret any more," says Elsa, when Watkins and Stockton have gone; "just sink into things. If anyone can tell me where I can find a nice single grave and bath. . . ."

Now it is Julian's turn to become excited. He is not prepared to accept things as they are. Elsa shall get away, in spite of being broke and fired, in spite of the petition and the threat of her father starving—Elsa shall go. It has just occurred to Julian that what Phipps said is true. "The security you buy with your freedom's no better than slavery."

"Between us we've got enough to get somewhere and last till I find a job," says Julian, standing by Elsa at the piano. "I could certainly make good at a ribbon counter. And, from my first pay day, your father becomes my charge and you're a free agent. Isn't it wonderful I've found out at last where I fit into your life? I never thought of myself as your servant. Your true and humble servant, Elsa. Don't look at me like that. I'm quite all right. Feel my forehead. [He snatches her hand and rubs the palm of it against his brow.] It's cool and moist, isn't it? Can't you understand? I'm not asking you to love me now! I'm not asking for any part of you. I'm just the means to your escape and that's all I want to be. Why won't you take my offer seriously?"

"I know what a different tune you'll be singing in the morning," answers Elsa.

"If I got myself fired tomorrow, would you believe me then?" demands Julian.

"But you're not going to get yourself fired, *and I'm going on earning my living*."

Elsa is putting out the lights when Julian springs suddenly to his desk and grabs up the entire pile of blue books standing there. He carries these to the fireplace and begins throwing them into the flames in double handfuls.

"Ever hear how the Greeks burned their ships behind 'em?" he cries. "See these exams? They're my job. I've just finished correcting them. I haven't turned in the grades. I haven't even corrected them."

Elsa springs to prevent the destruction of the blue books, but Julian throws her off. The last of them have gone into the fire when he casts himself sobbing at her feet, burying his face against her knees.

Outside there is a noise. Someone is knocking on the window. It is Harry Conway. He steps into the room and he and Elsa stand for a moment looking at each other. Now Julian realizes the truth.

"You love him, don't you?" he says to Elsa. "I hadn't thought of that. Well, I withdraw my offer."

Julian has gone now and Elsa has sunk down upon the sofa and is crying softly, to the distress of Conway.

"Please stop crying," he pleads. "I shouldn't have skipped out Sunday night. But I never could stand that kind of a row at home. I've been in Chicago trying to get things straight. Now I know that I care so much it doesn't matter whether you care or not. What I've let you in for, my poor darling!"

ELSA—Why did you have to come back tonight?

CONWAY—Are you sorry I came?

ELSA—Too much has been happening to me tonight.

CONWAY—If you still care for me?

ELSA—You know I do.

CONWAY—Then marry me! . . . I'll get a divorce. I need you so, Elsa! My God, how much I need you! And everything I've always missed in life. A living marriage and a living home! . . . I can make life pleasant for you. For your father, too. I swear I can make you happy. So happy you won't miss the rest. I mean Vienna and your career and all. . . . I may be a damned materialist, but a career can't be so different from any other racket. It's all right for Kreislers and Paderewskis, but, forgive me, darling, but how can you be sure you're in their class?

ELSA—I can't.

CONWAY—Or ever will be. And if you're not, what's the point?

ELSA—I don't know.

CONWAY—I'm offering you the best I've got to offer. And I'll stake you to the career if you want that more. So think!

ELSA—I can't think any more!

Conway—You've got to.

Elsa—You're making me choose again! It isn't fair!

Conway—I'm not pretending I'd be satisfied to share you with the public. I can't see that. That's why I'm making you choose. I've got my own job. I've got to be myself, in my own life, in my own home. . . .

Elsa—You're so definite, aren't you?

Conway—I know what I want as well as you do. I want you. Your talent aside, what are we, Elsa? A man and a woman in love with each other.

Elsa—I want something I can hang on to. I want something I can touch!

Conway—Happiness!

Elsa—I want that now!

Conway—Peace!

Elsa—That, too!

Conway—Security!

Elsa—Even that won't be so bad with you!

Conway (*taking her hands*)—Darling!

Elsa—Will you kiss me, please?

Julian has come quietly down the stairs and into the room. He walks slowly to the desk and takes his revolver from the drawer. He is facing them as he quotes—

"They told me, Heraclitus, they told me you were dead,
They brought me bitter news to hear and bitter tears to shed.
I wept as I remembered how often you and I—"

Excitedly Elsa calls to him to put the gun down. He pays no heed. He has burned his ships, he says, and there is no reason why he should not clean up the rest of the mess and go where he belongs.

Elsa would argue with Julian. Life, she reminds him, is the most precious thing any of them has got. That depends on whose life she selects, he answers. Conway would take a hand. If Julian should murder him it might satisfy his jealousy, but—

Julian has no thought of murder. He has backed into the hallway now and turned from them. "Elsa, I love you!" he mutters. Before they can reach him he has turned the revolver on himself and fired.

Elsa and Conway are kneeling over the body as Phipps and Brandt rush down the stairs.

"What are you doing here?" demands Phipps, sobering as he recognizes Conway.

"I came to see Elsa, and . . . What do we do? 'Phone for a doctor?"

PHIPPS—A doctor? We get the police. Coroner's inquest on this!

ELSA—Julian!

CONWAY—Can't it be hushed up?

PHIPPS—How?

CONWAY—I'm thinking of her. . . .

PHIPPS—So am I. "Miss Brandt will solemnly guarantee to attract no further untoward attention" . . . Whether she takes the leap or—

CONWAY—Call your police and get this over with.

PHIPPS (*going to door*)—All right. I'll try to locate the cop on this beat.

BRANDT—Elsa. Mein schaz. Mein liebe kind . . .

CONWAY—Elsa, darling . . . Steady now, steady.

PHIPPS—Hey! Officer! . . . Officer!

OFFICER—Did you hear a shot?

PHIPPS—Did I hear it! This is the house! . . . It's a suicide.

OFFICER (*coming in*)—A suicide, eh?

PHIPPS—Look for yourself.

OFFICER—Mr. Conway!

CONWAY—This is a damned unfortunate thing, officer. Don't bother these poor people any more than you have to.

OFFICER—Who are they?

CONWAY—Ottokar Brandt and his daughter, Elsa.

OFFICER—Teachers?

ELSA—No! A pianist. . . . A concert pianist. . . .

CONWAY—Just answer what he asks you!

ELSA—It's no good, darling. I'm not going to marry you. I'm not even going to see you again.

CONWAY—You don't mean . . .

ELSA—This is my life! Phipps knows it! Julian knew it!!

OFFICER—Is this her home?

ELSA—No. Vienna.

THE CURTAIN FALLS

THE LATE CHRISTOPHER BEAN

A Comedy in Three Acts

BY SIDNEY HOWARD

GILBERT MILLER, who has to a considerable extent taken the place of Charles Frohman as the most interesting and the most successful importer of plays to which a particular American audience can look with the fullest confidence, did not begin his Broadway season until late in October. And then he began it with a hit at his own theatre, the Henry Miller, on the 31st.

The play was a comedy, "The Late Christopher Bean," the idea and framework of which Sidney Howard had borrowed from a Paris success called "Prenez Garde a la Peinture," written by René Fauchois. His was not, however, an adaptation in the accepted sense. It was, in effect, a complete rewriting of the play in the terms of American folk comedy.

In place of rural France Mr. Howard established his characters in rural New England. Their motivations, their broader human characteristics and weaknesses, I assume, are much the same in the two plays. But their racial reactions and characteristics are as strongly contrasted as studies of Latin and Anglo-Saxon types would suggest.

With Pauline Lord starred and Walter Connolly a featured member of the cast, "The Late Christopher Bean" was an accepted success with its audiences from the first performance. Professional critics were generally enthused by the play without being what might be termed at all excited by it. The run continued through the season and the play received the third highest rating of the year's dramatic output in the vote of the Pulitzer Prize Committee.

As "The Late Christopher Bean" opens the scene revealed is that of the dining-room of an old house in a New England village. "The room is worthy of more tasteful furnishing than the Haggett family has given it. Mingled with the few old pieces is much of less merit and more recent date."

At the moment the room is in some confusion because the furnishings from Dr. Haggett's office, a desk, etc., have been moved in to get them out of the way of paper hangers and painters. A ladder, buckets, brushes and a paint sign also clutter the entry.

It is an early morning in October. Dr. Haggett, "an undistinguished rural medical man of fifty," is just returning from a round of calls. Mrs. Haggett hears him from upstairs and calls loudly to Abby to get the Doctor his breakfast, seeing he ain't had none.

The Doctor's daughter, Susan, "a pretty girl of nineteen," stands ready to help Abby, who is terribly upset this morning. Abby, it transpires, is about to leave the Haggetts after years of service and the thought is fairly disrupting the whole household.

Abby comes now with the Doctor's breakfast on a tray. "She is the 'help' of the Haggett family, a Yankee villager, aged vaguely between youth and maturity, of a wistful prettiness, simple and serious."

"I got strong coffee hot and ready for you, Dr. Haggett," calls Abby, as she enters. "Think of you going all this time on an empty stomach! Did everything come out all right?"

"Yes. Boy, eight pounds, three ounces, came out."

"Well, that's just lovely!" says Abby. "I expect the Jordans must be real pleased it's a boy! I expect most parents'd sooner have boys than girls, and I don't know as I blame 'em. You just sit there, Dr. Haggett, and, Susie, you fix your pa his coffee while I get the rest of his breakfast. [She starts toward the kitchen door, pointing to the newspaper and telegram on the table.] There's his Boston paper handy for him. And there's a telegram with it that just come."

The Doctor's telegram is from New York. "An admirer of the late Christopher Bean will do himself the honor of calling on you at noon on Thursday" it reads and is signed Maxwell Davenport.

It is a mystifying telegram to both the Doctor and Susan. They hadn't thought of Chris Bean for years. Chris Bean—who had painted all those pictures! At least, the Doctor is convinced, Chris thought they were pictures when he wasn't too drunk to think. But who is Maxwell Davenport?

Mrs. Haggett has come down the stairs. "Like her husband she is Yankee and they are about an age. Unlike him, however, she has assumed certain cityfied airs in dress and bearing which, so she feels, lift her above the standards of her native village."

At the moment Mrs. Haggett is greatly annoyed. The painter-paper hanger has not come for his stuff, when he promised to have it out this morning first thing, and Abby leaving today, too—

"I'd as soon you didn't speak about me leaving, if you've got no objection, Mrs. Haggett," protests Abby, arriving with the rest of the Doctor's breakfast.

"Well, you are leaving, ain't you?"

ABBY—Yes, I am. But you know I don't want to, and I wouldn't neither only it's the will of God. And the only way I can get through with it is if nobody speaks to me about it. But if you keep reminding me, I . . . I . . . (MRS. HAGGETT *looks up.* SUSAN *lays a warning hand on her mother's arm.* ABBY *just manages to control herself. She smiles bravely.*) What I want is to hear about Mrs. Jordan's baby. She didn't get married none too soon, did she? I should think when a baby comes that quick after a wedding you'd pretty near have to brush the rice off it. Was she in labor long? (*She returns to the table with a plate of butter and the syrup jug which she puts before the* DOCTOR.)

DR. HAGGETT—Not so long.

ABBY—Did she have just a terrible time? You look kind of washed out yourself, Dr. Haggett. Well, it couldn't have been more than four o'clock when they called you out. Seems like babies are always getting you up or keeping you up, don't it? (ADA HAGGETT, *a girl of twenty-six, who fancies her baby prettiness and babylike manner, comes down the stair.*)

SUSAN—If you feel so bad about leaving us, Abby, why don't you stay?

ABBY—You're all so good to me! I don't want to go. It's the will of God.

DR. HAGGETT—The first time I ever heard of the will of God sending a woman off to live in Chicago!

ABBY—It couldn't have been nothing less to make my poor brother's wife take sick and die and leave him with four little children and no woman in the house! You know it wouldn't be my way to will a thing like that!

DR. HAGGETT—Well, don't let's be going over it again. You're leaving us. We're sorry to have you go. We'll save our tears till the time comes for you to take your train. What time is it?

ABBY—The five o'clock to Boston.

SUSAN—We're going to miss you, Abby!

ABBY—And me? What about me leaving this place where I been so long? Fifteen years I been here! Fifteen years in my room back there! And all my things that I had so long. . . .

DR. HAGGETT—Don't keep on going over it!

ABBY—No, I don't want to go over it, either. I just can't stand . . .

She has flown to the kitchen. They'll never get another like Abby, Susan is convinced and the Doctor thinks it might be just as well. But Mrs. Haggett has no idea of getting along without help, even if there are three women in the house. She doesn't intend having people say Dr. Haggett's business has fallen off so bad he can't afford to keep help. She has no patience with the Doctor not being able to collect his bills. He shouldn't treat people who can't pay.

As for Abby's successor, Mrs. Haggett has already engaged a maid from Boston who isn't going to cost much more. It's in bad times that people have to keep up appearances most of all. And haven't they made every stitch of clothes they are going to wear in Florida?

"Well, the girls and you aren't going to Florida or any other place till times get better!" firmly announces the Doctor.

"Did I hear Pa say we can't go to Florida?" demands Ada Haggett, who has joined the group.

"Yes, you did, Ada," snaps the Doctor. "And it's not the first time either. Maybe I do sit by and let your Ma paint and paper up my office, and maybe your Ma is going to have a maid from Boston. Maybe. But as long as I can't collect the bills my patients owe me, there's no use of no more Florida talk! I take my stand on that!"

"Well, I take my stand, too, Milton Haggett, and I wouldn't be no mother if I gave it up," answers Mrs. Haggett.

If the Doctor has any interest in seeing his daughters married, Mrs. Haggett suggests, he will help them get to Florida. "Them Miami beaches is just alive with boys who don't give a thought to nothing but romance and getting married," says she.

Dr. Haggett is not convinced. His girls don't have to go to Florida to get married. And he doesn't see anything wrong about village boys, having been one himself. If it is because they have seen her in her swimming suit that is going to make Florida boys like Ada better than village boys, let Ada put her swimming suit on and invite the village boys in.

"If we stay here Susie'll get married before me because the boys here like her better than they like me," whines Ada, "and if she gets married before me I'll just die! I'll die! I know I'll die!"

"It's this forever having just enough and not one mite over for—" Mrs. Haggett starts to protest.

"Greed, Hannah! Greed!" interrupts the Doctor.

"Maybe I am greedy! It's only fools and wastrels who don't

try to get all they can out of life!"

"No man has ever called me greedy for money, Hannah. And I hope no man ever does. I'll go upstairs now and shave. . . ."

"I declare, if folks ain't peculiar," chimes in Abby, coming from the kitchen. "There I was crying and carrying on over going away and now you're doing the very same as me because you got to stay."

Warren Creamer, the village painter and paper-hanger, "a personable, self-satisfied youth in his early twenties," has come for his paint things and brought the girls each a present. To Ada a study in still life of a dead fish. To Susan a dead duck. Any kind of painting comes natural to Warren and these, he thinks, are real good.

Abby is the only one who appreciates Warren's paintings. Abby knows quite a lot about painting. As for Dr. Haggett, he is like the women of his family. Warren's work doesn't mean anything to him, except he wonders where he got the time to do it. Mrs. Haggett finds the idea that Warren is fixing to be a painter distressing. Nor is she impressed by his offer to do portraits of the girls.

But Warren has posed the girls and started his preliminary sketches. These are good enough to surprise all the Haggetts and the Doctor is keen to know where Warren picked up these painting tricks. From Chris Bean? The same Chris Bean that used to be a patient of Dr. Haggett's?

"Chris started me off on painting when I was a kid," explains Warren. "He'd let me follow him wherever he went and sit beside him and draw the same things he did. He gave me lessons, all I ever had. I try to remember what he taught me and practice it."

"Hope he didn't teach you to drink like he did!" snorts Mrs. Haggett.

"Well, I guess anything you learned from—" Abby would say more, but is frozen by a look from Mrs. Haggett.

For a moment Susan and Warren are left alone. It is long enough for Warren to explain that the only reason he is painting the portrait is because Susan is in it; that she must have known for a long time how he feels about her, and that the only way she can stop him talking about it is to promise to marry him.

Susan doesn't think she would be a good wife for an artist, even a good artist, but Warren is fairly convincing. He is kissing Susan by way of confirmation when Ada comes suddenly back from the kitchen and is forced to gasp her astonishment. Immediately she has called her father and mother to stop such goings on, and they have come running.

"There I was in the kitchen, Pa, with the new maid and Ma, and I came back and I caught him and Susie—"

"Don't tell 'em what I was doing," interrupts Warren, stepping undismayed to Susan's side. "I'd rather show 'em." And he kisses Susan again, with passion.

Mrs. Haggett would throw Warren and all his stuff out of the house. Warren is perfectly willing, but he thinks Susan should come with him, so they can get married. Susan decides that she shouldn't go just now, and Dr. Haggett thinks Warren would be wise to go alone until things simmer down.

With Warren out of the house and her mother and sister gone back to the kitchen Susan confesses that she does love Warren and sees nothing wrong in his intention of becoming an artist.

"What's wrong with artists?" she demands.

"Not a thing but the cost of food and lodging," admits Dr. Haggett.

"Not if he's a good one! And he will be a good one!"

"He's got conceit enough. But the best of them are poor providers, from all I hear, and these days—"

"These days!" explodes Susan. "That's all you ever say! These days! If it weren't for these days you and Ma wouldn't have anything against Warren, and Ma and Ada could go to Florida. . . ."

"And I could get a little peace—"

The doorbell has rung. Susan and her father have dashed upstairs. Abby goes to the door to admit Tallant, "a horn-rimmed, youngish, shabbily dressed New Yorker of the disarming, art loving variety."

Dr. Haggett is slow to understand who Tallant is and why he has called, when he discovers that he is not a patient. And doubly surprised to have Tallant explain that while he was motoring in the vicinity he realized that he had stumbled upon an opportunity to perform a duty that had been postponed much too long. Which would be the payment of a sacred debt he owes the Doctor.

"A matter of ten years ago you had as a patient a man whom I called and still call my dearest friend," explains Tallant.

"Did I now!"

"A man know by a good Yankee name. An excellent Yankee name, Christopher Bean."

Now the Doctor recalls the telegram. Of course this must be

the sender of the telegram. A statement that surprises Tallant also. He thinks he may remember, but he would like to see the telegram. Reading it, he remembers that he did send it. But it had taken him much less time than he had expected to get there.

Yes, Tallant was more than an admirer of Chris Bean, which leads Dr. Haggett to doubt that they are thinking of the same man. Chris was a likable chap and he used to think he was a painter, but—

"I always humored him about his pictures," explains the Doctor. "You've got to humor folks when they're sick as he was."

TALLANT—I know you did everything you could for him.

DR. HAGGETT—Well, I hope I did my duty by him. Of course, a case like his . . . This is no climate for tuberculosis. If he'd had the money to get himself out West he might have had some chance, if he'd quit drinking. But as it was, there wasn't much I could do.

TALLANT—We're all mortal, Doctor.

DR. HAGGETT—There's no denying that.

TALLANT—It delights me that you remember him with affection.

DR. HAGGETT—Oh, we none of us forgot him! Why, we were speaking of him just a few minutes past. My wife, she took a real fancy to him. He kind of appealed to her, I guess, seeing as we got no sons of our own, only two daughters. And him coming to live here, sick like he was and an orphan with no family. She took him right to her heart and gave him the old barn for his studio. He painted most everything round the place. They were terrible bad though, those pictures of his. (*He laughs reminiscently.*) Mebbe if he'd had some training . . .

TALLANT—Oh, very like. (*Then, more seriously.*) Recently though, Doctor, only the other day in fact, as I was going through an old desk of mine, I came across some letters Chris wrote to me while he was living here. And in the last of them—it's disgraceful I should have neglected it all these years—he spoke of your kindness to him and his gratitude and asked if I couldn't help him pay what he owed you.

DR. HAGGETT—Well, that's like Chris! Never a penny to his name and forever borrowing! He didn't even own a hat!

TALLANT—Let me see . . . the sum came to . . .

DR. HAGGETT—I don't remember!

TALLANT—Exactly a hundred dollars.

DR. HAGGETT—Mebbe so. Likely he asked me how much he

Photo by Vandamm Studio, New York.

"THE LATE CHRISTOPHER BEAN"

Abby: Would it really mean so much to all of you to have me hanging up there in an oil painting?

Mrs. Haggett: Would we want any one we didn't love in our dining-room?

(*Pauline Lord, Beulah Bondi and Walter Connolly*)

owed me, and likely I told him if ever he had a hundred he could spare . . .

TALLANT—Allow *me,* Doctor. (*He rises and hands the* DOCTOR *two fifty dollar bills.*) A little late, but paid in full.

DR. HAGGETT—Well, God Almighty!

TALLANT—And all my apologies for keeping you waiting.

DR. HAGGETT—My dear sir!

TALLANT—The debt's paid at last. I shall go home to New York a happier man.

DR. HAGGETT—I'll give you a receipt. (*Completely flabbergasted, he turns to his desk.*)

TALLANT—Oh, Doctor, please!

DR. HAGGETT—Would you allow me to shake you by the hand?

TALLANT—I should be honored.

Now the Doctor, vastly excited, has called in the family to meet this wonderful Mr. Davenport, who has forgotten his cards. With a flourish he introduces Mrs. Haggett and the girls and tells them excitedly of what Mr. Davenport has just told him about Chris Bean and what he has done in the name of his friendship for Chris. Such things don't happen every day. Such a devotion should be an example to them both, and let them never forget the name of Davenport.

Tallant, more or less covered with confusion, sees nothing unusual in what he has done. His friend had meant much to him. Is it possible that Chris had left them any of his pictures to remember him by? He knows what they thought of them and Chris had often told him that the boys of the village had laughed at him when they watched him painting. But they would have a special sentimental value to Mr. Tallant. Chris's letters had mentioned six or seven paintings that he had left. If Mr. Tallant could take these—

Mrs. Haggett thinks she can remember one that's out in the chicken house, but that, as the Doctor points out, must be in pretty sad condition. He had used it to mend a leak in the tar-paper roof.

"I was looking for something water-tight, and I found that picture. Fine, thick oil paint, you know, and there was no reason to set much store by it," the Doctor explains.

And there's another, he suddenly remembers, up in the attic in the corner behind the north dormer. That had been put there to stop a leak, too. Abby shall go fetch it.

Abby is of a mind to protest. What does the Doctor want to

do with the painting? Why should Mr. Davenport want to take it home with him? Because Mr. Davenport was Chris Bean's closest friend.

Abby goes reluctantly to look for the painting in the attic as Mrs. Haggett and Ada come from the chicken house with their "poultry-scarred loot." This sample is pretty dirty, but perhaps Abby can clean it with soap and a scrubbing brush—

"Oh, no, please!" protests Tallant. "I'd be afraid. I mean I'd rather clean it myself. . . . Don't you see, Doctor, what it will mean to me to bring this picture back to life? It will mean almost as though Chris himself—" He is deeply moved.

Now the Haggetts have remembered Ada's picture—the flower piece she had painted on the back of one of Chris Bean's that has been hanging on the wall of the dining room. But of course he wouldn't want that, after Ada had gone splotching—

To the contrary, Tallant is greatly impressed with Ada's talent and with the picture, even if she would make fun of it. "The exquisite texture of these buttercups is not to be under-rated!" says he. "Of course I don't mean that you won't do better things in the future, or that you won't go farther, higher! But here, already, I, the connoisseur, sense the spark of genius!"

Mr. Tallant would, if they were willing, like to buy Ada's picture for, say fifty dollars—well, say forty dollars. Which is quite a surprise to Ada. She could do one of those things a day.

"It strikes me kind of funny," admits Dr. Haggett, dubiously, "you coming in here and paying Chris Bean's bill and then offering my daughter forty dollars—"

"Fifty dollars!" corrects Mrs. Haggett.

"He said forty!"

"He said fifty first, and fifty's Ada's price!"

"I will, of course, pay fifty if you'll sell it," speaks up Tallant, peeling off the bills from his roll, "and you may be sure orders for more will follow."

Ada has taken the money despite a further mild protest by her father and Tallant has assured them of his great delight in discovering a new artist, when they remind him of the Chris Bean picture on the other side. He had, Tallant admits, quite forgotten that. Now he blows the dust from it and is obviously pleased. It is meant to be the old covered bridge up the back river, Ada explains.

Abby returns from the attic with the report that there are no pictures up there.

"But I know darn well!" insists Dr. Haggett.

"Mebbe the mice have et it," suggests Mrs. Haggett.
"It was on the left of the north dormer!"

ABBY—There's nothing there now but some tin cracker boxes Mrs. Haggett's saving.

DR. HAGGETT—But I tell you I'm positive!

ABBY—I've been over every inch of that attic, Doctor. I didn't find a thing but the old trundle bed used to be in the front room before you got the brass bed, and the trunk with your ma's pewter in it and the other trunk. . . .

DR. HAGGETT—I could have sworn! Well, it's too bad. That's all, Abby. (*He turns to* TALLANT.) I'm sorry, sir. I'd have liked to show you how much I appreciate what you've done, but there you are. No man can do better than his best. (ABBY *draws back, her gaze fixed on* TALLANT.)

TALLANT—I'm more than satisfied with what I've got, Dr. Haggett. And I repeat I'm sorry to have caused so much trouble. (*The ladies brush his apologies aside with low exclamations. He bows.*) Mrs. Haggett. Miss Haggett.

DR. HAGGETT—Mr. Davenport, your call this morning is going to stand out as one of the happiest memories of my medical career! (*The two men are in the entry.*)

TALLANT—Doctor, you and I are going to be much better acquainted. And it occurs to me that we might go into business together. Business which might be highly profitable to both.

DR. HAGGETT—I've got no capital!

TALLANT—It will require nothing more of you than what I might call friendly coöperation.

DR. HAGGETT—I've got a plenty of that! (*Laughter.*)

TALLANT—Then we're rich men, Dr. Haggett! We're rich men! (*They shake hands with more laughter and* TALLANT *goes.*)

MRS. HAGGETT—Well! (DR. HAGGETT *returns to the room.*) At this rate we'll mebbe get to Florida after all.

DR. HAGGETT—Well, after this morning, I'm not so sure you won't. Wish I knew what business he's got in mind.

ADA—I don't care what it is if it makes us rich!

DR. HAGGETT—Ada, that's no kind of talk for a daughter of mine! If there's one thing I can't abide it's greed for money!

Ada and her mother have gone to dress for their marketing. Dr. Haggett has suddenly discovered that the time is much later than he thought and is bustling to get started on his rounds.

Abby has helped him find his call book and he is starting for the Jordans' mumbling that that man Davenport's got his mind all off doctoring.

"If I was you, Dr. Haggett, I'd watch him careful," advises Abby.

"What makes you say that?"

"Strikes me it's always a good idea to watch folks careful when they know as much as he does."

"I declare, Abby, I think Mrs. Haggett's pretty near right about the way you meddle!" sputters the Doctor. "Didn't he send me a telegram about Chris Bean?"

Abby starts, but makes no reply. When the Doctor has left the house she finds the telegram on the desk. Mrs. Haggett and Ada come chattering down the stairs. Abby puts the telegram back and waits. When they have gone shopping she picks it up again. "This time she reads it through, pronouncing each word inaudibly to herself in an unaccountably warm glow of happiness."

Susan comes sobbing down the stairs. Abby stands with the telegram held against her heart. Now Susan, still sniveling, has recovered Warren's crushed sketch from the fireplace and is trying to smooth it out on the dining-room table.

ABBY—Susie!

SUSAN—Oh, Abby, I never knew I could be so miserable!

ABBY—Oh, folks can be awful miserable sometimes!

SUSAN—But look at poor Warren's drawing, all mussed up!

ABBY—He'll make another. Artists always do.

SUSAN—Abby, you haven't got anything against artists, have you?

ABBY—Me? No! No! Not me. . . . (*She smiles to herself on her way back to her kitchen as the curtain falls.*)

ACT II

A little later that morning the bell rings and Abby finds the Mr. Tallant she knows as Davenport returned. She sees no reason why she should let him in. Dr. Haggett is still on his rounds and Ada and Mrs. Haggett are in town shopping. But Tallant has come back to see Abby. He wants to thank her for being kind to a friend of his.

"You gave Chris Bean all the good things that have no name," he says. "All the warm, tender things he so sorely needed."

"What do you know about me?" demands Abby, really frightened.

"Only what he told me. Except for you I was the best friend he ever had."

"I never heard him name no Davenport," answers Abby, still suspicious. "He used to talk a lot about his friend Bert Davis! But I never heard of you."

"I'm Davis!"

Davenport, explains Tallant, is a professional name. He had taken it because he wanted a name people would remember. Also Bert Davis, being a lot like Chris, had got into trouble. The thought is rather pleasing to Abby. She likes to hear, too, that Chris often had spoken of her and that he was fond of her.

"He was the only man that ever took me serious and talked to me," Abby recalls, reminiscently. "He didn't talk so much. But what he said was awful pithy. And to think of you being Bert Davis! It certainly is a pleasure to make your acquaintance! I never expected to meet up with you. Don't you think we better shake hands on it? [They do.] Set down, Mr. Davis, and I'll set down with you. Mrs. Haggett don't favor the help setting in the setting-room, but she's cityfied that way. And she ain't home anyhow and what she don't know won't hurt her. [Her eyes shine as they take him in.] Bert Davis! My, don't that name bring things back, though!"

"Chris wrote me that you were the only one who ever liked his painting, or got what he was after," says Tallant.

That, too, pleases Abby. Chris had taught her many things. Mostly things to see. "Like the rust color the marshes get this time of year when the sky gets the color of that old blue platter. "That's cobalt blue. That's a painting term, cobalt blue," Abby continues, proudly. "And he showed me the old red barn and the covered bridge that he was forever painting and I was used to all my life and never noticed. And he taught me that old chairs may be more than just old chairs to be thrown away. That some of 'em may be real beautiful. He used to say those very words about the old doors in the brick houses up along the Common! That was when they begun taking the old doors out and putting in new ones ordered from Sears, Roebuck. And did you know that old brick houses ain't red but mostly green and brown and that moonlight and snow ain't white at all but all kinds of colors and that elm trees is mostly decorative when their leaves comes off? That's another painting term, decorative. He taught me! [Her reminiscence becomes more personal.] He taught me that a man can get drunk and not be no different only just more so and that everybody's got more good qualities than bad. Oh, he taught me lots! And I ain't never forgot none of it. I lived over and over that time he spent here. Over and over it ever since he died."

Tallant, approaching the subject cautiously, would know whether Chris Bean had left Abby much to remember him by. Nothing much beside her memories, Abby admits. But memories are important. Nobody can take them away, but perhaps something happens to them when they are taken away from the place they belong. That worries Abby. She is going away from there and she doesn't want to go. The Haggetts think it is because of them, but it isn't. It is because of her memories—the thought of not seeing the red barn any more, or the brick houses, or the covered bridge, or the hill pasture—

It was to these places he liked to paint that Abby used to take Chris hot coffee. Tallant remembers that once she knitted a sweater for him—

"I'm not ashamed," says Abby. "Only I'd sooner you wouldn't tell Doctor or Mrs. Haggett or the girls. You know how folks thought about him here—him being only an artist and all. And they never understood him. And they wouldn't have understood him no better for liking me! And I wanted to keep their good opinion and my place here with the Haggetts. But I'm not ashamed."

Again Tallant would know if there isn't something Chris has left. Little sketches or something—

Abby could show him something better than sketches if she wanted to. Once Chris had painted a portrait of her, life size. It has hung over her bed all these years. It is this portrait that worries Abby most when she thinks of its getting all smoked up in Chicago. It is out in her room and she would take him to see it—but the new maid is in the kitchen and Abby wouldn't like the maid to see her taking a man into her room. She'd tell Mrs. Haggett—

Tallant is disappointed. He hopes Abby will be able to come around to his hotel where they can finish their talk. And bring the portrait with her. Furthermore, if ever she is in need of money he, though not a rich man, would be glad to buy anything of Chris's that she has to sell. He would like to get all of Chris's works together, where they can keep each other company.

Abby could never think of selling anything of Chris's, but she might give his best friend—no, not the portrait—she'd have to think a long time about that—but—

Someone is heard at the kitchen door. Tallant escapes, on Abby's advice, before anyone sees him. The intruder is Warren Creamer. Susan comes from upstairs to greet Warren affectionately. They send Abby to watch the front. Abby is opposed to this sort of thing. There's bound to be a row. She is even more excited when Warren confesses that he has planned to sell his business for $500 and go to New York to study art. He won't go, however, without Susan, and he doesn't purpose waiting on the consent of her ma. If Susan likes him as well as she says she does she will take the chance.

It is Abby's idea that Warren needs a taking down, but she can't help admiring him. It is Warren's idea that Susan should give her clothes to Abby and be ready when he comes for Abby's things. Then she can go along as though she was going to see Abby off and he will meet them both in Boston.

Abby thinks she couldn't allow any such thing. It is her bounden duty to tell Mrs. Haggett. And if she does help the elopers it certainly won't be on Warren Creamer's account.

"When a girl gets in the state you got Susie in, she needs someone to look after her and see to it that she does get married and not just fly off the handle regardless! I've been in love! I know! [The doorbell rings. They freeze all three.] Better get along now, Warren Creamer, before you get caught!"

A gentleman named Rosen, "an oily and too affable Jewish gentleman," is at the door. He, too, would like to see Dr. Haggett. He, too, recognizes Abby. He has heard that Abby has an unusually kind nature and that she appreciates modern painting. He has seen the Old Brick Fronts on the Common. And the Red Barn. And now he has seen Abby—even if she isn't in red and white checked gingham.

Dr. Haggett, Mrs. Haggett and Ada have returned. Abby, puzzled by all the things that are happening around there, has gone back to the kitchen. Mr. Rosen has turned his attention to Dr. Haggett.

"Dr. Haggett," he begins, affably, "in the course of your professional career, you once had as a patient a young friend of mine. A painter [Dr. Haggett pricks up his ears.] with whom I confess I had personal difficulties. Ten years ago his death left me with that regret we all feel in such cases. Recently I have come across some letters. [Dr. Haggett shifts his chair forward, staring at Rosen in amazement.] Letters he wrote to me while he was living here under your care. They showed me how in a small way I might ease my conscience regarding him. Dr. Haggett, my friend Christopher Bean died owing you one hundred dollars. I have computed the interest on the unpaid bill at six per cent, and the total for ten years comes to exactly one hundred and sixty dollars. Allow me to offer you my check for the sum."

Dr. Haggett accepts the check and Mr. Rosen feels that now he can go back to New York a happier man. Dr. Haggett is prepared to believe that, and he also is most curious to know if, by any chance, Mr. Rosen is also interested in anything in the way of pictures that Mr. Bean might have left behind him?

Mr. Rosen is interested, but not in the collection of Bean souvenirs. He is a business man. If there are any pictures he would like to buy them. Mr. Rosen, in fact, is prepared to offer a thousand dollars for the lot!

A thousand dollars! Dr. Haggett is staggered. He is not saying a word against the offer. But he is placed in a position that is a little awkward because there has already been another man there to whom he had not sold, but practically given all the Chris Bean pictures—

ROSEN—You gave away "The Covered Bridge"! Dr. Haggett, you've been swindled!

DR. HAGGETT—You don't have to tell me that!

ROSEN—But what in God's name possessed you?

DR. HAGGETT—He sent me a telegram he was coming from New York.

ROSEN—What was his name?

DR. HAGGETT—I ain't much good at remembering names. . . . (*He fumbles through his pockets.*) I ought to have his telegram some place though. (*He finds the telegram on the desk.*) Here it is now. (*He reads.*) Maxwell Davenport. That was his name. Maxwell Davenport.

ROSEN (*staggered*)—Maxwell Davenport?

DR. HAGGETT—That's right. Yes.

ROSEN—You mean to say Maxwell Davenport let you give him . . .

DR. HAGGETT—I thought they weren't any good. He said they weren't.

ROSEN (*unable to believe his hearing*)—Davenport said that?

DR. HAGGETT (*holding out the telegram*)—Yes! Davenport! Here, (ROSEN *takes the telegram.*) if you don't believe me! Do you know him?

ROSEN—Do I know Davenport? Yes! Of course I know him!

But I never would have believed such a thing of him. (*He sniffs the smell of powder.*) Have you got witnesses?

DR. HAGGETT—I've got my wife and daughter.

ROSEN (*grinning and confidential*)—Then, I tell you, Doctor, this may not be so serious. I think I see how we can fix Davenport. He's the art critic on the New York *Tribune,* the best we've got down in the big city and everybody's looking up to him. Now he wouldn't hardly care to have it known what a dirty trick he played on you to get those pictures free when they're worth . . . (*He remembers discretion.*) a thousand dollars. So this is what we do. (*He extracts papers from his pocket and explains,* DR. HAGGETT *listening attentively.*) I've got here with me a bill of sale for what he took all made out in advance by my lawyer. (*The doorbell rings.*) You sign it and I give you my check for a thousand dollars. Then we get you and your wife and daughter and go down to the court house and swear out an affidavit about every word that great art critic said. Especially that the pictures were no good. You leave the rest to me. I think we can fix Mr. Davenport!

Now Abby has passed through the entry and admitted Maxwell Davenport, "an elderly and distinguished gentleman." Davenport has also called to see Dr. Haggett, and he, too, recognizes Abby. What luck! But Abby is getting a little tired of being recognized by strangers and retires precipitately to the kitchen.

Davenport introduces himself to Dr. Haggett before he sees Rosen. Now that he does see Rosen he is a little disgusted to find him there.

DAVENPORT—I might have known the scavengers would be gathering! I beg your pardon, Doctor, but this man, who exploits artists and treats their work like so much merchandise . . .

ROSEN—It's not the artists I exploit! It's the customers! And it's men like me who justify the existence of you art critics! Where yould you be, writing about your tactile values, your limpid shadows, your something or other highlights, if you didn't have us to create interest in art by building up prices?

DAVENPORT—You befoul the whole business of dealing in art with your tricks and forgeries, and . . .

DR. HAGGETT—Just a minute, please! This is my house and I got a right to know what's going on! You say you're Mr. Davenport. And he says you are! All right, you must be! But will you please tell me what this is all about?

DAVENPORT—It's about one of the world's great injustices, Dr. Haggett, which I am doing my small part to set right. You once had for your patient a poor boy, a painter . . .

DR. HAGGETT—Yes, I know. Chris Bean.

DAVENPORT—I'm glad, Doctor, that you remember him. Now this boy . . .

DR. HAGGETT—Died owing me a hundred dollars, and you've come to pay it!

DAVENPORT—No, Doctor! No! Don't say that Bean owed any man anything! It is we, all of us, who stand in everlasting debt to him! As the world must always stand in debt to its men of genius!

DR. HAGGETT—Genius? Chris Bean a genius?

DAVENPORT—If ever a genius lived and painted pictures! (*Then, more quietly:*) The object of my visit today is to gather any details that I may find concerning his life with you for a critical biography of him that I am writing.

DR. HAGGETT—You're writing a book about Chris Bean!

DAVENPORT—That is my occupation at the moment, yes.

DR. HAGGETT—Whatever gave you that idea?

DAVENPORT—Haven't you read of the sensation his pictures have been making in New York? (DR. HAGGETT *shakes his head dizzily.*) Haven't you seen the last *Atlantic Monthly?*

ROSEN—That only came out yesterday, Mr. Davenport.

DAVENPORT—Quite. Well, Dr. Haggett, art is long, and the world is often slow to recognize it. Only now, ten years after his death, has Christopher Bean had his first exhibition in New York. Only now do we realize that he was not merely the greatest American painter, but one of the great masters of all time.

DR. HAGGETT—Our Chris Bean was?

DAVENPORT—Your Chris Bean, who painted and drank and coughed his short life away here in this village. From which he wrote to his friend, Davis, alas, also dead, the exquisite group of letters published yesterday in the *Atlantic.*

DR. HAGGETT—Our Chris Bean! (*A pause. Then light dawns and he turns to* ROSEN.) So them's the letters you folks have been finding going through your desks!

ROSEN—You've guessed it, Doctor.

Mrs. Haggett has come in and met Mr. Davenport and Mr. Rosen, and before her amazement can be adjusted she has learned from Davenport that not only are folks paying money for Chris Bean pictures but that dealers cannot find enough to supply the demand. None of them has sold for less than five, and some for as high as ten, thousand dollars. Which makes Mrs. Haggett a little bit sick when she remembers—

Another telegram has arrived. This is from the Metropolitan Museum offering seven thousand, five hundred dollars for the choice of the Christopher Bean canvases! Dr. Haggett is desperate. Seven of the Bean pictures unaccounted for and he has no recollection of them!

"I must have them somewheres," insists Dr. Haggett. "There's two I can't account for just at the moment. But if he left seven I must have the rest. Did you ever hear of folks throwing away oil paintings? Valuable oil paintings? I'll have a look for 'em! I'll have a look and I'll find 'em! And when I do I'll pay 'em the honor they deserve! I'll hang 'em all here in my dining-room! And I don't know as I'm interested in selling 'em. Not now that I know what they're worth, I don't! At least . . . [With a glare toward Rosen.] At least, not for no small sums like I been offered! [He drops into his chair.] But now I'd like for you all to go away. And leave me to eat my dinner in peace. And talk matters over with my family. This is all kind of sudden, I've got to think."

Mr. Davenport will come back. He wants to see Dr. Haggett after dinner to get his recollections of Chris Bean. He will leave the copy of the *Atlantic Monthly* that Dr. Haggett may read the Bean letters.

The Haggetts are terribly upset. Which of them is to blame? Abby would not have them quarreling about that. Not on her last day. Ada is convinced that if the first man got the pictures under false pretenses they can get them back. But there is that fifty dollars that Tallant paid for Ada's picture!

Dr. Haggett might thrash Tallant—if he could. Or he might get a lawyer, though lawyers are expensive if you ain't sure of winning. And to think he let "that greedy crook" snatch ten and twenty thousand dollars out of his hands! Is Abby sure she searched the attic thoroughly?

Now Susan is back and excitedly drawn into the discussion. Is Susan sure she doesn't know anything about any more Chris Bean pictures? Susan can only remember the last time she saw them they were in the barn— She remembers showing them to Warren Creamer.

That's what has happened to them, explodes Dr. Haggett. Warren Creamer has stolen them! But now Mrs. Haggett has a confession to make. Warren Creamer didn't steal the pictures.

She burned them up. She put them on a bonfire and burned them! Eight or ten of them! Worth ten thousand dollars and over—

"You thought they were terrible pictures, too, Milton," protests Mrs. Haggett, defensively.

Ada has been to the attic and found nothing. Dr. Haggett has picked up the *Atlantic Monthly* and read from the Bean correspondence—

" 'Dr. H. takes conscientious care of me. He knows nothing of medicine but looks like a gargoyle and that amuses me.' " And further on—" 'This angel of devotion is both sister and nurse to me and more than both. I know that her care is adding months to my life, all the more because she, and only she, sees merit in what I paint. She is the single comfort I have found in my life here and in her own way she is beautiful.' "

"Well, I liked the boy and encouraged him," smirks Mrs. Haggett.

"But, Ma! That ain't you. It's Abby! 'When I go into the fields these chill autumn mornings she brings me out hot coffee to drink.' "

Suddenly the Doctor remembers that Chris Bean did paint one portrait while he was there. A portrait of Abby! And that has been hanging over her bed ever since! Let Ada go and get it.

Susan objects. If there is such a portrait it belongs to Abby!

Dr. Haggett insists that he doesn't intend to do anything unfair, but if it was left to Mrs. Haggett she would go right in Abby's room and take that portrait. After all, Abby's no artist's model and the Haggetts were paying her thirty dollars a month and keep while the portrait was being painted. Let Ada go in Abby's room and get the portrait, even if she has to tear down a part of the house to do it!

"I'm only a simple country doctor," protests Dr. Haggett. "I don't care for money. It's only for my loved ones I got to have it!"

Ada starts for the portrait but finds Abby in her room. Abby and the picture. Perhaps if they call Abby to set the table that will get her out of the way.

When Abby comes the Haggetts' interest in her is almost intense. Dr. Haggett would apologize for any rudeness of which he may have been guilty. Mrs. Haggett is very grateful that Abby wants to stay this last day and wait on them. It wouldn't seem natural with the new girl.

They have a time thinking of ways to keep Abby out of the

kitchen. No, they won't have any mustard pickles. No, nor any watermelon preserves, either. They just want to talk to Abby. They want to talk about the new girl. Does Abby think she really will be any good? Does she think—

Abby cannot be held longer. She has remembered her biscuits and she doesn't intend to let them burn. She is in the kitchen and for the moment they cannot think of any way to get her back. She's almost sure to catch Ada taking the portrait out of her room.

Ada is back but without the picture. She was just taking it off the hook when Abby came to see about the biscuits. Now they will just have to go ahead with dinner and wait their chances afterward.

New York is calling Dr. Haggett. The Knoedler Galleries would like to offer twelve thousand dollars for Chris Bean's picture of the covered bridge, if it is in good condition! And that's the one Ada painted her picture on and sold to Tallant for fifty dollars!

Now Abby has come from the kitchen with a soup tureen. "Well, I got dinner ready, folks," she says, cheerily. "You can set down now!" They do not move. Abby is mystified. "You can all set down," she repeats, "dinner's ready."

Mechanically the Haggetts move to their places. Mechanically Mrs. Haggett begins to serve the soup. Still wondering, Abby passes the soup from place to place. Nobody eats it. They are staring absently at nothing. All but the Doctor. His eyes are fixed on Abby. Abby looks into his face puzzled. The Doctor, lowering his gaze quickly, unrolls his napkin, tucks it in his coat and bows his head.

"For what we are about to receive, O Lord, make us truly thankful." The blessing is intoned as

THE CURTAIN FALLS

ACT III

In the late afternoon of that day Maxwell Davenport, calling on the Haggetts and finding Dr. Haggett out, meets Susan, and Susan has a favor to ask of him.

It is a secret favor in a way. Susan is thinking of eloping that afternoon and she needs the advice of an art critic. She is thinking of eloping with a boy who thinks he can paint, but Susan wants to be as sure as possible whether he should paint houses or pictures.

Mr. Davenport is willing to look at Warren Creamer's pictures and pass an opinion upon them. Susan shows him the dead duck and the salmon. They are, he agrees, individual at least. They make him want to see more of the young man's work, and Susan eagerly volunteers to act as guide. They are just leaving for Warren's place across the street when Dr. Haggett returns.

The Doctor is pretty tired. He has been all over the town looking for the scoundrel Tallant. He has heard that Tallant has been out painting, but he has not been able to find him. He has found, however, that the two Bean pictures Tallant took away from the Haggetts are in the vault at the bank and the bank refuses to let the Doctor have them.

Mrs. Haggett reports that there have been three more telephone calls from New York and seven more telegrams, but the Doctor doesn't want to hear about them.

"This kind of thing is no good for a man of my age!" he protests, as he holds up a trembling hand. "This morning I was a peaceful country doctor filled with gentle thoughts of a medical description and I coveted nothing, not even my collections! Look at me now! [The shaking hand again.] Hannah, if a patient came in with an appendix now I'd miss it so far I'd put his eye out! [He concludes desperately.] Once you get started on a thing like this, though, once you let it get a hold on you!"

The Doctor's chief concern at the moment is that Abby's train goes at five o'clock and she must not be permitted to take her portrait with her.

The portrait is the only one of the paintings they can be sure of getting their hands on. And he thinks he has thought of a way it can be done.

Abby, having noted the Doctor's distress when he came in, has been to the kitchen to get him a glass of milk and a cracker. She is so concerned she would like to heat up a pork chop for him.

"I never seen you in such a state, Dr. Haggett," says Abby, sympathetically. "It's all them New York folks coming here."

"And they're all coming back any minute, too!" sighs the Doctor.

Abby—Why do you bother with 'em, Dr. Haggett?

Dr. Haggett—Can't avoid responsibilities in this life, Abby. (*Then with unaccountable intention he adds:*) Wouldn't mind so much if this room looked right. It's that patch over the fireplace where Ada's picture was.

ABBY—I'll wash off where it's smoked.

DR. HAGGETT—There isn't time.

MRS. HAGGETT—You could hang up one of Warren Creamer's pictures.

DR. HAGGETT—Warren's pictures aren't big enough for that. We need something to cover up the whole place. A big picture.

ABBY—Well, then, I got nothing to suggest. (*She starts for kitchen.*)

DR. HAGGETT (*as though a thought struck him suddenly*)—Abby, haven't you got a picture Chris Bean painted of you before he died? (MRS. HAGGETT *starts.*)

ABBY—I got my portrait.

DR. HAGGETT—Well, if that isn't just the thing! We'll hang that there!

ABBY—Oh, Dr. Haggett!

DR. HAGGETT—Just till you go!

ABBY—I'd like very much to oblige. I certainly would like to oblige. But, Doctor . . . (*She is covered with embarrassment.*) Why, I couldn't have my portrait hanging in here! It wouldn't look right!

DR. HAGGETT—Why wouldn't it?

ABBY—What'd people say if they come into your dining-room and seen a picture of me hanging there, scraping carrots?

DR. HAGGETT—What do I care what people'd say? Ain't this a democracy? I'd rather have you there scraping carrots than half these society women who can't do nothing!

ABBY—But my portrait hasn't even got a frame, Dr. Haggett!

DR. HAGGETT—That don't matter either. Anything to cover up that patch!

MRS. HAGGETT—Don't refuse him, Abby!

Now the Doctor is piteously holding up his trembling hand again. Abby is quite overcome. She never could say no to Dr. Haggett, she admits, and goes to fetch the picture.

"A much better way than stealing it would have been," Dr. Haggett admits to Mrs. Haggett. "This has got to be done, but it's got to be done legitimate!"

Abby is back with the portrait, and worried because it has no frame. There is a frame on a picture of Dr. Haggett's mother upstairs that will just about fit, Mrs. Haggett thinks. Abby feels that such a frame would be doing too much honor to her portrait, but both the Doctor and Mrs. Haggett are insistent.

"Abby, if I put my mother's frame around your picture, it's

not for you to say that it isn't fitting," booms the Doctor.

Abby has gone to get Mother's picture and Dr. Haggett, a little conscience-stricken, decides he will give Abby something for her portrait. He will give her twenty-five dollars for it, though frankly, if it hadn't been for the telegrams and telephone calls he would not risk twenty-five cents on it.

Now Abby has brought Mother's frame and, with a little forcing, it just fits. And what a fine show it makes. Abby is quite impressed. She does wish Chris could see the picture now.

"All the time he was painting it he kept saying: 'Abby, this is my masterpiece I'm painting now,'" she says. "And when it was all done he thanked me. He thanked me, just like I'd done something for him. . . ." Her voice is choked, and her eyes misty. "Boys like him. . . . 'Tain't right for boys like him to die so young!"

"Don't cry, Abby. You'll have me crying, too," pleads Mrs. Haggett.

"You'll have us all crying," protests Dr. Haggett, blowing his nose stentoriously.

Now the Doctor has another idea. He thinks it would be fine if Abby, going away after all these years, would leave her portrait with them—

Abby can't quite grasp what he means. Leave her picture there for good! Go away without it! She couldn't think of that. Not for twenty-five or even fifty dollars! Not for anything could she do that.

"Oh, but I couldn't never see my way to giving up my portrait!" Abby protests.

"Abby, you amaze me!" The Doctor is peeved.

Abby—Well, I'm funny that way about things I had so long.

Dr. Haggett—You'd better think twice, Abby, before you refuse what I must say is a generous offer.

Ada—How'd it be, Abby, if we had a nice photograph made of it, and gave you that to keep with you in Chicago?

Mrs. Haggett—Now, ain't that a clever idea of Ada's, Milton! I declare, I never would have thought of it myself!

Abby—You've got me too upset to know what to do! I hadn't no idea you was so fond of me!

Mrs. Haggett—Abby!

Abby—No, I hadn't, Mrs. Haggett! I knew Susie was, but I hadn't no idea about you and Ada and the doctor! And it's awful hard for me to deny you, only . . .

Dr. Haggett—Then don't deny us, Abby! Say yes and shake hands on it!

Abby—I'll tell you! I'll get the photograph for you, Mrs. Haggett! I'll get it made in Chicago and send it back!

Dr. Haggett—But don't you see, Abby, it's the . . .

Ada—The color and all makes it so much . . .

Mrs. Haggett—No photograph'd ever give us the comforting feeling that we still had you with us!

Abby—Would it really mean so much to all of you to have me hanging up there in an oil painting?

Mrs. Haggett—Would we want anyone we didn't love in our dining-room?

Abby—But I got so used to looking at that portrait!

Dr. Haggett—Why, Abby! That's no better than sitting all day in front of a looking glass!

Abby—But it ain't me I see! It's . . . it's . . . it's the time when I was young! It's all how things used to be in the old days! It's . . . it's . . . (*But this is too private.*) I can't say it! Oh, I can't say it! (*The doorbell rings.*)

Mrs. Haggett—There's someone at the door!

Ada—Don't disappoint us, Abby!

Dr. Haggett—She won't! You know you won't, Abby! You'll say yes! Think! Fifty dollars!

Abby—Well, if you're all so bent . . . (*The doorbell rings again.*) If you're so bent on having it . . .

Mrs. Haggett—Now our own dear Abby's speaking!

Abby—No! I still got to think!

Dr. Haggett—Of course you have, Abby! And I want you to think! And I know you won't reach no wrong decision! You go set alone in your room for ten minutes. . . .

No one answering the bell, Tallant has let himself in. He is carrying a picture and the Haggetts gasp with astonishment. Abby's portrait catches his eye and for a moment he is conscious of nothing else.

"If you've come for my portrait, I can't let you have it," announces Abby, firmly. "I made up my mind I couldn't anyway, and now it looks like I got to make other arrangements."

Tallant would talk with Dr. Haggett alone. Abby has gone to the kitchen. Mrs. Haggett and Ada agree to retire, but they will not go far. If Tallant tries to take the Abby portrait they will be within call.

Tallant has no excuses to make for what he has done. His

getting the Bean pictures was "a simple business operation, carried through in the classic tradition of art collecting." And now he has another business proposition to make. Admitting that Abby's portrait is truly a masterpiece reminds him of it.

"You and I can hardly hope to reach that height," Tallant admits.

"You and I? What are you driving at?" demands the Doctor.

TALLANT—Corot. The name means nothing to you?

DR. HAGGETT—Not a thing.

TALLANT—Corot was a French painter of landscapes. He died in 1875. The bulk of his painting has been done since then. (DR. HAGGETT *is startled.*) The same is true of the late Cézanne. He died in 1906. I know a dozen excellent Cézanne's, all painted in the last year. (*He goes for the picture he brought in with him.*) I spoke this morning of a business partnership between us. Allow me . . . (*He exhibits.*) "The Hill Pasture," by the late Christopher Bean. (DR. HAGGETT *starts to take it from him.*) Careful! Don't touch it! It's not dry yet!

DR. HAGGETT—Where did you find it?

TALLANT—I didn't find it. I painted it.

DR. HAGGETT—What are you?

TALLANT—A forger. (*Light dawns on* DR. HAGGETT.) I see that you begin to understand. Those letters in the *Atlantic* tell us about the pictures Bean left here. The originals are lost. Thanks to my peculiar gifts, their loss needn't disturb us. (DR. HAGGETT *gasps.*) I assure you, Dr. Haggett, I'm offering you a gold mine. We have an absolute corner on Christopher Bean. Because you can not only vouch for my forgeries, but can also discredit my competitors in the trade. Have I made myself clear?

DR. HAGGETT (*mopping his brow*)—It's too risky!

TALLANT—Not at all!

DR. HAGGETT—It's criminal!

TALLANT—Perhaps, but no picture-collecting sucker ever admits that he's been stung, so . . .

DR. HAGGETT—I don't like the sound of it. I was all right this morning before you came in. I was respected by the world and at peace with myself and I was tempted by nothing and no man!

TALLANT—As I remarked this morning, we are all mortal. You have a wife and two lovely daughters . . .

DR. HAGGETT (*brightening*)—That's so! I have! And being tempted for your loved ones isn't as bad as if it was just on your own account! How much would I get from this scheme of yours?

Tallant—I thought twenty per cent.

Dr. Haggett—'Tain't worth it.

Tallant—I'll be liberal. Twenty-five.

Dr. Haggett—Not a cent under fifty!

Tallant—If you persist in letting your greed come between you and . . .

Dr. Haggett—*My* greed! Mine! (*A pause, then he adds craftily:*) You can't work this scheme of yours without my help. Because *I'm* in a position to discredit *you.*

Tallant (*holding out his hand*)—Dr. Haggett, it's done!

Mrs. Haggett has let Rosen in at the door. Rosen is a little surprised to find Tallant there, though he might have expected that. It is Tallant's suggestion that he come in with the just-organized firm and act as selling agent. Rosen, being honest for the moment, is not interested.

Now Rosen also has discovered the Abby portrait, but he isn't quite sure whether it is Bean's or Tallant's. Nor quite sure he can take even Dr. Haggett's word for it.

"Excuse me for doubting your word, Dr. Haggett," Rosen explains. "But in my profession we judge pictures by the company they keep."

Maxwell Davenport and Susan have returned. Davenport is asked to settle the doubt in Rosen's mind. He studies the Abby portrait carefully and speaks feelingly.

"And the man who painted this died miserably," he muses, looking up from the picture. "Here is all womanhood! Its nobility, its tenderness and its strength! This is beautiful as only . . . only . . . Damn comparisons! The thing's beautiful!"

"That's all I need to hear," declares Rosen. "Dr. Haggett, I'll give you seventy-five hundred for it."

Davenport is surprised, but Rosen is in earnest. He wants to show this original in his gallery, a one-man show for a month, and bring "all Duveen's customers to Lexington Avenue."

Dr. Haggett would like to sell, but he can't. Rosen raises his bid to ten thousand. Still the Doctor hesitates. And Abby's train leaving at five! Where *is* Abby?

Tallant thinks he will take a hand, acting as the Doctor's partner, but the Doctor will have none of that. And ten thousand ain't enough! Rosen goes to twelve thousand—and that's his limit! The Doctor wants forty! Comes down to thirty-five, and then to thirty!

Time is getting short. Susan is distressed. Mrs. Haggett

anxiously watches the kitchen door. Rosen goes up to seventeen thousand. The Haggetts order the protesting Susan to her room. And send Ada to the kitchen to keep Abby away. Thirty thousand or nothing says the Doctor.

Rosen goes to twenty! And a promise to pay cash in three days! The Doctor will take twenty-nine! Rosen offers twenty-three! Half down and the balance next day.

"Twenty-five on the same terms!" shouts the Doctor.

"Done!" answers Rosen, and Davenport cheers.

Dr. Haggett is on the verge of a nervous collapse. Ada is in from the kitchen to announce that the new maid is leaving. Who cares? The Haggetts will have a butler now! The doorbell rings. If it is a patient tell him the Doctor has retired from doctoring!

Warren Creamer has come for Abby's trunk. Davenport greets him jocularly as the boy marvel. This is news to Mrs. Haggett.

"I've been looking at his pictures, Mrs. Haggett," reports Davenport. "You produce talented painters in this village!"

"Are his pictures good, too?" demands Mrs. Haggett, hurrying over to the foot of the stairway. "Susie! Warren's here! Come in, Warren! Don't be afraid! We kind of changed our minds about artists since this morning."

The bill of sale is ready for Dr. Haggett to sign. Warren and Susan have gone to get Abby and the trunk. Dr. Haggett hastily signs the bill of sale and accepts Rosen's check as a first payment.

"How do I know I get the balance tomorrow?" demands Dr. Haggett.

"My God, it's in writing, isn't it?"

"Well, so long as you get that picture out of here before—"

"That's what I'm going to do," promises Rosen, taking the portrait out of the frame.

"Hannah," calls the Doctor, "watch that door—"

But Abby has already come through the door, dressed for her journey and carrying a handbag. She does not want to interrupt, but she has come to tell Dr. Haggett that as much as she hates to deny him—

The Doctor would stop her talking. He wants to thank her for changing her mind, and he would force the fifty dollars into her hands. Then Abby sees Rosen with her portrait—

Abby—What's that man doing there with my portrait?

Rosen (*blandly*)—Taking it to New York, Abby! To exhibit it! Where everybody will come to look at it! Could you let me have some string and wrapping paper?

ABBY (*wrenching free from* DR. HAGGETT)—What right have you got to take my portrait away?

ROSEN—Well, I never paid more for a right in my life!

ABBY—It belongs to me! (*Sensation.* TALLANT *is overjoyed.*)

ROSEN—How's that?

ABBY—It belongs to me!

DR. HAGGETT—What's come over you, Abby? Did anyone ask you to come in like this? What are you after in here anyway?

ABBY—I come in to say good-by and get my portrait, and I seen him fixing to go off with it!

DR. HAGGETT—But you just sold it to me!

ABBY—I never! I never!

MRS. HAGGETT—You got the money there in your hand, Abby!

DAVENPORT—Oh, Dr. Haggett! It can't be that you . . .

ABBY (*violently at the same time*)—Here! Take this money back! Go on, take it! You said you wanted my portrait to remember me by! I said I'd think about giving it to you! And I have thought! And I ain't never going to part with it! And now you're trying to sell it behind my back! I'd be ashamed!

MRS. HAGGETT—Abby!

ABBY—I would! I'd be ashamed! Of all the sharp, underhanded tricks!

DR. HAGGETT—This house is mine and everything in it's mine, and you're my paid help!

DAVENPORT—Good God, Dr. Haggett!

ABBY (*fortissimo*)—My portrait ain't yours!

DR. HAGGETT (*desperately*)—If you'd all step into the entry, Mr. Davenport, and leave me to explain things quietly to Abby, there won't be any more difficulty! Just five minutes, Hannah!

ROSEN (*protesting*)—Damn it, Doctor, I just gave you a check for . . .

DR. HAGGETT—Now don't you get upset, Mr. Rosen. There's just a little misunderstanding here! (*General murmurs as* MRS. HAGGETT *and he urge the company out and he closes the doors upon them. He mops his brow and turns to* ABBY. ABBY *moves close to her portrait.*) You're not showing much gratitude for all we've done for you, Abby, all these years!

ABBY (*at bay*)—I can't help that. I won't part with my portrait.

DR. HAGGETT—And I was just working up such a nice surprise for you!

ABBY—Well, I caught you at it! And I'd be ashamed!

DR. HAGGETT—You think I was trying to do something sneaky!

ABBY—Sneaky and greedy! I knew your wife and Ada was both greedy! But I never knew you was!

DR. HAGGETT (*hurt*)—Oh, Abby, how could you say that of me! When I was only trying to make some money for you! I don't mean that fifty! That was just for fun! I was really going to give you a thousand dollars! A thousand dollars, Abby!

ABBY—And you were going to get it by selling my portrait!

DR. HAGGETT—People in your circumstances have got no right to own things that are worth so much money!

ABBY—That may be! But my portrait's all I got in the world! The boy who painted it . . . Well, I ain't ashamed to say it now, it's so long ago. I loved him and I still love him! And he died just after he finished painting it, so it was the last thing he ever painted! That's why it means so much to me! It means all the happiness I ever had! And you know that I ain't had so much, Dr. Haggett! Now I guess I better go and catch my train!

Again Dr. Haggett would stop Abby. He would plead with her. Let her think of her poor brother and his children. Especially the children. Let her remember that she was being paid for all the time she set for that picture!

That isn't so. Abby worked every minute Chris was painting her. And it isn't true that she fed him Mrs. Haggett's coffee. Mrs. Haggett watched the coffee too closely. It was Abby's own coffee she saved for Chris. It was all she had to give him, her coffee was!

Now the Doctor is taking another tack. Honesty is the best policy. They want to pay twenty-five thousand dollars for the portrait. Let her take half and give him half!

"No!"

"Take fifteen thousand!"

"No!"

"Think what you could do for your brother's children with fifteen thousand!"

"No! No! I tell you!"

Nor twenty thousand! Nor even a million! Dr. Haggett gives up. Abby has turned lovingly back to the portrait. A new thought strikes her.

ABBY—He was so poor, Chris was. He never had no good coat

nor nothing warm, only that one sweater I knitted for him. He never had no warm room to sleep in nights nor nothing he needed, he was so poor! If he could have afforded to go away from here down South he needn't have died. I used to pray we'd get an early thaw just for Chris's sake. How is it a man can die so poor when he painted pictures that are worth so much?

DR. HAGGETT—Because nobody had any use for his pictures while he was living.

ABBY—I always liked 'em. That's why I kept so many. Not only just because he painted 'em. I thought . . .

DR. HAGGETT—You kept so many?

ABBY—Yes, I kept them!

DR. HAGGETT (*wetting his lips feverishly*)—How did you get them?

ABBY—Mrs. Haggett she put 'em on the bonfire and I took them off! (*She has again started for her handbag.*)

DR. HAGGETT—Where are they now?

ABBY—In my trunk. I rolled 'em up. But they're all right. I looked . . .

DR. HAGGETT—How many are there?

ABBY—There's seventeen of them. (DR. HAGGETT *gasps.*)

DR. HAGGETT—Seventeen, Abby? Did you say seventeen? (*He turns from her and runs to the entry door shouting:*) Hannah! Hannah!

Now they have all swarmed back into the room. There is a confusion of voices, a confusion of queries, a confusion of explanations. Seventeen new Christopher Beans? Even Davenport is all but bowled over.

Warren Creamer has come in with Abby's trunk on his shoulder. Dr. Haggett orders the trunk put down and opened. Let Warren cut the ropes. Let Abby get the pictures out. Now the Doctor has snatched the roll of canvasses out of Abby's hands. Now he is ready to talk business with Rosen. Let Davenport decide what these pictures are worth. What is one worth? Ten thousand dollars? Easily, agrees Davenport.

"Do you hear, Hannah? Easily ten thousand for the first one on the pile and there are seventeen of them!" The Doctor is shouting excitedly.

"We're rich, Ma! We're rich!" cries Ada.

Warren has roped up the trunk again. Now Abby is trying pitifully to edge into the Haggett group. Who is it the Doctor is aiming to sell the pictures to? The Doctor is too occupied to pay any attention to Abby.

"I saved those from burning and I thought they'd be mine to keep," suggests Abby, quietly.

Rosen would like to be sure this time who really owns the pictures. There is no doubt in Dr. Haggett's mind. Chris Bean had no family living. The paintings were left with Dr. Haggett against an unpaid bill! That's the answer.

Rosen had never thought of anything quite so big as this. A corner in Christopher Beans! Davenport, looking over the rest of the paintings, advises Dr. Haggett not to be in any hurry to sell. Even if he were, Rosen could not figure on buying. There might be a couple of hundred thousand dollars in those paintings.

Abby has been trying to say good-by, but no one will listen. The Doctor is too excited to notice her. So are Ada and Mrs. Haggett. Giving it up Abby turns to Warren.

"Well, I'll just go. I guess there ain't nothing else to do!" she says, plaintively.

Rosen is figuring on organizing a syndicate. He might get Schmidt in. And Goldstein! How about Dr. Haggett keeping the check Rosen gave him as a thirty-day option on the lot? The Doctor thinks before he can do that Rosen will have to set a price to cover all the pictures.

Abby has turned away from the group at the desk. Rosen is figuring on a price for the pictures and the others are looking over his shoulder.

"Well," mumbles Abby to herself, "if they're too busy to say good-by I can't make 'em. I ain't going to miss my train. I'll just get my portrait and—"

Davenport has stopped her. He would say a word to her about the portrait after she gets to Chicago. A work of art like that is a responsibility.

"It's yours, but it's yours in trust for the future," says Davenport. "Take it with you to Chicago by all means. But when you get there don't keep it where it won't be safe. Lend it to the Chicago Art Institute. You could go and see it every day, you know. Would you do that, Abby?"

"I'll think about it," says Abby.

Rosen has decided upon a figure. One hundred and eighty thousand dollars for the lot! But at first he had said two hundred thousand, Dr. Haggett protests. They turn to appeal to Davenport, who is still talking to Abby. He raises his hand to quiet them.

DAVENPORT—Please, Abby! I know it's more than a work of art to you. (MRS. HAGGETT *looks up.*) I know the bond that must have existed between you and Chris Bean when he painted it.

MRS. HAGGETT (*a supercilious sniff*)—Bond! Huh! Carryings on! If you call that a bond! (ABBY *looks at her, but turns back with her own dignity to answer* DAVENPORT.)

ABBY—Mr. Davenport, Chris was the only man ever asked me to marry him. (*Though the words are spoken quietly they fall like lead upon the room's sudden attention.*)

DR. HAGGETT—You . . . (*He moves toward her.*) You didn't marry him, though, Abby?

ABBY—He was so sick, I couldn't refuse him nothing. (*The idea strikes all present simultaneously.*)

DAVENPORT—Then you're his widow!

ABBY—I know I am!

DR. HAGGETT (*frenetic crescendo*)—She's got to prove it! She's got to prove it!! She's got to prove it!!! (WARREN *enters, picks up picture and bag and carries them out. This will not be noticed, however, except as adding to the general agitation. Everyone is talking at once and at the top of his or her voice, protesting to everyone else, and paying not the least attention to anyone else. This is what each one of them says:*)

DAVENPORT—I believe she can!

ABBY (*to one after the other and to all at once*)—Certainly I can! I got my marriage lines out in my . . . Do you want to see . . . ? And my wedding ring on a . . . Look! (*She jerks her ring on a ribbon from within her dress and holds it up so that all present can see.*) I wanted to hold folks' good opinion and my . . . But I don't care who knows it now! I'm Mrs. Christopher Bean, that's who I am, just as much as she's Mrs. Haggett and I never carried on with . . .

ROSEN (*at the same time*)—In that case these pictures belong to her! My God! I can't do business this way! If they don't know the difference between . . . Oh, I give it up!

MRS. HAGGETT (*snatching the roll of paintings from* ROSEN'S *lap*)—Well, she doesn't get these away from me! Not over my dead body she doesn't! If these pictures were mine to burn they're mine to keep and . . .

ADA (*at the same time, through gushing tears*)—Ma, does that mean Pa can't . . . ? Answer me, Ma! Aren't these pictures ours to sell? Oh, it isn't fair! It just isn't fair! I don't think it's . . .

DAVENPORT (*at the same time to* ABBY *in complete delight*)—And you never told! But, Abby, why didn't you? This is magnificent! And it's turning out just as Chris Bean would have . . . (*But, like* ROSEN, DR. HAGGETT *has given up. He gave up after that first glimpse of* ABBY'S *wedding ring. He turned from that to* ROSEN, *thrust the fatal check back upon him, snatched the pictures from his wife's arms and finally, if somewhat roughly, planted them in* ABBY'S.)

DR. HAGGETT (*barely audible above the din*)—There!

ABBY (*no more audible than her late employer*)—Oh, are you giving me back . . . ? (*But the confusion has not abated and it seems best for the curtain to fall without further explanation.*)

THE CURTAIN FALLS

WE, THE PEOPLE

A Drama in Twenty Scenes

By Elmer Rice

THE production of "We, the People" in January inspired a number of interesting debates. In some of them the writers who review plays for a living took active part. A majority of these found Mr. Rice too completely wedded to his convictions and prejudices. Propaganda, they argued, being one-sided, never offers satisfying material for the building of effective drama. Mr. Rice, they insisted, was suffering from gas pains and anger and had no moral right to pass on his distress to audiences gathered primarily in the hope of getting a bit of fun out of the theatre.

The opposition argued that in these days, times being out of joint, social problems are of such moment that they should be very freely discussed. If true drama is not to be found in the problems and perplexities of a distressed and unhappy people, then where can it be found? A grown-up theatre, they said, should welcome at least an occasional lapse from its adulteries and its romances. There are no more vital dramas to be discovered, or plots for dramas, than those taken from the lives of the people who really live on the hill, or across the tracks, or around the corner.

"We, the People" was not a satisfying commercial success. It stirred great enthusiasm with small audiences, but it found the larger public so concerned with the very problems set forth in the play that it was unwilling to add the depression of a theatre piece to its daily allotment.

From whatever angle it is accepted or rejected, "We, the People" remains a forcefully written, excessively timely and socially significant drama. It is, the editor is moved to think, too important a contribution to this particular theatre season to be denied a place among the important plays.

The first of the twenty scenes that make up the Rice drama is laid in the class room of a grade school in a large industrial city. Back of the teacher's desk there are lithographs of George Washington, "The Spirit of '76" and the "Battle between the 'Monitor' and the 'Merrimac.' "

Sitting in the front row of seats are Louis Volterra, a middle-aged Italian, and Tony, his thirteen-year-old son. "Both are shabbily, almost raggedly dressed." A moment's wait and they are joined by Helen Davis, Tony's teacher, "an attractive girl of twenty-four."

Helen has asked Tony to bring his father to see her. She has felt compelled to report the boy, not for any infraction of deportment or failure in his school work, but because he has acquired the habit of talking disloyally of his country to the other children.

"Every time we have a history or civics lesson," reports Helen, "Tony makes some disloyal remark. I've talked to him about it several times, but it doesn't seem to do any good."

Mr. Volterra can understand that Tony should talk about the bosses. He is himself opposed to the boss system. For some years he had owned his own shop. Then came the padrones with bigger shops and more machinery and put him out of business. At home Mr. Volterra often said that being a citizen is a big joke, because all a citizen does is vote for the bosses. All that he has told Tony is the truth, Volterra insists. Just what everybody knows.

"I don't agree with you at all," protests Helen. "I'm proud to be an American citizen and I don't understand why you should feel the way you do. I'm sure you're making your living here, bringing up your family, giving Tony an education—"

"Tony's a smarta kid, but he can' go to high school," interrupts Mr. Volterra. "Why can' smarta kid go to high school? Because his papa's poor shoemaker—because his papa maka twen'y dollar a week, workin' for padrone. W'en Tony's fourteen-year-old, he gotta go work for padrone—jussa lika his papa. He getta married and hava da kids and he see his leetla girl die, because he can' buya da milk, he can' paya for da doctor. He see his wife w'en she's t'irty-t'ree-year-old, she's lookin' lika ol', ol' gran'-mother, because she's work, work—never stop work."

"Well, I don't say that you haven't lots of reasons for being dissatisfied. But you must think there's some good in America; otherwise, I'm sure you wouldn't have come here."

"Me? You know why I'm comin' here? I run away from Eetaly in nineteen hun'red fourteen, because I don' wanna be a soldier. We have big meetings in Ancona. An' you know who's talkin' agains' war? Mussolini! In nineteen hun'red fourteen, Benito Mussolini is talkin' agains' war. Ha! An' now he gonna fight da whole worl'. [He points to the lithographs.] Soldiers! Battleships! In da school, too, you teacha da leetla kids war."

Again Helen is quick to defend her country and its schools. The children are taught the history of America but they are not taught to be warlike, and one of the things stressed at all teachers' meetings is the need of teaching the children loyalty and the principles of Americanism.

"I'm fond of Tony and proud of him," concludes Helen, "and I don't want to be obliged to go to the principal about this. Please think about it very carefully, won't you?"

"Sure. T'ank you, lady," replies Louis Volterra.

The Volterras have gone. Helen is sitting thoughtfully at her desk as the curtain falls.

The dining-room of the Davis home on the outskirts of town is small and not very tastefully furnished, but entirely livable. At the moment Frieda Davis, "a stout, pleasant-faced, middle-aged woman," is dividing her time between the dining-room and the kitchen, humming contentedly as she works, when her son Allen, a good-looking boy of seventeen, bursts into the room in an evident state of excitement.

Allen has passed the College Board with the very good mark of eighty-four point seven. This put him second in the whole list and he is greatly pleased. So is his mother; pleased and proud, too. So is his father, William Davis, a large man "in his fifties, but still vigorous," who has just arrived from the mills with his lunch box and the evening paper.

"You got a good head on your shoulders, young feller," agrees the elder Davis, with paternal pride, and adds, as he hugs the missus: "Well, mother, we didn't do so bad—a daughter teachin' school and a son at the state university. . . . In my day, only rich men's sons went to college."

Helen Davis, home from school, is the next to hear the good news about Allen and the eighty-four point seven average. Helen is even more pleased and proud than were her mother and father.

Allen has decided to go in for chemical engineering, and that choice is quite all right with the family, so long as he doesn't go and get himself blown up.

Helen is telling her father of the visit of the Volterras and of Louis Volterra's bitterness against the bosses. Davis is not surprised. He knows a lot of men at the plant like that, always belly-achin' and talking against the bosses.

Allen is for taking the men's side. Why should a few people have all the money and the rest have nothing? Allen wants to know.

"What have you got to kick about, I'd like to know," demands Davis, heatedly. "Ain't you goin' to college an' study to be an engineer? An' didn't Helen go through Normal School an' get a job teachin'? That ain't so bad for the children of a workin' man, is it? We own our own home an' we got a car an' a radio an' money in the bank. So where's the kick?"

"Sure, that's great for us. But what about all the ones that haven't got homes or cars or even jobs."

HELEN—That's the awful part of it: people without enough to eat. And especially growing children. I know there are some in my class that come to school hungry. No wonder they can't learn.

ALLEN—Yes, and we spend billions every year for battleships.

DAVIS—We gotta have protection, don't we? Do you want Japan or some other country to come in here and wipe us up? You better grow up a little bit an' find out what you're talkin' about before you begin talkin' so big.

ALLEN—Well, they'll never get me to go to war, I'll tell you that.

DAVIS—If the time ever comes, you'll go the same as all the rest.

ALLEN—Will I? Well, you just wait and see.

HELEN—Well, let's hope there won't be any more wars. Allen, you'd better get washed up now. Bert will be here any minute.

ALLEN—Oh, all right. Just the same, nobody can make me fight if I don't want to. (*He exits.*)

DAVIS—He better get over some of his ideas.

HELEN—He'll be all right, father. Once he gets to college, he'll outgrow all that. But with so many people having troubles, you can't help wondering whether things shouldn't be different.

DAVIS—Sure, don't I know that? I don't say everything is the way it should be. They laid off about another hundred men at the plant today.

HELEN—Oh, did they, father?

DAVIS—Yes. Some of them men with families, too. About a dozen of 'em come to me about it. Wanted to know what to do, an' couldn't I help them. "Well," I says. "Boys," I says, "I'm only a foreman aroun' here. I got no more to say about hirin' or firin' than a Chinaman." It's pretty tough, though, when a feller's been workin' at the same job for eight or ten years, to get his walkin' papers like that.

Davis and Helen have gone into an economic conference. Payments are piling up and Helen has been told at the teachers' meeting that she is not going to get her pay again this month, which makes five months since there has been a pay day. Davis is counting on paying something on the mortgage and there is the cost of getting Allen started at college to be figured on. That, with the car, the radio and the encyclopedia installments—

"I kinda hate to dig into that savin's bank account," worries Davis.

"Oh, you mustn't touch that, father," protests Helen, quickly. "We've got to keep that in case somebody gets sick or in case something unexpected happens."

Bert Collins, "a pleasant chap of twenty-seven, neatly dressed," is calling. Being Helen's young man Bert has come to supper. He, too, is properly impressed by Allen's record as a student.

The family has gathered around the supper table and Mrs. Davis is bringing in the soup tureen as the curtain falls.

In a public park, later that evening, Bert and Helen are in search of a bench in a reasonably dark spot, such as there used to be. They find one that will have to do, seeing that they have been walking a good two miles and are pretty tired.

As they sit down Bert draws Helen to him and, despite her modest protest that it is entirely too public a place, kisses her lingeringly upon the mouth. And then kisses her again, as a defiant right of engaged couples.

Bert and Helen are admittedly crazy about each other. Depressed, too, thinking of the little chance they have of getting married and having a place of their own to go to. It may be a little better at Helen's home after Allen goes to college, but she doubts it. There's always someone dropping in there.

BERT—I was wondering if, once in a while, we couldn't go up to my room and sit around there.

HELEN—Oh, I don't know, Bert. It would look sort of funny, wouldn't it?

BERT—Nobody would have to see us.

HELEN—But suppose somebody did? How would it look?

BERT—Well, I guess we'd better let it alone.

HELEN—It's not that I don't want to, dear.

BERT—Sure, I know, honey. (*A moment of silence.*) It just seems a shame that we can't ever be together, that's all.

HELEN—Well, we had a good time Sunday, Bert.

BERT—You bet we did! But that's all the more reason why I want more of you.

HELEN—It's about all I think about these days. I don't find it very easy to concentrate on irregular verbs and the principal exports of Brazil.

BERT—Well, I'm having plenty trouble keeping my books straight, too.

HELEN—If we only know for sure when we could get married—at least, it would give us something to look forward to. But this way—

BERT—Isn't there some way we could manage, Helen?

HELEN—Well, I don't see how, dear, do you?

BERT—I don't know.

HELEN—Everything is so uncertain. Besides, if we did get married, I might lose my job. They're getting very strict now about married teachers, with so many people out of work.

BERT—Anyhow, we want to raise a family.

HELEN—Yes. But Heaven knows when that will ever be.

Bert is worried about his job with Drew & Co., too. Not much chance for a fellow to get ahead in the banking business unless he happens to be one of the fellows on top. If Bert passes his examination as a certified public accountant that ought to help, but there still will be the family—

"I just got a letter from my mother this morning," reports Bert. "The farming game is getting worse and worse all the time. They can't even make it pay any more. I don't see how I can refuse to help them out, do you?"

"No, of course you can't, sweetheart," agrees Helen. "We've just got to hope for the best, that's all."

"I'm getting pretty tired of hoping."

"Yes, so am I."

A quarreling couple has passed. Perhaps if they did marry they would turn out to be like that, Bert suggests. But Helen is not worried. Now Bert has drawn her again into his arms and she is kissing him with a good deal of enthusiasm.

BERT—Helen, listen. Why do we have to wait until we get married?

HELEN—Oh, I don't know, Bert. We'd better.

BERT—Why? You don't want to wait, do you?

HELEN—I don't know.

Photo by White Studio, New York.

"WE, THE PEOPLE"

Helen: . . . It doesn't seem right that people who want to work can't find any work to do, and that their homes should be taken away from them. . . . A chance to live, that's all we want, that's all we ask for. That's all Allen wanted. Please help him to get it! Oh, please do! Don't let him die! Give him a chance to live!

(*Ralph Theodore, Blaine Cordner, Maurice Wells, David Leonard, Eleanor Phelps, William Ingersoll, Burr Caruth, Gladys Walker and Juliana Taberna*)

BERT—You know you don't. Do you?

HELEN—No. Only—

BERT—What?

HELEN—I don't know. I'd be afraid.

BERT—Why? What would you be afraid of?

HELEN—Somebody might find out. Then what would we do?

BERT—We could find a way so they wouldn't. I want you so much, darling.

HELEN—I know, dear. I want you, too. But I'm afraid—honestly I am.

BERT—Nobody would find out—not if we were careful.

HELEN—It's not only that. There are other things to think about, too.

BERT—What?

HELEN—Lots of things.

BERT—You mean a baby?

HELEN—Yes.

BERT—But, darling, if we're careful—

HELEN—Yes, I know.

BERT—There's nothing to be afraid of, dear—truly there isn't.

HELEN—No, Bert, I can't.

BERT—Well, if you don't want to—

HELEN—Oh, darling, I do want to—I do. It's only— (*Clinging to him.*) Oh, sweetheart, please don't be angry with me.

BERT—All right, sweetheart. Don't cry. I won't say any more about it.

HELEN—I can't help it that I'm a coward.

BERT—You're not, darling. I know how you feel about it. Just forget about it.

HELEN—You're so nice to me. Kiss me, dear.

They have embraced and separated. A passing policeman gives them no more than a glance.

They might as well go to a movie, suggests Bert. At least it will be warm there and they can hold hands. They are leaving the park, arm in arm, as the curtain falls.

Willard Drew's private office is a large room lavishly furnished. Mr. Drew in person is seated back of a wide desk telephoning. A stenographer who has been taking notes is at his side.

Mr. Drew is a busy man. He must cable Mallory of the Paris office. He must talk with Walter Applegate at once, even though Mr. Applegate is at home ill. He must not forget a meeting of the directors of the Applegate Harvester Company at 2:30.

Mr. Drew's telephone conversation with Applegate is concerned with the advisability of meeting the dividend on the preferred stock. Mr. Drew is positive it should be paid, even though it must be taken from surplus. If the dividend is passed the market is certain to react unfavorably.

"It's our duty to maintain public confidence," Mr. Drew tells Mr. Applegate over the phone. "Sure, I'm thinking just as much about the future as you are. You've got to cut wages. What kind of trouble? Not a bit. You leave the Federation of Labor end of it to Harry Gregg and me. Why, certainly they'll play ball. At a time like this, we've all got to pull together. But you can't maintain wages artificially in the face of falling commodity prices. It's bad business and it's bad economics. Well, it's a question of cutting twenty thousand men ten or fifteen per cent or of shutting off the income of a hundred thousand preferred stockholders. Of course, it's common-sense and it's what we've got to do. All right, Walter; take care of yourself. Better run down to Pinehurst for a week. Well, maybe I will. Good-by. [He hangs up.] It's about time we faced the realities of this situation. Labor has got to carry some of the burden."

"Yes, indeed, sir," agrees James Cunningham, the office manager.

"Look at those surtax schedules! Running up to sixty-five per cent. They're running wild, those fellows in Congress. They don't seem to realize that they're killing the goose that lays the golden egg. Do you know what will happen if this bill becomes law: it'll paralyze industry. You can't expect a man to give his time and his brains, if you take away all incentive from him."

"No, sir, you certainly cannot."

Mr. Drew has gone into the directors' meeting when Bert Collins arrives with a General Motors consolidated balance sheet that has been sent for. This, decides Bert, is a good time to sound out Mr. Cunningham as to the possibility of getting a little more money. Mr. Cunningham doesn't sound out at all favorably. In fact, he is rather surprised that Bert should even suggest an increase in wages at a time like this, when so many eager young men are without any jobs at all.

Winifred Drew, "a charming girl in the early twenties," is in looking for her father. She meets father's secretary, Jack Ingersoll. Ingersoll is interested in the plans for Miss Winifred's approaching wedding and amused to learn that she and Arthur, her fiancé, have compromised on having it at Westminster Abbey, though Arthur had been holding out for the embassy. And for the honeymoon Winifred expects to borrow her father's yacht, though she hasn't quite had the courage to suggest it up to now.

The telephone reveals that Winifred's mother is calling from London. Winnie talks with her while Mr. Drew is being summoned. Winnie is working very hard on Unemployment Relief, she tells her mother. And she is quite amazed to hear that mother is buying Titians again.

Mr. Drew is also surprised when he takes up the phone. Surprised and a little shocked that Lord Somebody should think of asking a half million even for a Titian these days. This is a buyers' market, Mr. Drew tells mother, and he happens to know that his Lordship is in financial difficulties. If she will let him do the buying he will get the painting for half.

Now Mr. Drew must get back to the directors' meeting, but not before Winifred has held him up for a five-thousand-dollar subscription for her Unemployment Relief Committee. Mr. Drew, having already given the mayor's committee a check for fifty thousand, is of a mind to protest, but doesn't.

Mr. Ingersoll is telephoning Mr. Collins to draw up a check for Miss Winifred for the five thousand dollars as the curtain falls.

The dining-room of the Collins home is typical of most farm house dining-rooms. Through the curtained windows at back there is visible a vista of bare, brown fields. The table is set for five.

Sarah Collins, "a white-haired, rather frail woman, dressed in her shabby best clothes and carrying a hymn book," is back from church. She has brought the Rev. Williamson, an elderly clergyman, with her. Mrs. Collins insisted on his coming, the Rev. Williamson explains to Stella, "a dark woman of forty, with faint traces of youthful beauty," who has been preparing the dinner.

"There's plenty to go around—such as it is," Stella answers.

"Well, at any rate, let us be thankful for plenty," suggests the pastor.

Both Rev. Williamson and Mrs. Collins are worried about these members of the flock. Sarah was not at morning service. Larry, who has driven over to Fayetteville to get Bert, hasn't been to church in ages and now young Donald will not go at all.

"Yes, I know," admits the Rev. Williamson. "I've watched them dwindle and dwindle. I've grown accustomed to preaching to empty pews."

"What are we coming to, Thomas? There's no faith any more,

no loyalty. What's to become of this generation?" asks Mrs. Collins.

"I wish that God had given me the wisdom to answer that. Sometimes I almost wonder if it can be that the old faiths and the old loyalties have lost their meaning. Look at your own family, Sarah. Both your boys were confirmed in my church, and Larry and Stella were married there. Why have they all drifted away? It's easy to blame them. It is more honest to question my own adequacy to fulfill their needs."

"It's all these new-fangled ideas that are to blame. People no longer respecting the Sabbath, people talking openly against the government. Foreigners over-running the land, until there seems to be hardly an American left. What's become of the America your forefathers and mine fought and died for? What's going to become of it?"

"Yes, what?"

"And our homes and families—what's going to become of them? I lived in peace with my husband, Thomas, for more than thirty years and when he went to his rest, I mourned him with all my heart. And now, here—in this house—quarreling, quarreling from morning until night. For years now—"

Bert Collins has come in the door. He is wearing his coat and hat and is carrying a package. His greetings are those of one of the family who has been a long time away. Mrs. Collins can't understand why Larry did not meet Bert. Fortunately Abe Winters happened to be there. Abe had given Bert a lift.

The talk turns from the family, which appears to be doing as well as could be expected, to general conditions, which are not good. Conditions in fact are pretty bad.

"The way prices have been dropping," the Rev. Williamson explains, "it doesn't pay the farmer to market his produce any more. Nobody's meeting his interest payments and we're all praying that the banks won't go under. The store-keepers are hard hit, too. They can't go on selling on credit forever and there doesn't seem to be any cash anywhere."

Steve Clinton, a young Negro, looks in from the kitchen. Steve has been putting in wood and wants to report. He is glad to see Mr. Bert there and he would be a little gossipy. Steve has heard the Applegate plant has laid off a lot more men, but he doesn't suspect that Applegate cares much. Applegate didn't get rich "by layin' awake nights thinkin' about the workin' man," allows Steve. And if the Scripture is right about a rich man's not havin' any more chance of gettin' into heaven than a camel through a needle's eye, Steve thinks it a mighty slim chance. He's seen a camel.

"Blessed are the poor, for theirs is the kingdom of heaven," concludes Steve, as Mrs. Collins sends him out. "Goin' to be pretty crowded up there."

There is some danger, thinks Mrs. Collins, that the Rev. Williamson has been encouraging Steve too much to speak his mind, but the pastor believes free speech to be educational. Besides he has a friendly feeling for the blacks. He is willing to admit to Bert that there has been considerable bad feeling between the whites and the Negroes lately. Southern Negroes have been gradually filtering in and, in some cases, taking the jobs of the whites. That has caused a good deal of ill will.

Stella is continuing preparations for dinner. She is not surprised that Larry failed to meet Bert. Larry probably found the applejack at Hanson's more interesting. Larry, it appears, has been drinking a good deal lately. Mrs. Collins is worried as well as Stella. With Larry uncertain the burden has fallen on Donald's shoulders, and now Donald is rebelling. If it had not been for Bert's help Mrs. Collins does not know what would have become of them all.

Donald, "a well-built boy of nineteen," has come from the barn. He has been killing a hog and is spattered with blood. Hog killing is common with Donald. It doesn't pay to market hogs, seeing they don't bring what it costs to feed them, so they kill them to eat. Donald wants to quit the farming business. He doesn't intend to work his guts out on a farm and end his days in a poorhouse.

Larry Collins has arrived. Larry is forty, but looks older. "His face is haggard and tense. He has obviously been drinking." Larry is also irritable. Catching sight of Donald he orders him to go clean himself up. When Steve comes from the kitchen, and would pick up casually his conversation with Bert, Larry flies into a rage and orders the Negro from the room. Larry may be low, but he doesn't propose to take anything from any damned nigger.

"You're all right, Larry," Bert assures his brother. "There's nothing the matter with you. Just snap out of it, that's all."

"Yeah, snap out of it!" snarls Larry. "That's what they told us in the army. That's a laugh, the army is. I got three medals for killing Germans. Did you ever try to eat a medal? But just ask some of them mam'selles over there if I'm a man."

Bert has gone to wash for dinner when Larry turns on Stella, accusing her of telling Bert all about him, about his not being a man, and about his drinking himself to death.

"Say, what do you want of me, anyhow?" demands Stella, spiritedly. "I'm doing the best I can. Who else would you get to look after you, I'd like to know. It's not my fault you had to go to war, is it? It's not my fault that you got gassed and shell-shocked and the government won't do anything for you. That's not what I got married for, to spend my life in the kitchen, with nothing to listen to, day in and day out, but your crazy talk."

Larry, red with anger, has grabbed Stella. His charges now are more intimate and more insulting. When Stella would resent them he slaps her across the mouth. Bert and Donald, coming upon the scene, both sense that something is wrong, but Stella assures them everything is all right. Let everybody sit down to dinner before everything gets cold.

The Rev. Williamson has risen at his place to say a blessing. "O Lord, in this hour of need, we turn to Thee for comfort and for guidance," the pastor intones, as the family bows its head. "Teach us the way; keep our feet from stumbling. Take the scales from before our eyes that we may see the light. Be merciful, O Lord, to these Thine erring children. Teach us not to despair but to put our trust in Thy divine benevolence. Let not hope depart from us. If the hour be dark, let it but be the darkness that precedes the restoring dawn. And instruct us, dear Father, to purge our hearts of anger and hatred and bitterness so that we may dwell together in peace and harmony and happiness. Amen."

As the Rev. Williamson takes his seat Stella suddenly bursts into tears and leaves the table. "The others sit in silence, not knowing whether or not to follow her."

"Well, do we eat or not?" demands Larry, harshly. He is pounding the table as the curtain falls.

Bert Collins' room is small and simply furnished. Helen Davis, partially dressed, her shoes on the floor, is lying full length on a disordered bed. Bert, his coat off, is sitting beside her. Between puffs of his cigarette he is telling Helen the news.

The big shot, Mr. Drew, is back from London. From all accounts and the pictures in the papers, the wedding of Winifred Drew was a complete success. The Duke of York was there and so was Lady Astor. "When you've got that kind of dough they will all turn out for you," is Bert's conviction.

Helen envies the beautiful bride, all her beautiful things and the grand times her money guarantees her. Think of how wonderful it would be for Bert if he married a girl like that.

For his part, Bert wouldn't trade so much as a very small mole back of Helen's ear for six Winifreds and a carload of ostrich feathers. By way of strengthening the boast he kisses the small mole. Bert is silly, but Helen, in his arms, is happily forgiving.

A noise in the hall is disturbing. Helen's heart is pumping. She never can get used to these meetings. It is all quite wonderful, Helen has been very happy, and does not regret anything, but she can't help worrying. What would happen if someone were to find out—

Bert is confident no one will find out. They have been so very careful. That time they had tried to register at a hotel and the clerk had said, rather pointedly, that there were no rooms—that was not very wise. But that is over—and they will not try anything like it again.

"If there were only some way," sighs Helen.

"It's not the way I want it to be, either, honey—you know that," protests Bert, gathering her into his arms. "I don't want to have to sneak you into my bedroom and be afraid that somebody might see us. I want a nice home with you in it and I want everybody to know that you're mine."

"Well, darling, we'll just have to wait for that. They've been discharging so many married teachers lately that I'm afraid to take a chance. If I were to lose my job now—"

Helen is worried, too, for fear she might have a baby. She wants a baby, too, which makes it worse.

Bert is very comforting and as reassuring as possible. Then he makes the discovery that, in place of the eleven-thirty they thought it was, the hour is nearer one. And what can they use as an excuse? It's a little late for the movies. Perhaps a dance? Anyway, they're engaged and there isn't anything, really, to be ashamed of.

Bert has taken a careful look down the hall. There seems to be someone moving about. Helen had better wait a minute, a minute in which there are more ardent farewell embraces. Then Bert finds the hall clear, switches off the light and Helen goes into the hall.

Now Bert has followed her out. There is the click of his key in the lock as the curtain falls.

At the Davises a few days later Mrs. Davis is humming a German Lied over the family mending when Helen bursts into the room with a smiling face and good news. The teachers have been given three months' back pay! Everybody is tremendously excited! The newspapers even sent photographers to the school to get pictures of the teachers standing in line to collect their checks.

A letter from Allen, in college, is also full of good news. Allen has passed his quarterlies with an honor in every subject and has been elected a member of the editorial board of the *Sentinel*, the undergraduate daily. . . .

Bert is coming for supper, and after supper he and Helen are going out, as usual. They have been staying out pretty late, Mrs. Davis thinks. Helen works so hard she needs more sleep.

The reason she has been coming home so late every night Helen thinks she had better tell her mother, even though it may worry her. She has been going to Bert's room.

"I just feel that I don't want to go on lying about it any more," says Helen. "Anyhow, you're my mother, and I want you to know about it."

"Ach, but, Helen, dear—"

"We love each other so, mother. Do you think it's so very wrong for us to try to get a little happiness?"

"I don't know what I should say, Helen. Everything is different nowadays." Mrs. Davis is in tears.

"Please don't be upset about it, mother. I wouldn't do it if I thought it was wrong, honestly I wouldn't. I've thought and thought about it and I can't believe that it's wrong for two people who really love each other to give way to their feelings."

"Ja, ja!" sighs Mrs. Davis, drying her eyes and scurrying into the kitchen as the head of the family comes into the room.

Davis is glad to hear Helen's good news about the back pay, and sorry to tell her that they are going to need it. There has just been another ten per cent cut in pay at the mill, and there's nothing to be done except to take it and keep mum. Helen's check will pay what is due on the mortgage and there will be a little to spare, but Davis doesn't think it right that she should be bearing so much of the load. One thing they can do is to bring Allen back from school. Davis wants Allen to have the education he has missed, but—

Helen doesn't think they should consider that. It would break Allen's heart just now, when he is doing so well and is so happy. She had rather give up the car, even though it is more than half paid for. They don't use it very much anyway.

Davis also thinks they might rent Allen's room. Might rent

it to Bert, though probably that would not look just right.

There will be ways of saving, Helen is sure of that. They will get along some way. And, as Davis admits, they are a lot better off than those fellows who have been laid off. Davis doesn't see how most of them are going to get through the winter.

"All right, Helen," agrees Davis; "we'll just put our shoulders to the wheel an' make the best of things."

"That's right, father," says Helen, kissing him. "And maybe, before long, things will begin to improve."

Helen has gone into the kitchen. Davis takes out his evening paper with a sigh and a "Well, what the hell!" He begins to read as the curtain falls.

It is evening at the Collins home. Mrs. Collins and the Rev. Williamson are waiting for Bert, who has been sent for. There has been trouble. Stella Collins, Larry's wife, has left him. Larry has come home at three o'clock one morning and found her gone. Donald, the son, had accused his father of being responsible and had been beaten and driven from the house as a result.

Nothing has been heard from Stella since then. She has been reported as being seen with a man named Odemira over near Winchester, and it was said she had told some one she and Odemira were going to settle in California.

Mrs. Collins thinks it is terrible of a woman to leave her husband and her child, but Bert can understand, and the Rev. Williamson thinks if they could see into Stella's heart they would find "not evil, but a longing for happiness."

Suddenly Larry comes in the door. He is wearing his hat and coat and he is looking for his pipe. He is a bit startled to find Bert there, but he doesn't want to talk to him. Larry doesn't want to talk to anybody. If they would know where he is going, he is going out to get drunk, and let any of them try to stop him!

Both Williamson and Bert do try, pleading with the angered man not to add to his mother's distress, but this serves only to increase his rage.

"Aw, let me alone, can't you? Let me alone, the whole lot of you!" Larry cries. "I don't want any prayer meeting held over me. What do you think I am, anyhow: a goddam, slobbering come-to-Jesus punk? You think I'm through, don't you? You think I'm licked, don't you, because that bitch ran out on me and everybody's giving me the laugh? My own son's giving me the laugh, the dirty little snot-nose—"

"Larry, wait a minute," protests Bert.

"Shut up, you! This is my shanty and I'm doing the talking. I'm all through, am I? I was good enough for the trenches, wasn't I? I was good enough for the rats and the cooties and the latrines. I was good enough to kill Germans and cough up gas and my goddam lungs along with it. But that's all over. The war's over. And they're through with me—they're all through with me: my wife and my son and Uncle Sam. They're all through with me—they can't be bothered. I'm just a no-account bum, that's all that I am—a low-down bastard that can't work and can't think straight and is no good for women. But just wait—just wait and see. I'll show them. I'll show them they can't make a bum out of me."

Larry has pushed by the restraining arm of Williamson and rushed from the house. A moment later Steve, the Negro, has come to tell them that Donald is there.

Donald has been hanging around outside in the cold until his father has left the house. He has just come back to say good-by to them. Donald has signed up with the marines and has to report first thing in the morning.

They try to dissuade him, but it is no use. Donald's mind is made up. He doesn't want to stay around there getting beat up every day and called dirty names. Anyway he's through with farming, through with working and sweating from sun-up till dark with nothing to show for it in the end, "with grain rottin' in the elevators and corn keepin' the kitchen stove a-goin'."

"I ain't forgettin' about grandma," explains Donald. "I'm gettin' twenty-one dollars a month pay, besides my keep. An' I figger I can send most of it to you. [To the others.] Gosh almighty, I don't see why a feller ain't got a right to see somethin' of the world. They'll give me a chance to improve my education and to learn a trade in the marines. I'll be fit for somethin' when I get through. An' meanwhile, I'll be travelin' around an' seein' things. They even let you pick out where you want to go. I picked out Haiti down in the West Indies."

Haiti? Now Steve joins the protest. Why should Donald pick out a place where white soldiers are shooting down colored folks in their country? What right have white folks to come plantin' themselves in the colored man's country and treat him like he didn't belong there?

They try to explain to Steve about the United States' investments in Haiti and the necessity of protecting them. The Negro can't see that, so they try to shut him up.

"I thought this was supposed to be a free country, Mr. Williamson, with everybody havin' the right to express his own opinion about things," protests Steve. "But I guess I've been on the wrong track. I guess if your skin don't happen to be white an' you've got nothin' in your pockets but holes, about all you're free to do is keep your mouth shut."

"That's what you'd better do in this house in the future," warns Mrs. Collins.

Now Donald has embraced his grandmother and is ready to go. He'll write as soon as he is settled. Let them send his mother his love, if they can find out where she is, and tell her where he is.

Donald has gone. The others are trying to comfort Mrs. Collins. "Sarah, I know how hard this is for you," begins the Rev. Williamson. But she stops him.

"No, Thomas. It's not hard for me. They were all soldiers in my family. I'm a Daughter of the American Revolution, you mustn't forget that. My country always comes first with me—it's bred in me. My father fought for the North. And in the Great War, I gave my son Larry to the cause of freedom. And now it's Donald turn. I shan't cry any more. It's just—it's just that it's a little hard to see them go. But it was just a moment's weakness—that's all."

They are all silent as the curtain falls.

The Davises have taken in a boarder. He is Fred Whipple, "a coarse-grained man of forty." He is sitting now in the armchair in the dining-room with his feet on another chair, doing a cross-word puzzle in the paper.

When Mrs. Davis comes from the kitchen Whipple roughly protests against the kind of food he has been getting. Mrs. Davis would like nothing better than to improve her table, but unfortunately there is no money for T-bone steaks. Everybody in her house gets enough to eat, that's the best she can promise.

When Helen comes Mrs. Davis thinks she looks tired. That's probably because Helen has been staying out late nights neckin' with the boy friend, ventures Whipple. That's what does it. Helen had better be marryin' that boy friend before he runs out on her. That's Mr. Whipple's advice.

"I guess you know your onions, all right," suggests Whipple, slyly. "Say, pretty classy linjeree you're wearin', kid. I saw some of it on the line this mornin'. Little Christmas present from the boy friend, is that it?"

The arrival of Davis shuts Whipple up for the moment. Helen

is glad to see her father. She wants to tell him the police have arrested Volterra, the father of Tony, and are going to deport him. They have found out that Volterra belongs to an anarchist society in Italy.

Davis doesn't think there is anything he can do about Volterra. The government is getting mighty strict, on account of all the unrest. "They've been roundin' up a lot of these foreigners an' sendin' 'em back to their own country."

"Well, I'm here to tell you it's about time they kicked all these Dagoes and Polacks the hell out o' here," says Mr. Whipple. "They shouldn't have let 'em in in the first place. We don't want a lot o' crummy foreigners in this country, stinkin' up the place an' takin' jobs away from Americans."

"Well, I'm not sayin' a feller should go around talkin' against the government," agrees Davis, " 'specially if he's a foreigner. But that's no reason for breakin' up a man's home an' takin' him away from his family."

"We were all foreigners originally," protests Helen. "Everybody in the United States is descended from people who came from other countries."

"I'm talkin' about all these wops and Jews. I suppose you'd like to marry some greasy dago and have a lot o' kids by him."

"All right, Fred, that's enough of that kind of talk," says Davis.

"If I was runnin' the government I'd shoot every goddam one o' the bastards at sunrise," concludes Mr. Whipple, passing out the door.

Davis has had about enough of Whipple. And about enough of having his home robbed of its peace and quiet. But, as Helen explains, so long as things are as they are they will have to put up with him.

Helen has still more bad news. The Northside Bank to which the Davis savings have been entrusted, has closed its doors.

Davis is distressed. Now there's nothing to fall back on if anything should happen. If he should get sick, or be hit by a truck—

Mr. Whipple is back to report the need of a plumber upstairs. With one glance at the Davises he thinks perhaps he is in a morgue.

Whipple has settled himself in the armchair and gone back to his paper as the curtain falls.

In the office of the *Sentinel* at the State University, a small and rather untidy room, the editorial board is in session. "It consists of six students and the faculty adviser. The students are Mark Brookwood, the chairman; Peter Hines, Daisy Costigan, Leo Schwartz, Allen Davis and Mary Klobutsko. Mary is a fair-haired Polish girl of sixteen. She speaks with a slight accent. The faculty adviser is C. Carter Sloane, who is in the early thirties."

Other business out of the way, the board is asked to settle the question about what stand they are going to take on military training. Hines moves that the matter be laid on the table. The *Sentinel* should stick to its business of reporting college activities and not meddle with policies established by the trustees and approved by a majority of the students.

Mary is opposed to that view. Listen to Hines and the *Sentinel* would print nothing but football scores. "This is a college, not a camp for training soldiers," protests Mary, with fire in her eye. "We come here to learn, to get educated, not to be preparing for wars. We don't want any more wars. We want to have peace in the world. How can you have peace in the world if you are going to teach boys in college to fight and be soldiers?"

Allen Davis is with Mary 100 per cent. It's up to them, who will do the fighting, to see that there isn't another war. Now's the time for them to take a stand against militarism. "We don't want to be trained for soldiers, we don't want to fight," insists Allen.

Schwartz is against military training because it gets him up too early in the morning. There are other views, mostly negative, and the motion to table is lost. On a motion by Allen that the *Sentinel* editorially oppose military training the opinion of Sloane, the faculty adviser, is sought. "This is a pretty important question and we'd like to have your opinion," says Brookwood, the chairman.

"All right," answers Sloane. "The way I look at it is this. A university should be something more than a place where you come to soak in a lot of facts. A college student should not only familiarize himself with the social system in which he is going to function, but he should learn to view it critically and with a certain amount of skepticism. Progress comes through change. We cannot hope for innovation and change from those who are past the prime of life. The impetus must come from youth. If we are against militarism, against war, against social and economic injustice and political corruption, we must make ourselves articulate, right here and now. I don't agree with Schwartz that protest is futile. I think that every voice that is raised has its effect.

My opinion is that if you have convictions, you shouldn't be afraid to express them."

The motion is carried. The meeting is adjourned. Hines thinks he will resign. They can't make a slacker out of him.

They have all gone now, except Mary and Allen. They linger to talk over the excitement of the meeting. They find they have a lot of ideas in common. Allen would also like to take Mary to the freshman dance. Mary has had three other invitations, and she has told Tommy Rogers she would go with him. But she had rather go with Allen, so she will tell Tommy she has changed her mind.

Mary and Allen have started a race to the library as the curtain falls.

Back in the Davis home a month later, Fred Whipple, the boarder, on his way out, stops to pass a few remarks with Helen. Whipple is off for a party well armed with ammunition he carries in a pocket flask. If Helen is going around to her boy friend's Whipple will walk her by there.

It won't do Helen any good to act the innocent, Whipple continues, when Helen resents his insinuations. He has seen her coming out of Bert's rooming house. He knows a thing or two. And she'd better be careful or there will be a little stranger one of these days. . . .

Davis is back from another job-hunting tramp. Nothing found. Nothing promising. He cannot get anywhere near Mr. Applegate, even though he knows him.

A moment later Allen Davis appears, smeared with coal dust. Allen has brought home some coal. He has been doing odd jobs for a coal dealer in Central Avenue, he explains, and taken his pay in coal. Allen, too, has been looking all day for a job and found none. He is ready to take anything so long as it is work. But there isn't any work.

"I see lots of people riding around in limousines, girls going around in fur coats and women wearing diamonds, having dinner in the big hotels. But try to get somebody to give you a chance to earn ten dollars a week."

There isn't any use talkin' against the rich, the elder Davis reminds his son. It may be wrong for some to have more than they can use and others to have to struggle to get enough to eat, as Helen says, but how are they going to change it?

"Well, I guess some way could be found of making guys like Applegate loosen up, so that some of the rest of us can have a chance to live," says Allen.

"I don't bear Applegate any hard feelin's," says Davis. "It ain't his fault that conditions are bad, any more'n it's mine. You can't blame a man for shuttin' down production when he's not gettin' any orders. It ain't common sense to keep a shop open when you're losin' money."

"Is it common sense to let people starve?" demands Allen, excitedly. "I'm not just talking about myself. All right, I wanted to go through college and I couldn't go. O.K. Just my tough luck, that's all. I'm ready to go to work. But where's the work? And it's not only you and me. It's millions all over the country."

"Well, it's general conditions."

"Then let's kick the general conditions in the pants and get some new ones."

Davis warns Allen not to be so free with his "kid's talk." He has heard enough of that and he doesn't want to hear any more.

"I won't starve. Not while there's any fight left in me," defiantly shouts Allen, as he goes into the hall.

Bert has come. As soon as they are alone Helen tells him of Whipple's discovery. Bert confesses his landlady has also become suspicious. This means that Helen must stop going to Bert's rooms, and that is a depressing thought for both of them.

"Well, maybe next summer, Bert, when you get your vacation we might be able to go to the country together for a week or so. Wouldn't that be nice?"

"Yes, it sure would. But next summer is a long way off."

They have settled down to a nice rough game of checkers as the curtain falls.

In the library of Willard Drew's home, "a comfortably furnished man's room, six men in dinner jackets are sitting in armchairs, all but one of them smoking cigars and sipping brandy from *verres ballons*. The men are Willard Drew, Elbert Purdy, Walter Applegate, Harry Gregg, Cleveland Thomas and Arthur Meadows.

The discussion at the moment is concerned with what the government should do with the agitators. Applegate is for putting a stop to them. Gregg, a United States senator, would remind his friends that not only agitators but a considerable number of good, plain, conservative Americans are also against war. Elbert Purdy, at the head of the State University, agrees with the Senator, believing, as he does, that peace must be established in the world if civilization is to endure. Drew, too, is for peace—but not peace at any price.

And that, Applegate is quick to insist, is the crux of the matter. Idealism is all very well, but the situation confronting them must be looked at from a practical angle.

"We've seen industry in this country slow down until it's damned near come to a standstill," says Applegate. "And why? Because we've let ourselves be led astray by a lot of this talk about internationalism. Our industries have come into competition with cheap labor and low standards of living in foreign countries and we have a lot of agitation against the tariff—"

"We've lent billions to foreign governments and when they don't pay we do not even make an effort to get them to toe the mark," interrupts Applegate. "What I say, charity begins at home. Let's have less talk about peace and good-will, and let's do something about protecting American industry and the American working-man. We're always worrying about the foreigners. We'd be a damned sight better off if we served notice on them that we mean business, and if we had an army and navy that was ready and willing to protect the interests of the American investor abroad."

"Yes, of course, we have to protect the American investor," agrees Senator Gregg, "but, on the other hand, we have to take into account the fact that there's a good deal of sentiment against our foreign policy being dictated by big business."

"The interests of business are the interests of the whole country," insists Drew. "When business prospers, everybody prospers."

Senator Gregg is willing to admit as much, but it isn't easy to convince the people of that fact. It is pretty hard also to convince the people that the appointment of Arthur Meadows, Willard Drew's new son-in-law, as Minister to Haiti, is not for the purpose of protecting the banking interests in Haiti.

"I think it's absurd to say that a man can't serve his country honestly because of his family connections," protests Meadows.

Now Winifred Drew has come for her husband and is ready to apologize for crashing the dinner party. With many compliments given and taken the Meadows depart, and the group returns to the consideration of the serious business for which they were called together.

This meeting was called, Willard Drew explains, for the specific purpose of drafting Elbert Purdy for the Presidency of the United States. And over Dr. Purdy's modest protests the idea is expanded.

"Don't say anything until you hear what we have to say," Drew requests of the startled Purdy. "I'll tell you how this thing originated. I was having lunch the other day with Harry and Walter, and we agreed that the one thing that this country needs is constructive leadership—a man in the White House whom the people can trust and respect and at the same time one who has broad vision and the qualities of statesmanship. Well, we got to mentioning this name and that, discussing personalities and qualifications, and the upshot of it all was that we agreed unanimously that you are the one man who fills the bill."

Dr. Purdy is deeply touched, but still considerably concerned about the possibility of his being the man for the job. Politics is not, nor ever has been, his job. And that, counters Applegate, is the very thing that speaks loudest in his favor. There are far, far too many professional politicians in Washington.

As for the Purdy campaign, everything has been, or will be, arranged. Senator Gregg will look after the political end and Applegate and Drew will take care of the finances. They already have the promise of the support of all the Vincent Thomas newspapers and periodicals and the free use of the Thomas broadcasting service.

PURDY—You make it difficult for me to refuse. Really, you know, I'm loathe to leave my post at the University. I'm at home up there on the campus. It's a cloistered life, and perhaps that's why I like it. I enjoy the society of my faculty and of my students. Scholarship is my first love.

GREGG—We know that, Elbert. We know it will be a sacrifice for you. But we feel that the country needs you and that you won't let personal considerations stand in the way. I don't mean to compare myself to you, either in importance or in ability, but I sacrificed a very lucrative partnership in Drew and Company because I felt that I could be serviceable in the Senate. And I know you'll look at it the same way.

PURDY—Well, I hope I am unselfish enough not to fail in the performance of a public duty.

DREW—Now, you're talking! Gentlemen, I have a toast to propose. Come on, Walter, get yourself a glass.

APPLEGATE—I'll drink it in water, if you don't mind. (*He fills a glass with water.*)

DREW (*raising his glass*)—To the next President of the United States!

APPLEGATE—Hear! Hear! (*They are drinking as the curtain falls.*)

The Davises are getting ready to move out of their home. The mortgage has been foreclosed. Allen is having some difficulty deciding what books and letters he wants to keep. Davis is tying the doors of the sideboard together. Helen is trying to sort the trash from the things they want to keep.

A committee is calling from the works. Workmen Fallon, Smith and Spandau have come to see Davis, following a meeting of the unemployed. They want him to head a parade to march out to the Applegate works "to kind o' call attention to how bad things are."

"We figgered that once we got out there we might get a chance to talk it over with Applegate," Fallon explains. "An' what we want you to do, Bill, is to kind o' lead the thing. We all decided that on account o' you workin' at the plant for all them years you'd be the right man to do it. You see, you're one o' the few that knows Applegate personally—"

Davis doesn't think it likely Applegate remembers him. He also resents his son Allen's breaking in with his radical opinions as to what he thinks of Applegate and his responsibilities. He turns to Helen for advice.

Helen thinks it possible that if Applegate has any human sympathy at all he will want to do something to help people who are starving.

"Sure, he'll give you lots of sympathy. But try and buy groceries with it," sneers Allen.

Detective Robert Marden has appeared at the door. He has come with a warrant for Allen's arrest. Allen is charged with stealing coal from the railroad yards, which explains to Davis where the Davis coal has been coming from.

DAVIS—So that's what you turned out to be, is it—a crook?

ALLEN—Yes, it is. I took the coal from the railroad company because we needed it to keep us warm. If that's being a crook, then I'm a crook. But who made me a crook? Is it my fault that I can't get a job? Is it my fault that the bank failed and that we're being put out of our home? Why don't they arrest the people that stole our jobs and our savings and our homes from us?

MARDEN—All through?

HELEN—Oh, can't you give him another chance? He won't do

it again.

MARDEN—It isn't up to me, miss. I've got nothing to say about it. There's been an awful lot of coal stolen from the yards lately and I guess the railroad company's decided it's about time they made an example of somebody. It's just his tough luck that it had to be him. Come ahead now, son.

ALLEN—All right, I'm ready. Good-by, ma. (*He kisses her.*)

MRS. DAVIS—Ach, Allen, Allen, why did you do it?

ALLEN—Good-by, Helen.

HELEN (*kissing him*)—We'll do everything we can to get you out of it, Allen.

ALLEN—Yes, a fat chance I've got. (*To* DAVIS.) Good-by.

DAVIS—I never thought I'd live to see my own son turn out to be a crook.

ALLEN—All right. You can think what you like of me. I don't care. (*He exits.*)

MARDEN—Well, folks, I'm sorry it had to be this way. But it's not my doing. (*He exits.*)

MRS. DAVIS (*sobbing*)—Ach, why did he do it? Why did he do it?

HELEN (*trying to comfort her*)—Don't, mother, don't! (*They exit.*)

FALLON—Bill, I guess we all know how you feel.

DAVIS (*turning to them*)—All right, boys, I'll go an' talk to Applegate. (*The curtain falls.*)

An eight-foot brick wall, pierced by double doors at the entrance to the works of the Applegate Harvester Company. A sign announcing that this is private property and that admission is not permitted except on business decorates one of the doors. Outside the fence is the public highway. Joe Callahan, watchman, is seated on a box just inside the doors smoking a pipe and reading a newspaper.

Sam Rogers, an employee, has come from the works and started down the road when he sees some sort of parade coming toward the gates. From afar off is heard the noise of an approaching crowd. Rogers, at Callahan's suggestion, goes into the works and brings out James Moulton, "an excitable little man," who is disturbed by the approach of the paraders.

"They look as though they were out for trouble," ventures Moulton. "Maybe we'd better 'phone for some State troopers."

"We don't need no State troopers," insists Callahan, still watching the parade. "They don't look as if they have any fight in 'em."

Moulton, however, orders that the guards in the plant be rounded up as a precautionary measure. A moment later the marchers have arrived at the doors, headed by Davis and the committee that waited on him at his home. There are several women in the crowd.

"Nearly all of the marchers carry slogans which consist merely of pieces of cardboard tacked to laths and crudely painted with such legends as 'Give us a chance, Mr. Applegate,' 'We want work,' 'Our children are hungry,' 'Give us jobs,' 'When do we eat?' 'Help men who are willing to work,' and numerous others of similar import."

At the doors Callahan bars the way. That's as far as the crowd can go, he informs Davis.

"We came out here to see Mr. Applegate and we want to see him," says Davis.

"I don't care what you came out for. I got orders not to let anybody in," answers Callahan.

Moulton, who has shrunk back against the office wall at sight of the crowd, steps forward to confirm the orders. The crowd boos lustily.

"We come out here representin' the unemployed, Mr. Moulton," explains Davis. "There's over two thousand men been laid off from this plant an' most of them are havin' a pretty hard time of it. We come out here to talk things over with Mr. Applegate an' see if somethin' can't be done about it."

"There's nothing to talk over," Moulton answers, sharply. "As soon as conditions improve, the men will be taken back."

"That may be a long ways off. What are we goin' to do in the meantime? We got families dependin' on us, Mr. Moulton—wives an' kids. How are we goin' to eat an' pay the rent?"

"That's not up to us. We can't do anything about that. Mr. Applegate isn't responsible for present conditions."

Davis is persistent. Moulton continues hard. The crowd continues to boo. Only Davis has any influence with them.

"If you don't mind my sayin' so, Mr. Moulton," protests Davis, finally, "this is a pretty lousy way to treat a bunch o' workin' men—not even givin' them a chance to get a hearin'."

"All right, go along now," orders Moulton, nervously. "You're just out here to make trouble, that's all."

"We'll make trouble for you, all right, you little pimp!" shouts a workman, pushing his way past Davis and spitting squarely in Moulton's face.

Moulton, almost inarticulate with rage and fear, shouts to Callahan for help. "Clean the goddam bastards out of here!" he yells.

Callahan has roughly forced Davis toward the gates. The crowd is booing, shouting, forcing itself forward. Four or five armed guards appear from inside the plant and help Callahan close the doors and bar them. The crowd grows noisier and is pushing and pounding on the doors.

"Stop them! Stop them! They'll break down the gate!" shrieks Moulton. "Look out! They're climbing over! Shoot them down!"

The heads of three or four of the paraders appear over the top of the wall. A guard orders them down, leveling his revolver at them, and they drop. The battering at the gate increases. Again the shrill voice of Moulton is ordering the guard to shoot before the gates are broken.

Suddenly several shots are fired. There are screams followed by a quiet muttering. Slogans that had been dancing above the wall disappear.

"That's it—shoot 'em down! That's right! That'll teach 'em! That'll teach the goddam bastards!" shrieks Moulton. The uproar grows as the curtain falls.

In his private office in the State University, President Purdy is at his desk reading telegrams. There is a great stack of them before him, and his secretary is bringing in more.

Mr. Purdy takes time out to answer the telephone. Willard Drew is talking and is very glad to report that his daughter Winifred and her baby are both doing well. It is an eight-pound boy and has been named for Dr. Purdy. Miss Innes, the Purdy secretary, is convinced that after the election there will be thousands of babies named after the doctor.

Two of the faculty, Professor Hirschbein and Professor Sloane, are waiting by appointment. Dr. Purdy sees Hirschbein first. It is about the professor having presided at a meeting of the Liberal Club the week before. That, Dr. Purdy informs the professor, represented a serious infraction of discipline.

"I presided at that meeting," explains Professor Hirschbein, a man in his early thirties, with a rather aggressive manner, "because, in my opinion, the Dean's ruling was an attempt to spare Mr. Walter Applegate the embarrassment of having that outrageous mass-murder at his plant ventilated."

"Murder is a strong word, Professor Hirschbein, and one which a member of a university faculty should use sparingly."

"Unfortunately, it is the only word which fits the facts."

"I cannot agree with you, Professor Hirschbein. I have discussed the matter at length with Mr. Applegate and I assure you that no one deplores the tragedy more than he does. He has given me his solemn assurance that whoever it was who gave the order to fire on the marchers, acted in excess of his authority. In fact, there seems to be reason for believing that the first shot was fired by someone in the crowd and that the guards merely were acting in self-defense."

"Well, I must congratulate Mr. Applegate upon having found so able and so learned an apologist."

The question, to Hirschbein, is entirely one of academic freedom. To Dr. Purdy the professor was guilty of a grave breach of discipline. Permission had not been granted by the Dean for outside speakers to address the Liberal Club.

"But why was permission refused?" demands Hirschbein. Because the speakers were known to be men of unorthodox economic views, who would attack not only Applegate, but the social system which he stands for and which protects him. I call that a free speech issue."

"Professor Hirschbein, there has never been, under my presidency, any restrictions upon freedom of speech in this University," replies Dr. Purdy. "But we have a grave responsibility to the youth who are entrusted to our care. This is an institution of learning and not a forum for political propaganda. We cannot sanction the use of university buildings, erected and supported by the state, for the purpose of disseminating doctrines which strike at the very existence of the state."

The Board of Trustees has decided, Dr. Purdy reports, in view of "certain apparently irreconcilable differences," to ask for Professor Hirschbein's resignation. No one regrets more than Dr. Purdy that—

Hirschbein—Oh, yes, I understand all that, Dr. Purdy. It's all being done in a spirit of friendship, I'm aware of that. I have a wife and two small children, Dr. Purdy. Do they have to suffer because I don't happen to believe that men seeking employment should be murdered in cold blood?

Purdy—I'm sure you'll have no difficulty in finding another post, Professor Hirschbein. You are an excellent teacher and a first-rate scholar.

Hirschbein—And being kicked out of State U will be a splendid recommendation to all the other boards of trustees.

PURDY—I asked the board to limit its action to a reprimand.

HIRSCHBEIN—I suppose they gave due consideration to the fact that I'm a Jew, didn't they?

PURDY (*rising*)—Professor Hirschbein, there is no distinction of race or creed in State U. This is a public university, dedicated to the service of all the citizens of the state. In behalf of the University, I thank you for the able performance of your scholastic duties and personally I wish you the best of luck. (*He extends his hand.*)

HIRSCHBEIN (*refusing the proffered hand*)—Why didn't you begin by saying: "We don't care to have any radicals around here"? That would have simplified matters. Good day.

PURDY (*as* HIRSCHBEIN *exits*)—Good day, Professor Hirschbein.

Professor C. Carter Sloane, a young man obviously of considerable family background, has passed Professor Hirschbein in the hall and knows that his colleague has been dismissed. He suspects that he is in for a dose of the same medicine.

The Trustees, however, have made a distinction, Dr. Purdy reports. Professor Sloane's participation in the meeting of the Liberal Club was confined to an expression of his personal opinion and, at Dr. Purdy's suggestion, the Trustees are prepared to let him off with an official reprimand.

"Well, Dr. Purdy, I appreciate your consideration and the kindness of the Trustees," replies Professor Sloane, "but if you'll permit me to say so, the point you make about Hirschbein and me seems to be a distinction without a difference. As far as I can see, our offenses are identical, and if you won't dismiss me, I'm afraid I'll have to ask you to accept my resignation."

"Mr. Sloane, I understand your gesture and I recognize the generosity which prompts it. But I urge you to reconsider. You are a very young man with every prospect of a fine academic career, if you do not allow yourself to be led astray by these shallow and specious doctrines which are abroad at the moment. You come of a distinguished family, which for centuries has played an important part in the building of America. You may not know it, but your grandfather taught me philosophy at Harvard."

"Yes, I do know it."

"No American scholar has ever matched his profound understanding of Plato. You have it in you to carry on the splendid tradition of your family. We want you here at State U. We hope that maturity will wean you away from your unsound theories. We all have worshiped false gods in our youth. State U needs men of character and of courage and of brilliant attainments. That is why I ask you not to act rashly."

"Thank you, Dr. Purdy," says Professor Sloane, as he rises to leave. "But if Hirschbein's conduct merits dismissal, so does mine. The fact that I'm descended from Cotton Mather has nothing to do with it."

In leaving Professor Sloane reminds Doctor Purdy that in the riot at the Applegate works William Davis, father of a former undergraduate and one of his best pupils, Allen Davis, was badly hurt. Dr. Purdy is sorry to hear that and he hopes Professor Sloane will take a day or two to think over his resignation and then come to see him again.

Professor Sloane feels that his mind is made up. However, he would like to congratulate Dr. Purdy on winning the Oregon primaries. It looks now as though he might have a majority on the first ballot.

"I am not politically ambitious, Mr. Sloane," Dr. Purdy insists. "I have consented to enter this campaign only with the hope of introducing, into the conduct of our public affairs, an element of enlightened liberalism."

"Yes, I'm sure of that. Good day."

Sloane has gone. Dr. Purdy's telephone is ringing. The Doctor and Mr. Applegate are exchanging health comparisons over the 'phone as the curtain falls.

Senator Gregg is at his desk in the Senate Office Building. Across the desk Walter Applegate is sitting, listening uneasily to the Senator's reports of disturbing activities.

Veterans are picketing the White House again. Senator Gregg has been rather impressed by their appearance. A lot of them look just like folks, and Gregg believes that, instead of running them out of Washington, as Applegate recommends, the authorities should be mighty careful how they handle them. Let Applegate remember that two of the men shot in the riot at his works were ex-service men. That may lead to a Congressional investigation.

"But, for God's sake, Harry, what is there to investigate," protests Applegate. "I've explained the whole thing to you, haven't I? Is it my fault that that fool secretary of mine lost his head? And I've told you that the guards never would have fired if they hadn't been attacked. I've sent checks to the families of all the men who were shot. I don't see what more I can do. Why don't you fellows here in Washington keep these Reds out of the country and run out the ones that are already in? That would put an end to all these riots and demonstrations."

Gregg is not so sure. The agitation isn't confined to the Reds. Right now there is a delegation representing a pacifist organization waiting to be seen.

"Well, sure, if you're going to listen to a lot of cranks and fanatics," says Applegate. "What do you want to do: scrap our army and navy and throw the country open to any foreign power that wants to walk in and take it away from us?"

"I'm talking about the temper of the country," answers Gregg. "The sentiment of the people is for peace. One reason that Purdy is getting so much popular support is that he's come out for world peace. And if he wins the Nobel peace prize, as he's likely to, it's going to mean that his nomination is assured."

Applegate is for peace, too, but, as an industrialist, he is not unmindful of the fact that if war should come every industry in the country would boom overnight and there would be jobs for everybody.

The delegation waiting to see Senator Gregg is composed of the Rev. Thomas Williamson, Professor Morris Hirschbein and four others. They represent the League for World Peace. They have come to protest, as the Rev. Williamson explains, that "war among civilized, Christian peoples is an anachronism."

"Senator, in the name of the people whom you serve, and in the name of the Master whom I serve, we ask you to advocate that our nation throw away its weapons, not in some dim future, but here and now," pleads Williamson.

The Senator is responsive. He, too, loves humanity. He, too, is for world peace. But—

"We must look before we leap, ladies and gentlemen. And so long as the other great nations of the world continue to pile up armaments, a regard for our national security demands that we shall not leave ourselves defenseless. Furthermore—"

Professor Hirschbein would like to interrupt with a few questions. Is it not a fact that Senator Gregg was formerly a member of the banking firm of Drew and Company, which has underwritten bond issues in many corporations engaged in the manufacture of munitions? Is it not a fact that Senator Gregg was formerly a director in at least three of these corporations?

"Professor Hirschbein, is it not a fact that you were recently dismissed from the State University for a serious infraction of discipline?" counters Gregg.

"Professor Hirschbein is speaking entirely for himself, Senator," declares a woman member of the delegation, giving Hirschbein a hard look.

"Ladies and gentlemen, I do not feel called upon to defend my public record," insists Senator Gregg, with fulsome candor. "It speaks for itself. It has been a great pleasure to receive you and I assure you that I shall continue to work unceasingly for the ends which we all have at heart."

With a chorus of soft "good-bys" the delegation has passed out. The Rev. Williamson has lingered to say a word for a young couple waiting to see the Senator. He has known them well and knows them to be deserving.

Albert Collins and his fiancée, Helen Davis, are hoping to interest Senator Gregg in the case of Allen Davis. They are hoping for a pardon. Allen is in the reformatory for stealing coal from the railroad—

"He's not a bad boy," pleads Helen; "really he isn't. He only did it because we've been having such a hard time lately. It's awful to think of his being there in the reformatory with all those criminals. I'm afraid it will ruin his chances for life."

Senator Gregg is sympathetic. It sounds like a most deserving case. But unfortunately it is a State court conviction and should be brought to the attention of the Governor. The Senator will be glad to look into the matter very carefully. The fact that Bert's brother is a shell-shocked veteran who has had to be sent to the State Insane Asylum, and that his nephew has been killed in Haiti, tend to increase the Senator's interest. He is always interested in the veterans.

A bell has summoned Senator Gregg to an important roll call. Helen and Bert, agreed that he certainly is a nice Senator, a prince, in fact, decide that, so long as they are in Washington, they might as well take a trip down to Washington's Home at Mount Vernon.

They have gone in search of a policeman to ask him the way as the curtain falls.

Mary Klobutsko is sitting on the bed in her "small, cheerless, meagerly furnished room," studying, when a knock at the door startles her. The caller is Allen Davis, "pale and shabby."

Allen has been given ten days off for good behavior and is out of the reformatory. He has come straight to Mary. Her letters and her visits have been the most cheering thing he has known in jail. He has left his bag at the station. His folks do not know yet that he is out.

Mary is overjoyed at seeing Allen. Glad to share her crackers and milk with him. Proud to report that she has been having quite a success making speeches to workers. Mary is a good speaker now. She had to give up her job in the candy factory because the foreman couldn't keep his hands off her. She is working now in a hotel kitchen peeling vegetables.

Mary had left college when Professor Hirschbein and Professor Sloane were dismissed. "I could not stay there, Allen," she explains. "It is only a place for hiding the truth from people, for making the students satisfied with the present conditions.

"Oh, Allen, I am so glad you are out of that place," cries Mary. "After I went to see you I cried for two days."

"You don't know what it was like, Mary. You can't imagine the things that go on in a place like that. Oh, God, it was awful. If I'd have had to stay there much longer, I think I would have killed myself, honest I do."

"Don't talk about it, Allen," pleads Mary, seizing both his hands. "You must forget about it."

"Yes, that's what I'm going to try to do. I suppose they'll be watching me now. I've got to report to some sort of probation officer every month. Well, no matter what happens, they'll never get me to go back to that place."

With the ten dollars they gave him when he left the reformatory Allen has spent six for a revolver. One of the fellows had told him where to get it. He does not intend to use it unless they try to send him back. But he refuses to throw it away as Mary begs him to do. Whatever happens he is going to see to it that he does not go back to jail.

Now there is the question of where Allen is going to live. He can't very well go back to his family. His father won't want him around. And they only have two little rooms and a kitchen, anyway.

MARY—Allen—
ALLEN—What?
MARY—Why don't you live here with me?
ALLEN—You mean—?
MARY—Yes.
ALLEN—Would you—would you really let me, Mary?

MARY—Yes.

ALLEN—Gee, that would be wonderful. I—I've never been with a girl.

MARY—I have never been with a boy, either.

ALLEN—I—Mary, I think you're— Oh, God! (*He takes her passionately in his arms as the curtain falls.*)

In a public square at night a crowd is gathered. From the base of a monument inscribed "To the memory of those who fell in the World War" speakers are addressing a small crowd. Mary Klobutsko is just finishing. She is followed by Mike Ramsay of the A.E.F. "Mike is going to tell you what he did for his country and what his country is doing for him," promises Jones, the chairman.

Mike had been caught in the draft. He trained at Camp Lee and went over there. He was at Château-Thierry, went over the top three times and got hit in the arm. After seven weeks in base hospital, account of blood poisoning, Mike was made a corporal and sent with the Army of Occupation into Germany. For two years now he has been looking for a job. Three times he has been arrested for vagrancy and let off because of his army record. He is just back from marching with the B.E.F. to Washington. All he got there was the bum's rush. Now Mike doesn't know what he is going to do.

Allen Davis is the next speaker. A policeman has sauntered in as Allen begins to speak. Allen, explains Jones, is talking as the son of a man who was a victim of the massacre at the Applegate Harvester Works. He is going to tell them what happens when unemployed workers go lookin' for jobs.

ALLEN—Yes, I'll tell you what happens. My father and I tramped around for months looking for work. And when we lost everything and I took some coal from the railroad yards to keep us from freezing, they sent me up for six months and told me that I'm a criminal. And when my father went out there to the Applegate plant to try to talk things over and get his job back, what happened to him? He got shot down like a dog by Applegate's hired gunmen, that's what happened. Yes, and that's what'll happen to all of you as long as you act like a lot of sheep. But you don't catch me taking it like that.

THE POLICEMAN—Hey, you, lay off that kind of talk.

ALLEN—I'll say anything I want to, and just try to stop me.

THE POLICEMAN—Yeah, well, you can it, or you'll get run in.

ALLEN—Shut up, you thug.

THE POLICEMAN—All right. That's enough out of you. Look out, youse— (*He blows his whistle and starts to push his way through the crowd. There is considerable resistance and the crowd protests volubly. Two more policemen hurry on.*)

ALLEN (*shouting above the noise*)—Don't let them stop you! Don't let them break up the meeting!

Two or three men try to impede the policemen, who are in the middle of the crowd. One of the policemen clubs a man, who falls to the ground. Allen goes on shouting inarticulately above the uproar. A shot is fired, and there is the sound of breaking glass, as the street light is extinguished. In the darkness, the struggle continues. Allen is still on the monument, shouting inaudibly. One of the policemen reaches him and pulls him down. Several shots are fired. The crowd scatters under the blows of the policemen. One of the crowd and a policeman are stretched on the ground. The curtain falls.

In the courtroom of Judge Cleveland Thomas the Judge's rostrum is faced by the desks of the Clerk and the Court Stenographer. There are a long table and a few chairs.

The case of the People against Allen Davis being called, Allen is led in and seated at the table. James Trowbridge, his attorney, and the State's Attorney are standing at the side.

"The defense has moved to set aside the verdict upon the ground that the guilt of the defendant was not established beyond a reasonable doubt," begins Judge Thomas. "I have carefully reviewed the evidence. The defendant claims that he was unarmed when he went to the meeting in Lincoln Square. He admits the ownership of the revolver which has been introduced into the evidence, but contends that he left it in the room of the girl, Mary Klobutsko. This contention is supported by the witness, Klobutsko. The inference is that the revolver was abstracted from the witness Klobutsko's room by the police and that the defendant is a victim of a police conspiracy. Against this must be weighed the testimony of Officer Klein and Sergeant Anderson, both of whom testified that they saw the defendant fire the shot which resulted in the death of Officer O'Leary and that the revolver was in his hand when they arrested him. This presents a clean-cut issue of fact and one which must be determined upon the basis of credibility. Officer Klein and Sergeant Anderson are men with long and honorable records and the efforts of the defense to discredit their testimony were without success. On the other hand, the testimony of the defendant and of his corroborating witness is open to the gravest suspicion. The defendant has a criminal record. His violent hostility to the police and his open threats against them have been testified to by a number of witnesses. His attitude throughout the trial was one of open defiance to the forces of law and order. In addition, he has admitted deflowering a virgin, under the age of consent. Under our statute this constitutes the crime of rape, one of the gravest offenses known to the law. And although the defendant was not on trial here for this crime, it must be taken into account as bearing upon his character and affecting his credibility. The witness Klobutsko is scarcely more reliable. Her emotional interest in the defendant casts considerable doubt upon her competence as a witness, ab initio. . . . The motion to set aside the verdict is therefore denied."

Attorney Trowbridge takes an exception. The defendant is called to the bar. Allen stands in his place.

"Have you anything to say before sentence is passed upon you?" demands Judge Thomas.

"I didn't do it. I was framed by the police," answers Allen, sullenly.

"Davis, it is not an easy task that confronts me," begins the Judge. "You are a young man, not yet out of your teens, and you stand before me convicted by a jury of the gravest of all crimes. In cold blood and with deliberate intent, you murdered an officer of the law in the performance of his duty. For such a crime one can never find justification, but in your case one looks in vain even for the usual palliating circumstances of ignorance, defective mentality or great privation. On the contrary, in your case, all the circumstances serve only to heighten the enormity of your offense. There is no hereditary taint in you nor are you a product of the slums, bred of some alien stock that brings with it from a less enlightened land embittered memories of oppression. You were born of sober, honest, hard-working parents, reared in comfort and with loving care. It was to have been expected of you that you would make something fine and worth-while of your life, that you would embrace the manifold opportunities which America offers to young men of brains and ability. And yet what have you done with your life? How have you used your talents and your opportunities? At nineteen, you are a hardened and a desperate criminal: a thief, a debaucher of a young girl and a murderer. You have shown respect neither for property, for womanly innocence nor for human life. An attempt has been made to excuse your offenses by depicting you as a victim of social injustice. To such a plea, I can turn only a deaf ear. You are the victim, not of society, but of your own vicious acts. . . . My duty is plain. You have been found guilty of murder in the first degree. The penalty is prescribed by the statute and it is mandatory upon me to impose it. Allen Davis, I sentence you to be hanged by the neck until you are dead. And may God have mercy on your soul."

The officer touches Allen's arm. Allen turns and mechanically follows him from the room as the curtain falls.

A mass meeting is being held. There is a small table on the stage of the auditorium. Behind the table a row of chairs is arranged. On the wall back of the chairs an American flag is spread. Presently the speakers of the evening file in and take their places. They are Sloane, Hirschbein, Trowbridge, Helen Davis, Mary Klobutsko and the Rev. Williamson. Bert Collins, pushing William Davis before him in a wheel chair, follows the speakers. Davis, shrunken and wan, has a blanket thrown across his knees.

As the audience quiets [the theatre audience represents the auditorium audience facing the speakers] the Rev. Williamson steps forward to explain the purposes of the meeting.

"Within the gray walls of the death house sits young Allen Davis awaiting his doom," begins Williamson. "We are here today to entreat you to unite with us in our efforts to stay the hand of the executioner and to afford the lad another opportunity to establish his innocence. The conviction of Allen Davis has led thousands of intelligent and liberal-minded men and women throughout the land to believe that the boy is the victim of anger and vindictiveness rather than the adjudged delinquent of wise and impartial justice. . . . It is not my intention to review the case in detail. Other speakers will describe graphically the atmosphere of hysteria in which the trial was conducted. They will tell you how men of liberal political opinions were rigorously excluded from the jury. They will point out to you that the judge, admittedly an able jurist, is the son of the proprietor of a group of influential newspapers, which pre-judged the case and stridently demanded the boy's conviction. They will show you that throughout the trial constant emphasis was laid upon the social and political philosophy of Allen Davis, so that one may almost say that he was tried for his opinions, rather than for the crime with which he was charged. Our first speaker is the sister of the condemned boy. Miss Helen Davis will say a few words to you."

Helen timidly takes her place at the speaker's stand. Her plea is for her brother's life. He is only nineteen, and though he may have said a lot of things he should not have said and done a lot of things he should not have done, this thing for which he has been convicted he did not do.

"He's a good boy, honestly he is," feelingly insists Helen. "He's had such a hard time of it. We've all been having a pretty hard time of it. I don't think it's our fault that things have turned out this way. We've all tried our best. I don't understand very much about politics and economics, although I did study them in normal school. But it seems to me that there should be some way of people getting just the few simple things that they want. It doesn't seem right that people who want to work can't find any work to do and that their homes should be taken away from them. And boys and girls who want an education and can't get it. Yes, and people not being able to get married and have children. Is it too much to ask: just to be allowed to live your own life in peace and quiet? . . . A chance to live, that's all we want, that's all we ask for. That's all Allen wanted. Please help him to get it, oh, please do. Don't let him die! Give him a chance to live!"

The Rev. Williamson echoes Helen's plea that Allen be given a chance to live as he introduces Mary Klobutsko, "a young woman who in every sense but a strictly legal one has the right to call herself the wife of Allen Davis."

Mary approaches the stand briskly and speaks with determination. Allen did not do the murder. They said at the trial that they found the revolver in his hand. The revolver was in Mary's room. The police came when she was not there and searched the room and found it.

"Why did they do this?" Mary cries. "I'll tell you why. Because when a policeman is killed somebody must be punished. If they cannot find the one who did it, then they must punish someone else. That is why they have punished Allen. And because he has been to prison for stealing coal. Yes, and I will tell you another reason why. Because he is not willing to submit to being poor. That is his crime. In America, you must not cry out. You must be meek, no matter what, no matter if you cannot find a way to live, no matter if you are starving, no matter if you are sent to prison. I was not born in America. I was born in Poland. In 1920, when I was a little girl, I came here. In Poland there was civil war and starvation. My father came here to find freedom and food for his family. To America, to the land of plenty. What did he find? He found starvation and death. Days he worked in a sweat-shop and nights he lived in a slum, until he coughed away his lungs and died. It is so with millions. They ask for bread and for peace and they are given only starvation and war. And they must not protest. If they protest, they are shot down and sent to prison. So that a few people can have a thousand times what they need, millions must live in darkness and hunger. And we must be silent. I shall not be silent, not as long as I live. Because my lover was not silent, they have told him he must die. Perhaps they will tell me that I must die, too. It is the only way they can make me be silent. Until then, I shall protest, protest, protest! And when my child is born, I shall teach it to protest, too. With my milk, it shall learn to protest. And we shall go on, thousands, millions, the poor and the oppressed everywhere, until we strike off our chains, until we free ourselves of our oppressors, until we win for ourselves the right to live.

Mary is sobbing hysterically as she leaves the stand and returns to her seat. The Rev. Williamson steps forward to echo again the prayer for help.

"As the servant of One Who made the weary and the heavy-laden His especial care, the fervent plea of this child moves me to a deep commiseration. Are we to waste these strong, eager, beautiful young lives—allow them to be ground out by cruelty and injustice?"

The next speaker is C. Carter Sloane, "a young man who comes of a brilliant and distinguished family, who resigned his post at the State University rather than allow his protesting voice to be stilled."

Calmly and in gentle, persuasive tones, Sloane reviews his own descent from immigrant stock; from that ancestor who had crossed in the *Mayflower;* from a second ancestor who, a hundred and fifty years later, affixed his signature to that document which held that all men were created equal; that they were endowed by their Creator with certain inalienable rights—

"Some of my forbears died to establish a union based upon those principles and others died to preserve that union." The voice of the speaker has taken on a ringing eloquence, as he turns and points to the flag on the wall. "I was taught to love and to venerate that flag. And I do love and venerate it. For to me it has always been a symbol of the ideals of freedom, of justice, of equality, of opportunity, of those unalienable rights of life, liberty and the pursuit of happiness. That is why I find it necessary to take this platform, in order that I may raise my voice against acts that are committed in contravention of those ideals and those rights, acts that deny the noble and humanitarian principles upon which our government was founded, and which besmirch this symbol in the eyes of all those who hold its true meaning dear. When you snuff out the life of an Allen Davis, when you murder him judicially, in an access of frenzy and of fear, you do more than take a human life. You proclaim to the world that America has forsaken justice for lynch-law, democracy for class-rule, and liberty for tyranny. I know Allen Davis. He was a student of mine—one of the best I ever had. A keen mind, sterling principles, a strong character, sound to the core, once you got past the volatile emotions and irrational enthusiasms of youth. It is of such young lives—Allen's and Mary's and Helen's and a dozen others I could name—that a strong and free people could be built. But what do we do with them? Mr. Williamson has told you: we waste them, squander them, throw them on the scrap-heap. The right to live, that is what Mary asks. That is all that any of them asks. And no social system that denies them that right has a claim to a continuance of its existence. In the name of humanity, ladies and gentlemen, in the name of common-sense, what is society for, if not to provide for the safety and well-being of the men and women who compose it? 'To promote the general welfare and secure the blessings of liberty'—you'll find it there, set forth in the preamble to the Constitution. Does that mean a denial of the rights of assemblage and of free speech? Does that mean millions without employment or the means to provide themselves with food and shelter? We are the people, ladies and gentlemen, we—you and I and every one of us. It is our house: this America. Let us cleanse it and put it in order and make it a decent place for decent people to live in!"

THE CURTAIN FALLS

PIGEONS AND PEOPLE

A Comedy in One Act

By George M. Cohan

MASTER COHAN was a trifle baffling as to mood when he wrote "Pigeons and People." It really isn't a play by any test of theatre rule or law of dramaturgy. It is a lark, a stunt, an amusing mystery.

"One left the theatre," wrote Percy Hammond, "convinced that he had been amused but unable to tell his neighbors much about the character that had most amused him."

"Trying to describe it [the play] will be like trying to make mashed potatoes out of rosebuds," declared Gilbert Gabriel.

"It is a rare piece of hocus-pocus which begins without a beginning, continues without a theme and stops without having arrived at a conclusion," Brooks Atkinson explained to his readers.

"Pigeons and People" is so typically Cohan in antic mood, and Cohan is so typically of the American theatre, that the comedy takes on an importance in the season's scheme that, presented under different auspices, it might not have achieved.

While in acting time it is as long as the average three-act play, "Pigeons and People" is played without intermission. "It represents," says Mr. Cohan, "a comic state of mind in continuous action." And it may very well represent a model in playwrighting form that shall hereafter be frequently adopted. The arbitrary three-act form is frequently open to criticism, and all playwrights are happy when they have been able to meet the test of the Aristotelian unities of time, action and place.

"Pigeons and People" was produced in mid-January and ran for nine weeks. Mr. Cohan then took it on tour, playing short engagements in many cities in the conviction that the best way an actor can help the road is to do his part in its reëstablishment.

As the comedy opens we are shown into the living-room of Joseph Heath's apartment in New York. It is a pleasantly furnished room with an alcove entrance at one side, separated from the main room by two small pillars. It is about six o'clock in the evening of an autumn day.

There is no one in the living-room, but a moment later a door is heard to slam outside the alcove. The slam is followed by the appearance of Joseph Heath, a smartly dressed young man of the alert business type, probably in his early thirties.

As he reaches the center of the room Heath turns expectantly and finds no one. He calls. A second later a man of medium build, an oldish man with a head of thinning white hair, wearing a soft shirt and collar, a soft hat and an overcoat that has seen considerable service, pauses beside one of the pillars and, upon Heath's further urging, advances hesitantly into the room.

This man is Parker. He is obviously not altogether at his ease. He has been studying his surroundings furtively as he has entered, and no move that Heath has made has escaped him.

Heath, the bustling, genial host, would have Parker make himself at home, throw off his coat, relax and otherwise be comfortable. But Parker, though profuse with his thanks, quite evidently prefers to stay as he is for the present. When Tokem, Heath's Japanese servant, is summoned to take the hats and coats Parker thinks he will keep his if they don't mind. He will be getting along shortly.

"Not until you've had a bite to eat," protests Heath.

"I don't want anything to eat," insists Parker. "Not a thing in the world. I'm much obliged."

Nor can he be induced to have so much as a cup of coffee. Or a drop of brandy. Not even a glass of champagne will tempt Parker. He really must be getting along. But, as Heath's urging continues, he agrees to stay a few minutes, hanging onto his coat and hat so they will be handy.

Heath lives alone, he explains, with only a housekeeper and a couple of other servants. His sister had lived with him up to a year ago. Then she married a young clergyman and moved to Albany.

"If I were a girl and felt that way about it, I don't think I'd get married at all," smiles Parker. "You're not married yourself, eh?"

"No. No. I'm single, I'm sorry to say," says Heath.

"What are you sorry about?"

"Well, you know—a bachelor's life. There's always something missing, I guess. Of course, the idea has its advantages, too."

"Yes," agrees Parker. "The trouble is so few fellows take advantage of the idea."

Parker is, to Heath, a very interesting man. An unusual man, too. It seems incredible to Heath that he and Parker had sat on a park bench talking for two solid hours. Yet that is what they did.

PARKER—Well, I guess I'd been sitting there yet if you hadn't come along.

HEATH (*lighting cigarette*)—Still talking to the pigeons, eh?

PARKER—No. They've gone to roost by now. Pigeons know when the day's done. They've got a lot of sense, those birds!

HEATH—You know it's wonderful the way you charm them—the way you talk to them. Do you suppose they really understand you?

PARKER—Sure they do, and I understand them. They're easier to understand than people. (HEATH *laughs.*) Well, they are. I ought to know a little something about pigeons. I've been hanging out with them for a long time now.

HEATH—I know you have. And there's hardly been a day this last month that I haven't gone into the park just to watch them flock around you. Hadn't you ever noticed me standing there taking it all in?

PARKER—Sure. Many a time.

HEATH—But I never got up courage enough to talk to you until this afternoon. Tell me, what did you think when I sat on the bench beside you?

PARKER—I thought at first you were a cop.

HEATH (*chuckles*)—A cop?

PARKER—Well, there's a lot of panhandlers around these days. Of course, I knew better when we got into conversation.

HEATH (*smiles*)—And what a conversation it developed into, eh?

PARKER—Well, of course, I didn't intend telling the story of my life when I started in, but—

HEATH (*interrupting him*)—I know you didn't. But once you did start, I made up my mind that I was going to hear it all. (*Smiles.*) And it wasn't so easy to get you to tell it—you know that, don't you?

PARKER (*smiles*)—To tell you the truth, I didn't think it'd be so easy to get anybody to believe it.

HEATH (*chuckles*)—And don't you think I believed it?

PARKER—Well, it doesn't seem like you'd go to all this trouble if you didn't. You certainly wouldn't bring me here to your home and treat me like this unless you were pretty well convinced. Anyway, that's the way it seems to me.

HEATH—And that's the way it is, Parker. I don't think I've

ever been so interested in anything as I am in your story.

PARKER—You mean that?

HEATH—I do. I mean about running away from life, as you call it. You've just been disappointed, that's all.

PARKER—That's it, is it?

HEATH—Yes. You've got the wrong angle on things, and you've got to get over it. God! If any man ever deserved a fresh start and a chance to get his feet stuck in the ground, you do. And I'm going to see that you get that chance. What do you think of that?

PARKER—I'm doing a lot of thinking. I've got plenty of thinking to do, believe me.

Heath would have Parker understand that he is not a professional philanthropist and Parker is quick to assure Heath that he is no subject for charity, either. He doesn't want anything from anybody. So far as he is concerned the world's all right and always has been all right. And as for the people in it—

Tokem has brought in a tray of coffee and sandwiches. Miss Giles, the housekeeper, has come in to see if everything is all right. A very attractive young woman, Miss Giles, and friendly. Especially when she smiles. Her smile is both interested and friendly when Heath tells her that Parker is to be their guest and that she should get the spare-room ready for him. Parker, explains Heath, is visiting the city and may be with them for some time. There has been a mixup with the railroad people and his baggage has gone astray. Miss Giles will kindly lay out some clean linen and anything else that Mr. Parker may need. Tokem, too, will be careful to see that Mr. Parker is well taken care of while he is with them.

Parker is a little stunned by all this attention. He would make sure that Heath is quite on the level about wanting him to stay.

"That's what I wish you'd do," insists Heath. "Give me a chance to talk to you for a day or two and see if I can't get your mind straightened out on this whole proposition. All you need is a little sound advice; just get your bearings and the world will look all different to you. Now you leave it to me. I'm very much interested, Parker. Terribly interested in your case."

"No, no, I couldn't do anything like that."

HEATH—Couldn't do what?

PARKER—Well, I couldn't impose on a man to that extent.

HEATH—Where's the imposition? Unless it's on my part.

This is all my thought, not yours. Now I'm insisting that you accept my hospitality. I want to round you to if I can. See here. I think yours is the most tragic story of a man's life I've ever heard.

PARKER—You do?

HEATH—I do. But it's comically tragic. You know I consider myself pretty lucky to have accidentally stumbled on to this opportunity.

PARKER—What opportunity?

HEATH—I mean, of trying to get you back where you belong. Can you imagine the kick I'm getting out of this? Don't you suppose it will be a real thrill when you come to me in a few days from now and say, "It's all right, Heath, I've found myself, thanks to you." And you know, I'll consider that I've done a damn fine job when that happens. And incidentally, it'll be one of the few really decent things I've ever done in my life.

PARKER—You don't say?

HEATH—Now come on, don't cheat me out of my chance to do it, please.

Parker is still unconvinced. Nor, in his present state of doubt, can he eat any of the sandwiches. Supposing, he protests, that everything he had told Heath in the park was just a pack of lies? Supposing he should turn out to be an impostor. What a damn fool that would make of Heath. Supposing he turned out to be a crook of some kind?

Heath only smiles at the suggestion, but the smile disappears as Parker reminds him that after all he [Parker] has admitted frankly using a phony name, that he has not said what part of the country he hails from and that he is determined to bury his identity with his past.

"You couldn't even check up on me," warns Parker. "You couldn't prove anything about me, even if you wanted to. I'll tell you something; and I'll be on the square with you, too. I wouldn't have believed that story I told you if I'd been you."

Heath, however, is satisfied. At least Heath insists that he is satisfied. No crook clever enough to invent such a story as Parker has told would turn around and warn the man who believed it to be on his guard. No crook would do that.

Which, argues Parker, is exactly what a clever crook might do, and for the very purpose of getting a man like Heath to believe in him.

Now it is plain from Heath's manner that he is becoming confused, even if he has not yet begun to worry. He still protests that he is not taking any chance where Parker is concerned. He is positive of that.

"All right," agrees Parker, laughing a little but quickly regaining his serious mood. "But remember, I warned you."

"Warned me?"

PARKER—Um hum. I mean in case— In case anything should happen.

HEATH—In case what should happen?

PARKER (*smiling*)—Now, you see. You're not sure of me at all. You're just trying to make yourself think you are.

HEATH (*disturbed*)—Well, of course, if you keep on talking this way and saying these things, why—(PARKER *is at the piano now getting his hat and coat.*) Here—what are you going to do?

PARKER—I'm going to get along.

HEATH—Oh, no, you're not. Give me that coat.

PARKER—Now wait a minute, Mr. Heath. You're a fine man, a decent man. But it takes just such a fellow as I am to appreciate the fact. Now I've had a lot of things happen to me in my time, but I want you to know that this meeting with you today and this little talk we've had have given me a lot of food for thought. More than all my other experiences put together, as a matter of fact. It's sort of changed my views on things. It's made me feel that—well, that maybe I've been a little bit wrong about people. You see, I'm in just about the same state of mind about things in general that you are about me. I mean by that that I'm a little bit befuddled. And so I want to get by myself and put pieces together, so to speak, and try and arrive at something that'll give me a better idea of what it's all about.

HEATH—An idea about what what's all about?

PARKER—This mad desire I have to tell you things. Things that I wouldn't tell anybody else in the world. I mean that. So before I break loose altogether I think I'd better get along.

HEATH (*visibly affected*)—Parker, you needn't be afraid to tell me anything. If it will relieve your mind at all to confide in me, go ahead. Shoot. I'll treat it with the strictest confidence. I give you my word of honor.

PARKER—Yeah?

HEATH—Absolutely.

Well, then, suggests Parker, suppose he should confess being a fugitive from the law? Suppose the police had been trying to hunt him down for years? Suppose he was wanted for a major crime? Would Heath hand him up? As an honest, law-abiding citizen, with a real sense of public duty he would have to, insists Parker.

Now Heath has begun to pace the floor slowly and to recapitulate the Parker suppositions before he answers. He is, as he understands it, to suppose that the story Parker told in the park was just an invention of the mind to stir interest; that having done that Parker had decided that he [Heath] was too big a damn fool to be taken advantage of and so confesses a criminal record. In those circumstances would he [Heath] or would he not hand Parker over to the authorities?

Heath, while he is talking, has worked his way over to a wall cabinet. Now he suddenly reaches in the cabinet and produces a revolver. Leveling it at the astonished Parker he commands him to hold up his hands.

Parker refuses for a moment to pay any attention. He can't take Heath seriously in this surprise rôle. But Heath is not to be talked out of another conviction. He follows Parker about the room until he has forced him to drop his hat and coat and elevate his hands.

"It takes two to play the game of 'who's the damned fool,'" says Heath, calmly keeping Parker covered; "you know that, don't you, Mr. Parker? And what's more you've got me right. I am a decent citizen, with a sense of responsibility and a respect for law and order. Now I don't know what your idea has been in telling me all this, but I'm going to find out."

"Then you don't believe the story I told you in the park, do you?"

"I don't know what to believe or disbelieve, now," answers Heath; "but I'm going to find out the truth before I turn you loose, you can bet on that."

Tokem, coming to answer the doorbell, is thoroughly surprised at what he finds. He is ordered to the door by his employer with instructions that if the caller is a Mr. Chase to let him in.

"I'm going to tell you something," interrupts Parker, a little contemptuously; "I had you tabbed for a smart fellow. You know that, don't you?"

"You had me tabbed for some sort of a 'come on,' that's about the size of it."

"And you had the nerve to ask me why I was so interested in pigeons!"

Frank Chase, another good-looking young man of the business

type and about Heath's age, comes quickly into the room. He cannot at first credit what he sees, but he obediently follows Heath's somewhat excited instructions that he pick up Parker's hat and coat and search the young man for firearms or other weapons. Perhaps they are playing amateur theatricals.

There being no guns on Parker he is permitted, even ordered, to lower his hands and sit down on the divan. And now Heath would tell Chase what has happened. He had met Parker in the park. He had listened to his story. He had brought him home. He had wanted to help him.

"I didn't ask you to help me," interrupts Parker. "I told you I wouldn't accept any help. Why don't you tell the man the truth?"

"Say, what the hell is this?" Chase wants to know.

PARKER (*to* CHASE)—I'll tell you what it is. This man came and sat beside me on a bench in the park today. He got into conversation and he asked me who I was. I told him I couldn't tell him who I was for the simple reason that any story I might tell him would be almost unbelievable. But he insisted. I told him a story. He said he believed it. I said I didn't believe he believed it. He said, "I'll prove it." I asked him how. He said, "Come to my home and I'll show you." Well, I came here with him. He offered me food, clothing, champagne. Promised to take an interest in me. Made all sorts of promises. He even introduced me to the servants here as an old friend of his. Ordered the spare room put in readiness for me right away. Said he wouldn't be satisfied unless I stayed here two or three days. What was I to think about that? What would any man think about such actions? I started to go and he wouldn't let me. I tried to alibi myself out of the house by telling him that I might be a crook or a fake. He laughed that off and still insisted that I stay. Finally I asked him how he'd feel if I turned out to be a murderer or something like that and he whipped out a gun and made me throw up my hands. That's the point we'd reached when you walked in. And that's the whole thing in a nut-shell.

CHASE (*to* HEATH)—Is that all true?

HEATH—Yes, it's true enough, but this fellow's painting the picture in a different . . .

PARKER—Oh, no, there are no "buts" or "ifs" about it. You know it's true; you know damn well it's true. And if you think I'm afraid to tell it to the police authorities, go ahead and ring 'em up and get 'em here. Get 'em here or fetch me to them—

I don't care. You'll find you'll have a little explaining to do on your own account before they're through listening to me. (*Over to* HEATH *now.*) And another thing. Now look here—you're so anxious to find out something about me. What do I know about you? Nothing—except that you said your name was Heath. And how do I know that? Not that I care, but how do I know? How do I know there isn't a catch to this somewhere—this good samaritan stuff of yours? You know that kind of thing isn't being done. Not regularly, it isn't.

Parker is indignant. He doesn't purpose being treated the way they have treated him and just let it go at that. Who, for instance, do they think they are? What's this new one's name? Chase? That doesn't mean a thing to Parker. What kind of a frame is this? This business of bringing him there and holding him? They don't expect to get away with that stuff, do they? Not in 1933!

Suppose he [Parker] turns out to be somebody pretty big. Supposing he should turn out to be one of the really big men of the country—what would they think of that? Of course, he had rather they would believe the story he told in the park, but if they don't want to that's their affair. Now let them call the cops. Parker can hardly wait to speak his little piece.

Heath and Chase are at least nonplussed. Heath would laugh the matter off if he could. He is laughing when he puts the revolver back in the cabinet and admits his defeat. Parker, he says, has won. He has had his little fun. Now let him go.

But Parker doesn't want to go. Certainly he doesn't want to be put out. No, sir. Parker has feelings. Parker has self-respect. And he is not kidding. He never kids. He's straightaway, is Parker. And he wants an apology. A complete apology.

"All right. I'm sorry. I apologize. Are you satisfied now?" asks Heath, looking a little helplessly at Chase.

"You call that an apology, do you?" protests Parker.

HEATH—Well, what kind of an apology do you want?

PARKER—I want to know what you're apologizing for.

HEATH—I don't know myself—I'm damned if I do. (*With a hopeless look at* CHASE.) You're too much for me. I don't get you at all.

PARKER (*defiantly following him up*)—Now no more cracks like that. That's about enough!

HEATH (*his blood up now*)—What! (PARKER *retreats.*)

CHASE—Here, wait a minute. Let me handle this, Joe. (*He comes between them.*) What are you looking for—trouble?

PARKER—Well, I've had plenty of trouble all my life.

CHASE—Oh, you think you can fight, eh?

PARKER (*after a pause*)—Yes, I can fight. I've been in a couple of battles.

CHASE—You have, eh?

PARKER (*snaps this up*)—Yes. (*Another pause.*) Suppose I were to tell you that I used to be a light-weight champion?

CHASE—*You* were?

PARKER—I didn't say I was. I said "suppose" I told you that?

CHASE (*half amused, half sore*)—Oh, shut up!

PARKER (*getting coat and hat*)—Is that so? I'll find out if there isn't some redress for a man in a case like this. I'll report this to Police Headquarters myself.

HEATH (*quickly going after him*)—Come here, Parker. What's the matter with you? Have some common sense.

CHASE—Oh, let him go, Joe. He's a nut!

PARKER (*to* CHASE)—I'm a nut, am I? Well, now you look here, you'll find I'm a pretty tough nut to crack.

Parker has started again for the door and again Heath has intercepted him. He wants Parker to know that he has not been talking to a couple of dubs. He and Chase happen to be smart fellows, a statement that does not impress Parker in the least. If they are smart what's their racket?

They are in no racket, Heath protests, producing a business card announcing that he is with the Consolidated Life Insurance Company of America. Chase also has a card. He is Franklyn Chase of Hall, Metcalf and Chase, one of the city's best known legal firms. So Parker can see that he is in pretty good company.

Still, Parker is not impressed. What do they mean by good company? A couple of swells? Well, he doesn't care who anybody is and he doesn't want anyone to care who he is. Parker wants to be liked for himself and not for what he might be. As for that, he could get some cards printed, too, if he wanted to.

Heath is disappointed that Parker doesn't believe that he and Chase are who they say they are. As for that, Parker was also disappointed that they did not believe he was who he said he was in the park. He is the one who has been picked for a criminal. He is the one at whom a gun has been pointed. And he had made no direct statements. He merely offered a supposition.

Well, Heath is ready to laugh that off, too. Everything should be all right now. He would like to shake hands with Parker and let everything go back to where it was.

Parker, after thinking it over, is also ready to shake hands with Heath. He is glad that Heath feels the way he does about it. Now, if everything is as it was, does the invitation to stay stand as it did?

Heath, a little hesitantly, agrees that it does—if Parker wants to stay—

"If I want to?" bristles Parker. "What do you mean—if I want to? Don't you want me to? It was your own idea, you know. The spare room, and all that."

"All right! All right!" shouts Heath. "I'll go through with it."

"Over my dead body you will," interposes Chase, butting into the argument. "Not a chance!"

Now they are all three at it again, Heath protesting that he knows what he is doing, Chase doubting it, and Parker insisting with increasing vehemence that if, as Chase sneers, they don't know who he is they will damned soon find out. With which statement Parker grabs the phone and asks for Police Headquarters.

Heath and Chase, startled by the call, are on Parker's back in an instant. After a tussle they take the 'phone away from him and Chase has to explain that the call was a mistake. Let Headquarters pay no attention to it.

Parker resents Chase's belligerency. Resents being held there while they swing more and more insults at him. But he doesn't want to talk any more about it. He is all upset and wants to go to his room. Where's the boy?

When Heath, staring foolishly at Parker, protests that he must first see if the room is all right Parker insists that it will be quite all right for him, whatever state it may be in.

Now Heath has dashed out and left Parker and Chase staring watchfully at each other, each trying to size the other up and each evidently mystified. Parker breaks the somewhat tense silence.

"Who the hell do you think you are?" he demands, suddenly, with a half laugh.

" 'Show me to my room'—for God's sake," laughs Chase derisively.

PARKER—You're a big lawyer, are you? A smart fellow! That's pretty good.

CHASE—I thought I'd met them all. But you lead the league, boy. I've got to hand it to you. (*Laughs.*) Used to be a light-weight champion. That's a good one, that is.

PARKER (*chuckling and attracting* CHASE's *attention*)—Come here. Come here a minute.

CHASE (*curiously*)—What?

PARKER—Come here! Come here! (*Looking around to make sure they're alone.*) Does he think I'm sore?

CHASE—I don't know. Aren't you?

PARKER—No. Why should I be? What about—huh? (*Good-naturedly.*) Are you sore at me?

CHASE—Well, I was for the moment. Yes, naturally.

PARKER—You're too smart a fellow for that. (*Pause.*) What was his idea, do you know?

CHASE—His idea about what?

PARKER—About bringing me here.

CHASE—I don't know. I guess it was on account of the story you told him in the park, whatever that was.

PARKER—Yeah? Well, why does he act so funny?

CHASE—Why does *he* act so funny?

PARKER—Yeah.

CHASE—What do you mean, why does he act so funny?

PARKER—Well, you too. Why do you act so funny?

CHASE—Say, are you trying to string me?

PARKER—No, I don't string. I'm straightaway.

CHASE—Yeah?

PARKER—Yeah.

CHASE—Well, what was your idea in trying to call in the police?

PARKER—He started to talk about the police, don't you remember? You heard him.

CHASE—Well, what were you going to say if you got them on the phone?

PARKER—What was I going to say? What do you think I was going to say? What could I say? Not a thing in the world! I was just going to talk to some of the boys down there, that's all.

CHASE—Oh, you know the boys at Police Headquarters, do you?

PARKER—Know them? Do I know the boys at Police Headquarters? (*Chuckles.*) Suppose I were to tell you something.

CHASE (*beating him to it*)—I know. I know. You used to be one of the biggest detectives in the country, is that it?

PARKER (*mock indignation*)—Used to be? What do you mean,

I used to be?

CHASE (*walks away on this*)—Oh, go to hell! Who do you think you're talking to?

PARKER (*following him over*)—Who do you think you're talking to?

CHASE—Just about the freshest proposition I ever met in my life.

PARKER—Is that so? (*Turns and starts for the phone again.*) Well, it won't take me two minutes to prove to you who I am. Just about two minutes, that's all. (*In phone.*) Hello! Get me Police Headquarters! Hurry it up!

CHASE (*rushing over to get phone*)—Say, what the hell—! Give me that phone! Give it to me, do you hear? What sort of a raving bug are you, will you please tell me? (*He gets the phone away from* PARKER.)

HEATH—What is it? What's the matter now?

PARKER—I don't know, he's at me again.

Now Chase must again tell Headquarters to pay no attention to the phone call. It was just a mistake. Heath has called Tokem to get Mr. Parker's hat and coat and Parker is going. Before he goes, however, Heath would have him take a check. A check made out to cash so he will have no trouble negotiating it. Heath is trying, he insists, to show that his heart is in the right place.

To Parker the check is adding insult to injury. Why should they want to make him feel like a beggar? A fine sport Heath has turned out to be.

"You're not even good enough sport to admit that I'm an innocent party to this whole affair," protests Parker, grabbing his coat from Tokem. "There I was sitting in the park minding my own business, hugging up to nature. I was as happy as a fellow could be. You come along with your joke sympathy and your phony promises and bring me here and mix me up with people again. And you had no right doing it. You ought to be ashamed of yourself for what you've done to me."

"Well, I'm awfully sorry you feel that way about it, Parker."

"Well, how did you expect me to feel about it? I told you I preferred the pigeons, didn't I?

Chase has begun to laugh again and that is too much for Parker. It just isn't fair to a fellow to be treated that way. It is a little more than he can stand. The next minute he is in tears. Heath and Chase think at first that Parker is pretending a grief he does not feel, but they are soon convinced the emotion is real and Heath, at least, is sympathetic.

Soon Parker has gained control of himself and is again ready to move on. But he will not take the check. He would hand it to Tokem as a tip. Heath, however, is quick to stop that, so Parker leaves the check on the table.

Parker is headed for the door when the bell rings. A moment later two attractive young women, Elinore Payne and Winnie Lloyd, have been shown in.

The girls are ready for dinner and a show. They are also ready for cocktails. Now they have noticed Parker with an interest that continues through the introductions. Parker, explains Heath, is an old friend who had just dropped in to say hello and is just leaving.

But Parker finds it hard to break away from such attractive company. He is easily urged, in fact, to stay and have a cocktail when Elinore pleads with Heath to make him stay.

"He's in a hurry," laughs Parker as Heath dashes upstairs to dress. "The whole world's in a hurry. We don't any of us know where we're going, but we're all in a hurry to get there, as the fellow says. Now I could understand pigeons being in a hurry, because they've got such a wonderful sense of direction. [This to Chase.] But strange to say, they're never in a hurry. [To Elinore.] They're never in a hurry."

It doesn't occur to Elinore that she has ever wondered about pigeons. As for that Parker doesn't believe the pigeons have ever wondered much about Elinore. Which makes it an even break. It is not easy for Elinore to understand Parker. In fact conversation is lagging and embarrassment increasing. Parker is unperturbed. He does think, however, and tells the girls so, that it was funny that Heath should have introduced him as an old friend when he hadn't set eyes on him until that very afternoon. The mystery implied is quite exciting to Winnie and Elinore.

Even after the cocktails have arrived, Parker is not content to let the matter of identity rest. Does he look like a highwayman? A bandit? A cutthroat, or anything like that? Nor will he be squelched by Chase, nor quieted with a cocktail. He doesn't want a cocktail. He hadn't asked for a cocktail. And he doesn't want to be made to feel like a beggar again, either. He has stood about as much—

A large, forbidding gentleman has walked in the door. His name is Gilroy. He has come to inquire what all the fuss is about. His authority is displayed in a detective's badge which he

Paul Hansen photo, New York.

"PIGEONS AND PEOPLE"

"You know, it's a long time since I sat between two beautiful girls like this," says Parker. ". . . Two beautiful girls, two beautiful hands. . . . The gentle touch of a woman's hand . . . Memories . . . Well, I guess that is about all life is made up of—just memories."

(*Alney Alba, George M. Cohan and Eleanor Audley*)

takes from his pocket. He would like to know who has been ringing up Police Headquarters from that number.

"Do you women know anything about it?" Gilroy demands.

"No, they don't know anything about it," quickly answers Parker. "I'll speak for them."

GILROY—You speak for yourself and wait until you're spoken to! You don't look so good.

PARKER—I feel all right.

GILROY—I'm not inquiring about your health. I was speaking to these two women.

PARKER (*correcting him*)—Ladies.

GILROY (*resenting the correction*)—Now don't you get sassy. I don't stand to be corrected by anybody. (*Turns to the girls.*) Do you ladies know anything about this telephone thing?

ELINORE—No, not a thing.

GILROY—You don't know anything about it, eh?

WINNIE—No, we just dropped in a few minutes ago.

GILROY (*seeing cocktails*)—Oh, I see. Just dropped in to get a cocktail, eh? Well, go ahead and drink 'em, I'm not looking. (*To* PARKER.) An apartment speakeasy, huh?

PARKER—You've got no right to talk like that, you know you haven't. What's the matter with you?

GILROY—Say, what do you think you are, a school teacher?

PARKER—I'm not saying what I am.

GILROY—Well, we'll find out what you are, and who you are.

CHASE—I wish to God you would!

GILROY (*turning to* CHASE)—Say! What was the reason for the argument you were having with this fellow when I walked in?

CHASE—He started a dozen arguments without any reason at all.

GILROY—Is that why you rang up Police Headquarters?

PARKER.—He didn't ring up Police Headquarters. I rang up Police Headquarters.

GILROY—Oh, you did, eh?

PARKER—Yes, and he grabbed the phone away from me twice.

GILROY—Is that right?

CHASE—Yes, because he had no reason for calling up Police Headquarters.

Gilroy would like to know who really lives in that house, but he will not let them send Tokem for Heath. He will do any sending that is necessary. Meantime they may as well all be seated.

Now Gilroy has rediscovered the cocktails. There are plenty of them. Must be quite a party. And the check Heath has left on the table. A check for $500! Where did that come from?

It is a check, Parker informs him, that Heath had offered him and that he had refused to take. He had refused to take it because they had tried to force it on him.

Gilroy can't quite understand that. If Parker had refused five hundred, how much did he want?

Gilroy has taken Tokem and gone to interview Heath, leaving an Officer McGuire on guard in the hall.

Now the girls' curiosity is feverish. What is the mixup all about anyway? Who is this Parker person?

Chase tells them of the meeting of Heath and Parker in the park; of Parker's "cock and bull story" and of Parker's "acting like a damn fool ever since."

Parker is quickly on the defensive. He has neither said nor done anything that was not straightaway, and everything they have said and done has been ridiculous. Here they have been trying to throw him out of the house, which is silly. The man to throw out is Gilroy, the detective. He has no right breaking into a man's house without a search warrant. Parker can prove that. If they think he doesn't know what he is talking about, give him the phone and he will show them—

Before Chase can interfere Parker is at the phone again calling Police Headquarters and insisting that he get it. Chase has another tussle with him to get the phone back.

Tokem has come for Chase, which leaves Parker alone with Winnie and Elinore, and right merrily does he try to entertain them. Recites the story of his meeting with Heath in the park and of the things that have happened to him since. That, Parker insists, is all his own fault. He never should have mixed in with people again.

"You know what this fellow Heath says to me this afternoon?" he asks, his mood becoming serious again. "He says: 'You're just disappointed, that's all.' He doesn't know how right he was. I am disappointed. Horribly disappointed. I'm more than disappointed. I'm heartbroken. That's what's the matter with me, I'm heartbroken."

Parker has sat down on the divan and drawn out his handkerchief. Now he is in tears again and the girls, wonderingly sympathetic, try to comfort him.

Winnie thinks perhaps if he would tell them the story he told

Heath in the park it would help. But Parker won't do that. They wouldn't believe it, anyway. Heath probably is telling it to the cop now. The cop will never believe it either.

They have sat down beside him now, and their proximity makes him sentimental.

"You know it's a long time since I sat between two beautiful girls like this," says Parker, reaching for a hand of each and noting their rings. "And it's a long time since I saw two such beautiful rings. Two beautiful girls, two beautiful rings, two beautiful hands . . . The gentle touch of a woman's hand. . . . Memories. . . . Well, I guess that's about all life is made up of—just memories."

ELINORE (*in his mood*)—It seems so, doesn't it?

PARKER (*smiling sadly*)—Yes. (*To* WINNIE.) What do you think?

WINNIE (*in the same mood*)—I think so.

PARKER (*to* ELINORE)—She thinks so, too. Well, we're all thinking anyway, aren't we? I'm thinking things about you. You're thinking things about me. All three of us sitting here thinking things about each other. It's wonderful, isn't it? (*A pause.*) You know there was something I was going to say to you two girls, but I guess I'd better not.

ELINORE (*interested*)—Oh, go on, Mr. Parker, say it.

WINNIE (*anxiously*)—Yes, please do. What was it?

PARKER—Well, suppose I were to ask you two girls to kiss me?

ELINORE (*indignantly*)—To what?

WINNIE (*indignantly*)—To kiss you?

PARKER—Well, what are you hollering about? I didn't ask you to kiss me. I said suppose I asked you to kiss me. I don't want you to kiss me. I don't want to be kissed. I just want to be left alone, that's all. I told that to Heath today when he sat beside me on the bench in the park. Did I ask you girls to come and sit beside me now? I did not. It was your own idea. There you are, you're just as unreasonable as your gentlemen friends. Trying to blame me for something you did yourselves. Oh, well, it's all right, let it go. It's my own fault for mixing in with people again. Well, I guess the only thing to do when a fellow gets all muddled up is to turn on the radio. (*He turns it on and the melody of "Strike Me Pink" comes over the air. He listens for a moment, smiles and then starts dancing about the room.*) There you are, that's life. That's what the boys and girls like, that's what they call having a good time. Tiring themselves all out.

Getting out of breath—bumping into everybody, wearing out their shoes and everything else.

Parker has danced around to Winnie and asked her to join him. Winnie doesn't want to dance. He dances on to Elinore. She is persuaded by Winnie to try it. Parker and Elinore are dancing a little wildly and Winnie is laughing at them when Heath, followed by Chase, Gilroy, Tokem and Giles, the housekeeper, return. Heath is immediately excited. Just what is the idea, he would like to know, as he deliberately steps between Elinore and Parker.

The idea, explains Parker, is that Elinore wanted to dance with him. He had asked Winnie to dance, but she had put Elinore off on him. That's the truth.

Now the police have interfered again. Gilroy will settle all this funny business by taking Parker with him. Which is quite all right with Parker. He will be happy wherever he is. It is his nature to be as happy one place as another.

The phone bell rings. Headquarters wants to know who was the last one to ring up. Gilroy would explain that he has got a new kind of guy there. Again Parker objects. He will do his own talking to Headquarters. And does.

Headquarters is puzzled and curt with Parker. Headquarters wants to know who Parker is and why. Parker is equally curt and defiant. He wants to know who this fellow Gilroy is and why. Perhaps he had better talk with the Commissioner. As a citizen and taxpayer he is certainly entitled to know something. Let him talk with the Commissioner—

After another tussle Gilroy manages to get the phone back. It's just a nuisance case, he assures Headquarters and can be handled.

"And I suppose now you're going to take credit for a big sensational arrest," sneers Parker, as the policeman puts up the phone. "Well, if I'm nailed there's the man deserves the credit. [Indicating Heath and continuing to Heath.] And I'll see that you get full credit for it, too, Mr. Heath. [To Gilroy.] And let me tell you something else. If you hand me up, don't be surprised if anything happens. Don't be surprised if a couple of your best friends and pals go up with me. Because I'm telling you now if I have to tell my story to the court I tell it all. Every bit of it. And I'm willing to do that now. I'm tired. Any man would be tired protecting a lot of people, so if you want to hand up your best friends and pals and be the laughing stock of every regular cop in town go ahead. I'm ready. Let's get the whole damn thing over with."

Gilroy is more worried than he would like to appear. Nor does he know exactly what to do next. Heath doesn't want to make any complaint against Parker. What, demands Parker, has he to complain against? There he was, sitting in the park, minding his own business— And he is perfectly willing to go back to the park and continue minding his own business. He will go back singing, too. Singing and dancing—

Gilroy has had enough. He won't hold them any longer. He lets Chase go on ahead to the dinner engagement with the girls. Heath stops behind to press the check on Parker. Parker will not take it. He's no beggar. He told them that. Let Gilroy take it.

Gilroy can't get Parker at all. He'd like to. He'd like to know something more about those two pals Parker had spoken about showing up. He doesn't believe the story Parker told Heath in the park. He doesn't believe any man likes pigeons better than people. And when he thinks of Parker's refusing Heath's check he has to laugh.

That laugh hurts Parker's feelings. He wants to bust out crying again. He does bust out crying again. Parker's human. He's no freak. He has the same sensibilities as Gilroy or anyone else. He is crying unrestrainedly when Heath comes back.

"What is it? What's the matter now?" Heath wants to know.

"His feelings are hurt," explains Gilroy.

HEATH (*crossing to divan*)—Now look here, Parker, you've got to listen to me. This is straight from the shoulder—man to man. I've never been so sorry about anything in my life as I am about this whole occurrence. I'm very unhappy about it. I feel guilty as the devil, I do honestly. I'm to blame—it's all my fault. I admit it. I admitted that to you, didn't I, Gilroy?

GILROY—Sure you did.

HEATH—I apologize, Parker. I offer a thousand apologies. Now will you please shake hands and tell me once and for all that you accept my apology. Come on, Parker, I've got to go—I've got people waiting—an important engagement. God, I've admitted everything.

PARKER (*getting over his cry*)—Will you admit one thing more?

HEATH—I'll admit anything. What is it?

PARKER—That you didn't believe the story I told you in the

park?

HEATH (*impatiently*)—But I did believe the story you told me in the park. (*To* GILROY.) I told you I believed it, didn't I, Gilroy?

GILROY—Sure you did.

PARKER—But do you still believe it—do you still believe it?

HEATH—Yes, yes, yes, I still believe it.

PARKER—Can I depend on that?

HEATH—Absolutely.

PARKER—You give me your word on that?

HEATH—I do. I give you my word.

PARKER (*rising and extending his hand*)—All right then, let's sake hands. (*They shake hands.*)

HEATH—Thanks, Parker. And there're no hard feelings.

PARKER—Not on my part.

HEATH—Fine.

PARKER—Am I back where I was with you?

HEATH—You bet you are, old boy.

PARKER—And does the invitation to stay here still go?

HEATH—What do you mean?

PARKER—You know what I mean. You asked me to stay here for a few days, didn't you? Don't you want to go through with it?

HEATH—All right, all right, I'll go through with it.

PARKER—Then why don't you have the boy show me to my room? What are you stalling for? I'm all tired out.

Tokem is called. Let him show Parker to his room and see that he is given every attention. Heath is determined to go through with his promise, even against the advice of Gilroy. There are further assurances of perfect understanding, there is more handshaking, and Heath and Gilroy are gone.

Now Tokem would make Parker comfortable. But Parker is not ready to be made comfortable. Nor ready to go to his room. He wanders over to the piano and sits down. He is singing a song about life when Giles, the housekeeper, reappears. Parker would talk with Giles. Just between the two of them Parker would like to know from Giles why, if she is as fond of Mr. Heath as he can see she is, she does not go to Heath and warn him of this other girl he thinks he is sweet on? Why should she accept defeat at the hands of this other woman? Let her tell Heath she loves him—

But, insists Giles, she does not love Mr. Heath. She certainly does not.

"Thank God—thank God—thank God!" ejaculates a thankful Parker, his mood becoming suddenly tender. "Miss Giles, don't you see that this was just my way of finding out if I had the right to say precisely what I'm going to say to you now. Suppose I were to tell you that from the moment I set eyes on you something here [Indicates heart.] some indescribable something, cried out, 'There she is, that's what you've been waiting for all your life.' Suppose I were to tell you that—"

But Miss Giles has leaped to her feet and is yelling lustily for Tokem. How dare Parker talk so to her? She would have Tokem show him to his room at once. Which is good news to Parker.

"Miss Giles, I congratulate you," he says to her, his mood again changing completely. "I heartily congratulate you. You've been tried and found true. This has all been my way of ascertaining as to whether or not my character reading of you was correct. I had you tabbed for a sensible, brainy, superior sort of person. Free from evil-mindedness, jealousy, deceit, and all the other nasty little traits so characteristic of housekeeping females. Why, you're not even frivolous, not even with me. And, my God! I'm a man who's worked magic with a thousand housekeepers in my time. Again I congratulate you, Miss Giles, and I shall make my report to Mr. Heath that you're certainly deserving of his implicit confidence, and any other little consideration he cares to show. And perhaps an increase in wages, who can tell?"

Giles is greatly relieved and rather thrilled by Parker's interest.

Tokem is next. Parker would like to go in with Tokem, share and share alike. By the time discovery's made Tokem will have had time to plant the stuff and Parker will be a thousand miles away. "All you have to do is play dead," promises Parker, "and we share and share alike. Where's the safe?"

Tokem is startled! Tokem is puzzled! Tokem no steal! Tokem has promised his mother! Tokem will neither go in with Parker, nor will he do the job himself. Tokem honest boy! Which gives Parker great pleasure.

"I congratulate you, my boy," Parker assures the still startled Jap. "You've been tried and found true. I shall make my report to Mr. Heath that you're an honorable, God-fearing, faithful little man. I shall also suggest that a few extra dollars be slipped into your envelope as an appreciation of that fact. You're a deserving lad. I congratulate you."

Tokem is also greatly pleased.

Now Dr. Frisby has arrived. He is a funny, nervous, apprehensive little man from upstairs. He had had a telephone call from Mr. Heath suggesting that he drop in and inquire of Giles about a Mr. Parker. He wants to talk to Parker about Parker, but Parker is much too modest a man to talk about himself.

"Let me understand this," says Parker, walking excitedly about Dr. Frisby. "You're Dr. Frisby from upstairs, and the fellow got you on the phone from the outside and asked you to come downstairs and find out what was the matter with me upstairs. Is that right?"

"Well, hardly that, no," answer the doctor, trying to dismiss the subject.

"You know, it's awfully funny to me," Parker goes on; "it must be twice as funny to you, being a doctor. The world's so topsy-turvy that the minute a man acts natural these days, they send for a doctor to come in and look him over."

Parker is interested, also, in finding out what kind of a doctor Dr. Frisby is. Does he specialize when he is faking, or is he just a general faker? Parker was a little afraid that Frisby might be a psychologist, a psychologist without a sense of humor, which it would be hard to imagine. The idea of being a psychologist is funny to start with.

Dr. Frisby would continue his investigations. He is sitting facing Parker and suggesting tests. Parker, refusing to be serious, had rather play "patty-cake" with the doctor. Parker knows what is happening. He knows that they all think he is a crackpot. Why?

"Because I act natural," explains Parker. "Because I shoot straightaway. Because I cannot conduct myself in direct contradiction to my nature. Because I won't trail along with this damn fool idea of taking the whole thing seriously."

FRISBY—Of taking what seriously?

PARKER—Life. As it's being lived today. Who is he? What's he got? How'd he get it? What day is it? What's the date? How's the weather? Stocks are up—stocks are down. Down with the rich. Pity the poor. God bless you, old pal. How are the folks? That's all there is to it, Doc. It's a fake. The whole thing's a fake. You know it's a fake as well as I do!

FRISBY (*chuckles*)—Well, all that may be very true, but what are we going to do about it?

PARKER—Do about it? Why side step it. Laugh at it. Run away from it, the same as I'm doing.

FRISBY—Run away from what?

PARKER—Life. The whole silly business. Live in your own world, Doc. Think your own thoughts and say them. I explained all that to him in the park today.

FRISBY—To whom?

PARKER—Heath. That's where I met him, in the park. That's where I told him my story. He said he believed it. I know now that he didn't believe it, or why should he have sent for you?

FRISBY—I see. I see.

PARKER—You see what?

FRISBY—Why do you keep saying: "You see what"?

PARKER—Well, why do you keep saying: "I see"? It's as fair for one as it is for another.

Dr. Frisby's assistant, an attractive young woman, has brought his visiting bag. She is one, Parker can see, who could be of great assistance to any doctor. But it would be just as well if she were a little cautious. Doctor's wives have been known to return from expected visits unexpectedly.

"Just answer me one little question before you go," pleads Parker, when the doctor would dismiss Miss Graham. "This is just between the three of us. Do you really love him or is this just sheer desperation?"

The doctor orders Miss Graham curtly to run along. His tone isn't a proper tone, Parker objects. No doctor should speak to his assistant as though she were no better than a slave. Parker has a mind to punish Dr. Frisby for that tone. He has his coat half off when Miss Graham screams and Giles and Tokem come running back.

"Is something the matter?" demands Giles, excitedly.

"Yes. Something's the matter with me," answers Parker. "At least everybody seems to think so. But the doctor's just about to tell us what it is. [To Frisby.] But I warn you now, Doc, examinations are a waste of time. I'll give you the report in advance. Steady pulse, normal pressure, strong heart, one hundred per cent physically fit. As to my mental condition, you can see for yourself. I'm gay, cheerful, happy as a bird. I laugh in the right place, cry in the right place. All the machinery in perfect running order, everything under control, and incidentally, having a hell of a good time. So long, Doc. Glad to have met you. Sorry I can't use you. Hope to see you again some time. Wish you the best of luck. [Going to Miss Graham.] Same to you, Miss Graham. Pleased to have met you. It's nice to know—

Be kind to the doctor and watch out for the wife. [To Tokem.] And now, my boy, if you'll be good enough to show me to my room, I'll spruce up a bit, brush off the garments, polish the nails, shine the shoes, and disguise myself as a dandy little dude."

"Doctor, do you think he's—" Miss Graham asks, as Tokem and Parker disappear.

"I don't know," confesses the doctor. "I couldn't say right now whether he's a very smart man or the biggest damned fool I ever met."

A moment later Parker has sent Tokem back to tell Miss Graham he wants to see her at once on an important matter. Dr. Frisby is indignant. Giles thinks perhaps she had better go. But Miss Graham decides to answer the summons herself. She will scream if she needs help.

The doorbell announces the arrival of Mrs. Dunlap, Heath's sister, a pleasant young woman a few years younger than Heath. She is surprised that she was not met at the station and that she is not expected. She had telegraphed from Albany. She is also surprised to hear that there is a man, a curious kind of a man, in the spare room. Since when has a sister been turned out to make room for a guest!

Tokem has gone to put Parker out of the spare room and Miss Graham has come back laughing. Dr. Frisby will never believe it when she tells him what it was Parker had wanted to see her about. He wanted her to go in partnership with him to shake down the doctor. And when she wouldn't do that he promised to speak to the doctor about raising her salary.

"Seems to be a little room trouble here of some kind," Parker is saying as he comes downstairs, followed by Tokem, and meets Mrs. Dunlap. "First the boy says it's my room. Now the boy comes and says it's your room. Of course I hate to be discommoded in this way but it brings back old times at that. [To Frisby.] It brings back old times, Doc. It's a long time since I was put out of a lady's room. [To Dunlap.] But it seems to me there ought to be room for all of us in this world. There's no room for an argument there. What is this, a rooming house? I thought it was a private home of some kind."

Mrs. Dunlap has come all the way from Albany to see her brother, she explains to Parker, but he finds it difficult to credit that news, knowing a good deal about brothers and sisters, and also something about Albany. And about husbands left in Albany. Of course he is perfectly willing to give up the spare room to the lady. Let Tokem take her luggage up and bring back his hat and coat. That's fair enough. Mrs. Dunlap says she hates to take the room. Very well, Parker will stay in it. But now Mrs. Dunlap has decided that she wants the room and that amuses Parker.

"I offer the room. You refuse the room. You fight for the room. I give you the room, and now you go to the room without a how-do-you-do—thank you—what have you, or anything else. Is that the way it's going to be?" Parker has followed Mrs. Dunlap to the stairs and sees her out. "There you are," he continues to the others, "that's life. That's gratitude. That's what I say. What's the use? Why try? It's a fake. The whole thing's a fake."

FRISBY—Say, what are you trying to do, make a fool out of life?

PARKER—Well, why should I permit life to make a fool out of me? That's what's the matter with life, Doc. It's had too much of its own way. Somebody's got to give it a battle. Why not I? You see, there's nothing straightaway. It's all curves, corners, indecision, confusion. Now there was a pretty good sample right there. (*Indicates.*) That girl there. She wanted the room. You know sooner or later we've got to come down to cases, or it'll get so nobody'll believe anything anybody says. And how are we going to cure it—just standing still—trailing along? The truth, that's the only cure. You're a doctor, you ought to know that. Now look, Doc. I'm satisfied that there isn't a problem of any kind that couldn't be settled in ten minutes, if we'd all quit stalling and trying to be so darned polite. And that takes in all problems, mind you, national, international, social, political, economic and otherwise. (*To* GRAHAM.) Now here's something they ought to teach in the public schools. Life was never supposed to be a riddle, an everlasting battle of wits. That wasn't the original idea; it couldn't have been. (*To them both.*) It's all because of this thing they call diplomacy. That's what's muddled us all up. And you know what diplomacy is. It's a fake business. It's conducted and controlled by a gang of professional sidesteppers, and they fight off common sense like the doctor here would fight a case of yellow fever. And for the very good reason that once common sense gets the upper hand of any argument, the diplomat's gone. He's lost his graft. He's out of work. And that's where he's going to find himself very shortly, you mark my words, because this whole thing's a mess. It's got to be cleaned up. We've got to find some straightaway fellow to do it. But don't look at me. I didn't build Radio City. I don't want the job. I'd rather string it out with the pigeons.

This whole adventure's a joke, Parker's agreed, but who is the joke on? Giles has rushed in to get Dr. Frisby. Mrs. Dunlap has fainted. Now they have all rushed upstairs to Mrs. Dunlap. Only Parker is left when Heath and Chase come in. They have left the girls in the car. Heath had been worried and had to come back. He is even more worried now when he hears that his sister is there and that she has fainted.

There is excitement now. Chase demanding to know what added thing Parker has contributed to make Mrs. Dunlap hysterical? And why doesn't Parker get out and go where he belongs? Chase would like to take Parker out on the sidewalk and kick hell out of him. Parker doesn't think he would like that, knowing exactly what Chase is up to.

Heath rushes in to suggest that Chase go tell the girls not to wait. He can't leave his sister. Parker has frightened the life out of her.

"Now what have you been up to?" Chase demands of Parker.

"I've been up to nothing up to now," answers Parker.

"You heard what he said, the woman's hysterical."

"So are you. So is he. So is everybody. Why blame me for a world condition?"

Miss Graham has come in excitedly looking for Dr. Frisby's bag. And gone out excitedly. The doorbell has rung and Tokem shows in Gilroy the detective.

"So you're still here, are you?" says Gilroy, catching sight of Parker.

"I knew you were going to say that," answers Parker, laughing. "He [Chase] said the same thing when he walked in. That's what's the matter with the whole works. You all say the same thing—you all do the same thing. You're making a fool out of the Declaration of Independence. The Great United States of America. They ought to call it the great united state of mind. You're just going through the motions—the daily exercise, if you ask me."

Gilroy has come back to return the check to Mr. Heath. Heath doesn't want it. Gilroy can't take it. Parker has refused it. It just goes round and round and nothing happens.

"That's the foreign war debt situation all over again," insists Parker. "They're all paying each other money and none of them know who they're collecting from. You know what I could do?

I could go over there and settle that whole thing, if I could get those babies to think straightaway. But you know why they won't think straightaway? They're too damned diplomatic for anything like that."

Gilroy thinks perhaps he had better take Parker along after all. On what charge? On a charge of disturbing the peace and being a public nuisance.

"All right," agrees Parker. "My counter charge is conspiracy —bribing an officer of the law. You've got a check in your pocket for five hundred dollars, signed by the man that brought me here. Why did he bring me here? Why does he want to get rid of me? Why the five hundred dollars? You want to contest it? Come on, I'll go with you."

Elinore and Winnie have come up from the car. Mrs. Dunlap, fit again, is down from her room. She would like to hear from her brother just who this Parker person is but, as Parker explains, Heath can only tell her the story he [Parker] had told him in the park and he doesn't believe the story he heard in the park.

"Come on, Parker. No more nonsense. Come along," calls Gilroy, and adds, a moment later: "Now listen. For the last time, are you going to go out of this house with me or not?"

"No, sir. Not a chance. Not with you. I'm willing to go, but not with you," says Parker. "If I go, I go alone. I want to be alone. That's the only time I'm happy is when I'm alone. . . . I can't get along with people. That's why I hang out with pigeons. I told him that too.

"I don't know how in God's name you put up with each other—on the square I don't. Why, it's a mad house, a monkey cage. You can't live in it and be yourself. Not if you have any convictions or strength of character. I couldn't stand the wear and tear of it. It's too much for me. And it's all so childish—the whole thing is so childish. Now look. There's the Police Department. Take a look at the Police Department. Organized to keep the peace. [To Gilroy.] Where do they keep it? Where is it? [To the others.] Isn't that good? [Laughing.] And the big doctor—the great reliever of pain—the great diagnostician. [To Frisby.] Diagnose my case, will you, Doc? Not a chance, is there? You bet there isn't. [To the others.] The old doc doesn't know right now whether I ought to be put in a strait jacket or sent to the United States Senate. [To Frisby.] Now do you, on the square? [To the others—indicating Chase.] It's just a guessing contest with these boys, that's all. And the lawyer. The great representative of justice. That's pretty good too. He wouldn't hesitate for a minute to take the meanest man in the world, defend him, and try to make him look like a public benefactor. [To Chase.] Now would you, on the square? [To the others.] Now isn't that childish? [Laughs. Looks at Mrs. Dunlap.] And preachers. And girls that marry preachers. Preachers in Albany and all other stops. Sermonizing. And what's the sermon? I ask you, what's the sermon? [Pointing above.] Is it what he preached, or is it diplomacy? [Laughs.] Why put up with it? Why take it seriously? Not I. I'm cured. [To Heath.] Well, I'm going. But when I go, just let me go. And don't snoop. Don't try to find out anything more about me at all, because I'm telling you now that anything you might find out about me would only confirm the story I told you in the park. So take my tip, play it my way. I don't care who anybody is. With me a pigeon's a pigeon, and the park's the park. And that's where you'll find me most any afternoon, in case you want to take another look. But remember, from now on I don't want to be disturbed. And just one parting word. Don't go telling any authors about me. These fellows that write books and plays—don't do that. Because I don't want to be written, not the way they write. There's no trick ending to me. I don't want to turn out to be anybody but just who I am."

FRISBY—Well, for God's sake, who are you?

PARKER (*smiles, indicating* HEATH)—I'm the fellow that told him the story in the park. (*To the others.*) And as far as I'm concerned that's the end of the story. If you want another chapter, you can fix it up yourselves. (*Chuckles.*) Well, I'm going. And I'm going alone. Yep, I'm going. (*A pause. Looks from one to another.*) Well, don't I even get the usual good-by?

ALL (*in unison*)—Good-by.

PARKER (*laughs heartily*)—There's another damn fool habit, you know, that hello and good-by. (*Mimics.*) Hello, good-by—hello, good-by. (*Laughs again.*) Who is he? What's he got? How'd he get it? What day is it? What's the date? How's the weather? Stocks are down. Stocks are up. (*Starting for the doorway.*) Down with the rich. Pity the poor. God save the King. (*As he exits.*) Merry Christmas. Happy New Year. It's a fake. The whole thing's a fake.

The outer door has slammed after Parker. Gilroy thinks perhaps he had better follow him and Heath agrees. Let Gilroy get the answer and let them know.

Dr. Frisby and Miss Graham have gone. Winnie and Elinore think they could stand a cocktail. Tokem is sent to shake them up, and the girls follow after.

Now Chase would know finally just how Heath happened to pick Parker up and why. But Heath is of no mind to go into that again. He only hopes Gilroy will find out something about him. He [Parker] would certainly make a great character in a story. Chase admits that much but insists there would have to be a trick ending of some sort to him.

They are both agreed that whoever Parker is he's somebody. That's certain. At which instant the phone bell rings. It's Gilroy, and what Gilroy has to say is exciting to Heath.

HEATH (*at phone*)—He did? . . . Himself? . . . No! . . . Well, how did you get him to prove it to you . . . (*Laughs.*) You don't mean it!

CHASE (*impatiently*)—What is it?

HEATH (*waving to* CHASE *to be quiet*)—Say, Gilroy, listen. Tell this to Chase, will you? Chase . . . Yes, wait, I'll put him on. (*Handing* CHASE *the phone.*) Here's your trick ending.

CHASE (*taking phone*)—Are you kidding?

HEATH—No. Go on and get it, it's a knockout.

CHASE (*in phone*)—Hello, Gilroy . . . Chase . . . Yes . . . No! . . . On the square? (*Laughs and looks at* HEATH *who is enjoying it hugely.*) Well, I'll be damned . . . (*Laughs.*)

HEATH—Can you beat it?

CHASE (*motions* HEATH *to be quiet*)—Well, I just said that I knew he was somebody . . . What? No, never. Not from us . . . Not a chance . . . Hold on a second, I'll put Heath on. (*Handing phone to* HEATH.) Here, talk to this fellow, will you, Joe?

HEATH (*in phone*)—Hello . . . Hello, Gilroy . . . What? . . . No, no, not a chance . . . You tell him for us that nobody will ever find out as far as we're concerned.

CHASE—Tell him we won't even tell the folks that are here.

HEATH (*nods to* CHASE, *speaking in phone*)—Listen, Gilroy. Tell him we won't even tell the folks that are here. And look. Tell him I'll mind my own business after this.

CHASE (*laughing*)—Tell him to tend to his own pigeons and you'll tend to yours.

HEATH (*laughing as he repeats into phone*)—Tell him I'll tend to my own pigeons and he can tend to his. (*Laughs.*) Yes, that's the idea, yes. (*He is still laughing and talking into the phone and* CHASE *is laughing also as the curtain falls.*)

ONE SUNDAY AFTERNOON

A Comedy in Two Acts

By James Hagan

THE production of "One Sunday Afternoon" in mid-February was one of the happier adventures of the theatre season. Obscurely written by James Hagan, actor-playwright-stage manager, whose previous efforts had not registered in these parts; obscurely produced by Leo Bulgakov, a Russian actor, and an associate, Leslie Spillers; obscurely cast with an actor named Lloyd Nolan, unknown to Broadway save in a very minor capacity, playing the leading rôle, the play was also greeted by a press divided in its opinions as to its worth as entertainment.

A few reviewers were inclined to shout its praises. The others would pass it by as a quite commonplace addition to the Broadway list. One section of the audience remained after the first performance to block the aisles and cheer. Other sections were in the usual hurry to reach the exits.

The public reception was also slow and uncertain. Business was just good enough to be tantalizing. There was no bankroll to sustain even so much of a run as might be necessary to make the public acquainted with the comedy. The actors were already on half salaries or less. And just as things began to look a little bright along came the Bank Holiday.

That week "One Sunday Afternoon" was withdrawn. The next week the head of the town's largest cut-rate theatre ticket agency, Matthew Zimmerman by name, having faith in Mr. Hagan's play as one his public would appreciate, revived the comedy at popular prices. It was still running successfully in late June, after having come within a single vote of tying the leader for the Pulitzer prize award as the best American play of the year.

The virtues of "One Sunday Afternoon" are found, as they usually are found in the popular drama, in its simplicity and human characterization. It is the story of people other people know and understand. It relates an adventure that awakens reminiscent recollections of similar personal adventures, experienced or imagined. And it happens to have been cast and directed by Mr. Bulgakov, whose training was with Stanislavsky and the Moscow Art Theatre, with judgment and skill.

At the opening of the play we are in the dentist's office of "Biff" Grimes "on Third Street, just around the corner from Market, in Hillsdale." It is a typical small-town dentist's layout, with a large window at the back of the office overlooking the street.

Facing the window is a dentist's chair of white enamel. Near it stand a gas tank and a small instrument cabinet. It is a Sunday afternoon in August, and Biff Grimes is discovered, his coat off, his collar off, his sleeves rolled up, reclining in the chair usually occupied by his patients.

"Biff is a large, coarse type of man, good-natured, past the middle span of life. In his younger days he would fight at the drop of a hat, but Biff's bark has always been worse than his bite."

At a small table in a corner of the office sits "Snappy" Downer, a thin, dried-up little man of about Biff's age. On the table is a quart whiskey bottle, half empty, and three or four glasses. Both Biff and Snappy have had a few drinks and are feeling it slightly. Snappy, who has had more than Biff, is remembering the songs of his youth, songs that were popular in the '90s. At the moment he is interested in the one about Bill Bailey—

"Won't you come home, Bill Bailey, won't you come home?"
She moans the whole day lo-hong.
"I'll do the washing, darling, I'll pay the rent,
I know I've done you wro-hong."

Biff comes in on the "wro-hong," finishing strong but a bit sour. They can't remember the next verse. Snappy would go back to letting darling pay the rent, but Biff votes for something new.

Snappy tries "Good-by, Dolly, I must leave you—though it—fight the foe—" Amy Grimes, calling from the next room, doesn't care for that one. Amy, in fact, would have them stop their noise, and she is not at all impressed by Biff's plea when he calls back that this is Snappy's first visit in a long time and that he is enjoying himself.

"The little woman doesn't understand," Biff explains. "Nothing artistic about her."

Snappy has an idea that it might be better if Biff were to sing something. Biff used to have a good voice. But Biff is not entertaining this afternoon. Snappy brought the bottle over and it is Snappy's party.

"Biff Grimes, the well-known dentist of Hillsdale, was entertained on Sunday afternoon by 'Snappy' Downer, the man who sells fish and crabs at Duncan's market." That is the way the news should read, so far as Biff is concerned.

Another little drink. Another little song. Another vigorous little protest from Amy. As respects Amy's protest Biff would have Snappy understand that he is boss in his own home. He'll drink when he wants to, and sing when he wants to.

Snappy tunes up "In the Good Old Summer Time—" but Biff doesn't care for that. Makes him quite angry, in fact. "Dear old summer time" brings up something to Biff and he doesn't want to hear it. That's all of that.

They go over to "Wait Till the Sun Shines, Molly," and, with Biff again coming in strong, manage to get through the entire song. There's a song, says Biff, that's both sweet and humble! Biff likes that kind of song.

Again Snappy would go back to "In the Good Old Summer Time," and again stands in danger of having his head punched. Biff has taken up "Meet me at St. Louie, Louie, meet at the Fair. Don't tell me those lights are shining anywhere's but there—" when Amy again interrupts. Amy, the intimation is plain, will be out there in a minute and if she does come they'll both be jounced right out of the house—

"You see what I have to put up with," says Biff, reveling in self-pity. "It's a shame. A man can't have a little peace and comfort but what his wife—" [He pauses while he pours himself a small drink.] "That's another thing—should be in the marriage laws. I'd say to all women when they get married—'Look here, you mind your own business and leave your husband alone' —right?"

"Right!" agrees Snappy.

Biff—Good old Snappy. We used to be kids together—remember Avery's Park—way back in—

Snappy—There was you and me and Beansy Miller and Hugo Barnstead.

Biff (*his eyes narrow*)—Yes—Hugo Barnstead.

Snappy—And Virginia Brush—you was stuck on her.

Biff—No, I wasn't—I was just—

Snappy (*teasing*)—Yes, you was, Biff—you was in love with her. And you used to sing— (*Sings.*) "In the good old summer time."

Biff (*forces a smile*)—Sure I used to sing that song—Virginia liked it.

SNAPPY—She was a swell girl—Hugo stole her away and she was yours.

BIFF (*his anger mounting*)—Hugo was just a plain everyday skunk. I never liked him. I bet I would have married Virginia if it hadn't been for him. He stole her. It's an awful thing for a skunk to steal another man's girl.

SNAPPY—I never did.

BIFF—It ain't right. Virginia never cared for him. I was the one she was nuts about. (*Pause—he is thinking.*) Hugo Barnstead! I'd like to get my two hands on him. What I wouldn't do to him.

SNAPPY (*maliciously*)—You're not jealous, are you, Biff?

BIFF—Say—Biff Grimes is too big a man to get jealous. I wouldn't get jealous just—haven't I got Amy? Haven't we been married for—shucks, I didn't care about Virginia—

SNAPPY—Yes, you did, Biff.

BIFF—No, I was just—

SNAPPY—What would you say if I told you they were in town? They are stopping at the hotel across the street—they're on their way to Oakley—I saw them.

BIFF—At the Majestic—Virginia and Hugo?

SNAPPY—Yes— They have a swell car— They must have plenty of money. Hugo's the president of a bank—so I heard.

BIFF—Yeh! (*Glances at the door.*) Did you see Virginia?

SNAPPY—Sure.

BIFF—How does she look?

SNAPPY—Swell—just like Queen Mary. Hugo looks bilious. You're the one she should have married, Biff.

BIFF—Well, maybe you're right. That dirty sneaking little— All my life Hugo Barnstead has stuck his nose around. I'll get even one of these days. Have a drink, pal.

SNAPPY (*pouring two drinks*)—Sure.

BIFF—Did Virginia say anything about me?

SNAPPY—I only saw them for a minute. (*They drink.*) You're a big man, Biff Grimes—you should have married her.

BIFF (*after a pause*)—You bet Biff Grimes is a big man.

SNAPPY—Too big for this town.

BIFF (*pulling himself up to his full height*)—You said it. Snappy—there comes a time in every man's life when he feels he needs a change—a change of everything. A man has to grow. Standing still warps him,—it warps him mentally and physically. When he wears out a suit of clothes he gets rid of it. When he outgrows a hat he gets a new one.—Growth, Snappy—growth—That goes for everything—even his wife.

SNAPPY—That's right.

BIFF—I need a change. Biff Grimes is a big man—I want to grow. I'm tired of being held back.

SNAPPY—You should have married Virginia—Biff. She would have made a swell wife.

BIFF—I know. (*Pause.*) I hate Hugo Barnstead.

SNAPPY (*soothing him*)—I know how you feel, Biff.

BIFF—Sure you do, pal—men always understand one another. (*Pause.*) Sing me a humble song, Snappy.

They are feeling their liquor as Snappy swings into "Good-by, little girl, good-by—" with fervor and a slight tremolo. Biff comes in with a bass "Bum-bum-bum" whenever it seems expected of him. They are pretty well through the first verse before Amy shuts them off long enough to demand to know whether or not Biff intends to go out or to continue being stuck in the house all day. Amy has slammed the door significantly.

"Let me give you a little advice, Snappy," advises Biff. "Never marry an old-fashioned woman, understand? When you pick out a woman you say, 'Are you old-fashioned?' If she says 'Yes' you say, 'Too bad—you'll never be able to grow'—"

They have another teeny-weeny drink and this time Snappy is permitted to get well into "In the Good Old Summer Time." It gives Biff an idea. He will put on his Sunday best and look up Hugo Barnstead, and when he meets him he will say to him, "Look here, Hugo Barnstead, I've got a bone to pick with you"—

The telephone is ringing. Whoever it is let Snappy tell them the doctor is out of town, instructs Biff. A man with a toothache? Let him come in next week. Biff never pulls teeth on Sunday unless it is a child.

A second call is from Dick Martin of the Majestic Hotel. Dick is pleading for a guest—an important guest—a Bank President. Biff doesn't care. Biff Grimes is important, too—

"Hey, what name did you say?" Biff was hanging up when he caught the name. "Hello—Dick— All right, I'll see him. Send him right over!" And to Snappy he adds, as he hangs up the phone: "Speak of a skunk and he sticks his nose around." It is Hugo Barnstead who has a toothache.

Snappy is worried. If Biff is going to pull Hugo Barnstead's tooth he thinks he will be going home, but Biff won't let him. Biff is pacing the office floor now, a malevolent look in his eye.

"I'll do it—I'll get even," he mutters. "He stole Virginia from me—and that's not all! . . . Hugo Barnstead coming to old Biff Grimes to have his tooth pulled—what a spot he picked—Bank President—I shoulda been a Bank President—something I could have been—the Mayor of this town or on the council. . . . I wonder what Virginia will say when she sees me. . . . Come on, Hugo Barnstead—Bank President—get your tooth pulled—"

Biff is himself singing gayly "In the Good Old Summer Time" as he picks up his white apron and goes into the other room. . . .

Hugo Barnstead is of the same age as Biff and Snappy, "though he has arrived at that point where he is crabbed and somewhat bald." His tooth is hurting him terribly, he explains to Snappy, and he has had the best doctors in America. Hugo has had seven teeth pulled in Pittsburgh and five filled in Detroit—

And then Biff comes. Biff Grimes! That's a surprise to Hugo. He didn't know Biff had gone on and become a dentist after all. It's been twenty-five years—

"Let's see," Hugo recalls. "Last time I saw you was when we had that trouble at the factory."

Hugo had wanted to wait until he got to Oakley, but Virginia insisted on his coming over. She must have known about Biff Grimes, too. Funny she didn't say anything about it! Hugo hopes Biff won't hurt! Anyway he wants gas.

It is evidently Biff's intention to give Hugo gas, whether he wants it or not. Snappy Downer will officiate with the face inhaler.

"You remember Snappy Downer," says Biff, as Hugo settles himself in the chair. "All of us used to be kids together. He owns a fish store—lot of experience with fish and crabs." Biff has set the face inhaler and begun to work the tank. "Now I want you to inhale deep—deep as you can." He has adjusted the nose piece and motioned to Snappy to hold it. There is an ugly black scowl on Biff's face. "Inhale," he commands. "Fill your lungs up—you're not getting any."

Hugo would indicate that he is doing quite well, but his nod is weak. Now he begins to laugh faintly.

"It has been a long time, hasn't it, Biff Grimes?" Hugo chuckles.

"What?"

HUGO—You and me—Schneider's Gardens—Virginia—

BIFF—Inhale.

HUGO—I remember it all—just like yesterday. . . . Thought

you were going to marry Virginia—but I fooled you. . . . I fooled you. . . . (*Faintly—laughs.*) I fooled you. . . . I fooled you, Biff Grimes.

BIFF (*quietly*)—Hugo Barnstead—I've got you right where I want you—you damn little crawling rat—

SNAPPY (*frightened*)—Biff!

BIFF—I've been waiting for this chance.

SNAPPY—Biff!

BIFF—Breathe! Breathe! (*He puts the mouthpiece on, then turns away with a cynical grin.*) I remember, Hugo Barnstead, you and the dirt you— Schneider's Gardens—yesterday—sure it was yesterday—Avery's Park—Amy and Virginia—we used to go over there—

SNAPPY (*looking down at* HUGO)—Avery's Park.

Biff is laughing loudly. Mechanically he picks up a pair of forceps. From the distance an orchestra can be heard softly playing "In the Good Old Summer Time." Amy is calling: "Yoo hoo, Virginia!"

"Avery's Park," mutters Biff, staring straight ahead of him as the light begins to fade. "Avery's Park"—

In the darkness the music and the girls' voices are mingled in a happy confusion as the curtain falls.

In a lane in Avery's Park bordered by trees and shrubs Amy Lind and Virginia Brush are sitting on a bench waiting expectantly. It is many years ago and both girls are dressed in blue, with flat straw hats and gloves. Virginia, the more aggressive of the two and a year or two older than Amy, is doing most of the watching up and down the path.

Virginia has seen the boys come in the Oak Street entrance and start for Mason's walk. At least she has seen Hugo Barnstead and she assumes that he has brought a friend, as he had promised. She had told Hugo she would meet him here. Amy feels Virginia has been quite forward, but she is eager to hear the details.

"Well, I was in the drugstore getting a belladonna plaster for Ma—when in he comes," recites Virginia. "I knew he was looking at me 'cause he rapped on the counter and coughed twice. Then he smiled—so I smiled. Then he winked—"

"Oh, Virginia! Weren't you horror-stricken?"

"For a second I was. I saw he was awfully good-looking so I winked back."

"Virginia!"

Virginia can see nothing wrong in a wink. Especially if a boy is awfully good-looking. A girl has to be up-to-date these days. If she's going to get a beau she can't be old-fashioned. She has got to be prepared to wink.

"Well, he waited outside for me and we walked down Meadow Street together," Virginia continues. "Oh, he was just swell. He had vanilla on him—smelt nice—he said, 'What's your name?' I didn't tell him—that would be brazen. So I said, 'What's yours?' He said, 'Hugo Barnstead.' Then he said, 'Can I meet you next Saturday afternoon?' I said, 'I don't see why you couldn't.' Then he said, 'I've got a friend. Have you got one?' I said, 'Yes,' thinking of you, of course. 'Good,' he said. 'This friend of mine is awfully swell-looking—tall and handsome.'

"Oh, golly—" giggles Amy.

Amy is worried. She never had met a boy before without a proper introduction. And if her mother knew that she was over in Avery's Park flirting—well, it would mean church twice the next Sunday for Amy. Church twice on Sunday, according to Amy's mother, is the only thing that can be depended upon to take sin away and purify a person. But of course Amy won't *have* to tell her mother— And she has promised to help Virginia out—just this once.

Now Amy is worried for fear Hugo's friend will not like her. Or won't think her dress is pretty. And Virginia's idea that he is likely to fall right in love with her at first sight is positively frightening. Amy would simply die! She'd fall down and die right on that spot if anything like that should happen to her. But Virginia is curious. She'd like to fall in love once just to see what it feels like.

As for that, Amy has had her adventures, too, though she wouldn't think of mentioning them except under promise of the strictest secrecy.

"When I was very young—of course that's a long time ago, you understand," Amy's confession runs. "It was in school. There was a boy. I don't know—he never looked at me and I never— [She looks at Virginia wistfully.] Virginia, did you ever have a feeling in your heart—something that you feel is going to happen and it doesn't—that's the way my heart was— [She touches her heart.] It wasn't love I know that— [Pause.] He never even noticed me. I could have been a stick in the mud as far as he was concerned. Virginia, this boy always seemed lonely somehow. Everybody had it in for him, even the teachers—they called him bully—but I know he wasn't. I saw him do a lot of good things—when the big boys picked on the smaller ones, he helped the little fellows out. I know he had a lot of good in him—good, that nobody else could see—that's why my heart—"

"Who was this boy?"

"You wouldn't know him—" insists Amy sheepishly.

"I might."

"Biff Grimes."

"Biff Grimes! You mean that big bully that hangs around Goldstein's drug store?"

"Yes."

"My mother has told me about him," says Virginia, accusingly.

"So has my mother, but I don't care," answers Amy.

"Why, Amy, he's terrible! The reputation—why, Amy, I'd be ashamed to mention his name. I heard that he drinks and smokes cigarettes."

"Of course, that was a long time ago," explains Amy. "Shucks, I'm over it now. He doesn't even know I'm alive."

Now the boys are in sight. Virginia can see them down the path looking first one way and then another. Now they have caught sight of her and are approaching. Hugo has got on a new suit and is wearing a red neck-tie. And the other fellow—

"Oh, my heavens— It's Biff Grimes!" explodes Virginia.

Amy would run if she could. She can't because the boys have seen them. Both their hearts are kerplunking, the girls admit. They are agreed that if the boys walk right on past and say nothing they will not say anything, either. Of course, if the boys say something then they will say something back. Otherwise they will just drop their eyes, which will show that they are good girls and not to be trifled with.

Now Hugo Barnstead and Biff Grimes have come in at the other end of the path. "Here they are!" Virginia whispers, warningly, casting her eyes down. "Our Father which art in Heaven—" prays Amy

Hugo and Biff are a couple of dandies of the period. They are twirling bamboo canes and chewing toothpicks. They would whistle to relieve their self-consciousness if they could, but though their lips pucker they can't manage a whistle.

Hugo (*nudging* Biff)—There they are.

Biff—I can see them.

Hugo—Swell, eh, Biff?

Biff—Swell, Hugo. Say, I know her—I've always wanted to

meet her. (*Glances over.*) Which is the one you've got picked out for me?

HUGO—The little one on the left.

BIFF—Nothing doing. I know that scrawny little thing—we used to go to school together.

HUGO—She ain't so bad.

BIFF—I'm telling you she's "skidoo"—if you can't pick out anything better than that then Biff Grimes does his own picking.

HUGO—Wait a minute, Biff.

BIFF—I pick the other one.

HUGO—That isn't fair.

BIFF—Twenty-three— Everything is fair to Biff Grimes. I've always wanted to meet her.

HUGO—But I got her first.

BIFF—Who has helped you out of a lot of scrapes?

HUGO—You, Biff—

BIFF—Then what are you kicking about—she's duck soup for me.

HUGO—Aw, gee, Biff. All right, we'll fix it.

BIFF (*nudging him*)—Say something.

HUGO—Well—all right. (BIFF *looks over to the girls and winks. They give him a sheepish smile.*)

BIFF—I winked at 'em, Hugo.

HUGO—Did they wink back?

BIFF—I don't think so. (*Nudges* HUGO.) Well—say something.

HUGO—Give me time. (*Looking over at girls, tips his hat.*) Hello—

VIRGINIA (*coyly*)—Hello— (*She nudges* AMY.)

AMY (*blurting out*)—'Lo—

HUGO—Nice afternoon.

VIRGINIA—Yes. (*Nudges* AMY.)

AMY—Yes. (HUGO *looks at* BIFF. BIFF *switches from one foot to the other.*)

BIFF—Say something familiar.

HUGO (*sees handkerchief*)—You dropped something.

VIRGINIA—What's that?

HUGO—You dropped something.

VIRGINIA—Oh— (*No, he won't pick it up.*) Thank you. (*She reaches down and gets it.*)

HUGO (*gulps*)—If the sun wasn't out it would be a nice day anyhow, wouldn't it?

VIRGINIA—That's right.

BIFF—Oh, hell—say something. They don't care about the sun.

HUGO—That's the way I start my conversation. They'll think you are up to date if you can talk about something in general.

BIFF (*sourly*)—They don't want to hear about that. They want to meet me.

Introductions are awkwardly managed, a little to the embarrassment of all four. Virginia is keen to further her acquaintance with Hugo, and would if Biff did not keep horning in and spoiling everything. Biff can't see Amy, even after they have established the fact that they were both at the John Marshall school. Amy, Biff recalls, was a funny-looking little thing, even then. Used to wear red flannel drawers—he remembers that. But she was good to him, too. He recalls one time she saved him from a licking in the principal's office and another time she helped him out with his arithmetic. Biff never was much at arithmetic. As Biff recalls it, although Amy was funny-looking she was real good at heart.

"I always liked you, Biff," confesses Amy, to Virginia's dismay. Amy might at least have waited. But Biff doesn't mind.

"That's all right," he comforts Amy. "I guess all the girls were stuck on me in those days."

The next moment Biff, ignoring Virginia's coldness, is gallantly offering a gum drop, which she will not have. She much prefers Hugo's horehound candy.

Then Biff has another idea. How about a little walk? How about an ice cream soda at Goldstein's. Wouldn't go so bad, eh?

"I like a college ice," admits Amy.

"Swell!" agrees Biff. "Say, Goldstein's got something new—I tried it last night. You'll rave about it. He says New York is going wild over it."

VIRGINIA—Yes—

BIFF—You know when New York goes wild over anything it must be good.

VIRGINIA—What is it?

HUGO—What is it, Biff?

BIFF—He spreads nuts all over the ice-cream.

VIRGINIA—I never heard of that before, did you, Amy?

AMY—No.

BIFF—That guy isn't dead—and Biff Grimes never lets the grass grow under his feet—New York style, that's me, every time— (*He steps forward to* VIRGINIA *and takes her arm, placing it under his own. He is all smiles.*) And you know, little girl—Virginia, that's the name, isn't it? Somehow I've always liked that name, Virginia— (HUGO *stands dumbfounded.* AMY *looks on.*) Do you know where they got it from? The state of Virginia. That's where Abraham Lincoln was born. I guess you didn't know that. Very few people do— (BIFF *is between the two girls.*) Yes, indeed! Too bad I haven't met you before, Virginia. Biff Grimes thinks you are the nicest little girl he's ever met— (AMY, *open-mouthed.* HUGO *watches carefully.*) And we won't sit up at the counter, either. Goldstein has chairs in the back. He did that at my suggestion. Gives the place sort of a sporty atmosphere—like New York. (*Looks around.*) Well, let's go. (*To* HUGO.) You can take the little girl, Hugo. (BIFF *bends to pick up cane.*)

HUGO (*smiles—passes quickly in front of* BIFF *to* VIRGINIA.) Sure—Biff— (*Takes* VIRGINIA.) You know, Virginia, I've wanted to take you to Goldstein's Drug Store for a long time.

VIRGINIA—Oh, Mr. Barnstead. (BIFF *turns and stares after* HUGO *and* VIRGINIA. *Pause.*)

AMY—I—I don't mind if you take me, Mr. Grimes.

BIFF (*starts off—takes* AMY'S *hand—runs off*)—Oh, sure—come on. (AMY *follows as the curtain falls.*)

Late that summer, on a sunny afternoon, Schneider's Garden, a typical German picnic ground, is alive with people. Groups are gathered at small tables under the trees. One family has arranged itself in a circle sitting on the ground and is laughing and talking while the men try to sing old German folk songs. The music of a merry-go-round in the near distance can be heard, and the occasional pop of guns in a shooting gallery.

Waiters are busy coming and going from the Schneider saloon with orders for beer, and an occasional "kummel und pig's-knuckles." The crowd, it appears, has been drawn by a retail merchants' picnic. There are to be raffles and other events of especial interest to the Mrs. Schnitzenmeyers and Mrs. Schutzendorfs.

There has already been a fight down by the bowling alleys. And that Grimes boy, the big bully, was in it, as usual. He should, thinks Mrs. Oberstatter, be run out of town, dot loafer.

"Dere vas a gang, und von of them say something to the Grimes boy—the Grimes boy already goes mit a new girl," reports Mrs. Oberstatter.

"Yah! Dot is dot Brush girl—such a nice girl, too. Yah! Yah! Yah!"

"Ven dot boy say something to the Grimes boy—the Grimes boy make out he hit him in the face und the udder boy fall down on the ground."

Amy Lind and Hugo Barnstead have come in and are sitting at a near-by table. Amy overhears Mrs. Oberstatter and knows that Biff is in trouble again. That is no surprise to Hugo. Biff is always in trouble. Schneider has threatened to put him out of the gardens if he ever gets in another fight.

Call for the raffle has taken the crowd to another part of the ground when Virginia Brush and Biff Grimes appear. It is evident that they have been quarreling. Virginia would move on to the raffle. Biff would stay where he is and order a sherry and egg. Virginia thinks Biff has had enough. Biff doesn't. Two sherry and eggs never hurt anyone.

"Biff Grimes, I want to tell you something," snaps Virginia. "I'm a respectable girl and I'm not in the habit of going with people that want to drink and fight. If you want to do that sort of thing you will kindly choose some other company."

"Will you kindly give me a chance to explain?" pleads Biff, querulously.

"There is nothing to explain."

BIFF—I didn't start the fight, did I?

VIRGINIA—Yes, you did—

BIFF—I did not. Do you think I am going to stand by and take an insult?

VIRGINIA—That boy didn't say anything.

BIFF—He did, too—I know what he said. When Biff Grimes takes his best girl to a picnic nobody is going to pass a remark. I heard what he said—

VIRGINIA—Aren't you gentleman enough to ignore it?

BIFF—No. I'm gentleman enough to take a slap at his nose.

VIRGINIA—If you ever do it again I'll walk away from you.

BIFF (*cooling down. Quietly.*)—I'm sorry I did it, Virginia—understand?

The waiter has brought Biff his sherry and egg and put it on the table. From the gardens appear two rowdies. They give Biff and Virginia a glance and pass on into the saloon.

BIFF (*looking after the rowdies*)—And if I've hurt your feelings I'm sorry about that— This will be the last, understand? (*She does not answer. He looks at her.*) Say, do you know I'm crazy about you— (VIRGINIA *looks the other way.*) Well, I am —I think of you all the time. Why, I could have a lot of girls but you are the only one that I care about. (*Pause.*) I guess I know how you feel. But seeing those fellows laugh and the remarks—I guess I lost my head. I guess I got jealous.

VIRGINIA—I don't see why you should get jealous over me.

BIFF—I can't help it. Ever since that day I first met you in Avery's Park—I've cared about you. You know that, Virginia— (*Pause.*) I guess you think I'm a fool.

VIRGINIA—Why don't you go with those other girls that you like to talk about?

BIFF—Because I want you.

VIRGINIA—Amy Lind likes you.

BIFF—Well, I don't care anything about her. You're the only one that I want, Virginia. Whenever I'm near you I just seem to forget everything.

VIRGINIA (*laughing*)—Don't be foolish!

BIFF—I'm not but I can't help it. I'd like to have a nice talk with you some time. There are a lot of things I want to tell you. You know I have ambitions and—

VIRGINIA (*cutting him off*)—I'm not interested. Besides you are not exactly my ideal, Mr. Grimes.

BIFF—What's the matter with me?

VIRGINIA—Well—maybe some day you'll find out.

BIFF (*crushed*)—I wish you would tell me now. I'll do anything you want me to do.

VIRGINIA (*laughing*)—I don't want you to do anything. (*Pause.*) And hereafter, Mr. Grimes—please don't call up my house. My mother doesn't know that I am going out with you and I don't want her to find out.

Biff suggests, as a further peace offering, that they go on an excursion to Lexington the next Sunday, but Virginia has an important engagement. It may be with Hugo Barnstead. If Biff has any idea that he is Virginia's steady he has another thought coming. She will go where she likes, and with whom she likes.

"Oh, Virginia, won't you give me a chance?" pleads Biff, seriously. "Honest, I'm crazy about you. I can't sleep night or day thinking about you. My brain keeps going 'round and when I know that you are meeting— (VIRGINIA *laughs merrily*—BIFF *clenches his fists.*) Hugo Barnstead won't cut me out."

"Listen to the little boy talk," smiles Virginia. "I thought you were a big man, Mr. Grimes. To hear you talk one would think you owned the world. I've heard of the great things you were going to do—so far I haven't seen anything."

Biff would remind Virginia that he is studying hard to be a dentist and that he has only four more years to go. When he is a dentist it is his intention to open a big shop right there in town with a big gold sign on it.

Virginia isn't interested. Even a little contemptuous. The next minute Biff's further pleading is interrupted by the appearance of Amy and Hugo. They have been looking everywhere for Virginia and Biff. At least Hugo had been looking everywhere for Virginia. Called her house and when her mother said she was out—

"You brought Amy," giggles Virginia.

"Yes, and we've been on the loop-the-loop three times," chirrups Amy.

"Yeah, and we went through the tunnel twice," says Hugo.

"Did you kiss her in the dark?" Virginia wants to know.

"No—he didn't kiss me," says Amy, as Hugo smirks. "Are you having a good time, Biff?"

"Swell!" says Biff.

The rowdies come out of the saloon. They are half drunk and looking for a fight. They sit at a near-by table and begin to talk in low tones. Virginia, sensing what is coming, suggests that they had better go. Biff, conscious of the boys at the other table, isn't easy to move. Biff isn't going to start anything. He can keep his mouth and his hands to himself. But—

"Funny how a cute little girl takes up with such rough people," sneers one of the boys. "You'd think she would pick up somebody that was decent."

Virginia has taken Hugo by the arm and Amy by the hand. She will not stand for Biff's fighting, she has told him that. If he does—

"Which girl are you referring to?" queries the second boy.

"Why—the swell-looking one—ain't she some cutie?"

"She looks cute enough for me."

"And what could you do with that cutie, eh?"

"I guess I could do more than chuckle her under the chin."

Hugo has started out with Virginia and Amy. Amy has pulled back to call a frightened plea to Biff. Biff has walked over to the two boys and is towering over them.

"That last remark—" he begins. "I don't like it!"

"What are you goin' to do about it?"

"Stand up!"

"What for?"

"I want to see how hard I can knock you down."

The girls are calling to Biff, to remind him of his promise. "If I'd promised God I wouldn't let that last remark go by," says Biff. And then to the boy: "I'm giving you one minute to get up."

The boys jump to their feet. One of them has produced a knife. Amy sees it and screams a warning to Biff. A waiter runs in yelling, "A fight, Schneider! A fight!"

Biff has swung on the boy and knocked the knife out of his hand. A second short blow sends him down and out. He turns to the other, but just in time to see him disappear in the gardens. Schneider has rushed in.

"So! Fight once more, huh? Raus mit him—" He has approached Biff but decided he needs assistance. "Come on, boys. Throw him out."

Two waiters close in on Biff, but get no farther. There is something about Biff's attitude that discourages them.

"Lay a hand on me and I'll drop you alongside of this punk," warns Biff. "I'll get out of here—by myself, see. And I don't need any help— Come on, Virginia."

"No! No! I never want to see you again, Biff Grimes!" rages Virginia, almost in tears. "I hate you! You're a bully! A big bully!"

"I'll see you over in Avery's Park Wednesday evening—at eight," says Biff. But Virginia does not hear. She is crying in Hugo's arms.

"So long, Biff," smiles Hugo.

Biff turns on his heels and goes out through the crowd as the curtain falls.

Back at the old meeting place in Avery's Park. Amy and Biff are sitting on the park bench. Biff, in his dull, blunt way, is trying to explain things to Amy. It isn't that he cares so much about Virginia's insulting him, but it's the way she did it that hurt.

"Any girl would have been proud to have a man protect her good name," says Biff, earnestly. "You know a girl has to have a man protect her good name. How is she going to hold up her head if she doesn't have a good name—you understand that—

Photo by White Studio, New York.

"ONE SUNDAY AFTERNOON"

Biff: . . . Amy, you are the first person that ever made me take back something. My feelings down here want to—I don't know—I'm glad I know you, Amy. . . . If I ask you something you won't mind? . . . Can I be your steady?

(*Frances Bruning and Lloyd Nolan*)

don't you, Amy?"

"Of course I do, Biff."

"That's all a girl can live on today is her good name. I never said a word out of the way to her all the time I was going with her. I always watched my step. I knew she came from good folks and nobody can say Biff Grimes took advantage of any girl— I'm not an angel, mind you. But I have a lot of respect for girls and I know a good one from a bad one. The bad ones live down on Pine Street."

"That isn't nice, Biff."

"I know it— I'm sorry I said that, Amy."

Biff hasn't seen Amy since the picnic in Schneider's Gardens. Tonight he has been waiting there in the park since eight o'clock and it's after nine now, and no Virginia.

There is one thing Amy would like to know, though Biff doesn't have to tell her if he doesn't want to. Still she would like to know if he really loves Virginia.

"Yes," admits Biff, after some hesitation. "Yes, I do love her. I guess maybe I got a little too crazy about her. She somehow was my ideal. You know every boy has an ideal, somebody that he cares for and when he cares for that somebody nothing else matters—it's sort of an ingrown pain. It starts in the pit of your stomach and works up to your neck. Well, that's the way I felt toward Virginia."

"I see," says Amy, meekly.

Biff, however, knows Virginia for what she is. There's nothing sincere about Virginia for one thing, and at heart she's just a "teaser." That's what rouses the devil in a fellow.

Biff knew that Virginia had been flirting with the boy he had taken a sock at in Schneider's Garden and he had been around to apologize to the fellow. Which proves to Amy that there is really a lot of good in Biff, only it has to be brought out.

"You know I don't mean anything wrong when I take a sock at a person," explains Biff. "Afterwards I feel awful sorry. Why, I'd do anything to help folks. I know the people in this town think I'm a bully but I ain't. I was taught to protect myself. When I was a kid—my old man used to say, "Sock 'em first, then afterwards ask them what they wanted."

Biff also remembers that he is sorry for some of the things he said to Amy the first time they met there at that bench. And he remembers all those things she used to do for him at school. He likes sitting there talking with Amy. Virginia could never sit down and talk that way.

Now Biff is wondering how Amy happened to come to the park this particular night. Perhaps she had a date with Hugo Barnstead. Biff's glad if she hadn't because he thinks Hugo is a pill. Well, it's a quarter past nine now and it looks like Virginia isn't coming. Perhaps Virginia had the date with Hugo.

It's a nice night. There's a moon coming up pretty soon. Everything is kinda still and quiet. Soon it will be fall. And then winter. Amy gets awful lonesome in the winter. And so does Biff.

"I like to walk over here in the evenings like this," muses Amy. "I like to look at the trees and the stars. I get tired sitting in the house. [Pause.] Ma's all right but—well, she doesn't believe in, that is, I can't talk to her the way I want to. You know, Biff, a girl has a lot of things she wants to tell—things that fall on her heart but— [She looks at Biff to see if he is grasping her meaning.] I suppose you'll laugh at me—please don't. They don't seem much, but to me they are mountains—you get awfully tired stifling things down. And when you can't tell things in your heart to somebody that is near, who are you going to tell them to? . . . I like to come over here alone because when my heart is full, I feel I can talk to the trees and the birds. Somehow I feel they understand. Do you see the way that big oak stands out? It looks deserted, but it isn't. There are birds hidden in that tree. She's like a big mother to them. Please don't laugh at me, but it's fun to watch them. Some of them are so naughty they fluster and bluster when she shakes them out in the morning. Others are grateful—they sing for her. And then in the evening, when the sun goes down, back they come—the good ones and the bad ones and she hides them under her leaves."

"I never looked at it from that point of view before," admits Biff.

Biff has ideas, too. He always wanted to talk to somebody like this, but he had an idea that if he did people would think that he was cuckoo. Biff is ambitious, too. He's got a new job over at the Phœnix Box Factory. He will have to give some of his money to the family but most of it is going to help him through Dental School. One day he is going to be mayor of that town.

Snappy Downer and his steady appear. They have been out for a walk and they have picked up a bit of news. Snappy can hardly wait to tell it. It's about Virginia Brush. And Hugo Barnstead. They have just been married!

The news percolates slowly through Biff's mind. His expression goes blank for a second. Then he snaps suddenly out of it.

"Hugo Barnstead!" he repeats. Then he smiles broadly. "Sure—well, I certainly worked hard to fix it up for that boy."

"I thought she was your steady," ventures Snappy, teasingly.

"Virginia Brush?" There is no telling Biff's true emotions by his tone. "No—she was a nice little girl—that's all. I guess everybody thought I was stuck on her—but I wasn't. That was just my little joke. [Laughs.] So, Snappy, when you see the gang you can say Biff Grimes is leading his own life and he's kinder walking clean."

"Sure. I saw Hugo this afternoon—he's going to work for his uncle in Toledo—got a swell job— He and the happy bride are leaving on the midnight. We're going to throw rice and everything. I hear they got a lower sleeper—"

"That's good."

Snappy and the steady have gone on. They are snickering as they pass out of sight. Biff is staring straight out at nothing. Amy puts her hand in his sympathetically.

AMY—I know. It hurts—doesn't it?

BIFF—I guess it does.

AMY—Sure it does. Your heart feels like it was all cut open and bruised—I know.

BIFF—Do you, Amy?

AMY—Yes.

BIFF (*bitterly*)—When he climbs into that sleeper I hope he breaks his damn legs.

AMY—Biff! You mustn't say that! It isn't nice.

BIFF—I can't help it.

AMY—You mustn't. Say you are sorry—please—

BIFF—All right—I'm sorry— Amy, you are the first person that ever made me take back something. My feelings down here want to— I don't know— I'm glad I know you, Amy. (*Pause.*) If I ask you something you won't mind?

AMY—What is it?

BIFF—Can I be your steady?

AMY—Do you want to?

BIFF—Yes.

AMY—All right, Biff.

BIFF—Can I call on you—I mean at your house?

AMY (*hesitating*)—I don't know, Biff—I'd like for you to but you see—

BIFF—I know—your mother—

AMY—She doesn't want anybody calling on me.

BIFF—I'll see you over here in the evenings then.

AMY—Yes—

BIFF—I guess I'll be going now. I just want what you said—I want to be alone.

AMY—All right, Biff.

BIFF (*gazing skyward*)—Sure is a pretty night. Looks like there's a million stars out.

AMY (*looking up*)—Yes—

BIFF—The old dipper stands out clear. (*Pause.*) Well, good night.

AMY—Good night, Biff. (*Neither makes a move to go.* AMY *turns to him and says softly:*) Would you like to kiss me?

BIFF (*staring at her*)—Yes— (*He gathers her into his arms, her arms going around his neck.*) Amy— (*They kiss.*) I'll walk down as far as the gate with you— (*They go off arm in arm.*)

THE CURTAIN FALLS

ACT II

Two years later, in the combination dining-room and kitchen of Biff Grimes' home on Twelfth Street, Oakley, Biff is sitting at the table, his shirt sleeves rolled up, several books in front of him. At a near-by sink Amy is just finishing the supper dishes.

There has been a letter from Amy's mother. The old lady has lost her house and she will have to come and live with them. Which worries Amy more than it does Biff.

Biff is in debt, but he will get out. He has only six months more at the Dental School. And he has nothing against Amy's mother, even if she had said some pretty nasty things to him when she discovered that he and Amy had been secretly married by a justice of the peace.

Amy would like to take a walk, now her work's done, but Biff feels he had better study, even if he has been at the factory all day. Which reminds him that they are switching Hugo Barnstead from the Toledo branch back to the Oakley factory.

Amy knew that, too. She had met Virginia on the street. Hugo and Virginia may be stopping in later. Biff is not pleased. He does not want to see them. If Hugo wants to talk to him let him see him at the factory. And he doesn't like the idea, also suggested by Virginia, that possibly Hugo will be able to do something for him at the factory. Biff can take care of himself.

Snappy Downer drops in. He is on his way to a burlesque show and thought Biff might want to go along. It's Billy Watson's Beef Trust and Snappy can hardly wait to have another look at the big blonde who used to stand on the end in green tights.

Hugo and Virginia come along a minute later. "Virginia is gorgeously dressed, wears a fur coat and muff. Hugo has grown a mustache and is very much the big business man."

Greetings are friendly and a little playful as far as Virginia is concerned. She is glad to find that Mr. Grimes is still the same big, manly fellow he used to be.

The talk settles into the usual comparative channels. Everybody's looking well. Virginia's dress is lovely. Biff is going to buy Amy a dress for her birthday, and it, too, will be an imported model.

Virginia and Hugo have been traveling a good deal. In New York they heard Caruso. They are thinking of taking an apartment on Chestnut Hill.

Biff thinks he and Amy may be moving to Chestnut Hill, too, when he gets his diploma. He has only six months more to go. Virginia thinks she may be Biff's first patient, but it is Hugo who is having trouble with his teeth. Hugo, however, doesn't intend to have anything to do with a novice dentist.

Hugo, it now appears, has come primarily to have a talk with Biff about factory conditions. His uncle has put him in charge with an idea that he can put through certain reforms. Fire a lot of useless help and double the output. Biff can be of use to Hugo in the plan. In fact Hugo would like Biff to give up his silly idea of becoming a dentist and become a regular business man.

HUGO—Forget your pride, Biff. You work along with me and you can make some more money.

BIFF—Let's get down to the point. What do you want?

HUGO—Well, what I am going to say is not going to affect you, understand.

BIFF—Yes.

HUGO—My uncle informs me that there are too many men laying off sick. That's what they say. I'm going to put a stop to it. The Phœnix Box Factory is paying its help to work, not to be sick. I'm going to clean out that place. Too much dead wood. We're not running an old man's home. Too many old timers.

BIFF—I've found the men good workers.

HUGO—Well, they're not. I'm going to cut down on the help. The rest will have to do more, that's all.

BIFF—Yes.

HUGO—You mingle with the men. You can keep your eyes open and see what's going on.

BIFF—I do my own work. I don't notice the others.

HUGO—But you can begin to notice them.

BIFF—I don't understand.

HUGO—For instance. This department where you are. Some are on the job, I suppose, others aren't. I want you to report to me. Now who would you suggest I get rid of?

BIFF—You mean get fired?

HUGO—Yes.

BIFF—In other words, Hugo, you want me to be the monkey in the clover?

HUGO—It's foolish to take that point of view.

BIFF—Spy work, eh?

HUGO—You see, Virginia. That's what I get for trying to help them out.

BIFF—I didn't ask you for any help. If you came here to-night to make a sneak out of me, you can get the hell out.

HUGO—Now he's insulting me without any reason. I came here ready—

AMY—No, no, Hugo, you don't understand—

HUGO—Oh, I understand.

VIRGINIA—Oh, stop it, Hugo. I think you've made a fool out of yourself.

HUGO—I haven't made a fool out of myself. I think Biff Grimes is too stubborn for his own good.

VIRGINIA—Oh, come on.

HUGO—Let me alone, Virginia. I want to tell you this, Biff Grimes—

BIFF—I don't want to hear anything.

HUGO—Very well. Come on, Virginia. I see Biff Grimes is still Biff Grimes. Always looking for trouble.

AMY—Oh, now, Hugo.

BIFF—I'm not looking for trouble.

HUGO (*to* BIFF)—Yes, you are. Don't forget that the Phœnix Box Factory pays you your living.

VIRGINIA (*between* HUGO *and* BIFF)—Stop it.

BIFF—I earn my wages and so do the rest of the men.

HUGO—What's the sense of talking to a man without brains. I'm going. Come on, Virginia. (HUGO *exits with* VIRGINIA.)

The Barnsteads' visit does not have a very good effect on Biff. Let Amy wait, he mutters, she will be doing just as nice things and wearing just as nice clothes as Virginia. And she will be living on Chestnut Hill, too. As for Hugo—"I ought to have taken a sock at him just for old times' sake," announces Biff.

Amy is a little worried. She thinks perhaps Biff is thinking of Virginia regretfully.

AMY—Tell me, Biff—are you happy?

BIFF—Sure—why, what would I do without you, honey? Guess I'd be like a ship in a storm. Wouldn't know which way to go.

AMY—I want you to be happy.

BIFF—I am. In six months I'm telling Hugo Barnstead and the Phœnix Box Factory to go to hell.

AMY—That's the stuff, Biff.

BIFF—I've got to work hard—harder than I have been. From now on every nickel means something.

AMY—I can attend to that, Biff.

BIFF—Sure you can.

AMY—Want to take that walk?

BIFF—No, I'd better stay here and work.

AMY—Just for a little while.

BIFF—No, Amy—you go— (*Pause.*) I've got to get this work done.

Amy goes into an inner room and reappears a moment later in a little faded jacket, pinning on her hat. She won't be long, she tells Biff, passing back of his chair and stopping to kiss him.

Amy turns at the door. A whimsical smile has spread over Biff's face as he gazes straight ahead. Then he turns suddenly to his books and digs into them feverishly as the curtain falls.

A few days later Mrs. Lind arrives at the Grimes'. It has been a blow to her, having to accept this help from Biff and Amy, but there didn't seem anything else to do after they foreclosed the house on her. They did not, fortunately, take it all away from her and she may get something from it later, but it will be a long time.

Amy is getting Mrs. Lind settled in the bedroom when Biff comes in from the factory. He is not happy. Finding himself alone he paces the room restlessly. Biff has lost his job.

Hugo Barnstead, the little rat, is at the bottom of it, of course. He had reported to his uncle Biff's refusal to do the spying Hugo wanted done and the uncle had demanded an explanation.

"For the last two days he's been riding me," reports Biff; "going out of his way to find things—yelling at me—trying to make me feel—it was only the thought of you, Amy, that held me back. I'd knocked his can clean up to the middle of his back. [Pause.] Funny when a fellow is decent and trying to make a living that a sneak steps on his neck—"

"Biff, tell me the truth—did you have words with Hugo?"

BIFF—Sure, I did.

AMY—Did you strike him?

BIFF (*pause*)—Well—

AMY—Tell me the truth.

BIFF—I didn't exactly strike him—I gave him a little shove—

AMY—That wasn't right and you know it.

BIFF—I know, Amy—but—

AMY—Biff—you can't. You can't quit that job.

BIFF—Huh?

AMY—Don't you see how we are fixed—you must go back.

BIFF—And have him bawl me out before everybody—make me feel like a fool! Say, I've got a little pride. I know it's been ground down. God, don't you think I'm human?—(*Controlling himself.*) I'm trying hard, Amy, to give you a little home. I know what you've been through, honey—I love you better than anything in this world—(*Bitterly.*) Hugo Barnstead—I'll get you one of these days.

AMY—Things were starting to look so beautifully for us—

BIFF—I know it, Amy.

AMY—If you went back and explained—

BIFF—I can't. (*Rises.*) Don't you see Hugo bawlin' me out and the others laughing—(*Walking around room.*) I kinda lost my head—something went wrong with the machinery—guess it was my fault. Hugo fired me. Wouldn't even give me my pay. I told him he had to give me my pay.

AMY—Oh, Biff—Biff—

BIFF—He's got to give me my pay—(*Pause.*) Threatened to call the cops—hell! I'm not afraid of the cops.

Now Amy has told Biff that her mother has arrived. That makes it look blacker than ever. Biff will just have to do something about that job. Or some job.

Amy has gone to her mother when Biff arrives at a momentous decision. He grabs his hat and coat and finds a revolver in a bureau drawer. He slips that in his pocket and is gone when Amy gets back. She thinks maybe he has gone to the grocery store for something.

A few minutes later there is a great commotion in the neighborhood of the factory, which is quite close to Biff's house. There is the screech of a police whistle and shouts of a crowd. Amy thinks perhaps someone is trying to hold up the bakery again.

Five minutes later Biff has dashed in, wild-eyed, breathless and hatless. Amy and her mother are in the bedroom. Now there is a sound of feet running up the stairs and two policemen burst open the door. One is carrying Biff's hat and gun.

Biff would laugh the matter off. He can't imagine what Charlie is talking about. When they begin to talk loud advising him to come with them quietly he changes his tone and begs them not to let his wife know.

First Policeman—Listen, Biff—you might just as well give in—

Biff—Listen, fellows—(*Breaks away—backs downstage.*)

Second Policeman (*following* Biff)—Hugo Barnstead wants you pinched—

Biff—Hugo Barnstead—always Hugo Barnstead—

Second Policeman—You took a punch at him, didn't you—that's assault and battery—charges—

Biff—I had a right to do that—

First Policeman—And he swears you tried to hold up the place—

Biff—I didn't.

First Policeman—You had this gun, didn't you?

Biff (*to* First Policeman)—For God's sake be quiet, will you—honest to God I wasn't going to hold up the factory. I got fired today. Hugo wouldn't give me my pay—it was coming to me—I worked for it and I worked hard—

First Policeman—You know what it means to carry a gun in this town—

Second Policeman—That's serious—

Biff (*between policemen in front of table*)—I just pulled it as a bluff—he had the whole force lined up against me. I don't mind three or four men but I can't lick fifty. I threw the gun down as soon as I got in the office—(*Pleading.*) You fellows know me—you've known me for years. I wouldn't steal anything from anybody—I was desperate I tell you—I only wanted what was coming to me.

FIRST POLICEMAN—We've got to arrest you, Biff—

BIFF (*edges around table*)—Honest to God, I wasn't going to hold up the place—just wanted to get into the office. Give me a break, will you—let me get out of here. I'll beat it out of town—nobody will know. (*Breaking down.*) I don't know why I took the gun—something snapped in my brain—I didn't know what I was doing—please, fellows—(*Keeping out of reach.*)

FIRST POLICEMAN—Sorry, Biff.

BIFF—I'll do anything—honest I will.

FIRST POLICEMAN—We can't—you were seen—Hugo has the whole factory against your word.

SECOND POLICEMAN—His uncle means something—

FIRST POLICEMAN—It's tough for you, Biff—

BIFF—It ain't myself I'm thinking of—I don't give a damn about myself, it's Amy—this will about kill her—please, boys—

FIRST POLICEMAN—Sorry, Biff—we can't—

SECOND POLICEMAN—Come along.

The bedroom door opens and Amy is standing there. Biff breaks suddenly into a loud laugh. Well, well—it certainly is awful nice of Matt and Charlie to come for him this way. The police department is giving a clam bake, Biff explains to Amy, and they want him to be on the committee. They want him to go down now and arrange things.

"All right, let's go," calls Biff, his voice growing husky as he steps between the policemen. "I'll be back in a little while—a little while, honey."

"All right, Biff!"

"Wait for me."

"I'll wait."

Amy stands for a second with a puzzled expression on her face. Then she rushes to the window and what she sees causes her to gasp.

"Biff! Biff!" she screams.

The lights fade out as the curtain falls.

It is evening in Avery's Park two years later. Amy is there with her mother, sitting on the bench. Toby, the lamplighter, shuffles in, puts on the gaslight, and shuffles out.

This is the day Biff is coming home, but his wire didn't say on what train. Amy went down to the 5:45 but he wasn't on that. It is probable that he will get off at the junction and if he does he is sure to come through the park. Amy can't go back home. She must wait for him. In which case Mrs. Lind decides that she will go on home and warm up the supper. She has some packing to do, too. She is going to her sister's next day.

Toby has shuffled in again. He has just finished his twenty-three lights. It would be a pretty dark park if it weren't for Toby.

In the distance there is a cheerful whistle. This would be Biff. He comes down the path now and stops. For a second he and Amy stare at each other:

"Hello, Amy."

"Biff!" Amy sits a little weakly on the bench.

BIFF—Yep—it's me. (*Pause.*) What are you doing—(*Pause.*) Just goin' over to the house. Dropped off at the junction. Could have made the 5:45 but I didn't want anybody at the station to see me.

AMY (*quietly*)—I know—

BIFF (*sheepishly*)—Something told me you would be here—don't know, just something. (*Pause.*) Nice over here tonight—spring.

AMY—Yes—spring.

BIFF—Smells good—the earth—the trees. Everything seems to be waking up. New life coming in. (*There is an awkward pause between them.* BIFF *whistles softly.*) Got out at twelve o'clock. The warden was a prince of a chap. Shook hands and—and—(*Pause.*) Glad to see me, Amy?

AMY—You know I am, Biff.

BIFF—Feels good to see you—feels good to be back. Two years— (*Looking around.*) Seems more like ten.

AMY—Biff—I'm so glad to see you.

BIFF—Same here— Guess I would have been all shot to pieces if I hadn't gotten your letters. The thought of you waiting—I just somehow—somehow—(*There is a break in his voice—he catches himself.*)

AMY—It's all right, Biff.

BIFF (*laughs*)—I knew you would be waiting over here—s'funny—(*He takes her hand and holds it.*) Thank you, Amy, for all your kindness—all your goodness.

AMY—That's all right, Biff.

BIFF—You all right, Amy? (*Laughs.*)

AMY—Yes—I'm all right, Biff—it was just seeing you—

BIFF—Sure, I understand—nice of your mother to slip us that money when the house was sold.

AMY—Yes— She's leaving for Sedalia tomorrow.

BIFF—Is she?

AMY—Yes.

BIFF—Learned a lot since I've been away—(*Sits on arm of bench.*)

AMY—Yes—

BIFF—S'funny—the same moon, the same stars, the same rain comes down on us all. It doesn't know whether you're a crook, or an angel—a cock-eyed Chinaman— It doesn't give a damn. It just says, "Here I am—I'm yours, what the hell are you going to do about it"—it's good too. It never gives any pain or heart-aches—there isn't any worry in it. Never takes anything from you but gives everything. (*Pause.*) You know, Amy—there's a lot of good in people if we look for it. The trouble is—we don't look for it. We just go through life saying, "I'm O.K. and the other guy is all wrong. When you lie in a bunk at night with nothing but men around—it is different—you can feel it. There seems to be an understanding.

AMY—I know, Biff.

BIFF—Sure you do—you always know. (*He pats her hand.*) Quiet—isn't it?

AMY—Yes.

From a distance a phonograph can be heard playing "Let the Rest of the World Go By." It reminds Biff that it will probably be just as well if they let this town go by. He is thinking they will try Hillsdale.

"There's something big coming up for Biff Grimes and his wife. I can feel it in my bones—Biff Grimes is going to be Bigg Grimes— Yessir—there ain't going to be nothing too good for Biff Grimes and family.—God, it feels good! (*Pause.*) Want to go home, honey?"

"Yes."

"All right."

Biff has gathered Amy into his arms as she rises. "I love you, Amy," he says. "I think you are the loveliest lady in the world. I love your hair—your eyes—your mouth—"

"I love you, too, Biff—" He has kissed her fervently.

"Look at the old sky—must be a million stars out—moon is up full—spring!" Biff muses happily. "Let's walk home!"

They are walking off arm in arm. The gramophone music can still be heard. The lights fade.

Back in Biff Grimes' dentist shop in Hillsdale. Hugo is still under gas. Biff holds the forceps and is staring at nothing, as he repeats: "Avery Park!"

Snappy Downer has dropped the mouthpiece and is thoroughly frightened. If this is the time Biff is to start pulling Hugo's tooth it is also the time Snappy is going home. Snappy can't stand the sight of blood—

The door has opened and Virginia Barnstead breezes in. "She has become a coarse type of person, a washed-out blonde, extravagantly dressed but overdone."

"Well, if it isn't my old-time sweetheart himself," is Virginia's cheery greeting.

Biff is still in something of a daze. His greeting of Virginia is casual. He is ready to agree with her that the world does move.

"And here you are—the big dentist of Hillsdale," goes on Virginia. "Say, have you pulled old Goofy Jake's tooth yet?" Biff has forgotten Hugo, the tooth and the gas, but his brain is clearing quickly. He turns to his dental chair and extracts Hugo's molar.

"Will you do me a favor?" calls Virginia. "Will you put him out of his misery? . . . Let him alone. He's half dead anyway."

Biff is shaking Hugo violently. A moment later the patient has come to, muttering, "Biff, you're a fool—a fool—" Biff hands him a glass of water and he rinses his mouth.

"God, what an awful taste!" exclaims Hugo. "You here, Virgie?"

"Yes, nature's child," answers Virginia, through a cloud of smoke from her cigarette. "Did you think you were going to crash the pearly gates?"

Hugo is out of the chair and ready to go. He could find the time to show them all the cavity from which the offending tooth has been removed, but Virginia puts a stop to that. She has been hearing about those teeth morning, noon and night until she is ready to yank them out herself without any gas.

There is no charge. Hugo is surprised to hear Biff say that. Puzzled to be invited to call again.

"Perhaps you'll examine me some time, Dr. Grimes," suggests Virginia. "Say, by the way, how's your wife?"

"Very well."

"Still married, or don't you work at it?"

"Mrs. Grimes is still Mrs. Grimes," Biff replies, quietly.

"Well, God knows what I've suffered married to this death

house buzzard," sneers Virginia.

"Now, Virgie, I'm a good man."

"Good for what?"

"I'm going home," says Snappy Downer. "I don't feel so good," and he disappears.

Now the Barnsteads have gone. For a moment Biff is lost in thought. "He is like a man waking from a bad dream. At first the dream was pleasant but it turned into a nightmare. He is glad he is awake. Realizing that he was about to make an awful blunder he stands half ashamed—"

Now Biff has taken off his apron and hung it up. Suddenly he breaks into a loud laugh. Amy comes quickly into the room. "She is dressed in her Sunday best, a sweet-faced, gray-haired lady."

Amy—For heaven's sake, Biff Grimes, if you don't stop making that noise—

Biff—I've got something to tell you.

Amy—You ought to be ashamed of yourself—drinking and raising this racket—

Biff—Yes, ma'am—I am—

Amy (*looking around*)—Where's Snappy?

Biff—Gone.

Amy (*sharply*)—Where did you get that whiskey, young man?

Biff (*like a spanked boy*)—I had it.

Amy—Now I don't mind your taking a drink, Biff, but you make such a fool of yourself.

Biff—Yes, ma'am, I do.

Amy—Are you ready to go out?

Biff—Yes—

Amy (*fixing her gloves*)—Well, get your hat. Sunday afternoon and everybody out.

Biff—Amy—

Amy—What's the matter, Biff—

Biff (*taking her in his arms*)—Do you know that you are very sweet and beautiful. I love you.

Amy—I love you too, Biff—

Biff—And that new car you've wanted—say, you're going to get a better one. Tomorrow you're going to get the finest car in Hillsdale.

Amy—Our old car is getting terrible-looking—

Biff—Why, I wouldn't let you be seen in it. (*Pause.*) Say, there's a brand new taxi standing across the street—let's see if it's still there. (*He goes to the window and looks out—calls.*) Hey, taxi! Drive up to that front door and wait there. Biff Grimes and his best girl are going for a ride—(*He comes back and sweeps her off her feet—into his arms. She tries to protest but he holds her tight.*)

AMY—Biff, put my skirt down—

BIFF (*starting for the door*)—Hell, let them look! Biff Grimes' girl has the best legs in town. (*The taxi is honking as they go out.*)

THE CURTAIN FALLS

THE PLAYS AND THEIR AUTHORS

"Both Your Houses." A drama in three acts by Maxwell Anderson. Copyright, 1932, 1933, by the author. Copyright and published, 1933, by Samuel French, New York.

This is Maxwell Anderson's fourth appearance with the authors of best plays contained in these yearbooks. He made his début as co-author with Laurence Stallings of "What Price Glory" (1924-25) and was later represented by his own "Saturday's Children" (1926-27) and by "Gypsy" (1928-29). He had been a university professor and an editorial writer before he took to playwrighting with "White Desert" in 1923. In recent years he has done considerable writing for the motion pictures in Hollywood. He was born in Atlantic, Pa.

"Dinner at Eight." A drama in three acts by George S. Kaufman and Edna Ferber. Copyright, 1932, by the authors. Copyright and published, 1932, by Doubleday, Doran & Co., Inc., New York.

George Kaufman and Edna Ferber were represented in the year book of 1924-25 by "Minick" and in 1927-28 by "The Royal Family." Mr. Kaufman had previously been a frequent contributor, first as co-author with Marc Connelly of several plays, beginning the season of 1921-22 with "Dulcy." He was co-author of "June Moon" (1929-30) with Ring Lardner, of "Once in a Lifetime" (1930-31) with Moss Hart, and "Of Thee I Sing" (1931-32) with Morrie Ryskind and the Gershwins. He did "The Butter and Egg Man" (1925-26) on his own. He was born in Pittsburgh, Pa., and was dramatic editor of the New York *Times* before quitting newspaper work for playwrighting.

Miss Ferber, a Kalamazoo, Mich., girl and also a former newspaper writer, is one of the most successful of American novelists, her most recent work being "They Brought Their Women." The enormously popular "Show Boat" was also hers. So far she has stood out successfully against the lure of Hollywood money, letting others fashion the screen adaptations of her plays.

"When Ladies Meet." A comedy in three acts by Rachel Crothers. Copyright, 1932, by the author. Copyright and published, 1932, by Samuel French, New York.

Rachel Crothers made her first appearance as a Best Plays author the season of 1920-21 with "Nice People." Later she was represented by "Mary the 3d" (1922-23). To the issue of 1928-29 she contributed "Let Us Be Gay," and in 1930-31 "As Husbands Go." Miss Crothers was born in Bloomington, Ill. The daughter of parents devoted to the profession of medicine, she elected in her school years to become associated with the theatre. She has been a successful dramatist for many years, was the organizer of stage war reliefs in 1918 and last winter organized the Stage Relief Fund by the aid of which some 6,000 unemployed actors and their families were helped through the depression.

"Design for Living." A comedy in three acts by Noel Coward. Copyright, 1933, by the author. Copyright and published, 1933, by Doubleday, Doran & Co., New York.

Noel Coward, at 33, is quite an old man so far as his theatre adventures go. He began as a boy actor when he was 10, after having been sent away to school when he was 8 from the parish of Teddington, near London, where he was born. His father and mother kept a music shop, selling sheet music, records and probably saxophones. When he was going on 12 he joined a company organized for rural England by the late Charles Hawtrey. His playmates in that organization included the Gertrude Lawrence for whom he later wrote "Private Lives," Estelle Winwood and Flora Sheffield, all three known to American playgoers. Coward played many parts during his juvenile days, and wrote several plays, but nothing much came of either activity. He joined the Artists' Rifles at the outbreak of the war, when he was 18, and came home disgusted with the whole business. Shortly after that he began an upward climb with his first play, "I'll Leave It to You," which eventually carried him through the success of "The Young Idea," "The Vortex," and a series of Charlot revues. For several of these he wrote songs, sketches and dialogue, did the staging and took part in the performance. His recent triumphs have included the motion picture, "Cavalcade," made from a historical revue he wrote for Drury Lane and concededly the screen's greatest achievement to date; "Private Lives," a farce comedy success the stock companies dote on, and this "Design for Living," the outstanding commercial success of New York's last season.

"Biography." A comedy in three acts by S. N. Behrman. Copyright, 1932, 1933, by the author. Copyright and published, 1933, by Farrar & Rinehart, Inc., New York.

S. N. Behrman is another of the playwrights who drags himself back from Hollywood occasionally to see one of his plays produced on Broadway. A season ago it was "Brief Moment," which Francine Larrimore played the better part of the season, and which was included in the 1931-32 volume of this series. Like most of his scenario writing colleagues, Mr. Behrman does not care a lot for the movies, but knows what he likes in the way of money. He was born in Worcester, Mass., took naturally to study and kept at it until he was through Clark, Harvard and Columbia universities with a collection of degrees. He wrote "The Second Man" for the Theatre Guild, collaborated with Kenneth Nicholson on a number of plays, and wrote "Serena Blandish" and "Meteor" by himself.

"Alien Corn." A drama in three acts by Sidney Howard. Copyright, 1932, by the author. Copyright and published, 1933, by Charles Scribner's Sons, New York.

"The Late Christopher Bean." A comedy in three acts, founded upon "Prenez Garde a la Peinture" by René Fauchois. Copyright, 1932, 1933, by the author, under the title of "Muse of All Work." Copyright and published, 1933, by Samuel French, New York.

Sidney Howard this year achieves the distinction of being the first playwright to have two dramas in the same volume of the year book of American drama. The editor tried with some persistence to jocky Mr. Howard out of this honor, thinking thus to make room for one more American author, but the fact remained to face him down that "Alien Corn" and "The Late Christopher Bean" were, in his judgment, two of the best plays of the year and he could think of no legitimate excuse for leaving either out. Mr. Howard's last appearance with a best play was in the book representing the season of 1926-27, when he wrote "The Silver Cord." Previous to that he had won the Pulitzer prize in 1924 with "They Knew What They Wanted," which was included in the issue of 1924-25. Mr. Howard was born in Oakland, California, in 1891, and was graduated from the University of California in 1915. He studied drama with Prof. George Pierce Baker at Harvard, and left that class to enlist in the World War as an ambulance driver at the Soloniki front. Later he transferred to the air forces and was in command of a combat squadron at armistice time. He has done some special assignment newspaper and magazine work and written one novel, "The Labor Spy."

"We, the People." A drama in twenty scenes by Elmer Rice. Copyright, 1933, by the author. Copyright and published, 1933, by Coward, McCann, Inc., New York.

This is Mr. Rice's third appearance in these volumes, he having written the Pulitzer award drama, "Street Scene," included in the issue of 1928-29, and "The Left Bank," 1931-32. Mr. Rice was born in New York, 1892, hated the law which his parents insisted he should prepare to follow and took to playwrighting with "On Trial" in 1914. Later he wrote the first expressionistic drama, "The Adding Machine," to boast an American background. Last year he scored two successes, both of which he personally financed and staged, "The Left Bank" and "Counselor-at-Law." In spite of which he is, he says, through with producing.

"Pigeons and People." A comedy in one act by George M. Cohan. Copyright, 1932, by the author.

Having come honestly by his eminence as an American theatrical institution, George M. Cohan deserves a place in any year book of American drama. It happens, however, that the years of his greater achievements as a dramatist were those preceding the publication of the first volume of the Best Plays series in 1919. He is included in a new volume covering the decade from 1909 to 1919 (Mantle-Sherwood), issued last spring, as the adapter of "Seven Keys to Baldpate," an outstanding comedy success of 1913-14. Mr. Cohan was born in Providence, R. I., July 4, 1878, and has spent fifty of his fifty-five years in and about the theatre. He is the most versatile of native authors and composers, a man of many talents. His first full-length play was "The Governor's Son" (1899), which he expanded from a sketch played for years by the Four Cohans, the quartet including his father Jere, his mother Helen, his sister Josephine and his lively stepping, vocally nasal self. His first "$2 show," which lifted him into the legitimate field, was "Little Johnny Jones" (1904); his first straight comedy "Popularity," which failed in 1906; his first straight comedy success "Get Rich Quick Wallingford;" his biggest comedy success "Seven Keys to Baldpate." Both "Wallingford" and "Baldpate" were adaptations.

"One Sunday Afternoon." A comedy in three acts by James Hagan. Copyright, 1932, by the author. Copyright and published, 1933, by Samuel French, New York.

James Hagan is the mysterious stranger of this year's playwright group. He literally "sneaked in on rubbers," and is still moving about more or less noiselessly. His comedy, "One Sunday Afternoon," had been for sale several years before it finally was produced. Once it was offered to Paramount as a talking picture possibility and for a few hundred dollars. Paramount could not see it. After its production as a play Paramount paid $26,000 for the motion picture rights. Asking Mr. Hagan for essential facts of biography brought forth the information that he was a newspaper man, working on the old New York *World* and the St. Louis *Post-Dispatch* and being fired from both. He did a black-face act in a medicine show, but was not very funny, even to the doctor. The show was helped out of Elgin, Ill., by the police. Hagan was stage manager for Henry Miller and later for Arthur Hopkins. He has written two other plays, "Guns" and "Trimmed." Both, he feels positive, were quite awful. Recently he was hired to write motion picture scenarios, but his contract expired, he says, before RKO knew he was on the lot.

PLAYS PRODUCED IN NEW YORK

June 18, 1932—June 17, 1933

(Plays marked with asterisk were still playing June 17, 1933)

MAN CRAZY

(8 performances)

A comedy in three acts by Stephen Sanford. Produced by Paul Gilmore at the Cherry Lane Theatre, New York, June 18, 1933.

Cast of characters—

Dick Stout....................Thad Sharretts
Christine Parks....................Elsia Michael
Edward, a Butler....................Vincent Mallory
Robert Archer....................James Hale
Helen Archer....................Dorothea Mallory
Kenneth Williams....................Frances Arnold
Ford Mallory....................Fredric Cali
Olive Williams....................Sylvia Singer
Clara Mallory....................Eloise Ferrier
Mrs. J. Jennings Parks....................Dolores Leon
Vernon Armstong....................Jack Stern
A Maid....................Evelyn Finkles
Acts I, II and III.—Seaview Country Club.

During Mr. Gilmore's season at the Cherry Lane Theatre the following were played for one, two and three-week engagements: "Almost a Husband," "As We Love," "Black Ace," "Minister in Hell," "Uptown West," "The Devil's Daughter," "Dumb Luck," "The Havoc," "Redwoods," "Things We Do," "Marriage," "Sickness of Youth," "Muddy Doorsteps," "House of Hate." "Charming Rascal" had a seventh month run.

THE WEB

(24 performances)

A play in two acts by Frederick Herendeen. Produced by Charles H. Abramson and Jess Smith at the Morosco Theatre, New York, June 27, 1932.

Cast of characters—

Warden Sullivan....................Frank Shannon
Kelly....................John Bohn

Professor Warren.............................William Ingersoll
Moto Ishada.............................Harold DeBecker
Marian Warren.............................Elizabeth Day
Lett Hollins.............................Sherling R. Oliver
Robert Clark.............................Edmund Mack
Rocky Flint.............................Curtis Karpe
Red Slade.............................Joseph McCoy

Act I.—Scene 1—In the Heart of the Everglades. 2—The Home of Professor Warren. 3—In the Attic. 4—The Living-room. Two Hours Later. Act II.—The Same. Ten Seconds Later.

Entire Action of the Play Takes Place in the Everglades, Florida.

Staged by Frank McCormack; settings by Nicholas Yellanti.

Professor Warren and Moto Ishada have spent thirty years in the Everglades of Florida seeking to stimulate the growth of human organisms by practicing on spiders. They have succeeded in developing a spider as big as a small man when two desperate criminals escape from a nearby prison—the spider grabs them and hangs them in its web. Marian Warren, a young and beautiful ward of the professor's and Robert Clark, a fresh reporter, are scared something terrible.

THE LINGERING PAST

(13 performances)

A play in three acts by Leonard J. Tynan. Produced by the Seven Arts Guild Players at the Provincetown Playhouse, New York, June 29, 1932.

Cast of characters—

Ben Morland.............................Frank J. Marshall, Jr.
Irene Weller.............................Elizabeth King
Kate Gardner.............................Mara Keval
Mrs. Laura Pond.............................Esther Solveig
Simon Weller.............................Charles Angelo
Miss White.............................Anna Ray
Ira Powell.............................John E. Riley
John Gardner.............................Howard McCulley
Nancy Gardner.............................Frances Tannehill
Sam Belden.............................George A. Lawrence
Bobby Watt.............................Robert Emory
Clara Smith.............................Henrietta Appleby
Janice.............................Dona Fairchild
George Williams.............................Edmund Hale
Riley.............................George Spelvin

Acts I, II, III.—John Gardner's Home in The Country, North of the New York-New Jersey State Line.

Staged by Edwin Hopkins; settings by George Segare.

Laura Pond divorced John Gardner and gave him their infant daughter Nancy to rear. John married Kate, who brought Nancy up as her own child. When Nancy is ten years old Laura Pond, seeking rest from her job as a night club entertainer, answers the advertisement of a summer resort and finds it to be run by her former husband and his new wife. She also finds her daughter

Nancy and wants her back. She does not get her, because her past rises up and smites her.

DESTRUCTION

(1 performance)

A tragedy in six episodes by Bertha Wiernik. Produced by the American Classic Players at the Chanin Auditorium, New York, June 30, 1932.

Cast of characters—

Josiah Amon....................Kirk Brown
Della....................Kathleen Costa
Eleazur....................Claude Tonsick
Mira....................Ruth Guion
Rita....................Virginia Dean
"Dr. Porzowsky"....................Joseph King
Mrs. Kerlington....................Diana Park
Comrade Crown....................Harry Tebbutt
Butler....................Louis Milner

Episodes I, IV, V—Living-room of Amons, Chicago. Episode II—Mrs. Kerlington's reception room. Episode III—Communist mass meeting, interior of lyceum. Episode VI—Josiah's study room.

Staged by Howard Sinclair.

Eleazur Amon, son of Josiah, a minister of God, is temporarily lured away from the faith of his fathers. Becoming interested in communism through a certain Dr. Porzowsky, young Amon is led to a declaration in a communist mass meeting that he no longer believes in a capitalistic world or in God. Josiah appears dramatically and snatches his son from the burning Reds. Eleazur returns penitently to his home.

THE CHAMELEON

(8 performances)

A comedy in three acts by Adam Gostony, adapted from Hungarian by Giza H. von Hessen. Produced by Lionel A. Hyman at the Masque Theatre, New York, July 18, 1932.

Cast of characters—

Aunt Regina....................Delephene Eaton
The Nurse....................Frances Armstrong
A Patient....................Hazel O'Connell
The Attendant....................Robert Walker
The Interne....................Earl Eby
Wanda Alba....................Virginia Byron
Doctor Peter....................Allen Forth

Acts I, II, and III.—A Convalescing Room in Doctor Peter's Sanatorium.

Staged by Lionel A. Hyman.

Wanda Alba, enamored of Dr. Peter, manages an entrance to his sanatorium on a ruse. Threatened with the failure of her scheme Wanda invents other ruses, finally insisting that she is suffering an acute attack of appendicitis. The Doctor operates, falls in love with Wanda's appendix and is thus snared into marriage.

THE DEVIL'S LITTLE GAME

(8 performances)

A play in three acts by Joseph Jay Ingerlid. Produced by Alexander Burke at the Provincetown Theatre, New York, August 1, 1932.

Cast of characters—

Joe....................Victor Morgan
Jeanette....................Ann Shearer
Eddie....................Edward J. Schneider
Millie....................Sydelle Bry
Parsons....................John O. Hewitt
Mac....................Jerry Sylvestre
Sloppy....................Edward B. Latimer
Dan....................W. Messenger Bellis
Phil....................Charles Atken
Edna....................Ruth Fields
Marcus....................Leslie Morson
Jane....................Constance Martin
Lippo....................Lee Sanford
Tramp....................J. S. McLaughlin
First Policeman....................Otto Barthel
Second Policeman....................Edmond Hale

Acts I, II, and III.—Cheap Speakeasy in Lower New York.
Staged by Stuart Beebe.

A cashiered divinity student finds himself in a cheap speakeasy in lower New York where the Devil confuses his choice between two feminine lights o' love. Gangsters plot murders and an absconding bank cashier is finally captured.

CHAMBERLAIN BROWN'S SCRAP BOOK

(10 performances)

A vaudeville type of revue produced by Chamberlain Brown at the Ambassador Theatre, New York, August 1, 1932.

Charles Schofield and Almira Sessions.
Ina Hayward
Vinton Haworth and Ray Hedge ("Myrt and Marge" radio sketch).
Terry Carroll and Company.
"Harlemade," featuring Ernest Whitman, 3 Flashes of Lightning, Lillian Ridley, William Andrews, Percy Verwaynen.
Leda Lombard.
"Memories," with Helen Bertram, Nancy McCord, Frazer Coleman and the Ritz Quartette.

Florence Auer.
"In a Radio Station."
Barre Hill, Stella De Mette, Charles Hedley.
Priscilla Knowles and Company in "East Lynne."
"That New Gang of Mine," Ethel Norris and Jonathan Hole.
Smith Ballew and Orchestra.
"The Community Players," with Valerie Bergere and Company.
Charles Hedley and Cecile Sherman, with Paul Taubman at the Piano.
Mae Dix.
Dorothy MacDonald.
"Taken from Life."
Kate Woods Fiske.
Staged by Charles Schofield and Robert Lively.

A potpourri of vaudeville strung together on so slender a thread of plot the Actors' Equity Association permitted its showing on Sunday nights.

PAGE PYGMALION

(13 performances)

A comedy in three acts by Carl Henkle. Produced by the A. I. M. (Alan Morrill) Productions Corp., at the Bijou Theatre, New York, August 3, 1932.

Cast of characters—

Tony Walder....................................Carleton Young
John Coates.................................Robert Emmett Keane
Sally Gray....................................June Clayworth
Percy Drury....................................Percy Helton
Henry Sewell................................Thomas Coffin Cooke
Elvira Sewell..................................Aline McDermott
Mrs. Brownell..................................Claire Whitney
Helen Brownell....................................Doris Eaton

Acts I, II, and III.—A Room in Tony Walder's Studio Apartment in New York.
Staged by Paul Porter.

Tony Walder, son of wealthy Oklahomans, establishes a studio in New York. He falls in love with Sally, the model for his statue of the Goddess of Love, but feels that he is obligated to marry Helen Brownell. His cousin, John Coates, to correct the situation, takes advantage of an alcoholic party to substitute Sally for the statue, bring her to life and let her tell the truth about those present. This eliminates Helen and convinces Tony that he was right about Sally all the time.

DOMINO

(7 performances)

A romantic comedy in three acts adapted by Grace George from the French of Marcel Achard. Produced by William A. Brady at the Playhouse, New York, August 16, 1932.

Cast of characters—

Lorette....................................Jessie Royce Landis
Christine....................................Joan Carr
Louise....................................Geraldine Wall
Mirandole....................................Walter Kingsford
Domino....................................Rod La Rocque
Heller....................................Robert Loraine
Cremone....................................Geoffrey Kerr

Act I.—Christine's Apartment in Paris. Acts II and III.—Heller's Villa in St. Cloud.

Staged by Stanley Logan; settings by Livingston Platt.

Before Lorette married Heller she had known Cremone, who signed his letters François. After she married Heller he finds one of François' letters and becomes wildly jealous. Fearing he may discover that Cremone is François, Lorette hires an adventuring youth named Domino to pretend that he is François. He is to let Heller punch his head if necessary and disappear, thus relieving Heller of all suspicion. The plot works until Lorette really falls in love with Domino and prefers him to either husband or lover.

SMILING FACES

(33 performances)

A musical comedy in two acts by Harry Clarke; music by Harry Revel; lyrics by Mack Gordon. Produced at the Shubert Theatre, New York, August 30, 1932.

Cast of characters—

Helen Sydney....................................Barbara Williams
George Black....................................Bradford Hatton
Robert Bowington....................................Roy Royston
Perkins....................................Boyd Davis
Arthur Lawrence....................................Charles Collins
Amy Edwards....................................Hope Emerson
First Assistant....................................Ray Romain
Second Assistant....................................Tom Romain
Peggy Post....................................Dorothy Stone
Monument Spleen....................................Fred Stone
Sybilla Richter....................................Isabel O'Madigan
Cordonia Potts....................................Adora Andrews
Horatio Dalrymple....................................Ali Youssoff
Edward Richter....................................Eddie Garvey
Mildred McKay....................................Doris Patson
A Waiter....................................Bradford Hatton
A Bellhop....................................Harold Offer
A Gangster....................................Thomas Sternfeld
A Minister....................................Rex Coover
A Bishop....................................Carl Duart

Act I, Scenes 1, 2, 3, 4—Robert Bowington's Home, Southampton, L. I. 5—Ballroom of Country Club. Act II.—Grand Hotel, Havana, Cuba.

Staged by R. H. Burnside.

The motion picture company of which Monument Spleen is a director invades the Long Island estate of Robert Bowington.

The leading lady is Peggy Post, engaged to young Bowington's friend, Arthur Lawrence. They cannot be married because Peggy is not in the Social Register. Bowington tries to fix that by marrying Peggy, giving her a Social Register standing and then turning her over to Arthur. Later he decides to keep her in the family, and Arthur marries Mildred McKay instead.

HERE TODAY

(39 performances)

A comedy in three acts by George Oppenheimer. Produced by Sam H. Harris at the Ethel Barrymore Theatre, New York, September 6, 1932.

Cast of characters—

Jeffrey Windrew....................................Geoffrey Bryant
Gertrude....................................Elizabeth Taylor
Philip Graves....................................Donald Macdonald
Claire Windrew....................................Sally Bates
Mrs. Windrew....................................Charlotte Granville
Stanley Dale....................................Charles D. Brown
Mary Hilliard....................................Ruth Gordon
Spencer Grant....................................Paul McGrath

Acts I and III.—Windrew House at Nassau, the Bahamas. Act II.—Beach of the Windrew House.

Staged by George S. Kaufman; settings by Raymond Sovey.

Mary Hilliard and Stanley Dale find themselves in Nassau, the Bahamas, after a party in New York. There Mary meets her ex-husband, Philip Graves, who is trying to confirm his engagement to Claire Windrew, the restless daughter of the Boston Windrews. Mary and Stanley, volunteering to help Philip, manage to lie him into Social Register connections and to blacken the reputation of his rival. At which point Mary decides that she wants Philip back and all the work has to be done over. Philip and Mary are finally reunited and Claire takes her Bostonian.

BALLYHOO OF 1932

(95 performances)

A musical comedy in two acts by Norman B. Anthony, music by Lewis E. Gensler, lyrics by E. Y. Harburg. Produced at the 44th St. Theatre, New York, September 6, 1932.

Principals engaged—

Willie Howard
Eugene Howard
Bob Hope
Tom Harty

Donald Stewart	Vera Marche
Ralph Sanford	Gloria Gilbert
Paul Hartman	Dorissa Nelova
Jeanne Aubert	Rasch Girls
Lulu McConnell	Lucille Clay Osborne

Staged by the Messrs. Anthony, Gensler, Connolly and Patterson; settings by Russell Patterson.

Principal songs—"Thrill Me," "Riddle Me This" and "Falling off the Wagon."

BEST YEARS

(45 performances)

A comedy in three acts by Raymond Van Sickle. Produced by Elizabeth Miele at the Bijou Theatre, New York, September 7, 1932.

Cast of characters—

Emma Davis....................Mary Horne
Mrs. Davis....................Jean Adair
Madge Davis....................Marjorie Lytell
Milt Stotter....................Thomas Reynolds
Floss Reynolds....................Leona Powers
Cora Davis....................Katherine Alexander
Tommy Craven....................Fred Sherman
Fred Barton....................Harvey Stephens
Dr. Graffis....................Thomas Findlay
Mr. Craven....................Daniel Poole

Acts I, II, and III.—Living-room of the Davis Home.
Staged by Priestly Morrison; settings by Rollo Wayne.

Cora Davis is the patient and devoted slave of her mother, a whining hypochondriac. Cora gives up her suitors one by one and loses hope of ever having a home of her own. Fred Barton, the best loved of her sweethearts, returns to town determined to marry Cora and break the spell of her mother's domination. Cora is strengthened to rebellion by Fred's encouragement and Mother suffers a stroke from which she does not recover.

THE MAN WHO RECLAIMED HIS HEAD

(28 performances)

A drama in three acts by Jean Bart. Produced by Arthur Hammerstein and L. Lawrence Weber at the Broadhurst Theatre, New York, September 8, 1932.

Cast of characters—

Jean....................Richard Barrows
Fernand Demoncey....................Romaine Callender
Paul Verin....................Claude Rains
Linette Verin....................Evelyn Eaton

Curly....Carleton Young
Mimi....Janet Rathbun
Margot....Emily Lowry
Pierre....Paul Wilson
Jack....Allen Nourse
Adele Verin....Jean Arthur
Henri Berthaud....Stuart Casey
Gendarme....C. Ellsworth Smith
Waiter....Allen Nourse
Antoine....Paul Wilson
Baron de Montford....Lionel Braham
Chonchon....Dennie Moore
Lulu....Janet Rathbun
Danglas....Richard Barrows
Maid....Lucille Lortel
Charlot....Alexander Cross
Maniac....Marshall Hale
Maid....Kay Miller
Beppo....Edward T. Colebrook
Old Lady....Marie Hunt
Station Master....Daniel Hamilton
English Officer....David Hughes
Nichette....Kay Miller
Sister Sophie....Marjorie Dalton
Sister Rose....Mona Moray
Marchand....Paul Wilson
Louis....Ray Harper
Messenger....Alexander Cross
Soldier of the Foreign Legion....James J. Coyle
French Soldier....Richard Bowler
Picard....Allen Nourse
Market-women—Marie Hunt, Marjorie Dalton, Kay Miller.
Peddlers—William Boren, Julien Garfield, Daniel Hamilton, Roger Paul Craig.
Midinettes—Hester Holm, Rita Agostini, Tucker McGuire.
Spectators—Burton Mallory, Ray Lawrence, Milton Owen, Robert Neff.

Act I.—Faubourg St. Germain, Boulevard Clichy. Act II.—St. Cloud—Auteuil—Quai d'Orsay. Act III.—Donneville—St. Cloud—Faubourg St. Germain.

Staged by Herbert J. Biberman.

Paul Verin, an ugly little man of Clichy, has married Adele, a pretty girl. Paul is a radical socialist, a newspaper writer. When he discovers that Adele is restless and unhappy, being denied money and a good time, Paul sells his services to Henri Berthaud, a politician with an eye on the premiership of France. At the outbreak of war Paul advises Berthaud to desert his party and vote for war. As a result Berthaud wins the premiership and takes Adele as his mistress. Paul hurries back from the front, severs Berthaud's head from his body and would kill himself were it not for the plight of his 4-year-old daughter.

COUNSELLOR-AT-LAW

(First return engagement 104—second, 16 performances)

A play in three acts by Elmer Rice. Run resumed at the Plymouth Theatre, New York, September 12, 1932.

Cast of characters—

Bessie Green....Dorothy Day
Henry Susskind....Jules Garfield
Sarah Becker....Malka Kornstein
A Tall Man....Victor Wolfson
A Stout Man....Jack Collins
A Postman....James Mullin
Zedorah Chapman....Doris Underwood
Goldie Rindskopf....Angela Jacobs
Charles McFadden....J. Hammond Dailey
John P. Tedesco....Sam Bonnell
A Bootblack....William Vaughn
Regina Gordon....Ann Teeman
Herbert Howard Weinberg....Harry Mervis
Arthur Sandler....Conway Washburne
Lillian Larue....Sue Moore
An Errand Boy....Buddy Proctor
Roy Darwin....Jack Leslie
George Simon....Paul Muni
Cora Simon....Mary Servoss
A Woman....Jane Hamilton
Lena Simon....Jennie Moscowitz
Peter J. Malone....T. H. Manning
Rigby Crayfield....John Crump
Johann Breitstein....John M. Qualen
David Simon....Ned Glass
Harry Becker....Martin Wolfson
Richard Dwight, Jr....David Vivian
Dorothy Dwight....June Cox
Francis Clark Baird....Elmer Brown

Acts I, II, III.—Law offices of George Simon, mid-town New York.
Staged by Elmer Rice; settings by Raymond Sovey.

The summer of 1932 Paul Muni, who created the rôle of George Simon in "Counsellor-at-Law," went to Hollywood to fulfill a motion picture contract. Otto Kruger, who had been playing the rôle in Chicago, came on to replace him in New York while Harry Mervis took Kruger's place in Chicago. In July the play was withdrawn for the summer. When the run was resumed in September Muni returned to his old rôle and several members of the Chicago company were substituted for those of the original company. These included Mary Servoss, Ann Teeman, Dorothy Day and Doris Underwood. During the winter the play was sent on tour, with Muni again the star, and ended its season with a second return to New York for a two-weeks engagement beginning May 15, 1933, at the Forty-sixth Street Theatre. For original cast and production see "Best Plays of 1931-32."

CLEAR ALL WIRES

(93 performances)

A comedy in three acts by Bella and Samuel Spewack. Produced by Herman Shumlin at the Times Square Theatre, New York, September 14, 1932.

Cast of characters—

First Chambermaid..........Ludmilla Toretzka
Second Chambermaid..........Anna Ouzoroff
Porter..........Alexander Lapteff
Pettingwaite..........Charles Romano
Renke..........Egon Brecher
Mackenzie..........Philip Tonge
Kate Nelson..........Dorothy Tree
Menzies..........John Hoysradt
Kostya..........Ari Kutai
"Lefty" Williams..........Harry Tyler
Peasant..........Peter Lopoukin
Soldier..........Aaron Pett
Sozanoff..........John Melvin Bleifer
New Woman..........Alla Cutlerova
Buckley Joyce Thomas..........Thomas Mitchell
Eugenie Smirnova..........Pauline Achmatova
Prince Tomofsky..........Eugene Sigaloff
Dolly Winslow..........Dorothy Mathews
Professor Sverdin..........John Hamsa
Commissar of Foreign Affairs..........George Ermoloff
Graustein..........Alexander Danaroff
Volchok..........Alexander Lapteff
Cogan..........Alexander Markoff
Rubinstein..........Jacques Neradoff
Nurse..........Nina Dolgova
Chairman of Tapestry Delegation..........Nicholas Busanovsky
Conductress..........Tamara Kirillin
Conductor..........Serge Antonoff

Acts I, II and III.—Room in the Hotel Savoy, Moscow.
Staged by Herman Shumlin; settings by Aline Bernstein.

Buckley Joyce Thomas, chief of the foreign news service of the Chicago Press, is relieved of his berth in Paris when he becomes too actively interested in Dolly Winslow, sent abroad by his boss to have her voice cultivated. Transferred to Moscow, Thomas takes Dolly with him and for a fortnight spends a lively time dodging cables from the home office tracing Dolly and trying to fire him. To reëstablish himself with the boss Thomas plots an alleged attempted assassination of the last of the Romanoffs, takes the bullet himself when the Soviet Foreign Minister gets in the way, is a hero for a day and then exposed. Then he goes to China for Hearst.

FLYING COLORS

(188 performances)

A revue in two acts by Howard Dietz, music by Arthur Schwartz. Produced by Max Gordon at the Imperial Theatre, New York, September 15, 1932.

Principals engaged—

Clifton Webb
Charles Butterworth
Philip Loeb
Buddy Ebsen
Larry Adler
Jay Wilson

George Kirk	Imogen Coca
June Blossom	Monette Moore
Tamara Geva	Jean Sargent
Patsy Kelly	Albertina Vitak
Vilma Ebsen	Helen Carrington

Albertina Rasch girls

Staged by Howard Dietz; settings by Norman Bel-Geddis.

Principal songs—"Alone Together," "Shine on Your Shoes" and "Louisiana Hayride."

LILLY TURNER

(24 performances)

A play in three acts by Philip Dunning and George Abbott. Produced by Abbott-Dunning, Inc., at the Morosco Theatre, New York, September 19, 1932.

Cast of characters—

Dave Turner.............James Bell
Doc McGill.............Granville Bates
Mrs. McGill.............Clare Woodbury
Lilly Turner.............Dorothy Hall
Frederick.............Robert Barrat
Dr. Hawley............. Joseph Creahan
Bob Cross.............John Litel
Truckman.............Percy Kilbride
Hotel Manager.............Emmett Shackleford
Bell Boy.............Warren Bryan
Policeman.............Byron Shores

Act I.—Scene 1—Store entrance to "Doc McGill's Free Health Exhibit." 2—Front of Lecture Platform. 3—Back of Lecture Platform. Act II.—Back of Lecture Platform. In Another Town. Act III.—Hotel Room.

Staged by Philip Dunning and George Abbott; settings by Livingston Platt.

Lilly Turner, the Venus doing poses with Doc McGill's Health Exhibit and married to Dave, barker and property man, shares her favors with Frederick, the German strong man of the troupe. Frederick, crazed by love of her, is put away in a sanitarium and Lilly next imagines herself truly in love with Bob Cross, his successor. She is ready to run away with Bob, because Dave won't stop drinking, when Frederick escapes from the sanitarium and comes to get her. Finding both Dave and Bob in Lilly's room Frederick knocks Bob out and throws Dave through the office skylight. Dave's need of her convinces Lilly that she really loves him more than any of the others and she sends Bob away. Frances Fox Dunning wrote the original story.

THE BUDGET

(7 performances)

A comedy in three acts by Robert Middlemass. Produced by Harry Askin and Hugh Ford at the Hudson Theatre, New York, September 20, 1932.

Cast of characters—

Betty Harper....................................Mary Lawlor
Peter Harper....................................Lynne Overman
Calpurnia.......................................Olive Burgoyne
Benjamin Kaplan.................................Nicholas Adams
Claude Knowles..................................Raymond Walburn
Elsie Knowles...................................Olive Reeve-Smith
Theodore Roosevelt Smith........................Paul C. Floyd
Mrs. Mullens....................................Clara Palmer
Mr. Mullens.....................................John M. Kline
Miss Mullens....................................Virginia Curley
Acts I and II.—Porch of the Harper Home. Act III.—Living-room of the Harper Home.
Staged by Hugh Ford.

Peter Harper, laid off for two months during the depression, has $750 in the bank. By a strict budgeting Peter believes he can get through the two months and still make a payment of $325 on his house. Then his wife's sister and her husband come to visit, the cook's husband settles down on them and the bank in which they had the $750 closes its doors. They try to rent the house, but the mosquitoes drive a prospective tenant away. In the end Peter gets another job.

TRIPLETS

(3 performances)

A comedy in three acts by Mark Linder. Produced by the author at the Masque Theatre, New York, September 21, 1932.

Cast of characters—

Ruthie..Olga C. Hansen
Marie Schindelheim..............................Fernanda Eliscu
Heinrich Schindelheim...........................Chester Clute
Lawrence O'Day..................................Jack C. Connolly
Essie Schindelheim..............................Helen Glenn
Bessie Schindelheim.............................Ruth Edell
Tessie Schindelheim.............................Alney Alba
Jim O'Day.......................................James Eby Jr.
Jerry O'Day.....................................John A. Willarde
John O'Day......................................Stanley Marlowe
Patricia O'Day..................................Marguerite Tebeau
Dr. Ludwig Strouse..............................William Dorbin
Judge Dalton....................................Kirk Brown
Leader of the Band..............................J. S. McLaughlin
Acts I, II and III.—Carbondale, Pa.
Staged by Walter Wilson; settings by Ned Crane.

The O'Day triplets marry the Schindelheim triplets and sign an agreement that if their marriages are without issue in two years they will separate. They quarrel, threaten to quit and are finally reconciled when the three Schindelheim girls present the three O'Day boys with three babies each.

ONLY THE YOUNG

(4 performances)

A comedy in three acts by Cecil Lewis. Produced by Robert Gross and Fred Fisher at the Sutton Show Shop, New York, September 21, 1932.

Cast of characters—

Delia....................Beverly Bayne
Ronny....................Theodore St. John
Kit....................Elizabeth Young
Squirrel....................Hilda Spong
John....................Barry Townley
Roger Arkwright....................Leslie Denison
Miriam....................Maud Ainsle

Acts I, II and III.—Living-room of a villa on the Italian Lakes.
Staged by Ralph McBane.

Both Ronny and his father, John, are in love with Delia, who is the father's mistress. In seeking a solution of the tangle through a frank discussion it is revealed that Ronny is not John's son, which so shocks Ronny that his whole viewpoint is changed and he falls in love with another girl.

THE STORK IS DEAD

(27 performances)

A farce comedy in three acts by Hans Kottow, adapted from the Viennese by Frederic and Fanny Hatton. Produced by A. H. Woods, Manager, at the 48th St. Theatre, New York, September 23, 1932.

Cast of characters—

Comte Rene de Gaumont....................Ross Alexander
Paul de Gaumont....................Fred Stewart
Lola Faubert....................Ninon Bunyea
Lucien Bridier....................Mark Smith
Madame Bridier....................Nana Bryant
Suzanne Bridier....................Ethel Norris
Max....................Frank Woodruff
Jerome....................Robert Vivian
Madelaine....................Eva Farrell
Hortense....................Phyllis Holden

Act I.—Scenes 1 and 2—Rene de Gaumont's Bedroom in His Paris Apartment. Acts II and III.—Suzanne's Sitting-room and Bedroom in the Bridiers' House Just Outside of Paris.
Staged by A. H. Van Buren.

Comte Rene de Gaumont is living with Lola but must marry Suzanne in order to replenish his fortunes with her dowry. Lola kicks up a fuss and forces Rene to sign an agreement that he will be a husband in name only to Suzanne for three months, threatening to break up the marriage if he doesn't. Rene has a hard time explaining his apparent aversion to Suzanne, who is eager to know the facts of life. Finally he determines to defy Lola, who astonishes him by announcing her engagement to his cousin.

SUCCESS STORY

(121 performances)

A play in three acts by John Howard Lawson. Produced by the Group Theatre, Inc., at the Maxine Elliott Theatre, New York, September 26, 1932.

Cast of characters—

Sarah Glassman....................................Stella Adler
Dinah McCabe....................................Ruth Nelson
Jeffery Halliburton..............................William Challee
Raymond Merritt..............................Franchot Tone
Rufus Sonnenberg.............................Morris Carnovsky
Sol Ginsberg....................................Luther Adler
Marcus Turner....................................Art Smith
Agnes Carter....................................Dorothy Patten
Harry Fisher....................................Russell Collins
Miss Farley....................................Margaret Barker

Acts I, II and III.—Private Office in the New York Headquarters of Raymond Merritt Company, Inc., Advertising and Sales Counsel.
Staged by Lee Strasberg; settings by Mordecai Gorelik.

Sol Ginsberg is an assistant statistician in the advertising firm of the Raymond Merritt Company, Inc. A product of the East Side of New York who has established his efficiency by hard work and application, Sol is viciously resentful of the capitalistic class represented by Raymond Merritt. Gradually Ginsberg rises to a position of importance, marries the mistress of his employer and becomes in fact the dominant head of the firm. Still he is not satisfied. His soul's unrest is violently disturbing to him. He has cast aside Sarah Glassman, the Jewish girl who loves him and with whom he had shared his youthful ideals. In a struggle for the possession of a revolver, Sarah shoots Ginsberg dead.

BELMONT VARIETIES

(8 performances)

A vaudeville revue in two acts by Helen and Nolan Leary and Sam Bernard 2nd. Music and lyrics by Serge Walter, Alvin Kaufman, Charles Kenny, Henry Lloyd, Mildred Kaufman and Robert Burk. Produced by Richard Herndon at the Belmont Theatre, September 26, 1932.

Principals engaged—

M. Maurice	Maryon Dale
Roy Benson	Marion Young
Leo Henning	Marjorie Enters
Lucien La Riviere	Jane Dudley
Philippe Borgia	Mauricette Ducret
Gustavo Carrasco	Lilyan Astaire
Mura Dehn	Shawni Lani

Staged by Max Scheck and Sam Bernard 2nd.

"Belmont Vanities" ran from September 6 to October 2. "Cosmo Vanities," "an enlarged and revised edition of 'Belmont Vanities,'" opened October 21 and later the title was changed to "Manhattan Vanities."

EARL CARROLL VANITIES

(87 performances)

A revue in two acts, dialogue by Jack McGowan; music and lyrics by Harold Arlen and Ted Koehler. Produced by Earl Carroll at the Broadway Theatre, New York, September 27, 1932.

Principals engaged—

Will Fyffe	Helen Broderick
Milton Berle	Harriet Hoctor
Andre Randall	Josephine Huston
Edwin Styles	Lillian Shade
John Hale	Marcelle Edwards
Andre Renaud	Beryl Wallace
Max Wall	Helene Callahan
Keith Clark	Gay Orlova
Lester Crawford	The Jackson Girls

Staged by Earl Carroll; settings by Vincente Minnelli.

Principal songs—"My Darling," "Along Came Love" and "Love Is My Inspiration."

BIDDING HIGH

(23 performances)

A comedy drama in three acts by Lois Howell. Produced by Joe De Milt at the Vanderbilt Theatre, New York, September 28, 1932.

Cast of characters—

Jimmy Stevens..King Calder
Mrs. Crane..Maud Edna Hall
Edward Crane..Carleton Macy
Myra Crane..Nedda Harrigan
Mark Ellis..Ivan Miller
Sylvia Crane..Shelah Trent
Acts I, II and III.—Living-room of the Crane Home in Englewood, New Jersey.
Staged by John Hayden; settings by William Mensching.

Sylvia Crane, courted by Jimmy Stevens and thrown into contact with Mark Ellis, takes Ellis because he is rich. Ellis really preferred Sylvia's sister Myra until Sylvia lied to him, by insisting Myra was engaged to Stevens. Jimmy, hurt by the cheating Sylvia, swears that so long as she is for sale he will make enough money to buy her back. Which he does by becoming a successful bootlegger. Ellis, losing his money, agrees to divorce Sylvia when she runs away to Reno with Jimmy, and Myra waits expectantly.

THE OTHER ONE

(16 performances)

A drama in three acts by Henry Myers. Produced by Thomas Kilpatrick at the Biltmore Theatre, New York, October 3, 1932.

Cast of characters—

Jim..George Baxter
Doctor..Frank Andrews
Martha..Lida MacMillan
Claire..Helen Ford
Mrs. Flood..Florence Vroom
Mr. Flood..George Nash
Grandfather..Fuller Mellish
Acts I, II and III.—Studio and Living-room in Jim's Home.
Staged by Harold Winston; settings by Cleon Throckmorton.

Claire's twin sister, Christine, is dead by her own hand. Claire, long suppressed by the more vivid personality of her sister, hopes now to recover the love of Jim, Chris's husband, whom she has always wanted. Jim marries Claire, but when she begs to be taken away from the house in which Jim and Christine spent their honeymoon he confesses that he is held there by his dead wife's influence. There is an intimation that the soul of Chris returns to inhabit the body of Claire in the end.

OL' MAN SATAN

(24 performances)

An allegory in three acts and thirty-seven scenes, with incidental music by Donald Heywood. Produced by Shillwood Productions at the Forrest Theatre, New York, October 3, 1932.

Cast of characters—

Satan	A. B. Comatheire
Saul	Dan Michaels
Peter	Lionel Monagas
Ma Jackson	Georgette Harvey
Josh	Phyllis Hunt
Maggie	Edna Thomas
Gabriel	Mike Jackson
Moses	Laurence Chenault
Noah	Hayes L. Pryor
David	Walter Richardson
Sister Bright	Alice Ramsey
Sister Crabtree	Tressie Legge
Teacher	Lorenzo Tucker
Number Three Imp	Freeman Fairley
Becky	Mary Jane Watkins
Soldier	Kolly Mitchell
First David Temptress	Hilda Offley
Second David Temptress	Bee Freeman
Keeper of Souls	Herbert Ellis
Farmer	Fred Miller
Paul	Walter Robinson
James	DeKoven Thompson
John	James McPheeters
Disciple	Taylor Gordon
"	Luther Henderson
"	David Bethe
"	James McPheeters
Noah's Temptress	Clyde Faison
Jezebel	Florence Lee
Maggie's Protector	Arthur McLean
Sister Johnson	Ismay Andrews
Hunchback	James Cook
Blind Man	Ralph Ramson
Mother	Helen Nelson
Procuress	Alice Ramsey
Racketeer	Wandolf Saunders
Jezebel	Florence Lee
Murderer	Lionel Monagas
Primrose	Ellen Baylor
Merrie	Cleo Harris

Staged by William A. Shilling; settings by Continer and Golding.

Mammy Jackson's children have gone to camp meeting, leaving one small boy at home. Mammy tries to interest the boy by telling him the story of Satan, visualized in a series of episodes having to do with man's temptation and frequent defeat by

Jezebel, Intemperance, Pride, Greed and other allegorical figures. Confusion in the end, with Satan still finding work for idle preachers of many faiths and panaceas to take over.

NONA

(31 performances)

A romantic farce in three acts by Gladys Unger. Produced by Peggy Fears at the Avon Theatre, New York, October 4, 1932.

Cast of characters—

Joe.....Millard F. Mitchell
Otto Vogel.....Hans Hansen
Miriam Skidwell.....Patricia Calvert
Mr. Compton.....Dudley Hawley
Dolly Armstrong.....Ellen Southbrook
Anna.....Jane Ferrel
Henry Cade.....Arthur Margetson
A Young Man With a Toupee.....John McCloskey
Nona.....Lenore Ulric
Rocco.....Aristides de Leoni
Lyle D. Armstrong.....Russell Hicks
An Old Lady.....Genevieve Dolaro
A Photographer.....Bernard Susman
A Handsome Young Man.....Warren Sterling
A Pullman Porter.....Oscar Polk
The Station Master.....Harlan Briggs

Act I.—Artists' Room of Symphony Hall, Philadelphia. Act II.—Nona's Private Car—Somewhere in Colorado. Act III.—Waiting-room of a Railway Station.

Staged by Burk Symon; settings by P. Dodd Ackerman.

Henry Cade, a well-born and rich Philadelphian, falling in love with Nona, a temperamental German dancer, applies for the job of her accompanist under the name of Enrico Finale. Nona, pestered by many accompanists, hires Cade with the understanding that he will not try to make love to her so long as he is in her employ. Which forces her to discharge the handsome fellow quickly in the second act, follow him through a snowstorm to a railway station and agree to marry him on the spot.

AMERICANA

(77 performances)

A revue in two parts by J. P. McEvoy; music by Jay Gorney, Harold Arlen, Herman Hupfeld and Richard Meyers; lyrics by E. Y. Harburg. Produced by Lee Shubert at the Shubert Theatre, New York, October 5, 1932.

Principals engaged—

George Givot	Lillian Fitzgerald
Albert Carroll	Francetta Malloy
Don Barclay	Peggy Cartwright
Gordon Smith	Lloyd Nolan
Rex Weber	Georgie Tapps
Ralph Locke	Allan Mann

The Musketeers
Charles Weidman Dancers
Doris Humphrey Dance Group
Alfredo Rode's Tzigane Orchestra
Staged by Harold Johnsrud; settings by Albert R. Johnson.

Principal songs—"Brother, Can you Spare a Dime," "Five Minutes of Spring" and "Whispering for a Kiss."

WHEN LADIES MEET

(First engagement 173 performances; return, 18 performances)

A comedy in three acts by Rachel Crothers. Produced by John Golden at the Royale Theatre, New York, October 6, 1932.

Cast of characters—

Mary Howard....................................Frieda Inescort
Jimmie Lee..Walter Abel
Mrs. Bridget Drake.............................Spring Byington
Walter Manners...................................Robert Lowes
Rogers Woodruff.................................Herbert Rawlinson
Pierre..Auguste Aramini
Claire Woodruff...................................Selena Royle
Act I.—Balcony of an Apartment in West 10th Street, New York.
Acts II and III.—Mrs. Bridget Drake's Place in Connecticut.
Staged by Rachel Crothers.

"When Ladies Meet" ran from October 6, 1932, to March 4, 1933. After a brief tour it was brought back to New York for a return engagement again at the Royale, starting May 15, 1933. See page 105, this volume.

CRIMINAL AT LARGE

(161 performances)

A mystery play in three acts by Edgar Wallace. Produced by Guthrie McClintic at the Belasco Theatre, New York, October 10, 1932.

Cast of characters—

Messenger..James Vincent
Sergeant Ferraby, C.I.D.......................Geoffrey Wardwell
Sergeant Totty, C.I.D...........................Walter Kingsford
Chief Detective Inspector Tanner, C.I.D.........William Harrigan
Warder Wilmot.....................................Neville Percy
Briggs..Perry Norman

Lord Lebanon....................................Emlyn Williams
Kelver....................................David Glassford
Gilder....................................Robert Middlemass
Brooks....................................Scott Moore
Lady Lebanon....................................Alexandra Carlisle
Rawbane....................................St. Clair Bayfield
Isla....................................Katherine Wilson

Act I.—Chief Inspector Tanner's Room at Scotland Yard. Acts II and III.—At Mark's Priory.

Staged by Guthrie McClintic; settings by Cleon Throckmorton.

Murders at Mark's Priory—first that of a chauffeur and later that of a physician—completely baffle Scotland Yard, and particularly Inspector Tanner, in charge of the investigation. On a visit to the scene of the crime Tanner encounters Lady Lebanon, an imperious aristocrat tracing the Lebanon line back to days when England had no history; her weakling son, Lord Lebanon, and a beautiful niece, Isla. Both Isla and Lord Lebanon are frightened of their lives. Tanner finally solves the problem by discovering that practically all the Lebanons are mad, especially his lordship.

PEACOCK

(7 performances)

A comedy in three acts by Leonard Ide. Produced by George Fawcett at the 49th Street Theatre, New York, October 11, 1932.

Cast of characters—

Suzanne de Brulard....................................Virginia Curley
Pauline....................................Kate Mayhew
Dr. Raymond La Salle....................................Charles Campbell
Andre....................................Philip Leigh
Roger de Brulard....................................George Fawcett
Felix Doumarai....................................Alfred Kappeler
Clothilde de Martin....................................Percy Haswell
Comtesse Leontine D'Alvay....................................Helen Raymond
Eugenie Maubran....................................Dorothy Tennant
Diane Girard....................................Rena Parker
Jules Perret....................................Rupert LaBelle

Acts I, II and III.—De Brulard's Home, Fifty Miles from Paris.

Staged by George Fawcett.

M. de Brulard, aging and ill, is slowly slipping away from life when his grandniece, rummaging through his papers, comes upon the letters of three former mistresses. Upon these she calls in a polite form of blackmail, inviting them to spend a week-end with M. de Brulard and, later, to assist her in restoring him to health by handing back some of the money he had given them in his days as a gay boulevardier. Money in hand M. de Brulard gets out his old striped trousers, his frock coat and gardenia and goes on a spree that restores both his health and spirits and he is off to Syria on a minor diplomatic mission at the play's close.

I LOVED YOU WEDNESDAY

(63 performances)

A play in a prologue and three acts by Molly Ricardel and William Du Bois. Produced by Crosby Gaige at the Harris Theatre, New York, October 11, 1932.

Cast of characters—

Jardinier....................Edward La Roche
Renee....................Anna Lubowe
Victoria Meredith....................Frances Fuller
Randall Williams....................Humphrey Bogart
Dr. Mary Hansen....................Jane Seymour
Philip Fletcher....................Henry O'Neill
Tom....................Harry Gresham
Freddy....................Robert Henderson
Wyn Terrell....................Fred Irving Lewis
Cynthia Williams....................Rose Hobart
Joe....................Edward La Roche
Eddie....................Henry Bergman
Ralph....................Eddie Sexton
Gene....................Ken Harvey
Fritz....................Philip Van Zandt
Dino....................Ralph Simone
Eustace....................Henry Fonda
Jennifer....................Mary Alice Collins
Peggy....................Anna Lubowe
Viola....................Jean Briggs
Nicholas....................Guy Hamilton

Prologue—Corner of the Luxembourg Gardens in Paris. Acts I and III.—Vicki's Apartment in the East Fifties. Act II.—The Bar at Joe's, New York.

Staged by Worthington Miner; settings by Raymond Sovey.

Victoria Meredith and Randall Williams, students, have been intimate friends in Paris for several months when Randall's wife calls him home. Victoria had not known about the wife. Five years later in New York Victoria is a great dancer and Randall a successful architect. They meet. Randall wants to leave his wife, Cynthia, and renew his friendship with Victoria. Victoria agrees, but later, after a talk with Cynthia, reconsiders and Randall again goes back to Cynthia.

THE GREAT LOVER

(23 performances)

A romantic comedy in three acts by Leo Ditrichstein and Frederic and Fanny Hatton. Revived by O. E. Wee and Jules J. Leventhal at the Waldorf Theatre, New York, October 11, 1932.

Cast of characters—

Mr. Stapleton....................Leo Kennedy
Maestro Cereale....................William Ricciardi

Dr. Mueller....................Clyde Veaux
Faranald....................Richard K. Keith
Ward....................Gustav Bowhan
Carl Losseck....................Curtis Karpe
Sparapani....................Leo Leone
Jean Paurel....................Lou Tellegen
Carlo Sonio....................Grant Gordon
Posansky....................Alexis Polianov
Ethel Warren....................Ilse Marvenga
Giulia Sabittini....................Mme. Marguerita Sylva
Madame Trellerbeinbrich....................Elsa Leon
Kartzag....................Leroi Operti
Bianca Sonio....................June Mullin
Mrs. Schuyler....................Julia Johnson
Mrs. Van Ness....................Alice Frost
Dr. Stetson....................Maurice J. Morris

Act I.—Manager's Office, Gotham Opera House. Act II.—Paurel's Dressing-room. Act III.—Paurel's Rooms at Hotel.
Staged by Gustave Bowhan.

Paurel, at one time a fêted baritone, is singing at 46 with what is left of his voice and making love to a young prima donna who agrees to marry him because he can advance her career. She is in love with young Sonino, Paurel's rival, but Paurel will not give her up. Sonino takes Paurel's place in "Don Giovanni" and scores a triumph. Paurel finally is forced to relinquish his claim and is consoled by other loves. Produced first by Leo Ditrichstein in New York, November, 1915.

RENDEZVOUS

(21 performances)

A play in three acts by Barton MacLane. Produced by Arthur Hopkins at the Broadhurst Theatre, New York, October 12, 1932.

Cast of characters—

Private Stull....................Tom Fadden
Private Kelley....................Jackson Halliday
Private Vincent....................E. J. Ballantine
Private Oakley....................Barton MacLane
Lieutenant Hanley....................Jack Davis
The Sergeant....................Henry Shelvey
Regan....................Murray Alper
Detective Sullivan....................Charles Kennedy
Porter....................William Maxwell
Kane....................Nolan Leary
Carey....................John Monks, Jr.
Carlson....................Rand Leyman
Mitchell....................Clement Wilenchick
Miller....................Arthur Marlowe
Boyle....................Ross Hertz
Lawton....................Larry Clark
Morgan....................Frank Curry
Judge Horton....................Robert Lowe
Holden....................Jack Clifford
Madge....................Ruth Fallows
Counselor Costello....................Henry Sherwood
Boss Potter....................Dean Borup
Calgano....................Jerome Cowan

Tony Rossalino....................................Neill O'Malley
Officer Murphy....................................George W. Smith
Guard....................................Thomas Dillon
Warden....................................Paul Caldwell
Matron....................................Frances Meade
Priest....................................James Clairton
Act I.—A Dugout in France. Act II.—A Warehouse in America. Act III.—A Death House.
Staged by Arthur Hopkins; settings by Cleon Throckmorton.

Private Oakley, disillusioned by the war, organizes a squad of ex-service men and takes on a beer racket. Inspired by a poetic buddy and a John Neidhart verse, Oakley decides to sacrifice his life to a great deed and die. He orders his gang to kidnap the town's three most corrupt men, a political boss, a judge and a criminal lawyer. The boss shoots himself. The Judge dies of fright. A rival gang shoots its way in. Oakley is wounded. The rival's girl, inspired by Oakley, turns on her own crowd and kills their leaders. Oakley and the girl go to the chair content. They have done some good and found each other.

BLACK SHEEP

(4 performances)

A comedy in three acts by Elmer Rice. Produced by Elmer Rice at the Morosco Theatre, New York, October 13, 1932.

Cast of characters—

Mary Thompson Porter....................................Jean Adair
Dorothy Woods....................................Helen Brooks
Elizabeth....................................Harriet Russell
Alfred Porter....................................Edward Downes
Henry Porter....................................Dodson Mitchell
Penelope Porter....................................Jane Hamilton
Thompson ("Buddy") Porter....................................Donald Macdonald
Kitty Lloyd....................................Mary Philips
A Taxi Driver....................................James Carroll
Helena Abercrombie....................................Anne Shoemaker
Milton Abercrombie....................................Fred Herrick
Bertha Belknap....................................Frederica Going
Acts I, II and III.—Living-room of the Porter Home in New York.
Staged by Elmer Rice; settings by Raymond Sovey.

Buddy Porter, a wild son, after seven years of wandering the earth and developing a talent for writing realistic fiction, returns to his middle-class home in New York, bringing with him Kitty Lloyd, an inspiration with whom he has been living for five years. Buddy as a son is unwelcome. Buddy as a celebrity is fawned upon. He makes advances to his brother's fiancée, looks feverishly upon the housemaid, and is in pretty much of a mess until Kitty manages to get him away to South America to write another story.

MEN MUST FIGHT

(35 performances)

A play in three acts by Reginald Lawrence and S. K. Lauren. Produced by Joseph P. Bickerton, Jr., at the Lyceum Theatre, New York, October 14, 1932.

Cast of characters—

José....................Edgar Barrier
Albert....................J. Malcom Dunn
Mrs. Chase....................Laura Treadwell
Peggy Chase....................Erin O'Brien-Moore
Madame Seward....................Alma Kruger
Robert Seward....................Douglass Montgomery
Laura Seward....................Janet Beecher
Edwin Seward....................Gilbert Emery
Lieut. Chase....................Kent Smith
Evelyn Clyde....................Lauralee Skinner
Siebert....................Percy Moore

Acts I, II and III.—Upstairs Living-room of Seward Home, Fifth Ave., New York City.

Staged by Arthur Sircom; settings by Raymond Sovey.

Laura Seward, wife of Secretary of State Seward, whom she married after the Great War, work together as pacifists until, in 1940, the United States gets into trouble with the United South American states, backed by Japan. Seward goes military for his country. Laura continues a pacifist. Robert Seward, following his mother's lead, refuses to fight, declaring his right to be as strong for principle as the other Sewards, which forces his supposed father to tell him that he is not a Seward, but the son of a British aviator killed in the Great War. Robert absorbs the shock and decides to become an aviator like his father, marries his sweetheart and is off for the front.

THE GOOD EARTH

(56 performances)

A play in ten scenes adapted by Owen and Donald Davis from a novel by Pearl Buck. Produced by the Theatre Guild at the Guild Theatre, New York, October 17, 1932.

Cast of characters—

Wang Lung....................Claude Rains
Wang Lung's Father....................Henry Travers
The Gatekeeper of the House of Hwang....................Homer Barton
A Peach Vendor....................Conrad Cantzen
A Beggar....................William Franklin
The Old Lord....................Harold Thomas
His Son....................A. Francis Karll

The Fifth Lady..Marel Foster
A Slave..Joan Hathaway
Cuckoo..Marjorie Wood
The Ancient Mistress of the House of Hwang..........Kate Morgan
O-Lan..Alla Nazimova
Wang Lung's Uncle..........................Sydney Greenstreet
Wang Lung's Aunt..Jessie Ralph
Ching..Clyde Franklin
Wang Lung's Son..Freddy Goodrow
Two Strangers..{ Jack Daniels
Vincent Sherman
A Tall Beggar..Harry M. Cooke
A Poor Man..Albert Hayes
Another Poor Man..Conrad Cantzen
A Young Speaker..Vincent Sherman
The Rich Man..Homer Barton
The Fool Child..Helen Hoy
Lotus..Sabene Newmark
A Slave..Nola Napoli
A Doctor..Mark Schweid
Yi Ling, the Maker of Coffins.................. Donald Macmillan
Wang Lung's Eldest Son..Harry Wood
The Bride..Geraldine Kay
A Taoist Priest..Philip Wood
Priests from the Temple of Buddha..............{ Harry Barfoot
M. W. Rale

Scenes 1, 4 and 8—Wang Lung's Farm House. 2—Great House of Hwang. 3, 6 and 10—Wang Lung's Land. 5—Gates of the Great House of Hwang. 7—Outside the Wall of a Rich Man's House. 9—Court of the Great House.

Staged by Phillip Moeller; settings by Lee Simonson.

Wang Lung, Chinese peasant farmer, takes to wife O-Lan, slave in the House of Hwang. Together they work and till the rice fields. O-Lan bears Wang Lung three children, urges him to buy more and more land, as his silver accumulates. In time of famine Wang Lung and his family trek to the south. During a revolutionary outbreak a rich man's jewels come into O-Lan's possession. Back home Wang Lung buys more land, coming finally into possession of the Great House of Hwang. With opulence comes vanity. Wang takes as a second wife Lotus, a Tea House girl. When O-Lan dies Wang is penitent and chastened in spirit and goes back to the soil to work out his destiny.

ABSENT FATHER

(88 performances)

A play in three acts by Francis De Witt. Produced by James E. Kenney and Joseph Levitt at the Vanderbilt Theatre, New York, October 17, 1932.

Cast of characters—

Larry (Lawrence Carter Boyden)....................Joseph Cotten
Riggs..Alexander Frank
Anne (Mrs. Oliver Townsend)....................Kathryn Givney
Oliver (Oliver Townsend, Senior)..................Clyde Fillmore

Ollie (Oliver Townsend, Junior)..................Edward Crandall
Julie (Julia Boyden)..........................Patricia Barclay
Gloria (Princess DeMauriac)..........................Lea Penman
Janice (Janice Joy)..............................Barbara Weeks

Acts I, II and III.—Living-room of the Townsend Penthouse, Park Avenue, New York.

Staged by Lionel Bevans; settings by Yellenti.

The Oliver Townsends are living in a Park Avenue penthouse with three children by former marriages. Mr. Townsend is the father of a son by his first wife, now a Countess, who in the interim has married and divorced Mrs. Townsend's former husband, and borne him two children. Mr. Townsend's son thinks to marry Mrs. Townsend's daughter, but gets drunk and elopes with a cigarette girl instead. Sober, young Townsend refuses to divorce his wife and she meets the family's threat of disinheritance with a counter threat of blackmail. The Countess is called in to straighten matters out.

THINGS THAT ARE CÆSAR'S

(4 performances)

A tragedy in three acts by Paul Vincent Carroll. Produced by the Abbey Theatre Irish Players under the management of Alber & Wickes, Inc., at the Martin Beck Theatre, New York, October 17, 1932.

Cast of characters—

Peter Hardy..................................Michael J. Dolan
Julia Hardy....................................Maureen Delany
Alice Brady.......................................Ria Mooney
Phil Noonan..................................Barry Fitzgerald
Terrence Noonan...................................Denis O'Dea
Eilish Hardy......................................Kate Curling
Rev. Father Duffy...............................F. J. McCormick
Josephine Noonan....................................May Craig
Doctor Downey.....................................P. J. Carolan

Acts I and III.—Royal Arms Bar Parlor, on the outskirts of Dundalk. Act II.—A private parlor.

Julia Hardy, slave to her religion, ruler of her home and family, is determined to marry her daughter Eilish to a chosen suitor. Eilish is opposed to the marriage. So is her free-thinking father. The father dies, the marriage is ordered and dominant Julia is triumphant.

THE FAR-OFF HILLS

(13 performances)

A comedy in three acts by Lennox Robinson. Produced by the Abbey Theatre Irish Players at the Martin Beck Theatre, New York, October 18, 1932.

Cast of characters—

Patrick Clancy.....P. J. Carolan
Marian.....Eileen Crowe
Dorothea ("Ducky").....Ria Mooney
Anna ("Pet").....Kate Curling
Oliver O'Shaughnessy.....Barry Fitzgerald
Dick Delaney.....Michael J. Dolan
Harold Mahony.....F. J. McCormick
Susie Tynan.....Maureen Delany
Pierce Hegarty.....Arthur Shields
Ellen Nolan.....May Craig
Acts I and III.—Clancy Drawing-room. Act II.—Pet's and Ducky's bedroom.

Marian Clancy thinks she wants to become a nun until her sisters make it possible and the man she had wanted to marry is freed of an insane wife. Being made available marriage also becomes less attractive to the prospective groom. "The far-off hills are always green."

MADEMOISELLE

(103 performances)

A play in three acts adapted by Grace George from a French play by Jacques Deval. Produced by W. A. Brady at the Playhouse, New York, October 18, 1932.

Cast of characters—

Madame Galvosier.....Alice Brady
Lucien Galvosier.....A. E. Matthews
Valentin.....Frank Rothe
Helene.....Lillian Savin
Christine Galvosier.....Peggy Conklin
Mademoiselle.....Grace George
Maurice Galvosier.....Thomas Beck
Therese.....Garda Olesen
Georges Boutin.....Harold West
Edouard.....Kenneth Treseder
Juliette.....May Marshall
Acts I, II and III.—Home of the Galvosiers, Paris.
Staged by Clarence Derwent; settings by Livingston Platt.

Madame and Lucien Galvosier, he a leading criminal lawyer and she a flighty wife, follow a modern custom of neglecting their adolescent offspring, Christine and Maurice. Christine's chaperon, Mademoiselle, discovers Christine to be carrying a child and plans for its surreptitious birth both to save Christine's honor and to still her own consuming maternal cravings. Christine becomes a mother and returns to society. Mademoiselle quits her job and goes to adopt the child.

Mr. Brady revived "Little Women" during the Christmas holiday when "Mademoiselle" was not using the stage.

THE PASSIONATE PILGRIM

(5 performances)

A play in three acts by Margaret Crosby Munn. Produced by Howard Inches at the 48th Street Theatre, New York, October 19, 1932.

Cast of characters—

Anne Hathaway....Emily Ross
John Richardson....Donald Wilson
Taverner....Alan Wallace
William Shakespeare....Albert Van Dekker
Bailly....Charles Henderson
Sir Thomas Lucy....Thomas F. Tracey
Peter Dumpser....Burford Hampden
Robert Armin....Charles W. Homer
Nicholas Tooley....Wilbur Cox
Hemings....John Bryan
Mistress Elizabeth Vernon....Ara Gerald
Florian....Percival Vivian
Earl of Southampton....George Macready
Lady Bridget Manners....Beverly Roberts
Countess of Rutland....Wauna Midwell
Earl of Essex....Leslie Dennison
Earl of Pembroke....Donald Wilson
Phillida....Norville Barry

Prologue—Forest Glade in Charlcote Park. 1582. Act I.—Scene 1—Interior of the Home of Shakespeare. 1586. 2—Entrance to the Country Seat of the Earl of Southampton. Act II.—Scene 1—Inner Court of the London House of the Earl of Southampton. 1598. 2—Southampton's Cabinet. Act III.—Garden of the Country House of the Earl of Southampton at Titchfield.

Staged by Howard Inches.

Will Shakespeare, caught poaching on the estate of Sir Thomas Lucy, is forced to marry Anne Hathaway to keep out of jail, his captors hoping this will cause him to settle down. A few years later Shakespeare follows a band of wandering players to London and there achieves some fame as playwright and poet. Meeting Elizabeth Vernon in the home of his patron, the Earl of Southampton, Shakespeare falls desperately in love with her, making her his Dark Lady of the Sonnets. Elizabeth is at first favorably impressed, but later decides to return to her real love, who is Southampton, and Shakespeare goes back to Anne and his children in Stratford.

KEEPING EXPENSES DOWN

(12 performances)

A comedy in three acts by Montague Glass and Dan Jarrett. Produced by Dimitri Tiomkin at the National Theatre, New York, October 20, 1932.

Cast of characters—

Julius Bruckliner.......................................Joe Greenwald
David Gordon.......................................William Tannen
Harris Fishbein.......................................Louis Sorin
Esther Fein.......................................Alice Burrage
Isaac Blintz.......................................Solly Ward
Moskin.......................................Samuel Schneider
Kent J. Goldstein.......................................Bernard Gorcey
Max Fein.......................................Wm. E. Morris
De Witt C. Rubensohn.......................................Raymond Bramley
Miss Ross.......................................Patricia Quinn
Thornbusch.......................................Arthur Jarrett

Acts I, II and III.—Office of Fishbein & Blintz, Realtors.
Staged by Dan Jarrett.

Harris Fishbein and Isaac Blintz, realtors, advertise for an heir to a piece of property they have sold and to which they must clear the title. Dan Thornbusch answers the ad. Other comic complications embrace bankers and brokers and are topped by the discovery that Thornbusch is also a cheater.

THE NEW GOSSOON

(14 performances)

A comedy in three acts by George Shiels. Produced by the Abbey Theatre Irish Players at the Martin Beck Theatre, New York, October 21, 1932.

Cast of characters—

Ellen Cary.......................................Maureen Delany
Luke Cary.......................................Denis O'Dea
Peter Cary.......................................Michael J. Dolan
Ned Shay.......................................P. J. Carolan
May Kehoe.......................................May Craig
Rabit Hamil.......................................F. J. McCormick
Sally Hamil.......................................Eileen Crowe
John Henly.......................................Arthur Shields
Biddy Henly.......................................Kate Curling

Acts I, II and III.—Carys' kitchen.

Luke Cary, about to come of age and take over his dead father's farm, anticipates his day of independence by "borrowing" five of his mother's sheep, selling them for enough to buy himself a motorcycle and an aviator's suit with which he goes scooting over the surprised countryside in search of women and whisky. Becoming involved with Biddy Henly, a flirt, it takes hard but sensible May Kehoe to get Luke out of trouble.

During the engagement of the Irish Players revivals were made of Sean O'Casey's "Juno and the Paycock," Lennox Robinson's "The White-headed Boy" and "Crabbed Youth and Age," J. M. Synge's "Playboy of the Western World" and "The Shadow of the Glen," Lady Gregory's "The Rising of the Moon," and T. C. Murray's "Birthright," plays recorded in previous volumes of "The Best Plays."

A single performance was given of "Œdipus Rex" in the adaptation by William Butler Yeats on Sunday, January 15. This in association with the Theatre Guild, with F. J. McCormick as Œdipus, Eileen Crowe as Jocaster, Barry Fitzgerald as Creon and Arthur Shields as Messenger.

DINNER AT EIGHT

(232 performances)

A comedy in three acts by George S. Kaufman and Edna Ferber. Produced by Sam H. Harris at the Music Box Theatre, New York, October 22, 1932.

Cast of characters—

Millicent Jordan	Ann Andrews
Dora	Mary Murray
Gustave	Gregory Gaye
Oliver Jordan	Malcolm Duncan
Paula Jordan	Marguerite Churchill
Ricci	Cesar Romero
Hattie Loomis	Margaret Dale
Miss Copeland	Vera Hurst
Fosdick	Clarence Bellair
Carlotta Vance	Constance Collier
Dan Packard	Paul Harvey
Kitty Packard	Judith Wood
Tina	Janet Fox
Dr. J. Wayne Talbot	Austin Fairman
Larry Renault	Conway Tearle
The Bellboy	Robert Griffith
The Waiter	James Seeley
Max Kane	Samuel Levene
Mr. Hatfield	William McFadden
Miss Alden	Ethel Intropodi
Lucy Talbot	Olive Wyndham
Mrs. Wendel	Dorothy Walters
Jo Stengel	Frank Manning
Mr. Fitch	George Alison
Ed Loomis	Hans Robert

(Note—Margaret Sullavan succeeded Marguerite Churchill as Paula in March and was succeeded by Jane Wyatt in May.)

Act I.—Scene 1—Upstairs Sitting-room in the New York House of Mr. and Mrs. Oliver Jordan. 2—Oliver Jordan's Office. 3—Home of the Packards. 4—Jordan Sitting-room. Act II.—Scene 1—Larry

Renault's Apartment. 2—Dr. Talbot's Office. 3—Butler's Pantry in the Home of the Jordans. 4—Sitting-room. Act III.—Scene 1—The Packard Home. 2—Renault's Apartment. 3—Jordan Drawing-room.

Staged by George S. Kaufman; settings by Livingston Platt.

See page 61.

THE ANATOMIST

(8 performances)

A play in three acts by James Bridie. Produced by Frank Conroy at the Bijou Theatre, New York, October 24, 1932.

Cast of characters—

Amelia Dishart....................................Audrey Ridgwell
Mary Belle Dishart....................................Eunice Osborne
Walter Anderson....................................Leslie Barrie
Jessie Ann....................................Molly Pearson
Robert Knox, M.D....................................Frank Conroy
Augustus Raby....................................Denis Gurnsy
Landlord of the Three Tuns....................................Barlowe Borland
Mary Paterson....................................Paula Bauersmith
Janet....................................Bernard Ostertag
Davie Paterson....................................George Tawde
William Burke....................................Jack McGraw
William Hare....................................Ralph Cullinan

Acts I and III.—Disharts' Drawing-room. Act II.—Scene 1—Three Tuns Tavern. 2—Lobby at Dr. Knox's Rooms.

Staged by Thomas Wood Stevens.

Walter Anderson, student surgeon, quarrels with his sweetheart, Mary Belle Dishart, who accuses him of being more deeply in love with his profession and his favorite anatomist, the great Dr. Knox, than he is with her. In his disappointment young Anderson gets drunk, consorts with a beautiful jezebel, Mary Paterson. The same night Miss Paterson is murdered by body snatchers. Her body is recognized in the dissecting room next day by Anderson. The shock drives him temporarily from surgery, exposes other similar murders and threatens the popularity and career of the great anatomist.

THE GIRL OUTSIDE

(8 performances)

A play in five scenes by John King Hodges and Samuel Merwin. Produced by Alfred E. Aarons at the Little Theatre, New York, October 24, 1932.

Cast of characters—

Frederick P. Dorne....................................Charles Richman
Mrs. William Dorne....................................Helen Strickland

Garrison Dorne..Horace Braham
Doctor Hudson..Sydney Riggs
The Girl..Lee Patrick

Scenes 1 and 4—Frederick Dorne's Apartment Uptown. 2 and 3—Garry's Basement Room Downtown. 5—Ethel's Room.

Staged by Priestly Morrison; settings by P. Dodd Ackerman.

Garrison Dorne, living and composing in Greenwich Village because he will not accept charity from his Uncle Frederick, finds a girl who has fainted on his doorstep, takes her inside and nurses her back to health. Discovered by his mother the girl lies to save Garrison, saying they are married. With this assurance mother invites her home, where she meets and induces Garrison to make up with Uncle Fred and everything looks pretty rosy at the finish.

LILIOM

(35 performances)

A play in seven scenes and a prologue adapted by Benjamin Glazer from the original of Ferenc Molnar. Revived by the Civic Repertory Theatre, Inc., at the Civic Repertory Theatre, New York, October 26, 1932.

Cast of characters—

Marie..Beatrice de Neergaard
Julie..Eva Le Gallienne
Mrs. Muskat..Beatrice Terry
Liliom..Joseph Schildkraut
("Liliom" Is the Hungarian for "Lily" and the Slang Term for "a Tough")
Servant Girl..Margaret Love
Captain..Robert H. Gordon
Plain Clothes Policeman..Joseph Kramm
Mother Hollunder..Leona Roberts
"The Sparrow"..Walter Beck
Wolf Berkowiz..Howard da Silva
Young Hollunder..Burgess Meredith
Linzman..Charles Ellis
First Mounted Policeman..David Turk
Second Mounted Policeman..Tonio Selwart
Doctor..Harold Moulton
Carpenter..Donald Cameron
First Policeman of the Beyond..Nelson Welch
Second Policeman of the Beyond..Richard Waring
The Richly Dressed Man..Paul Leyssac
The Poorly Dressed Man..Robert F. Ross
The Old Guard..Landon Herrick
The Magistrate..Sayre Crawley
Louise..Florida Friebus

Peasants, Townspeople, etc.

Prologue—An Amusement Park on the Outskirts of Budapest. Scene 1—A Lonely Place in the Park. 2, 3 and 5—Tin-Type Shop of the Hollunders. 4—Railroad Embankment. 6—A Courtroom in the Beyond. 7—Before Julie's Door.

Staged by Eva Le Gallienne; settings by Aline Bernstein.

Eva Le Gallienne, returning from a Sabbatical year in Europe, reëstablished the Civic Repertory Theatre in Fourteenth St. with a revival of "Liliom." The play was first produced by the Theatre Guild at the Garrick Theatre, New York, April 20, 1921. Excerpts from the text are included in "The Best Plays of 1920-21." Miss Le Gallienne was the original Julie and Joseph Schildkraut the original Liliom in America.

DANGEROUS CORNER

(206 performances)

A play in three acts by J. B. Priestly. Produced by Harry Moses at the Empire Theatre, New York, October 27, 1932.

Cast of characters—

Maud Mockridge.....Jane Wheatley
Olwen Peel.....Mary Servoss
Frieda Chatfield.....Jean Dixon
Betty Whitehouse.....Barbara Robbins
Charles Stanton.....Stanley Ridges
Gordon Whitehouse.....Cecil Holm
Robert Chatfield.....Colin Keith-Johnston
Acts I, II and III.—Living-room of the Chatfield country home.
Staged by Elsa Lazareff; settings by Woodman Thompson.

Robert and Frieda Chatfield are giving a dinner at which Maud Mockridge is chief guest. During the after-dinner chat Mrs. Chatfield passes cigarettes in a musical cigarette box. Olwen Peel remarks having seen the box at the home of Martin Chatfield, Mrs. Chatfield's brother-in-law, now dead. Miss Peel could not have seen the box at Martin's, insists Mrs. Chatfield, because it was not given to Martin until the day he shot himself, and no one but Gordon Whitehouse saw him that day. From which casual remark a drama develops exposing most of the group as liars and adulterers. If the conversation had been permitted to pass that one dangerous corner there would have been no exposures—and no drama.

THE SURGEON

(5 performances)

A play in three acts by Anthony Young. Produced by the Mirror Players at the Belmont Theatre, New York, October 27, 1932.

Cast of characters—

Helen Strong.....Carolyn Wills
Parkway.....Marriott Wilson
Lo Chatterton.....Paul Barrett

Reverend Allgood....................................David Baylor
Dr. Victor Strong..................................Michael Randolf
Christine Hart.......................................Helen Marley
The Nurse..Julia McGhan
Jim Cook...Joseph L. Brandt
The Voice of Conscience..........................Stephen Juriste
Doctors, Internes, Nurses, Ladies and Gentlemen Guests, Maid, are played by Milo Martin, Ramon Marien, Blanche Gordon, Ann Smith, Walter Kybitz, Charlotte Kybitz, Marion Wilcox, Joan Chapman, Grace Renee, Helen Murray, Zenith Meyers, Carlotta Hoff, Bresci Thompson, Emil Hurst, Stanley Rash, Stanley B. Robinson and Mildred Bell.

Acts I, II and III.—Operating Room in Hospital and Dr. Strong's Drawing-room.

Staged by Stephen Van Gluck; settings by Ward and Harvey Studios.

Victor Strong, plastic surgeon, boasts his ability to make the ugliest of God's humans beautiful. He is opposed by the Rev. Allgood, who is convinced that when God makes people ugly He knows what He is doing, and His work should not be tampered with. Dr. Strong, however, makes a beautiful woman of Christine Hart and then falls in love with her. When he learns that she is the wife of a felon and scandal threatens he would back hurriedly out of the mess and Miss Hart smears her face with acid that she may be ugly again.

TELL HER THE TRUTH

(11 performances)

A musical farce in three acts by R. P. Weston and Bert Lee, adapted from "Nothing But the Truth" by Frederick Isham and James Montgomery; music by Jack Waller and Joseph Tunbridge; lyrics by the authors. Produced by Tillie Leblang at the Cort Theatre, New York, October 28, 1932.

Cast of characters—

Dick..Ray Walburn
Office Boy...Lou Parker
Maclean..Hobart Cavanaugh
Mr. Ralston.....................................Andrew Tombes
Mr. Parkin......................................William Frawley
Bobbie..John Sheehan, Jr.
Polly...Thelma White
Helen...Edith Davis
Mrs. Ralston..................................Margaret Dumont
Gwen..Lillian Emerson
Ethel...Louise Kirtland
Martha...Molly O'Doherty

Act I.—A Real Estate Office. Acts II and III.—Interior of the Ralston home.

Staged by Morris Green and Henry Thomas.

Principal song—"Sing, Brother."

"Nothing But the Truth" was first produced with William Collier as the star at the Longacre Theatre, New York, September 14, 1916. It was revived, with music, in 1927 as "Yes, Yes, Yvette." The story revolves about the adventure of Bobbie Bennett, who wagers $10,000 that he will tell nothing but the absolute, unvarnished truth for twenty-four hours.

THERE'S ALWAYS JULIET

(20 performances)

A comedy in three acts by John Van Druten. Revived by the Messrs. Shubert at the Ethel Barrymore Theatre, New York, October 27, 1932.

Cast of characters—

Leonora Perrycoste....................Violet Heming
Florence....................Lillian Brennard Tonge
Dwight Houston....................Roger Pryor
Peter Walmsley....................John Graham Spacey
Acts I, II and III.—Leonora's sitting-room in a flat in the West End of London.
Staged by John Van Druten.

Produced originally by Gilbert Miller at the Empire Theatre, New York, February 15, 1932, with Edna Best as Leonora and Herbert Marshall as Dwight Houston. See "Best Plays of 1931-32."

CARRY NATION

(First engagement 17 performances; return, 13. Total 30)

A play in fifteen scenes by Frank McGrath. Produced by Arthur J. Beckhard at the Biltmore Theatre, New York, October 29, 1932.

Cast of characters—

Aunt Judy....................Fannie Belle de Knight
George Moore....................John Parrish
James Campbell....................Myron McCormick
Mary Campbell Moore....................Gertrude Garstin
Charles Gloyd....................Byron McGrath
Sam....................Buddy De Loach
Mrs. Gloyd....................Frieda Altman
Dr. Hull....................Ernest Pollock
Miss Sicat....................Minna Adams
David Nation....................Leslie Adams
Carry Nation....................Esther Dale
Mrs. Noble....................Mildred Natwick
Daniel Dent....................Donald Foster
Mrs. Cain....................Daisy Belmore
A Brute....................Clarence E. Smith
Mart Strong....................Joshua L. Logan

Constable Gano....................................James Stewart
Mayor Washbrook..............................Arthur C. Morris
O. L. Day...Charles E. Arnt
A Salesman...Kenneth Berry
Kiowan Youths..............Frank M. Thomas, Jr., Rufus Peabody
Sporting Girls........................Barbara O'Neil, Lilian Okun
Senator..John F. Morrissey
The Mayor of Kiowa..........................Alfred Dalrymple
Mrs. Skoll...Nina Varesi
Skoll..Luther Williams
Jailor...Walter Eviston
Landlord..Harry Bellaver
Leader of the Vigilantes.............................Karl Swenson
The Woman With a Whip.......................Roberta Hoskins
The Woman With a Club...............................Bela Axman
Louis Sauerberger..............................Frederick Kemp
A Whiskey Drinker.....................................Leslie Hunt
Mrs. Klopp..Katherine Emery
Miss Sheriff...Helen Huberth
Mrs. McHenty..Mary Jeffery
Chairman..Robert Allen

Scene 1—Farmhouse in Kentucky. November 25, 1846. 2—In Front of the Moore Home in Missouri. April, 1857. 3, 4—Room in the Home of Dr. Gloyd in Holden, Missouri. June, 1868, and 1877. 5—Interior of the Christian Church in Medicine Lodge, Kansas. July, 1899. 6—Room in the Nation Home in Medicine Lodge. 7—Front Room of Mart Strong's Saloon in Medicine Lodge. 8—O. L. Day's Drug Store in Medicine Lodge. February, 1900. 9—Street in Kiowa, Kansas. August, 1900. 10, 11—Jail in Kiowa. 12—Room in Stagg's Hotel, Enterprise, Kansas. 13—Louis Sauerberger's Saloon, Topeka, Kansas. 14—Room in the Home of Mrs. Klopp in Kansas City, Missouri. June, 1903. 15—Town Hall, Waterville, Tennessee. May, 1910.

Staged by Blanche Yurka; settings by Charles Boss.

A biographical drama that goes back of the career of Carry Nation to the months preceding her birth to a weak-minded mother and a father who was a religious fanatic. The biography continues through her first marriage to a drunkard named Gloyd, and her second marriage to the small-town preacher, David Nation. Carry, enlisting in the war on rum, smashes and closes up joints in Medicine Lodge, Kiowa and Enterprise, Kansas. She is jailed by scheming authorities, whipped by vigilantes. As an old and broken woman she passes out of the picture on the stage of the Town Hall in Waterville, Tenn., where she made her last address in May, 1910.

THE LATE CHRISTOPHER BEAN

(224 performances)

A comedy in three acts adapted by Sidney Howard from the French of Rene Fauchois. Produced by Gilbert Miller at the Henry Miller Theatre, New York, October 31, 1932.

Cast of characters—

Dr. Haggett.......................................Walter Connolly
Susan Haggett.....................................Adelaide Bean

Abby....................................Pauline Lord
Mrs. Haggett....................................Beulah Bondi
Ada Haggett....................................Katherine Hirsch
Warren Creamer....................................William Lawson
Tallant....................................George Coulouris
Rosen....................................Clarence Derwent
Davenport....................................Ernest Lawford

Acts I, II and III.—Dining-room of the Haggetts' house, not far from Boston.

Staged by Gilbert Miller; settings by Aline Bernstein.

See page 238.

CAMILLE

(15 performances)

A play in five acts by Alexander Dumas, fils, new version by Edna and Delos Chappell and Robert Edmond Jones. Revived by Delos Chappell, Inc., at the Morosco Theatre, New York, November 1, 1932.

Cast of characters—

Marguerite Gautier....................................Lillian Gish
Prudence Duvernoy....................................Cora Witherspoon
Olympe....................................Helen Freeman
Nanine....................................Mary Morris
Nichette....................................Leona Boytel
Anais....................................Edna James
Armand Duval....................................Raymond Hackett
M. Georges Duval....................................Moffat Johnston
Baron De Varville....................................Frederic Worlock
Gaston Rieux....................................Lewis Martin
Comte De Giray....................................Ian Van-Wolfe
Gustave....................................Ian Van-Wolfe
Saint Gaudens....................................Robert Le Sueur
The Doctor....................................Moffat Johnston
Arthur....................................Paul Stephenson
Guests, Servants and Others: Harriett Ingersoll, Betty Upthegrove, Lillian Bronson, William James, Bartlett Robinson, Richard Kendrick.

Act I.—Marguerite's Drawing-room. Paris. Act II.—Marguerite's Boudoir. Act III.—Auteuil. Act IV.—Gambling-room at Olympe's. Paris. Act V.—Marguerite's Bedroom. New Year's Day.
The Play Is Presented in the Manner of 1878.

Staged and designed by Robert Edmond Jones.

The most notable revivals of "Camille" made in the American theatre the last thirty years was one featuring Margaret Anglin and Henry Miller in 1903, that of a new version prepared by Edward Sheldon for Ethel Barrymore in 1917, when Conway Tearle was the Armand, and that made by Eva Le Gallienne at the Civic Repertory Theatre in January, 1931, on which occasion Morgan Farley was the Armand. The version used for the presentation of Lillian Gish as Marguerite Gautier was prepared for a week of gala performances in the old opera house at Central City, Colo., on the occasion of its anniversary in July, 1932.

INCUBATOR

(7 performances)

A play in three acts by John Lyman and Roman Bohnen. Produced by Arthur Edison and George Burton at the Avon Theatre, New York, November 1, 1932.

Cast of characters—

Mrs. Morton, the Matron............................Claire Devine
Coon..James H. Dunmore
Horst...Alfred A. Webster
Whitaker..Chas. H. Cline
Fred Martin.....................................Charles Eaton
Jimmie..Frank Collins
Burman..Henry Howard
Greek...Alfred A. Browne
Sap...Geo. Offerman, Jr.
Five-Eyes.......................................Larry Ellinger
Jew...Muni Diamond
Crip..Sam Byrd
Miles...Warren McCollum
Hick..Neil Malloy
Fat...Sonny Taubin
Bert..Richard De Angelis
Olsen...Vincent York
Jamison...Leslie King
Mrs. Martin.....................................Eeda Von Buelow
Mrs. Dalton.....................................Marie D. Shotwell

Act I.—Scene 1—Recreating and Dressing Quarters, State Training School for Boys. 2—Corner of the Dormitory. Acts II and III.—Basement.

Staged by George Burton.

Fred Martin is sent to the State Training School when he is convicted of having "borrowed" and accidentally smashed an automobile. When he is rebellious he is put to work on the coal pile. When he is transferred to a dormitory he falls in with other potential criminals, learns the tricks of crime and crooks, and goes out of the institution embittered and an enemy of society.

WHISTLING IN THE DARK

(122 performances)

A melodramatic farce in three acts by Laurence Gross and Edward Childs Carpenter. Revived by O. E. Wee and J. J. Leventhal at the Waldorf Theatre, New York, November 3, 1932.

Cast of characters—

Hildar..Gertrude Ritchie
Joe Salvatore...................................Clyde Veaux
Slim Scanlon....................................Edwin Redding
Herman Lefkowitz................................Arthur S. Ross
Charlie Shaw....................................Charles McClelland

Jacob Dillon....................................Leo Kennedy
Cossack....................................Anthony Ross
Benny....................................Curtis Karpe
Wallace Porter....................................Bernard Granville
Toby Van Buren....................................Eleanor King
Cap O'Rorke....................................William Balfour
Police Sergeant....................................William Melville

Acts I, II and III.—Living-room in Jacob Dillon's House Near Spuyten Duyvil.

Staged by Gustave Bowhan and Charles McClelland.

A popular-priced revival of the farce produced originally by Alexander McKaig at the Ethel Barrymore Theatre, New York, January 19, 1932, with Ernest Truex playing the chief part of Wallace Porter, novelist. See "Best Plays of 1931-32."

* MUSIC IN THE AIR

(First engagement 144 performances. Return, 91 performances)

A musical comedy in two acts; book and lyrics by Oscar Hammerstein II; music by Jerome Kern. Produced by Peggy Fears at the Alvin Theatre, New York, November 8, 1932.

Cast of characters—

Herman....................................Charles Belin
Tila....................................Edna Hagan
Dr. Walther Lessing....................................Al Shean
Sieglinde....................................Katherine Carrington
Karl Reder....................................Walter Slezak
Burgomaster....................................Marty Semon
Pflugfelder....................................Robert Williamson
Town Crier....................................Ivan Arbuckle
Heinrich....................................Cliff Heckinger
The Apothecary....................................Anton Lieb
Widow Schreimann....................................Lydia Van Gilder
Priest....................................George Spelvin
Frau Pflugfelder....................................Gabrielle Guelpli
Hans....................................Edward Hayes
Cornelius....................................Reinald Werrenrath
Ernst Weber....................................Nicholas Joy
Uppmann....................................Harry Mestayer
Marthe....................................Dorothy Johnson
Frieda....................................Natalie Hall
Bruno....................................Tullio Carminati
Lilli Bohm-Kirschner....................................Ivy Scott
Hulde....................................Desha
Stout Mother....................................Belle Sylvia
Stout Father....................................Earl Edem
Stout Boy....................................George Hermans
Waiter....................................Eric Berlenbach
Zoo Attendant....................................Alfred Russ
Herr Kirschner....................................Alexis Obolensky
Tenor....................................Alexander McKee
Sophie....................................Kathleen Edwards
Assistant Stage Manager....................................Paul Donah
Brandel....................................Frank Dobert
Anna....................................Marjorie Main
Tessie....................................Ann Barrie
Lena Baum....................................Claire Cole

Act I.—Scene 1—*Leit Motif*—Dr. Walter Lessing's Home, Edendorf, Bavaria. 2—*Etudes*—Karl Reder's Classroom. 3—*Pastoral*—

On the road to Munich. 4—*Impromptu*—Ernst Weber's Office, Munich. Act II.—Scene 1—*Sonata*—The Zoo. 2—*Nocturne*—Frieda's Suite, Munich. 3—*Caprice*—Sieglinde's Room. 4—*Rhapsody*—Star Dressing-room. 5—*Intermezzo*—Stage and Orchestra Pit. 6—*Humoresque*—Star Dressing-room. 7—*Rondo*—Edendorf.

Staged by Oscar Hammerstein II and Jerome Kern; settings by Joseph Urban.

In Edendorf Dr. Walther Lessing, the old music master, has written a song to which Karl Reder has fitted words and a title, "I've Told Every Little Star." In Munich is Ernst Weber, an old school-fellow of Dr. Walther's, so Karl, the Doctor and Karl's sweetheart, the Doctor's daughter, Sieglinde, go to Munich with the Edendorf Walking Club hoping to get the song published. In Munich they run into adventure, Karl being taken over by Frieda, a prima donna, and Sieglinde being preferred by Bruno, a playwright who has quarreled with Frieda. The song is published but after a little the three Edendorfians are glad to get back to the quiet and simplicity of their village.

Principal songs—"I've Told Every Little Star," "And Love Was Born," "We Belong Together."

THE SILENT HOUSE

(16 performances)

A melodrama in four acts by John G. Brandon and George Pickett. Revived by Lee Shubert at the Ambassador Theatre, New York, November 8, 1932.

Cast of characters—

Mateo....................James MacDonald
Ho-Fang....................Harold de Becker
Philip Barty....................Stephen Appleby
Benson....................Frederic Leslie
George Winsford....................Gavin Muir
Dr. Chan-Fu....................Howard Lang
H'wang....................Raymond O'Brien
Jacob Herrington....................Arthur Bowyer
T'mala....................Jane Bramley
Señor Leon Peroda....................Louis Tanno

Acts I, II and IV.—Morning-room of Richard Winsford's House on Barnes Common, London, Known as "The Silent House." Act III.—Chinese Room of the Red House, Barnes.

Staged by Carl Hunt.

A revival of a mystery play produced in February, 1928. (See "Best Plays, 1927-28.")

THE DARK HOURS

(8 performances)

A tragedy in five scenes by Don Marquis. Produced by Lodewick Vroom at the New Amsterdam Theatre, New York, November 14, 1932.

Cast of characters—

Caiaphas, the High Priest	Herbert Ranson
Annas, His Father-in-Law	Fuller Mellish
Machir, a Beggar, Witness Against Jesus	Marshall Hale
Malchus, a Servant to the High Priest	Irving Beebe
Mary Magdalene	Eleanor Goodrich
Judas	Hugh Miller
Ezekiel, a Priest	Bert C. Wood
The Segan of the Temple	Larry Johns
Reuben (Scribes, Witnesses Against Jesus)	David Kerman
Abidah (Scribes, Witnesses Against Jesus)	Richard Warner
A Singer	George Heller
Voice of Jesus	———
Simon (Peter) (Disciples)	Marc Loebell
John (Disciples)	House Jameson
Andrew (Disciples)	Richard Abbott
James (Disciples)	H. Craig Neslo
Phillip (Disciples)	Donn Bonhoff
Thomas (Disciples)	LeRoy Bailey
Bartholomew (Disciples)	Angus Duncan
Judean Woman	Evelyn Este
Leper	John C. Hickey
Man Born Blind	Albert Berg
First Citizen	Robert Bruce
Second Citizen	J. P. Corr
First Pilgrim	Harold Brent
Second Pilgrim	John Beaver
A Galilean	Michael Cisney
Second Officer of the Temple	Paul Jones
Third Officer of the Temple	Walker Thornton
Maid Servant	Clara Mahr
Levi (Citizens of Jerusalem)	Victor Beecroft
Jonas (Citizens of Jerusalem)	George Bleasdale
Joseph (Citizens of Jerusalem)	Bernard Savage
Gershon (Citizens of Jerusalem)	Joseph Singer
Abishua, a Priest	Richard Abbott
Servant of Abishua	Harold Baumstone
Nahash (Witnesses Against Jesus)	Charles Jordan
Garmite (Witnesses Against Jesus)	H. H. McCollum
Pilate	Charles Bryant
Centurion (Roman Soldiers)	Bram Nossen
Marcus (Roman Soldiers)	Herbert Delmore
Caius (Roman Soldiers)	Walker Thornton
Blind Man	Peter Pann
Messenger from Herod	Earl White
Procla, the Wife of Pilate	Ruth Vonnegut
Lazarus	Ian Bowers
Barabbas	Herbert Gubelman
Mary, the Mother of Jesus	Georgia Graham
First Thief	J. D. Stradley
Second Thief	Michael Cisney
First Priest	Lee Baxter
Second Priest	Martin Sloane
Scribe	Sam Martin
Mark	Homan Bostock
The Cripple	Alfred Jenkin
The Samaritan Woman	Paula Verdin

Mary Cleophas....................Estelle Scheer
The Beggar....................Maurice Manson
First Roman Soldier....................Don Baker
Second Roman Soldier....................Edward Acuff
Third Roman Soldier....................Charles Adams
Fourth Roman Soldier....................Ernest Hartman

Scene 1—In the House of Caiaphas, the High Priest, on the Evening Before the Crucifixion. 2—In the Garden of Gethsemane. 3—In the House of Caiaphas. 4—At the Palace of Pilate. 5—Golgotha.

Staged by Marjorie Marquis; settings by Cleon Throckmorton.

A rewriting of the story of the crucifixion beginning with the decision of Caiaphas, the High Priest, to bring about the arrest of Jesus on the charge of his having claimed divine powers. Judas, tortured by doubts and misunderstandings, accepts the bribe and betrays the Savior in Gethsemane. The trials before the Sanhedrin and Pilate follow, preceding the scene of Golgotha.

RUTH DRAPER

(24 performances)

A series of character sketches by Ruth Draper. Produced by the Actors-Managers, Inc., at the Ritz Theatre, New York, November 14, 1932.

Sketches—

Opening A Bazaar
An Italian Lesson
Showing the Garden
In County Kerry
A Southern Girl at the Dance
In a Church in Italy
In a Railway Station on the Western Plains
A Dalmatian Peasant on the Hall of a New York Hospital
A Class in Greek Poise
Love in the Balkans
The Débutante
Three Women and Mr. Clifford
Three Generations in a Court of Domestic Relations
On a Maine Porch

Miss Draper's first engagement from November 14 to November 20 included 8 performances and the proceeds were given to nine charitable organizations. Her second engagement, from December 12 to December 24, was for the benefit of the Gibson Emergency Relief and the Stage Benefit Funds.

DEAR JANE

(11 performances)

A comedy in a prologue and three acts by Eleanor Holmes Hinkley. Produced by Eva Le Gallienne at the Civic Repertory Theatre, New York, November 14, 1932.

Cast of characters—

PROLOGUE

Joshua Reynolds....................................Paul Leyssac
Dr. Samuel Johnson..............................Howard da Silva
James Boswell.....................................Robert H. Gordon
David Garrick.......................................Joseph Kramm

THE PLAY

Henry Austen.......................................Richard Waring
Mrs. Austen..Beatrice Terry
James Austen.......................................Donald Cameron
Cassandra Austen.................................Eva Le Gallienne
Mr. Edgeworth.......................................Walter Beck
Mrs. Mitford...Margaret Love
Jane Austen.....................................Josephine Hutchinson
Tom Lefroy..Robert F. Ross
James Digweed.......................................Nelson Welch
Charles Powlett.....................................Harold Moulton
Mrs. Powlett..Leona Roberts
Sir John Evelyn..................................Joseph Schildkraut
Hickson..David Turk
Milliner...Beatrice de Neergaard
Mary Russel Mitford..................................Ruth Russell
Guests—Misses Pleadwell and Hare. Messrs. Bissel, Bower, Leonard, Sacks, Pollock, Valentis, Jacobson.
Dancers—Misses Beck, Dare, Goodman, Crosby, Campbell. Messrs. Cotsworth, Ballantyne, Marks, Wilkes.
Maids—Misses Relda, Johnson.
Servants—Merrs. Scourby, Hampshire.

Prologue—Cheshire Cheese, London, December 16, 1775. Act I.—Scene 1—Steventon Parsonage, Hampshire, 1798. 2—Basingstoke Ballroom. Act II.—Scene 1—Milliner's Shop, Bath. 2—Pumproom, Bath. Act III.—Evelyn Park, Marlboro Downs.

Staged by Eva Le Gallienne.

A biographical drama in which Jane Austen, a simpering, sweet child, puts aside two lovers, James Digweed and Tom Lefroy, and falls in love with Sir John Evelyn. Jane is eager to marry Sir John until she realizes that he has no interest in her literary ambitions. That, says she, is not love, and runs away from Sir John.

SINGAPORE

(24 performances)

A melodrama in three acts by Robert Keith. Produced by John Henry Mears at the 48th Street Theatre, New York, November 14, 1932.

Cast of characters—

Ah Qui....................H. L. Donsu
A Hindu Peddler....................Frank De Silva
Ricksha Boys....................Richard Wang, Marshall De Silva
Herbert Boerham....................J. W. Austin
Captain Robertson....................Lionel Ince
Malaya....................Suzanne Caubaye
Eric Hope....................Donald Woods
Hilda Armstrong....................Louise Prussing
Sir Almoktasim, Sultan of Selernerak....................Edward Raquello
Yvonne de Lacretelle....................Elizabeth Mears
Native Dancers....................{ Ann Caruth / Miriam Louis }
Tom Tom Player....................J. Marshall De Silva
Podah Singh....................Frank De Silva
Punchirah....................John De Silva

Acts I, II and III.—Living-room of Eric Hope's Bungalow in Singapore, Malay Straits Settlement.
Staged by Lee Elmore; settings by Edward Eddy.

Hilda Armstrong, engaged to marry Eric Hope, goes through with the ceremony so she can be near her lover, Sir Almoktasim, Eric's employer in Malay Straits Settlement. Seeking then to be rid of Eric so she may marry Sir Almoktasim Hilda gives a dinner at which trained cobras are a feature. One is supposed to strike Eric, but strikes Hilda instead.

CHRYSALIS

(23 performances)

A play in ten scenes by Rose Albert Porter. Produced by Martin Beck in association with Lawrence Langner and Theresa Helburn at the Martin Beck Theatre, New York, November 15, 1932.

Cast of characters—

Elizabeth Cose....................Lily Cahill
Michael Haverill....................Osgood Perkins
Lyda Cose....................Margaret Sullavan
Mary....................Gilberte Frey
Blondie....................Fan Bourke
Honey Rogers....................Elisha Cook, Jr.
Eve Haron....................June Walker
Louis....................E. Kazan
Don Ellis....................Humphrey Bogart
Mrs. Reilly....................Hazel Hanna
Mrs. Thomas....................Jessie Graham
Mrs. Haron....................Kathleen Comegys
Nat Davis....................Frank Layton
Miss Haskel....................Lalive Brownell
Guard....................Russell Thayer
Booboo....................Harry D. Southard
Cook....................Alvin Barrett
Molly....................Georgie Lee Hall
Lil....................Jean Macintyre
Ray....................Mary Orr
Bee....................Henrietta Kaye
Katie....................Kathleen Comegys

Mabel....................................Phyllis Loughton
Lottie....................................Florence Heller
Nettie....................................Wilhelmina Barton
Mary....................................Beta Rothafel
Becky....................................Kathryn McClure
Flaggerty....................................Arling Alcine
Judge Halman....................................Thurston Hall
Patrons of "Louie's"..............Toni Sorel, Jock Munro, George Kinsey and Harold Woodall
Pianist....................................Edmund Ziman

Scenes 1, 4, 7 and 10—Living-room in the Cose House. 2—"Louie's." 3—Hallway in a Tenement. 5—Room in Rose Manor. 6—House of Refuge. 8—Rose Manor—Recreation Room. 9—Hideaway Flat Near Hell's Kitchen.

Staged by Theresa Helburn; settings by Cleon Throckmorton.

Lyda Cose, thrilled with the adventure of life and rebellious of restraint, quits college and defies her mother, a stiff-necked and shallow society woman, to send her back. Investigating life on her own, Lyda goes out to get drunk with Don Ellis; elects to become Ellis' mistress; meets Honey Rogers, a thief, and his girl, Eve; is later asked to help get Honey out of jail and Eve out of reform school and becomes involved with the police in this adventure. Honey and Eve kill themselves to avoid capture and Lyda is returned to society.

THE PERFECT MARRIAGE

(13 performances)

A play in three acts by Arthur Goodrich. Produced by William Caryl at the Bijou Theatre, New York, November 16, 1932.

Cast of characters—

Bernard Catalan....................................George Gaul
Suzanne, His Wife....................................Edith Barrett
Georges Fleury....................................George Baxter
Louise Morel....................................Fay Bainter
Henri, the Son (in Acts I and III) }
Henri, the Father (in Act II) }..............Harold Gould
Henri, the Son (in Act II)....................................Jackie Kelk

Acts I, II and III.—Home of Bernard Catalan, in Auvergne, France.

Staged by Melville Burke; settings by Rollo Wayne.

Bernard Catalan, playwright, and Suzanne, his wife, are celebrating their golden wedding after fifty years of what their friends insist is a perfect marriage. Bernard invites Georges Fleury, a famous actor who played in his first success, and Louise Morel, former secretary to Bernard, invites herself. With the quartet assembled Louise dares them all to go back and reënact the scenes of their meeting forty-five years before. They take the dare and reveal the actor Fleury as Suzanne's lover, with Louise and Bernard equally friendly. After which the Catalans forgive each other and return to their peaceful ways.

CRADLE SNATCHERS

(6 performances)

A play in three acts by Russell Medcraft and Norma Mitchell. Revived by Max Rudnick at the Liberty Theatre, New York, November 16, 1932.

Cast of characters—

Susan Martin....................................Florence Moore
Ethel Drake....................................Alice Ann Baker
Kitty Ladd....................................Jasmine Newcombe
Anne Hall....................................Jean May
Elinor....................................Christy Sloane
Francine....................................Nancy MacGregor
Jackie....................................Luba Malina
Henry Winton....................................Converse Tyler
George Martin....................................William Corbett
Roy Ladd....................................George Lessey
Howard Drake....................................Joseph Holicky
Oscar Nordholm....................................Maury Tuckerman
Paul....................................Edward Tracy
Jose Vallejo....................................David Morris

Act I.—Ethel Drake's apartment, New York City. Acts II and III.—Kitty Ladd's Summer Home, Glen Cove, L. I.
Staged by Russell Medcraft.

The original production of "Cradle Snatchers" was made by Sam Harris at the Music Box Theatre, New York, September 2, 1925. See "Best Plays, 1925-26."

A MIDSUMMER NIGHT'S DREAM

(27 performances)

A comedy in six acts by William Shakespeare. Revived by the Shakespeare Theatre Company at the Shakespeare Theatre, New York, November 17, 1932.

Cast of characters—

Theseus....................................Charles Dingle
Egeus....................................Harry Joyner
Lysander....................................Irving Morrow
Demetrius....................................Leslie Austen
Philostrate....................................Russell Rhodes
Quince....................................Maurice Greet
Snug....................................Hugh F. Noall
Bottom....................................Curtis Cooksey
Flute....................................Percival Vivian
Snout....................................Ian Maclaren
Starveling....................................Robert Hamilton
Hippolyta....................................Grace Halsey Mills

Hermia....................................Frederica Going
Helena....................................Carolyn Ferriday
Oberon....................................Donald Somers
Titania....................................Ruth Vivian
Puck, or Robin Goodfellow....................Paula Trueman
Peaseblossom..............................Ann Middleton
Cobweb...................................Hanna, Marie Barrie
Moth......................................Audrey Kettle
Mustard Seed..............................Jane Marsh
Attendants on Theseus and Hippolyta { Catherine Ann Carr, Nora Novik, Jacqueline Hoyt, Judith Lawrence, Florence Robinson, Vilma Hoover, Paul Hirsch, Curtis Conwaye }
Singing Fairy..............................Rose D. Fox
Staged by Percival Vivian.

During the season of the Shakespeare Theatre Company, playing at popular prices, 249 performances of the Poet's works were revived. These included "Midsummer Night's Dream," with a total of 27 performances, "Merchant of Venice" with 29, "Macbeth" 27, "Julius Cæsar" 25, "Twelfth Night" 19, "As You Like It" 16, "Taming of the Shrew" 15, "Hamlet" 18, "Comedy of Errors" and "Much Ado About Nothing" 6 each, "Othello" 13, "Merry Wives of Windsor" 15, "Romeo and Juliet" 15, "The Tempest" 10, "King Lear" 8.

THE GOOD FAIRY

(68 performances)

A comedy in three acts by Ferenc Molnar, English text by Jane Hinton. Revived by O. E. Wee and J. J. Leventhal, Inc., at the Forrest Theatre, New York, November 17, 1932.

Cast of characters—

Head Waiter..............................John Eldredge
Konrad...................................Robert T. Haines
Lu ....Ada-May
Dr. Metz.................................Thomas A. Braidon
Dr. Sporum...............................Charles A. Francis
Karoline.................................Hilda Plowright
Law Clerk................................John Lynds
Underwaiter..............................Salo Douday
Act I.—Private Dining-room in a hotel. Acts II and III.—Dr. Sporum's office.
Staged by Lionel Bevans; settings by Joseph Urban.

Produced originally by Gilbert Miller at the Henry Miller Theatre, New York, November 24, 1931, with Helen Hayes as Lu. See "Best Plays of 1931-32."

AUTUMN CROCUS

(210 performances)

A play in three acts by C. L. Anthony. Produced by Lee Shubert in association with Basil Dean at the Morosco Theatre, New York, November 19, 1932.

Cast of characters—

Gentleman in Gay Braces........................Francis Lederer
Lady in Buttoned Boots........................Evamarie Hechtl
Lady With the Lost Underclothes..................Minna Phillips
Lady in Spectacles............................Patricia Collinge
Lady With the Baedeker........................Eda Heinemann
Young Lady Living in Sin.......................Patricia Calvert
Young Gentleman Living in Sin..................Lowell Gilmore
Reverend Gentleman.......................Charles H. Croker-King
Thirsty Lady..................................Margaret Arrow
Thirsty Gentleman............................Robert C. Fischer
Maid...Polly de Loos
Crocus-Gatherer...............................Eleanor Hausman

Acts I, II and III.—At the Rote Hirsch Inn in the Austrian Tyrol.
Staged by Basil Dean; settings by Rollo Wayne. After the London production designed by G. E. Calthrop.

The Lady in Spectacles, on a holiday in the Tyrol, falls desperately in love with the Gentleman in Gay Braces, who is the youthful and handsome keeper of an inn. He, also attracted, reminds her that she is still beautiful at 35, and that life is slipping by. He is married, but still free to love. The Lady in Spectacles thinks she will stay over in the Tyrol and let love awaken her spinster heart to the joy of living, but thinks better of it, on the advice of a friend, and continues her holiday in Munich.

FIREBIRD

(42 performances)

A play in three acts by Lajos Zilahy adapted by Jeffrey Dell. Produced by Gilbert Miller at the Empire Theatre, New York, November 21, 1932.

Cast of characters—

A Messenger.......................................Ernest Gann
The Hall Porter...............................John Daly Murphy
A Schoolgirl.....................................Mab Maynard
Postman...Lewis Dayton
Janos..Harry Plimmer
Zoltan Balkanyi.....................................Ian Keith
Mrs. Aranyosi...............................Evelyn Beresford
Karola Lovasdy...............................Judith Anderson
Andor Lovasdy...............................Henry Stephenson
Mr. Halasz...Edgar Kent
Alice.......................................Margot Stevenson

Mariette Lovasdy....................................Elizabeth Young
Mlle. Mousquet....................................Andree Corday
A Street Musician....................................Eugene Fila
A Tenant....................................Paul Allen, Jr.
Boriska....................................Helen Crane
Pfeiffer....................................Louis Polan
Theatre Attendant....................................James Roper
Girl Tenants....................................Mary Heberden, Katherine Locke
Policeman....................................Wylie Adams
Ambulance Men....................................Frederick Macy, George Grayson
Doctor....................................Arthur Metcalf
Police Inspector....................................Reginald Mason
Police Officer....................................Colin Hunter
Photographer....................................Robert Baldon
Police Commissioner Szentesi....................................Montagu Love
Szamosi....................................Le Roi Operti
Clerk at Police Headquarters....................................Harold Martin
Jolan Rosza....................................Nita Naldi
Anni....................................Whitney Bourne

Prologue and Act I.—Scene 1—Entrance Hall of an Apartment House in Budapest. 2—Commissioner Szentesi's Office. Acts II and III.—Room in the Lovasdys' Home.

Staged by Gilbert Miller; settings by Aline Bernstein.

Karola Lovasdy meets a popular actor, Zoltan Balkanyi, as a tenant of her husband's apartment building in which the Lovasdys also live. Finding Balkanyi's attentions distasteful Mme. Lovasdy seeks to have the actor ejected, but fails. Three months later Balkanyi is found shot dead in his apartment. A woman seen going through the halls is suspected. As circumstantial evidence encircles her Mme. Lovasdy confesses the murder. The Police Commissioner does not believe her story and proceeds with the investigation, finally uncovering Mariette Lovasdy, the Lovasdy daughter, as the murderess.

MORAL FABRIC

(32 performances)

A comedy in three acts by G. N. Albyn. Produced by the Playwrights' Guild at the Provincetown Playhouse, New York, November 21, 1932.

Cast of characters—

Fred Williams....................................Joe Bates Smith
Elsa....................................Mimi Rose
Jessica Bryce....................................Anne English
Isabel Morley....................................Edna M. Holland
William Carlton....................................Jos. N. P. Wilson
Grace Thompson....................................Alma Brock
Lowell Hardy....................................Harry Holbrook

Acts I, II and III.—Isabel Morley's Studio Apartment.

Staged by John F. Grahame; settings by Bernard Brooks.

Lowell Hardy, an upright person, is candidate for mayor of his town and opposed by the gang headed by William Carlton.

Carlton, a smooth article, conspires with Hardy's friend, Edna Holland, to have Hardy photographed in the act of accepting a bribe. Hardy and Edna fool the gangsters, however, and Hardy is elected.

THE BARRISTER

(8 performances)

A play in three acts by Sydney Stone. Produced by Sydney Stone at the Masque Theatre, New York, November 21, 1932.

Cast of characters—

Besson....................Pacie Ripple
Mona Latimer....................Emily Ross
Ronald Waring....................Robert Leslie
Arthur Wickham....................Edgar Mason
Connie Denmore....................Helen Kingsley
Flora Trevisson....................Jeannette Fox-Lee
Freddy....................Jack Edwards
Police Constable Reynolds....................Henry Hawkins
Harrod....................Stapleton Kent

Acts I, II and III.—Library of Ronald Waring's Chambers, Temple Court, London.
Staged by Sydney Stone.

Mona Latimer, loving Ronald Waring, is intent on marrying him. Ronald, however, insists on marrying Flora Trevisson instead. To prevent this Mona produces a bunch of Ronald's warmest letters, a brother steals them for blackmail purposes, Ronald shoots brother and tosses him out the window, and Harrod, the butler, who really is from Scotland Yard, overlooks practically everything.

THE DUBARRY

(87 performances)

An operetta in two acts adapted by Rowland Leigh and Desmond Carter from the German of Paul Knepler and J. M. Willeminsky; music by Carl Millocker, arranged by Theo Mackaben; lyrics by Rowland Leigh. Produced by Morris Green and Tillie Leblang at the George M. Cohan Theatre, New York, November 22, 1932.

Cast of characters—

Margot....................Pert Kelton
Madame Labille....................Lolita Robertson
Gwen May....................Iris Newton
Marquis De La Marche....................Robinson Newbold
Comte DuBarry....................Percy Waram
Elise....................Melba Forsythe
Jeanne....................Grace Moore
Rene Lavallery....................Howard Marsh

Hubert Oronais....................................Alexis Sandersen
La Jeune Moreau....................................Len Saxon
Landlady....................................Mildred Gethins
Comte Bordeneau....................................Harold Crane
Prince de Soubise....................................Fenton Barrett
Baron Chamard....................................Charles Angelo
Comte Fragonard....................................James Philips
Therese....................................Roberta Pierre
Didine....................................Helen Withers
Madame Sauterelle....................................Helen Raymond
Sophie....................................Vivian Vernon
Ninon....................................Patricia Clarke
Josephine....................................Marion Santry
Violet....................................Mildred Manning
Maitre Cascal....................................Craig Williams
Maid to Madame DuBarry....................................Ethel Britton
Duc de Choiseul....................................Max Figman
La Canargo....................................Joyce Coles
Maréchale de Luxembourg....................................Nana Bryant
Comte Lammond....................................John Clarke
Louis XV....................................Marion Green

Dorathea Burke Ballet.

Act I.—Scene 1—Workroom in Madame Labille's Hat Shop. 2—Near Port Maillot. 3—Rene's Garret. 4, 6—In Front of DuBarry's House. 5—DuBarry's Dining-room. 7—Salon of Madame Sauterelle. Act II.—Scene 1—Jeanne's Boudoir in DuBarry's House. 2—Rene's Study. 3—House of La Maréchale de Luxembourg. 4—Near the House of La Maréchale. 5—On the Road to Versailles. 6—Louis XV's Salon in the Palace of Versailles. 7—A Corner of a Garden. 8—Gardens of the Palace Luciennes.

Staged by Morris Green and Rowland Leigh; settings by Vincenti Menelli.

Jeanne, working in the millinery shop of Madame Labille, falls in love with Rene Lavallery and goes to live with him. Rene has no money either. Suspecting Jeanne of flirting with the Comte DuBarry Rene tosses her out and she stops for a while in Madame Sauterelle's house of pleasure. There DuBarry finds her and makes her his wife, an arrangement that continues until the King Louis XV catches sight of her and issues a summons. So well pleased is he with the DuBarry visit that Louis makes her Mme. Pompadour's successor.

Principal songs—"I Give My Heart," "If I'm Dreaming," "Jeanne."

GEORGE WHITE'S MUSIC HALL VARIETIES

(First engagement 48 performances. Second edition 24. Total 72.)

A revue by William K. Wells and George White; songs by Irving Cæsar and others. Produced by George White at the Casino Theatre, New York, November 22, 1932.

The principals—

Harry Richman	Barre Hill
Bert Lahr	Loomis Sisters

Peggy Moseley	Vivian Fay
Herr Al Gordon	Mullen Sisters
Joseph Donatella	Betty Kean
Lili Damita	Helen Gordon
Eleanor Powell	Helen Arnold

Staged by George White and Russell Markert.

CORNELIA OTIS SKINNER

(24 performances)

A series of character sketches by Cornelia Otis Skinner. Produced by James F. Reilly at the Lyceum Theatre, New York, November 22, 1932.

1. In the Bois de Boulogne—1853.
2. In the Gardens of Compiègne—1858.
3. An Ante Room of the Tuileries—1865.
4. After the Defeat at Sedan—1870.
5. Visit of Condolence by Queen Victoria to Eugenie After the Death of the Prince Imperial in the Zulu War—1879.
6. The Hotel Continental—1919.

Miss Skinner also revived "The Wives of Henry VIII" and several of her character sketches formerly given in New York, including: Old Embers, A Southern Girl in the Sistine Chapel, Homework, Motoring in the '90's, In a Telephone Booth, Sailing Time, The Eve of Departure, In a Gondola, A Lady Explorer.

JAMBOREE

(28 performances)

A play in three acts by Bessie Beatty and Jack Black based on a book, "You Can't Win" by Jack Black. Produced by Elizabeth Miele at the Vanderbilt Theatre, New York, November 24, 1932.

Cast of characters—

Sing....................Peter Goo Chong
Marguerite....................Wanda Howard
Bull....................John Alexander
Julie....................Olivia Wrightson
First "Bar Fly"....................Jack Clifford
Second "Bar Fly"....................Wesley Givens
A Gambler....................Al Guin
A Sucker....................Charles Craig
Justice of the Peace Beasley....................Roger Bacon
Colonel Poe....................Howard Morgan
Foot-'n'-Half George....................Frank Dae
Sanctimonious Slim (Sanc)....................Carroll Ashburn
Jack (The Kid)....................Lee Ellsworth
Al Sheets....................Carleton Macy
Blackie....................Barry Macollum
Mary Howard, Salt Chunk Mary....................Marie Kenney
Breeze....................Ruth Chorpenning
Cheyenne Lizzie....................Patsy Klein

Spot....................Walter Roach
Mimi....................Elizabeth Parks
Mike....................T. C. Connor
Jonathan Schorr....................Dodson Mitchell
A Deputy Marshal....................Jack Clifford
A Spokesman....................John McNulty
Gamblers, Dance Hall Girls and Other Habitués of the Board of Trade Hotel and Bar Played by Ruth Gibson, Richard Ewell, Signa Andres, George C. Mantell, Sheelagh Kennedy, Renée Cartier.

Acts I, II and III.—Mary's Living Quarters, the Board of Trade Hotel and Bar in Pocatello, Idaho.

Staged by Charles Friedman; settings by Philip Gelb.

Salt Chunk Mary Howard ran the Board of Trade Hotel and Bar in Pocatello, Idaho, in the early nineties. She acted as a fence and was a friend of crooks. Once a year she went on a jamboree and tried to clean up the town. Being sound at heart in the play she takes under her protection Marguerite, headed for sin, and Jack, headed for jail. Jack has helped with a robbery and is charged with a murder. Mary manages an escape for Jack and Marguerite, after she has discovered that the boy is her own son, reported dead to her when she was in jail.

* TAKE A CHANCE

(227 performances)

A musical comedy in two acts by B. G. De Sylva and Laurence Schwab; additional dialogue by Sid Silvers; music by Herb Brown Nacio and Richard Whiting; additional songs by Vincent Youmans. Produced by Schwab and De Sylva at the Apollo Theatre, New York, November 26, 1932.

Cast of characters—

Duke Stanley....................Jack Haley
Louie Webb....................Sid Silvers
Toni Ray....................June Knight
Wanda Brill....................Ethel Merman
Kenneth Raleigh....................Jack Whiting
Andrew Raleigh....................Douglas Wood
Consuelo Raleigh....................Mitzi Mayfair
Mike Caruso....................Robert Gleckler
Thelma Green....................Josephine Dunn
Butler....................George Pauncefort
Actors and Actresses in Kenneth Raleigh's Revue, "Humpty Dumpty": Oscar Ragland, Sara Jane, John Grant, Louise Seidel, Lee Beggs, Al Downing, Andrew and Louise Carr.

Act I.—Scene 1—Mike's Place. 2—Bedroom in a Hotel. 3—Stage of Embassy Theatre. 4—Raleigh Town House. Act II.—Scene 1—Outside of Stage Door, Embassy Theatre. 2—Opening Night of the Revue, "Humpty Dumpty."

Dancers, Ritz Quartette, The Admirals

Staged by Edgar MacGregor; settings by Cleon Throckmorton.

Duke and Louie are likable crooks. Toni Ray is a pal who is trying to make them behave. Especially after she meets and loves Kenneth Raleigh, a Harvard boy producing a show. The crooks rob Kenneth, who thinks Toni helped them. There is considerable trouble until Kenenth's revue, "Humpty Dumpty," with Toni as the prima donna, proves a success.

On June 5 Ole Olsen and Chic Johnson, having bought an interest in the show, replaced Jack Haley and Sid Silvers in the leading comedy rôles. At the same time Barbara Newberry replaced June Knight and Doris Groday took over Mitzi Mayfair's dancing part.

Principal songs—"Eadie Was a Lady," "Smoothie," "Turn Out the Lights," "I've Got Religion."

* GAY DIVORCE

(232 performances)

A musical comedy in two acts by Dwight Taylor, based on an unproduced play by the late J. Hartley Manners; musical adaptation by Kenneth Webb and Samuel Hoffenstein; music and lyrics by Cole Porter. Produced by Dwight Deere Wiman and Tom Weatherly at the Ethel Barrymore Theatre, New York, November 29, 1932.

Cast of characters—

Robert....Gordon Taylor
Guy....Fred Astaire
Teddy....G. P. Huntley, Jr.
Gladys....Jean Frontai
Vivian....Helen Allen
Doris....Mary Jo Mathews
Barbara....Joan Carter-Waddell
Phyllis....Eleanor Etheridge
Joan....Joan Burgess
Joyce....Dorothy Waller
Waiter....Eric Blore
Ann....Billie Green
Hortense....Luella Gear
Mimi....Claire Luce
Porter....Martin Cravath
Tonetti....Erik Rhodes
Pat....Pat Palmer
Diana....Mitzie Garner
Claire....Edna Abbey
Elaine....Jacquie Simmons
Edith....Ethel Hampton
Evelyn....Grace Moore
Beatrice....Bobby Sheehan
Elizabeth....Evangeline Raleigh
Mr. Pratt....Roland Bottomley

Prologue: Guy's London Flat. Act I.—Seaside Hotel. Act II.—Scenes 1 and 3—Mimi's Suite. 2—A Hotel Corridor.

Staged by Howard Lindsay; settings by Jo Mielziner.

Mimi, seeking to divorce Mr. Pratt, a frigid scientist, goes with her lawyer to an English seacoast village where she is to meet and be caught with a professional co-respondent. Guy, in love with Mimi, is also at the resort and accidentally becomes possessed of the password by which Mimi is to recognize the co-respondent. Mimi accepts the surprised Guy as the man engaged to compromise her and a hectic evening is spent in her apartment, with a chorus of hotel attachés serving as witnesses.

Principal songs—"Night and Day," "I've Got You on My Mind," "Mr. and Mrs. Fitch."

THE MAD HOPES

(12 performances)

A comedy in three acts by Romney Brent. Produced by Bela Blau at the Broadhurst Theatre, New York, December 1, 1932.

Cast of characters—

Hilton Hope....................................John Halloran
Geneva Hope....................................Jane Wyatt
Charlemagne....................................Harold Webster
Claude Hope....................................Rex O'Malley
Eugenie....................................Harriet Eells
Mrs. Clytemnestra Hope....................Violet Kemble Cooper
Henry Frost....................................Harry Ellerbe
Lady Ingleby....................................Doris Rich
Sheriff....................................Raymond O'Brien
Comte Rene D'Entain....................Marcel Journet, Jr.
Josephine....................................Ina Rorke
Bedford....................................Charles Wellesley
Maurice Klein....................................Pierre Watkin
Acts I, II and III.—The Château Sans-Souci at Nice.
Staged by Bela Blau; settings by Albert R. Johnson.

Clytemnestra Hope is a flighty, irresponsible person of lovable qualities. Completely down on her luck, with neither money nor food in the house, Mrs. Hope is still a grand lady who manages to fascinate the wealthy friend of an American house guest. Henry Frost, staying with the Hopes and paying his way because he loves Geneva, invites Maurice Klein to stop by and Maurice ends by buying the Hope property and marrying Mrs. Hope as well.

THE GREAT MAGOO

(11 performances)

A drama in three acts by Ben Hecht and Gene Fowler. Produced by Billy Rose at the Selwyn Theatre, New York, December 2, 1932.

Cast of characters—

Tante....Charlotte Granville
Sailor Burke....Victor Kilian
Jackie....Dennie Moore
Harry Costello....Jack Hazzard
Pauline....Muriel Campbell
Inspector....Charles Henderson
Nicky....Paul Kelly
Dowager....Violet Barney
Moe Weber....Harry Green
Julie Raquel....Claire Carleton
Gypsy Dancer....Della Lorraine
Fatima Twins.... { Evelyn Gaile / Mildred Stansill }
Sam....Millard Mitchell
Dummy Nolan....Joe Ploski
Waiter....Emil Hoch
Rathskeller Girls.... { Mildred Stansill / Evelyn Gaile }
Hanratty....Percy Kilbride
Weber's Band....Louis Savarese, Wally Curtis, Vic Piemonte, Al Savarese, John Porpora, Al Gentile, Eddie Bergman, John Sylvester
Mr. Ritchie....Gilbert Douglas
La Sylphe....Violet Barney
Mario....Juan Varro
Harry Aarons....Joseph Greenwald
Wench....Ronnie Madsen
Mr. McGinnis....Lloyd Pickney
Leo McCafferty....John Butler
Professor Jonas....Joe Fields

Dancing Girls, Amusement Seekers, etc.

Act I.—Scene 1—Coney Island. 2—On the Boardwalk. 3—Back Room of the Rathskeller. Act II.—Scene 1—Jackie's Bedroom, Coney Island. 2—Weber's Apartment, New York City. 3—La Sylphe's Rehearsal Studios. Act III.—Scene 1—Flea Circus. 2—Julie's Chamber.

Staged by George Abbott; settings by Hermann Rosse.

Nicky, a Coney Island barker, and Julie Raquel, who does the Salome dances, are in each other's blood. Even after Nicky cheats and lies to Julie, driving her to accept the attentions of Moe Weber, the bandman, and others, and after Nicky has been driven into the gutter by one experience after another with other girls, they find each other and make it up.

WALK A LITTLE FASTER

(119 performances)

A revue in two acts with music by Vernon Duke; lyrics by E. Y. Harburg; sketches by S. J. Perelman and Robert MacGunigle. Produced by Courtney Burr at the St. James Theatre, New York, December 7, 1932.

The principals—

Bobby Clark
Paul McCullough
John Hundley
Donald Burr
Dave Fitzgibbons
Jerome Andrews

Owen Coll	Katherine Hall
Jerry Norris	Dorothy McNulty
Lloyd Harris	Bernice Lee
Beatrice Lillie	Dorothy Fitzgibbon
Patricia Dorn	Albertina Vitak
Evelyn Hoey	Sue Hicks

Kay Lazelle

Staged by E. M. Woolley; dances by Albertina Rasch; settings by Boris Aronson.

Principal songs—"April in Paris," "Off Again, On Again," "Where Have We Met Before."

* BIOGRAPHY

(219 performances)

A comedy in three acts by S. N. Behrman. Produced by The Theatre Guild, at the Guild Theatre, New York, December 12, 1932.

Cast of characters—

Richard Kurt....................Earle Larimore
Minnie....................Helen Salinger
Melchior Feydak....................Arnold Korff
Marion Froude....................Ina Claire
Leander Nolan....................Jay Fassett
Warwick Wilson....................Alexander Clark
Orrin Kinnicott....................Charles Richman
Slade Kinnicott....................Mary Arbenz

Acts I, II and III.—Marion Froude's Studio in New York City.
Staged by Philip Moeller; settings by Jo Mielziner.

See page 172.

ALICE IN WONDERLAND

(127 performances)

A play in two parts adapted by Eva Le Gallienne and Florida Friebus from "Alice in Wonderland" and "Through the Looking Glass" by Lewis Carroll. Produced at the Civic Repertory Theatre, New York, December 12, 1932.

Cast of characters—

PART I

Alice....................Josephine Hutchinson
White Rabbit....................Richard Waring
(Freddy Rendulic and Doris Sawyer)
Mouse....................Nelson Welch
Dodo....................Joseph Kramm
Lory....................Walter Beck
Eaglet....................Robert H. Gordon
Crab....................Landon Herrick
Duck....................Burgess Meredith

Caterpillar.......................................Sayre Crawley
Fish Footman.......................................Tonio Selwart
Frog Footman.......................................Robert F. Ross
Duchess.......................................Charles Ellis
Cheshire Cat.......................................Florida Friebus
March Hare.......................................Donald Cameron
Mad Hatter.......................................Landon Herrick
Dormouse.......................................Burgess Meredith
Two of Spades.......................................David Marks
Five of Spades.......................................Arthur Swenson
Seven of Spades.......................................Whitner Bissell
Queen of Hearts.......................................Joseph Schildkraut
King of Hearts.......................................Harold Moulton
Gryphon.......................................Nelson Welch
Mock Turtle.......................................Lester Scharff
Cook.......................................Howard da Silva
Knave of Hearts.......................................David Turk
Clubs.......................................Jacobsen, Lloyd, Green, Dwenger
Hearts.......................................Tittoni, Ballantyne, Cotsworth, Pollock, Fox, Scourby, Milne, Marsden, Leonard

PART II

Red Chess Queen.......................................Leona Roberts
Train Guard.......................................Robert H. Gordon
Gentleman Dressed in White Paper.......................................Robert F. Ross
Goat.......................................Richard Waring
Beetle.......................................Florida Friebus
Hoarse Voice.......................................David Turk
Gnat.......................................May Sarton
Gentle Voice.......................................Agnes McCarthy
Tweedledum.......................................Landon Herrick
Tweedledee.......................................Burgess Meredith
White Chess Queen.......................................Eva Le Gallienne
Sheep.......................................Margaret Love
Humpty Dumpty.......................................Walter Beck
White Knight.......................................Howard da Silva
Horse { Front Legs.......................................Robert F. Ross
Horse { Back Legs.......................................Wm. S. Phillips
Old Frog.......................................Sayre Crawley
Shrill Voice.......................................Adelaide Finch
Singers.......................................Ruth Wilton and Adelaide Finch
Marionettes Worked by English, Beck, Snaylor, Nurenburg, Hill, Tittoni, Marsden, Bauer, Pollock, Under the Direction of A. Spolidoro.

Part I.—Alice at Home. The Looking Glass House. White Rabbit. Pool of Tears. Caucus Race. Caterpillar. Duchess. Cheshire Cat. Mad Tea Party. Queen's Croquet Ground. By the Sea. The Trial. Part II.—Red Chess Queen. Railway Carriage. Tweedledum and Tweedledee. White Chess Queen. Wool and Water. Humpty Dumpty. White Knight. Alice Crowned. Alice With the Two Queens. The Banquet. Alice at Home Again.

Staged by Eva Le Gallienne; dances by Ruth Wilton; settings by Irene Sharaff.

A faithful transcription of incidents from the well-loved children's classic, read mostly by their elders. On January 30 Miss Le Gallienne transferred "Alice" to the New Amsterdam Theatre in the hope of building up a fund that would help save her repertory idea. Expected subsidies had failed her.

THE SHOW-OFF

(119 performances)

A comedy drama in three acts by George Kelly. Revived by Jules J. Leventhal and O. E. Wee at the Hudson Theatre, New York, December 12, 1932.

Cast of characters—

Clara...Beatrice Maude
Mrs. Fisher...Jean Adair
Amy...Frances McHugh
Frank Hyland...Gus D'Ennery
Mr. Fisher...Charles Martin
Joe...Warren Ashe
Aubrey Piper...Raymond Walburn
Mr. Gill...D. Bagnell Rae
Mr. Rogers...Charles Sugah-Turner

Acts I, II and III.—The Big Room at Fishers'.
Staged by Raymond Walburn; settings by Philip Maltese.

"The Show-off" was produced originally at the Playhouse February 5, 1924. It was selected as one of the "Best Plays of 1923-24." The part of Aubrey was played originally by the late Louis John Bartels. Helen Lowell was the Mrs. Fisher. Raymond Walburn of the above cast played Piper with the Chicago company.

THE METROPOLITAN PLAYERS

(5 performances)

Five short plays. Produced by Mabel Rowland and Jay Strong at the Chanin Auditorium, New York, December 13, 1932.

The plays—

"The Family Exit," by Lawrence Langner, played by Sardis Lawrence, Antoinette Rochte, Thomas Dillon, Milton McClenaghan, Alice Griswold, Aubrey Beattie, Beverly Sitgreaves.

"Counsel's Opinion," by Roland Pertwee, played by Eleanor Steele, Robert Neff, Alan Brooks, Virginia George, John Monks, Sardis Lawrence.

"Saturday It Rained," adapted by Paul Gallico, played by Louise Groody, Ruth Gilbert, Doris Witherby, Virginia French, Evelyn Behning, Sardis Lawrence.

"The White Dress," by Ruth Welty, played by Joan Sudlow, Marion Brent, Mary George, Cele McLaughlin, Ann Sawyer, Cherry Goda, Elizabeth Devery, Kay Dorney, Ruth Foster, Marie Lindley, Alice Griswold, Rose Struli, Charlotte Smith, Octavia Freis, Georgia Simmons.

"The Way Out," by Ruth Giorloff, played by Glenn Hunter, Sardis Lawrence, Thomas Dillon.

"The March Heir," by Robette Hughes, played by Hall Clovis, Jack Easton, Elizabeth Sinclair, Robert Neff, Beverly Sitgreaves, Antoinette Rochte.

RED PLANET

(7 performances)

A play in three acts by John L. Balderston and J. E. Hoare. Produced by Laurence Rivers, Inc., at the Cort Theatre, New York, December 17, 1932.

Cast of characters—

Ray Fanshawe....................Bramwell Fletcher
Admiral Sir Reginald Battersby, K.C.B....................Eugene Powers
Bolt....................Wilfred Seagram
Mary Fanshawe....................Valerie Taylor
Maid....................Madelaine Vaughn
John Morrison....................Percy Moore
The Right Hon. A. D. Randall, P.C....................Richard Whorf
Parliamentary Secretary to Mr. Randall....................Wallace Widdecombe
The Lord Chancellor....................Thomas Louden
The Prime Minister....................Oswald Yorke
Sir James Valentine....................Louis Hector
The Count de Reinach....................Walter Armin
Linton....................Tod Waller
The Archbishop of Canterbury....................Leonard Willey
First Newsboy....................Walter King
Second Newsboy....................David Hughes
Joe....................Harry Green
Kate....................Beatrice Miller
Herbert Calder....................Henry Herbert
Members of Parliament: C. E. Smith, William Reinecker, Alistaire Johnson, Richard Walsh, E. Norris, Wallace Banfield, John Wheeler, Bertram Millar, Frederick Raymond. Speaker: Edward Trevor. Clerks: Charles Buroughs, Marshall Brown, Wilber Cox.
Ensemble: Marie Pape, Joy Douglas, Beryl Douglas, Tucker McGuire, Dorothy Howard, Ethel Ashby, Helen Wynn.

Act I.—Laboratory of the Fanshawes. Act II.—Scene 1—Chancellor of the Exchequer's Room in the Treasury. 2—Study in Lambeth Palace. 3—Office of the Count de Reinach. 4 and 6—A London Street. 5—Annex to the Laboratory. 7—Laboratory. 8—House of Commons. 9—Prime Minister's Ante-Room. 10—Outside Buckingham Palace. Act III.—Scene 1—Laboratory. 2—Westminster Abbey.

Staged by Burk Symon and Chester Erskin; sets by Lee Simonson.

Ray and Mary Fanshawe are scientists who have completed so powerful a short-wave radio set that they believe they have established contact with Mars. The day they receive answering signals they are sure of it. A code is worked out and information sought from the Martians as to their progress in science and religion. Word comes back that the Martians hold to the teachings of Jesus Christ. Ray Fanshawe, an atheist, refuses to accept the statement. Mary Fanshawe, a sincere religionist, is deeply moved. When the news is given to the world a spiritual revolution follows. Then a third scientist, a misshapen little man named Calder, appears to expose a hoax. He would arrange God's neglect of him. He has been sending the answers from Mars from another super-radio set which an avalanche in the Alps has just destroyed. To prevent complete exposure Mary Fanshawe blows up the Fanshawe's laboratory, her husband, Calder and herself.

LUCRECE

(31 performances)

A play in six scenes by André Obey; translated by Thornton Wilder; musical setting by Deems Taylor. Produced by Katharine Cornell at the Belasco Theatre, New York, December 20, 1932.

Cast of characters—

First Soldier....William J. Tannen
Second Soldier....George Macready
Tarquin....Brian Aherne
Collatine....Pedro de Cordoba
Brutus....Charles Waldron
First Narrator....Blanche Yurka
Lucrece....Katharine Cornell
Julia....Kathleen Chase
Emilia....Joyce Carey
Sidonia....Harriet Ingersoll
Marina....Brenda Forbes
Second Narrator....Robert Loraine
Valerius....George Macready
First Servant....Francis Moran
Second Servant....Barry Mahool
Third Servant....Charles Thorne

Citizens, Soldiers, Servants

Scene 1—Collatine's Tent. Scenes 2 and 6—A Room in Collatine's House. Scenes 3 and 4—Lucrece's Room. Scene 5—Before the Curtain.

Staged by Guthrie McClintic; settings by Robert Edmond Jones.

Lucrece, at home while her noble lord, Collatine, is at the siege of Ardea, is surprised by a visit of the generals of her husband's army and caught innocently spinning with her maids. Few of the other generals' wives were so discreetly employed. Brutus, boasting of his friend's wife in honoring Collatine, so fires the imagination of Tarquin, the king's son, that he determines to test the virtue of the chaste Lucrece. Forcing his attentions upon the unhappy wife he so humiliates her that she conceives self-destruction as the only means of reclaiming her honor. Her accusations against Tarquin and her suicide bring about a rising of the people.

ANYBODY'S GAME

(29 performances)

A play in three acts by Paul Barton. Produced by Elizabeth Miele at the Bijou Theatre, New York, December 21, 1932.

Cast of characters—

Peggy Blake.......................................Emily Lowry
Lulu Corliss.......................................Edna Hibbard
Helen Martin.......................................Neville Westman
Ed Delaney.......................................Paul Stanton
Bill Cassidy.......................................Walter Roach
Jimmy Craig.......................................Sam Wren
Sid Lewis.......................................Louis Sorin
Dennis Gibbs.......................................Calvin Thomas
Sebastian Palukas.......................................Edward Colebrook
Laura Hale.......................................Charlotte Andrews
Fritz Klinghopper.......................................Joseph Greenwald
Greta Swinberg.......................................Vanda Norin
A Little Stranger.......................................Marian Warring-Manley

Acts I, II and III.—Reception Room of the Delaney Advertising Agency.

Staged by Theodore J. Hammerstein; sets by Philip Gelb.

Jimmy Craig, unemployed, tries selling stockings from door to door. He drifts into the Delaney Advertising agency when a new space buyer is expected. Coached by Peggy Blake, an old sweetheart now secretary to the agency, Jimmy permits Delaney to mistake him for the expected expert and blunders dumbly into a succession of triumphs in copywriting, slogan-coining and popular appeal. He is temporarily won over by the office vamp, Lulu Corliss, but returns to Peggy in the end and is taken into the firm.

TEATRO DEI PICCOLI

(129 performances)

Vittorio Podrecca's Italian marionette troupe. Presented by S. Hurok at the Lyric Theatre, New York, December 22, 1933.

The singers—

Emilio Cabello	Lia Podrecca
Thea Carugati	Mario Serangeli
Giuseppe Costa	Dario Zani
Augusto Galli	Irma Zappatta
Carlo Pessina	Rosina Zotti

Manipulators and operators: The families of—Gorno, Dell'Acqua Possidoni, Forgioli, Borgogni, Donati, Braga, Rosagni, Vanelli and Gabutti.

During the season there were puppet shows produced by Tony Sarg, Sue Hastings and the Yale Puppeteers. The latter played from December 6, 1932, through to June 7, 1933, at a Lilliputian Lyceum in 46th Street, building up a considerable and loyal following.

HONEYMOON

(76 performances)

A comedy in three acts by Samuel Chotzinoff and George Backer. Produced by Harold Stone at the Little Theatre, New York, December 23, 1932.

Cast of characters—

Mrs. Leslie Taylor....Katherine Alexander
Nicola....Joseph Spurin-Calleia
Bob Taylor....Thomas Mitchell
Katie....Elizabeth Bruce
Joan Chapman....Rachel Hartzell
Sam Chapman....Ross Alexander

Acts I and III.—Sitting-room of Mrs. Taylor's House in Paris. Act II.—Mrs. Taylor's Boudoir.

Staged by Thomas Mitchell; settings by Raymond Sovey.

The Leslie Taylors are in Paris on their honeymoon. They quarrel violently. The Sam Chapmans are going through a similar unhappiness. Mr. Chapman and Mrs. Taylor decide to cheat fate by going out together. After a day and a night of night-club exhilaration they are sobered and cured. Mrs. Taylor decides to go back to Mr. Taylor and Mr. Chapman is happily forgiven by Mrs. Chapman.

CYRANO DE BERGERAC

(16 performances)

A comedy in five acts by Edmond Rostand adapted by Brian Hooker. Revived by Walter Hampden at the New Amsterdam Theatre, New York, December 26, 1932.

Cast of characters—

Cyrano de Bergerac....Walter Hampden
Christian de Neauvillette....John D. Seymour
Comte de Guiche....Reynolds Evans
Ragueneau....Whitford Kane
Le Bret....Ernest Rowan
Ligniere....William Sauter
Carbon de Castel-Jaloux....C. Norman Hammond
Vicomte de Valvert....Gordon Hart
A Marquis....Robert C. Schnitzer
Another Marquis....Lewis McMichael
Montfleury....Gerald O'Neill
Bellerose....W. Messenger Bellis
Jodelet....Cyrus H. Staehle
Cuigy....Joseph V. de Santis
Brissaille....Harold Williams
A Busybody....P. J. Kelly
A Musketeer....Arthur Stenning
D'Artagnan....John Marquand
A Spanish Officer....Howard Galt

A Cavalier....................................Spencer Kimbell
A Porter....................................J. P. Wilson
A Man....................................Wilfred Jessop
Another Man....................................Murray D'Arcy
A Guardsman....................................Edward E. Hale
A Citizen....................................Henry Warwick
His Son....................................Robert B. Mantell, Jr.
A Pickpocket....................................Harvey Sayers
Betrandou, the Fifer....................................Walter Plinge
A Capuchin....................................George Thorp
Pages....................................Edwin Ross, James R. Pray
Roxane....................................Katharine Warren
Her Duenna....................................Mabel Moore
Lise....................................Evelyn Goodrich
An Orange Girl....................................Esther Mitchell
A Flower Girl....................................Evelyn Venable
A Soubrette....................................Alice Dalton
A Comedienne....................................Laura Barrett
Another Comedienne....................................Helen O'Connor
Mother Marguerite de Jesus....................................Joanna Dorman
Sister Marthe....................................Margaret Watson
Sister Claire....................................Mildred Vail
A Nun....................................Eliza Connolly
A Little Girl....................................Mary Alice Dill

Cadets of Gascoyne: John Marquand, Henry Warwick, Spencer Kimbell, Wilfred Jessop, W. Messenger Bellis, Edward E. Hale, Guy Collins.

Poets: Gordon Hart, P. J. Kelly, Cyrus H. Staehle, Harvey Sayers, Pickering Brown.

Intellectuals and Précieuses: Alice Dalton, Mary Dill, Bessie Beatty, Helen O'Connor, Laura Barrett, Wanda Geib and Phyllis Sallee.

Act I.—Hotel de Bourgoyne. Act II.—Bakery of the Poets. Act III.—Roxane's Kiss. Act IV.—Cadets of Gascoyne. Act V.—Cyrano's Gazette.

Staged by Walter Hampden; sets by Claude Bragdon.

Mr. Hampden's original production of "Cyrano" was made in November, 1923, with Carroll McComas as the Roxane. The last previous revival in New York was staged in 1928 with Ingeborg Torrup the Roxane.

SHUFFLE ALONG OF 1933

(17 performances)

A musical comedy in two acts and eight scenes by Flournoy E. Miller; music by Eubie Blake; lyrics by Noble Sissle. Produced by Mawin Productions, Inc., at the Mansfield Theatre, New York, December 26, 1932.

Cast of characters—

Edith Wilkes....................................Lavada Carter
Taxi Ben....................................Marshall Rodgers
Mrs. Jones....................................Edith Wilson
Cæsar Jones....................................Mantan Moreland
A Customer....................................Louise Williams
Dave Coffey....................................George McClennon
Tom Sharp....................................Noble Sissle
Steve Jenkins....................................Flournoy Miller
Harry Walton....................................Clarence Robinson
Alice Walker....................................Vivienne Baber

Sam....................Howard Hill
Farmer Taps....................Taps Miller
Sheriff....................Joe Willis
Summons Server....................James Arnold
Stenographer....................Catherine Brooks
Office Boy....................Herman Reed
Telephone Girl....................Ida Brown
Shipping Clerk....................Romaine Johns
Waiter....................Adolph Henderson
At the Piano....................Eubie Blake

Act I.—Scene 1—City Square—Jimtown, Mississippi. 2—Jones' Cabin. 3—U-Eat-Em Molasses Factory. Act II.—Scene 1—City Square. 2—Sugar Cane Field. 3—Office of U-Eat-Em Molasses Factory. 4—Ben's Taxi Stand. 5—Roof of U-Eat-Em Molasses Factory.

Staged by Walter Brooks; settings by Karl Amend, dances by Davis and Carey.

The usual colored revue libretto, this one having to do with the financing of a molasses factory.

THE LITTLE BLACK BOOK

(8 performances)

A comedy drama in three acts by Harold Sherman. Produced by American Plays and Players, Inc., at the Selwyn Theatre, New York, December 26, 1932.

Cast of characters—

Mrs. Gideon Tremper....................Clara Palmer
Lulu May Porter....................Virginia Stevens
H. D. Porter....................Jonathan Hole
Rev. Orville Sweetman....................Howard Kyle
Mrs. Eunice Sweetman....................Emma de Weale
Daniel Sweetman....................Bernie Neary
Timothy Sweetman....................Robert Mayors
Mort Pierce....................Donald Foster
Claudia Pierce....................Audrey Davis
Mr. Sternberg....................Herbert Heywood
Colonel Shutes....................Arthur Griffin
Henry C. Roland....................Russell Hicks
Tony Mazetti....................Douglas MacPherson
Officer Ward....................Jerome Cowan
Senator Thompson....................Dodson Mitchell

Acts I, II and III.—Porter Apartment, Washington, D. C.
Staged by Karl Nielsen; settings by Louis Kennel.

The H. D. Porters, recently come to live in Washington, D. C., are overwhelmed by visits from their neighbors and also a proposition made by a local political boss that Porter take a hand in a political graft having to do with the withdrawal of liquor from bonded warehouses. Porter comes into possession of a little black book that contains the names of most of the Washington politicians whose records are vulnerable and this helps him a lot when he is arrested on a trumped-up charge of theft.

RADIO CITY MUSIC HALL

Inaugural program produced under the personal direction of S. L. (Roxy) Rothafel, December 27, 1932.

Order of exercises—

Symphony of the Curtains, Caroline Andrews, soloist.
Dedication, by Robert T. Haines.
"Sept. 13, 1814," with Taylor Holmes as Francis Scott Key.
Impressions of a Music Hall, the Wallendas, the Kiutas.
In the Spotlight, Eddie and Ralph, "Sisters of the Skillet."
Radio City Ballet, Patricia Bowman première danseuse.
Fräulein Vera Schwarz of the Stats-Opera, Berlin.
Kirkwhite and Addison, dancers.
The Tuskogee Choir, William L. Dawson, Director.
Ray Bolger, Dancer.
Herald Kreutzer, Interpretive Dancer.
Radio roxyettes, Russell Markert, Director.
Doctor Rockwell, Monologist.
Night Club Revels, by the Company.
Excerpts from "Carmen," with Titta Ruffo.
Doctor Rockwell.
Martha Graham.
Minstrelsy, with De Wolf Hopper, Weber and Fields and the Company.

An audience of 6,000 attended the inaugural exercises of the Rockefeller Center Music Hall. A week later a second auditorium, the "Roxy," devoted exclusively to motion pictures and an accompanying stage show, was dedicated. Soon thereafter the music hall policy was abandoned and both theatres devoted to motion pictures.

* GOODBYE AGAIN

(200 performances)

A play in three acts by Allan Scott and George Haight. Produced by Arthur J. Beckhard at the Masque Theatre, New York, December 28, 1932.

Cast of characters—

Anne Rogers....................Sally Bates
Kenneth Bixby....................Osgood Perkins
Waiter....................Harold Bassage
Bellboy....................Myron McCormick
Maid....................Nell Burt
Julia Wilson....................Katherine Squire
Chauffeur....................James Stewart
Elizabeth Clochessy....................Dortha Duckworth
Arthur Westlake....................Hugh Rennie
Harvey Wilson....................Leslie Adams
Mr. Clayton....................Alfred Dalrymple
Theodore....................Jackie Kelk

Acts I, II and III.—Double Bedroom in the Hotel Statler, Cleveland.

Staged by Arthur J. Beckhard; settings by Tom Adrian Cracraft.

Kenneth Bixby, novelist and lecturer, is in Cleveland on a tour. With him is Anne Rogers, his secretary and best friend. Suddenly appears Julia Wilson, a slightly hysterical married woman who remembers a first love affair with Kenneth, and is now of a mind to resume what she considers her rightful job as his inspiration. Kenneth tries to be rid of Julia and gets himself into a mess which seems likely to result in divorce for Julia and the loss of Anne for Kenneth. But life, Anne, Kenneth and the lecture tour go on.

On June 3 Osgood Perkins and Sally Bates were succeeded by Bert Lytell and Lora Baxter.

20TH CENTURY

(152 performances)

A comedy in three acts by Ben Hecht and Charles MacArthur based on a play by Charles B. Milholland. Produced by George Abbott and Philip Dunning at the Broadhurst Theatre, New York, December 29, 1932.

Cast of characters—

Porter.....Frank Badham
Grover Lockwood.....James Spottswood
Anita Highland.....Dennie Moore
Train Secretary.....Ross Hertz
Owen O'Malley.....William Frawley
Conductor.....Granville Bates
Oliver Webb.....Matt Briggs
Flannagan.....Alfred Webster
Pullman Conductor.....William Worth
Dr. Johnson.....Clare Woodbury
Matthew Clark.....Etienne Girardot
First Beard.....Hans Hamsa
Second Beard.....Edward La Roche
Oscar Jaffe.....Moffat Johnston
Waiter.....Ernest Hunter
Sadie.....Florence Edney
Lilly Garland.....Eugenie Leontovich
George Smith.....Roy Roberts
First Detective.....Joseph Crehan
Second Detective.....J. Ascher Smith
Max Jacobs.....Henry Sherwood
Gateman.....Robert Sloane
Reporter.....Cliffman Jewel

Act I.—Observation Car on the Twentieth Century Limited. Acts II and III.—Scenes 1 and 2—Twentieth Century En Route. 3—Grand Central Station, New York.

Staged by George Abbott; settings by Cirker and Robbins.

Lilly Garland, picture star, is on a 20th Century train coming east from Chicago. Oscar Jaffe, New York theatre manager, having quarreled with Lilly, both as star and sweetheart, injects himself into an adjoining compartment in the hope of making up with her. He needs her name to a contract to help him mollify his bankers. Jaffe meets on the train two German Passion Play actors, signs them to act the Passion Play with Lilly as the Magdalen and induces a traveling churchman to back the show. At Cleveland the police take the backer off to send him back to the asylum from which he has escaped and Jaffe is again in the market, with Lilly as a star.

GIRLS IN UNIFORM

(12 performances)

A drama in three acts and ten scenes by Christa Winsloe adapted by Barbara Burnham. Produced by Sidney Phillips at the Booth Theatre, New York, December 30, 1932.

Cast of characters—

Fräulein von Nordeck, Headmistress		Roberta Beatty
Excellency von Ehrenhardt, Manuela's Aunt		Jean Newcombe
The Grand Duchess, Patroness of the School		Charlotte Walker
Countess Kernitz, Court Lady		Ethel Jackson
Fräulein von Bernberg	Mistresses	Rose Hobart
Fräulein von Gaerschner	Mistresses	Edith Gresham
Fräulein von Kesten	Mistresses	Jane Seymour
Mademoiselle Alaret	Mistresses	Andre Caron
Miss Gibson	Mistresses	Velma Roberts
Fraulein von Atams	Mistresses	Mathilde Baring
Manuela von Meinhardis	Pupils	Florence Williams
Marga von Rasso	Pupils	Wauna Lidwell
Ilse von Treischke	Pupils	Margaret Oliver
Ilse von Westhagen	Pupils	Florence McGee
Lilli von Kattner	Pupils	Marcella Abels
Oda von Eldenslehen	Pupils	Lily Marne
Edelgard Countess Mengsberg	Pupils	Helen Claire
Anneliese von Beckendorf	Pupils	Rose Lieder
Mia von Wollen	Pupils	Dana Hughes
Paula von Bley	Pupils	Barbara Hunter
Freda	Pupils	Ruth Gilbert
Jose	Pupils	Charlotte Silton
Greta	Pupils	Jonatha Jones
Frau Alden, Ballet Mistress		May Ediss
Frau Lehmann, the Portress		Hope Landen
Martha, Wardrobe Mistress		Clara Thropp
Manni, Nurse		Jessamine Newcombe
Johanna, Chambermaid		Elizabeth Upthegrove

Pupils: Cathleen Barrett, Sarita Coffyn, Marjorie A. Cushman, June Cox, Olive Corn, Renah Homer, Nancy Hughes, Sonya Jaffe, Janet Lord, Thelma Lynn, Edith Lyon, Jean McIntyre, Wanda Perry, Beverly Roberts, Gretchen Rochelle, Ruth Ryan, Sonya Staff and Elizabeth Townsend.

Act I.—Scenes 1 and 3—Reception Hall. 2—Wardrobe Room. 4—Dormitory. Act II.—Scenes 1 and 3—Girls' Common Room. 2—Fräulein von Bernberg's Room. Act III.—Scene 1—The Sick Room. 2—The Reception Hall. 3—Fräulein von Bernberg's Room. A Town in the North of Germany.

Staged by Frank Gregory.

Manuela, motherless daughter of a Prussian army officer, is placed in a girls' school dedicated to the severe restrictions of the old Prussian military régime. Lonesome and starving for affection, Manuela conceives a great love for the gentlest of her teachers, Fräulein von Bernberg. Her tongue loosened by a light punch at a class supper Manuela boasts her love. The Headmistress, reading unhealthy motivations into the girl's declarations, disgraces her with punishments and Manuela kills herself through shame.

SAINT WENCH

(12 performances)

A comedy in three acts by John Colton. Produced by Helen Menken at the Lyceum Theatre, New York, January 2, 1933.

Cast of characters—

Nadja Nikolaivna....................Jean Fullarton
Josef Tzigardis....................Russell Hardie
Mara Nikolaivna....................Helen Menken
Kristan, the Wolf....................Edward Leiter
Vaso, the Hermit....................Bernard Jukes
Guardsman....................John Burke
Councilman Nikola....................Philip Lord
Milika....................Margaret Linden
Reka....................Miriam Battista
Ilija....................Thomas Hamilton
Jena Tzigardis....................Mrs. Jennings Hine
Archbishop....................John Krikoff
Acolyte....................Master Rene Poucil
Acolyte....................Master Harry McKean
A Bottle Woman....................Florence Gerald
A Blind Girl....................Lorraine Jailet
A Man With a Twisted Foot....................J. Francis Robertson
A Poppy Eater....................Paula MacLean
A Man With a Curved Spine....................John Burke
A Boy With Devils....................John Drew Colt
A Man With Wooden Limbs....................Frank Diaz
A Voyager From Caspia....................Wilfred Clarke
The Duchess Icara of Barabia....................Anne Ravel
Her Child....................Ann Middleton
Mrs. Blowsybell....................Mabel Kroman
Priests of the Bed, Guardsmen, Gypsies, Wedding Guests, Town Folk.

Act I.—Home of Councilman Nikola Inside the Walled Town of Trabia, Seventeenth Century. Acts II and III.—Upper Room in the House of Josef Tzigardis.

Staged by Charles Hopkins; settings by Robert Redington Sharpe.

Mara Nikolaivna, afterward to become Saint Mara of Trabia, is betrothed to Josef Tzigardis who is about to take holy orders. While Josef is away Mara meets Kristan the Wolf, a bandit, in the woods and is surprised. After Josef returns and he and Mara are married Mara cannot get Kristan out of her thoughts, or her room. Josef, who is patiently understanding, lives to see Mara turn saint and acquire even greater healing powers than he ever had.

FANTASIA

(7 performances)

A drama in three acts by John Eldon Fillmore. Produced by the Provincetown Playhouse Guild at the Provincetown Theatre, New York, January 3, 1933.

Cast of characters—

Paul Kemble, as Beggar Paul Kemble, as Playwright Milton Senator Caldwell Paul Kemble, as Producer	Richmond Cooper
Belle Kemble Mother Mrs. Nolan Mrs. Ward	Lillian Shrewsbury
Street Girl Martha Benn Elaine Sargeant Countess de Marq Miss Patricia	Frances Armstrong

Supporting cast—Wendel K. Phillips, Lawrence Menkin, Wilton Graff, Frederick Flint, Elbert Drew, Charles Brown, Joan Meyer, Dorothy Nodine, Sylvia Tree, Grace Carney, Katherine MacDonald, Betty Doyle, Sarah Ellen Glass, Elaine Eldridge, Max Beck, Muni Diamond, Valerie Shinn, Ralph Young, Claron Drayd, Wilton Flint, and Miriam Treisman.

Act I.—Scene 1—Side street. 2, 4—Paul Kemble's Living-room. 3—Scene from Kemble's Play. Act II.—Scenes 1, 3 and 5—Kemble's Living-room. 2—Kemble's visual recollections. 4—Senator Caldwell's office. Act III.—Scene 1—Street. 2, 4—Living-room. 3—Kemble's Office. 5—Side street.

Staged by Donald Lamotte Hathway; settings by Bernard Brooks.

Among other experimental ventures at the Provincetown Theatre were productions of "Crescendo," by Donald Lamotte Hathway, and "A Temporary Husband," of anonymous authorship.

A GOOD WOMAN, POOR THING

(8 performances)

A comedy in three acts by Dillard Long. Produced by John H. Potter at the Avon Theatre, New York, January 9, 1933.

Cast of characters—

Picks	Johnnie Brewer
Bill Smith	Arthur Margetson
Edward	W. J. McCarthy
Philomena	Gwen Day Burroughs
Lelia	Irene Purcell
Christine	Millicent Hanley
John	John Williams

Acts I, II and III.—Bill Smith's Home Somewhere in the Country.

Staged by Arthur Sircom; settings by Aline Bernstein.

Lelia, having divorced a husband in Paris, returns to New York all set to marry Bill Smith. Which she does, over the fairly mild protests of Christine, Bill's mistress. Lelia and Bill are rapturously happy for a few months, after which they quarrel and separate until the theatre's reconciliation hour.

LATE ONE EVENING

(8 performances)

A play in two acts by Audrey and Waveney Carten. Produced by Harry C. Bannister at the Plymouth Theatre, New York, January 9, 1933.

Cast of characters—

Nurse....................Eva Leonard-Boyne
Hospital Attendant....................H. Craig Neslo
Pauline Murray....................Ursula Jeans
Doctor....................H. Langdon Bruce
Victor Franklin....................John Buckler
Anesthetist....................Isadore Marcil
Lady Murray....................Winifred Harris
Laura....................Audrey Ridgwell
Maid....................Ernestine de Becker
Mrs. Green....................Daisy Belmore
Michael....................Edward Ryan
Mr. Higgins....................Ralph Roberts
Porter....................Gilbert Squarey
1st Nurse....................Estelle Scheer
2nd Nurse....................Vera Fuller-Mellish
Paul....................Roman Arnoldoff
General Coulsden....................Edward Emery
Mrs. Coulsden....................Alice May Tuck
Geoffrey Dennis....................Don Bonhoff
Donald....................Richard Carey
George Dorsett....................Hugh Buckler
Countess Voronzoff....................Enid Romany
Maid....................Isabel Keightley
Hotel Manager....................Richard Warner
Hotel Attendant....................Don Bonhoff
Betty....................Helen Deddens
Phillip....................Dennis Gurney
Fritz....................Hans Hansen
Bartender....................Ernest Robert
Wardress....................Antoinette Rochte
Warder....................Orville Harris

Act I.—Scene 1—London Nursing Home. 2—Lady Murray's Drawing-room, London. 3—Lodging House in Bloomsbury. 4—Waiting-room in a London Hospital. Act II.—Scenes 1 and 6—Café St. Pol, French Riviera. 2—Victor Franklin's Villa at Cannes. 3—Hotel Bedroom at Biarritz. 4—Café in Montmartre. 5—Prison Cell.

Staged by Cecil Humphreys; settings by Edward Eddy.

Pauline Murray is run down by Victor Franklin's automobile. In hospital they agree that inasmuch as both have been living wasted lives they declare a new deal, take each other for better or worse and start over. Under this agreement Victor's old talent as a novelist is restored and Pauline is happy with her husband and her son. Son dies and with Victor's prosperity comes a return to the bad old life and a further defeat for both. Pauline threatens to leave Victor when, by picturing for her the life she would lead if she kept her threat to be even with him, the novelist is able to win her back to still another start.

TWO STRANGE WOMEN

(15 performances)

A play in three acts by Edwin B. Self. Produced by A. C. Mester at the Little Theatre, New York, January 10, 1933.

Cast of characters—

Greatgrandma Jenkins............................Lida McMillan
Grandma Jenkins.................................Maude Durand
Judge Whiffle...............................John Daly Murphy
"Mel" Jenkins......................................John Griggs
Harry Martin...................................Houston Richards
"Pap" Jenkins......................................Seth Arnold
Grace Martin...................................Jacqueline Logan
Robert Skinner.................................Douglas Gilmore

Acts I, II and III.—Jenkins' Fishing Ranch on a Canyon of the Dix River in Kentucky.

Staged by Egon Brecher; settings by David S. Gaither.

The Jenkinses run a fishing ranch in Kentucky. Their cabin is on a steep bank high above the Dix River. The Harry Martins, city folk, come to fish. Helen, the wife, takes a fancy to Mel Jenkins, the strong son of the Jenkins family. He falls desperately in love with her and when she makes him believe she loathes her husband he takes that worthy for a boat ride and pushes him into the river, where he drowns. Convinced thereafter that Mrs. Martin was only making a fool of him Mel insists on giving himself up to the authorities. Whereupon Greatgrandma Jenkins, who has taken no part in any conversation for eighteen years, rises up and pushes Mrs. Martin through a door from which she falls into the river and is killed.

FOOLSCAP

(13 performances)

A comedy in three acts by Gennaro Curci and Eduardo Ciannelli. Produced by John R. Sheppard and Frank A. Buchanan at the Times Square Theatre, New York, January 11, 1933.

Cast of characters—

George Bernard Shaw..........................Frederic Worlock
Luigi Pirandello..........................Eduardo Ciannelli
Dr. Harrold..........................Henry O'Neill
Nurse..........................Cynthia Latham
Shakespeare..........................Geoffrey Kerr
Francesca da Rimini..........................Peggy Hovenden
Cleopatra..........................Alice Reinheart
Marc Antony..........................Robert Wallsten
Eve..........................Rosamund Merivale
Helen of Troy..........................Katherine Hastings
Menelaus..........................Gorris Nels
Photographer..........................Arnold Preston
Assistant Photographer..........................Francis Carter
Orderly..........................William Dorbin
Martina..........................Diane Bori
Pierce..........................Arthur Bowyer
Servant..........................Allen Nourse
Prof. Bluttner..........................Bennett Southard
The Stranger..........................Alan Marshal
Octavius..........................George Tawde
Lunatic..........................Richard Whorf
Electrician..........................Charles S. Brown
Property Man..........................Frank Conlan
Another Lunatic..........................Harold Bolton
Second Orderly..........................William Orville

Act I.—Ward Outside the Surgery. Acts II and III.—The Stage.
Staged by Geoffrey Kerr; settings by David S. Gaither.

George Bernard Shaw and Luigi Pirandello were motoring near London when their attention was distracted by the sudden appearance of a young man who looked like Shakespeare and who waved to them from a high wall. The Shaw and Pirandello cars went into a head-on collision and the dramatists were carried into the institution for repairs. Recovering consciousness they discover they are in a sanitarium for the well-to-do insane. The fellow who imagines he is Shakespeare is running a theatre with a company composed of Francesca da Remini, Marc Antony, Cleopatra, Eve, Helen of Troy and God. Shaw and Pirandello write a play for the company and there is much fun at rehearsals.

PIGEONS AND PEOPLE

(70 performances)

A play in one act by George M. Cohan. Produced by the author at the Sam H. Harris Theatre, New York, January 16, 1933.

Cast of characters—

Joseph Heath..........................Walter Gilbert
Miss Giles..........................Olive Reeves-Smith
Franklyn Chase..........................Paul McGrath
Gilroy..........................Edward Nannery
Dr. Frisby..........................Reynolds Denniston
Parker..........................George M. Cohan

Tokem....................Arvid Paulson
Elinore Payne....................Eleanor Audley
Winnie Lloyd....................Alney Alba
McGuire....................Howard Hull Gibson
Miss Graham....................Lucille Sears
Mrs. Dunlap....................Janet Rathbun
Staged by Sam Forrest.

See page 311.

BIG NIGHT

(7 performances)

A play in three acts by Dawn Powell. Produced by The Group Theatre, Inc., at the Maxine Elliott Theatre, New York, January 17, 1933.

Cast of characters—

Myra Bonney....................Stella Adler
Ed Bonney....................Lewis Leverett
Winnie Murphy....................Phœbe Brand
Delicatessen Boy....................Herbert Ratner
Bob Tuttle....................Grover Burgess
Bert Schwartz....................J. Edward Bromberg
Fargo....................Roman Bohnen
Mrs. Fargo....................Eunice Stoddard
Eugene....................Clifford Odets
Chet Davies....................Russell Collins
Ladies in Evening Dress.................... { Ruth Nelson / Dorothy Patten
Acts I, II and III.—Bonney Apartment in Tudor Terrace.
Staged by Cheryl Crawford; settings by Mordecai Gorelik.

Ed Bonney, eager to secure the advertising business of Bert Schwartz of Fortune Stores, Inc., organizes a home-drinking party for Bert. Myra Bonney, Ed's wife, had known Schwartz when she was a cloak model and had been obliged to repulse him frequently and with force. Now Ed insists that for the sake of the business Myra must be nice to Bert. Which she is. Next morning Ed gets the contract, but Myra goes out into the world on her own, pretty disgusted with her husband.

AS HUSBANDS GO

(148 performances)

A comedy in three acts by Rachel Crothers. Revived by O. E. Wee and J. J. Leventhal, Inc., at the Forrest Theatre, New York, January 19, 1933.

Cast of characters—

Lucile Lingard....................Alice Frost
Ronald Derbyshire....................Leslie Denison

Emmie Sykes...Sue Keller
Hippolitus Lomi.....................................Ben McQuarrie
Charles Lingard.....................................Joseph King
Maitre D'Hotel......................................Arthur Mack
Waiter..Bruno Wick
Wilbur..Norman Williams
Christine...Mathilda Baring
Peggy Sykes...Marjorie Lytell
Jake Canon..Robert Foulk
Katie...Margo Fiske

Prologue—A Café in Paris. Acts I, II and III.—Living-room in the Lingard House, Ten Miles from Dubuque, Iowa.

Staged by Rachel Crothers.

Selected as one of the ten best plays of 1930-31. First produced by John Golden at the John Golden Theatre, New York, March 5, 1931. See "Best Plays of 1930-31."

PARDON MY ENGLISH

(46 performances)

A musical comedy in two acts by Herbert Fields, music by George Gershwin and lyrics by Ira Gershwin. Produced by Alex A. Aarons and Vinton Freedley at the Majestic Theatre, New York, January 20, 1933.

Cast of characters—

Mr. Preston...Tony Blair
Mrs. Preston..Eleanor Shaler
Robin...Jack Davis
College Student.....................................Robert Spencer
Another College Student.............................William Lilling
Schultz...Cliff Hall
Girl..Betty Hamilton
Johnny Stewart......................................Carl Randall
Gerry Martin..Barbara Newberry
McCarthy..Harry T. Shannon
Gita..Lyda Roberti
Michael Bramleigh...................................George Givot
Commissioner Bauer..................................Jack Pearl
Dr. Richard Carter..................................Gerald Oliver Smith
Ilse Bauer..Josephine Huston
Magda...Ruth Urban
Anna..Wilma Roeloff
Inn-Keeper..George Shields
Karl..John Cortez
Heinrich..Jack Carver

Ladies of the Ensemble, Gentlemen of the Ensemble, Schuhpladlers: Joe Gerhei, Hans Kiendl, Mack Gassl, Alex Atzenbeck, Joe Wagner, Max Seidl.

Act I.—Scene 1—Beer Garden in Dresden. 2—Street. 3—Living-room in the Home of Commissioner Bauer. 4—Police Station. 5—Garden of Bauer's Home. Act II.—Scene 1—Inn at Schandau. 2—Front of Bauer's House. 3—American Bar. 4—Den. 5—Garden of Bauer's Home.

Staged by George Hale; book directed by John McGowan; settings by John Wenger.

Once there were a couple of thieves in Vienna. One was named McCarthy and the other Gita. And a kleptomaniac named

Michael Bramleigh. As well as a couple of American dancers whose names were Johnny Stewart and Gerry Martin. Well, the police arrested Gerry and Johnny, thinking they were Mc and Gita. So Michael, the kleptomaniac, married Ilse, the daughter of the chief of police.

WE, THE PEOPLE

(49 performances)

A play in twenty-one scenes by Elmer Rice. Produced by Elmer Rice at the Empire Theatre, New York, January 21, 1933.

Cast of characters—

Tony Volterra.....Egisto Visser
Louis Volterra.....Charles La Torre
Helen Davis.....Eleanor Phelps
Frieda Davis.....Grace Mills
Allen Davis.....Herbert Rudley
William Davis.....Ralph Theadore
Albert Collins.....Blaine Cordner
Willard Drew.....Pierre Watkin
A Stenographer.....Mildred Quigley
Jack Ingersoll.....Randolph Hale
James Cunningham.....George Pembroke
Winifred Drew.....Mildred Baker
Sarah Collins.....Katherine Emmett
Stella Collins.....Valerie Valaire
Thomas Williamson.....William Ingersoll
Steve Clinton.....Frank Wilson
Donald Collins.....Fred Herrick
Larry Collins.....Carol Ashburn
Mark Brookwood.....Charles H. Davis
Leo Schwarz.....Marvin S. Borowsky
Peter Hines.....Sam Byrd
Daisy Costigan.....Jane Hamilton
Mary Klobutsko.....Juliana Taberna
C. Carter Sloane.....Maurice Wells
Fred Whipple.....Gregory Deane
Isabella Volterra.....Maria Sermolino
Harry Gregg.....George Christie
Arthur Meadows.....Howard Miller
Elbert Purdy.....Thomas F. Tracey
Walter Applegate.....Calvin Thomas
Cleveland Thomas.....Walter N. Greaza
George Fallon.....Arthur Ritchie
Luke Smith.....Jean Sidney
Herman Spandau.....Jules J. Bennett
Robert Marden.....Forrest Taylor
James Moulton.....House Jameson
Joe Callahan.....Glenn Coulter
A Clerk.....David Appelbe
Edna Inness.....Alice John
Morris Hirschbein.....David Leonard
Luther Weeks.....Harry Moore
Ellis Jones.....Orrin Burke
Mike Ramsay.....Harry Bellaver
James Trowbridge.....Burr Caruth
Passers-by: Frieda Altman, Lawrence Ellinger, Harry Fischer, Alan Hale, Carlton Moss, Clement O'Loghlin, Birrell Rawls, Florence Robinson, Phil Sheridan, Gladys Walker.

Scene 1—Class Room in a Grade School. 2, 7, 10, 12 and 14—Davis Home. 3—Public Park. 4—Drew's Private Office. 5, 8 and 13—Collins Home. 6—Albert's Room. 9—Office of *The Sentinel* at the State University. 11—Drew's Home. 15—Entrance to the Applegate Plant. 16—Purdy's Private Office. 17—Gregg's Office in the Senate Office Building in Washington. 18—Mary Klobutsko's Room. 19—Public Square. 20—Court Room. 21—Public Auditorium.

Staged by Elmer Rice; settings by Aline Bernstein.

See page 271.

DOROTHY SANDS

(2 performances)

An illustrated lecture on styles in acting by Dorothy Sands. Produced by James B. Pond at the Booth Theatre, New York, January 22 and January 29, 1933.

Illustrations—

Lillian Gish, Leonore Ulric and Nazimova in the Sleepwalking Scene from "Macbeth"
Pauline Lord in "Anna Christie"
Haidee Wright, Ethel Barrymore, Laurette Taylor and Mae West as Lady Macbeth
Millamant in "The Way of the World"
Almahide in "The Conquest of Granada"
"Buy a Broom" song of Mme. Vestris
Nellie Denver in Arthur Henry Jones "The Silver King"
Last Act of Shaw's "Candida"

DESIGN FOR LIVING

(135 performances)

A play in three acts by Noel Coward. Produced by Alfred Lunt, Lynn Fontanne and Noel Coward at the Ethel Barrymore Theatre, New York, January 24, 1933.

Cast of characters—

Gilda....................Lynn Fontanne
Ernest Friedman....................Campbell Gullan
Otto....................Alfred Lunt
Leo....................Noel Coward
Miss Hodge....................Gladys Henson
Mr. Birbeck....................Philip Tonge
Photographer....................Ward Bishop
Grace Torrence....................Ethel Borden
Helen Carver....................Phyllis Connard
Henry Carver....................Alan Campbell
Matthew....................Macleary Stinnett

Act I.—A Studio in Paris. Act II.—A Flat in London. Act III.—A Penthouse in New York.

Staged by Noel Coward; settings by G. E. Calthrop.

See page 134.

MARATHON

(5 performances)

A play in three acts by Isabel Dawn and Boyce de Gaw. Produced by Joseph Bernard at the Mansfield Theatre, New York, January 27, 1933.

Cast of characters—

April Jones....Isabel Dawn
Charlie Baker....Paul Guilfoyle
"Too Soon" Decker....Robert Strange
Ropey....Millard F. Mitchell
Mops....W. W. Shuttleworth
Gilly Bray....Frank Rowan
Rose Malloy....Franka Moore
Gertie Hicks....Claire Nolte
Minna Geckel....Ruth Chorpenning
Liz Briggs....Ruth Conley
Sonia Markoff....Czarr Romanyi
Señor Alvarez....Pierre de Ramey
Dolores Alvarez....Julie Chandler
Leo Berry....Reed McClelland
Luis Borkofski....Ivan Triesault
Jimmy Dugan....Arthur Marlowe
Light Collector....Jerome Cowan
Eddie Hicks....Don Wyatt
Val Owen....Jack Klendon
Devlin....William E. Morris
Nurse....Roberta Gleckler
Medical Attendant....George Spelvin
Marathon Dancers: Rosa Malvin, Bernice Moore, Louis Malvin, Earnest Van Renssler, Charles Oddo, Gerry O'Connell.
Acts I, II and III.—A dance hall in New York.
Staged by Clyde North; settings by P. Dodd Ackerman.

April Jones loses her job as a Childs waitress. With a sick husband to take care of April enters a marathon dancing contest hoping to win enough to move West. Gilly, the partner she picks up, means April no good, and the manager of the marathon is also after her. April eludes them both by selling her story to the *Daily News* for $500. Gilly tries to hold up Decker, the dance manager, and is killed.

BAD MANNERS

(8 performances)

A comedy in three acts by Dana Burnet and William B. Jutte. Produced by William A. Brady, Ltd., by arrangement with Dwight Deere Wiman at the Playhouse, New York, January 30, 1933.

Cast of characters—

Tami.....H. L. Donsu
Craig Baldwin.....Bert Lytell
Marian Lane.....Leona Maricle
Don Baldwin.....William David
Lois Aiken.....Margaret Sullavan
Jerry Dilworth.....Harold Vermilyea
Porter.....Franklin West

Acts I, II and III.—Craig Baldwin's apartment in New York City.
Staged by William A. Brady, Jr., and Dwight Deere Wiman.

Craig Baldwin, an architect wasting his life with wine and women, talks it out with Lois Aikin, fiancée of his best friend. As a result of the talk Lois breaks her engagement at the altar and accepts Craig's invitation to occupy the guest room in his apartment on a purely platonic basis. They are agreed that the world places too much importance on sex and will banish it from their lives. After a month they acknowledge their need of each other, which relationship later produces all the irritations of marriage. On the brink of a separation they decide to patch up their quarrel and get married.

EVENSONG

(15 performances)

A play in three acts by Edward Knoblock and Beverly Nichols, adapted from a novel by Beverly Nichols. Produced by Arch Selwyn and Sir Barry Jackson at the Selwyn Theatre, New York, January 31, 1933.

Cast of characters—

Scott.....Claude Disney-Roebuck
Tremlowe.....Beatrix Fielden-Kaye
Arthur Kober.....Jacob Ben-Ami
Pauline Lacey.....Jane Wyatt
Irela.....Edith Evans
Donald Gage.....Owen Davis, Jr.
John.....Holland Bennett
Julius Rosenberg.....Walter Armin
Dr. Campbell.....Hugh F. S. Casson
Duchess of Rockstone.....Marjorie Chard
Gen. Sir Ronald Hinchcliffe.....Reginald Carrington
Lady Hope Martineau.....Christine Lindsay
Capt. Hon. Percy Bragge.....Brian Buchel
Rose Belcher.....Freda Gaye
Mr. Freddie Parks.....Fotherinham Lysons
Tom.....Willard Dashiell
1st Elderly Lady.....Jane Evans
2nd Elderly Lady.....Nellie Malcolm
Mr. Stamper.....Walter Fitzgerald
Attendant at Opera.....Frederick Jordan
Baba Letoile.....Leyla Georgie
Pablo Sovino.....Dennis Val-Norton
Princess Stephanie Rabnitz.....Gladys Hanson
Daphne Carruthers.....Florence Selwyn

Sir Geoffrey Filmer............................William J. Tannen
Laura Payne....................................Valerie Ziegler
Major Dennis Foss....................................John Dunn
Señora De Carranza..................................Zolya Talma
Señor De Carranza...........................Leopoldo Gutierrez
Señor Luis Moreno....................................Luis Bruno
Archduke Theodore............................Frederick Leister
Nurse Phillips......................................Hilda Spong
Guests: Doris Crandall, Natalie Davis, Alice Griswold, Joan Hamilton, Florence Heller, Natalie Hess, Jean Howard, Helen Judge, Virginia Ann Kaye, Mary Melhado, Mary Morrison, Margot Stevenson, Ripples Swann, Harry Warwick.

Act I.—Irela's Music Room, Charles Street, Mayfair, London. Act II.—Artiste's Room at the Opera. Act III.—Irela's apartment, Paris. Staged by Paul Smythe.

Irela, Queen of Song, having come upon the years when even the best voices break, is holding desperately to her fading glories and her position of dominance. A vain, sensitive, selfish person, her possessiveness envelops her niece, Pauline Lacey, come from Canada to be her secretary, and all the members of her household. Irela publicly insults a rival, Baba Letoile, belittles her faithful manager, Kober, and finally breaks her promise to marry an old flame, Archduke Theodore, to organize a concert tour in America.

FACE THE MUSIC

(Original run 165 performances. Return 32. Total 197)

A musical comedy in two acts by Irving Berlin and Moss Hart. Revived by Producing Associates, Inc., at the 44th Street Theatre, New York, January 31, 1933.

Cast of characters—

Hal Reisman..............................Robert Emmett Keane
Kit Baker.......................................Nancy McCord
Pat Mason, Jr.....................................John Barker
Mrs. Meshbesher...................................Mary Boland
Her Footman......................................Peter Sargent
Miss Eisenheimer..................................Margot Adams
Martin Van Buren Meshbesher...................Charles Lawrence
Mr. O'Rourke....................................George Anderson
A Sister Team.........................Inez Goetz, Colleen Ward
Pickles...Margaret Lee
Joe..Jack Good
Louis...Don Costello
Mme. Elise.......................................Dorothy Drum
Her Assistant..................................Martha Tibbetts
Postman...Daniel Sullivan
May..Pat O'Keefe
Rodney St. Clair...................................John Ehrle
Rivington..Oscar Polk
Sheriff...Frank Dobson
Mr. O'Ryan.......................................Don Costello
Stage Doorman...................................George Marshall
Detective..Thomas Arace
Bartender..Bob Baldwin
Prosecuting Attorney...............................John Ehrle
Judge Furioso..................................Thomas Reynolds

The Albertina Rasch Dancers: Betty Eisner, Leading Dancer; Vera Fredericks, Captain; Janet Carver, Peggy Dell, Martha Merrill.
Staged by Hassard Short and George S. Kaufman; settings by Albert R. Johnson; dances by Albertina Rasch.

Principal songs—"Let's Have Another Cup of Coffee," "Soft Lights and Sweet Music," "I'll Say It's Spinach," "Roof in Manhattan."

See "Best Plays of 1931-32."

LA NATIVITE

(2 performances)

A ritualistic drama in one scene arranged by Natalie Hays Hammond. Produced by the Stage Alliance at the Guild Theatre, New York, February 5, 1933.

Cast of characters—

The Virgin Mary....................................Martha Graham
Angel....................................Joane Woodruff
First Child Angel....................................Sidney Brenner
Second Child Angel....................................Lucy Newman
First Deacon....................................Kenneth Bostock
Second Deacon....................................William Matons
Third Deacon....................................Colfax Sanderson
Fourth Deacon....................................John Beaver
Fifth Deacon....................................Harold Baumstone
Archbishop....................................John Glenn
Bishop....................................John O'Shaughnessy

This short ritualistic drama was given at the Altar of the Cathedral just before the hour of midnight, Christmas Eve. It was a part of the Church ceremony and ends with the Mass.
Staged by Martha Graham; settings by Alice Laughlin.

One of six miracle plays selected from ancient religious ceremonies of the Eleventh, Thirteenth and Fifteenth centuries and arranged for the stage by Natalie Hays Hammond. The others included "The Miraculous Birth and the Midwives," "Les Trois Rois," "Les Trois Maries," "The Lamentation of the Virgin Mary" and "The Magdalen." Other performers taking part in the presentations were Peter Railey, Lillian Shapero, Paul Leyssac, Georgia Graham, Dorothy Bird, Mary Rivoire and Alma Kruger.

ONE WIFE OR ANOTHER

(3 performances)

A comedy in three acts by Percy Shaw and T. Wigney Percyval. Produced by Actors and Authors, Associated, at the Provincetown Playhouse, New York, February 6, 1933.

Cast of characters—

Major Roderick Humphries....Fred Leslie
Banks....Arthur Bowyer
Rita Derrick....Kathleen Chase
Harold Penniman....Gerald Hamer
Margaret Penniman....Betty Young
Jimmy Derrick....Ray Clifford
Marcia Stockton....Ernita Lascelles
Philip Stockton....Herbert Ranson
Jessica Tremaine....Ruth Edell

Acts I and II.—Stockton's country home. Act III.—Hunting lodge in the Berkshires.

Staged by Herbert Ranson; settings by Bernard Brooks.

At a Stockton house party Philip Stockton confides to Marcia, his wife, that he would like her to divorce him that he may take up with the younger and more excitable Jessica Tremaine. Marcia refuses to oblige unless, after a month's experiment, Philip and Jessica can truthfully report that they are still of the same mind. During the month Mrs. Stockton also tries to rearrange the marriages of the Pennimans and the Derricks. Wives are traded, but without success. Philip also is glad to come back to Marcia at the end of his month with Jessica.

LOW BRIDGE

(3 performances)

A play in three acts dramatized by Frank B. Elser from Walter D. Edmonds' novel, "Rome Haul." Produced by the Players Theatre at the Fifty-seventh Street Playhouse, New York, February 9, 1933.

Cast of characters—

Lucy Gurget....Marion Wall
Sol....John Guerin
Fortune Friendly....Michael Kelly
Samson Weaver....Charles Berry
Stark....Joseph Ptagek
Buscerk....Alec Tulmann
Andy Hikes....Morris Sikora
Luke....Edward Cooney
Jotham Klore....Royce Ward
Molly Larkins....Margaret O'Donnell
Dan Harrow....Thomas Paradine
Abel Marsters....Herbert Fischer
Nancy Cashdollar....Kathleen O'Connell
Elvira Quackenbush....Cornelia Smith

Staged by William J. O'Neill.

BEFORE MORNING

(28 performances)

A melodrama in three acts by Edna and Edward P. Riley. Produced by Albert Bannister and John G. Norman at the Ritz Theatre, New York, February 9, 1933.

Cast of characters—

Jenny.....Maud Turner
Doris.....Alice Burrage
Joyce.....Norvell Barry
Leo Bergman.....Clyde Fillmore
Ben Ayoub.....Jules Epailly
Elsie Manning.....Jessie Royce Landis
Horace Barker.....John Litel
Neil Kennedy.....Louis Jean Heydt
James E. Nichols.....Hugh Buckler
Dr. Gruelle.....McKay Morris
Mrs. Nichols.....Louise Prussing
Acts I, II and III.—Elsie Manning's apartment.
Staged by William B. Friedlander; settings by Karle Amend.

Elsie Manning, actress, returns to her apartment after the theatre with Horace Barker, a business man of Detroit who wants to marry her. Elsie, having a young daughter, is of a mind to accept Barker, but in doubt as to whether she should tell him she has been living with James E. Nichols, banker. That night Nichols, returning unexpectedly, is seized with a heart attack and dies. Friends get the body to a sanitarium before the police are called. Dr. Gruelle of the sanitarium, finding Nichols' will, leaving $200,000 to Elsie, tries to blackmail her for half of it on threat of charging that she had poisoned Nichols. Mrs. Nichols is drawn into the plot and revealed finally as the real poisoner.

THE MONSTER

(38 performances)

A drama in three acts by Crane Wilbur. Revived by Jules J. Leventhal and O. E. Wee at the Waldorf Theatre, New York, February 10, 1933.

Cast of characters—

Skipworth Mackenzie.....Harry Short
Caliban.....Ernest R. Whitman
Alvin Bruce.....Grant Gordon
Julie Cartier.....Suzanne Caubaye
Rigo.....Curtis Karpe
Dr. Gustave Ziska.....De Wolf Hopper
Acts I, II and III.—Home of Dr. Ziska.
Staged by Frank McCormack; settings by Savoy Studios.

In the original production of "The Monster," August, 1922, the late Wilton Lackaye played the rôle assigned De Wolf Hopper in the revival. See "The Best Plays of 1922-23."

THE SOPHISTICRATS

(2 performances)

A farce comedy in three acts by Kenneth Phillips Britton. Produced by Shepard Traube at the Bijou Theatre, New York, February 13, 1933.

Cast of characters—

Arthur....................Ben Lackland
Gertrude....................Marjorie Jarecki
Carson....................Coburn Goodwin
Walters, Sr....................Doan Borup
Watts....................Carl Benton Reid
Rollo....................Forrest Orr
Babe....................Mildred Van Dorn
Lamont....................Robert Allen
Bettina....................Marion Evensen
Charlotte....................Jessamine Newcombe
Markowski....................Frank Stringfellow
Nell....................Helen Brooks
Beach....................Lewis Martin

Acts I, II and III.—Nell Newsome's sitting-room, Danfield.
Staged by Shepard Traube; settings by Isaac Benesch.

Nell Newsome is a passionate poetess whose verse is in great demand by publishers and whose wisecracks are town talk in Danfield, near New York. Nell, her home the center of the village head-hunters, is led to pretend an intimate friendship with a touring novelist, Lewis Beach, and slightly embarrassed when the celebrity walks in on her. Beach is glad to help her carry out the deceit, but when he demands payment in the flesh Nell is forced to confess that she is a cheat. She knows only the passion she puts into words. She marries Arthur Walters, son of the village publisher, who gets her out of the mess by paying back the money Beach has borrowed from her friends.

FOUR O'CLOCK

(16 performances)

A melodrama in three acts by Nan O'Reilly and Rupert Darrell. Produced by E. H. O'Connor at the Biltmore Theatre, New York, February 13, 1933.

Cast of characters—

Donna Mason.....Ara Gerald
George Mason.....William Balfour
Mrs. Hinchcliffe.....Sarah Strong
Robert Hudson.....Jack Harwood
Marcia Irwin.....Mary Tupper Jones
Iverlutey Jacobs.....Florence Lee
Sylvia Grey.....Betty Worth
Trumbull.....Jerome Haynor
Henry Willis.....Charles Benjamin
Wallace Irwin.....William Janney
Salo.....Phillip Tully
Eduardo Canneli.....Marc Loebell
Cyrus Webster.....Herbert Warren
Chief of Homicide Squad.....Harry Wilson
Police Commissioner.....Eugene Weber
Hennesey.....Reed Carlton
Police Reporter.....Rupert Darrell

Act I.—Kitchen in the Home of the Masons. Acts II and III.—Apartment of Donna Mason, now known as Donna Madison.
Staged by Rupert Darrell.

Donna Mason, involved in an affair with a boy who kills himself after stealing $25,000 from his bank to give to her, is pictured in the tabloids with her daughter. The daughter kills herself through shame and Donna, becoming Donna Madison, devotes her life to getting even with Cyrus Webster, publisher of the tabloid. In a blackmail trap set for Webster Donna is killed and mystery surrounds her murder.

MELODY

(79 performances)

A musical romance in three acts and thirteen scenes by Edward Childs Carpenter; lyrics by Irving Cæsar; music by Sigmund Romberg. Produced by George White at the Casino Theatre, New York, February 14, 1933.

Cast of characters—

ACT I

Jean Blanchon.....Harrison Brockbank
Mariette.....Mildred Parisette
Leon Tabar.....Milton Douglas
Henri Fanchery.....Carl Rose
Lizette.....Marjorie Dille
Tristan Robillard.....Everett Marshall
Francois Trapadoux.....Hal Skelly
Jacqueline Grimaud.....Vivian Fay
Sergeant Perecin.....Frederick B. Manatt
Andree De Nemours.....Evelyn Herbert
Lise.....Valerie Bergere
Compte Gustave De Nemours.....Victor Morley
Pierre, Vicompte DeLaurier.....George Houston
Antoine.....Jerome Daley
Camille.....Peggy Moseley
Claire Lolive.....Rose Louise
Bridesmaids: Hope Dare, Alma Saunders, Georgia Ellis, Lois Eckhart,

Hazel Boffinger, Hilda Knight, Peggy Moseley, Johanna Allen, Toni Chase.
Lazare....................................Frederick B. Manatt

ACT II

Max DeLaurier....................................Milton LeRoy
Pierre, Vicompte DeLaurier....................................George Houston
Compte Gustave De Nemours....................................Victor Morley
Designer....................................David Morton
Dress Models: Hazel Boffinger, Lois Eckhart, Hilda Knight, Peggy Moseley, Johanna Allen, Georgia Ellis, Hope Dare, Toni Chase.
Butler....................................Glenn Graham
Andree, Vicomptess DeLaurier....................................Evelyn Herbert
Francois Trapadoux....................................Hal Skelly
Angelique Normand....................................Venita Varden
Eugenie Revelle....................................Jeanne Aubert
Ninon Revelle....................................Louise Kirtland

ACT III

A Clerk....................................Neil Moore
Phœbe Jones....................................Ina Ray
Anstruther....................................Harrison Brockbank
Francois Trapadoux....................................Hal Skelly
George Richards....................................Walter Woolf
Sabine Pataille....................................Mildred Parisette
Vivienne Grandet....................................Marjorie Dille
Paula DeLaurier....................................Evelyn Herbert
Toby....................................Milton Douglas
Bob....................................Charles Fowler
Marie....................................Consuelo Flowerton
Boris....................................Michael Dalmatoff
Waiter....................................Jack Saltzman
Shabby Man....................................Lyle Evans
Eugenie Revelle....................................Jeanne Aubert
Louis LeBeau....................................Carlos Roca

Act I.—Scenes 1 and 5—Quarters of Concierge in Mansion of Compte Gustave De Nemours, Paris. 2—Library. 3—Grand Salon. 4—Faubourg St. Honoré in front of Mansion. Act II.—Terrace of Gustave's Château, Loos, France. Act III.—Scene 1—Corridor, Universal Radio Building, New York. 2—Penthouse Apartment of Francois Trapadoux, Radio Building. 3—Street near Etoile, Paris. 4, 5 and 7—Café L'Auberge du Coq d'or in the Bois, Paris. 6—Sidewalk Café, Paris.

Musical numbers staged by Bobby Connolly; settings by Joseph Urban.

Principal song—"Give Me a Roll on a Drum."

Andree De Nemours, loving Tristan Robillard, poor composer, is obliged to marry the Vicompte DeLaurier. She comes to give her love to Tristan on her wedding night and he composes a song to her. Tristan is killed in the wars. Andree lives to rear a family and years and years after her granddaughter meets George Richards, nephew of Tristan's oldest and best friend, and they duplicate the old romance.

* ONE SUNDAY AFTERNOON

(143 performances)

A play in a prologue, two acts, and an epilogue by James Hagan. Produced by Leo Peters and Leslie Spiller at the Little Theatre, New York, February 15, 1933.

Cast of characters—

Biff Grimes...Lloyd Nolan
Snappy Downer.......................................Percy Helton
Hugo Barnstead...................................Rankin Mansfield
Virginia Brush.....................................Mary Holsman
Amy Lind.......................................Francesca Bruning
Mrs. Oberstatter..................................Eeda von Buelow
Mrs. Schitzenmeyer...............................Marion Frederic
Mrs. Schutzendorf...................................Rita Collins
Waiter..Boris Batt
Waiter...Fred Steinway
Otto..Leo Hoyt
Mr. Schneider.......................................Ernst Robert
Rowdy..Everett Ripley
Rowdy...Karl Swenson
Snappy's Girl Friend..................................Sara Arms
Mrs. Lind..Janet Young
Charlie Brown.....................................Wm. J. Nelson
Matt Hughes...Byron Shores
Lamplighter....................................Maurice Mitchell

Prologue and Epilogue: Biff Grimes' Dental Office. Act I.—Scenes 1 and 3—Avery's Park (Thirty Years Earlier). 2—Schneider's Gardens. Act II.—Scene 1—Mrs. Lind's Home. 2 and 3—Biff Grimes' Home. 4—Avery's Park.

Staged by Leo Bulgakov.

See page 341.

CONQUEST

(10 performances)

A play in three acts by Arthur Hopkins. Produced by the author at the Plymouth Theatre, New York, February 18, 1933.

Cast of characters—

Eva Locke...Jane Wyatt
Branch...Charles Brown
Frederick Nolte, Jr. (Fritz)...................Raymond Hackett
Frederick Nolte, Sr...............................Henry O'Neill
John Palmer....................................Harvey Stephens
Helen Nolte....................................Judith Anderson
Cornelius Garvan..................................Hugh Buckler
Dr. Thomas Wilson...................................Boyd Davis
Pierrette.......................................Bernice Elliott

People of Masquerade: Dorothy Young, Tania Redfield, Suzanne Freeman, Bernice Richmond, Katherine Lowry, Joyce Hill, Louis MacMichael, James MacColl, Henry Lase, Clement Wilenchick, Edward Toledano.

Acts I, II and III.—The Nolte Home in a Connecticut Town.

Staged by Arthur Hopkins; settings by Raymond Sovey.

Frederick Nolte, Sr., German manufacturer, proud of his family name and what it stands for in business, sends his son to Germany to prepare himself to take over the business. The day the son leaves his mother sells her Nolte stock, betraying the business into the hands of unscrupluous merger interests headed by Cornelius Garvan. The shock kills the elder Nolte. His widow marries Garvan. Two years later the son returns to America, hears the voice of his father calling upon him to avenge his death and succeeds in working the ruin of Garvan. Having laid his father's restless ghost young Nolte marries Eva Locke and dedicates his life to the rebuilding of the Nolte honor.

ALIEN CORN

(98 performances)

A play in three acts by Sidney Howard. Produced by Katharine Cornell at the Belasco Theatre, New York, February 20, 1933.

Cast of characters—

Ottokar Brandt....................Siegfried Rumann
A Piano Tuner....................Ludwig Steiner
Mrs. Skeats....................Jessie Busley
Stockton....................E. J. Ballantine
Watkins....................Richard Sterling
Elsa Brandt....................Katharine Cornell
Phipps....................Charles D. Brown
Julian Vardaman....................Luther Adler
Skeats....................Charles Waldron
Harry Conway....................James Rennie
A Chauffeur....................James Vincent
Muriel Conway....................Lily Cahill
A Policeman....................Francis Moran

Acts I, II and III.—Living-room of the House Occupied by Elsa Brandt and Her Father on the Campus of Conway College for Women in a Small Town a Few Hours West of Chicago.
Staged by Guthrie McClintic; settings by Cleon Throckmorton.

See page 205.

AMERICAN DREAM

(39 performances)

A dramatic trilogy by George O'Neil. Produced by the Theatre Guild, Inc., at the Guild Theatre, New York, February 21, 1933.

Cast of characters—

THE FIRST PLAY, 1650

Roger Pingree....................Lee Baker
Martha....................Josephine Hull
Daniel Pingree....................Douglass Montgomery
Luke Pingree....................Wilton Graff
An Indian....................Frank Verigun
Lydia Kimball....................Gale Sondergaard
Celia....................Gertrude Flynn

THE SECOND PLAY, 1849

Daniel Pingree....................Stanley Ridges
Susannah....................Leona Hogarth
Abbie Pingree....................Helen Westley
Ezekial Bell....................Claude Rains

THE THIRD PLAY, 1933

Daniel Pingree....Douglass Montgomery
Gail Pingree....Gale Sondergaard
Henri....Sanford Meisner
Vladimir....Manart Kippen
Beth Harkness....Edith Van Cleve
Richard Biddle....Philip Barber
Eddie Thayer....Stanley Ridges
Sarah Culver....Helen Westley
Mrs. Schuyler Hamilton....Josephine Hull
Lindley P. Carver....Spencer Barnes
Julius Stern....Lester Alden
Murdock....Erskine Sanford
Amarylis....Gertrude Flynn
Tessa Steele....Mary Blair
Lincoln Park....Wilton Graff
Mrs. Harry Tsezhin....Mary Jeffery
Harry....Frank Verigun
Jake Schwarz....Samuel Goldenberg

Staged by Philip Moeller; settings by Lee Simonson.

In 1650 Roger Pingree, Puritan, turns Daniel, his son, out of the house because the boy refuses to accept his father's dictation in religious and family matters. In 1849 the grandson, Daniel Pingree 2d, resenting the mess his people have made of the mills and the working conditions in them, goes West seeking a new start, leaving his wife and mother where they are. In 1933 the third Daniel Pingree has become a parlor Communist and taken to drink. Invading a cocktail party organized by his wife to celebrate their wedding anniversary Daniel curses out his ancestors and his wife's decadent friends and shoots himself through the heart.

BLACK DIAMOND

(16 performances)

A play in one act by Stanley Kimmel. Produced by Donald Lamotte Hathway at the Provincetown Playhouse, New York, February 23, 1933.

Cast of characters—

Mrs. Phillips....Kate McComb
Minnie Gleason....Celia Haskell
Len Phillips....Ralph Young
Seed....James H. Dunmore
Bill Phillips....Lewis Leverett
Mead Gleason....Schuyler McGuffin
Sheriff....Hendrik Booraem
Laura....Margaret Barker
Tad Jones....Judd Carrel
Mike McDonnell....Lawrence Menkin

Outside the Phillips home in Herrin, Ill.
Staged by Ralph MacBane; settings by Wendell K. Phillipps.

While her husband is away in Kentucky Laura McDonnell loans Bill Phillips books and helps him to improve his mind.

When McDonnell returns he suspects the worst and is ready to shoot Bill. During trouble at the mine McDonnell is shot, Laura's brother Tad is hung on suspicion and Bill and Laura leave town hoping to find peace and happiness in new surroundings.

HANGMAN'S WHIP

(11 performances)

A play in three acts by Norman Reilly Raine and Frank Butler. Produced by George Kondolf and Merlin Taylor in association with William A. Brady, Jr., at the St. James Theatre, New York, February 24, 1933.

Cast of characters—

Prin	Montagu Love
Kurt von Eltz	Ian Keith
Judith	Helen Flint
Ballister	Barton MacLane
Jakey	Harold DeBecker
Fenton	William Sharpe, Jr.
M'Bala	Malongo
Baaswami Chief	Clarence Redd
Basonga Chief	Hubert Brown
Native Porters	Masamba Tom Jetter

Acts I and II.—The Saloon of the "Dei Gratia." Act III.—Scene 1—The Deck of the "Dei Gratia." 2—The Saloon of the "Dei Gratia."

Staged by Robert Bell; settings by Livingston Platt.

Prin, a beast of a trader who has ruled the Congo, black and white, for many years, has a pretty wife, Judith, whom he has "bought" for the price of her debts. Judith loves Kurt von Eltz, who can't escape either the hold the tropics have put upon him or Prin's influences. Ballister, hard-boiled American, takes a hand, defies Prin and would have Judith for himself. Realizing in the end the woman is not for him Ballister helps Judith and Kurt escape. He is killed in a native attack. Prin is grimly defending his compound as the play ends.

LOUISIANA

(8 performances)

A play in prologue and three acts by J. Augustus Smith. Produced by George L. Miller for The Negro Theatre Guild, at the 48th Street Theatre, New York, February 27, 1933.

Cast of characters—

THE PROLOGUE

Aunt Hagar....................................Laura Bowman
Ebenezer....................................Lionel Monagas

THE PLAY

Amos Berry....................................J. Augustus Smith
Myrtle Simpson....................................Edna Barr
Brother Zumee....................................James Davis
Sister Marguerite....................................Trixie Smith
Thomas Catt....................................Morris McKenney
Sister Knight....................................Alberta Perkins
Brother Zero....................................Fred Bonny
Deacon August....................................Paul Johnson
Ebenezer....................................Lionel Monagas
Brother Dunson....................................A. B. Comathiere
Sister Zuzan....................................Carrie Huff
Sister Gaghan....................................Ruth Morrison
Sister Lauder....................................Harriet Daughtry
Bou Bouce....................................Bennie Small
Marcon....................................Pedro Lopez
Aunt Hagar....................................Laura Bowman
Members of the Flat Rock Baptist Church: Jennie Day, Gladys Booker, Herminie Sullivan, Lillian Exum, Edith Woodby, Mabel Gant, Marion Hughes, Madeline Smith, Theresa Harris, Dorothy St. Clair, Eleanor Hines, Marie Remsen, Pauline Freeman, Annabelle Smith, Jacqueline Ghant, Annabelle Ross, Harriett Scott.
Voodoo Dancers: Cherokee Thornton, James Davis, Arthur McLean, DeWitt Davis, Rudolph Walker, Marvin Everhart, Jimmie Cook, Irene Bagley, Sally Timmons, Beatrice James, Marie Remsen.

Prologue—Clearing in a Cypress Swamp. Act I.—Cottage of Elder Amos Berry. Act II.—Flat Rock Washfoot Baptist Church. Act III.—Aunt Hagar's Cabin.

The Action of The Play Is Laid in a Colored Settlement Near Bayou-la-Fouche, Louisiana.

Staged by Samuel J. Park.

In a colored settlement hard by Bayou-la-Fouche, Louisiana, Amos Berry is the pastor of a Baptist flock and Aunt Hagar represents the thinning adherents of the Voodoo faith. Conflict between the two is stirred when Amos' niece, Myrtle Simpson, comes home from school and attracts the favorable attention of Thomas Catt, the community's dive keeper. Thomas, knowing Amos once served time on a chain gang, has blackmailed the preacher for years. Now he would take the niece. Between the forces of God and those of Aunt Hagar's Voodoo controls Thomas is blinded by lightning and sunk in quicksand.

A SATURDAY NIGHT

(40 performances)

A comedy in three acts by Owen Davis. Produced by William A. Brady at the Playhouse, New York, February 28, 1933.

Cast of characters—

Sally....................................Elizabeth Young
Ted....................................Richard Jack
Jim Langdon....................................Hugh O'Connell
Marguerite Langdon....................................Peggy Wood
Annie....................................Jane Corcoran
Lena....................................June Webster
Peter Cary....................................Owen Davis, Jr.
Bill Cary....................................Warren McCollum
Fred Dorris....................................Robert Courtleigh
Anthony Kirk....................................Joseph Striker
Dick Carrington....................................Arthur Margetson
Doctor Morton....................................Addison Pitt

Acts I, II and III.—The Living-room of the Langdons' Duplex Apartment, New York City.

Staged by Melville Burke; settings by Livingston Platt.

Marguerite Langdon, celebrating a late-thirty birthday, plans to go to a "Scandals" with her husband, Jim, and afterward to a night club. Before she can start her son, 15-year-old Ted Langdon, is brought home with a sprained ankle from a basketball game. A few hours later 17-year-old Sally Langdon, having gone out without permission and with the wrong young man, comes home slightly tipsy and quite sick. During the excitement Dick Carrington, who has long been in love with Mrs. Langdon, proposes that she divorce Jim and marry him, and Jim, having disappeared after learning of a job disappointment, returns to admit that he has not always been faithful to Marguerite. Making a final choice, Marguerite sticks to Jim and the children.

RUN, LITTLE CHILLUN

(126 performances)

A Negro folk drama in four scenes by Hall Johnson. Produced by Robert Rockmore at the Lyric Theatre, New York, March 1, 1933.

Cast of characters—

Ella....................................Edna Thomas
Children
Organist....................................Esther Hall
Bessiola Hicks....................................Marietta Canty
Jeems Jackson....................................Jimmie Waters
Other Children: Henri Wood, Bennie Tattnall, Nell Taylor, Edna Commodore
The Rev. Sister Luella Strong....................................Olive Ball
Sister Mattie Fullilove....................................Mattie Shaw
Sister Flossie Lou Little....................................Bertha Powell
Brother Bartholomew Little....................................Ray Yeates
Brother Esau Redd....................................Walter Price
Sister Mahalie Ockletree....................................Rosalie King
Sister Judy Ann Hicks....................................Pauline Rivers
Sisters Lulu Jane Hunt and Susie May Hunt, Lulu Hunt, Carolyn Hughes

Brother George W. Jenkins.......................Edward Broadnax
Brother Jeremiah Johnson.............................Milton Lacey
Brother Goliath Simpson..............................Service Bell
The Rev. Jones....................................Harry Bolden
Jim...Alston Burleigh
Sulamai...Fredi Washington
Elder Tongola......................................Harold Sneed
Brother Moses...Jack Carr
Mother Kanda.......................................Olga Burgoyne
Reba..Waldine Williams
Sister Mata..Ethel Purnello
Brother Lu-Te.....................................James Boxwill
Brother Jo-Ba.......................................Gus Simons
Pilgrim Choir—Sopranos: Jean Cutler, Effie McDowell, Bessie Guy, Irma Allen, Katherine Ahnor, Lucile Dickson, Blanche Eckles. Altos: Lavetta Albright, Marietta Canty, Amy Goodwin, Dorothy Perry, Rosalie King. Tenors: Arthur Walker, George White, Carrington Lewis, Jimmie Waters, Charlie Frye, Milton Martin, Perrin Knight. Baritones: Service Bell, George Clark, Ernest Shaw, Milton Lacey. Basses: Ernest Baskett, Oliver Hartwell, Edward Broadnax, Ernest Brown.
Pilgrims—Eneida Hamlet, Ray Polite, Alma Reynolds, Rosina Weston, Paul Smellie, Assotta Marshall.
Novitiates—Evelyn Davis, Alice Grant, Eva Evelyn, Jack Meredith, Emma Sealy, Annie Jennings, H. J. Williams, Mayme Davis.
Tansadi Tongole (Tongola's Dancers)—Esther Hall, Irene Ellington, Nell Taylor, Alice Magee, Dorothy Boxwill, Maggie Carter, Odelle Ricks, Larri Laurier, Clarence Yates, Bruce Nugent, O. Portier, E. Wilson, R. Alday, E. Adderly, J. Baker, A. Ferguson, A. Adderly, L. Stirrup, J. Nealy, W. Polhamus, O. Gordon, A. McCullough, R. Branch, J. Gordon, M. Sands, E. Cæsar, C. Gibson, R. Braithwaite.

Scene 1—Parsonage. 2—Meeting Place of the New Day Pilgrims. 3—Toomer's Bottom. 4—Hope Baptist Church.
Staged by Frank Merlin.

In a Southern town there is a contest in soul-saving between the New Day Pilgrims, encamped on one side of the river and observing pagan rites, and the Hope Baptists who are holding the fort for the Christian God. Jim, son of Pastor Jones, though married, is lured over to the New Pilgrim side by Sulamai, a devastating sinner. But next act he is lured back to the Baptists and Sulamai is stricken in Rev. Jones' revival meeting and Jim is saved to his wife.

FORSAKING ALL OTHERS

(110 performances)

A comedy in three acts by Edward Roberts and Frank Cavett. Produced by Arch Selwyn at the Times Square Theatre, New York, March 1, 1933.

Cast of characters—

Dent..Harlan Briggs
Mrs. Paula La Salle..........................Cora Witherspoon
Jefferson Tingle.....................................Fred Keating
Shepherd Perry...............................Donald Macdonald
Mary Clay......................................Tallulah Bankhead

Dottie Winters....................Nancy Ryan
Arthur Smith....................Roger Sterns
Dillon Todd....................Anderson Lawlor
Constance Barnes....................Millicent Hanley
Elinor Branch....................Ilka Chase
Susan Thomas....................Barbara O'Neil
Hooker Mason....................George Lessey
The Reverend Duncan....................Robert Hudson
Eddie....................Harry Anderson

Act I.—Mary Clay's House, New York. Act II.—Scene 1—Mary Clay's House. 2—A Back Room at Charlie's. Act III.—Room at Charlie's.

Staged by Thomas Mitchell; settings by Donald Oenslager.

On the eve of Mary Clay's marriage to Dillon Todd Constance Barnes, who had done the continent with Dillon the season before, returns and figuratively files a prior claim on the groom. Dillon in a weak moment marries Constance and sends Mary word that he will not be able to keep his appointment at the altar. Next day Dillon is sorry and would renew his engagement. Mary is open minded about it and willing to forget until she suddenly realizes that it is Jefferson Tingle she has really loved all the time. She takes Jeff and Dillon is left waiting.

OUR WIFE

(20 performances)

A comedy in three acts by Lyon Mearson and Lillian Day. Produced by Thomas J. R. Brotherton and Abe H. Halle at the Booth Theatre, New York, March 2, 1933.

Cast of characters—

Margot Drake....................Rose Hobart
Jerry Marvin....................Humphrey Bogart
Concierge....................Michelette Burani
Barbara Marvin....................June Walker
Elisabetta....................Miriam Battista
Antonio Di Mariano....................Edward Raquello
First Agente....................Raymond O'Brien
Second Agente....................Juan Varro

Acts I and III.—Paris Apartment of Jerry and Margot. Act II.—Villa on an Island in the Bay of Naples.

Staged by Edward C. Lilley.

Jerry Marvin and Margot Drake, companionable writers, are living together in Paris and supporting Barbara, Jerry's wife, in New York. Barbara decides to join them in Paris in the hope she may win Jerry back. Jerry and Margot escape to an island in the Bay of Naples, and Barbara tags along. Looks like a bust for a few scenes, and then Jerry and Margot decide to divorce Barbara and get married.

STRIKE ME PINK

(105 performances)

A revue in two acts and twenty-nine scenes by Ray Henderson and Lew Brown; additional dialogue by Mack Gordon. Produced by Henderson and Brown at the Majestic Theatre, New York, March 4, 1933.

Principals engaged—

Jimmie Durante	Hope Williams
Hal Le Roy	Lupe Velez
Roy Atwell	Ruth Harrison
Eddie Garr	Carolyn Nolte
George Dewey Washington	Wilma Cox
Alex Fisher	Gracie Barrie
Frank Conlon	Dorothy Dare
Johnny Downs	Barbara McDonald
Milton Watson	M. Vodnoy
Aber Twins	Will Vodery Singers

Staged by Henderson and Brown; settings by Henry Dreyfuss. Dances arranged by Seymour Felix; sketches directed by Jack McGowan.

Principal songs—"Let's Call It a Day," "It's Great to Be Alive," "Strike Me Pink."

* BOTH YOUR HOUSES

(First engagement 72. Return 32. Total 104.)

A drama in three acts by Maxwell Anderson. Produced by the Theatre Guild, Inc., at the Royale Theatre, New York, March 6, 1933.

Cast of characters—

Marjorie Gray....................Aleta Freel
Bus....................Mary Philips
Eddie Wister....................Robert Shayne
Solomon Fitzmaurice....................Walter C. Kelly
Mark....................Oscar Polk
Simeon Gray....................Robert Strange
Levering....................Morris Carnovsky
Merton....................John Butler
Dell....................William Foran
Sneden....................Jerome Cowan
Miss McMurtry....................Jane Seymour
Wingblatt....................J. Edward Bromberg
Peebles....................Russell Collins
Farnum....................John F. Morrissey
Alan McClean....................Shepperd Strudwick
Ebner....................Joseph Sweeney

Acts I, II and III.—Office of the Chairman of the Appropriations Committee and Committee Room, House Office Building, Washington, D. C.

Staged by Worthington Miner; settings by Arthur P. Segal.

The original run of "Both Your Houses," starting March 6, 1933, was for nine weeks at the Royale. It closed May 6 and, after a short engagement in Philadelphia, returned to Broadway for two weeks at the Ethel Barrymore Theatre. When the engagement of "The Mask and the Face" ended June 10 the Theatre Guild moved the Anderson play to the Guild Theatre for a limited engagement.

See page 25.

YOUNG SINNERS

(72 performances)

A comedy in three acts by Elmer Harris. Revived by Thomas Kilpatrick at the Ambassador Theatre, New York, March 6, 1933.

Cast of characters—

Madge Trowbridge	Maida Carrell
Bud Springer	Paul Clare
Betty Biddle	Virginia Lloyd
Jimmy Stephens	David Morris
Butler	John Bramhall
Constance Sinclair	Dorothy Appleby
Mrs. Sinclair	Hilda Spong
Baron von Konitz	Alfred Hesse
Gene Gibson	Jackson Halliday
John Gibson	Percy Moore
Trent	Arthur Bower
Manager of Apartment House	Ralph Sumpter
Alice Lewis	Dorothy Dianne
Tom Maguire	Frank Shannon
Maggie Maguire	Paddy Reynolds
Tim	Freddie Stange

Act I.—Scene 1—The Sinclair Winter Home, Palm Beach. 2—Gene's Apartment, New York. Acts II and III.—The Living-room at Gene's Camp, Adirondacks.

Staged by Carl Hunt.

Originally produced by the Shuberts at the Morosco Theatre, New York, November 28, 1929, where it had a run of 229 performances. Revived by George Sharp at the New Yorker Theatre, New York, April 20, 1931, with a run of 249 performances and a return engagement of 40. Dorothy Appleby played Constance in the original cast and in both revivals. Raymond Guion played Gene in the original cast and Jackson Halliday was the Gene in the two revivals.

See "Best Plays of 1929-30" and "1930-31."

THE CHERRY ORCHARD

(30 performances)

A comedy in four acts by Anton Tchekov; translated by Constance Garnett. Revived by Eva Le Gallienne at the New Amsterdam Theatre, New York, March 6, 1933.

Cast of characters—

Lopahin (Yermolay Alexeyevitch)................Donald Cameron
Dunyasha................................Beatrice de Neergaard
Epihodov (Semyon Pantaleyevitch)................Nelson Welch
Firs....................................Sayre Crawley
Madame Ranevsky (Lubov Andreyevna)............Alla Nazimova
Anya................................Josephine Hutchinson
Varya................................Eva Le Gallienne
Charlotta Ivanovna..........................Leona Roberts
Gaev (Leonid Andreyevitch)....................Paul Leyssac
Semyonov-Pishtchik..........................Walter Beck
Yasha................................Robert H. Gordon
Trofimov (Pyotr Sergeyevitch)..................Harold Moulton
A Tramp................................Robert F. Ross
A Stationmaster..........................Howard da Silva
A Post-Office Clerk..........................Robert F. Ross
Nurse................................Agnes McCarthy
Visitors and Servants—The Misses Manners, English, Nurenberg, Martin, Snaylor and Messrs. Simonson and Wilkes.

Acts I and IV.—A Room in the House on the estate of Madame Ranevsky. Act II.—The Open Country. Act III.—Living-room.

Staged by Eva Le Gallienne; settings by Aline Bernstein.

Produced originally in New York at the Fifty-ninth Street Theatre by F. Ray Comstock and Morris Gest as one of five Russian plays on the Moscow Art Theatre program in January and February of 1923. James B. Fagan produced George Calderon's translation at the Bijou Theatre, New York, March 5, 1928. Eva Le Gallienne added the Garnett translation to her Civic Theatre repertory in 1928. See "Best Plays of 1927-28, 1928-29, 1929-30."

THE LADY REFUSES

(7 performances)

A comedy in three acts by Saxon Kling. Produced by H. Clayborne at the Bijou Theatre, New York, March 7, 1933.

Cast of characters—

Henriette................................Blanche Gordon
Mary................................Mary Manson
Hank Parkes................................Edward Bracken
Nancy Whitehouse Parkes Rogers....................Cecil Spooner
Jacques Castel................................Lou Tellegen
Jerome Parkes................................Charles Bryant
Mathers................................Thomas V. Morrison

Belinda Rogers....................................Helene Wincere
Harry Rogers......................................Paul Byron
Act I.—Jacques Castel's Apartment in Nice, France. Acts II and III.—The Rogers Home in New York.
Staged by Saxon Kling.

Nancy Rogers, twice divorced, in Nice for a vacation, meets Jacques Castel, owner of the apartment she thinks she has rented. Jacques would take Nancy to Italy for a trip. The day Nancy is ready to go Jerome Parkes, her first husband, arrives to make overtures for a remarriage. Nancy, thinking favorably of the proposal, returns to New York and meets Harry Rogers, her second husband, who also wants to remarry her. Along comes Jacques from France and Nancy goes back to Italy, as planned.

LONE VALLEY

(3 performances)

A play in three acts by Sophie Treadwell. Produced by the author at the Plymouth Theatre, New York, March 10, 1933.

Cast of characters—

Joe..Alan Baxter
Lottie...Mab Maynard
Lasly...Ian Wolfe
Grainger...Charles Kennedy
Mary..Marguerite Borough
Ella...Virginia Tracy
Lyman..Oliver Barbour
Acts, I, II and III.—Sitting-room of a Little Cottage on the Outskirts of an Isolated Ranching Community Called Lone Valley.
Staged by Sophie Treadwell; settings by Raymond Sovey.

Mary, representing the eternal Magdalen, has been living in a house of ill repute in a Southwestern city. She inherits a ranch from an aunt and goes there to recuperate from a hospital experience. She finds the ranch linked in various ways with a variety of frustrated humans, including Joe, a bound-boy working for Grainger, flint-hearted sheriff. Mary accepts Joe's slightly hysterical love, is threatened with arrest by Grainger, refuses to marry Joe and moves on. Joe is threatening to follow her at the play's end.

RIDDLE ME THIS

(70 performances)

A comedy in three acts by Daniel N. Rubin. Revived by O. E. Wee and Jules J. Leventhal, Inc., at the Hudson Theatre, New York, March 14, 1933.

Cast of characters—

Dr. Ernest Tindal.....Franklyn Fox
Mrs. Ruth Tindal.....Hazel Drury
McKinley.....Frank Allworth
Dr. Scully.....Earl Redding
Alcock.....Edwin Redding
Duffy.....George Graves
Brown.....Anthony Ross
Mrs. Ward.....Gertrude Ritchie
Kirk.....Taylor Holmes
Mrs. Alvin.....Jean Newcomb
Frank Marsh.....Warren Ashe
Vera Marsh.....Virginia Stevens
Jack Reed.....Howard Hall
Julia Reed.....Sondra Arleaux

Act I.—Mrs. Tindal's Bedroom. Acts II and III.—Office at Police Headquarters.
Staged by Robert Burton and Howard Hall.

"Riddle Me This" was produced originally by John Golden in February, 1932 ("Best Plays 1931-32"), with Frank Craven and Thomas Mitchell in the chief rôles.

THE BEST PEOPLE

(67 performances)

A comedy in three acts by David Gray and Avery Hopwood. Revived by O. E. Wee and Jules J. Leventhal, Inc., at the Waldorf Theatre, New York, March 15, 1933.

Cast of characters—

Marion Lenox.....Mary Frances McHugh
Lord Rockmere.....Kenneth Treseder
Miss Tate.....Mary Lewis
Bronson Lenox.....John T. Dwyer
Mrs. Lenox.....Maida Reade
Bullock.....Robert Vivian
George Grafton.....Thomas A. Braidon
Bertie Lenox.....Derek Fairman
Leo.....Joseph Burton
Millie.....Betty Garde
Henry.....King Calder
Alice O'Neill.....Thelma Paige
Footman.....Roy Stuart

Acts I and III.—Library in Home of Bronson Lenox, New York.
Act II.—Private Dining-rooms in Broadway Restaurant.
Staged by Lionel Bevans.

Produced originally by Charles Frohman, Inc., at the Lyceum Theatre, New York, in August, 1924 ("Best Plays 1923-24"), "The Best People" enjoyed a run of 143 performances. The following year it was played in San Francisco by the Henry Duffy company for 342 performances, which was a record for San Francisco.

MARILYN'S AFFAIRS

(1 performance)

A comedy in three acts by Arthur Ebenhack. Produced by John Paffrath, Inc., at the Mansfield Theatre, New York, March 15, 1933.

Cast of characters—

Mrs. Royden....................................Gertrude Mudge
Marilyn Royden....................................Loretto Shea
Dora Paden....................................Linda Eder
Tony Martino....................................Stanley Marlowe
Dan Callahan....................................Lynn Edwards
Cortez....................................Santos Ortega
Robert Culver....................................George Junior
Marie....................................Viola Kane
Adolph Blerkmeyer....................................William Bonelli
Commissioner Hammond....................................George Taylor

Act I.—Scene 1—In a Taxi. Scene 2—A Shoe Repair Shop. Acts II and III.—Marilyn Royden's Penthouse Apartment.

Staged by Arthur Ebenhack; settings by Vail Scenic Construction Co.

Marilyn Royden, taking another drink from her silver flask, bets Dora Paden that she can make any man propose to her within twenty-four hours after meeting him. Her first tests include Tony Martino, who runs a shoe-repair place; Dan Callahan, a young Irish policeman, and Cortez, a taxi driver. Marilyn, taking another drink from her flask, invites all three to a party, finally settles on Cortez as the man she loves and discovers that he is none other than the son of Commissioner Hammond of the police.

THREE-CORNERED MOON

(76 performances)

A comedy in three acts by Gertrude Tokonogy. Produced by Richard Aldrich and Alfred de Liagre, Jr., at the Cort Theatre, New York, March 16, 1933.

Cast of characters—

Mrs. Rimplegar....................................Cecilia Loftus
Kenneth Rimplegar....................................Ben Lackland
Douglas Rimplegar....................................John Eldredge
Ed Rimplegar....................................Elisha Cook, Jr.
Elizabeth Rimplegar....................................Ruth Gordon
Donald....................................Richard Whorf
Dr. Alan Stevens....................................Brian Donlevy
Kitty....................................Eunice Stoddard
Jenny....................................Paula Bauersmith

Acts I, II and III.—Entrance Hall and Dining-room of the Rimplegar Home in Brooklyn.

Staged by Alfred de Liagre, Jr.; settings by Arthur P. Segal.

The Rimplegars, well-to-do Brooklynites, discover their widowed mother has invested the family money and lost it. None of them is fit to work at any useful job. They take what they can get and with the aid of Dr. Alan Stevens, who is friendly and pays $25 a month for a room, they manage to get through. Elizabeth, in love with Donald, a poet too sensitive to work, turns finally to Dr. Stevens, realizing, as they say in Russia, that love is not a potato. You can't eat it. It is Stevens, stout heart and good provider, who wins and holds her affections.

MASKS AND FACES

(1 performance)

A comedy in three acts by A. J. Minor. Produced by Paul E. Martin at the Liberty Theatre, New York, March 18, 1933.

Cast of characters—

De Witt Keith....William Roselle
Potter....Edward Broadley
Herbert Baxter....Edgar Nelson
Gloria Sprague....Kathleen Lowry
Kenneth Ritchie....Allen B. Nourse
Geraldine Keith....Ann Deighton
Schuyler Ewing....Gordon Richards
Frances Ballou....Enid Romany
Elliot Williams....Donald Foster

Acts I, II and III.—Living Hall in the Keith Home, New York City.
Staged by Paul Martin.

Frances Ballou, psychiatrist, is called in to help straighten out the mental quirks of Geraldine Keith, who believes she is in love with another man, a phantom lover who always takes her husband's place whenever the husband embraces her. Dr. Ballou advises the husband to find out who the imagined lover is and then depart. First Elliot Williams, then Schuyler Ewing is suspected of being the man. Ewing, liking the doctor, is fairly distressed but stays close to the Keith house for a week. At the end of that time Mrs. Keith's hallucination has righted itself, and she is eager for her husband's return.

FAR-AWAY HORSES

(4 performances)

A comedy in three acts by Michael Birmingham and Gilbert Emery. Produced by Sidney Harmon and James R. Ullman at the Martin Beck Theatre, New York, March 21, 1933.

Cast of characters—

Nana....................................Josephine Williams
Ellen....................................Edna Hagan
Nancy Duffy....................................Eleanor Daniels
Tom....................................Bernie Neary
Celia....................................Leona Hogarth
Cathleen....................................Lillian Savin
Tim....................................Barry Macollum
Patrick....................................Bruce Macfarlane
Mary....................................Marion Barney
Sheila Donovan....................................Katharine Walsh
Rosie Duffy....................................Cele McLaughlin
Mrs. Mooney....................................Jessie Graham
Seumas....................................Thomas Chalmers
Ed Whalen....................................Clarence Rock
Mr. Greene....................................J. M. Clayton
Expressman....................................Horace McMahon

Acts I, II and III.—Kitchen of the O'Hara Home on the Banks of the Hudson River.

Staged by the authors; settings by Syrjala.

Mary O'Hara, with a brood of six children and an amiable but uncertain drinking millman for a husband, goes to Ireland to collect a legacy, finds there is none and comes home on borrowed money. Oldest daughter Ellen, determined to lift the O'Haras out of milltown depths, saves her money and spends it on the family when daughter Cathleen comes home with an unemployed husband and an expected baby. Mrs. O'Hara sells the O'Hara cottage for four hundred dollars which she entrusts to oldest son Patrick who buys himself a few drinks and a second-hand car. The O'Haras are still a mess at the play's end.

RAW MEAT

(1 performance)

A play in three acts by Myla Jo Closser and Homer Little. Produced by the Provincetown Playhouse Guild at the Provincetown Playhouse, New York, March 22, 1933.

Cast of characters—

Joe Drake....................................Margaret Hatfield
Peter Drake....................................Jean Clarendon
Babs Walker....................................Betty Upthegrove
Lenny O'Neil....................................John Clymer
Junior....................................Thomas Beck
Fergus....................................Alfred Jenkin
Hiram Hall....................................Hal Don
Birbal....................................James Dunmore
Earl Bonaparte....................................Lawrence Menkin
Ann....................................May Marshall

Staged by William A. Williams; settings by Hugh Mason.

Junior Drake, son of two famous explorers, distresses his parents by preferring the milder sport of amateur photography. Dismissed as a coward, Junior is at home when a circus lion escapes. Junior captures the beast single handed while several professional lion tamers, including his father and mother, are scouring the surrounding estates for it.

THE NEW YORK IDEA

(3 performances)

A play in four acts by Langdon Mitchell. Revived by the Snarks, Ltd., at the Heckscher Theatre, New York, March 22, 1933.

Cast of characters—

Philip Phillimore..............................Sterling T. Foote
Mrs. Phillimore (his mother)..................Leonie A. Danforth
The Rev. Matthew Phillimore (his brother).......Theodore Steinway
Grace Phillimore (his sister)...................Margaret G. Brett
Miss Heneage (his aunt).......................Amy B. Groesback
William Sudley (his cousin)....................Harold W. Gould
Mrs. Vida Phillimore (his divorced wife).............Olivia Bird
Brooks (her footman)...........................Philip Kobbe
Benson (her maid)...............................Janet Brower
Sir Wilfrid Cates-Darby...................Van Henry Cartmell
John Karslake..............................Charles E. Maxwell
Mrs. Cynthia Karslake (his divorced wife)..........Lois S. Coffin
Nogam (his valet)................................Robert Irwin
Tim Fiddler..................................George H. Darrell
Thomas (the Phillimore's family servant).....Drelincourt M. Martin
Staged by Arthur Sircom.

Originally produced by Minnie Maddern Fiske and the Manhattan Company at Milwaukee, October 9, 1906, subsequently opening at the Lyric, New York, November 19, 1906, with Mrs. Fiske in the rôle of Cynthia Karslake. Other notables in the Fiske cast were George Arliss, Emily Stevens, William B. Mack and John Mason.

THE PARTY'S OVER

(48 performances)

A comedy in three acts by Daniel Kusell. Produced by the author at the Vanderbilt Theatre, New York, March 27, 1933.

Cast of characters—

Mrs. Theodore Blakely..........................Effie Shannon
Theodore Blakely.............................George Graham
Maid...Hilda Plowright
Phylis Blakely..................................Peggy Conklin
Martin...Ross Alexander
Bruce Blakely................................Harvey Stephens

Clay Blakely.....Geoffrey Bryant
Mrs. Patricia Henley.....Katharine Alexander
Betty.....Claire Trevor
Beulah.....Georgette Harvey
Oglethorpe.....G. Albert Smith

Act I.—Living-room of Blakely Home. Act II.—A Hotel Bedroom, a Lunchroom in New Haven and Blakely Home. Act III.—Blakely Home, and Bruce Blakely's Office.

Staged by Howard Lindsay; settings by Cirker and Robbins.

Bruce Blakely, the inspiration and support of his father and mother, sister and brother, rebels modesty when his sister brings home an insipient crooner as a husband and Brother Clay marries a waitress in New Haven and adds her to the family. Bruce's rebellion becomes acute when he falls in love with Mrs. Patricia Henley and his business goes to pieces in the depression. He informs his parasitic relatives that the party's over and leaves all save his parents to fend for themselves.

HER TIN SOLDIER

(2 performances)

A comedy in three acts by Frederick Rath. Produced by William A. Brady and Frederick Rath at the Playhouse, New York, April 6, 1933.

Cast of characters—

Mark Mitchell.....Ralph Locke
Miss Rogers.....Hazel O'Connell
Mrs. Powers.....Ethel Jackson
Jerry Powers.....Harry Ellerbe
Corporal Harvey.....Thomas Hamilton
Mrs. Henderson.....Maude Odell
John Rand.....William R. Randall
Claire Rand.....Emily Lowry
Bob Marlowe.....Edmund MacDonald
Oscar.....Curtis Karpe
Gwen Olcott.....Charlotte Wynters
Waldo Wayne.....Charles Quigley
Flaherty.....John Kearney
Tito.....Richard Wang
Skipper.....Henry Wade
Tommy.....Buddy Mangan

Prologue, Acts I and III.—Mark Mitchell's Office in the Mitchell Theatre. Act II.—Lounge aboard the Yacht "Gwendolyn."

Staged by Milton Stiefel; settings by Livingston Platt.

Claire Rand, impulsively married to Waldo Wayne, movie hero, is eager to divorce him that she may marry Bob Marlowe, West Point cadet. In looking for a professional co-respondent she selects Jerry Powers, captain of ushers at the Mitchell Theatre and an imitation West Point cadet himself. Jerry and Claire are to be caught in a compromising situation aboard a yacht.

After many interruptions Jerry determines to teach Claire a lesson, as a result of which she next day ditches Bob and marries Jerry.

HUMMING SAM

(1 performance)

A musical comedy in two acts by Eileen Nutter, music by Alexander Hill. Produced by Allan K. Foster at the New Yorker Theatre, New York, April 8, 1933.

Cast of characters—

Humming Sam	Gertrude "Baby" Cox
Uncle Ned	Speedy Smith
Totem	Alonza Bozan
Hot Cakes	Bunny Allen
1st Jockey 2nd Jockey	The Two Chesterfields
Harlem Dan	Robert Underwood
Louise Lovelle	Louise Lovelle
Esmaraldae	Dorothy Embry
Emmaraldae	Catherine Brooks
Mamaraldae	Mary Mason
Yellow, George	Lionel Monogas
E. Bolton	Lorenzo Tucker
Mr. Conners	John Lee
Mike	Sandy
Madge Carter	Madeline Belt
Cæsar Cicero	Jones & Allen
Mr. Carter	Al Watts
Mae Carter	Flo Brown
Freddie Marlowe	Cecil Rivers
Nina May	Edith Wilson
Clara	Hannah Sylvester
Drum Major	J. Mardo Brown
Miss Jitters	Louise Cook

Act I.—Scene 1—Stables At a Race Track in Kentucky. 2—Exterior of the Track. 3—Home Stretch. Act II.—"Bogoo Inn," Kentucky.

Staged by Carey and Davis.

A version, in sepia, of the "In Old Kentucky" story in which Humming Sam, the best jockey in all America, rides Boogoo to victory in the Kentucky Derby to the joy of Madge Carter and the consternation of a couple of gambling villains.

FOR SERVICES RENDERED

(21 performances)

A play in three acts by W. Somerset Maugham. Produced by Sam H. Harris at the Booth Theatre, New York, April 12, 1933.

Cast of characters—

Charlotte Ardsley....................................Jean Adair
Gertrude....................................Mabel Gore
Sydney Ardsley....................................Leo G. Carroll
Gwen Cedar....................................Elizabeth Risdon
Ethel Bartlett....................................Lillian Kemble Cooper
Lois Ardsley....................................Jane Wyatt
Wilfred Cedar....................................Walter Kingsford
Eva Ardsley....................................Fay Bainter
Collie Stratton....................................Henry Daniell
Leonard Ardsley....................................Richie Ling
Dr. Prentice....................................David Glassford
Howard Bartlett....................................Perry Waram

Act I.—Terrace of the Ardsleys' House, Rambleston, Kent, England. Act II.—Dining-room. Act III.—Drawing-room.

Staged by Robert B. Sinclair; settings by Livingston Platt.

Fifteen years after the signing of the Armistice the Ardsleys of Rambleston, Kent, face many problems. Sydney Ardsley, blinded in the war, is the especial charge of his spinster sister, Eva, whose lover was killed at the front. His second sister, Ethel, having married out of her class during the war excitement, is patiently watching her husband drink himself to death. A third sister, Lois, is being pursued by a married war profiteer, who offers her a season on the Riviera and an allowance. Sydney's mother, told that she will die within three months of cancer, refuses an operation, and his friend, Collie Stratton, an officer discharged from the navy and a failure in business, kills himself. To complete the evening Eva, who had hoped to marry Stratton, loses her mind and Lois runs away with the profiteer.

THE 3-PENNY OPERA

(12 performances)

An operetta in three acts by Bert Brecht; music by Kurt Weill; adapted into English by Gifford Cochran and Jerrold Krimsky. Produced by John Krimsky and Gifford Cochran at the Empire Theatre, New York, April 13, 1933.

Cast of characters—

Legend Singer....................................George Heller
Jonathan Peachum....................................Rex Weber
Mrs. Peachum....................................Evelyn Beresford
Polly Peachum....................................Steffi Duna
Capt. Macheath....................................Robert Chisholm
Jenny Diver....................................Marjorie Dille
Filch....................................Herbert Rudley
Matthew....................................Anthony Blair
Crooked Finger Jack....................................Burgess Meredith
Walter....................................Harry Bellaver
Robert....................................George Heller
Jimmy....................................Francis Kennelly
Wing....................................H. L. Donsu

Reverend Kimball....................................John Connolly
Sheriff Brown..Rex Evans
Beggar..Harry Hornick
Vixen...Mary Heberden
Trull...Eugenie Reed
Madame..Lotta Burnell
Tawd..Hilda Kosta
Dolly...Ruth Thomas
Betty...Lilian Okun
Molly Brazen..Jean De Koven
Smith...Gerald Hamer
Constable...Arthur Brady
Lucy Brown..Josephine Huston
Constables: Clyde Turner, Larry Larkin, James Harvey.
Beggars: Tom Morgan, Harold Imber, Gus Alexander, Thomas Murphy, Richard Bengali, Morton Ulman, Louis Halperin, Jack Carstairs, Geraldine Lunby, Lillian Ardell, Barbara Winchester, Ellen Love, Corine Anderson.

Prologue—Fair in Soho. Act I.—Scenes 1 and 3—Mr. Peachum's Beggars' Establishment. 2—Stable in Soho. Act II.—Scene 1—Stable in Soho. 2—Brothel in Turnbridge Alley. 3—Old Bailey Gaol. Act III.—Scene 1—Mr. Peachum's Beggars' Establishment. 2—Old Bailey Gaol.

Staged by Francesco von Mendelssohn; settings by Cleon Throckmorton and Caspar Neher.

A German version of John Gay's eighteenth-century "Beggars' Opera" with an entirely new musical setting. The story is practically the same, following Captain Macheath's wooing and wedding of Polly Peachum, his betrayal to the police by Polly's father, his escape and recapture and his final conviction and sentence to die on the gallows. He would have died, too, if the soft-hearted authors had not decided at the last minute to provide a happier ending by having him pardoned by the king. "The Beggars' Opera" in an original version was imported by George C. Tyler in 1920, and by Jones and Green in 1928.

STRANGE GODS

(9 performances)

A drama in three acts by Jessica Ball. Produced by Samuel Wallach at the Ritz Theatre, New York, April 15, 1933.

Cast of characters—

Mrs. Williams.......................................Mary Horne
Jason Williams......................................Richard Ewell
Sam Williams..Ralph Theadore
Lem Highsmith.......................................Herbert Heywood
Zillah Carrington...................................Vera Allen
Arthur Carrington...................................Donald Randolph
Ulysses...Fred Miller
Benjamin Lassiter...................................John B. Litel

Act I.—Scene 1—Outside the Williams Cabin, the pine barrens of West Florida. 2—Carringtons' Lodge. Acts II and III.—Williams' Sitting-room.

Staged by Priestly Morrison; settings by P. Dodd Ackerman.

Zillah Carrington had her choice of two Harvard men, Arthur Carrington, scientist, and Benjamin Lassiter, lawyer. Taking Carrington she followed him dutifully into the pine barrens of Florida where he went in search of a rare species of butterfly. Zillah becomes interested in a young Florida "cracker," Jason Williams, and spurs his interest in learning. Carrington, realizing his love has grown cold and hurt in his vanity when Jason also first captures the wanted butterfly, shoots himself. Jason, fearing knowledge of the suicide will hurt Zillah, tries to lead the authorities into believing he is the murderer. He is cleared by the discovery of a note left by the suicide. Lassiter, the lawyer, conducts his case and incidentally retrieves Zillah.

THE MIKADO

(16 performances)

Operetta in two acts by W. S. Gilbert; music by Arthur Sullivan. Revived by the Civic Light Opera Company at the St. James, New York, April 17, 1933.

Cast of characters—

The Mikado of Japan....William Danforth
Nanki-Poo....Roy Cropper
Ko-Ko....Frank Moulan
Pooh-Bah....Herbert Waterous
Pish-Tush....Allen Waterous
Yum-Yum....Hizi Koyke
Pitti-Sing....Ethel Clarke
Peep-Bo....Mabel Thompson
Katisha....Vera Ross
Ladies of the Mikado's Suite: Martha Wallace, Leone Krauss, Frances Sinclair, Mildred Cory, Helen Ryan, Ruth Dawson, Mildred Guthins, Pearle Wible.
The Mikado's Body-guard: Thomas Green, Donald Smith, Frederick Grieve, John Willard.
Ensemble of School-girls, Nobles, Guards, Coolies: Frances Baviello, Frances Moore, Gertrude Waldon, Paula Rodes, Victoria Menou, Mary Hennessey, Olga Schumacher, Adele Story, Patty Gray, Pearl Olmstead, Vera Muller, Catherine Cale, Marjorie DeVoe, Geraldine Olive, Rebecca Wilkison, Adel DeSyova, Harrison Fuller, Frank Clarke, Gus Loring, Thomas Green, Donald Smith, Frederick Grieve, Bert Melrose, Basil Prock, Hobson Young, John Willard, John Cardini, Norman Van Embuigh, Rudolph Glaisek, Leo Nash.
Kiddies: Donna Leon Ard, Iris Posner.

Act I.—Court-yard of Ko-Ko's Official Residence. Act II.—Ko-Ko's Garden.

Staged by Milton Aborn.

During this engagement Milton Aborn also revived "HMS Pinafore," "Trial by Jury," "Yeoman of the Guard," and "Patience." Records of their previous revivals will be found in preceding volumes of "The Best Plays."

THE COMIC ARTIST

(21 performances)

A play in three acts by Susan Glaspell and Norman Matson. Produced by The Comic Artist, Inc., at the Morosco Theatre, New York, April 19, 1933.

Cast of characters—

Luella McClure.......................................Lea Penman
Eleanor Rolf...Blanche Yurka
Stephen Rolf...Richard Hale
Karl Rolf..Robert Allen
Nina Rolf..Lora Baxter

Acts I and III.—Living-room of Stephen and Eleanor's Old House on Cape Cod. Act II.—Scene 1—Stephen's Studio in the Barn. 2—Kitchen Steps.

Staged by Arthur Beckhard; settings by Cleon Throckmorton.

Stephen and Eleanor Rolf are living happily on Cape Cod. Stephen's younger brother, Karl, a successful comic artist, brings his wife Nina to visit. Nina and Stephen had known each other intimately in Paris before Karl had married Nina. They are drawn again into each other's arms. Eleanor forces Stephen to choose between his women. He sticks to Eleanor. Nina threatens to throw herself into the sea but doesn't. Like his most populaı comic strip character, Karl is "socked" in the last picture, but recovers Nina and is ready for the next strip.

UNTO THE THIRD

(4 performances)

A comedy in three acts by J. N. Gilchrist. Produced by the author at the Bijou Theatre, New York, April 20, 1933.

Cast of characters—

Wordley..Wallace Erskine
John...Edward Broadley
Muriel Case..Loretto Shea
George Talbot..Sam Wren
Mrs. Lucien Case, Jr.................................Gwen Day Burroughs
Lucien Case, Sr......................................Seth Arnold
Lucien Case, Jr......................................Robert Conness
Rufus Hatch..Robert Crozier
James Case...Milton Parsons
Edward...Edward Hartford

Acts I, II and III.—Living-room of the Case Home in Boston.

Staged by J. N. Gilchrist.

For many years Lucien Case, Sr., a hard and pious New Englander, has ruled his family and his son's family with an iron hand.

Muriel Case, his granddaughter, is the only one with spirit enough to stand up against him. Muriel meets and loves George Talbot, son of the Governor of Maine and a political enemy of Grandfather Case. Grandfather tries to prevent the union. Muriel out-lies and out-tricks him. Grandfather gives her a new Ford for her honeymoon trip.

LITTLE OL' BOY

(12 performances)

A drama in three acts by Albert Bein. Produced by Henry Hammond, Inc., at the Playhouse, New York, April 24, 1933.

Cast of characters—

Tommy Deal.....Garson Kanin
Pee Wee.....Richard Segal
Mr. Sanger.....William Lynn
Chock.....Lionel Stander
Mr. Leach.....Leo Curley
Dewey Hunter.....Tom Fadden
Ossie Prater.....Josef Lazarovici
Little Deadman.....Roy LeMay
Monitor.....Clem Wilenchick
Roy Wells.....John Drew Colt
Johnny Hamilton.....Warren Bryan
Robert Locket.....Edwin Philips
Horsethief.....Thomas Fischer
Ed Sweet.....Muni Diamond
Brownie.....Charles Powers
Pieface.....Edward Craven
Enoch Bryant.....Jimmy Fallon
Possum.....Frank M. Thomas, Jr.
Jimmy Green.....Joseph McGarrity
Wagon-Driver.....Randolph Echols
Hyacinth (Mrs. Sanger).....Ara Gerald
Carrol.....Harold Grau
Red Barry.....Burgess Meredith
Smithy.....Otto Frederick
Tall Boy.....Coleman Norton
Penitentiary Guard.....Jack Howard
Boys—Lew Amster, Henry DeKoven, Alex Ferency, Saul Gellis, Fred Kaufman, George Leland, Boris Vodeski, Joe Zito.

Acts I and II.—Scenes 1 and 2—Cottage D of a Reform School in the Middle West. Scene 3—Behind the Blacksmith's Shop. Act III.—Scene 1—A Barn. Scene 2—Cottage D.

Staged by Joe Losey; settings by Mordecai Gorelik.

Red Barry, graduate of six jails and tough, is sent to reform school and assigned to Cottage D. Cottage D boys are in a jam. Robert Locket has written a letter of protest to the Governor, and there is a search on for the writer. When Barry is accused Locket, inspired by hero worship, confesses. Barry seeks to repay Locket by making a fighting man of him. Together they make a break for liberty and are trailed by a posse. Locket is shot. Barry is recaptured and sent to a penitentiary.

MAN BITES DOG

(7 performances)

A farce in three acts by Don Lochbiler and Arthur Barton. Produced by Theron Bamberger and Bernard Klawans at the Lyceum Theatre, New York, April 25, 1933.

Cast of characters—

STAFF OF *The Daily Tab*

Doc Sanger, Managing Editor........................Leo Donnelly
Jake Zimmel, City Editor........................Raymond Walburn
Pete Schultz, News Editor........................Victor Kilian
Vic Kane, a Reporter........................Don Beddoe
Joe Barringer, a Reporter........................Millard Mitchell
Clarence Brophy, a Reporter........................John Griggs
Ike Gomberg, Police Headquarters Reporter..............Jay Adler
Snake Barlum, a Photographer........................Owen Martin
Freddy, an Office Boy........................Leo Needham
Miss Binswanger........................Lillian Herlein

OTHER CHARACTERS

Renee Brennan........................Dennie Moore
Joe Brennan........................Jack Stone
Helen Lee........................Gertrude Flynn
Trendle........................Charles Walton
McIntosh........................Horace McMahon
Armistead........................Phil Sheridan
Dr. Haas........................W. Francis Robertson
Lieutenant Zurbe........................James Kearney
Sergeant Burke........................Lawrence O'Brien
Emmett........................Martin Gabel

Acts I, II and III.—News Room of *The Daily Tab* in an American City.

Staged by Arthur Barton.

Doc Sanger, managing editor of a struggling tabloid, starving for sensations, is favored by the fates when Renee Brennan shoots her prizefighter husband in the office of the Sanger paper. Sanger capitalizes the sensation, hides the body, gets out an extra, helps Renee get tight, dresses her up as an Indian princess to give color to the story and then discovers Brennan is not dead but sleeping off his liquor. Making it necessary for Renee to shoot him again.

NINE PINE STREET

(28 performances)

A play in six scenes and an epilogue by John Colton and Carleton Miles, based on a play by William Miles and Donald Blackwell. Produced by Margaret Hewes at the Longacre Theatre, New York, April 27, 1933.

Cast of characters—

Clara Holden.......................................Helen Claire
Annie.......................................Barna Ostertag
Mrs. Holden.......................................Janet Young
Mrs. Powell.......................................Eleanor Hicks
Edward Holden.......................................Robert Harrison
Effie Holden.......................................Lillian Gish
Warren Pitt.......................................Raymond Hackett
Mrs. Carrie Riggs.......................................Roberta Beatty
Capt. James Tate.......................................John H. Morrissey
Miss Littlefield.......................................Catherine Proctor
Miss Roberts.......................................Jessamine Newcombe
Dr. Powell.......................................William Ingersoll
Lieut. Middleton.......................................James Hollicky
Rev. Appleton.......................................James P. Houston
Ernestine.......................................Andree Corday
Martin Lodge.......................................Neil McFee

The action takes place in the Holden Home, New Bedford, Mass.
Staged by A. H. Van Buren; settings by Robert Edmond Jones.

Effie Holden, a sweet and religious-minded creature, is so emotionally disturbed by the death of her mother, whom she adored, and her father's rather quick marriage with Mrs. Riggs, that she is led to bash in her stepmother's head with a flatiron and hammer her father into kingdom come with a knotted walking stick. Brought to trial Effie makes no other defense than that she was not at home, but had gone by a street-car to an appointment with her fiancé, Warren Pitt. She is, partly through the influence of her church, acquitted and thereafter lives for twenty-odd years in the old Holden home, defying and mystifying these neighbors who still believe she is guilty. The play is generously based on the Lizzie Borden murder case which was a Fall River, Mass., sensation forty years ago.

SPRINGTIME FOR HENRY

(16 performances)

A comedy in three acts by Benn W. Levy. Revived by Thomas Kilpatrick at the Ambassador Theatre, New York, May 1, 1933.

Cast of characters—

Miss Jones.......................................Mady Correll
Mr. Dewlip.......................................Henry Hull
Mr. Jelliwell.......................................Gavin Muir
Mrs. Jelliwell.......................................Edith Atwater
Miss Smith.......................................Dorothy Appleby

Acts I, II and III.—Henry Dewlip's flat in London.
Staged by Carl Hunt.

Produced originally at the Bijou Theatre, New York, by Kenneth Macgowan and Joseph Verner Reed, with Leslie Banks, Nigel Bruce and Helen Chandler in the cast. ("Best Plays, 1931-32.")

BEST SELLERS

(53 performances)

A play in three acts adapted by Dorothy Cheston Bennett from Edouard Bourdet's "Vient de Paraitre." Produced by Lee Shubert at the Morosco Theatre, New York, May 3, 1933.

Cast of characters—

Ambrose....................Joseph Allenton
Henri....................Philip Cary Jones
Bragayon....................Edgar Barrier
Mr. Felix....................Roman Bohnen
Fournier....................Ernest Truex
Gilbert Marechal....................Ian Keith
Julian Mosca....................George Coulouris
Bourgine....................Ralph Locke
Olivet....................Frederick Voight
Jacqueline....................Peggy Wood
Photographer....................John Adair
Naomi....................Hildur Ouse

Act I.—Offices of Julian Mosca. Act II.—Scene 1—Fournier's Study. 2—Sitting-room of Mosca's Villa. Act III.—Fournier's Study.

Staged by F. Cowles Strickland; settings by Rollo Wayne.

Marc Fournier, a Treasury clerk, has turned his wife's diary, relating her adventures with an early love affair, into a novel. The novel is submitted for the Zola prize and, because of trade intrigues, is given the prize. Fournier is placed under contract by a publisher, gives up his Treasury job and starts on a second book. Discovering his inspiration gone the publisher insists that Jacqueline Fournier submit herself to another love affair and keep another diary for the sake of her husband's career. Jacqueline reluctantly agrees and Fournier's jealousy is aroused. He gives up his contract, takes his wife back to Orleans and resumes his job at the Treasury. There he finds he is able to write a novel based on his jealousy. So does his rival. And a third observer makes a play of the same plot.

HILDA CASSIDY

(4 performances)

A play in three acts by Henry and Sylvia Lieferant. Produced by Robert Stephens, Inc., at the Martin Beck Theatre, New York, May 4, 1933.

Cast of characters—

Tony....................Joseph Olney
Tom Cassidy....................Howard Phillips

Max Holman.....George Greenberg
Mrs. Kimmel.....Josephine Deffry
Hilda Cassidy.....Stella Adler
Mrs. O'Brien.....Jeanne Wardley
Mamie Kimmel.....Sylvia Field
Francis Foley.....Gregory Deane
Connie Dugan.....Harry Hanlon
Danny Sheridan.....Charles Moyer
Nevins.....Fred Knight
Herman Bauer.....Max Beck
Mrs. Miller.....Frieda Altman
Marty O'Brien (Act II).....Jackie Clark
Kelly.....William Mercer
Claire Cassidy (Act II).....Edna Hagan
Leo O'Brien (Act II).....Bobbie Thomas
Ruffo.....George Spelvin
Marty O'Brien (Act III).....Edward Emerson
Claire Cassidy (Act III).....Margaret Barker
Leo O'Brien (Act III).....David Morris

Act I.—Scene 1—Yard of a Tenement on 3rd Avenue in New York City. 2—Backroom of Tom Cassidy's Cigar Store. 3—Yard. 4—Cassidy Living-room. Act II.—Scenes 1 and 3—Backroom of Tom Cassidy's Cigar Store. 2—Yard. Act III.—Backroom of the Store.

Staged by Marcel Strauss; settings by Tom Adrian Cracraft.

Tom Cassidy marries Hilda when he is in love with Mamie Kimmel. Later he goes back to Mamie. Hilda is convinced that if she has a child she can hold Tom. Ten years later Tom is devoted to his 10-year-old daughter, but still loyal to Mamie Kimmel. He has advanced from bookmaker to bootlegger. Hilda, realizing that she has lost, sends Tom to live with Mamie. Later he is arrested for selling liquor to soldiers and spends several years in prison. Out of prison in 1928 Tom finds Hilda and his daughter waiting. Also Mamie. He cannot change his loyalties. His daughter is in love with a racketeer. He would stop her marrying him. Hilda feels differently. She had given up her husband to the woman he loved; she will make the same sacrifice for her daughter.

IT HAPPENED TOMORROW

(11 performances)

A comedy in three acts by Leo A. Levy and D. Frank Marcus. Produced by the authors at the Ritz Theatre, New York, May 5, 1933.

Cast of characters—

Ronald Ramsbo.....France Bendtsen
Willa Welso.....Winifred Cahoon
Captain Boda Gardo.....Grenna Sloane
General Edna Millraine.....Ina Rossiter
Mehitabel Leoni.....Helen Raymond
Colonel Domba.....Donald Reed
Ivy Leoni.....Frances Sage

Eric Billodi....................................Alan Ward
Moda Ramsbo....................................Ann Deighton
Dr. Kurt Etsbo....................................Barry Townly
Mr. Lobb....................................Ashley Cooper
The Doctor's Assistant....................................Alfred Jenkin
The Robot....................................Egron Ivleps
The Escaped Convict....................................Marjory Hays

Acts I, II and III.—The Chancellor's study in the Palace of the Dictatrix of the United Provinces of Mythica.

Staged by D. Frank Marcus; settings by Herbert Ward and Walter Harvey.

Mehitabel Leoni, Dictatrix of the Kingdom of Mythica, is so violently opposed to war that she issues a decree against the birth of boy babies. When boys are born they are to be immediately spirited out of the country and Dr. Etsbo, the country's chief physician, is to stick to laboratory experiments until he is able to control the sex of expected infants. The doctor does some experimenting with the wife of a high official and she presents the state with twin boys. Things like that continue to happen until nearly 11 o'clock.

* ANOTHER LANGUAGE

(53 performances)

A comedy in three acts by Rose Franken. Revived by Arthur J. Beckhard at the Waldorf Theatre, New York, May 8, 1933.

Cast of characters—

Mrs. Hallam....................................Margaret Wycherly
Mr. Hallam....................................Wyrley Birch
Harry Hallam....................................William Pike
Helen Hallam....................................Esther Dale
Walter Hallam....................................Hal K. Dawson
Grace Hallam....................................Genevieve Frizzel
Paul Hallam....................................Herbert Duffy
Etta Hallam....................................Maude Allan
Victor Hallam....................................Glenn Anders
Stella Hallam....................................Patricia Collinge
Jerry Hallam....................................John Beal

Acts I and III.—The Hallam Home on the West Side. Act II.—Stella's and Victor's Apartment on the upper East Side.

Staged by Arthur J. Beckhard; settings by Cleon Throckmorton.

Produced originally April 25, 1932, "Another Language" achieved a run of forty-three weeks. Following a road tour it was brought back for a supplementary spring engagement with Patricia Collinge replacing Dorothy Stickney as Stella Hallam, Esther Dale following Margaret Hamilton as Helen Hallam and Genevieve Frizzel in place of Irene Cattell as Grace Hallam. Excerpts from the play were included in "The Best Plays of 1932-33."

THE MASK AND THE FACE

(40 performances)

A comedy in three acts translated from the Italian of Luigi Chiarelli by W. Somerset Maugham. Produced by The Theatre Guild, Inc., at the Guild Theatre, New York, May 8, 1933.

Cast of characters—

Elisa Zanotti	Shirley Booth
Giorgio Alamari	Donald McClelland
Marta Setta	Dorothy Patten
Cirillo Zanotti	Leo G. Carroll
Wanda Sereni	Alice Reinheart
Marco Miliotti	Ernest Cossart
Piero Pucci	Charles Campbell
Savina Grazia	Judith Anderson
Count Paolo Grazia	Stanley Ridges
Luciano Spina	Humphrey Bogart
Andrea	Manart Kippen
Giacomo	William Lovejoy
Teresa	Joan Marion

Acts I, II and III.—Room in the Villa Grazia on the Lake of Como.

Staged by Philip Moeller; settings by Lee Simonson.

Count Paolo Grazia, in a philosophical discussion with Cirillo Zanotti, makes the boast that any man who failed to kill a wife who deceived him would be ridiculous. Finding the Countess Grazia entertaining a lover in her rooms the same evening the Count tries to strangle her but cannot. Tries to shoot her but cannot. Ends by banishing her from the country and announcing to the police that he has killed her and thrown her body in the lake. Arrested, tried and convicted Count Grazia returns home months later and is received as the hero of the countryside. A woman's body has been found in the lake and is being buried as that of the Countess when the banished lady suddenly returns. Again the Count would take steps, but is overcome by his love for his wife. A reconciliation is effected to the strains of the Chopin funeral march being played at the services of the wrong woman.

A Chester Bailey Fernald version of "The Mask and the Face" was produced by Brock Pemberton at the Bijou Theatre, New York, September 10, 1924.

$25 AN HOUR

(22 performances)

A comedy in three acts by Gladys Unger and Leyla Georgie, based on outline by Erno Balogh. Produced by Alfred Aarons and Thomas Mitchell at the Masque Theatre, New York, May 10, 1933.

Cast of characters—

Miss Minners....................................Natalie Browning
Anna Olson....................................Catherine Field
Mrs. Rosenwasser....................................Helena Rapport
Claude de Rozay....................................Georges Metaxa
William....................................Stanley Harrison
Cornelius....................................William Bowers
Hope Belmore....................................Cyrena Smith
Mr. Menaker....................................Ralph Sanford
Germaine Granville....................................Olga Baclanova
Lucy....................................Jean Arthur
Mr. Barton....................................Paul Huber

Acts I, II and III.—Music Studio of Claude de Rozay in New York City.
Staged by Thomas Mitchell; settings by Livingston Platt.

Claude de Rozay, disappointed in an operatic career, takes up teaching at $25 an hour. Susceptible ladies flock to his studio. Rozay is in chains to Germaine Granville, his mistress. When she is ordered to Paris Germaine leaves cold little Lucy to watch over Rozay. Lucy, being an operatic agent in disguise, reëstablishes Rozay's confidence in himself as a singer and completely captures his affections as a man. Before Germaine can stop them Lucy and Rozay are engaged to be married.

THEY ALL COME TO MOSCOW

(20 performances)

A comedy in three acts by John Washburne and Ruth Kennell. Produced by The Players Theatre at the Lyceum Theatre, New York, May 11, 1933.

Cast of characters—

Dunya Sulich....................................Natasha Boleslavsky
Earl Collins....................................Thomas Paradine
Jim Hardy....................................Maurice Manson
Laura....................................Marjorie Dalton
Kolenko....................................Michael Dalsky
Betty Granfield....................................Lillian Walters
Molly Mintz....................................Aileen Poe
Natalya Brikin....................................Tamara
Dmitri Nekrasov....................................Cornel Wilde
John McNair....................................Jack Davis

Joseph Lebetz....................................Boris Marshalov
Andrey Brikin....................................Clifford Odets
Mary Collins.....................................Marie Nevills
Diana Richardson.................................Olga Krolow
Dr. Sergey Strogov...............................Rani Jovanowitsch
Victor Markov....................................Cecil Clovelly
An O.G.P.U. Officer..............................Roger G. Moore
An O.G.P.U. Officer..............................George Spelvinsky

Acts I, II and III.—Living-room of Diana Richardson's Apartment in Moscow.
Staged by William J. O'Neill; settings by Tom Adrian Cracraft.

John McNair, American engineer in Russia helping the Soviet with the five-year plan, falls in love with Natalya Brikin, assigned to him as a secretary. Andrey Brikin, Natalya's husband, would divorce Natalya that she may honorably give herself to McNair. Natalya loves her hubsand too much to leave him, and McNair is too honorable to take her otherwise. Joseph Lebetz, plotting against McNair and Brikin, tries to make capital of the situation but fails.

* JUNE MOON

(41 performances)

A comedy in three acts by Ring Lardner and George S. Kaufman, music and lyrics by Ring Lardner. Revived by Thomas Kilpatrick at the Ambassador Theatre, New York, May 15, 1933.

Cast of characters—

Fred Stevens.....................................Thomas Gillen
Edna Baker.......................................Emily Lowry
Paul Sears.......................................Fred Irving Lewis
Lucille..Edith Van Cleve
Eileen...Lee Patrick
Maxie..Harry Rosenthal
Goldie...Virginia Lloyd
A Window Cleaner.................................John Bramhall
A Man Named Brainard.............................Milano Tilden
Benny Fox..Ross Hertz
Mr. Hart...Leo Kennedy
Miss Rixey.......................................Mady Correll

Prologue—In a Parlor Car. Act I.—Paul Sears' Place. Acts II and III.—Room at Goebel's.
Staged by Milano Tilden and Carl Hunt.

Beginning in October, 1929, "June Moon" ran for 273 performances in New York and was afterward played in the major cities. Two members of the original cast were engaged for this revival, Lee Patrick and Harry Rosenthal. Rosenthal was made the star of the company. ("Best Plays of 1929-30.")

CANDIDE

(8 performances)

A dance drama adapted from the Voltaire novel by Charles Weidman; music arrangement by Genevieve Pitot and John Coleman; narrative by Ian Wolfe. Produced by Michael Meyerberg at the Booth Theatre, New York, May 15, 1933.

Cast of characters—

Master of Ceremonies.................................Jose Limon
Baron Thunder.................................Gene Martel
Baroness.................................Katharine Manning
Cunegonde.................................Eleanor King
Candide.................................Charles Weidman
Dr. Pangloss.................................John Glenn
Paquette.................................Cleo Atheneos
Martin.................................William Matons
Staged by Charles Weidman.

Excerpts loosely taken from the Voltaire novel and fitted to dance forms. Following his banishment with Cunegonde from the rose garden Candide takes up with the Bulgarian army, which raids the Castle for rape and plunder. Candide fares forth to Spain for an adventure with the priests and the inquisition. On to South America Candide comes upon the gold-worshiping country of Eldorado and later continues on to Paris for joy and gayety.

OF THEE I SING

(First engagement, 441 performances. Return, 32. Total, 473.)

A musical comedy in two acts by George S. Kaufman and Morrie Ryskind, music by George Gershwin, lyrics by Ira Gershwin. Return engagement at the Imperial Theatre, New York, May 15, 1933.

Cast of characters—

Louis Lippman.................................Sam Mann
Francis X. Gilhooley.................................Harold Moffet
Maid.................................Vivian Barry
Matthew Arnold Fulton.................................Dudley Clements
Senator Robert E. Lyons.................................George E. Mack
Senator Carver Jones.................................Edward H. Robins
Alexander Throttlebottom.................................Victor Moore
John P. Wintergreen.................................William Gaxton
Sam Jenkins.................................George Murphy
Diana Devereaux.................................Betty Allen
Mary Turner.................................Lois Moran
Miss Benson.................................June O'Dea
Vladimir Vidovitch.................................Tom Draak
Yussef Yussevitch.................................Sulo Hevonpaa
The Chief Justice.................................Ralph Riggs

Scrubwoman....................................Leslie Bingham
The French Ambassador..........................Florenz Ames
Senate Clerk....................................Martin Leroy
Guide...Ralph Riggs
The Dave Allman Band: Dave Allman, Ronald Perry, Walter Hinger, Milton Hollander, Frank Miller, Pete Shance, Jake Vander Muelen and Sidney Tropp.

Act I.—Scene 1—Main Street. 2—Hotel Room. 3—Atlantic City. 4—Madison Square Garden. 5—Election Night. 6—Washington. Act II.—Scenes 1 and 4—White House. 2—Capitol. 3—Senate. 5—Yellow Room.

Staged by George S. Kaufman; singing and dancing ensembles by Georgie Hale; settings by Jo Mielziner.

Principal songs—"Who Cares," "Of Thee I Sing," "Love is Sweeping the Country."

"Of Thee I Sing" toured during the winter of 1933 and was brought back to New York for a supplementary engagement at the Imperial Theatre with but one important change in cast. Betty Allen succeeded Grace Brinkley as the Diana Devereaux. In June Harriette Lake replaced Lois Moran for the last week. For original cast see "Best Plays 1931-32."

IT'S A WISE CHILD

(34 performances)

A comedy in three acts by Laurence E. Johnson. Revived by O. E. Wee and J. J. Leventhal, Inc., at the Hudson Theatre, New York, May 16, 1933.

Cast of characters—

Alice Peabody.......................................Alice Frost
Mrs. Stanton...................................Gertrude Ritchie
Bertha...May Vokes
Bill Stanton....................................George Walcott
Roger Baldwin...................................Joseph Striker
Joyce Stanton...................................Geraldine Brown
Jim Stevens...Ivan Miller
Otho Peabody......................................John Carmody
G. A. Appleby......................................Harlan Briggs
Cool Kelly..Hugh Cameron

Acts I, II and III.—Living-room in the Stanton Home.

Staged by Harlan Briggs.

Staged by the late David Belasco in August, 1929, "It's a Wise Child" collected a record of 378 performances in New York before being sent on tour. ("Best Plays of 1929-30.") In this revival the only member of the original cast is Harlan Briggs, who staged the comedy after the Belasco model.

GHOSTS

(6 performances)

A drama in three acts by Henrik Ibsen. Revived by George H. Brennan at the Sutton Theatre, New York, May 23, 1933.

Cast of characters—

Jacob Engstrand....................John Ravold
Regina Engstrand....................Joan Cordes
Pastor Manders....................Stuart Beebe
Mrs. Helen Alving....................Hilda Englund
Oswald Alving....................Donald Somers
Acts I, II and III.—Living-room in Mrs. Alving's Country Home, Rosenvold, overlooking one of the large fjords of Western Norway.
Staged by George H. Brennan.

"Ghosts" was first produced in New York January 5, 1894, with Ida Jeffreys-Goodfriend playing Mrs. Alving at the Berkeley Lyceum Theatre. Mary Shaw first played Mrs. Alving in a Chicago production in 1903, with Frederick Lewis the Oswald, and in New York with the Washington Square players in 1917, with Jose Ruben the Oswald. The Actors' Theatre presented Lucille Watson in the Alving rôle in 1926, with Ruben again the Oswald. The play ran for thirty-four performances on this occasion. Mrs. Fiske revived "Ghosts" in January, 1927, with Theodore St. John as the Oswald.

Other experimental productions at the Sutton Theatre during the season included those of "Cinderella's Brother," "The Mighty Conlon," and "Ann Adams, Spinster."

UNCLE TOM'S CABIN

(24 performances)

A melodrama in three acts dramatized by G. L. Aiken and revised by A. E. Thomas; from the novel by Harriet Beecher Stowe. Revived by the Players' Club at the Alvin Theatre, New York, May 29, 1933.

Cast of characters—

Eliza....................Elizabeth Risdon
George Harris....................Pedro de Cordoba
Shelby....................Malcolm Duncan
Haley....................Lyster Chambers
Harry....................Roy Le May
Aunt Chloe....................Cecilia Loftus
Uncle Tom....................Otis Skinner
Phineas Fletcher....................Edward MacNamara
Marks....................John Daly Murphy
Waiter....................W. B. Taylor

Tom Loker.......................................John C. King
Marie..Sylvia Field
Nurse......................................Eleanor Goodrich
Eva...Lois Shore
St. Clare.................................Ernest Glendinning
Aunt Ophelia..................................Minnie Dupree
Topsy...Fay Bainter
Mr. Wilson..................................George Christie
Overseer.......................................Earl Mitchell
Gumption Cute...............................Gene Lockhart
Skeggs, the Auctioneer......................Harold W. Gould
Clerk...John Kramer
Simon Legree..............................Thomas Chalmers
Adolph..John Knight
First Bidder..................................Francis H. Day
Second Bidder................................Edwin T. Emery
Third Bidder...................................Harold McGee
Cæsar......................................Burford Hampden
Aunt Hagar.....................................Kate Mayhew
Major Mann....................................Wright Kramer
George Fisk....................................Frank Wilcox
Sambo...Ben Lackland
Quimbo.......................................Harry Gresham
Singers: Harry Gilbert, James Stanley, Paul Parks, Frederick Jagel, T. H. Montgomery, Joseph Cummings Chase, Raymond Thayer, Samuel Merwin, John Barnes Wells.
Southern Ladies, Planters, Slaves, etc.: Alice MacKenzie, Florence Short, Kathleen Lockhart, Essie Emery, Katherine Doyle, Amy Groesbeck, Janice O'Connell, Elizabeth Dewing, Nancy Levering, Mrs. Edward D. Dunn, Patricia O'Connell, Oswald Hering, Grenville Vernon, Owen Culbertson, George Riddell, Richard Hoffmann, William Fisher, Oswald Marshall, Russell Crouse, Harold Staton, Edward Delaney Dunn.
Soprano Soloist, Patricia O'Connell.

Act I.—Scene 1—Dining-room. 2—Uncle Tom's Cabin. 3—Tavern by the River. 4—Ohio River. 5—Handsome Parlor. 6—Garden. 7—Tavern by the River. Act II.—Scene 1—Eva's Chamber. 2—Quaker Kitchen. 3—Rocky Pass in the Hills. 4—Study. 5—Garden. 6—Eva's Chamber. 7—Street in New Orleans. 8—Handsome Chamber. 9—Auction Mart. Act III.—Scene 1—Street in New Orleans. 2—Rude Chamber. 3—Roofless Shed. 4—Rude Chamber. 5—Street in New Orleans. 6—Roofless Shed.

Staged by Earle Booth; settings by Donald Oenslager; musical program prepared by Edward T. Emery and directed by Harry Gilbert.

Originally produced in Troy, N. Y., in 1853, "Uncle Tom's Cabin" enjoyed a run of seventy-seven years, according to the records of Elizabeth Corbett. There were no performances of record in 1930. In 1901 William A. Brady staged a revival with Wilton Lackaye, Theodore Roberts, Artie Hall and Emily Rigl in the cast at the Academy of Music, New York, which ran for twenty weeks. Four years before, in St. Paul, Jacob Litt revived the old drama with Louis James and Julia Arthur in the cast.

* TATTLE TALES

(20 performances)

A revue in two acts by Frank Fay and Nick Copeland; music and lyrics by Howard Jackson, Edward Ward, Leo Robins, Ralph

Ranger, George Waggoner, Willard Robison, Edward Eliscu, Eddie Bienbryer and William Walsh. Produced at the Broadhurst Theatre, New York, June 1, 1933.

Principals engaged—

Frank Fay	Barbara Stanwyck
Nick Copeland	Lillian Reynolds
James Mack	Dorothy Dell
Ray Mayer	Evelyn Page
John Dyer	Edith Evans
Beauvell	Miss Tova
William Hargrave	Betty Doree
Les Clark	Mary Barnett
Don Cumming	Betty Nylander

Staged by Frank Fay; musical numbers arranged by John Lonergan, Danny Dare and LeRoy Prinz.

A revue assembled by Mr. Fay in California and played across country to New York.

FLY BY NIGHT

A comedy in three acts by Richard F. Flournoy. Produced by Charles E. Sullivan at the Belmont Theatre, New York, June 2, 1933.

Cast of characters—

Harry...Frank Shannon
First Man...Al Berg
Second Man...Anthony Ross
Billie...David Morris
Toby...Edgar Nelson
Irene...Florence Arlington
Bunny...France Bendsten
Ruth...Ruth Nugent
Bob...Alan Bunce
Jim...Paul Guilfoyle
Hortense...Arlien Marshall

Acts I, II and III.—Dressing-rooms of the Ruth Clark Stock Company, a Theatrical Repertoire organization under a canvas tent.
Staged by Murray Phillips.

Ruth Clark is the star and owner of a traveling tent show. Her husband and manager, Jim Clark, is a drunk and a would-be wife beater. Resenting Jim's references to Ruth Bob, who loves the gal, hits Jim so hard he falls against an iron pole and is killed. Harry, sympathetic prop man, hides Jim's body and when the tent blows down in a storm a few hours later it looks as though Providence killed Jim and cleared the way for Ruth and Bob to be happy.

*SHOOTING STAR

(8 performances)

A play in three acts and eleven scenes by Noel Pierce and Bernard C. Schoenfeld. Produced by Crosby Gaige and Kenneth Nash at the Selwyn Theatre, New York, June 12, 1933.

Cast of characters—

Aaron Fleischer	Robert C. Fischer
Flo Curtis	Lee Patrick
Olive O'Casey	Violet Barney
Jackson Macy	Roland Drew
Ed Fleischer	Philip Van Zandt
Julie Leander	Francine Larrimore
Hannah	Harriet MacGibbon
Spittoon Man	Gene Moore
Tom Blair	Barry O'Neill
Chris	Joseph Downing
Bill	George Cowell
Johnson	Forrest Taylor, Jr.
Miss Frothingham	Beverly Sitgreaves
Herman Mordecai	Samuel Goldenberg
Carl Hoffman	Henry O'Neill
Edna Judd	Cora Witherspoon
Gareth Judd	Van Lowe
Hank Morrisey	Walter Baldwin
Grantland North	George Houston
Mat Hardy	Robert Gleckler
Katie	Edith Shayne
Nora	Mary Alice Collins
Emmett	Barry Mahool
Malcolm Craig	Vincent York
Asst. Stage Manager	William Sharpe, Jr.
Allister	Scott Moore
Mrs. Honeycut	Helen Crane
Mrs. Mercer	Harriet MacGibbon
Leo Bennett	Frank Wilcox
Ella	Engel-Sumner
Second Maid	Mathilde Baring
Bell-Boy	Gilbert Squarey
Reporter	Oliver Barbour

Act I.—Scene 1—Stage of Bijou Theatre. Beardstown, Illinois. 2—Stage of the Palace Theatre. Heather, Montana. 3—Ante-Room of Herman Mordecai's Office. New York. 4—Mordecai's Office. Act II.—Scene 1—Library at Edna Judd's House. New York. 2 and 3—Living-room in Julie's Apartment. New York. 4—Julie's Dressing-room in the Hoffman Theatre. New York. Act III.—Scene 1—Julie's Dressing-room in a Pennsylvania Town. 2—Loggia of Julie's Home in Westchester. 3—Hotel Room in New York.

Staged by Bela Blau; settings by Raymond Sovey.

Julie Leander, ingénue of a Western stock company, sees Duse play Camille in Chicago and is fired with great ambitions. To advance her career she marries her manager. Two years later she leaves him and their child to go to New York. In New York she becomes the star and the mistress of Herman Mordecai. In two years she is famous. She leaves her manager for a handsomer man, socially prominent Grantland North, who in time leaves her. Julie acquires a play about a Carrie Smith who curses her

way through a four-year run. This, with her disappointments in love, drives Julie to drugs and drink and she finally dies of an overdose of stimulants.

* THE CLIMAX

(7 performances)

A play in three acts by Edward J. Locke; incidental music by Joseph Carl Briel and Rachmaninoff. Revived by Harold Hevia at the Bijou Theatre, New York, June 13, 1933.

Cast of characters—

Luigi Golfanti....................................Guy Bates Post
Pietro Golfanti....................................George Heller
John Raymond....................................Matthew Smith
Adelina von Hagen....................................Norma Terris

Acts I, II and III.—Within the Four Walls of Luigi Golfanti's Home.

Staged by Ronald T. Hammond.

"The Climax" was produced originally by Joseph Weber April 12, 1909, and revived by Mr. Weber in 1910, with Ann Swinburne in the heroine's rôle. It was revived by the Shuberts in January, 1919, with Eleanor Painter the soprano, and in May, 1926, by Sam Wallack with Dorothy Francis as the heroine. The play has been in the Guy Bates Post repertory in various parts of the world. The story is of Adelina, beautiful niece of the music master, Luigi Golfanti, who is led by Dr. Raymond to believe that she has lost her voice. The doctor would discourage Adelina's ambitions for a career so she will marry him. Later Adelina recovers her voice and sings more gloriously than before.

STATISTICAL SUMMARY

(Last Season Plays Which Ended Runs After June 18, 1932.)

Plays	*Number Performances*	*Plays*	*Number Performances*
Another Language	344	Of Thee I Sing	441
Bridal Wise	128	Reunion in Vienna	264
Cat and the Fiddle	395	Show Boat	180
Counsellor at Law	292	That's Gratitude	204
Face the Music	165	A Thousand Summers	51
Hey Nonny Nonny	32		

LONG RUNS ON BROADWAY

To June 18, 1933

Plays	*Number Performances*	*Plays*	*Number Performances*
Abie's Irish Rose	2,532	Kiki	600
Lightnin'	1,291	Blossom Time	592
The Bat	867	Show Boat	572
The Ladder	789	The Show-off	571
The First Year	760	Sally	570
Seventh Heaven	704	The Green Pastures	640
Peg o' My Heart	692	Strictly Dishonorable	557
East Is West	680	Good News	551
Irene	670	The Music Master	540
A Trip to Chinatown	657	The Boomerang	522
Rain	648	Blackbirds	518
Is Zat So	618	Sunny	517
Student Prince	608	The Vagabond King	511
Broadway	603	The New Moon	509
Adonis	603	Shuffle Along	504
Street Scene	601	Bird in Hand	500

PULITZER PRIZE WINNERS

"For the original American play performed in New York which shall best represent the educational value and power of the stage in raising the standard of good morals, good taste and good manners."—The Will of Joseph Pulitzer, dated April 16, 1904.

In 1929 the advisory board, which, according to the terms of the will, "shall have the power in its discretion to suspend or to change any subject or subjects . . . if in the judgment of the board such suspension, changes or substitutions shall be conducive to the public good," decided to eliminate from the above paragraph relating to the prize-winning play the words "in raising the standard of good morals, good taste and good manners."

The committee awards to date have been:

1917-18—Why Marry? by Jesse Lynch Williams
1918-19—None
1919-20—Miss Lulu Bett, by Zona Gale
1920-21—Beyond the Horizon, by Eugene O'Neill
1921-22—Anna Christie, by Eugene O'Neill
1922-23—Icebound, by Owen Davis
1923-24—Hell-bent fer Heaven, by Hatcher Hughes
1924-25—They Knew What They Wanted, by Sidney Howard
1925-26—Craig's Wife, by George Kelly
1926-27—In Abraham's Bosom, by Paul Green
1927-28—Strange Interlude, by Eugene O'Neill
1928-29—Street Scene, by Elmer Rice
1929-30—The Green Pastures, by Marc Connelly
1930-31—Alison's House, by Susan Glaspell
1931-32—Of Thee I Sing, by George S. Kaufman, Morrie Ryskind, Ira and George Gershwin
1932-33—Both Your Houses, by Maxwell Anderson

PREVIOUS VOLUMES OF BEST PLAYS

Plays chosen to represent the theatre seasons from 1909 to 1933 are as follows:

1909-1919

"The Easiest Way," by Eugene Walters. Published by G. W. Dillingham, New York; Houghton Mifflin Co., Boston.

"Mrs. Bumpstead-Leigh," by Harry James Smith. Published by Samuel French, New York.

"Disraeli," by Louis N. Parker. Published by Dodd, Mead and Co., New York.

"Romance," by Edward Sheldon. Published by the Macmillan Co., New York.

"Seven Keys to Baldpate," by George M. Cohan. Published by Bobbs-Merrill Co., Indianapolis, as a novel by Earl Derr Biggers; as a play by Samuel French, New York.

"On Trial," by Elmer Reizenstein. Published by Samuel French, New York.

"The Unchastened Woman," by Louis Kaufman Anspacher. Published by Harcourt, Brace & Howe, Inc., New York.

"Good Gracious, Annabelle," by Clare Kummer. Published by Samuel French, New York.

"Why Marry?" by Jesse Lynch Williams. Published by Charles Scribner's Sons, New York.

"John Ferguson," by St. John Ervine. Published by the Macmillan Co., New York.

1919-1920

"Abraham Lincoln," by John Drinkwater. Published by Houghton Mifflin Co., Boston.

"Clarence," by Booth Tarkington.

"Beyond the Horizon," by Eugene G. O'Neill. Published by Boni & Liveright, Inc., New York.

"Déclassée," by Zoe Akins.

"The Famous Mrs. Fair," by James Forbes.

"The Jest," by Sem Benelli. (American adaptation by Edward Sheldon.)

"Jane Clegg," by St. John Ervine. Published by Henry Holt & Co., New York.

"Mamma's Affair," by Rachel Barton Butler.

"Wedding Bells," by Salisbury Field.

"Adam and Eva," by George Middleton and Guy Bolton.

1920-1921

"Deburau," by H. Granville Barker. Published by G. P. Putnam's Sons, New York.

"The First Year," by Frank Craven.

"Enter Madame," by Gilda Varesi and Dolly Byrne. Published by G. P. Putnam's Sons, New York.

"The Green Goddess," by William Archer. Published by Alfred A. Knopf, New York.

"Liliom," by Ferenc Molnar. Published by Boni & Liveright, New York.

"Mary Rose," by James M. Barrie.

"Nice People," by Rachel Crothers.

"The Bad Man," by Porter Emerson Browne. Published by G. P. Putnam's Sons, New York.

"The Emperor Jones," by Eugene G. O'Neill. Published by Boni & Liveright, New York.

"The Skin Game," by John Galsworthy. Published by Charles Scribner's Sons, New York.

1921-1922

"Anna Christie," by Eugene G. O'Neill. Published by Boni & Liveright, New York.

"A Bill of Divorcement," by Clemence Dane. Published by the Macmillan Company, New York.

"Dulcy," by George S. Kaufman and Marc Connelly. Published by G. P. Putnam's Sons, New York.

"He Who Gets Slapped," by Leonid Andreyev. Published by Brentano's, New York.

"Six Cylinder Love," by William Anthony McGuire.

"The Hero," by Gilbert Emery.

"The Dover Road," by Alan Alexander Milne.

"Ambush," by Arthur Richman.

"The Circle," by William Somerset Maugham.

"The Nest," by Paul Geraldy and Grace George.

1922-1923

"Rain," by John Colton and Clemence Randolph.

"Loyalties," by John Galsworthy. Published by Charles Scribner's Sons, New York.

"Icebound," by Owen Davis. Published by Little, Brown & Company, Boston.

"You and I," by Philip Barry. Published by Brentano's, New York.

"The Fool," by Channing Pollock. Published by Brentano's, New York.

"Merton of the Movies," by George Kaufman and Marc Connelly, based on the novel of the same name by Harry Leon Wilson.

"Why Not?" by Jesse Lynch Williams.

"The Old Soak," by Don Marquis. Published by Doubleday, Page & Company, New York.

"R.U.R.," by Karel Capek. Translated by Paul Selver. Published by Doubleday, Page & Company, New York.

"Mary the 3d," by Rachel Crothers. Published by Brentano's, New York.

1923-1924

"The Swan," by Ferenc Molnar. Published by Boni & Liveright, New York.

"Outward Bound," by Sutton Vane. Published by Boni & Liveright, New York.

"The Show-off," by George Kelly. Published by Little, Brown & Company, Boston.

"The Changelings," by Lee Wilson Dodd. Published by E. P. Dutton & Company, New York.

"Chicken Feed," by Guy Bolton. Published by Samuel French, New York and London.

"Sun-Up," by Lula Vollmer. Published by Brentano's, New York.

"Beggar on Horseback," by George Kaufman and Marc Connelly. Published by Boni & Liveright, New York.

"Tarnish," by Gilbert Emery. Published by Brentano's, New York.

"The Goose Hangs High," by Lewis Beach. Published by Little, Brown & Company, Boston.

"Hell-bent fer Heaven," by Hatcher Hughes. Published by Harper Bros., New York.

1924-1925

"What Price Glory?" by Laurence Stallings and Maxwell Anderson.

"They Knew What They Wanted," by Sidney Howard. Published by Doubleday, Page & Company, New York.

"Desire Under the Elms," by Eugene G. O'Neill. Published by Boni & Liveright, New York.

"The Firebrand," by Edwin Justus Mayer. Published by Boni & Liveright, New York.

"Dancing Mothers," by Edgar Selwyn and Edmund Goulding.

"Mrs. Partridge Presents," by Mary Kennedy and Ruth Warren.

"The Fall Guy," by James Gleason and George Abbott.

"The Youngest," by Philip Barry. Published by Samuel French, New York.

"Minick," by Edna Ferber and George S. Kaufman. Published by Doubleday, Page & Company, New York.

"Wild Birds," by Dan Totheroh. Published by Doubleday, Page & Company, New York.

1925-1926

"Craig's Wife," by George Kelly. Published by Little, Brown & Company, Boston.

"The Great God Brown," by Eugene G. O'Neill. Published by Boni & Liveright, New York.

"The Green Hat," by Michael Arlen.

"The Dybbuk," by S. Ansky, Henry G. Alsberg-Winifred Katzin translation. Published by Boni & Liveright, New York.

"The Enemy," by Channing Pollock. Published by Brentano's, New York.

"The Last of Mrs. Cheyney," by Frederick Lonsdale.

"Bride of the Lamb," by William Hurlbut. Published by Boni & Liveright, New York.

"The Wisdom Tooth," by Marc Connelly. Published by George H. Doran & Company, New York.

"The Butter and Egg Man," by George Kaufman. Published by Boni & Liveright, New York.

"Young Woodley," by John Van Druten. Published by Simon and Schuster, New York.

1926-1927

"Broadway," by Philip Dunning and George Abbott. Published by George H. Doran Company, New York.

"Saturday's Children," by Maxwell Anderson. Published by Longmans, Green & Company, New York.

"Chicago," by Maurine Watkins. Published by Alfred A. Knopf, Inc., New York.

"The Constant Wife," by William Somerset Maugham. Published by George H. Doran Company, New York.

"The Play's the Thing," by Ferenc Molnar and P. G. Wodehouse. Published by Brentano's, New York.

"The Road to Rome," by Robert Emmet Sherwood. Published by Charles Scribner's Sons, New York.

"The Silver Cord," by Sidney Howard. Published by Charles Scribner's Sons, New York.

"The Cradle Song," by John Garrett Underhill. Published by E. P. Dutton & Company, New York.

"Daisy Mayme," by George Kelly. Published by Little, Brown & Company, Boston.

"In Abraham's Bosom," by Paul Green. Published by Robert M. McBride & Company, New York.

1927-1928

"Strange Interlude," by Eugene G. O'Neill. Published by Boni & Liveright, New York.

"The Royal Family," by Edna Ferber and George Kaufman. Published by Doubleday, Doran & Company, New York.

"Burlesque," by George Manker Watters. Published by Doubleday, Doran & Company.

"Coquette," by George Abbott and Ann Bridgers. Published by Longmans, Green & Company, New York, London, Toronto.

"Behold the Bridegroom," by George Kelly. Published by Little, Brown & Company, Boston.

"Porgy," by DuBose Heyward. Published by Doubleday, Doran & Company, New York.

"Paris Bound," by Philip Barry. Published by Samuel French, New York.

"Escape," by John Galsworthy. Published by Charles Scribner's Sons, New York.

"The Racket," by Bartlett Cormack. Published by Samuel French, New York.

"The Plough and the Stars," by Sean O'Casey. Published by the Macmillan Company, New York.

1928-1929

"Street Scene," by Elmer Rice. Published by Samuel French, New York.

"Journey's End," by R. C. Sheriff. Published by Brentano's, New York.

"Wings Over Europe," by Robert Nichols and Maurice Browne. Published by Covici, Friede, New York.

"Holiday," by Philip Barry. Published by Samuel French, New York.

"The Front Page," by Ben Hecht and Charles MacArthur. Published by Covici, Friede, New York.

"Let Us Be Gay," by Rachel Crothers. Published by Samuel French, New York.

"Machinal," by Sophie Treadwell.

"Little Accident," by Floyd Dell and Thomas Mitchell.

"Gypsy," by Maxwell Anderson.

"The Kingdom of God," by G. Martinez Sierra. Published by E. P. Dutton & Company, New York.

1929-1930

"The Green Pastures," by Marc Connelly (adapted from "Ol' Man Adam and His Chillun," by Roark Bradford). Published by Farrar & Rinehart, Inc., New York.

"The Criminal Code," by Martin Flavin. Published by Horace Liveright, New York.

"Berkeley Square," by John Balderstone. Published by the Macmillan Company, New York.

"Strictly Dishonorable," by Preston Sturges. Published by Horace Liveright, New York.

"The First Mrs. Fraser," by St. John Ervine. Published by the Macmillan Company, New York.

"The Last Mile," by John Wexley. Published by Samuel French, New York.

"June Moon," by Ring W. Lardner and George S. Kaufman. Published by Charles Scribner's Sons, New York.

"Michael and Mary," by A. A. Milne. Published by Chatto & Windus, London.

"Death Takes a Holiday," by Walter Ferris (adapted from the

Italian of Alberto Casella). Published by Samuel French, New York.

"Rebound," by Donald Ogden Stewart. Published by Samuel French, New York.

1930-1931

"Elizabeth the Queen," by Maxwell Anderson. Published by Longmans, Green & Co., New York.

"Tomorrow and Tomorrow," by Philip Barry. Published by Samuel French, New York.

"Once in a Lifetime," by George S. Kaufman and Moss Hart. Published by Farrar and Rinehart, New York.

"Green Grow the Lilacs," by Lynn Riggs. Published by Samuel French, New York and London.

"As Husbands Go," by Rachel Crothers. Published by Samuel French, New York.

"Alison's House," by Susan Glaspell. Published by Samuel French, New York.

"Five-Star Final," by Louis Weitzenkorn. Published by Samuel French, New York.

"Overture," by William Bolitho. Published by Simon & Schuster, New York.

"The Barretts of Wimpole Street," by Rudolf Besier. Published by Little, Brown & Co., Boston.

"Grand Hotel," by Vicki Baum.

1931-1932

"Of Thee I Sing," by George S. Kaufman and Morrie Ryskin; music and lyrics by George and Ira Gershwin. Published by Alfred Knopf, New York.

"Mourning Becomes Electra," by Eugene O'Neill. Published by Horace Liveright, Inc.

"Reunion in Vienna," by Robert Emmet Sherwood. Published by Charles Scribner's Sons, New York.

"The House of Connelly," by Paul Green. Published by Samuel French, New York.

"The Animal Kingdom," by Philip Barry. Published by Samuel French, New York.

"The Left Bank," by Elmer Rice. Published by Samuel French, New York.

"Another Language," by Rose Franken. Published by Samuel French, New York.

"Brief Moment," by S. N. Behrman. Published by Farrar & Rinehart, New York.

"The Devil Passes," by Ben W. Levy. Published by Martin Secker, London.

"Cynara," by H. M. Harwood and R. F. Gore-Browne. Published by Samuel French, New York.

WHERE AND WHEN THEY WERE BORN

Abbott, George	Hamburg, N. Y.	1895
Abel, Walter	St. Paul, Minn.	1898
Aborn, Milton	Marysville, Cal.	1864
Adams, Maude	Salt Lake City, Utah	1872
Adler, Stella	New York	1904
Aherne, Brian	King's Norton, England	1902
Akins, Zoe	Humansville, Mo.	1886
Alexander, Katherine	Arkansas	1901
Alexander, Ross	Brooklyn, N. Y.	1904
Allanby, Peggy	New York	1905
Allen, Viola	Huntsville, Ala.	1869
Ames, Robert	Hartford, Conn.	1893
Ames, Winthrop	North Easton, Mass.	1871
Anders, Glenn	Los Angeles, Cal.	1890
Anderson, Judith	Australia	1898
Anderson, Maxwell	Atlantic City, Pa.	1888
Andrews, Ann	Los Angeles, Cal.	1895
Anglin, Margaret	Ottawa, Canada	1876
Anson, A. E.	London, England	1879
Anspacher, Louis K.	Cincinnati, Ohio	1878
Arliss, George	London, England	1868
Arthur, Julia	Hamilton, Ont.	1869
Astaire, Fred	Omaha, Neb.	1899
Atwell, Roy	Syracuse, N. Y.	1880
Atwill, Lionel	London, England	1885
Bainter, Fay	Los Angeles, Cal.	1892
Bankhead, Tallulah	Huntsville, Ala.	1902
Banks, Leslie J.	West Derby, England	1890
Barbee, Richard	Lafayette, Ind.	1887
Barrett, Edith	Roxbury, Mass.	1904
Barrie, James Matthew	Kirriemuir, N. B.	1860
Barry, Philip	Rochester, N. Y.	1896
Barrymore, Ethel	Philadelphia, Pa.	1879
Barrymore, John	Philadelphia, Pa.	1882
Barrymore, Lionel	London, England	1878

Bates, Blanche	Portland, Ore.	1873
Baxter, Lora	New York	1907
Beatty, Roberta	Rochester, N. Y.	1900
Beecher, Janet	Chicago, Ill.	1884
Behrman, S. N.	Worcester, Mass.	1893
Ben-Ami, Jacob	Minsk, Russia	1890
Bennett, Richard	Cass County, Ind.	1873
Bennett, Wilda	Asbury Park, N. J.	1894
Berlin, Irving	Russia	1888
Best, Edna	Sussex, England	1900
Binney, Constance	Philadelphia, Pa.	1900
Blackmer, Sidney	Salisbury, N. C.	1896
Boland, Mary	Detroit, Mich.	1880
Bondi, Beulah	Chicago, Ill.	1892
Bordoni, Irene	Paris, France	1895
Brady, Alice	New York	1892
Brady, William A.	San Francisco, Cal.	1863
Brady, William A., Jr.	New York	1900
Braham, Horace	London, England	1896
Brian, Donald	St. Johns, N. F.	1877
Brice, Fannie	Brooklyn, N. Y.	1891
Broadhurst, George H.	England	1866
Bryant, Charles	England	1879
Buchanan, Jack	England	1892
Buchanan, Thompson	Louisville, Ky.	1877
Buckler, Hugh	Southampton, England	1886
Burke, Billie	Washington, D. C.	1885
Burton, Frederick	Indiana	1871
Byington, Spring	Colorado Springs, Colo.	1898
Byron, Arthur	Brooklyn, N. Y.	1872
Cagney, James	New York	1904
Cahill, Lily	Texas	1885
Cahill, Marie	Brooklyn, N. Y.	1871
Calhern, Louis	New York	1895
Cantor, Eddie	New York	1894
Campbell, Mrs. Patrick	England	1865
Carle, Richard	Somerville, Mass.	1871
Carlisle, Alexandra	Yorkshire, England	1886
Carminati, Tullio	Zara, Dalmatia	1894
Carpenter, Edward Childs	Philadelphia, Pa.	1871
Carr, Alexander	Russia	1878
Carroll, Earl	Pittsburgh, Pa.	1892

Carter, Mrs. Leslie	Lexington, Ky.	1862
Catlett, Walter	San Francisco, Cal.	1889
Cawthorne, Joseph	New York	1868
Chandler, Helen	Charleston, N. C.	1906
Chaplin, Charles Spencer	London	1889
Chatterton, Ruth	New York	1893
Cherry, Charles	England	1872
Churchill, Burton	Toronto, Can.	1876
Claire, Ina	Washington, D. C.	1892
Clarke, Marguerite	Cincinnati, Ohio	1887
Cliffe, H. Cooper	England	1862
Clifford, Kathleen	Charlottesville, Va.	1887
Clive, Colin	St. Malo, France	1900
Coburn, Charles	Macon, Ga.	1877
Coghlan, Gertrude	England	1879
Coghlan, Rose	Petersborough, England	1850
Cohan, George M.	Providence, R. I.	1878
Cohan, Georgette	Los Angeles, Cal.	1900
Colbert, Claudette	Paris	1905
Collier, Constance	Windsor, England	1882
Collier, William	New York	1866
Collinge, Patricia	Dublin, Ireland	1894
Collins, José	London, England	1896
Colt, John Drew	New York	1914
Conklin, Peggy	Dobbs Ferry, N. Y.	1912
Connolly, Walter	Cincinnati, Ohio	1888
Conroy, Frank	London, England	1885
Cook, Joe	Evansville, Ind.	1890
Cooper, Violet Kemble	London, England	1890
Cornell, Katharine	Buffalo, N. Y.	1900
Corrigan, Emmett	Amsterdam, Holland	1871
Corthell, Herbert	Boston, Mass.	1875
Cossart, Ernest	Cheltenham, England	1876
Courtenay, William	Worcester, Mass.	1875
Courtleigh, William	Guelph, Ont.	1869
Coward, Noel	England	1899
Cowl, Jane	Boston, Mass.	1887
Craven, Frank	Boston, Mass.	1880
Crews, Laura Hope	San Francisco, Cal.	1880
Crosman, Henrietta	Wheeling, W. Va.	1865
Crothers, Rachel	Bloomington, Ill.	1878
Cumberland, John	St. John, N. B.	1880

Dale, Margaret	Philadelphia, Pa.	1880
Dalton, Charles	England	1864
Daly, Blyth	New York	1902
Daniels, Frank	Dayton, Ohio	1860
Dawn, Hazel	Ogden, Utah	1891
Day, Edith	Minneapolis, Minn.	1896
De Angelis, Jefferson	San Francisco, Cal.	1859
Dean, Julia	St. Paul, Minn.	1880
De Cordoba, Pedro	New York	1881
Dillingham, Charles B.	Hartford, Conn.	1868
Dinehart, Allan	Missoula, Mont.	1889
Dixey, Henry E.	Boston, Mass.	1859
Dodson, John E.	London, England	1857
Doro, Marie	Duncannon, Pa.	1882
D'Orsay, Lawrence	England	1860
Dressler, Eric	Brooklyn, N. Y.	1900
Dressler, Marie	Cobourg, Canada	1869
Drew, Louise	New York	1884
Dunn, Emma	England	1875
Dunning, Philip	Meriden, Conn.	1890
Dupree, Minnie	San Francisco, Cal.	1875
Edeson, Robert	Baltimore, Md.	1868
Eldridge, Florence	Brooklyn, N. Y.	1901
Ellis, Mary	New York	1900
Elliston, Grace	Wheeling, W. Va.	1881
Ellinger, Desirée	Manchester, Vt.	1895
Elliott, Gertrude	Rockland, Me.	1874
Elliott, Maxine	Rockland, Me.	1871
Eltinge, Julian	Boston, Mass.	1883
Emery, Gilbert	Naples, New York	1875
Emerson, John	Sandusky, Ohio	1874
Errol, Leon	Sydney, Australia	1881
Ervine, St. John Greer	Belfast, Ireland	1883
Fairbanks, Douglas	Denver, Colo.	1883
Farnum, William	Boston, Mass.	1876
Farrar, Geraldine	Melrose, Mass.	1883
Faversham, William	Warwickshire, England	1868
Fenwick, Irene	Chicago, Ill.	1887
Ferber, Edna	Kalamazoo, Mich.	1887
Ferguson, Elsie	New York	1883
Field, Sylvia	Allston, Mass.	1902

Fields, Lew	New York	1867
Fields, W. C.	Philadelphia, Pa.	1883
Fischer, Alice	Indiana	1869
Fiske, Minnie Maddern	New Orleans, La.	1867
Fontanne, Lynn	London, England	1882
Forbes, Robertson, Sir J.	London, England	1853
Foster, Claiborne	Shreveport, La.	1899
Foster, Norman	Richmond, Ind.	1907
Foster, Phœbe	New Hampshire	1897
Foy, Eddie, Jr.	New Rochelle, N. Y.	1906
Franklin, Irene	St. Louis, Mo.	1878
Frederick, Pauline	Boston, Mass.	1884
Friganza, Trixie	Cincinnati, Ohio	1870
Frohman, Daniel	Sandusky, Ohio	1850
Gahagan, Helen	Boonton, N. J.	1902
Garden, Mary	Scotland	1876
Gaxton, William	San Francisco, Cal.	1893
Gaythorne, Pamela	England	1882
George, Grace	New York	1879
Gerald, Ara	New South Wales	1902
Gillette, William	Hartford, Conn.	1856
Gillmore, Frank	New York	1884
Gillmore, Margalo	England	1901
Gish, Dorothy	Massillon, Ohio	1898
Gish, Lillian	Springfield, Ohio	1896
Gleason, James	New York	1885
Glendinning, Ernest	Ulverston, England	1884
Golden, John	New York	1874
Gottschalk, Ferdinand	London, England	1869
Greenstreet, Sydney	England	1880
Grey, Katherine	San Francisco, Cal.	1873
Groody, Louise	Waco, Texas	1897
Haines, Robert T.	Muncie, Ind.	1870
Hale, Louise Closser	Chicago, Ill.	1872
Hall, Bettina	North Easton, Mass.	1906
Hall, Laura Nelson	Philadelphia, Pa.	1876
Hall, Natalie	North Easton, Mass.	1904
Hamilton, Hale	Topeka, Kansas	1880
Hampden, Walter	Brooklyn, N. Y.	1879
Hanson, Gladys	Atlanta, Ga.	1887
Harding, Lyn	Newport, England	1867

Name	Birthplace	Year
Harrigan, William	New York	1893
Harris, Sam H.	New York	1872
Harrison, Richard B.	London, Ontario	1864
Hayes, Helen	Washington, D. C.	1900
Hazzard, John E.	New York	1881
Hedman, Martha	Sweden	1888
Heggie, O. P.	Australia	1879
Heming, Violet	Leeds, England	1893
Herbert, Evelyn	Brooklyn, N. Y.	1900
Herne, Chrystal	Dorchester, Mass.	1883
Hobart, Rose	New York	1906
Hodge, William	Albion, N. Y.	1874
Hopkins, Arthur	Cleveland, Ohio	1878
Hopkins, Miriam	Bainbridge, Ga.	1904
Hopper, De Wolf	New York	1858
Hopper, Edna Wallace	San Francisco, Cal.	1874
Holmes, Taylor	Newark, N. J.	1872
Howard, Leslie	London, England	1890
Hull, Henry	Louisville, Ky.	1893
Hunter, Glenn	Highland Mills, N. Y.	1896
Huston, Walter	Toronto	1884
Hutchinson, Josephine	Seattle, Wash.	1898
Inescort, Frieda	Hitchin, Scotland	1905
Irving, Isabel	Bridgeport, Conn.	1871
Irwin, May	Whitby, Ont.	1862
Janis, Elsie	Delaware, Ohio	1889
Joel, Clara	Jersey City, N. J.	1890
Johann, Zita	Hungary	1904
Jolson, Al.	Washington, D. C.	1883
Kaufman, George S.	Pittsburgh, Pa.	1889
Keane, Doris	Michigan	1885
Kelly, Walter C.	Mineville, N. Y.	1875
Kennedy, Madge	Chicago, Ill.	1890
Kerrigan, J. M.	Dublin, Ireland	1885
Kerr, Geoffrey	London, England	1895
Kershaw, Willette	Clifton Heights, Mo.	1890
Kosta, Tessa	Chicago, Ill.	1893
Kruger, Alma	Pittsburgh, Pa.	1880
Kruger, Otto	Toledo, Ohio	1895

Lackaye, Wilton	Virginia	1862
Larimore, Earl	Portland, Oregon	1899
Larrimore, Francine	Russia	1898
La Rue, Grace	Kansas City, Mo.	1882
Lauder, Harry	Portobello, England	1870
Lawrence, Gertrude	London	1898
Lawton, Thais	Louisville, Ky.	1881
Lean, Cecil	Illinois	1878
Lederer, Francis	Karlin, Prague	1906
Le Gallienne, Eva	London, England	1900
Leiber, Fritz	Chicago, Ill.	1884
Leontovich, Eugenie	Moscow, Russia	1894
Levey, Ethel	San Francisco, Cal.	1881
Lewis, Mabel Terry	London, England	1872
Lillie, Beatrice	Toronto, Canada	1898
Logan, Stanley	Earlsfield, England	1885
Loraine, Robert	New Brighton, England	1876
Lord, Pauline	Hanford, Cal.	1890
Lorraine, Lillian	San Francisco, Cal.	1892
Lou-Tellegen	Holland	1881
Lowell, Helen	New York	1866
Lunt, Alfred	Milwaukee, Wis.	1893
Mack, Andrew	Boston, Mass.	1863
Mack, Willard	Ontario, Canada	1873
Mackay, Elsie	London, England	1894
MacKellar, Helen	Canada	1896
Marlowe, Julia	Caldbeck, England	1870
Marshall, Herbert	London, England	1890
Matthews, A. E.	Bridlington, England	1869
Matthison, Edith Wynne	England	1875
Maude, Cyril	London, England	1862
McClintic, Guthrie	Seattle, Wash.	1893
McIntyre, Frank	Ann Arbor, Mich.	1879
Meek, Donald	Glasgow, Scotland	1880
Meighan, Thomas	Pittsburgh, Pa.	1879
Melba, Nellie	Melbourne, Australia	1866
Menken, Helen	New York	1901
Mercer, Beryl	Seville, Spain	1882
Merivale, Philip	Rehutia, India	1886
Miller, Gilbert	New York	1884
Miller, Marilyn	Findlay, Ohio	1898
Mitchell, Grant	Columbus, Ohio	1874

Mitchell, Thomas .... Elizabeth, N. J. 1892
Mitzi (Hajos) .... Budapest 1891
Moore, Grace .... Del Rio, Tenn. 1901
Moore, Victor .... Hammonton, N. J. 1876
Moran, Lois .... Pittsburgh, Pa. 1909
Morgan, Helen .... Danville, Ill. 1900
Morgan, Ralph .... New York City 1889
Morris, McKay .... San Antonio, Texas 1890
Muni, Paul .... Lemberg, Austria 1895

Nash, Florence .... Troy, N. Y. 1888
Nash, Mary .... Troy, N. Y. 1885
Nazimova, Alla .... Crimea, Russia 1879
Nielsen, Alice .... Nashville, Tenn. 1876
Nolan, Lloyd .... San Francisco, Cal. 1903
Nugent, J. C. .... Miles, Ohio 1875
Nugent, Elliott .... Dover, Ohio 1900

O'Connell, Hugh .... New York 1891
Olcott, Chauncey .... Providence, R. I. 1862
O'Neill, Eugene Gladstone .... New York 1888
O'Neill, Nance .... Oakland, Cal. 1875
Overman, Lynne .... Maryville, Mo. 1887

Painter, Eleanor .... Iowa 1890
Pawle, Lenox .... London, England 1872
Pemberton, Brock .... Leavenworth, Kansas 1885
Pennington, Ann .... Philadelphia, Pa. 1898
Perkins, Osgood .... Boston, Mass. 1892
Philips, Mary .... New London, Conn. 1901
Pickford, Mary .... Toronto 1893
Pollock, Channing .... Washington, D. C. 1880
Post, Guy Bates .... Seattle, Wash. 1875
Power, Tyrone .... London, England 1869
Powers, James T. .... New York 1862
Pryor, Roger .... New York City 1901

Quartermaine, Leon .... Richmond, England 1876

Rains, Claude .... London, England 1889
Rambeau, Marjorie .... San Francisco, Cal. 1889
Rathbone, Basil .... Johannesburg 1892
Reed, Florence .... Philadelphia, Pa. 1883

Rennie, James	Toronto, Canada	1890
Revelle, Hamilton	Gibraltar	1872
Richman, Charles	Chicago, Ill.	1870
Ring, Blanche	Boston, Mass.	1876
Ring, Frances	New York	1882
Robson, May	Australia	1868
Ross, Thomas W.	Boston, Mass.	1875
Royle, Selena	New York	1905
Ruben, José	Belgium	1886
Rumann, Siegfried	Hamburg, Germany	1879
Russell, Annie	Liverpool, England	1864
Sanderson, Julia	Springfield, Mass.	1887
Sands, Dorothy	Cambridge, Mass.	1900
Santley, Joseph	Salt Lake City	1889
Sawyer, Ivy	London, England	1897
Scheff, Fritzi	Vienna, Austria	1879
Schildkraut, Joseph	Bucharest, Roumania	1896
Scott, Cyril	Ireland	1866
Segal, Vivienne	Philadelphia, Pa.	1897
Selwyn, Edgar	Cincinnati, Ohio	1875
Serrano, Vincent	New York	1870
Shannon, Effie	Cambridge, Mass.	1867
Shepley, Ruth	New York	1889
Sherman, Lowell	San Francisco, Cal.	1885
Sherwood, Robert Emmet	New Rochelle, N. Y.	1896
Sidney, George	New York	1876
Sidney, Sylvia	New York	1910
Sinclair, Arthur	Dublin, Ireland	1883
Sitgreaves, Beverly	Charleston, S. C.	1867
Skelly, Hal	Allegheny, Pa.	1891
Skinner, Otis	Cambridgeport, Mass.	1857
Smith, Ben	Waxahachie, Texas	1905
Smith, Queenie	New York	1898
Sothern, Edward H.	New Orleans, La.	1859
Spong, Hilda	Australia	1875
Stahl, Rose	Montreal, Canada	1872
Standing, Sir Guy	London	1873
Starr, Frances	Oneonta, N. Y.	1886
Stone, Fred	Denver, Colo.	1873
Stone, Dorothy	New York	1905
Strudwick, Sheppard	North Carolina	1905

Sullavan, Margaret	Norfolk, Va.	1910
Sydney, Basil	London	1894
Taliaferro, Edith	New York	1892
Taliaferro, Mabel	New York	1887
Tanguay, Eva	Middletown, Conn.	1878
Taylor, Laurette	New York	1884
Tearle, Conway	New York	1878
Tell, Alma	New York	1892
Tell, Olive	New York	1894
Terris, Norma	Columbus, Kansas	1904
Thomas, Augustus	St. Louis, Mo.	1859
Thomas, John Charles	Baltimore, Md.	1887
Tobin, Genevieve	New York	1901
Tobin, Vivian	New York	1903
Toler, Sidney	Warrensburg, Mo.	1874
Tone, Franchot	Niagara Falls, N. Y.	1907
Truex, Ernest	Red Hill, Mo.	1890
Tynan, Brandon	Dublin, Ireland	1879
Ulric, Lenore	New Ulm, Minn.	1897
Varesi, Gilda	Milan, Italy	1887
Victor, Josephine	Hungary	1891
Waldron, Charles	New York	1877
Walker, June	New York	1904
Walker, Charlotte	Galveston, Texas	1878
Walter, Eugene	Cleveland, Ohio	1874
Warfield, David	San Francisco, Cal.	1866
Warwick, Robert	Sacramento, Cal.	1878
Ware, Helen	San Francisco, Cal.	1877
Waterous, Herbert	Flint, Mich.	1863
Webb, Clifton	Indiana	1891
Weber, Joseph	New York	1867
Welford, Dallas	Liverpool, England	1874
Westley, Helen	Brooklyn, N. Y.	1879
Westman, Nydia	White Plains, N. Y.	1906
Whiffen, Mrs. Thomas	London, England	1845
White, George	Toronto, Canada	1890
Whiteside, Walker	Logansport, Ind.	1869
William, Warren	Aitkin, Minn.	1896
Williams, Hope	New York City	1901

Wilson, Francis	Philadelphia, Pa.	1854
Wiman, Dwight Deere	Moline, Ill.	1895
Winwood, Estelle	England	1883
Witherspoon, Cora	New Orleans, La.	1891
Wood, Peggy	Brooklyn, N. Y.	1894
Wright, Haidee	London, England	1868
Wycherly, Margaret	England	1883
Wyndham, Olive	Chicago, Ill.	1886
Wynward, Diana	London, England	1906
Wynn, Ed.	Philadelphia, Pa.	1886
Yurka, Blanche	Bohemia	1893
Zabelle, Flora	Constantinople	1885
Ziegfeld, Florenz, Jr.	Chicago, Ill.	1867

NECROLOGY

June 15, 1932—June 18, 1933

Charles S. Abbe, actor, 73. Fifty years on stage; started at Boston Museum; afterward in companies of Edwin Booth and Charles Frohman; played with Maude Adams, Annie Russell, Bertha Kalich, Alfred Lunt and Billie Burke. Born South Wyndham, Conn.; died Darien, Conn., June 16, 1932.

Lydia Barry (Mrs. George Felix), actress, 56. Favorite as singing comedian in vaudeville; with her father, Billy Barry, formed team of Barry and Fay. Born Brooklyn, New York; died Rumson, New Jersey, July 3, 1932.

Dennis Neilson-Terry, actor-manager, 36. Descendant of two famous British theatrical families; son of Fred Terry and Julia Neilson, nephew of the late Ellen Terry; came to New York in 1925 in "The Crooked Friday" and "The Offense"; last of the Terrys. Born London; died Bulawayo, South Africa, July 12, 1932.

Jessie Millward, actress, 75. Daughter of Charles Millward, English writer of pantomimes; London début in 1881 in "The Love Chase"; came to America with Sir Henry Irving 1884 to play Pauline in "Called Back"; Marguerite to Irving's Faust in 1894; original Lady Algy with William Faversham in "Lord and Lady Algy"; member of Charles Frohman's Empire Stock Co.; married John Glendinning. Born London, England; died London, July 13, 1932.

Florenz Ziegfeld, producer, 64. Held unique place in the theatre for thirty years as creator of the modern revue; staged first "Follies" in 1907; first theatrical activity in 1893 during World's Fair; managed Sandow, Strong Man; married and managed Anna Held; established "Midnight Frolic" on roof of New Amsterdam; married Billie Burke. Born Chicago, Ill.; died Los Angeles, Cal., July 22, 1932.

Peter Lang, actor and singer, 73. Veteran character actor; began career with Portland, Me., stock company; with Bostonians in 1889; subsequently supported James K. Hackett, Mary Nash, Katharine Cornell, Frances Wilson and others; member Daniel Frohman Lyceum Company; was rehearsing in "Another Language" when he died. Died New York City, August 20, 1932.

Wilton Lackaye, actor, 69. Many years popular romantic actor; first appearance at Star Theatre, New York, in 1883 as Lucentio in "Francesco da Rimini"; with the late Lawrence Barrett; played with Fanny Davenport, Nance O'Neill, and other prominent stars; outstanding hit Svengali in "Trilby"; a founder of Equity. Born Loudon County, Virginia; died New York City, August 22, 1932.

John Craig, actor and manager, 64. Managed Boston Castle Square Company for many years; Peggy Wood, Alfred Lunt, Charles Bickford and Warren William received early training there; member of an Augustin Daly Shakesperian company; once leading man for Minnie Maddern Fiske. Born Columbia County, Tenn.; died Woodmere, L. I., New York, August 23, 1932.

Sir Gilbert Parker, novelist and playwright, 69. Wrote "The Vendetta," "No Defense," "The Seats of the Mighty"; for eighteen years a member of the British Parliament; directed publicity for Great Britain in the United States during the World War; knighted in 1902; spent ten years in Hollywood. Born Camden East, Ontario, Canada; died London, September 6, 1932.

Camille d'Arville (Crelin), actress and singer, 69. Light opera star; American début 1888 in "The Queen's Mate" dividing honors with Lillian Russell; later joined Bostonians; original Maid Marian in "Robin Hood"; in vaudeville after 1901. Born Overrysel, Holland; died San Francisco, September 10, 1932.

Lillian Millicent (Peg) Entwistle, actress. Prominently cast in "The Mad Hopes," "Tommy," "The Great God Brown" and "Getting Married." Died Hollywood, September 18, 1932.

Eva Davenport (Mrs. Neil O'Brien), actress and singer, 74. Played in many light operas at Casino Theatre with Jefferson de Angelis, Lillian Russell, Edwin Stevens, Harry Macdonough, Jennie Weathersby and others, and in many Gilbert and Sullivan revivals; last tour with De Wolf Hopper in "The Student Prince." Born London, England; died White Plains, New York, September 26, 1932.

Anthony Paul Kelly, dramatist and scenario writer, 37. Writer of scenarios and adapter of plays to screen purposes; wrote "Three Faces East" and "The Battle Royal"; member of

American Legion. Born Chicago; died New York City, September 26, 1932.

Norman Forbes-Robertson, actor, manager and playwright, 74. Brother of Sir Johnston Forbes-Robertson and well-known English actor for fifty-seven years; played with Henry Irving, Wilson Barrett, Madame Modjeska, Mr. and Mrs. Kendal, Mrs. Langtry and Ellen Terry; accompanied Sir Henry Irving to America; in 1889 came over with the Kendals. Born London, England; died London, September 29, 1932.

John R. Rogers, press agent, 92. Connected with the theatre seventy years; agent for Mary Anderson and later for Minnie Palmer whom he married and promoted in "My Sweetheart" in London. Born Cincinnati, Ohio; died New York City, October 7, 1932.

Jessie Bonstelle, actress, 66. Director of Detroit Civic Theatre; developed many stage and screen stars; début in "Bertha the Sewing Machine Girl" with Augustin Daly; played stock in Rochester and Syracuse; directed stock companies in Buffalo, Toronto, Rochester and Detroit. Born Greece, New York; died Detroit, October 14, 1932.

Emmett Corrigan (Antoine Zilles), actor, 61. First appearance Baltimore in "Esmeralda" at 14; member of original Empire Theatre stock company; played in "Men and Women," "The Girl I Left Behind Me," "The Lost Paradise," "Shenandoah"; later in "Ben Hur," "The Prince of India" and "Cameo Kirby." Born Amsterdam, Holland; died Los Angeles, October 29, 1932.

William Morris, theatre booking agent, 59. Leading independent vaudeville agent in America for many years; president and founder of Jewish Theatrical Guild. Born Schwartzenau, Germany; died New York City, November 1, 1932.

Alexander Clark, comedian, 66. First appearance in "Pinafore"; prominent in support of Willie Collier, Lillian Russell, Fay Templeton and Lulu Glaser. Born Bordentown, New Jersey; died New York City, November 10, 1932.

Anton Van Rooy, singer, 62. Metropolitan Opera bass-baritone; American début 1898. Born Rotterdam, Holland; died Munich, Germany, November 27, 1932.

Eugene Brieux, dramatist, 74. Member French Academy and a Commander of the Legion of Honor in France; plays best known in America included "Damaged Goods," and "The

Red Robe." Born Paris, France; died Nice, France, December 6, 1932.

Lon (Laurence) Hascall, actor, 60. A feature of Hammerstein vaudeville and revues for many years; last appearance in New York was in "Lysistrata." Born Grand Rapids, Michigan; died New York City, December 13, 1932.

Max Rogers, actor, 59. German dialect comedian; first appeared in 1885 at National Theatre, Bowery; with his brother Gus long identified with series of vaudeville comedies: "The Rogers Brothers in Wall Street," "In Central Park," "In Harvard," etc. Retired fifteen years ago. Born New York. Died Far Rockaway, New York, December 26, 1932.

Jack Pickford (Jack Smith), actor and producer, 36. Brother of Mary Pickford and well known on stage and screen; first appeared with Mary and their sister Lottie en tour; played in early Biograph productions with Mary and Dorothy and Lillian Gish; married Olive Thomas who died; Marilyn Miller and Mary Mulhern, from both of whom he was divorced. Born Toronto, Canada; died Paris, France, January 3, 1933.

Barry Conners, playwright and actor, 49. Actor for many years; since 1930 with Fox in Hollywood writing continuities; Broadway productions include "The Patsy," "Hell's Bells" and "Girl Trouble." Born Oil City, Pa.; died Hollywood, January 5, 1933.

Mollie Fuller, actress, 68. Musical comedy star and member of the vaudeville team of Fuller and Golden; stage début Boston at 13; played in E. E. Rice's "Evangeline" at 17; starred in Hallen and Hart shows. Born Boston, Mass.; died Hollywood, January 5, 1933.

Paul Dickey, actor, playwright and scenario writer, 48. Supported many stars including Robert Edeson in "Strongheart" and Henrietta Crosman in "Sham"; served as lieutenant in bombing squadron during World War; wrote (with Charles Goddard) "The Misleading Lady," "Miss Information," "The Ghost Breaker" and with Mann Page "The Back Slapper" and "The Red Trail." Born Chicago; died New York City, January 8, 1933.

Elisabeth Marbury, author and authors' representative, 76. Leading play broker of late nineties; encouraged talent of many famous playwrights and actors including Clyde Fitch, J. M. Barrie (whom she persuaded to adapt "The Little Minister" for Maude Adams), and Elsie deWolfe; brought plays of

Oscar Wilde to American stage. Born New York City; died New York City, January 22, 1933.

John Galsworthy, novelist and playwright, 65. Wrote twenty-one long and six short plays, including "Justice," "The Skin Game," "Loyalties," "Old English," "Escape" and "The Roof"; awarded Nobel prize for literature in 1932; received "Order of Merit" from the King of England. Born Coombe, England; died Hampstead, January 31, 1933.

James Bernard Fagan, actor, playwright and producer, 59. Plays included "The Earth," "And So to Bed" and "The Improper Duchess"; as actor was two years each with F. R. Benson and Sir Herbert Beerbohm Tree; organized Oxford Playhouse at Oxford University. Born Glasgow; died Hollywood, February 17, 1933.

James J. Corbett, actor, 66. Starred by William A. Brady in "Gentleman Jack" and "The Naval Lieutenant"; played vaudeville in dramatic sketch and monologue. Born San Francisco; died Bayside, New York, February 18, 1933.

Brigham Royce, actor, 69. Début with Marie Wainwright in 1890; played with James K. Hackett, Julia Arthur, William Hodge, Modjeska, Rose Coghlan; last appearance with William Collier in "On the Quiet." Born Memphis, Tenn.; died Baltimore, Md., March 2, 1933.

Ernest Temple Thurston, novelist and dramatist, 53. English playwright; wrote many plays including "The Blue Peter," "Judas Iscariot" and "The Wandering Jew." Born Cork; died London, March 19, 1933.

Jefferson de Angelis, comic opera comedian, 74. Started stage career of sixty years in vaudeville 1874; member New York Casino company and later one of famous triumvirate composed of De Wolf Hopper, Digby Bell and De Angelis; headed his own world touring opera company in the early eighties; remembered in "The Wedding Day" with Della Fox and Lillian Russell, and in "Fantana"; last stage appearance in "Apron Strings" in 1930. Born San Francisco; died Orange, N. J., March 20, 1933.

Patrick Kearney, playwright, 36. Best known as author of "Old Man Murphy," "A Man's Man" and "A Regular Guy"; dramatized Dreiser's "American Tragedy" and Sinclair Lewis' "Elmer Gantry." Born Columbus, Ohio; died New York City, March 28, 1933.

Don Mullally, actor, playwright and director, 48. Wrote and staged "Conscience," "Laugh That Off," "The Camels Are

Coming," "Maggie" and "Desert Flower"; co-author "Coastwise Annie," and "Noble Experiment"; staged "Love, Honor and Betray"; built and operated theatre at Woodstock, N. Y.; in vaudeville ten years; wrote many scenarios. Born St. Louis, Mo.; died Duarte, Cal., April 1, 1933.

Wilson Mizner, playwright, 56. Noted wit and author; first play, "The Only Law"; wrote with Paul Armstrong "The Deep Purple," "The Greyhound" and "Alias Jimmie Valentine"; wrote many scenarios. Born Benicia, Cal.; died Los Angeles, April 3, 1933.

Earl Derr Biggers, author and playwright, 48. Foremost writer of mystery and detective plots; created "Charlie Chan," used extensively in motion pictures; wrote novel "Seven Keys to Baldpate," a musical comedy, "See-Saw," "Three's a Crowd" (with Christopher Morley) and "A Cure for Curables" (with William Hodge). Born Warren, Ohio; died Pasadena, Cal., April 5, 1933.

Eva Clara Lang, actress, 48. Best known as stock player. Started with O. D. Woodward in Kansas City and Denver; toured in "Under Two Flags"; appeared with John Holliday, her husband, in "The Dancer" and "Dancing Mothers." Born Columbus, Ohio; died Los Angeles, April 6, 1933.

J. Ranken Towse, dramatic critic, 88. Critic of the *New York Evening Post* for fifty-four years; wrote "Sixty Years in the Theatre." Born Streatham, Surrey, England; died Streatham, April 11, 1933.

Fred Terry, actor, 69. Member of famous British theatrical family; first stage appearance at fifteen at Haymarket Theatre, London; subsequently played in most of the principal cities of United Kingdom and United States; managed and played with wife, Julia Neilson, in "Sweet Nell of Old Drury," "The Argyle Case," "The Popinjay," "The Scarlet Pimpernel" and many Shakespeare plays. Born London, England; died London, April 17, 1933.

William Courtenay, actor, 57. Leading man with Richard Mansfield; played with Lyceum and Empire stock companies; Milton and Dolly Nobles; co-starred in "Pals First," "General Post" and "Cappy Ricks"; with Doris Keane in "Arsene Lupin" and "Romance"; played opposite his wife, Virginia Harned, in "Iris," "Camille" and "The Light That Lies in Woman's Eyes"; last appearance 1931 in "The Inside Story." Born Worcester, Mass.; died Rye, New York, April 20, 1933.

Joseph Kilgour, actor, 69. Created leads in "The Easiest Way" and "The Lion and the Mouse"; noted for portrayal of stage millionaires; supported Mrs. Fiske, Henrietta Crosman and Mrs. Leslie Carter; appeared in many motion pictures. Born Ayr, Ontario, Canada; died East Islip, L. I., April 20, 1933.

Frederick Kerr (Frederick Grinham Keen), actor and stage director, 74. Noted stage and screen comedian for more than half a century; supported Lily Langtry, Sir John Hare and Mrs. Patrick Campbell; started film career at 72 in screen version of "The High Road"; wrote "Revelations of a Defective Memory"; father of Geoffrey Kerr. Born London, England; died London, May 2, 1933.

Albert H. Perry, actor, 63. Supported James K. Hackett, Mrs. Leslie Carter, Olga Nethersole and Bertha Kalich; was in Theatre Guild productions of "Ned McCobb's Daughter" and "Heartbreak House"; first appearance with William Gillette in "Secret Service." Born Detroit, Michigan; died St. George, Staten Island, May 6, 1933.

Ernest Torrence, actor and vocalist, 54. As a young man concert pianist and leading baritone Savoy Opera Co., London; known in America in musical comedy and motion pictures; best remembered on Broadway in "The Night Boat," "The Only Girl" and "Peggy"; in pictures in "Tol'able David" and his last screen play, "I Cover the Waterfront." Born Edinburgh, Scotland; died New York, May 15, 1933.

Lee Wilson Dodd, author and playwright, 54. Most successful plays: "His Majesty, Bunker Bean," "Pals First," "The Changelings," "The Return of Eve," "Speed" and "A Strong Man's House"; associate professor in drama department Yale University at time of death. Born Franklin, Pa.; died New York City, May 16, 1933.

Arthur Forrest, actor, 74. Began stage career under management of Mrs. John Drew, the elder, in Philadelphia; with Charles Wyndham two years in London; several years with Lester Wallack and Daniel Frohman stock companies; supported Lily Langtry, Kate Claxton, Mme. Januschek and Richard Mansfield. Born Baireuth, Germany; died New York City, May 16, 1933.

Elmer Grandin, actor, 72. Début "Pinafore" 1879; last performance in Canadian production of "Applecart"; said to have been first "Abraham Lincoln," 1890; with Chrystal Herne and Dustin Farnum in "The Squaw Man"; with Tyrone Power in "Thais"; with Olive Wyndham and Wallace Eddinger in "The Only Son"; with Henry Kolker in "The Greyhound." Died Patchoque, New York, May 19, 1933.

James M. Bradford, actor, 89. Long theatrical career including stage association with Edwin Booth, Barrett, McCullough and the Davenports; served with Union forces during the Civil War and spent five months in Andersonville prison. Born Cincinnati; died Akron, Ohio, June 8, 1933.

Winchell Smith, actor, producer, stage director and playwright, 61. Produced "Turn to the Right," "Lightnin'," "Three Wise Fools," etc., with John Golden; in association with Arnold Daly introduced plays of Bernard Shaw to America; first play "Brewster's Millions," written with Byron Ongley 1906; own plays included "The Fortune Hunter" and "The Only Son"; twenty-nine others written with collaborators include "Polly of the Circus," "Via Wireless," "The New Henrietta" and "The Boomerang"; last work directing "The Vinegar Tree" 1930. Born Hartford, Conn.; died Mill Stream, Farmington, Conn., June 10, 1933.

THE DECADES' TOLL

(Players of Outstanding Prominence Who Have Died in Recent Years)

	Born	*Died*
Bacon, Frank	1864	1922
Belasco, David	1856	1931
Bernhardt, Sarah	1845	1923
Coghlan, Rose	1851	1932
Crabtree, Charlotte (Lotta)	1847	1924
Crane, William H.	1845	1928
Drew, John	1853	1927
De Koven, Reginald	1861	1920
De Reszke, Jean	1850	1925
Ditrichstein, Leo	1865	1928
Duse, Eleanora	1859	1924
Galsworthy, John	1867	1933
Goodwin, Nathaniel	1857	1920
Fiske, Minnie Maddern	1865	1932
Hawtrey, Sir Charles	1858	1923
Herbert, Victor	1859	1924
Lackaye, Wilton	1862	1932
Mantell, Robert Bruce	1854	1928
Miller, Henry	1858	1926
Morris, Clara	1848	1925
O'Neill, James	1850	1920
Patti, Adelina	1843	1919
Rejane, Gabrielle	1857	1920
Russell, Lillian	1861	1922
Shaw, Mary	1860	1929
Smith, Winchell	1862	1933
Terry, Ellen	1848	1928
Ziegfeld, Florenz	1869	1932

INDEX OF AUTHORS

INDEX OF PLAYS AND CASTS